Discoveries in Gaming and Computer-Mediated Simulations:

New Interdisciplinary Applications

Richard E. Ferdig
Research Center for Education Technology – Kent State University, USA

Information Science
REFERENCE

Senior Editorial Director:	Kristin Klinger
Director of Book Publications:	Julia Mosemann
Editorial Director:	Lindsay Johnston
Acquisitions Editor:	Erika Carter
Development Editor:	Michael Killian
Production Editor:	Sean Woznicki
Typesetters:	Keith Glazewski, Jennifer Romanchak, Milan Vracarich Jr. & Michael Brehm
Print Coordinator:	Jamie Snavely
Cover Design:	Nick Newcomer

Published in the United States of America by
Information Science Reference (an imprint of IGI Global)
701 E. Chocolate Avenue
Hershey PA 17033
Tel: 717-533-8845
Fax: 717-533-8661
E-mail: cust@igi-global.com
Web site: http://www.igi-global.com

Library of Congress Cataloging-in-Publication Data

Discoveries in gaming and computer-mediated simulations : new interdisciplinary applications / Richard E. Ferdig, editor.
       p. cm.
  Includes bibliographical references and index.
  Summary: "This book explores and promotes a deep conceptual and empirical understanding of the roles of electronic games and computer-mediated simulations across multiple disciplines, building a significant bridge between research and practice on electronic gaming and simulations"--Provided by publisher.
   ISBN 978-1-60960-565-0 (hardcover) -- ISBN 978-1-60960-566-7 (ebook) 1. Computer games. 2. Electronic games. I. Ferdig, Richard E. (Richard Eugene)
  GV1469.15.D57 2011
  794.8--dc22
                                        2011013280

British Cataloguing in Publication Data
A Cataloguing in Publication record for this book is available from the British Library.

All work contributed to this book is new, previously-unpublished material. The views expressed in this book are those of the authors, but not necessarily of the publisher.

For Cherilyn, Owen & Ethan

Table of Contents

Section 1
Design of Games and Simulations

Patrick O'Shea, Harvard University, USA
Rebecca Mitchell, Harvard University, USA
Catherine Johnston, Harvard University, USA
Chris Dede, Harvard University, USA

Jan L. Plass, New York University, USA
Bruce D. Homer, CUNY, USA
Catherine Milne, New York University, USA
Trace Jordan, New York University, USA
Slava Kalyuga, University of New South Wales, Australia
Minchi Kim, Purdue University, USA
Hyunjeong Lee, University of Seoul, Korea

Miguel Sicart, IT University of Copenhagen, Germany

Carrie Heeter, Michigan State University, USA
Brian Magerko, Georgia Tech University, USA
Ben Medler, Georgia Tech University, USA
Joe Fitzgerald, Michigan State University, USA

Section 2
Learning Outcomes of Games and Simulations

Section 3
New Theoretical Considerations of Games and Simulations

Section 4
Creating and Living in Virtual Worlds

Detailed Table of Contents

Section 1
Design of Games and Simulations

Chapter 1
> *Patrick O'Shea, Harvard University, USA*
> *Rebecca Mitchell, Harvard University, USA*
> *Catherine Johnston, Harvard University, USA*
> *Chris Dede, Harvard University, USA*

While utilizing GPS-enabled handheld computing units, we have developed and studied augmented reality (AR) curricula to help middle school students learn literacy and math. In AR, students move around an outdoor physical environment, interacting with virtual characters and artifacts on their handheld computer. These invisible objects and characters provide clues to help solve a mystery, guiding the students through a process of inquiry and evidence building. The first AR curriculum we developed, Alien Contact! is based on a scenario where aliens have crash landed near the students' middle school. Students, working in teams, learn math and literacy skills in the course of determining why the aliens have come to earth. This study describes the design heuristics used during the initial development and deployment of Alien Contact!, the results of two formative evaluations of this curriculum, and the impact these findings have had on revising our design heuristics for a subsequent AR curriculum about beached whales, called Gray Anatomy.

Chapter 2
> *Jan L. Plass, New York University, USA*
> *Bruce D. Homer, CUNY, USA*
> *Catherine Milne, New York University, USA*
> *Trace Jordan, New York University, USA*
> *Slava Kalyuga, University of New South Wales, Australia*
> *Minchi Kim, Purdue University, USA*
> *Hyunjeong Lee, University of Seoul, Korea*

We argue that the effectiveness of simulations for science education depends on design features such as the type of representation chosen to depict key concepts. We hypothesize that the addition of iconic representations to simulations can help novice learners interpret the visual simulation interface and improve cognitive learning outcomes as well as learners' self-efficacy. This hypothesis was tested in two experiments with high school chemistry students. The studies examined the effects of representation type (symbolic versus iconic), prior knowledge, and spatial ability on comprehension, knowledge transfer, and self-efficacy under low cognitive load (Study 1, N=80) and high cognitive load conditions (Study 2, N=91). Results supported our hypotheses that design features such as the addition of iconic representations can help scaffold students' comprehension of science simulations, and that this effect was strongest for learners with low prior knowledge. Adding icons also improved learners' general self-efficacy.

Chapter 3

This article presents a typology for classifying computer games designed to create ethical gameplay. Ethical gameplay is the outcome of playing a (computer) game in which the players' moral values are of relevance for the game experience. The article explores the different types of designs that create these types of experiences, and how they are characterized. The author provides an analytical framework for classifying games according to the experience they create and how they create it. The article is informed by both game design theory and postphenomenological philosophy, and it is intended to provide a theoretical framework for the study of the design of ethical computer game experiences.

Chapter 4

Achiever and Explorer player types are well known in MMOs and educational games. Players who enjoy being a winner, but dislike hard challenges ("Self-Validators") are a heretofore ignored but commonly occurring player type. Self-Validators worry about and are distressed by failing. They can simply avoid playing overly difficult games for entertainment. But in a required learning game, Self-Validators' excessive worry about failing can interfere with learning. The authors consider whether and how eight very different modern games accommodate Explorers, Achievers, and Self-Validators and discuss implications for entertainment and learning game design and research. Seven of eight diverse games analyzed primarily served either the Explorer or Achiever player type. Self-Validators were partially accommodated in some Achiever-oriented games, through user-selectable difficulty. Design with all three types in mind would encourage inclusion of features that enable players to optimize their preferred style of play.

Recommendation systems are key components in many Web applications (Amazon, Netflix, eHarmony). Each system gathers user input, such as the products they buy, and searches for patterns in order to determine user preferences and tastes. These preferences are then used to recommend other content that a user may enjoy. Games on the other hand are often designed with a one-size-fits-all approach not taking player preferences into account. However there is a growing interest in both the games industry and game research communities to begin incorporating systems that can adapt, or alter how the game functions, to specific players. This article examines how Web application recommendation systems compare to current games that adapt their gameplay to specific players. The comparison shows that current games do not use recommendation methods that are data intensive or collaborative when adapting to players. Design suggestions are offered within this manuscript for how game developers can benefit from incorporating the lesser used recommendation methods.

Market 3D engines have all the capabilities needed for developing full-featured 3D simulation and game environments. However, for those in education and small-business, it remains a formidable task to acquire the resources needed to purchase or create a development platform with cutting-edge capabilities. Leveraging existing and open-source software libraries can greatly enhance the main application development, freeing developers to focus more on the application concept itself rather than the needed supporting pieces. This chapter explores the nuances of successfully mixing core code with these third-party libraries in creating a fully functioning development environment. Many steps with accompanying checks-and-balances are involved in creating a game engine, including making choices of what libraries to use, and integrating the core code with third-party libraries. By offering insights into our open source driven process, we help inform the understanding of how game engines may be generated for other educational and small-budget projects.

Section 2
Learning Outcomes of Games and Simulations

A growing body of research suggests that computer games can help players learn to integrate knowledge and skills with values in complex domains of real-world problem solving (P. C. Adams, 1998; Barab et al., 2001; Gee, 2003; Shaffer et al., 2005; Starr, 1994). In particular, research suggests that *epistemic games*—games where players think and act like real world professionals—can link knowledge, skills, and values into professional ways of thinking (Shaffer, 2006). Here, we look at how a ten hour version of the epistemic game Urban Science developed civic thinking in young people as they learned about urban ecology by role-playing as urban planners redesigning a city. Specifically, we ask whether and how overcoming authentic obstacles from the profession of urban planning in the virtual world of a role playing game can link civic values with the knowledge and skills young people need to solve complex social and ecological problems. Our results from coded pre- and post-interviews show that players learned to think of cities as complex systems, learned about skills that planners use to enact change in these systems, and perhaps most important, learned the value of serving the public in that process. Two aspects of the game, *tool-as-obstacle* and *stakeholders-as-obstacle*, contributed to the development of players' civic thinking. Thus, our results suggest that games like Urban Science may help young people—and thus help all of us—identify and address the many civic, economic, and environmental challenges in an increasingly complex, and increasingly urban, world.

Chapter 8

Learning as Becoming: Values, Identity, and Performance in the Enaction of Citizenship
    Yam San Chee, Nanyang Technological University, Singapore
    Swee Kin Loke, University of Otago, New Zealand
    Ek Ming Tan, Nanyang Technological University, Singapore

In this chapter, we share a model of game-based learning for use in the context of classroom learning in school. The model is based on the dialectic interaction between game play and dialogic engagement with peers and teacher on one hand and a developmental trajectory of competence-through-performance on the other. It is instantiated in the context of a learning program related to citizenship education using the computer game Space Station Leonis. We argue for the importance of values in all learning, based upon a theory of becoming citizens that is founded on process philosophy. We relate values to dispositions as articulated manifestations of values and describe how the Leonis learning program helps to achieve dispositional shifts befitting citizenship education in a globalized and multi-cultural world.

Chapter 9

    B. J. Gajadhar, Eindhoven University of Technology, The Netherlands
    Y. A. W. deKort, Eindhoven University of Technology, The Netherlands
    W. A. IJsselsteijn, Eindhoven University of Technology, The Netherlands

This chapter presents an empirical study of social setting as a determinant of player involvement in competitive play. We conceptualize player experience as roughly comprising of components of involvement and enjoyment. Involvement relates to the attentional pull of games encompassing feelings of immersion, engagement, and flow. Enjoyment taps into the fun and frustration of playing. A few recent studies indicate that co-players boost player enjoyment, yet the effect on involvement is still largely unknown. In line with enjoyment, involvement could increase with the sociality of settings. On the other hand, the presence of others provides a potential distracter and threat to involvement in games. Results of an experiment where social setting was manipulated within groups indicated that players' involvement remains constant or even increases with mediated or co-located co-players compared to solitary play. Hence, co-players do not break the spell of a game, but become part of the magic circle.

Chapter 10

Literature suggests that games can support learning in schools by enabling creative problem solving, allowing dynamic resource allocation, providing a motivating, immersive activity, and supporting explorations of identity. A descriptive, inductive study was carried out to identify how high school students make use of the video game interface and its representations. Results demonstrate that specific cues direct attention, helping to focus efforts on new or underutilized game tasks. In addition, consistent and well-organized visualizations encourage learning and collaboration among students by providing shared referential resources and scaffolding coordinated sequences of problem solving acts during gameplay. Conversely, when affordances are inconsistently represented, students' focus can shift from problem solving at the goal level (game strategy, etc.) to problem solving at the game interface level (which is frustrating their goals). In general, the design of game representations and behaviors can help guide or hinder student learning.

Chapter 11

The experience of a successful adolescent learner will be described from the student's perspective about learning the video game Dance Dance Revolution (DDR) through selected passages from a phenomenological interview. The question driving this investigation is, "Why did she sustain engagement in learning?" The importance of this question came out of the need for background on how to create an afterschool program that was to use DDR as an after school activity that might engage adolescents and tweens to become more physically active and reduce the risk of adult obesity, and to increase bone density for these developing young people through playing the game over time. The difficulty of creating this program was the risk that the students would not sustain engagement in the activity, and we would not have a viable sample for the bone density adolescent obesity study. Implications of this study include understanding the potential construction of learning environments that motivate and sustain engagement in learning and the importance of identity construction for teachers to motivate and engage their students. In addition to the analysis of sustained engagement through the four socio- and cultural-cognitive theories, four major principals were extracted from the operationalized themes into a framework for instructional design techniques and theory for engaging learners for game design, training, and in classroom learning.

Section 3
New Theoretical Considerations of Games and Simulations

Modding communities are particularly ripe environments for rethinking what it means to be IT literate in the contemporary world. Mods are, as we argue, computational literacy artifacts, exemplifying not merely computer literacy but also the ability to understand and use computational models and processes to conceptualize and solve problems. In this article, we describe modding practice in the context of the best-selling computer game to date: World of Warcraft. By analyzing such activities as a form of computational literacy practice "in the wild," we demonstrate how modding illustrates what it means to be technically literate in the contemporary participatory sociotechnical world. Based on our analysis, we argue for reconsideration of computer literacy as computational literacy, authorship as collaborative and negotiated rather than individually achieved, and digital media literacy practice as one involving design and production, not merely passive or critical consumption.

Video game developers make multimillion dollar decisions based on hunches, personal experience, and iteration. A theoretical model of video game player behavior – how one chooses, plays, and evaluate games – can provide an important framework for these decisions. According to social cognitive theory, one's behavior can be understood as the result of expected outcomes resulting from direct and observational learning processes. Video game players use symbolic representations (quality perceptions) of their direct and observed experiences with video games to build expectations of whether playing a specific video game will satisfy their needs. A series of in-depth interviews and a subsequent survey with students of a large mid-western university was conducted to enumerate groups of similar players (player types), and video game quality perceptions. Both concepts were used to provide empirical evidence for a model to predict video game playing. Results show that, in prediction models, the best player types are those that include player type-specific quality perceptions.

Game designer Nick Fortungno's keynote speech at the Meaningful Play conference talked about the conundrum of whether serious games can or even should be fun. Fortugno looks back at historical works of popular culture that exerted transformative effects on society. He examines three current persuasive games and offers his thoughts on what it will take for a game to achieve societal transformation.

Chapter 15

As serious games gain momentum in the academic arena, no doubt more educators and instructional technologists will begin considering the possibility of making their own games for instruction. As developers of instructional resources, instructional technologists need to steer clear of producing more 'video' games, and instead, developing more 'serious' games that incorporate both learning and assessment. The research community needs to learn from tested processes and best practices to avoid repeating old mistakes. The model for serious game making presented in this article has been used successfully for the creation of an award winning project, and will now be shared for the benefits of fellow researchers, educators, and instructional technologists.

Section 4
Creating and Living in Virtual Worlds

Chapter 16

Video games are becoming more popular; there has been a particular rise in interest and use of massively multiplayer online role-playing games (MMORPGs). These games utilize avatar creation; avatars can be seen as the technological instantiation of the real person in the virtual world. Little research has been conducted on avatar creation. Although it is has been anecdotally postulated that you can be anything you want online, there is a dearth of research on what happens when participants are told to create avatars, particularly avatars within given contexts. In this study, we used the Second Life avatar creation tool to examine what would happen when participants were told to create avatars as heroes, villains, their ideal self, and their actual self. Data analyses reveal that characters often refuse to change permanent aspects of their features, instead modifying only temporal aspects. This research has provided support for the quantitative review of avatar characteristics as predictors of vignette groupings.

We report results of an experiment on prices and demand in a fantasy-based virtual world. A virtual world is a persistent, synthetic, online environment that can be accessed by many users at the same time. Because most virtual worlds are built around a fantasy theme, complete with magic, monsters, and treasure, there is considerable skepticism that human behavior in such environments is in any way "normal." Our world, "Arden," was designed to test whether players in a typical fantasy environment were economically "normal." Specifically, we tested whether fantasy gamers conform to the Law of Demand, which states that increasing the price of a good, all else equal, will reduce the quantity demanded. We created two exactly equivalent worlds, and randomly assigned players to one or the other. The only difference in the two worlds was that the price of a single good, a health potion, was twice as high in the experimental world than in the control. We allowed players (N = 43) to enter and play the environment for a month.

Chapter 18

Catherine Norton-Barker, Cornell University, USA
Margaret Corbit, Cornell University, USA
Richard Bernstein, Cornell University, USA

Immersive virtual worlds structured for education have the potential to engage students who do not respond well to traditional classroom activities. To test the appeal and usability of virtual environments in the classroom, four ninth grade science classes in a rural Upstate New York school were randomly assigned to learn an introductory genetics unit for three class periods in either an online, multi-user, virtual world computer environment or in a traditional classroom setting using lecture, worksheets, and model building. The groups were then reversed for a second three-day trial. Quizzes were given before, at midpoint, and at the end of the study. Both groups demonstrated significant knowledge gain of the genetics curriculum. This study demonstrates that self-directed learning can occur while exploring virtual world computer environments. The students were enthusiastic about using virtual worlds for education and indicated a strong preference for a variety of teaching methods, which suggests that offering mixed modalities may engage students who are otherwise uninterested in school.

Chapter 19

Sabine Trepte, Hamburg Media School, Germany
Leonard Reinecke, Hamburg Media School, Germany
Katharina-Maria Behr, Hamburg Media School, Germany

Who do people want to be in virtual worlds? Video game players can create their avatars with characteristics similar to themselves, create a superhero that is predominantly designed to win, or chose an in-between strategy. In a quasi-experimental study, players were expected to prefer their avatars to have their sex, but to create avatars with gender attributes that best meet the requirements of the game. In the main study, participants created an avatar they would like to play with by choosing from a list of (pre-tested) masculine and feminine avatar features. Additionally, participants chose their avatars' biological sex. The results reveal a mixed strategy: On the one hand, the avatar's features are chosen in accordance with the game's demands to facilitate mastery of the game. On the other hand, players strive for identification with their avatar and thus prefer avatars of their own sex. Participants rated those game descriptions and gaming scenarios more entertaining which require avatar features in line with their own sex role.

The purpose of this qualitative inquiry is to extend the investigation of perceptions and experiences of users creating avatars for interactions in online learning environments. Using Linden Lab's *Second Life*, volunteers created three-dimensional representations of themselves, called avatars, under the premise of participating in a hypothetical online class. Avatar creation sessions were book-ended with pre- and post- interviews focused on participant perceptions of various elements of self-representation and interactions as situated in online environments. Human computer interactions (HCI) of avatar creation were also explored. Findings indicate users created avatars that mirrored their respective physical appearances as closely as possible and were collectively adamant in feeling morally obliged to do so.

Preface

INTRODUCTION

Electronic gaming and computer-mediated simulations have risen to the forefront of research and practice in many fields ranging from education to sociology and from computer science to business. Researchers and practitioners argue some very interesting and important points. First, there is research emerging that suggests games and simulations help audiences teach and learn. Inquiries have ranged from learning K-12 content to the impact of videogames on violent behaviors. Regardless of the positive or potential negative construct, there is evidence of a connection between the input of games and/or simulations and a desired or undesired output. If such evidence exists, it is important and critical to understand more about the connections and the constructs.

Second, there is a wealth of popular press—and some academic literature—that highlights the common occurrence of games and simulations in the lives of people essentially throughout the lifespan. Many young children play games daily; elderly audiences often use simulations for physical and mental rehabilitation. Again, if games and simulations have become so ubiquitous, researchers, practitioners, and even policymakers want to know more about how to harness their potential.

This book sets out to capture a snapshot of some important things we know about games and computer-mediated simulations. This is not meant to be a handbook of everything that has been written about games and simulations. On the contrary, this tome was created to highlight the work that has emerged through a year-long snapshot of articles published in a leading, peer-reviewed journal. This chapter begins with a brief background about the journal, and then provides an overview and summary of the 20 chapters in this book. In doing so, it describes the four main themes throughout this book and how the chapters have pushed the field related to that theme. The chapter concludes with some recommendations and goals for future research, policy, and practice.

IJGCMS

The *International Journal of Games and Computer-Mediated Simulations* (IJGCMS) was launched in 2009 (http://www.igi-global.com/ijgcms). The journal is devoted to the theoretical and empirical understanding of electronic games and computer-mediated simulations. The journal is interdisciplinary in nature; it publishes research from fields and disciplines that share the goal of improving the foundational knowledge base of games and simulations. The journal publishes critical theoretical manuscripts as well as qualitative and quantitative research studies, meta-analyses, and methodologically-sound case studies.

The journal also includes book reviews to keep readers on the forefront of this continuously evolving field. Occasional special issues from the journal provide deeper investigation into areas of interest within either gaming or simulations.

One main goal of this peer-reviewed, international journal is to promote a deep conceptual and empirical understanding of the roles of electronic games and computer-mediated simulations across multiple disciplines. A second goal is to help build a significant bridge between research and practice on electronic gaming and simulations, supporting the work of researchers, practitioners, and policymakers.

There are at five guiding principles supporting this mission as well as the editorial policy of IJGCMS. The first important principle is quality and rigor. IJGCMS follows a double-blind review process to ensure anonymity and a fair review. Research articles that are published may contain either quantitative or qualitative data collection & analyses. However, articles using either method must present data to support and justify claims made within the article. Articles that simply summarize data without presenting it or the analytical techniques used, are not considered. Theoretical manuscripts are also published. However, these theoretical reviews must create new knowledge by synthesizing and critiquing past research. Simple summaries of existing literature without thoughtful and considerate analyses are not considered.

A second important principle is the notion of IJGCMS as an interdisciplinary journal. There are numerous fields and disciplines that undertake research related to games and simulations. Psychology, Education, History, Journalism, Literature, Computer Science, Engineering, Fine Arts, and Medicine are just a few of the areas where one could find gaming and simulation research. Unfortunately in academia, the notion of standing on the shoulders of giants has often meant taken a historical perspective on one's line of research. Gaining a historical backing is an important part of moving the field forward; however, failing to consider parallel work in other fields is failure to address and accept the complex natures of games and simulations. IJGCMS publishes articles from any discipline as long as the content of the work is related to games and simulations. Including multiple fields helps researchers recognize their similarities as well as introducing them to colleagues from distinctly different backgrounds.

In addition to having an interdisciplinary focus, a third principal of this journal is its international focus. There are over 18 countries represented on the Editorial Board of IJGCMS. There is no justifiable reason why our research should have disciplinary OR geographical boundaries. Drawing on work from international authors provides two interesting opportunities. First, readers are able to see one topic from multiple perspectives. For instance, how are researchers from various countries working on science simulations? Second, readers are able to see variations across countries. For instance, what are the current research topics and sets of expertise in various countries around the world?

Innovation is a fourth principle guiding the work of IJGCMS. Gaming and simulation researchers often create new concepts and technologies in their work. IJGCMS is a journal where authors who create new tools and techniques go to publish their findings; it is also a resource for readers who want to keep up with the latest and most cutting edge technologies. Special, focused issues with guest editors will also promote in-depth analyses at conceptual or technological innovations (proposals for special issues are welcomed at any time).

Finally, IJGCMS is focused on implications. Developing a strong research foundation for games and simulations is important, but only to the extent that the research impacts others. One of the main items reviewers are asked to consider when reviewing for IJGCMS is: "What are the implications of this work on other research, policy, and practice?" Each article author is asked to include direct implications for others working in similar areas, regardless of whether they be researchers, practitioners, or policy-makers.

Recommended topics for the journal include (but are not limited to) the following:

- Cognitive, social, and emotional impact of games and simulations
- Critical reviews and meta-analyses of existing game and simulation literature
- Current and future trends, technologies, and strategies related to game, simulation development, and implementation
- Electronic games and simulations in government, business, and the workforce
- Electronic games and simulations in teaching and learning
- Frameworks to understand the societal and cultural impacts of games and simulations
- Impact of game and simulation development use on race and gender game and simulation design
- Innovative and current research methods and methodologies to study electronic games and simulations
- Psychological aspects of gaming
- Teaching of games and simulations at multiple age and grade levels

During its inaugural year, IJGCMS had three 'regular' or general issues and one special issue. Some work in gaming and simulations gets published in journals like IJGCMS. However, a tremendous amount of cutting-edge research in this area is first presented at conferences. In an attempt to capture these findings, IJGCMS often partners with conferences and organizations to create special issues focused on the leading research from the conference. The special issue for 2009 was from a conference called *Meaningful Play* (http://meaningfulplay.msu.edu/) held at Michigan State University. According the website, Meaningful Play "is a conference about theory, research, and game design innovations, principles, and practices. Meaningful Play brings scholars and industry professionals together to understand and improve upon games to entertain, inform, educate, and persuade in meaningful ways."

IJGCMS' editorial board consists of four separate groups (http://www.igi-global.com/ijgcms).

1. The international advisory board consists of a panel of leading experts from around the world. The advisory board provides insight and helpful recommendations to the editor; they are also available for suggestions and recommendations of future journal goals and special issues.
2. IJGCMS has a panel of associate editors. Each submission goes to one associate editor. Having a smaller number of associate editors has provided a way to maintain consistency in reviews.
3. Submissions also then go to two editorial review board members. As such, each submission receives three double-blind, peer reviews. The associate editor and the editorial review board members are matched as closely as possible based on the topic of the submission and the expertise of the reviewer. However, the reviews are double-blind. In other words, the authors do not know the identity of the reviewers assigned to their paper, nor do the reviewers know the author.
4. Finally, IJGCMS publishes a book review with almost every issue. The fourth group is a panel of co-book review editors who help select books, solicit reviewers, and edit reviews.

Journal special issues are also peer-reviewed. This can be done in a number of different ways. Often, for conference special issues, submissions are reviewed once at the submission stage, where they are accepted or rejected for presentation. Accepted papers are then offered the chance to submit for journal submission, where they are again reviewed either by the conference review panel or IJGCMS' own review board.

The four issues for 2009 produced a total of 20 peer-reviewed papers. In preparing this book, authors were given the opportunity to update their paper with new data, new findings, or related articles since the original publication of their paper. The purpose and goal of this book is to highlight the work of those authors, presenting findings that will impact the field of gaming and simulations in multiple ways.

The book itself is divided into four sections, which represent the four main themes that emerged upon a closer analysis of the chapters. As with most categorization schemes, chapters can cut across multiple themes. However, these themes help present a coherent look at some of the cutting-edge research in this area.

- Section 1: Design of Games and Simulations
- Section 2: Learning Outcomes of Games and Simulations
- Section 3: New Theoretical Considerations of Games and Simulations
- Section 4: Creating and Living in Virtual Worlds

It should be noted that the purpose of this summary is to highlight the main ideas identified in each chapter. It is not intended to take away from the rich insights or deep conversations included in each chapter. For instance, one of the goals of IJGCMS is to publish articles that directly impact policy, research, and practice. Each chapter in this book contains a rich description of the 'so what?' for those working in various fields. A thorough reading of each chapter will provide such detailed information.

Section 1: Design of Games and Simulations

As previously indicated, there are multiple fields that are interested in games and simulations. Design is an area of games and simulations that is often addressed regardless of whether the conversation originates in computer science or psychology. During 2009, there were six articles that focused prominently on design.

Lessons Learned about Designing Augmented Realities (O' Shea, Mitchell, Johnston, & Dede)

In this chapter, O'Shea and his colleagues discussed the design and development of an augmented reality curriculum. Their project, *Alien Contact!*, was created to teach math and literacy to middle and high school students. The technology enables students' real world position to correlate with the virtual location in the simulation. Working in teams, students must explore the world and collect data to determine why the aliens have landed. Evaluation of the curriculum has provided evidence that students are more motivated during the implementation of the content, but there were significant logical limitations. Given these limitations, the authors then report on the development of *Gray Anatomy*, a subsequent augmented reality curriculum. This is really the core of what this chapter can offer educators and developers. Augmented reality presents important educational opportunities, but developers must consider cognitive overload, unintended competition, the need to have flexible roles, helping students find multiple answers vs. the 'correct one', the length of the curriculum, and how to get classroom teachers involved. The authors conclude that having educators recognize student-owned technologies will also help implementation.

Design Factors for Effective Science Simulations: Representation of Information (Plass, Homer, Milne, Jordan, Kalyuga, Kim, & Lee)

Plass et al. proposed that the effectiveness of science education simulations depend on important design features. Using this hypothesis, they ran two experiments with high school chemistry students. They did indeed find that design features can help scaffold student comprehension. They also noted this was particularly true for learners with low prior knowledge. The authors provide three important findings for our field. First, learner's prior knowledge needs to be considered in selecting representations in the simulation. Second, adding iconic representations can increase both comprehension and learner self-efficacy, particularly for students with low-prior knowledge. Third, iconic representations may be more suited than symbols to reducing cognitive load, due in part to the close relation to the referent they represent.

Beyond Choices: A Typology of Ethical Computer Game Designs (Sicart)

Sicart explored a typology for classifying games designed to create ethical game-play. Ethical game-play, according to the author, is the experience in which the outcomes require moral reflection beyond statistics or probability. Sicart presents a typology that includes open ethical design where players can influence the game through their values, and closed design where they cannot. In open design, there are open systems where the game adapts to the player values and open world where the world adapts. In closed design, Sicart presents subtracting, where the player interprets the game as an ethical experience (cued by design) and mirroring, where the player is forced to adopt the values of the game character. Given this framework, Sicart demonstrates the need to understand the ethical player, the ethical multiplayer, and the design methods around these complex issues.

Game Design and the Challenge-Avoiding, Self-Validator Player Type (Heeter, Magerko, Medler & Fitzgerald)

Heeter et al. argued that there are well-recognized player types such as *achievers* and *explorers*. Achievers are those who are motivated by extrinsic reward. Explorers, conversely, play because of curiosity and learning. However, the authors argue that there is another player type that is often ignored—that of the *self-validator*. Self-validators like extrinsic rewards, but unlike achievers, they dislike losing so much that they would prefer an easy challenge. Using eight games as examples, the authors then discuss the design features that might appeal to the different types of players. One main outcome of their work includes the need for designers and producers to play off these types, while not discouraging them. A second is the need for more research on the role of adaptive games.

Using Recommendation Systems to Adapt Game-Play (Medler)

In this chapter, Medler argued that most game systems are designed in a one-size fits all approach. Conversely, there are a number of Web-based adaption systems that many users are already used to (e.g. Amazon's recommendation function). These systems include content recommendations (what did you do before?), collaborative recommendations (what do your friends like?), and hybrid recommendations that do both. The challenge for game-play, according to the author, is game-play requires constant and continuous adaptation. Further, game-play adaptation is used to challenge users (rather than recommend), is created implicitly (rather than asking users), and gathers/filters data in real time. In the end, Medler argues that game-based models have yet to take seriously the possibility of memory-based and complex collaborative-based filters. Exploring these features will lead to improved adaptive game-play.

Leveraging Open Source Technology in 3D Game Engine Development (Stowell, Scoresby, Coats, Capell & Shelton)

Stowell et al. informed readers about how game engines may be generated for educational projects. In the chapter, they discussed the 'nuances' of mixing core code with third party libraries to create fully functioning development environments. They conclude with a list of suggested practices for the use of open source libraries to develop 3D game engines. Their main findings suggest that using such libraries is a good practice, but it involves keeping abreast of updates and changes from other developers. Using the libraries can be important for budget considerations, but require learning throughout the process.

Section 2: Learning Outcomes of Games and Simulations

Although the word "learning" is often thought of as K-12 or post-secondary content, learning can also mean what happens in out-of-school contexts. Learning can also define outcomes beyond content, to focus on skills, attitudes, and behaviors. During 2009, there were five chapters that focused prominently on learning outcomes.

Promoting Civic Thinking through Epistemic Game Play (Bagley & Shaffer)

Bagley and Shaffer wrote about their interest in games and civic thinking. According to the authors, developing civic thinking goes beyond merely disseminating facts and information. It includes being guided by civic, social, and ecological values while applying real world skills to learning problems and opportunities. They proposed games as a way to provide a context for learning civic thinking. Using a game called *UrbanScience*, the authors guided students through urban planning through a series of mentored activities including a site visit, a survey, meetings, plans, and final proposals. Results from a study of middle school-age players found that gaming can provide a way by which students engage with complex civic problems. The authors content that students learned by understanding the concepts of *tool-as-obstacle* and *stakeholders-as-obstacle*. The resulting implications are that developers consider building non-player-characters with pro-social obstacles and then get teachers to engage such games to help students address an increasingly complex world.

Learning as Becoming: Values, Identity, and Performance in the Enaction of Citizenship Education through Game Play (Chee, Loke & Nanyang)

Chee et al. addressed the topic of citizenship in their study. They share a model of game-based learning using Space Station Leonis to teach students about citizenship education. Leonis includes a game, curriculum materials, learning processes, and then formative and summative assessments. The research participants from a government secondary school played the game, used a wiki, and then completed the formative assessments. Students were also asked to create an end-of-program campaign artifact to advocate for a certain position on a 'hot-topic.' The findings revealed that the program contributed to shaping students' values in educationally-preferred directions. Their work provides evidence of the use of games and simulations for dispositional shifts that are important for life in a globalized and multicultural world. Finally, they provided evidence of the possible positive outcomes of game-based learning in classroom contexts.

Rule of Engagement: The Presence of a Co-Player Does not Hinder Gamers' Focus (Gajadhar, deKort, & Ijsselstejn)

Recognizing the increasingly social aspect of digital gaming, Gajadhar et al. explored player experience, particularly as it related to enjoyment and involvement. Drawing on notions of flow, immersion, and engagement, the authors set out to study whether a player's focus was decreased with the involvement of others. Participants in this experience played *WoodPong*, and then completed a set of self-report measures around enjoyment, involvement, and social presence. The results indicated that additional players did not impact immersion, engagement, or flow. If anything, the authors argued that the increased social setting may have improved some outcomes. Their conclusion is that all models of game-play experience should take into account social play setting.

Game-Based Representations as Cues for Collaboration and Learning (Sharritt & Suthers)

Sharritt and Suthers were interested in how high school students used commercial game interfaces in game settings. Their particular interest was how the visualizations and behaviors of the game interfaces impacted collaboration and activity to support learning. In their study, three video games were selected and then played by two students using a single computer. Their results demonstrated key features necessary for learning. Consistency in game behaviors was critical to success, as was participant scaffolding. Inconsistent behaviors led students away from problem-solving and goal achievement. Feedback was also important, triggering new strategies from players. Such feedback also reduced uncertainty for participants. Finally, game representations helped with cognitive offloading, helping players learn how to accomplish their goals.

Designing Learning Activities for Sustained Engagement: Four Social Learning Theories Coded and Folded into Principals for Instructional Design through Phenomenological Interview and Discourse Analysis (Dubbels)

Dubbels used a qualitative approach to understand the experiences of an adolescent female as she learned about the video game "Dance Dance Revolution." His approach was to examine the game as an after school activity for helping teens become more physically active. Dubbels suggested the experience led to four main principles of play, including play as subjunctive mode, desirable activities, space, and desirable groups. In the end, the author argued that to sustain engagement, we must find a way to use these game experiences to help students turn play into meaningful experiences that resemble real-world rites of passage/initiation.

Section 3: New Theoretical Considerations of Games and Simulations

Many of the articles published at IJGCMS focus on practical outcomes or empirical evidence to support hypotheses. There is an important need for articles that use both practice and data to push our theoretical beliefs about games and simulations. During 2009, there were four articles that aimed to push our theoretical beliefs and models of games and game-play.

Computational Literacy in Online Games: The Social Life of Mods (Steinkuehler & Johnson)

In addition to research on playing games or developing games from scratch, Steinkuehler and Johnson argued for the importance of understanding user modding with existing games. Such an examination, they suggest, provides an important medium for studying computational literacy in the 21st century. As important, it helps move the research and practice field from computer to computational literacy. The authors provided two examples—*Auctioneer* and *Quark*—to highlight how modding can be done through an informal joint application-development model or through a single individual utilizing a reusable component model. Steinkuehler and Johnson end the piece by recommending that modding not only happens 'in the wild', it should happen in educational practice as a way of informing computational literacy, as a means of improving collaborative programming, and as a way to potentially bridge the digital divide.

What Players Like about Video Games: Prediction of Video Game Playing through Quality Perceptions and Player Types (Weber & Shaw)

In this chapter, Weber and Shaw described a need to understand more about how people select, play, and evaluate video games. They used two different research studies to specifically explore a theoretical link between motivations of video game play and operational features of video games. They hypothesized that quality perceptions and player types would predict video game playing, and that the combination of the two would better predict than each of the predictors alone. In study one, they interviewed participants about their game-play experience and their quality perceptions of game-play. In study two, 422 students were surveyed about their experience and perceptions of game-play. Their studies reported small to medium evidence about the predictability of quality perceptions, player types, and game-play. The implications are that developers and designers should clarify player types and features related to those types. As important, there are specific quality perceptions that might be most important for specific player types.

Play of Persuasion: Why "Serious" Isn't the Opposite of Fun (Fortugno)

Fortugno asked an important question about whether games need to be fun. He argued that in traditional game design, the answer is always yes. However, in serious game design, people wanted to be serious by substituting compelling or engaging for fun. Using examples from both the past and present, Fortugno makes the case that serious games can be fun. The implications for designers is that they should understand their goals (e.g. persuasion vs. attracting players), and then examine what game players do.

Researching and Developing Serious Games as Interactive Learning Instructions (Loh)

Loh strongly articulated a need for game developers to learn from tested procedures to avoid repeating mistakes of past developers. He includes a model that has been successfully tested and used in the production of serious games. That model includes a ten-step process focusing on the target audience, funding, writing game narratives, beta-testing, and efficacy assessment. Loh's main argument is that researchers do need to apply learning theories to game development, but they also need to avoid media 'no significant difference' studies in the process. A final important recommendation is the need for collaboration not just between researchers, but also between game developers, designers, educators, and players.

Section 4: Creating and Living in Virtual Worlds

One of the most popular areas of study in many fields relates to life online. The tremendous growth of online environments ranging from *Facebook* to immersive 3D worlds like *Second Life*, provide unique opportunities to explore how people represent themselves when given the opportunity to do so electronically. During 2009, there were five articles that focused prominently on life in virtual worlds.

Visual Analyses of the Creation of Avatars (Black, Ferdig, DiPietro, Liu & Whalen)

There has been a well-documented increase in popularity of multi-player gaming known as MMORPGs. In these MMORPGs, the game players use avatar to traverse their virtual worlds. The authors of this chapter argued that little work has been done in the area of avatar research. In their study, they gave students four different scenarios, asking them to create a hero avatar, a villain avatar, an avatar that most looked like themselves, and then an avatar that represented their ideal self. The researchers then used visual analyses to examine photos of the real person compared with their avatar. The findings indicated participants created avatars that most looked like themselves when they were asked to create hero or villain representations. Conversely, participants looked most unlike themselves when they were told to create an ideal or actual self representation. Finally, in all cases, participants refused to change enduring traits, changing only temporal things like hair color. This work provides insight into future avatar research, suggesting we need to learn more about how people represent themselves online.

A Test of the Law of Demand in a Virtual World: Exploring the Petri Dish Approach to Social Science (Castronova, Bell, Cummings, & Falk)

Castronova et al. reported on an economics experiment in a fantasy-based virtual world. The authors tested the Law of Demand, or the idea that when prices go up (keeping all else equal), demand will go down. The authors argue that they have found skeptics who believe a fantasy context invalidates human behavioral theory. Their study provides evidence to the contrary. They found evidence that such a demand exists in the virtual world; as such, they provide justification for the importance of continued, greater, and more sustained economic and social experiments within a social world. Additionally, they provide substantial cause for the continuing use of massive virtual worlds for researching human behavior.

Virtual Worlds for Teaching: A Comparison of Traditional Methods and Virtual Worlds for Science Instruction (Norton-Barker, Corbit, & Bernstein)

The goal of this study was to test the appeal and usability of gaming in four ninth-grade science classrooms. Groups of students were placed in an online world or in a traditional curricular environment; after a set period of time, the groups switched. The environment, called 'Jumping Genes', lets students master fundamental concepts while also needing to collaborate with others to succeed. The study found that students were enthusiastic about learning genetics in a virtual environment. Perhaps more importantly, students who were otherwise uninterested in school (and in science) were motivated to participate and engage in learning activities. Finally, according to the authors, this study provides evidence that a significant amount of learning can occur in virtual worlds.

Playing Myself or Playing to Win? Gamers' Strategies of Avatar Creation in Terms of Gender and Sex (Trepte, Reinecke & Behr)

Trepte et al. addressed the topic of avatars and gamers' strategies as they relate to gender and sex. The authors questioned why gamers select various attributes of their avatars, particularly relating to gender and sex. Their research provides an important look at both avatar choice and resulting enjoyment from game players. In their main study, participants received five game descriptions and were asked to create an avatar they wanted to play with using pre-tested attributes (e.g. leadership, beauty, etc.). They found players wanted characters they could identify with and yet were willing to manipulate those characters so they could achieve mastery of the game. The authors shed light on the fact that players want avatars like themselves as long as that does not prevent game success.

Investigating Perceptions of Avatar Creation for Use in Educational MUVEs (DiPietro)

DiPietro authored a study of the creation of avatars. DiPietro's early work examined what choices people will make when given the opportunity to create an avatar and when given a specific scenario. This new study followed that line of questioning and used qualitative inquiry to investigate the creation of avatars for interactions in virtual worlds. DiPietro found that users created avatars that mirrored their physical appearances and felt morally obliged to do so. There are obvious implications for teachers who may or may not ask participants to create realistic avatars, particularly for the first-world biases that might follow. A second major implication is the need for more research in understanding how avatar creation and use impacts online interactions.

Conclusion

The work that has been published on games and simulations in IJGCMS is continuing to advance research, policy, and practice. In conclusion, one could ask, what can we learn about the current state of the field from these twenty publications? Listed below are some of the key findings from each of these studies (by chapter number).

1. Augmented reality is an important new and effective medium for designers.
2. Game and simulation designers could increase their outcomes by considering the ways in which representations occur.
3. Game play can and does involve opportunities for ethical considerations. Designers can use this to their advantage, but should not ignore it.
4. There are multiple game player types; designers should consider the ways in which they can adapt game-play for certain users.
5. Adaptive game-play is a promising new area, but to be effective, designers should consider what Web adaptation models have already discovered.
6. 3D open source technologies are not problem-free, but designers could improve budgets and time-to-production with their use.

7. Game developers can use non-player-characters and other design features to help students address and understand civic engagement.
8. Games can be used to positively influence the dispositions and values of students.
9. Multi-player gaming does not decrease participant focus or flow.
10. Consistency, feedback, and the appropriate use of representations through game interfaces can positively impact student learning and cognitive overload/offloading.
11. Games and game-play can be used as hooks to help students then help students understand and explore real-world rites of passage.
12. Computational--rather than just computer--literacy is an important goal for designers and educators. Modding can be an important way to understand computational literacy.
13. Player types and quality perceptions are, at least at some level, predictive of game-play.
14. Serious gaming can be fun.
15. Game design research needs to move past media comparison studies.
16. People generally create avatars that look like themselves when put into scenarios rather than when told to create avatars like themselves.
17. Participants have similar human behaviors in fantasy worlds as they do in real life.
18. Students who are unmotivated to participate and engage in learning often change their mind when presented with virtual worlds.
19. Players often want avatars to represent themselves, as long as that does not interfere with their chances of winning.
20. Players often feel morally obligated to create avatars that look like themselves.

Richard E. Ferdig
Research Center for Education Technology - Kent State University, USA

Section 1
Design of Games and Simulations

Chapter 1
Lessons Learned about Designing Augmented Realities

Patrick O'Shea
Harvard University, USA

Rebecca Mitchell
Harvard University, USA

Catherine Johnston
Harvard University, USA

Chris Dede
Harvard University, USA

ABSTRACT

While utilizing GPS-enabled handheld computing units, we have developed and studied augmented reality (AR) curricula to help middle school students learn literacy and math. In AR, students move around an outdoor physical environment, interacting with virtual characters and artifacts on their handheld computer. These invisible objects and characters provide clues to help solve a mystery, guiding the students through a process of inquiry and evidence building. The first AR curriculum we developed, Alien Contact! is based on a scenario where aliens have crash landed near the students' middle school. Students, working in teams, learn math and literacy skills in the course of determining why the aliens have come to earth. This study describes the design heuristics used during the initial development and deployment of Alien Contact!, the results of two formative evaluations of this curriculum, and the impact these findings have had on revising our design heuristics for a subsequent AR curriculum about beached whales, called Gray Anatomy.

INTRODUCTION

Researchers are starting to study how AR modalities for learning aid students' engagement and understanding (Dunleavy, Dede, & Mitchell, in press; Klopfer & Squire, 2008; Klopfer, Yoon, & Perry, 2005; Klopfer, Yoon, & Rivas, 2004). This article explores the background of AR, describes the Handheld Augmented Reality Project (HARP) at Harvard University, explains the results from formative evaluations of the first AR curriculum created through HARP, and delineates how the lessons learned from this evaluation impacted the development of a subsequent AR curriculum.

THEORETICAL FRAMEWORK

The theory that learning occurs most effectively in authentic setting is not new. Hendricks (2001) stated that complex social interactions are at the heart of learning. Brown, Collins, and Duguid (1989) more precisely defined this thinking through their belief that individuals' interactions with their social teams lead to their adoption of learned behaviors. This phenomenon, which Hendricks called situated cognition, is different from practices in traditional educational settings. There is ample research to substantiate that social interactions are important for accomplishing challenging learning tasks. Bandura (1977), Vygotsky (1978), and Scaife and Bruner (1975) found that observation of and assistance from others at times precedes and always interacts with human cognitive development. Bandura (p.12) highlights the importance of "symbolic, vicarious, and self-regulatory" processes in social learning. As compared to a psychological view where learning is a matter of an individual "performing responses and experiencing their effects." Bandura elaborates on his theory that learning is a social process, explaining that we learn everything vicariously before we learn it directly because it is the only way we can "acquire large, integrated patterns of behavior without having to form them tediously by trial and error. The harder the task to be learned, the more we must learn it through observation first.

Hendricks (2001) found evidence to support the idea that practices based on situated cognitive theory can have significant impacts on immediate learning. Klopfer et al. (2004) focused on the use of technology to facilitate situated learning environments—particularly through the use of handheld and wearable computing devices. Through the use of *participatory simulations* they found that

students were more motivated, engaged, and excited by the process of participatory learning than they are by more traditional means of learning.

Motivation concerns the selective direction, energizing, and regulating of behavior patterns (Ford, 1992). It is central to persistence in learning and to producing positive outcomes (Ryan & Deci, 2000). Vygotsky (1978) found that, even before behavior sets in, through motivation we decide where we direct attention. There are different types of motivation, and they have different impacts on learning and sustaining learning (Ryan & Deci). Extrinsic motivation ranges from, at one end, a sense that our behavior is controlled by others who do things to regulate our behavior, to the other end, where we have a sense that we are in control of our own actions and get support from outside actors but little direct regulation of our behavior (Ryan & Deci). Most of the incentives to succeed academically in postsecondary education are designed to stimulate various forms of extrinsic motivation. For example, in a competitive classroom, some students' suboptimal performance, made explicit through student rankings and bell curves, serve as extrinsic motivators for other students to achieve.

There is strong evidence that cooperative learning is better for stimulating intrinsic motivation than competitive learning (Gehlbach, 2007). Classrooms that focus on cooperative learning make students responsible for one another's outcomes (Gehlbach). Social learning approaches may be more likely to foster intrinsic motivation, the form of motivation most likely to positively influence persistence, because it is the most self-directed form of behavior regulation and taps into our innate desire and capacity to seek out challenge and explore (Ryan & Deci, 2000). Later research by Klopfer et al. (2005) substantiated these earlier findings as to the impacts of simulations. More recently, Rosenbaum, Klopfer, and Perry (2007) placed their participatory simulations within the context of augmented reality.

AUGMENTED REALITY

Squire and Jan (2007) define augmented reality as "games played in the real world with the support of digital devices (PDAs, cellphones) that create a fictional layer on top of the real world context" (p. 6). Squire and Jan focus on place-dependent AR games, which require participants to come to specific locations to work through the game. Alternatively, place-independent AR games are designed to overlay game elements on a map of any physical location.

In AR environments, students interact with virtual and physical objects, people, and environments. Unique capabilities of AR include the amplification of real world environments, the ability of team members to talk face-to-face while interacting simultaneously in the virtual environment, and the capacity to promote kinesthetic learning through physical movement through sensory spatial contexts. In the form of AR that we studied, students utilize GPS-enabled wireless devices that allow them to engage with virtual information superimposed on the physical world. For example, a student may be guided by a map of Washington DC on their handheld to walk to the Lincoln Memorial. When they arrive, an image may appear of the memorial itself containing architectural specifications, or a movie may become accessible that talks about famous events in history that have occurred at this location, or they will be asked to perform a particular task. By infusing digital resources throughout the real world, augmenting students' experiences, improving their recognition of patterns, critical features, background information, and reinforcing what they are learning through multiple sensory experiences (i.e., hearing about the memorial from an expert, seeing it with their own eyes, and even possibly touching a feature of the memorial itself while seeing that feature explained up close on their handheld device). Unique capabilities of AR include the amplification of real world environments, the ability of team members to talk face-

to-face while interacting simultaneously in the virtual environment, and the capacity to promote kinesthetic learning through physical movement through sensory spatial contexts.

In addition, the current software developed to facilitate the delivery of AR curricula allows authentic team interactions and collaboration. This is due to the fact that the technology provides individuals within a team of students the ability to take on different roles within the augmented reality environment, thus allowing each individual to interact with the virtual elements in different ways than their teammates. While students may arrive at the same physical location as their group, a different artifact, interview, or task will appear on their handheld device than on their teammates who holds a different role. This is more authentic as a collaborative tool due to the fact that individual students within a team must collaborate and share information in order to progress through the game. The frequently seen suboptimal practice that team work is *turned over* to an individual student within the team to complete is not possible with this pedagogical approach; each individual must participate for the team to be successful.

THE HANDHELD AUGMENTED REALITY PROJECT

HARP is part of a three-year federal grant through the U.S. Department of Education Star Schools Initiative. HARP is a collaborative effort between Harvard University, the University of Wisconsin, and the Massachusetts Institute of Technology to study the efficacy of AR technology and curricula for the instruction of math and language arts at the middle-school level.

This project has as its primary objective to design and study engaging and effective augmented reality learning environments using wireless handheld computers equipped with GPS receivers. In order to do this, HARP personnel have developed an AR curriculum called *Alien Contact!* and a subsequent curriculum called *Gray Anatomy* that incorporates many of the lessons learned from formative evaluations of the earlier curriculum.

ALIEN CONTACT! CURRICULUM

We designed *Alien Contact!* to teach math and literacy skills to middle and high school students (Dunleavy et al., in press). This narrative-driven, inquiry-based AR simulation is played on a Dell Axim X51 handheld computer and uses GPS technology to correlate the students' real world location to their virtual location in the simulation's digital world (Figure 1).

As the students move around a physical location, such as their school playground or sports fields (Figure 2), a map on their handheld displays digital objects and virtual people who exist in an AR world superimposed on real space (Figure 3). When students come within approximately 30 feet of these digital artifacts, the AR and GPS software triggers video, audio, and text files, which provide narrative, navigation, and collaboration cues as well as academic challenges.

In *Alien Contact!* the students are presented with the following scenario: Aliens have landed on Earth and seem to be preparing for a number of actions, including peaceful contact, invasion, plundering, or simply returning to their home planet, among other possibilities. Working in teams (four pupils per team), the students must explore the augmented reality world, interviewing virtual characters, collecting digital items, and solving mathematics and literacy puzzles to determine why the aliens have landed. Each team has four roles: chemist, cryptologist, computer hacker, and FBI agent. Depending upon his or her role, each student will see different pieces of evidence. In order to successfully navigate the augmented reality environment and solve various puzzles, the students must share information and collaborate with the other members of their team. As students collect this data, they will discover different possibilities for why the aliens may have landed. It is up to the students to form hypotheses based upon the data collected. At the end of the unit, the students orally present their findings as a team to the class and support their hypothesis with data collected in the field (Figure 4).

In order to keep the game space uncluttered, only the current and next interactions are shown on the map at any one time. This reduces confusion pertaining to the order of the game, and clarifies where the students should progress to next. This is done through a *triggering* mechanism built into the game development editor. Each character or object with which the students interact activates the next character or object to appear in the progression and deactivates the previous character or object.

Figure 1. Dell Axim & GPS receiver

Figure 2. Students exploring school grounds

In its full form, *Alien Contact!* is a six-day, multidisciplinary curriculum that includes two days dedicated to playing the game, and four days interspersed to introduce concepts, allow for analysis and synthesis of data gathered during the game days, and enable students to develop and present their hypothesis for why the aliens have come to Earth. This curriculum is based on Massachusetts state standards and fosters multiple higher-order thinking skills. In designing this unit, HARP personnel targeted concepts in math and literacy typically difficult for middle school students to master. Using the spring 2005 8th grade MCAS test as a reference to determine high-need areas, project personnel focused primarily on aspects of ratio, proportion, and indirect measurement (Math Standard 6.M.3, 8.M.4, 8.N.3) in combination with how English vocabulary has been influenced by Latin and Greek languages (ELA Standard 4.18, 4.21, 4.24). However, other Math and ELA standards are embedded within the unit, such as reading graphs (Math 6.P.6, 8.D.2) and conducting team discussions and presentations (ELA 2.4, 3.8, 3.9, 3.11, 3.13).

This game also aligns with other standards. The Partnership for 21st Century Skills, a state-level, public-private partnership geared at making U.S. public education relevant in the 21st century,

Figure 3. Handheld display of digital objects on school grounds

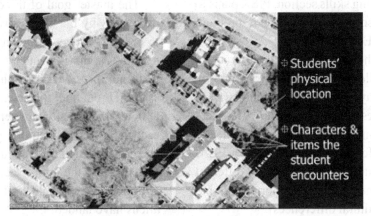

Figure 4. Students presenting their hypothesis

has recognized education's role in building social capital through education and how challenging this will be. The Partnership for 21st Century Skills believes key skills students need include: global awareness and civic literacy; communication and contextual learning; and leadership, ethics, and social responsibility (Hardy, 2007). The Organization for Economic Cooperation and Development (OECD) has included new measures in its Programme for International Student Assessment (PISA), a 42 country comparative study conducted every three years on the skills that 15-year-olds are developing in school. In 2003, PISA added a problem-solving section to its international assessment designed to assess cross-disciplinary, problem-solving skills. In future iterations of the problem-solving skills section, PISA plans to include an assessment of collaborative problem solving skills (OECD, 2008).

In addition, the game content and structure are designed to allow for multiple entry points on which teachers may build in future iterations (Dunleavy et al., in press). The design allows teachers the flexibility to emphasize: (1) different academic standards; (2) different content areas (math, ELA, science, social studies/history); and (3) different current events (energy crisis, oil shortage, global nuclear threat, cultural differences).

This design rationale is three-fold: (1) build in multiple entry points for teachers; (2) build in mathematical and linguistic patterns that, when recognized, reveal the ubiquity and mystery of mathematics and language; and (3) build in multiple layers of complexity that will engage and challenge students regardless of ability and will provide teachers opportunities for differentiation. As students engage in the mathematics and literacy of the content, the curriculum attempts to capitalize on some of the inherent properties of these fields that are fascinating (e.g., mapping latitude and longitude, ancient languages, and cultures) regardless of the standards that are targeted.

AR in general and *Alien Contact!* specifically incorporates several elements from popular video games that increase learning and engagement: (1) narrative and setting; (2) differentiated role playing; (3) master goal divided into subtasks; (4) interactivity; (5) choice; and (6) collaboration. In *Alien Contact!* the narrative and setting is the unfolding saga of the aliens' interactions with Earth. To infuse this situation with challenge and invite curiosity, each student's differentiated role is presented with an alternate, incomplete view of the game space. For example, when presented with a piece of alien spacecraft debris, each team member is given a different dimension of the wreckage to measure or a unique clue as to how to measure it. If the students do not collaborate, they will not be able to solve the problem and advance to the next stage of the game (Figure 5).

The master goal of the curriculum unit is to discover why the aliens have landed. However, in order to collect sufficient evidence to form a hypothesis, the students must successfully complete multiple subtasks requiring math and literacy skills. Throughout the scenario, the students interact with virtual characters, digital items, and each other to navigate the game space. Choice and collaboration are embedded within the entire unit. Finally, the entire scenario is open ended, with multiple possible explanations for why the aliens have landed.

Figure 5. Students collaborating to measure a physical object used in the AR gamespace

FORMATIVE EVALUATION

During the fall of 2006 and the spring of 2007 early iterations of the *Alien Contact!* curriculum were implemented for the purposes of conducting formative evaluation of the format. As there was no existing design for developing in-practice AR curriculum, much of this formative evaluation was intended to develop the heuristics for developing appropriate and effective AR curricula. The methodology and results of this pilot formative evaluation are described in depth by Dunleavy et al. (in press); however, for clarity purposes, the methodology and findings of this study are described here.

Utilizing a multiple case studies design, a series of data collection techniques were implemented at three sites (selected through convenience sampling) in order to gather in-depth information on how students and teachers perceived the AR curriculum. These data sources (including observations, formal interviews, informal interviews, and Web site postings) provide rich, contextual data that allowed for triangulation of results.

These data were qualitatively analyzed within each site using a structured-coding scheme that followed an initial open-coding process. The initial open coding resulted in 30 descriptive codes, which were then analyzed iteratively using pattern matching analysis. The analysis from each case study was then used for cross-case analysis to determine if there were similarities across implementations in usage and perceptions.

RESULTS

Through the analysis of case study data from the initial formative evaluation, Dunleavy et al. (in press) documented high student engagement during the implementations of the *Alien Contact!* AR curriculum. According to Dunleavy et al. "high motivation and engagement seems logical and almost a given during an activity that has students go outside with handheld computers and search for clues about aliens, it was nonetheless a critical threshold that needed to be reached during this first year of the AR design development."

Students and teachers reported several factors that played a role in motivating them throughout the curriculum implementation. Among the most common factors mentioned by both teachers and students were the use of the GPS-enabled handhelds themselves, the ability to collect data outside, and the interdependence of the roles within the team dynamic. In addition, teachers focused on how the AR curriculum engaged previously disengaged students (Figure 6).

However, in addition to the increased motivation, Dunleavy et al. (in press) also found significant logistical limitations in implementing AR curricula. In particular, hardware and software issues, particularly due to GPS errors, interfered with the seamless integration of this technology. Another issue dealt with the substantial management and technical support required to maintain the instructional process and the technology—a problem deemed to be *prohibitive* in any effort at scalability. Also of concern were findings of substantial cognitive overload on the part of students involved with the AR curriculum. Students and teachers indicated that learning the technology while also trying to work relatively complex

Figure 6. Students engaged in the AR game

Figure 7. Students playing the boardgame control curriculum

content problems caused confusion and led to some students giving up before completing tasks.

Another result from the research was the discovery of unanticipated competition between teams. Due to the linear nature of the learning path (that is, all students moved from one character to another in an identical and predictable progression), student teams were able to visually see where other teams were within the progression. Therefore, each team had the sense that they were either *ahead* or *behind* other teams in the game space. This led to student teams hurrying through the activities in order either keep pace or pass other students, whom they viewed as their competition. As would be expected, this resulted in students missing valuable information within the game space.

An additional unanticipated finding was a desire on the part of the students to know the *right* answer. As would be expected with students at the middle-school level, especially with those accustomed to commercially available games designed to provide closure, participants expressed a strong desire to know why the aliens were actually here at the end of the game (this was usually articulated through the focus group interactions). In most cases, the ambiguity of the

game's multi-hypothesis nature was difficult for these students to accept.

It is important to note that current implementations of the *Alien Contact!* curriculum are validating the findings from the formative evaluation—particularly where the issues of technical and logistical support are concerned. Students appear to be motivated by the AR curriculum; however, competition between student groups is present in nearly every implementation, and the issue of having the right answer continues to persist.

FURTHER EVALUATION

Building upon the formative evaluation conducted by Dunleavy et al. (in press), further research is being conducted to study the impact that *Alien Contact!* has on academic achievement and affect. Through a pre-test/post-test, control-group design, it will be possible to draw preliminary conclusions about how effective this version of an AR curriculum can be in an educational setting.

Data for this analysis is being collected during the spring of 2008. The control curriculum is identical to the *Alien Contact!* AR curriculum in terms of content, however, it is played inside using a board game rather than outside using the handheld computers (Figure 7).

MODIFICATIONS BASED ON FORMATIVE EVALUATION

HARP personnel responded to the results from the formative evaluations to better design a subsequent AR curriculum called *Gray Anatomy*. This section will describe the initial version of this new curriculum and the changes that were made to our AR design template based on the findings of the formative evaluations discussed previously.

Gray Anatomy

Gray Anatomy, just as is the case with *Alien Contact!,* is a scenario-based AR curriculum. As the game begins, students are presented with a scenario in which a gray whale has beached itself. Working in teams, the students must interview virtual characters, inspect virtual objects, and work through mathematics and language arts problems to determine what occurred and why the whale beached.

Similarly to *Alien Contact!,* this curriculum also focuses on middle-school, Massachusetts state math and language arts standards. In this case, the math standards revolve around data analysis, statistics, and probability (MCAS standards 6.D.1 and 8.D.3) and the ELA standards include thematic identification and support (MCAS standards 11.3 and 11.4), understanding a text (MCAS standard 8.19), and support hypotheses with evidence from text (MCAS standard 8.24). Additional standards that are touched upon are numbers and number sense (MCAS math standards 8.N.10 and 8.N.11), vocabulary and concept development (MCAS ELA standard 4.17), formal and informal English (MCAS ELA standard 6.6), questioning, listening, and contributing (MCAS ELA standard 2.4), and oral presentation (MCAS ELA standards 3.9, 3.11, and 3.12).

As with *Alien Contact!,* this curriculum incorporates the previously mentioned video game characteristics that increase learning and engagement. However, several substantial changes have been made to the game play in response to the results from evaluating *Alien Contact!'s* design.

Cognitive Overload

The most difficult of the concerns identified by evaluations of *Alien Contact!* was the issue of cognitive overload. Due to the fact that the overload was caused by difficulties synthesizing several tasks, each of which was relatively complex in and of itself and was dependent on the individual student, it was difficult to develop solutions to address the problem. For this reason, several steps were taken to mitigate complexity of the tasks required in the *Gray Anatomy* curriculum.

The first step taken was to limit the number of characters or objects that any student would interact with during a given time period. Initially, the *Alien Contact!* curriculum incorporated far too many characters and objects. Through the formative evaluation conducted by Dunleavy et al. (in press) as well as lessons learned through subsequent implementations of the AR curriculum, we determined that between five and six items or characters per AR session is optimal for progressing through the game in a timely, efficient, and effective manner. For this reason, each of the two game days involved with *Gray Anatomy* include a maximum of six interactions.

In addition in attempting to limit the scope of the interactions that any individual student might have, we also made efforts to limit the opportunities to misunderstand directions for given tasks. The *Alien Contact!* curriculum depends to a great extent on providing written textual directions to students. In many of these cases, the content required at least one scroll to complete the reading of the directions. Following several of the principles of game design for effective learning laid out by Gee (2003), it was decided to focus on using multimedia for the delivery of directions and content though the game. According to the work of Gee, by leveraging the technological capabilities of the handheld computers themselves, the AR games pace can effectively provide multimodal meaning (i.e., use materials other than text to provide meaning). In addition, by providing materials in other formats than simply through text, the curriculum can address semiotic principles (i.e., identifying and appreciating the interrelations between multimedia elements in a complex system) (De Oliveira & Baranauskas, 2000).

More tangentially, in response to a perceived need for greater clarity throughout the game, a new design paradigm was implemented for *Gray*

Anatomy. As HARP staff did not have any previous experience designing AR curricula, this first effort was done without a roadmap. In essence, project staff designed the process for developing an AR curriculum through the process of developing the AR curriculum itself. Based on lessons learned from this *bootstrapping* design strategy, a more structured development process utilizing a storyboarding approach was implemented for the development of *Gray Anatomy*. This process involved multiple meetings among HARP staff during which the broad strokes of the story involved with the curriculum were outlined. In these meetings, we decided that there would be various possible theories to why the whale would have beached, one of which would be a *correct* response. Documents were developed to guide the formulation of these different theories, and each member of the HARP team designed one set of evidence that can confirm or deny individual theories using these guides to assure consistency across the different answers.

Competition

The other major unanticipated issue seen throughout our evaluations of *Alien Contact!* was the competitive interactions among the student teams when playing the game. As was discussed earlier, this was generally due to the fact that all students followed the same path of characters and objects, and thus each team could see which other teams were ahead or behind them in that progression. On its face, competition is not necessarily a negative thing to build into a game; however, in this instance, it did have negative repercussions. Because of the competition, students who wished to *win* would rush through the individual interactions that make up the game and would miss important information that they needed to progress through subsequent characters or to identify possible support data for individual hypotheses.

In order to undercut this competition across teams, the HARP staff developed a nonlinear path

through the game. Instead of each character/object triggering the next character to appear along a proscribed path, an entry-point character will trigger all of the other characters in the game. This entry-point character will direct the students on the scope and sequence of the game playing experience and will inform them that each team must visit all of the other characters within the game space during the course of the AR event. The path through which the students progress can be determined by them, thus making it less likely that student teams will see other teams as ahead or behind them.

Modifications Based on Other Considerations

In addition to the modifications that were made based on our evaluation findings, there were also several modifications that came about due to informal analysis of the *Alien Contact!* curriculum and implementations that took place after the formative evaluation was conducted.

Flexible Roles

The first change occurred due to difficulties that were caused by the hard coding of four roles within the *Alien Contact!* curriculum. As was mentioned previously, students were placed into teams of four, with each of the students within a team taking on one of four roles (chemist, cryptologist, computer hacker, and FBI agent). However, the relative inflexibility of this system caused difficulty when there were a number of students that was not divisible by four. What would be done with any *excess* students? In implementations of *Alien Contact!* these additional students would be allocated to teams and would duplicate one of the four roles (thus a team might have two chemists). Obviously, this is not optimal due to the fact that the content was developed to assure that each of the students within a team would receive unique information that would need to be shared with other members of the team in order for the team to be successful. Having two students playing one role, although expedient, created a situation where the additional student was not necessary to the team's success.

In order to combat this situation, *Gray Anatomy* was designed with a flexible role structure. The AR editing software and the needs of the curriculum design still dictated the hard coding of roles within the game space. However, HARP personnel decided that two different versions of the game would be created. The first version would have three students in each team. Each of these three students would take on one of the following roles: marine biologist, oceanographer, and reporter. The second version of the game would entail two students pairing together to play the game. These two students would play the game as the marine biologist and oceanographer.

In keeping with the design paradigm used within *Alien Contact!*, the reporter would receive unique information within the three-person version of the game. The fact that this information would be necessary to progress through the game effectively created the problem of how to allocate the reporter's information to the participants within the two-person version of the game. The solution for this was to have the reporter incorporated as a character the paired students would interact with within the game space itself. Thus, each of the two students would still be receiving all of the information that any student working within the three-person version would see, while allowing the flexibility to accommodate any number of students without the need of duplication of roles.

Correct Answer

Another issue that was present within most of the implementations of the *Alien Contact!* AR game was a desire on the part of the students to know the correct answer to the question of why the aliens had come to earth. Manifesting itself within the focus team interviews that followed the full implementation of the curriculum, students asking for the *right* answer lead to discussions of the need to use data to support hypotheses in ambiguous situations. Although this is a valuable lessons for students to learn, and one that *Alien Contact!* attempts to convey, one of the strengths of many commercially available games is that they build to a climax and then offer closure (whether this is on a small scale based on individual tasks within a game or on a larger scale as the structure of the entire game). For this purpose, HARP personnel decided that *Gray Anatomy* would include such a correct answer.

This, however, presented its own unique challenge, as there is no explanation widely accepted in the scientific community as to why whales beach themselves. In a game based on having students answer this question, it is not appropriate to offer a solution as correct if the wider scientific community cannot support such an assertion. Such an act would provide students a false sense of the real world and would be impossible to support ethically.

The solution that the HARP staff decided on was to have a series of "crackpot theories" that were viable sounding, but which each had a "fatal flaw" that made them impossible to have actually caused the beaching. Thus, whichever theory was not fatally flawed could be seen as the correct answer to the simulation. HARP staff developed three theories, two of which are fatally flawed. These theories, along with the corresponding characters used to support or debunk them, make up the suite of interactions that each team of students has over the course of two days of outdoor AR interactions.

Redesigned Control

In order to do rigorous research into the efficacy of both AR curricula as an instructional strategy, we use a pre-test/post-test control group research design. As such, a board game version of the AR game is developed to act as the control curriculum to determine what value, if any, the technology adds. All content was the same as would be found in the AR curriculum, and the team dynamics remained the same. This board game consists of an 8x8 checkerboard, around which student teams move game pieces. Each of the 64 squares on the checkerboard corresponds to an envelope on a tri-fold poster demonstration board. According to where they were in the game, the team is directed to open a particular envelope, which holds cards that deliver the role-based content for that interaction. In addition, the teams are directed to move their game pieces to the corresponding next square on the checkerboard.

Using the version of the board game initially developed for *Alien Contact!*, HARP staff determined that the design of the board game made it unnecessary to interact with the actual checkerboard for all but the most ancillary activities. In order to make the interface more interactive and engaging, the board game portion of this control curriculum was redesigned. The new version of the board game includes a foam board image of a neighborhood with puzzle-piece shaped, yellow spaces interspersed throughout the image. As students move through the game, they receive puzzle pieces that show them with whom or what they were interacting with next and in which envelope that character's or object's information would be found. This redesign dramatically improved the *feel* of the board game and has created a situation where the students need to interact with the board, making the control curriculum more similar in its format to the AR curriculum.

Shorter Curriculum

Another modification made to the curriculum template for *Gray Anatomy* was to switch from a six-day to a five-day schedule. The *Alien Contact!* curriculum follows a staggered indoor/outdoor pacing. As was discussed earlier, four of the six days within the *Alien Contact!* curriculum are dedicated to work in a traditional classroom setting.

Each day immediately following the two game days are dedicated to analyzing and synthesizing the data that were gathered during the gameplay. This had the consequence of creating an awkward schedule that required more than one academic week for completion.

This awkwardness of the schedule led to a switch to a five-day curriculum plan for *Gray Anatomy*. Rather than having an analysis and synthesis day following each of the two game days, there is only one analysis day following two straight game days. It is postulated that this change will have dual benefits. The first benefit is to create a schedule that works within a single academic week. The second benefit is to create a more focused analysis opportunity.

Curriculum Focus

Another issue that has been addressed for *Gray Anatomy* was the focus on integrating the different content areas more meaningfully. *Alien Contact!* can be implemented as a math curriculum, an ELA curriculum, or a combination of math and ELA. The decision to split the combined curriculum and only implement that math or ELA content areas was made in order to facilitate the ability to recruit individual teachers for the project. If a math teacher wished to implement *Alien Contact!*, however, there was no corresponding ELA teacher to conduct those sections of the curriculum, so it would be more difficult to recruit teachers. The focus for Gray will be on an integrated math and ELA curriculum rather than on separate math and ELA. This is in line with skills that students need in their future work, which is interdisciplinary. It also significantly reduces logistical problems or need for so much technical support of setting up two different games.

Teacher Involvement

Finally, there is discussion about how to get the teachers themselves more involved in the delivery of the curriculum rather than having it be something that the research team comes in and does. It was never intended that the research team would teach the content itself, as the future of AR lies in its ability to be a seamless part of the learning environment run by the in-service teachers. With implementations of *Alien Contact!* it has been necessary for the research team to play a relatively large role in managing the content. In order to mitigate this for *Gray Anatomy* implementations, the game will be played fully with teachers before the students play so they themselves are engaged in situated learning and learn the process involved. This has the indirect benefit of getting buy-in from the teachers both for the technology and for the process of situated learning. Second, the HARP team is considering ways (both technological and non-technological) to have teachers gather feedback from students after the first outdoor day so they can more closely track individual student's progress and give them formative feedback to improve their experience for the second outdoor day.

CONCLUSION

The development and deployment of AR technologies is still in its early stages. Since these types of curricula incorporate nascent technology, taking the long view about their potential for student learning is appropriate. As Dede (2005) asks when discussing the learning styles associated with "Millennial" students, "What new forms of neomillennial learning styles might emerging media enable?" (p. 8). We know that students will increasingly bring learning strengths and preferences to the classroom derived from the ever more sophisticated and pervasive use of cell phones. This trend implies that instructional designs merging physical and virtual environments hold great promise for building on learners' emerging skills and inclinations. Our early research is promising in demonstrating AR can enhance student mo-

tivation, involvement, and excitement; and our current studies are examining the extent to which learning outcomes are enhanced over comparable control curricula.

As a field, instructional designers are at the beginning of identifying best practices for developing effective AR curricula. Systematically building on findings from early studies such as our work will not only improve later AR curricula, but also may lead to improvements in the technology itself, particularly as AR moves to its eventual target device, the cell phone. By migrating this emerging interactive medium from custom, school-supported PDA/GPS technologies to standardized, commercial-provider-supported, cell phone technologies, educators can realize the advantages of using ubiquitous, powerful devices students could bring from their homes to classroom settings.

AR can reach its full potential only when this leveraging of student-owned technologies is realized. Any instructional design that depends on school-based personnel maintaining and managing complex, custom sets of equipment has inherent weaknesses. Maintenance and management is time consuming, and the equipment is prone to obsolescence; the total cost of ownership by the school system is substantial when this includes initial purchase, maintenance, technical personnel, and replacement costs. Beyond those issues, if educators are responsible for equipment evolution, this will dramatically slow the advance of AR technologies. Compared to large telecommunications companies rapidly enhancing their equipment to gain market share in the lucrative cell phone market, educators have neither the technical capacity nor the competitive incentives to rapidly improve AR devices.

We estimate that, within a year or two, the next generation of cell phones can deliver the types of AR developed in our studies. Such a migration in AR infrastructure will require a substantial shift in how teachers and administrators treat cell phone usage in school settings. At present, many educators see cell phones as a barrier to effective instruction because of their potential to distract students' attention and to facilitate cheating. Once schools go beyond banning cell phones, or reluctantly accepting smart phone technology as a necessary evil, to instead developing ways to incorporate these powerful devices for the improvement of student learning, then educators will have a commercially supported learning infrastructure with which students are already familiar and fluent, paid for and maintained external to education, and available for learning inside of classrooms and out. AR is a fulcrum for leveraging this evolution.

REFERENCES

Bandura, A. (1977). *Social learning theory.* NJ: Prentice Hall.

Brown, J. S., Collins, A., & Duguid, P. (1989). Situated cognition and the culture of learning. *Educational Researcher, 18,* 32-42.

De Oliveira, O. L., & Baranauskas, M. C. C. (2000). Semiotics as a basis for educational software design. *British Journal of Educational Technology, 31*(2).

Dede, C. (2005). Planning for neomillennial learning styles. *Educause Quarterly, 28*(1), 7-12.

Dunleavy, M., Dede, C., & Mitchell, R. (in press). Affordances and limitations of immersive participatory augmented reality simulations for teaching and learning. *Journal of Science Education and Technology.*

Ford, M. (1992). Summary of motivational systems theory. In *Motivating humans* (pp. 244-257). Newbury Park, CA: Sage.

Gee, J. P. (2003). *What video games have to teach us about learning and literacy.* New York: Palgrave Macmillan.

Gehlbach, H. (2007, April 30). *Liking and co-operation.* PowerPoint slides on self perception presented in *T405 Social Dimensions of Teaching and Learning,* Cambridge, MA: Harvard Graduate School of Education.

Hardy, L. (2007). Children at risk: Graduation day. *American School Board Journal, 194*(9), 18-20.

Hendricks, C. (2001). Teaching causal reasoning through cognitive apprenticeship: What are results from situated learning? *The Journal of Educational Research, 94*(5), 302-311.

Klopfer, E., & Squire, K. (2008). Environmental detectives: The development of an augmented reality platform for environmental simulations. *Educational Technology Research and Development, 56*(2), 203-228.

Klopfer, E., Yoon, S., & Perry, J. (2005). Using Palm technology in participatory simulations of complex systems: A new take on ubiquitous and accessible mobile computing. *Journal of Science Education and Technology, 14*(3), 285-297.

Klopfer, E., Yoon, S., & Rivas, L. (2004). Comparative analysis of Palm and wearable computers for participatory simulations. *Journal of Computer Assisted Learning, 20,* 347-359.

Organization for Economic Co-Operation and Development (OECD). (2008). *What PISA assesses.* Retrieved April 30, 2007, from http://www.oecd.org/pages/0,3417, en_32252351_32235918_1_1_1_1_1,00.html

Ryan, R., & Deci, E. (2000). Self-determination theory and the facilitation of intrinsic motivation, social development, and well-being. *American Psychologist, 55*(1), 68-78.

Scaife, M., & Bruner, J. S. (1975, January). The capacity for joint visual attention in the infant. *Nature, 253,* 265-266.

Squire, K. D., & Jan, M. (2007). Mad city mystery: Developing scientific argumentation skills with a place-based augmented reality game on handheld computers. *Journal of Science Education and Technology, 16*(1), 5-29.

Vygotsky, L. S. (1978). *Mind in society. The development of higher psychological processes.* Cambridge, MA: Harvard University Press.

Chapter 2

Design Factors for Effective Science Simulations:
Representation of Information

Jan L. Plass
New York University, USA

Slava Kalyuga
University of New South Wales, Australia

Bruce D. Homer
CUNY, USA

Minchi Kim
Purdue University, USA

Catherine Milne
New York University, USA

Hyunjeong Lee
University of Seoul, Korea

Trace Jordan
New York University, USA

ABSTRACT

We argue that the effectiveness of simulations for science education depends on design features such as the type of representation chosen to depict key concepts. We hypothesize that the addition of iconic representations to simulations can help novice learners interpret the visual simulation interface and improve cognitive learning outcomes as well as learners' self-efficacy. This hypothesis was tested in two experiments with high school chemistry students. The studies examined the effects of representation type (symbolic versus iconic), prior knowledge, and spatial ability on comprehension, knowledge transfer, and self-efficacy under low cognitive load (Study 1, N=80) and high cognitive load conditions (Study 2, N=91). Results supported our hypotheses that design features such as the addition of iconic representations can help scaffold students' comprehension of science simulations, and that this effect was strongest for learners with low prior knowledge. Adding icons also improved learners' general self-efficacy.

What makes computer animations and simulations effective instructional tools for learning science? We currently see a growing excitement about using simulations, microworlds, and games to learn and teach, yet there are also voices who are concerned about the potentially high cognitive

DOI: 10.4018/978-1-60960-565-0.ch002

load involved in learning from such exploratory environments (Kirschner, Sweller, & Clark, 2006). Evidence is mounting that the effectiveness of visual environments for learning depends on a variety of design factors, including the information design and interaction design of the materials, and the level of cognitive load they impose. This paper will focus on one of these design factors, namely the type of representation chosen by the designer to depict key concepts in the simulation.

There is a wealth of research suggesting that the design of learning materials, including instructional simulations, must be consistent with the nature of human cognitive architecture and take into account limitations of our perceptual and cognitive systems (Mayer, 2001, 2005; Plass, Homer, & Hayward, 2009; Sweller, 1999). One such limitation is the capacity of working memory (Miller, 1956). Cognitive load theory (CLT) describes two different sources of cognitive load for learning materials that compete for the limited working memory resources of learners: *intrinsic cognitive load* and *extraneous cognitive load* (Sweller, 1999). Intrinsic load refers to the processing of essential information and is determined by the complexity of the material to be learned. Intrinsic load is often described as the level of element interactivity in learning materials, i.e., as the number of items a learner has to hold in working memory in order to comprehend the material. Extraneous load refers to processing non-essential information and is determined by the design of the instruction and the presentation of the materials, which includes the instructional format as well as the format of the representation of information (Sweller, 1999). Instructional designers aim to reduce extraneous cognitive load, especially in situations when intrinsic cognitive load is high.

Much of the research on cognitive load has been done on verbal materials or combinations of visual and verbal materials, showing that in order to be effective, temporal and spatial arrangements of the information, as well as the modality of the verbal information (e.g., narration versus on-screen text) must be taken into account (Brünken, Steinbacher, Plass, & Leutner, 2002; Brünken, Plass, & Leutner, 2003; Kalyuga, Chandler, & Sweller, 1999; Mayer, 2001; Rieber, 1991; Sweller, 1999). However, verbal and visual materials differ in significant ways that affect the amount of cognitive effort required to process information in these two formats. Whereas verbal information consists of discreet symbolic representations that are processed sequentially, visual information is inherently relational and its elements can be encoded simultaneously (Clark & Paivio, 1991). Because we are interested in identifying design factors for effective simulations, we focus in the present paper on cognitive load induced by visual materials.

Recent research in cognitive science and neuroscience has dramatically improved our understanding of how visual information is processed. Current working memory models include separate cognitive systems – the visuo-spatial sketchpad and the phonological loop – for processing visual and verbal information (Baddeley, 1986). There is a large body of research on the processes involved in the perception and comprehension of visual information (Levie, 1987; Winn, 1994), and for specific types materials, such as charts, graphs, and diagrams, effects of the design of visual displays on comprehension are well understood (Shah & Hoeffner, 2002; Winn, 1991). Researchers have studied the comprehension of graphics and pictures (Schnotz & Kulhavy, 1994; Willows & Houghton, 1987) and how learning scientific information from diagrams, maps, and charts can be more effective than learning from text (Guthry, Weber, & Kimmerly, 1993; Hegarty & Just, 1993; Kosslyn, 1989; Levie & Lentz, 1982; Mandl & Levin, 1989; Shah & Carpenter, 1995; Winn, 1991). Much less empirical research is available on the design of educational simulations.

LEARNING FROM ANIMATIONS AND SIMULATIONS

There has been significant interest in the use of simulations and animations in education. Initial research was concerned with the comparison of the educational effectiveness of animations, i.e., visualizations that change over time, to that of static visualizations (Höffler & Leutner, 2007). Reviews of this research have not been able to identify overall benefits of animations over static pictures. Instead, they suggest that a more appropriate approach is to ask under what conditions and for whom one type of visualizations might be more effective than the other (Betrancourt, 2005). Other reviews have found that learner variables such as prior knowledge moderate the effectiveness of these representations, with low prior knowledge learners benefiting more from static images, and high prior knowledge learners benefiting more from dynamic visualizations (Kalyuga, 2006). In some cases, research has even shown that dynamic visualizations can interfere with learners' performance of relevant cognitive processes, resulting in *worse* learning outcomes compared to non-animated, static visualizations (Schnotz, Böckler, & Grzondziel, 1999). There are also indications that the effectiveness of a particular animation depends on the design of the visualization, especially the appropriateness of the design for the specific learning goal and related tasks (Schnotz & Bannert, 2003).

In comparison to animations, which do not allow for significant user interactions, simulations can represent complex dynamic systems in which learners can manipulate parameters to explore and observe the behavior of a system (Gogg & Mott, 1993; Towne, 1995). This exploratory nature of simulations allows learners to engage in processes of scientific reasoning, i.e., problem definition, hypothesis generation, experimentation, observation and data interpretation (De Jong & van Joolingen, 1998; Kim & Hannafin, 2010a; Towne, 1995). Therefore, simulations have the

potential to allow learners to understand scientific phenomena and transfer knowledge to novel situation better than other visual representations. In addition, while learners experience difficulties interpreting information from multiple representations such as text, pictures, and animation, the dynamic visualizations of system behavior in simulations can assist learners in interpreting concurrent changes in variables by revealing the underlying computational model (de Jong, 1991; Van der Meij & de Jong, 2006).

Although there are advantages to using simulations, learning from interactive simulations can also impose high cognitive load because some learners may not possess the required knowledge, cognitive abilities or metacognitive skills necessary to pursue scientific reasoning through simulations (Kim & Hannafin, 2010b; De Jong, & van Joolingen, 1998). Even though the integration of information in a simulation can help learners understanding the dynamic relationship between variables and representations, cognitive resources are required to relate the multiple changes that occur simultaneously in the various representations within a simulation (Van der Meij & de Jong, 2006). The integration of multiple representations may therefore result in high cognitive load (Lowe, 1999; Van der Meij & de Jong, 2006). Lowe (2003) attributes this added cognitive load to the changes in the form of representation, position of visual entities, and inclusion (appearance and disappearance) of visual components, which add to the visual complexity of simulations. Such a high degree of visual complexity may interfere with extraction and integration of relevant information from dynamic representation and incorporation of the information into learner's prior knowledge (Lowe, 2003).

In order to optimize the information design and interaction design of simulations, it is useful to identify design principles that are based on an understanding of how our cognitive architecture processes information. Several design factors for effective simulations for science learning have already been identified (Plass, Homer, & Hayward, 2009). For example, one line of research has investigated how learners can be supported to overcome the challenges imposed by the scientific reasoning processes (De Jong & van Joolingen, 1998). In particular, this research focused on providing direct and timely access to domain knowledge (Elshout & Veenman, 1992; Leutner, 1993) and the activation of learner's prior knowledge to assist the integration of experimental outcomes from simulation (Lewis, Stern & Linn, 1993). Research has also focused on methods of clearly communicating learning goals by providing different assignments (de Jong et al, 1994; Swaak, van Joolingen & de Jong, 1998). Research on metacognition in learning from simulations investigated the use of metacognitive scaffolds to support hypothesis generation (Quinn & Alessi, 1994; Shute & Glaser, 1990; van Joolingen & de Jong, 1991), and how to provide metacognitive support to monitor learning and discovery processes (Gruber, Graf, Mandl, Renkl & Stark, 1995; Njoo & de Jong, 1993).

Other research on design factors has examined questions related to the difficulty of the information presented, investigating, for example, the effect of the number of variables in the simulation model (Quinn & Alessi, 1994) and how learning is affected by the available level of control over variables (Rieber & Parmley, 1995). This line of research also showed that the interactivity afforded by simulations, especially the possibility to manipulate the content of the visualization by adjusting parameters, improved learning (Chandler, 2004; Hegarty, 2004; Plass, Homer, Milne, & Jordan, 2007; Plass et al., 2009; Rieber, 1990; Wouters, Tabbers, & Paas, 2007), and increased intrinsic motivation (Rieber, 1991).

In summary, research on learning from simulations has shown that the cognitive load imposed by the dynamic and often complex content and by the requirements of interacting with the simulation may pose significant challenges for learners (Plass et al., 2009). Several design factors have

been identified to address this issue, especially related to the difficulty of the simulations and to the support of learners' scientific inquiry and metacognition, and the impact of different levels of learner control and interactivity. Our research aims at identifying load-reducing design features that are related to the information design, or visual design, of simulations. In the present research, we focus on the question of how the type of representation of key concepts in a simulation affects cognitive and affective learning outcomes. We are also interested in the question of how learner characteristics may moderate the effects of representation type.

REPRESENTATION OF KNOWLEDGE

In science education, important information is often presented visually, e.g., in charts, graphs, or diagrams, both amongst experts and for relative novices in a classroom setting. There are many advantages to representing information visually, however, the interpretation of visual representations requires a certain amount of domain-specific knowledge and visual literacy. Representations that are most efficient for experts may be difficult to comprehend for novice learners. This suggests that the particular format of visual representations should be considered when designing materials for novice learners.

Schnotz distinguishes two types of representations for his *Integrative Theory of Text and Picture Comprehension*, namely descriptive and depictive representations (Schnotz & Bannert, 2003). Descriptive and depictive representations are similar to the symbols and icons identified in Peirce's (1955) classification of signs that increase in complexity and abstraction: *icons* (depictive representations), which are the most basic, rely on physical resemblance to convey meaning, and *symbols* (descriptive representations) are abstract, arbitrary and rely on social conventions for meaning[1]. Deacon (1997) argues that the different types of representations (i.e., icon, index, and symbol) correspond to a developmental trajectory through which learners progress whenever acquiring symbolic representation in a new domain. A learner's developmental state affects how a sign is actually interpreted, with a true understanding of symbols not being possible until a certain level of knowledge has been acquired (Homer & Nelson, 2005). Instructional simulations are often designed by domain experts and use abstract, symbolic representations that assume domain-specific knowledge that may be lacking in novice learners. Novices may actually benefit more from the use of basic, iconic visual representations in simulations.

This research suggests that for novices in a particular domain, iconic visual representations may be more easily understood that symbolic representations, and therefore, icons should be incorporated into the design of visual materials for novice learners who possess low prior knowledge in the domain. Yet, what are the possible consequences of adding icons to a display that already represents the information in symbolic format, i.e., as numbers and words? From a computational perspective of visual complexity, adding any visual elements to a visual display would lead to a more complex visual display. Because of this increased level of visual complexity, a higher amount of cognitive resources would be required to process this information. From a computational perspective, therefore, adding icons to the simulation would increase cognitive load and, in turn, reduce learning. Yet, from an information design perspective informed by a cognitive load approach, adding icons that represent key concepts in the simulation display (for example, depicting temperature as burners and pressure as weights, see Figure 2) should enhance learning, especially for students with low prior knowledge. From this perspective, adding icons provides learners with representations that they can better relate to their prior knowledge.

Our prior research provides preliminary findings on this issue. We have found that adding iconic representations of key information in a computer-based simulation was one of the design features that affected the cognitive load imposed by interacting with the simulation and improved learning outcomes (Lee, Plass, & Homer, 2006). This is consistent with previous research that showed a different effectiveness of written and pictorial instructions (Carlson, Chandler, & Sweller, 2003). Carlson et al. found that written and pictorial instructions were equally effective for building simple molecular models. However, for building complex molecules the pictorial directions (i.e., iconic representations) were more effective for students than the written directions (i.e., symbolic representations). These results indicate that pictorial, iconic representations reduced cognitive load compared to the written, symbolic information, freeing cognitive resources and allowing students to solve complex tasks. Research has also found that feedback in simulations is more effective when it is provided in graphical rather than textual form (Rieber, 1996; Rieber, Tzeng, & Tribble, 2004; Rieber et al., 1996)

LEARNER CHARACTERISTICS

The cognitive load generated by processing visual representations depends not only on the design of the visual displays, but also on characteristics of specific learners, and, in particularly, their prior knowledge (e.g., Kalyuga, 2006; Lee et al., 2006; Mayer & Sims, 1994; Plass, Chun, Mayer, & Leutner, 2003). Prior knowledge, i.e., organized knowledge structures from long-term memory, can reduce working memory limitations by chunking several bits of related information together into a single, higher-level element (Chi, Glaser, & Rees, 1982). Prior knowledge in the domain of the subject matter being taught is one of the strongest predictors of learning outcomes in most learning environments, a phenomenon recently described in terms of an *Expertise Reversal Effect* (Kalyuga, 2006; Kalyuga, Ayres, Chandler, & Sweller, 2003). In accordance with general cognitive studies of expert-novice differences (e.g., Chase & Simon, 1973; De Groot, 1965), studies on the expertise reversal effect have found that many instructional design techniques that are highly effective with less knowledgeable learners, lose their effectiveness and can even have negative consequences when used with more experienced learners, and vice versa.

A number of studies of individual differences in learning from text and visual displays have demonstrated that the instructional advantages of diagrams depend on student domain-specific knowledge and experience (e.g., Hegarty & Just, 1989; Lowe, 1993; Schnotz, Picard, & Hron, 1993). Less knowledgeable learners can have difficulty processing visual information because of the limited capacity of working memory and a lack of background knowledge required to easily interpret the visual information. Cognitive load increases when novice learners have to interpret the meaning of symbolic representations that implicitly assume prior domain-specific knowledge. Acquiring sufficient knowledge in a domain reduces working memory load and allows for effective learning from more abstract, symbolic representations by tapping into relevant schematic representations already held in long-term memory.

THE PRESENT STUDIES

The studies presented here were conducted to investigate the impact of adding iconic representations of key information to a simulation of the Kinetic Theory of Heat. These simulations were designed for high school chemistry with the goal of fostering students' science learning as well as increase their science-related self-efficacy. Self-efficacy, i.e., learners' predictive judgment of their efficacy of performing a task (Bandura, 1986), relates to self-regulation (Zimmerman, 2000) and is a predictor of learning success (Pajares, 1996). We had found in our previous research that the RAPUNSEL game, which was developed to teach middle school students how to program, was able to improve students' computer-related self-efficacy (Plass et al., 2007). We argue that RAPUNSEL was able to increase self-efficacy by allowing even low prior-knowledge learners to successfully program. In the current study, therefore, we proposed that the addition of icons would make the chemistry simulations more comprehensible for low prior-knowledge learners and therefore improve their self-efficacy.

For the current study, we were therefore interested in the effect of iconic representations on learning outcomes, both the comprehension of the principles of Kinetic Theory as well as the transfer of this knowledge to new situations. In addition, we were interested whether adding iconic representations would affect learners' self-efficacy. Of particular interest was the interaction of design features and learner characteristics. The expertise reversal effect would predict that adding iconic representations to simulations would be effective only for novice learners and would become less effective as learners' levels of expertise increased. Adding redundant, iconic representations can help novices learn by providing a context for interpreting the visual information. Therefore, we expected that adding iconic representations to symbolic information would improve learning for low-prior knowledge learners, but will have little or no effect on high-prior knowledge learners. We also included a measure of spatial ability into the design of the study in order to examine possible moderating effects of this learner variable. We hypothesized that icons would assist learners with low prior knowledge, as well as learners with low spatial ability.

Study 1

Participants and Design

The participants for this study (N = 80; approximately 40% female) came from a large public high school in rural Texas. A majority of the students were of Hispanic decent (88%) with the remaining students being White (non-Hispanic) (10%), African-American (1%) or "other" (1%). The students ranged from 16-18 years of age (M = 17) and had not studied any materials related to the simulation content (i.e., kinetic theory of heat). Participants were randomly assigned to one of two treatment conditions: One group received the simulation with symbolic representations only, i.e., without icons (SYMB), the other group received the same simulations with added icons for key information (ICON), see Figure 1 and Figure 2.

Materials

The computer-based instructional materials included two versions of a simulation of the *Ki-netic Theory of Heat* designed using Flash MX 2004 software (Macromedia, 2004), which was delivered on a web page and viewed by learners on desktop PCs. The versions varied in their type of representation (*symbolic* versus *iconic*). In the *symbolic* version of the simulation, essential information was presented in symbolic format (e.g., numbers were given to indicate pressure and temperature), while in the *icon* version, iconic representations were added to represent the same essential information. Figures 1 and 2 are screenshots from the *Kinetic Theory of Heat* simulations with and without icons.

Independent variables included demographics and learners' prior knowledge, spatial ability, and self-efficacy. The computer-based *demographic questionnaire* asked students about their age, gender, ethnicity, and prior chemistry experience. The *knowledge pre-test*, also administered on the computer, consisted of 8 items. Two short-answer questions tested general knowledge of situations that involve properties of gas, and 6 multiple-choice questions tested for knowledge of kinetic theory of heat. Learners received up to

Figure 1. Screen shot from the Low-Load Kinetic Theory simulation without chart, with symbolic representations

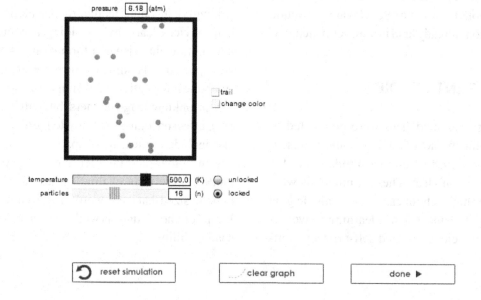

Figure 2. Screen shot from the Low-Load Kinetic Theory simulation without chart, with added iconic representations

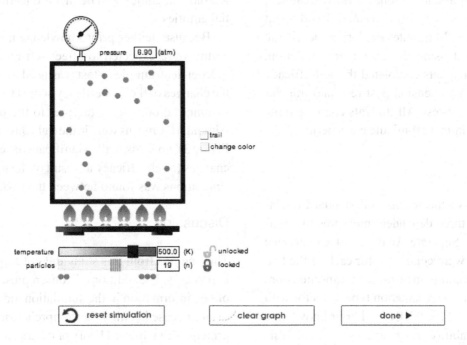

two points for each open-ended question and one point for each correct multiple-choice item. Two raters scored the short answers. When their scores differed, the raters resolved their disagreements through discussions of the merit of the response. Learners' *spatial ability* was assessed using a paper-and-pencil version of the water-level task (Piaget & Inhelder, 1956), in which participants were shown 6 pictures of empty bottles in different orientations and were asked to draw what the water level would look like if the bottles were half-full of water. The degree to which the drawn line deviated from the horizontal line was recorded and an average "deviation" score was calculated for each participant. Learners' pre-treatment *self-efficacy* was assessed using a computer-based 11-item scale adapted from Jinks and Morgan (1999).

The dependent measures included a comprehension test, knowledge transfer test, and a test of learners' self-efficacy. The *comprehension post-test* included 10 item multiple-choice questions that tested learners' understanding of the kinetic theory of heat. Learners received one point for each correct answer. The *knowledge transfer post-test* consisted of 6 open-ended items in which learners were asked to provide written explanations of different phenomena and real life applications of the kinetic theory. Learners received up to two points for their response to each question. Two scorers rated the written responses, using the method described above for the knowledge pre-test. Learners' post-treatment *self-efficacy* was assessed using the same measure as the pre-test.

Procedure

Participants were tested in groups of approximately 15-20 students in grades 11 and 12. The study took place in a science classroom with each participant working on an individual computer. Participants were first provided with an overview of the study, and all students consented to participate. They then completed the demographics questionnaire, knowledge pre-test, self-efficacy pre-test, and water level task. Participants were then randomly assigned to one of the two treatment conditions (i.e., *iconic vs. symbolic*) and spent approximately 20 minutes exploring the kinetic theory of heat using the computer simulation. Finally, participants completed the self-efficacy post-test, comprehension post-test, and transfer knowledge post-test. All students completed the procedure within a 50-minute class period.

Results

Table 1 shows the means and standard deviations for all three dependent measures by treatment group. Separate Analyses of Covariance (ANCOVA) were conducted for each of the two learning outcome measures (comprehension, transfer), with representation type as factor with two levels (SYMB, ICON) and prior knowledge and spatial ability as covariates. The analysis model included interactions between prior knowledge and representation type and spatial ability and representation type.

For comprehension, there was only a significant main effect of prior knowledge, $F(1, 74) = 20.48$, $MSE = 161.23$, $p < .001$, partial eta squared $\eta^2_p = .22$. Similarly, the only statistically significant finding for transfer was a main effect of prior knowledge, $F(1, 74) = 12.05$, $MSE = 31.72$, $p = .001$, partial eta squared $\eta^2_p = .14$. In other words, learners with higher prior knowledge comprehended the simulation better and were able to provide more answers to transfer questions than learners with low prior knowledge. Adding icons

to the simulations did not have an impact on learning outcomes, and neither did learners' spatial abilities.

Because neither prior knowledge nor spatial ability were expected to affect self-efficacy, an independent samples t-test was used to compare the changes of the self-efficacy scores for the two treatment groups from the pre- to the post-test. Although the means were in the right direction (see Figure 3), no statistically significant difference in changes to self-efficacy as result of the use of the simulations was found between the two groups.

Discussion

The findings from this study did not support our hypotheses: The addition of iconic representations of key information in the simulation did not lead to an increase in either the comprehension of the principles of Kinetic Theory or the transfer of this knowledge to new situations. In addition, although the directions of the means of the changes to self-efficacy were as expected, with self-efficacy scores decreasing after use of the simulations without icons and self-efficacy scores increasing after use of the simulation with icons, these differences were not statistically significant.

What may have led to these findings? Previous research has shown that methods to reduce extraneous load were only necessary when the overall load of the learning task was high (Plass et al., 2009). Likewise, we only expect spatial ability to impact learning outcomes when the overall learning task is difficult (Plass et al., 2003). It is

Table 1. Mean (SD) Scores for Knowledge Pre-test, Comprehension and Transfer Post-tests, and Change to Self-efficacy (post-test minus pre-test) by Simulation Design Condition, for Low Cognitive Load Simulation (no chart)

	Knowledge Pre-Test	Comprehension Post Test	Transfer Post Test	Self-Efficacy Change
No Icon (N =38)	4.78 (1.60)	9.92 (3.42)	2.85 (1.71)	-.51 (4.02)
Icon (N = 42)	3.97 (1.50)	9.57 (3.01)	2.54 (1.82)	.42 (4.61)

Figure 3. Self-efficacy changes for Low-Load simulations by treatment group (iconic vs. symbolic)

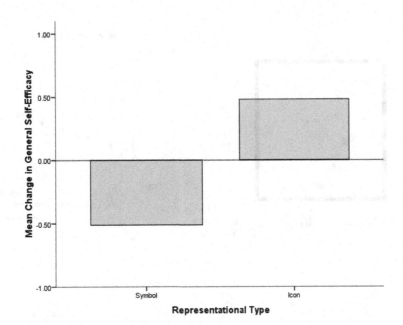

possible that the cognitive load experienced by students during learning with this simulation was not very high. We therefore decided to increase the load induced by the learning activity by adding a second representation of the simulation content. This second representation was a chart, commonly found in simulations, which displayed the results of the learners' explorations of the simulation on the right side concurrently with the changes to the simulation on the left. Prior research has shown that processing of multiple representations that were dynamically linked placed high demands on learners' cognitive processing (Van der Meij & de Jong, 2006; Plass et al., 2009). Study 2 was a replication of Study 1 with these revised materials that induced higher cognitive load.

Study 2

Participants and Design

The participants for this study (N = 91; approximately 40% female) came from a large public high school in rural Texas. A majority of the students were of Hispanic decent (88%) with the remaining students being White (non-Hispanic) (10%), African-American (1%) or "other" (1%). The students ranged from 16-18 years of age (M = 17) and had not studied any materials related to the simulation content (i.e., kinetic theory of heat). Participants were randomly assigned to one of two treatment conditions: One group received the simulation with chart and with symbolic representations only, i.e., without icons (SYMB), the other group received the same simulation with chart with added icons for key information (ICON), see Figure 4 and Figure 5.

Materials

The computer-based instructional materials included the same two versions of a simulation of the *Kinetic Theory of Heat* as in study 1, with the addition of a chart to the right of the simulation. The two versions varied in their type of representation (*symbolic* versus *iconic*).

Figure 4. Screen shot from the High-Load Kinetic Theory simulation with chart, with symbolic representations

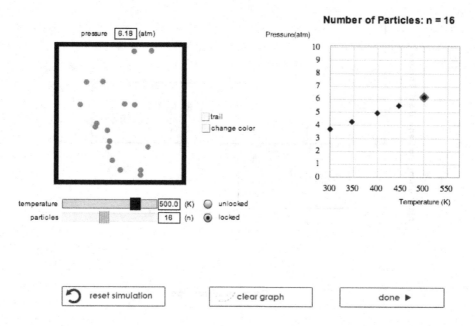

Figure 5. Screen shot from the High-Load Kinetic Theory simulation with chart, with added iconic representations

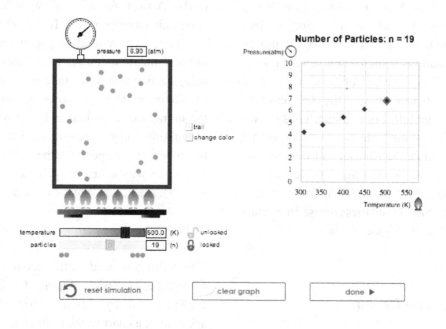

Independent variables included the same demographic questionnaire and measures of learners' prior knowledge, spatial ability, and self-efficacy as in study 1.

The dependent measures included the same comprehension test, knowledge transfer test, and measure of learners' self-efficacy as study 1.

Procedure

As in study 1, participants were tested in groups of approximately 15-20 students in grades 11 and 12. The study took place in a science classroom with each participant working on an individual computer. The procedure used for this study was the same as in study 1, with the exception of the treatments, as described above.

Results

Table 2 shows the means and standard deviations for all three dependent measures by group. Separate Analyses of Covariance (ANCOVA) were conducted for each of the two learning outcome measures (comprehension, transfer), with representation type as factor with two levels (SYMB, ICON) and prior knowledge and spatial ability as covariates. The analysis model included interactions between prior knowledge and representation type and spatial ability and representation type.

For comprehension, there were significant main effects of representational type, $F(1, 85) = 5.91$, $MSE = 40.96$, $p < .05$, partial eta squared $\eta^2_p = .065$; of prior knowledge, $F(1, 85) = 5.17$,

$MSE = 35.87$, $p < .05$, $\eta^2_p = .06$; and of spatial ability, $F(1, 85) = 7.52$, $MSE = 52.18$, $p < .01$, $\eta^2_p = .08$. A significant interaction was found for representational type and prior knowledge, $F(1, 85) = 5.03$, $MSE = 34.91$, $p < .05$, $\eta^2_p = .06$. The interaction of representational type and spatial ability failed to reach significance. Figure 6 illustrates the interaction of pre-test scores and treatment condition for the comprehension test. In both conditions, post-test comprehension scores increased with higher pre-test scores, however, this difference between high and low scores was less in the icon condition.

For transfer, the only significant finding was a main effect of prior knowledge, $F(1, 85) = 10.82$, $MSE = 27.82$, $p = .001$, $\eta^2_p = .11$. The relatively low scores the students received on the transfer post-test, with an average score of 2.5 out of a maximum possible of 12, suggests that there may be a floor effect for transfer.

The comparison of the changes of the self-efficacy scores of the two treatment groups from pre- to post-test showed that self-efficacy increased for learners using the simulations with icons, and decreased for learners who received the simulation without icons, see Figure 7. These differences are statistically significant, $t(87) = -1.90$, $p < .05$ (one-tailed), $d = .40$, which is considered a medium to small effect.

Discussion

Study 2 tested hypotheses on how computer simulations can be designed to optimize cognitive

Table 2. Mean (SD) Scores for Knowledge Pre-test, Comprehension and Transfer Post-tests, and Change to Self-efficacy (post-test minus pre-test) by Simulation Design Condition, for High Cognitive Load Simulation (with chart)

	Knowledge Pre-Test	Comprehension Post Test	Transfer Post Test	Self-Efficacy Change
No Icon (N = 45)	4.53 (1.52)	10.18 (2.87)	2.64 (1.51)	-.20 (2.17)
Icon (N = 46)	4.13 (1.42	10.28 (2.97)	2.28 (1.87)	.93 (3.33)

Figure 6. Relation between prior knowledge and comprehension for iconic and symbolic conditions

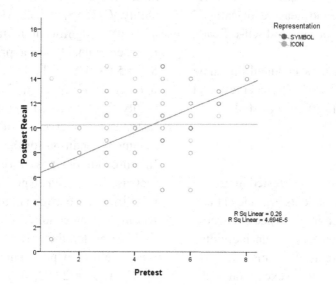

Figure 7. Self-efficacy changes for High-Load simulations by treatment group (iconic vs. symbolic)

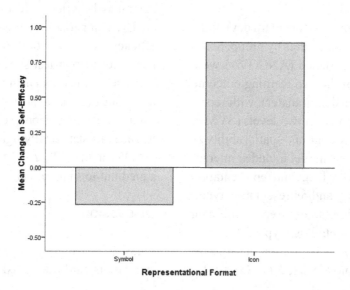

load and increase learning outcomes. Of particular interest was how the representation type of visual information in the simulation interacts with learners' levels of prior knowledge and spatial ability. Empirical evidence was obtained by allowing high school students with different levels of knowledge of chemistry and different levels of spatial ability to interact with different versions of a simulation of the kinetic theory of heat.

The analysis of the comprehension test results showed that adding icons increased learning for all learners, independent of their prior knowledge or spatial ability. The interaction of prior knowledge and representation type indicates that learners with low prior knowledge especially benefited from the simulation with added icons. Learners with high prior knowledge still benefited, but less so than those with low prior knowledge, which is in line with our predictions.

The analysis also revealed that learners with high spatial ability overall comprehended the simulation better than learners with low spatial ability, which is in line with prior research on the effect of spatial ability on multimedia learning (Plass, Kalyuga, & Leutner, 2010). These patterns were not replicated for the transfer test, but the low mean scores on this test suggest a floor effect.

GENERAL DISCUSSION

What makes computer animations and simulations effective instructional formats for learning science? Our research suggests that design factors such as the type of representation of key concepts in the simulation affect the effectiveness of computer simulations when cognitive load is high, and that individual difference variables such as prior knowledge moderate these effects.

The results from the simulations with higher cognitive load, which included a chart with the data points obtained in the simulation, show that adding iconic representations resulted in an overall improvement of comprehension of the content of the simulation. In addition, we found that especially learners with low prior knowledge benefited from the added icons, whereas learners with high prior knowledge benefited less from icons or may even have found them distracting. This is in line with the expertise reversal effect, which has been observed under a variety of conditions, and which states that materials that are effective for novice learners are often not effective for learners with high prior knowledge, and vice versa. Translated to our study, learners with low prior knowledge comprehended the kinetic theory of heat better when learning from a simulation with icons added. This effect is much smaller for

learners with higher prior knowledge. We should note that since none of the learners had studied the topic of Kinetic Theory of Heat before, even high prior knowledge learners in this study were far from being experts on the topic. We therefore did not see a complete reversal of the effectiveness of the two simulations, which one might expect if this study were replicated, for example, with chemistry majors in a college setting.

Perhaps even more interesting than the results for learning outcomes are our findings for the changes learners' perceived self-efficacy. Adding icons to the simulation not only increased learners' comprehension of the chemistry concepts, but also improved their perception of their own ability to learn. In contrast, simulations without icons, representing information only symbolically, resulted in a reduced perception of learning ability. The type of information representation in this simulation affected learners' self-assessment of their ability to learn chemistry, specifically, icons appear to have improved the learnability of the materials. This is particularly promising for students that are in traditionally less privileged environments to learn science and have limited exposure to science practice and inquiry (Lee, Buxton, Lewis, & LeRoy, 2006).

This research has important implications for simulation design as well as for theory development. For simulation design, this research provides suggestions on how the design of simulations for science education can be improved. Our results show that learners' prior knowledge needs to be considered in selecting the representation type of key information in the simulation. For learners with low prior knowledge, adding iconic representations can result in improved learning, especially comprehension. It is important to note that due to the nature of the materials, the exposure time to the simulations was with approximately 20 minutes relatively short. It is intriguing that despite this very short treatment time, and despite the relatively small change in the treatments, consisting only of the addition of icons, improvements of comprehension as well as learners' self-efficacy were found for students who received simulations with icons compared to the students who learned from simulations without icons.

On the theoretical side, our research shows that comprehension was improved when iconic representations of key information were added to the simulation display, even though this meant that the visual complexity of the display increased. Iconic representations are more closely related to the referent they represent, allowing learners to more easily to perceive the structural relations of the content (Schnotz & Bannert, 2003). In comparison, symbols such as verbal codes are arbitrary representations of content, in which structural relations must be represented through propositions. Such propositions require additional mental effort by the learner in order to be processed. The sign used to represent key information in a simulation, then, appears to affect the cognitive load experienced by students learning with the simulations.

Further studies are required to replicate these results with other materials, including subject areas that are either more or less intrinsically difficult, and with learners with different levels of prior knowledge. In one follow-up study we conducted, we compared the effect of iconic representations in narrated visualizations on learners with different levels of cognitive development (Homer & Plass, 2009). 186 middle- and high school students were randomly assigned to the iconic or the symbolic version of narrated visualizations of two chemistry topics: Kinetic Molecular Theory (Day 1) and Ideal Gas Laws (Day 2). This study found a main effect of prior knowledge on learning and no effects for icons on Day 1. However, on Day 2, we found a three-way interaction between prior knowledge, age group and icons. The interaction revealed that icons were effective for all middle school students. For high school students, icons were effective for learners with low prior knowledge, but not for high school students with high prior knowledge. These findings suggest that the expertise reversal effect can be mediated by cognitive development, not just prior knowledge in a specific subject matter (Homer & Plass, 2009).

These findings also need to be replicated in both the more controlled setting of a laboratory and in authentic educational settings where multiple sources of scaffolds dynamically interact (e.g., teacher, peers, and tools, Kim & Hannafin, 2010a; Kim, Hannafin, & Bryan, 2007). Further work should also look at how icons influence learning with simulations over longer durations (e.g., over time in an actual chemistry class). In addition, research should examine the effects of exposure to a series of related simulations, and should include measures of cognitive load other than learning outcomes.

In summary, the findings from the two studies presented here further support the idea that icons can facilitate learning and increase self-efficacy in visual learning environments, particularly for low prior knowledge learners, and especially under high cognitive load conditions. This provides an example of a design principle for effective simulations for science learning, which suggests that the design of simulations must take into account the representation type used for key concepts of the content.

ACKNOWLEDGMENT

The authors would like to thank the students and teachers who participated in this research. We would also like to express our gratitude to Juan Barrientos, Reneta Lansiquot, Yoo Kyung Chang, Andrew Gallegos and Pamela Young for their assistance with data collection and coding. The research presented in this paper was supported in part by the Institute of Education Sciences (IES), U.S. Department of Education (DoEd) through Grant R305K050140 to Jan L. Plass, Bruce D. Homer, Catherine Milne, and Trace Jordan at New York University. The content of this publication does not necessarily reflect the views or policies of IES or DoEd, nor does any mention of trade names, commercial products, or organizations imply endorsement by the U.S. Government. Correspondences should be addressed to Jan L. Plass by e-mail at jan.plass@nyu.edu or by mail at CREATE, New York University, 239 Greene St. Suite 300, New York, NY, 10003, USA.

REFERENCES

Baddeley, A. D. (1986). *Working memory*. New York, NY: Oxford University Press.

Bandura, A. (1986). *Social foundations of thought and action. A social cognitive theory*. Englewood Cliffs, NJ: Prentice Hall.

Betrancourt, M. (2005). *The animation and interactivity principles in multimedia learning*. New York, NY: Cambridge.

Brünken, R., Plass, J. L., & Leutner, D. (2003). Direct measurement of cognitive load in multimedia learning. *Educational Psychologist, 38*, 53–61. doi:10.1207/S15326985EP3801_7

Brünken, R., Steinbacher, S., Plass, J. L., & Leutner, D. (2002). Assessment of cognitive load in multimedia learning using dual-task methodology. *Experimental Psychology, 49*, 109–119. doi:10.1027//1618-3169.49.2.109

Carlson, R., Chandler, P., & Sweller, J. (2003). Learning and understanding science instructional material. *Journal of Educational Psychology, 95*(3), 629–640. doi:10.1037/0022-0663.95.3.629

Chandler, P. (2004). The crucial role of cognitive processes in the design of dynamic visualizations. *Learning and Instruction, 14*, 353–357. doi:10.1016/j.learninstruc.2004.06.009

Chase, W. G., & Simon, H. A. (1973). Perception in chess. *Cognitive Psychology, 4*, 55–81. doi:10.1016/0010-0285(73)90004-2

Chi, M. T. H., Glaser, R., & Rees, E. (1982). Expertise in problem solving. In Sternberg, R. (Ed.), *Advances in the psychology of human intelligence* (*Vol. 1*, pp. 17–76). Hillsdale, NJ: Erlbaum.

Clark, J. M., & Paivio, A. (1991). Dual coding theory and education. *Educational Psychology Review, 3*(3), 149–210. doi:10.1007/BF01320076

De Groot, A. D. (1965). *Thought and choice in chess*. The Hague, The Netherlands: Mouton.

De Jong, T., van Joolingen, W., Scott, D., de Hoog, R., Lapied, L., & Valent, R. (1994). SMISLE: System for multimedia integration simulation learning environments . In de Jong, T., & Sarti, L. (Eds.), *Design and production of multimedia and simulation based learning material* (pp. 133–167). Dordrecht, The Netherlands: Kluwer Academic Publishers.

de Jong, T., & van Joolingen, W. R. (1998). Scientific discovery learning with computer simulations of conceptual domains. *Review of Educational Research, 68*(2), 179–201.

Deacon, T. W. (1997). *The symbolic species: The co-evolution of language and the brain* (1st ed.). New York, NY: W. W. Norton.

Elshout, J. J., & Veenman, M. V. (1992). Relation between intellectual ability and working method as predictors of learning. *The Journal of Educational Research, 85*(3), 134–143. doi:10.1080/0022067 1.1992.9944429

Gogg, T. J., & Mott, J. R. (1993). *Improve quality & productivity with simulation*. Norcross, GA: Industrial Engineering Management Press.

Gruber, H., Graf, M., Mandl, H., Renkl, A., & Stark, R. (1995). *Fostering applicable knowledge by multiple perspectives and guided problem solving*. Paper Presented at the Conference of the European Association for Research on Learning and Instruction, Nijmegen, The Netherlands.

Guthrie, J. T., Weber, S., & Kimmerly, N. (1993). Searching documents: Cognitive processes and deficits in understanding graphs, tables, and illustrations. *Contemporary Educational Psychology*, *18*, 186–221. doi:10.1006/ceps.1993.1017

Hegarty, M., & Just, M. A. (1993). Constructing mental models of machines from text and diagrams. *Journal of Memory and Language*, *32*(6), 717–742. doi:10.1006/jmla.1993.1036

Höffler, T., & Leutner, D. (2007). Instructional animation versus static pictures: A meta-analysis. *Learning and Instruction*, *17*, 722–738. doi:10.1016/j.learninstruc.2007.09.013

Homer, B. D., & Nelson, K. (2005). *Seeing objects as symbols and symbols as objects: Language and the development of dual representation.* Mahwah, NJ: Erlbaum.

Homer, B. D., & Plass, J. L. (2010). Expertise reversal for iconic representations in science simulations. *Instructional Science*, *38*, 259–276. doi:10.1007/s11251-009-9108-7

Jinks, J., & Morgan, V. (1999). Children's perceived academic self-efficacy: An inventory scale. *Clearing House (Menasha, Wis.)*, *72*, 224–230. doi:10.1080/00098659909599398

Kalyuga, S. (2006). *Instructing and testing advance learners: A cognitive load approach.* New York, NY: Nova Science.

Kalyuga, S. (2008). Relative effectiveness of animated and static diagrams: An effect of learner prior knowledge. *Computers in Human Behavior*, *24*, 852–861. doi:10.1016/j.chb.2007.02.018

Kalyuga, S., Ayres, P., Chandler, P., & Sweller, J. (2003). Expertise reversal effect. *Educational Psychologist*, *38*, 23–31. doi:10.1207/S15326985EP3801_4

Kim, M. C., & Hannafin, M. J. (2010a). Scaffolding problem solving in technology-enhanced learning environments (TELEs): Bridging research and theory with practice. *Computers & Education*. doi:.doi:10.1016/j.compedu.2010.08.024

Kim, M. C., & Hannafin, M. J. (2010b). Scaffolding 6th graders' problem solving in technology-enhanced science classrooms: A qualitative case study. *Instructional Science*. doi:.doi:10.1007/s11251-010-9127-4

Kim, M. C., Hannafin, M. J., & Bryan, L. A. (2007). Technology-enhanced inquiry tools in science education: An emerging pedagogical framework for classroom practice. *Science Education*, *91*(6), 1010–1030. doi:10.1002/sce.20219

Kirschner, P. A., Sweller, J., & Clark, R. (2006). Why minimal guidance during instruction does not work: An analysis of the failure of constructivist, discovery, problem-based, experiential and inquiry-based teaching. *Educational Psychologist*, *41*, 75–86. doi:10.1207/s15326985ep4102_1

Kosslyn, S. M. (1989). Understanding charts and graphs. *Applied Cognitive Psychology*, *3*(3), 185–225. doi:10.1002/acp.2350030302

Lee, H., Plass, J. L., & Homer, B. D. (2006). Optimizing cognitive load for learning from computer-based science simulations. *Journal of Educational Psychology*, *98*(4), 902–913. doi:10.1037/0022-0663.98.4.902

Lee, O., Buxton, C., Lewis, S., & LeRoy, K. (2006). Science inquiry and student diversity: Enhanced abilities and continuing difficulties after an instructional intervention. *Journal of Research in Science Teaching*, *43*(7), 607–636. doi:10.1002/tea.20141

Leutner, D. (1993). Guided discovery learning with computer-based simulation games: Effects of adaptive and non-adaptive instructional support. *Learning and Instruction*, *3*(2), 113–132. doi:10.1016/0959-4752(93)90011-N

Levie, W. H. (1987). Research on pictures: A guide to the literature . In Willows, D. M., & Houghton, H. A. (Eds.), *The psychology of illustration: I. Basic research* (pp. 1–50). New York, NY: Springer.

Levie, W. H., & Lentz, R. (1982). Effects of text illustrations: A review of research. *Educational Communication & Technology Journal, 30*(4), 195–232.

Lewis, E. L., Stern, J. L., & Linn, M. C. (1993). The effect of computer simulations on introductory thermodynamics understanding. *Educational Technology, 33*, 45–58.

Lowe, R. (1993). Constructing a mental representation from an abstract technical diagram. *Learning and Instruction, 3*(3), 157–179. doi:10.1016/0959-4752(93)90002-H

Lowe, R. K. (1999). Extracting information from an animation during complex visual learning. *European Journal of Psychology of Education, 14*(2), 225–244. doi:10.1007/BF03172967

Lowe, R. K. (2003). Animation and learning: Selective processing of information in dynamic graphics. *Learning and Instruction, 13*(2), 157–176. doi:10.1016/S0959-4752(02)00018-X

Macromedia. (2004). *Flash MX 2004* [Software application]. Mountain View, CA.

Mandl, H., & Levin, J. R. (1989). *Knowledge acquisition from text and pictures*. Amsterdam, The Netherlands: Elsevier.

Mayer, R. E. (2001). *Multimedia learning*. New York, NY: Cambridge

Mayer, R. E. (2005). *The Cambridge handbook of multimedia learning*. New York, NY: Cambridge.

Mayer, R. E., & Sims, V. K. (1994). For whom is a picture worth a thousand words? Extensions of a dual-coding theory of multimedia learning. *Journal of Educational Psychology, 86*(3), 389–401. doi:10.1037/0022-0663.86.3.389

Miller, G. A. (1956). The magical number seven, plus or minus two: Some limits on our capacity for processing information. *Psychological Review, 63*, 81–97. doi:10.1037/h0043158

Njoo, M., & De Jong, T. (1993). Exploratory learning with a computer simulation for control theory: Learning processes and instructional support. *Journal of Research in Science Teaching, 8*, 821–844. doi:10.1002/tea.3660300803

Pajares, F. (1996). Self-efficacy beliefs and mathematical problem solving of gifted students. *Contemporary Educational Psychology, 21*, 325–344. doi:10.1006/ceps.1996.0025

Peirce, C. S. (1955). Logic as semiotic: The theory of signs . In Buchler, J. (Ed.), *The philosophical writings of Peirce* (pp. 98–110). New York, NY: Dover Books.

Piaget, J., & Inhelder, B. (1956). *The child's conception of space*. London, UK: Routledge & Paul.

Plass, J. L., Chun, D. M., Mayer, R. E., & Leutner, D. (2003). Cognitive load in reading a foreign language text with multimedia aids and the influence of verbal and spatial abilities. *Computers in Human Behavior, 19*(2), 221–243. doi:10.1016/S0747-5632(02)00015-8

Plass, J. L., Goldman, R., Flanagan, M., Diamond, J., Song, H., Rosalia, C., & Perlin, K. (2007). *RAPUNSEL: How a computer game designed based on educational theory can improve girls' self-efficacy and self-esteem*. Paper presented at the 2007 Annual Meeting for the American Educational Research Association (AERA), Division C-5: Learning Environments, in Chicago.

Plass, J. L., Homer, B. D., & Hayward, E. (2009). Design Factors for Educationally Effective Animations and Simulations. *Journal of Computing in Higher Education, 21*(1), 31–61. doi:10.1007/s12528-009-9011-x

Plass, J. L., Homer, B. D., Milne, C., & Jordan, T. (2007). *Optimizing cognitive load in simulations for science education*. Paper presented at the 2007 Annual Meeting for the American Educational Research Association (AERA), Division C-4: Science, in Chicago.

Plass, J. L., & Kalyuga, S. (2010). Individual differences and cognitive load theory. In Plass, J. L., Moreno, R., & Brünken, R. (Eds.), *Cognitive Load Theory*. New York, NY: Cambridge University Press.

Quinn, J., & Alessi, S. M. (1994). The effects of simulation complexity and hypothesis-generation strategy on learning. *Journal of Research on Computing in Education, 27*, 75–91.

Rieber, L. P. (1990). Using computer animated graphics with science instruction with children. *Journal of Educational Psychology, 82*(1), 135–140. doi:10.1037/0022-0663.82.1.135

Rieber, L. P. (1991). Effects of visual grouping strategies of computer-animated presentations on selective attention in science. *Educational Technology Research and Development, 39*(4), 5–15. doi:10.1007/BF02296567

Rieber, L. P. (1996). To teach or not to teach? Comparing the use of computer-based simulations in deductive versus instructive approaches to learning with adults in science. *Journal of Educational Computing Research, 13*(4).

Rieber, L. P., & Parmley, M. W. (1995). To teach or not to teach? Comparing the use of computer-based simulations in deductive versus inductive approaches to learning with adults in science. *Journal of Educational Computing Research, 13*(4), 359–374. doi:10.2190/M8VX-68BC-1TU2-B6DV

Rieber, L. P., Smith, M., Al-Ghafry, S., Strickland, B., Chu, G., & Spahi, F. (1996). The role of meaning in interpreting graphic textual feedback during a computer-based simulation. *Computers & Education, 27*(1), 45–58. doi:10.1016/0360-1315(96)00005-X

Rieber, L. P., Tzeng, S., & Tribble, K. (2004). Discovery learning, representation, and explanation within a computer-based simulation: Finding the right mix. *Learning and Instruction, 14*, 307–323. doi:10.1016/j.learninstruc.2004.06.008

Schnotz, W., & Bannert, M. (2003). Construction and interference in learning from multiple representation. *Learning and Instruction, 13*(2), 141–156. doi:10.1016/S0959-4752(02)00017-8

Schnotz, W., Böckler, J., & Grzondziel, H. (1999). Individual and co-operative learning with interactive animated pictures. *European Journal of Psychology of Education, 14*, 245–265. doi:10.1007/BF03172968

Schnotz, W., & Kulhavy, R. W. (1994). *Comprehension of graphics*. Amsterdam, The Netherlands: North-Holland/Elsevier Science Publishers.

Schnotz, W., Picard, E., & Hron, A. (1993). How do successful and unsuccessful learners use texts and graphics? *Learning and Instruction, 3*, 181–199. doi:10.1016/0959-4752(93)90003-I

Shah, P., & Carpenter, P. A. (1995). Conceptual limitations in comprehending line graphs. *Journal of Experimental Psychology. General, 124*(1), 43–61. doi:10.1037/0096-3445.124.1.43

Shah, P., & Hoeffner, J. (2002). Review of graph comprehension research: Implications for instruction. *Educational Psychology Review, 14*, 47–69. doi:10.1023/A:1013180410169

Swaak, J., Van Joolingen, W., & De Jong, T. (1998). Supporting simulation-based learning- The effects of model progression and assignments on definitional and intuitive knowledge. *Learning and Instruction, 8*(3), 235–252. doi:10.1016/S0959-4752(98)00018-8

Sweller, J. (1999). *Instructional design in technical areas*. Camberwell, Australia: ACER Press.

Towne, D. M. (1995). *Learning and instruction in simulation environments*. Englewood Cliffs, NJ: Educational Technology Publications.

Van der Meij, J., & deJong, T. (2006). Supporting students' learning with multiple representations in a dynamic simulation-based learning environment. *Learning and Instruction, 16*(3), 199–212. doi:10.1016/j.learninstruc.2006.03.007

Willows, D. M., & Houghton, H. A. (Eds.). (1987). *The psychology of illustration – Vol. I basic research*. New York, NY: Springer-Verlag.

Winn, W. (1991). Learning from maps and diagrams. *Educational Psychology Review, 3*(3), 211–247. doi:10.1007/BF01320077

Winn, W. (1994). Contributions of perceptual and cognitive processes to the comprehension of graphics . In Schnotz, W., & Kulhavy, R. (Eds.), *Comprehension of graphics* (pp. 3–27). Amsterdam, The Netherlands: Elsevier. doi:10.1016/S0166-4115(09)60105-9

Wouters, P., Tabbers, H. K., & Paas, F. (2007). Interactivity in video-based models. *Educational Psychology Review, 19*(3), 327–342. doi:10.1007/s10648-007-9045-4

Zimmerman, B. J. (2000). Attaining self-regulation: A social cognitive perspective . In Boekaerts, M., Pintrich, P., & Zeidner, M. (Eds.), *Self-regulation: Theory, research, and applications* (pp. 13–39). Orlando, FL: Academic Press.

ENDNOTE

[1] Peirce (1955) identified indices, which obtain meaning from temporal or spatial proximity to their referent, as a third type of sign. We did not include them in the review, as they did not apply to our research.

Chapter 3
Beyond Choices:
A Typology of Ethical Computer Game Designs

Miguel Sicart
IT University of Copenhagen, Germany

ABSTRACT

This article presents a typology for classifying computer games designed to create ethical gameplay. Ethical gameplay is the outcome of playing a (computer) game in which the players' moral values are of relevance for the game experience. The article explores the different types of designs that create these types of experiences, and how they are characterized. The author provides an analytical framework for classifying games according to the experience they create and how they create it. The article is informed by both game design theory and postphenomenological philosophy, and it is intended to provide a theoretical framework for the study of the design of ethical computer game experiences.

INTRODUCTION

In his Game Developers Conference talk "Exploration: From Systems to Spaces to Self" (Hocking, 2007), game developer Clint Hocking argued that computer games can be experienced not only as explorations of systems of rules and game world spaces, but also of the players' subjectivities, that is, the construction of our self, who we are and how that is expressed in a series of ethical values with which we relate with others and the world. Hocking's central example was Ultima IV (Origin

Systems, 1985), a game that encouraged players to explore the values they were playing by.

The main question developers like Hocking pose are: how do games explore the ethics of their players? How are computer games designed to create this type of ethical exploration? This article will present a typology that can be used to classify games according to how they appeal to their players' ethics. This typology will argue that there is such a thing as ethical gameplay, and that there are sufficient recurring design elements in computer games to justify a typology of ethical gameplay designs. Computer games can create deep ethical experiences, which, as this article will argue, can be categorized according to abstract game design concepts.

Though this article may be of interest to game designers, the intended audience is academics with an interest in the formal analysis of computer games as designed objects and how they engage players in ethical experiences. Nevertheless, the typology presented here can be used in specific design practices as a reference framework, or even as an inspirational tool. The topics discussed will expand these possible uses and expansions of the typology in the closing section of the article.

The conceptual model of how ethical gameplay is created by means of general design choices can help elucidate the role of computer games in our ethical landscape, further arguing for the recognition of computer games as not only a form of entertainment, but also a medium capable of contributing with its expressive capacities to the shaping of contemporary culture. This being said, I will not directly address the ubiquitous issue of violence and computer games. Directly addressing this issue is a side path from the essence of this article.

My goal is to introduce the concept of ethical gameplay, understood as the morally relevant outcome of the experience of a game system by an ethical agent. This concept will be used to argue for a typology of ethical design principles based on the analysis of a number of computer games. These games were chosen for their relevance in terms of ethical discourses created by means of their procedural rhetoric (Bogost, 2007), not necessarily by the ethical motives of their theme, or game world. The games used as illustrations of this typology create ethical experiences primarily by means of game design, that is, by the way the game system, its rules and mechanics, its affordances and constraints (Norman, 2002) affect the player experience of the fictional world (Juul, 2005). This typology is inspired by the work of Järvinen (2008) and Bjork and Holopainen (2005), even though my scope is narrower, since the intention

is to present a typology of game designs that can potentially cue ethical gameplay.

Ethical gameplay is a concept inspired by the works on gameplay by Bateman and Boon (2006), Salen and Zimmerman (2003), and Juul (2005). This tradition will be put in the perspective of phenomenology (Gadamer, 2004) and postphenomenology (Ihde, 1990, 1995; Verbeek, 2005), and so ethical gameplay will consider both player and game system ethics as an integral part of the ludic activity.

Computer games that appeal and challenge our ethical values are a step towards the expressive maturity of the medium. Computer games challenge what we think and who we are and by understanding how they do so, we can imagine new ways of describing, developing, and playing computer games, incorporating ethics as a gameplay challenge.

DEFINING ETHICAL GAMEPLAY

Ethical gameplay is the ludic experience in which regulation, mediation, and/or goals require from the player moral reflection beyond the calculation of statistics and possibilities. This type of gameplay requires the understanding of games as objects with values embedded in their design (Latour, 1992; Winner, 1986), that establish a mode of relation with the player, limiting their agency in the game world with a pre-determined, designed purpose; it also requires the understanding of players as moral agents, capable of using ethical reflection to act upon choices in game experience. The implications of this perspective for the analysis of games as cultural objects are significant: not only game design is ethically relevant, but also play is a moral action.

The player I will invoke here is a an implied, model player (Eco, 1978), one that has experience playing games, and that has the ethical maturity to understand games not only as means for entertainment, but also as expressive medium (Bogost,

2007). This implied player engages in the ludic experience with the intention of exploring the game system, but also the player's own values. An ethical player is a condition for ethical gameplay, but it is the game system that will determine the relevance of the player's values for the game experience.

One approach to describing the values of a game design, according to Nissenbaum (2001), would be to "study the complex interplay between the system or device, those who built it, what they had in mind, its conditions of use, and the natural, cultural, social, and political context in which it is embedded, for all these factors may feature in an account of the values embodied in it" (p. 120). Science and Technology Studies (Akrich & Latour, 1992) used this methodology to describe the importance of values in the way technologies shape our interaction with the world (Flanagan, Belman, Nissembaum, & Diamond, 2007). Nevertheless, from a philosophical perspective, it is necessary to establish an ontology of the object before we can talk about values. That is, we need to understand what games are before we can assign values to it, and project them to the player experience.

Don Ihde's postphenomenology provides arguments for understanding ethical gameplay as related to the game object projected to the player experience. In Ihde's perspective, "there are no neutral technologies, or, positively put, all technologies are non-neutral … they are transformational in that they change the quality, field and possibility range of human experience, thus they are non-neutral" (Ihde, 1995, p. 33). Since technologies—in this case computer games—are intended to create human experiences, such as gameplay, then games are non-neutral, and as such we can analyze their values as intended experiences.

This analysis needs to be in form of the experience of the game, since "technologies have to be understood phenomenologically, that is, as belonging in different ways to our experience and use of technologies, as a human-technology relation…" (ibid, p. 34). It is in this perspective where design becomes moral, and we can think about ethical gameplay as the experience of a moral system: "Design ethics requires that artifacts be treated as members of the moral community, conceived as the community in which morality assumes a shape. Things carry morality because they shape the way in which people experience their world…" (Verbeek, 2005, p. 217). Within this postphenomenological perspective, then, games should be understood as objects that create experiences by limiting the agency of an ethical being, and because they do so, they ought to be ethically analyzed.

The elements that are present in the experience of ethical gameplay are three: the game world, the game rules, and the game mechanics. The game world should be understood as the semantic wrapper of the game system, the combination of fiction and simulation (Aarseth, 2005). I am using the term "semantic" in its classic, semiotic meaning, that is, "the general study of the interpretation of signs" (Honderich, 1995, p. 820). Game rules are the formal structure of the game, the boundaries in which play takes place, freely accepted by players and unbreakable (Salen & Zimmerman, 2004). Game mechanics are the actions afforded by the system to the player so the player can interact with the game state and with other players (Järvinen, 2008). Players experience a game world constrained by rules, and interact with(in) it by means of game mechanics (see also Juul, 2005). Since that world is designed to create a number of behaviors, we can describe the game as an ethical technology, and the act of playing, a moral action.

For example, in Grand Theft Auto: Vice City (Rockstar North, 2002), players can drive a car, pick up a prostitute, have "sex" with her to increase the maximum health from 100 to 125 units, and then kill her to recover the money. From a formal perspective, a number of rules create that gameplay experience: players have a maximum of 125 health units, but only 100 in normal conditions; if players are in a specific location, inside a car, close to a character of a specific type, a sequence will trigger granting them 125 health units in exchange for some game tokens; if computer-controlled agents lose their hit points, they die, leaving a certain amount of money. In the semantic level, this flowchart of actions is represented, as I have previously described, with cars, prostitutes, sex, money and murder simulations (Frasca, 2003). The player that experiences ethical gameplay will interact with this system, and relate to it by means of its semantic layer, but will take all of the elements into consideration in the process. In this sense, ethical gameplay is a process of ethical interpretation of the game—a hermeneutics of play (Aarseth, 2003).

Hermeneutical phenomenology (Gadamer, 2004) connects the player as moral agent and the experience of ethical gameplay. Gadamer's reflections on the work of art illustrate how experiencing ethical gameplay occurs: "in the experience of art we see a genuine experience (Erfahrung) induced by the work which does not leave him who has it unchanged…" (p. 86). Players engage with the game system mediated by the semantic layers of the game, but this mediation is not absolute; players are not blinded by the semantics—they understand the procedural aspects of their experience, the ergodic (Aarseth, 1997) requirements of the system. The semantic layer should be understood as a facilitator for player interaction with the game system, a method of reducing the cognitive friction of interacting with such a complex system (Cooper, 2004, p. 19).

Playing is inserting the self in a structure experienced as a world: "The player experiences the game as a reality that surpasses him…this is all the more the case where the game is itself 'intended' as such a reality" (Gadamer, 2004, p. 109). But play is also to interpret the conditions for play (Gadamer, 2004) by means of the semantic layer of the game. Semantics, as stated before, is understood as the "interpretation of signs," and in this case is the interpretation of the game system and the afforded mechanics by means of the game world as fiction and simulation.

Players create the game in play by interacting with a game system which state is communicated by means of a simulational system (Retaux &

Rouchier, 2002). This creation is a co-creation; players are also created by the game system as subjects to that game. Since this process involves an ethical being in the experience of understanding, then ethics becomes a principle at play.

Ethical gameplay, then, has to be seen not only in light of the game system, nor as exclusively dependent of the game world; ethical gameplay is a process of decision-making constrained by morally relevant technologies, and mediated by a game world that translates the principles of those technologies into behavioral patterns that can be understood by players. But, since the game world is a means for conveying information to the player, we cannot analyze ethical gameplay exclusively in terms of the game world, but in the ways the game world is interactive. In this sense, ethical gameplay is an experience of a system mediated by a game world; in postphenomenological fashion (Ihde, 1990), it would be schematized as follows:

player $\rightarrow$ (game world - game system)

In classic postphenomenology, hermeneutical relations, those in which "we are involved with the world via an artifact, but the artifact is not transparent…the artifact…provides a representation of the world" (Verbeek, 2005, p. 126), are schematized as:

I $\rightarrow$ (technology-world) (ibid).

In computer games, it is the game world which acts as a representation of the game system. Simulation is informational mediation of an abstract system towards the player. Ethical gameplay is then the hermeneutical experience of that combination, (world-system), by a reflective being. The modalities of design for ethical gameplay should then be understood as the modes in which the (game world—game system) mediation is constructed, with the intention of being experienced by an ethical agent.

In this section the basics for understanding ethical gameplay is presented. The next section will present a typological categorization of ethical gameplay in computer games.

A TYPOLOGY OF DESIGNS FOR ETHICAL GAMEPLAY

The goal of game design is to create interesting gameplay. The comparative analysis of different game designs can result in typologies of game designs (Aarseth & Elverdam, 2007). For example, Björk and Holopainen (2004) apply the concept of design patterns to the analysis of games, with the intention of influencing the ways games are designed. By invoking design patterns, the authors provide us with a formal tool for describing games. There is a crucial difference between these typologies, though: game design patterns can be used to solve specific design problems, while Aarseth and Elverdam's are a descriptive tool for existing games. Presented here is the typology closer to the latter.

A typology that categorizes computer games depending on how they create ethical gameplay is presented here. This typology is a descriptive, analytical tool, meant to facilitate game research, and perhaps even inspire game designers. They are meant to provide clear, overarching types for classifying design for ethical gameplay.

The two dominant modalities of design for ethical gameplay are open games and closed games. This terminology is inspired by Eco's (1989) theories on the open and the closed work. The metaphor of the open/closed in game studies has a long tradition in different fields. Suits (1978) writes about open and closed games depending on the properties of the game when played, while Juul (2005) uses the terminology to explain the differences between games of emergence and games of progression.

In this case, open design refers to that in which the player can bring her own values to the game experience, and the game system will react accordingly to those values. Open design allows players to let their ethical values modify the game

experience. On the opposite side, closed design limits ethical player agency, but focuses on creating a strong ethical experience: players cannot affect the world with her values, but they are affected by the game's designed values. These types are not mutually exclusive. In fact, they can appear in the same game, with the goal of creating an intended ethical experience at a given time in the game. Any game can apply any of these methods at any given time, to explore different possibilities in the ethical experience of the player.

According to this typology, some games will tend to be open, while some others will tend to be closed. Nevertheless, we will find instances of closed ethical gameplay design in open games, and vice versa. This typology, then, can be used both as a general description of the dominant type of ethical gameplay design present in a game, and as a categorization tool of the different gameplay sequences, or moments, that constitute a game system as a whole.

Open ethical design is dominant in those games that encourage players to elaborate their own ethical systems, and apply them to the experience. Open ethical design encourages players to play by and with their own values.

Multiplayer games tend to be predominantly open ethical designs, since they require players that create codes of conduct and behaviors for playing with others according to interpretations of the rules. For example, Eve Online (CCP Games, 2003) does not force any value system on players. The forums and online communities in Eve thrive with stories of heists, coups, and piracy—tales of survival and corporate loyalty illustrate the open ethics of the game, where players are given a world to live by their own values.

An extreme case of open ethical multiplayer game is A Tale in the Desert, where players could vote their own laws, which would then be implemented by the developers as rules and mechanics. Effectively, players of A Tale in the Desert created a world where they lived by their values, and the world adapted to their ethics.

Open ethical design is also present in other types of multiplayer games, like Wario Ware: Smooth Moves (Intelligent Systems, 2007), or Dance Dance Revolution (Konami, 1999) series. In these games, the social experience is often more important than the gameplay. These games are mediators for the simultaneous presence of different individuals enjoying a shared ludic experience. In this sense, these games do not punish poor performances beyond the systemic losing condition, and they encourage, by means of design, the presence of a collective ethical decision of playing by the rules and enjoying the experience.

As a comparison, Counter-Strike (Valve, 2000) is very punishing: once the player is killed, the player has to wait in spectator mode, watching others play, until the level is over. Most team-based competitive multiplayer first person shooters present similar handicaps. Competition is driven by the game design. On the other hand, the multiplayer version of Dance Dance Revolution encourages simultaneous competition: regardless of player performance, songs will be played until the end, when the scores will reflect the difference in performance quality. In the single player version, bad performance is punished with the abrupt end of the song. These multiplayer social games are designed to encourage the creation of a communitarian ethics in which players care not only for winning, but also for maintaining the good spirits and flow of the game experience (Smith, 2006).

Open ethical multiplayer design, then, is focused on encouraging players to create the values they play by with other agents, values that are then respected and encouraged by the game system, in terms of influence in the world, or specific game rules tailored for that type of values.

Open ethical design is also possible in single player games. In Fable (Lionhead Studios, 2005), for example, player's actions and their values are acknowledged by the game system, and reflected upon in the game world: non player characters will modify their behaviors depending on the values the player has lived by. Essentially, open ethical

designs in single player games allows players to explore variations of moral positions, and reflects them in the way the world, or the narrative, are experienced. Of course, the game is designed with a number of embedded values that do not allow total freedom. In fact, there is never such thing as total ethical freedom for players: a game will always encourage modalities of play and interactions it considers morally good. Games are always ethically relevant systems, since they constraint the agency of an ethical being.

Single player games with open ethical structures, then, focus the ethical experience in the player agency within the world. For example, Deus Ex (Ion Storm, 2000) is a game built around ethical player agency: the player can explore both a game world and a story, and both are deeply intertwined with the player's ethical agency. Deus Ex, like any game that presents dominant open ethical design, makes players play by their own values, giving choices not only strategic, but also moral meaning.

Open ethical design can present different subtypes. Open ethical design can affect the game system or the game world, or both. If the values the player affords to the game affect the game system, we will have open ethical system design. In Knights of the Old Republic (Bioware, 2003), depending on the values the player adopts, different powers will be available. These powers imply different modes of agency in the game world, which implies a different system design. Similarly, in Bioshock the amount of resources a player has at the player's disposal depends on how the player interacts with the game world, and those resources modify the space of possibility of the player.

Open ethical design can also relate to the game world, understood loosely as the fictional element of the game (Juul, 2005). Open ethical world design defines the modes in which the game world is affected by the player values. In Fable, non player characters will react differently to the player depending on the player's actions, which will provide constant feedback to the player on the player's moral status. Furthermore, in that game the avatar changes appearance also depending on the palyer's moral decisions, providing even more ethical feedback to the player's values. In Deus Ex, on the other hand, it is the way the story unfolds that shows the world reaction to the player actions: depending on the choices of the player, the player will explore a dominant branch of the narrative, and on occasions will experience another branch of the narrative. The way the player relates to the characters and to these narratives will show this modality of open ethical design.

Open ethical design is the general design type that allows players to afford their values, to a certain extent, to the game world or to the game experience. Most computer games that have attempted to create ethical gameplay inspired by open design characteristics, yet it is not the only type of design available for creating ethical gameplay.

Closed ethical designs restrict ethical agency in the game world, yet encourage players to reflect about the values of their gameplay experience. In closed ethical designs, the game world and the game experience are moral in nature, yet the player cannot do anything to alter the values of the game. The game is morally static, and the player has to accept its values in order to experience the game. This acceptance does not mean a passive position of the player towards the game system. As a matter of fact, it requires from players to be active ethical agents: closed ethical design requires ethical players, and creates a ludic experience specifically tailored for them.

Closed ethical design is based on the assumption that the player, as a moral being, will relate to the game system by means of the player's own ethical values, yet the player will accept the values of the game world or the game fiction in order to enjoy the ludic experience. This means a tension between the player as an ethical agent in the game system, and the values the game system is designed to enforce. This tension builds the game as a designed ethical experience.

For example, a game like Grand Theft Auto: San Andreas (Rockstar North, 2004) has a rather unlikable main character, which has to commit all kinds of gruesome crimes in order to proceed in the game. Players cannot change the characters' ethics, nor influence the world. Players are tied to the values of the game system. Parts of the enjoyment of the game is the system exploration, but also the process of letting go on moral restraints and build this character inside the game, experiencing what cannot be accepted by a moral agent outside the game. It is in this tension between the ethical agent outside of the game and the ethical being in the game were the interest of closed ethical design shows.

There are two types of closed ethical designs: substracting and mirroring, each referring to a particular combination of design choices and intended or interpretable player experience. Substracting closed design is a category based on Fumitu Ueda's thoughts on the design process behind Ico (Ueda & Kaido, 2002). This approach implies substracting from the game design all those elements that do not directly support the core gameplay, enhancing those elements crucial to the game experience. In my appropriation of the term "substracting," I use it to define those game designs in which the game system expects a moral agent that will play the game as an ethical experience, yet that system is not designed to reinforce the ethics of the player. Substracting closed design forces players to experience their morals in a world that does not react to these values. The player is left alone to understand and evaluate the ethics of the experience. Substracting means relieving the game from openly addressing ethical discourses, while encouraging the player to morally reflect about the meaning and consequences of the player's actions.

Shadow of the Colossus is an example of substracting closed design: in this game, players are asked to slay 16 colossi to revive a dead girl. The game does not build any type of moral argumentation around the actions the player has to take. In a strict sense, the game consists of 16 boss fights that act as connecting threads of a story told, by allusion, through non-interactive cut scenes. Players are devoid of any backstory, meaning, or sense of consequence of their actions towards the game world. Yet the game is designed to become an ethical experience.

Central to the experience of the game are the colossi. These beasts places are symbols of the space they inhabit. The colossi are not necessarily aggressive as there are no cues given to the player as to their ethical alignment, nor there any information on the morals of the player character's motivations; there is no sense of good and evil, of the morally good or bad. Everything moral is substracted from the game. The question becomes: why is it then, an ethical design?

There are elements in the design of the game that can be interpreted as signs towards a moral agent, as hints towards a reflection on the ethics of the gameplay. When the player finally slays a colossus, a non-interactive sequence triggers: the colossus dies, the player falls to the ground, a shadow stems from the dead colossus, the shadow penetrates the player's body, almost killing the player. The player then wakes up to an improved stamina, but the looks of the avatar degrade, as if reflecting some kind of illness. These two apparently contradictory elements, the enhanced systemic agency and the visual feedback through the avatar, send contradictory messages to the player. On one hand, the player is progressing in the game; on the other, the player's avatar is showing symptoms of suffering. These contradictory messages can be interpreted as cues that appeal to the player's repertoire (Juul, 2005), the paleyr's capacity to understand both the rules of the system, to create strategies, and the semantics of the game world as means for informing the player about the game state and its progression.

As a substractive closed design, Shadow of the Colossus detaches itself from any moral reasoning, yet it induces moral thinking in the player. In other words, it requires a moral agent that can interpret the game world from an ethical perspective in order for some elements of the game

to make sense. Substractive designs require and appeal to a moral player to complete the ethical meaning of the game, beyond the basic gameplay requirements.

Mirroring design is the opposite of subtracting and this type of games place the ethical meaning of the game at the center of the experience, forcing players to actions of intense moral nature. Closed mirroring design projects the ethical experience from the game to the player, who is forced to accept a set of values more or less explicitly described by the game. Mirroring closed design forces players to adapt to the values of the game, but provoking them as reflective ethical beings, making the adoption of that external set of values a core part of the ethical gameplay experience.

Manhunt (Rockstar North, 2003) is an example of closed mirroring design. In this game, players have to commit gruesome acts of violence in order to survive. As a matter of fact, players are rewarded on their violence: the bloodier the execution, the more points are awarded. The game is encouraging players to commit these murders by rewarding players with a high score, a classic method to get players attached to game strategies. Incidentally, the game is much harder to play if not committing these vile acts. The game is balanced so that the player has to commit those acts in order to survive, as any other type of violence will likely end up in the death of the player. This design choice reinforces the need of the player to focus on strategies based on executions, further insisting on Manhunt as a game of tactical gore.

In Manhunt, the mirroring structure is designed to create a disgust effect in the player. There is nothing attractive in the executions: they are brutal, unpleasant, and crude. But it is in these executions where the gist of Manhunt can be found: the game is about experiencing disgust, about enacting the extreme opposite ethical values as any sane human would enforce. And doing so by interacting with a system designed to reach an end state if the user does not follow those values. Manhunt is a game that explores our commitment to a game we are encouraged to despise, mirroring the values acted in the game to our actions needed to play the game.

Another mirroring closed design is Super Columbine Massacre RPG (Ledone, 2006). In this independent title, players control the two perpetrators of the Columbine murders. The game is an old school role-playing game, in which combat takes place in turns, and the violence is abstracted to the tactical choice of the right weapons at the right time. As opposed to Manhunt, Super Columbine Massacre RPG is not a realistic game, so its mirror structure is not reinforced directly by aural feedback. The fact that the graphics are cartoonish, for such a serious topic, brings forth a substantial element for reflection in players. But it is precisely in the mental connection between players' cultural knowledge and the mechanics and aesthetics of the game where it becomes a mirror ethical experience. Players know about the Columbine events, yet they play this game where they have to control the murderers. The ethical tension in this case is between players as cultural beings, and their in game actions. This game, following all gaming conventions, encourages the player to reflect about the Columbine events. In Super Columbine Massacre RPG, players have to experience Columbine through the eyes of the killers. By manipulating the general emotional attachment that players have to avatars and characters, this game forces players to think about the meaning of the actions; actions that are resonant of the actual Columbine murders. In that gameplay, the game becomes an ethical experience.

Mirroring structures are rather problematic—they are very effective in games with focused gameplay, or in gameplay sequences in which affecting and challenging the players' values is a fundamental design goal. However, it could be argued that it can lead to numbing or a certain habituation to unethical actions. Even though it is beyond the scope of this article, this issue will be briefly addressed.

Mirroring designs demand a mature player that has developed a set of ethical values that apply to her experience of computer games. This mature player will understand that the unethical actions she has to perform in order to progress in the game are designed and intended to create a specific effect. This awareness is fundamental for a successful, ethically sound mirroring design. Closed mirroring designs can be used sparingly to create strong ethical engagement in players. But their continuous use may be too demanding on the players' values, hence making the ethical arguments of the game weak. Players, as ethical agents, will reflect and react at the values of the game, and that reaction will make ethical gameplay become a meaningful experience.

A typology of ethical gameplay design is then constituted by two arch-types: open ethical design, in which player agency influences to some extent elements of the game world, or the game system; and closed design, where the player's ethical position does not influence the game world, or the game system. Each of these has two different types: open system design, open gameworld design, closed ethical substracting design, and closed mirroring design. All these design types create ethical gameplay, understood as the ethical experience of a morally relevant system by an agent, on different degrees. Any game that creates ethical gameplay will have a dominant type, yet it is possible to have gameplay sequences where other ethical design types are present.

In a postphenomenological sense, open ethical system designs make the game system adapt to players choices, relating the values the agent plays by with the extent of her agency in the system:

(ethical player) $\Leftrightarrow$ (game system $\Rightarrow$ game world)

Open ethical world designs adapt the game world to the values of the player, providing feedback to the players values by means of world adaptation to the palyer's agency.

(ethical player) $\Leftrightarrow$ (game world - game system)

Substracting designs require ethical agents that bring their values as a part of the gameplay experience, yet neither the game world, nor the game system reacts to those values. This implies that, on occasions, players can be oblivious to the ethical message of the game, if they do not understand their interaction as ethically relevant. The game will nevertheless cue them to interpret the game as an ethical system. But the game nevertheless projects certain need for interpretation that players need to decode in an ethical fashion.

(ethical player) $\Rightarrow$ (ethical game world/system)

Mirroring designs force players into a system of values at the core of the ethical gameplay. Reflection is only possible as a reaction, or consequence, of the values imposed by the system. On occasions, the reflection appeals to the ethical agent as a human being, and not only an ethical player:

(ethical being) $\Leftrightarrow$ (ethical player) $\Leftarrow$ (ethical game world/system)

This typology can be modeled in Figure 1.

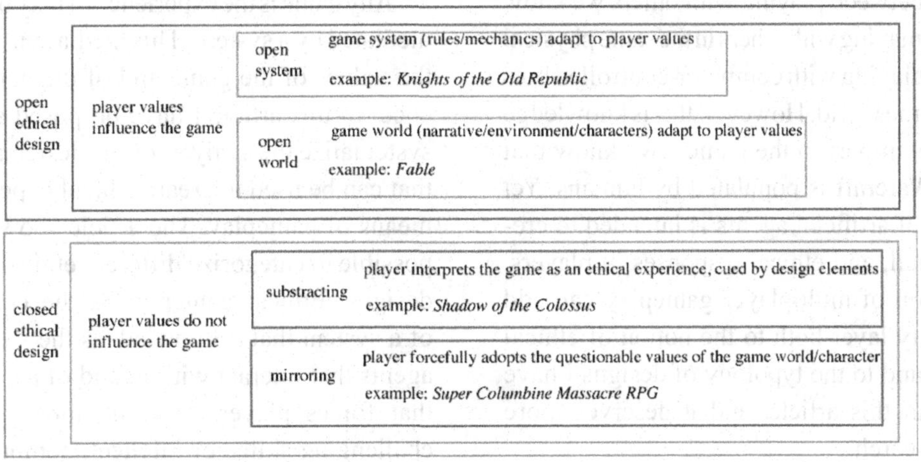

CONCLUSION

This article is titled "Beyond Choices" to break one of the assumed conventions in ethical gameplay design. As evidenced by those games which insist on being called "moral experiences," such as Fable or Knights of the Old Republic, players have to have choices to create experiences about morals. While taking choices is a good vehicle to explore morals, ethics is a greater topic which is concerned with how we interpret good and evil, who we are, and who do we want to become. This article has presented a typology for classifying games depending on how they are designed to provoke these reflections. Some games offer choices as a tool for exploring values, like open ethical designs, while others rely more on taunting the ethical agent that is playing the game, forcing them to reflect about what is actually happening in the game—the meaning of the ludic actions.

This article is an introduction to the topic of designing ethical gameplay. With this typology, I provide an initial framework to categorize the variety of approaches to ethical gameplay experiences that computer games can take. Used as an inspirational tool, this typology allows the comparison between different types of ethical gameplay and their implications. A designer has now a conceptual

Figure 1.

framework where a designer's work, as well as others, can be classified and compared.

This typology is also systematizing implicit knowledge. Game designers like Koster (2005) or Rollings and Adams (2003) have introduced the importance of ethics for game design, and its possible potential. This article intended to pick up that challenge and provide a coherent, systematic categorization of games based on their design for ethical gameplay.

Yet, there is more work to be done, especially in two domains for ethical gameplay to take place, we need to understand the ethical player. Ethical player should be understood here as a philosophical anthropology: who is an ethical player, and how is the palyer characterized? There has been interesting works on both the deviant ethical players, like cheaters (Consalvo, 2007), and a general perspective on players as ethical agents (Sicart, 2006). But we do not know who the ethical player is, and worse, how to effectively communicate with the player. Discovering and describing an ethical player model is an urgent task in the research of ethical gameplay, and once it is completed, it will allow the introduction of ethical parameters in the design, evaluation, and research on computer games.

Closely related to the understanding of the ethical player would be a mapping of the ethical significance of multiplayer play, both online and co-present. Moral intuition dictates that there is difference between playing with others we know are human, playing with others in the same physical space, and playing with computer-controlled bots populating the world. However, this is knowledge that players import to the game—we know that World of Warcraft is populated by humans. Yet the design of artificial agents is intended to create emotional, and ethical responses in players. The question of multiplayer gameplay can add a complexity layer both to the notion of ethical gameplay, and to the typology of designs I have presented in this article, and it deserves more detailed research.

The second domain that needs further work is related with specific design methods. As I have mentioned, Järvinen, Holopainen, Björk, and other game designers that have developed methods for designing games inspire this article. The next step in the process initiated by this typology is to complement it with a design methodology: what are the patterns, procedures, methods and techniques that can be used to create these games.

This method will have to draw not only on the formal aspects of games, but also on their relation with the aesthetic aspect. Järvinen's RAM (2008), Hunicke, LeBlanc, and Zubeck's MDA (2005), or the Values at Play project (www.valuesatplay. org) should be inspirational projects. The goal is to develop a set of practices and methods that allow the creation of games that incorporate ethical gameplay as one of their core characteristics. For instance, substractive design games require providing subtle information to the player regarding the ethical nature of the gameplay experience. Shadow of the Colossus does so by conflicting messages: the avatar looks ill, but the gameplay relevant characteristics, like stamina, improve. A player invested in understanding the ethical dimension of the game can pick up on that tension between the mechanics/dynamics and the aesthetics, and explain it by means of ethical thinking. Thus, the player becomes empowered to explore the moral meaning of the game and her being in that experience.

Any game is the experience of play by an agent, mediated by a system. This mediation determines the values of the game and of the game experience. In this article I have proposed a model to systematize the analysis of the design techniques that can be used to create ethical experiences by means of gameplay. The article shows that it is possible to categorize different ethical gameplay designs. Ethical gameplay is the consequence of a system that acknowledges the values of the agents that interact with it, and of a game world that forces players to think morally. Beyond challenging skills, or intellect, computer games have the possibility of making players experience ethical dilemmas, and make their game exploration a process of self-understanding. Beyond choices, ethical gameplay holds the promise of what computer games can express.

REFERENCES

Aarseth, E. (1997). *Cybertext: Perspectives on ergodic literature.* Baltimore, MD: Johns Hopkins University Press.

Aarseth, E. (2003). Playing research: Methodological approaches to game analysis. *Digital Arts and Culture Conference Proceedings,* RMIT University, Melbourne.

Aarseth, E. (2005). Doors and perception: Fiction vs. simulation in games. *Digital Arts and Culture Conference Proceedings,* IT University of Copenhagen.

Aarseth, E. & Elverdam, C. (2007). Game classification and game design. Construction through critical analysis. *Games and Culture, 2*(1), 3-22.

Akrich, M. & Latour, B. (1992). A summary of a convenient vocabulary for the semiotics of human and nonhuman assemblies. In W. Bijker & J. Law (Eds.), *Shaping Technology/Building Society* (pp. 259-264). Cambridge, MA: MIT Press.

Bateman, C. & Boon, R. (2006). *XXI century game design.* Hingham: Charles River Media.

Björk, S. & Holopainen, J. (2005). *Patterns in game design.* Hingham: Charles River Media.

Bogost, I. (2007). *Persuasive games.* Cambridge, MA: MIT Press.

Caillois, R. (1956). *Man, play and games.* Illinois: University of Illinois Press.

Consalvo, M. (2007). *Cheating.* Cambridge, MA: MIT Press.

Cooper, A. (1999). *The inmates are running the asylum.* Indianapolis: Sams Publishing.

Eco, U. (1978). *The role of the reader: Explorations in the semiotics of texts.* Bloomington, IN: Indiana University Press.

Eco, U. (1989). *The open work.* Cambridge, MA: Harvard University Press.

Flanagan, M., Nissenbaum, H., Diamond, J., & Belman, J. (2007). A method for discovering values in digital games. *Situated Play DiGRA 07 Conference Proceedings,* Tokyo.

Frasca, G. (2003). Simulation versus narrative: Introduction to ludology. In M. J. P. Wolf & B. Perron (Eds.), *Video/Game/Theory.* London: Routledge.

Fullerton, T., Swain, C., & Hoffman, S. (2005). *Game design workshop. Designing, Prototyping, and Playtesting Games.* San Francisco: CMP Books.

Gadamer, H-G. (2004). *Truth and method.* New York: Continuum.

Hocking, C. (2007). *Exploration - From systems to spaces to self.* Talk at the Game Developers Conference, San Francisco, CA, USA.

Honderich, T. (1995). *The oxford companion to philosophy.* Oxford: Oxford University Press.

Hunicke, R., LeBlanc, M., & Zubek, R. (2005). *MDA: A formal approach to game design and game research.* Retrieved April 11, 2009, from http://www.cs.northwestern.edu/~hunicke/MDA.pdf

Ihde, D. (1990). *Technology and the lifeword.* Bloomington, IN: Indiana University Press.

Ihde, D. (1995). *Postphenomenology. Essays in the Postmodern Context.* Evanston, IL: Northwestern University Press.

Järvinen, A. (2008). *Games without frontiers: Theories and methods for game studies and design.* University of Tampere Pres, Tampere. Retrieved April 11, 2009, from http://acta.uta.fi/english/teos.phtml?11046

Juul, J. (2005). *Half real*. Cambridge, MA: MIT Press.

Koster, R. (2005). *A theory of fun for game design*. Scottsdale: Paraglyph Press.

Latour, B. (1992). Where are the missing masses? - The sociology of a few mundane artifacts. In W. Bijker & J. Law (Eds.), *Shaping technology/building society* (pp. 225-58). Cambridge, MA: MIT Press.

Nissenbaum, H. (2001, March). How computer systems embody values. *Computer, 34*(3), 118-120.

Norman, D. (2002). *The design of everyday things*. Cambridge, MA: MIT Press.

Retaux, X. & Rouchier, J. (2002). Realism vs. surprise and coherence: Different aspect of playability in computer game. Essay presented at *Playing with the Future: Development and Directions in Computer Gaming*, Manchester.

Rollings, A. & Adams, E. (2003). *On game design*. Indianapolis, IN: New Riders.

Rouse, R. (2005). *Game design, theory, and practice*. Plano, TX: Wordware Publishing.

Sicart, M. (2006). *Computer games, players, ethics*. Copenhagen, IT: University of Copenhagen.

Smith, J. (2006). *Plans and purposes: How videogame goals shape player behavior*. Copenhagen: IT University of Copenhagen.

Suits, B. (1978). *The grasshopper*. Ontario: Broadview Press.

Sutton-Smith, B. (1997). *The ambiguity of play*. Cambridge, MA: Harvard University Press.

Ueda, F. & Kaido, K. (2002). Game design methods of Ico. Presented at the *Game Developers Conference 2002*, San Jose, CA, USA.

Verbeek, P-P. (2005). *What things do*. Pennsylvania: Pennsylvania State University Press.

Winner, L. (1986). *Do artifacts have politics? The whale and the reactor: A search for limits in an age of high technology* (pp. 13-39). Chicago: University of Chicago Press.

Zimmerman, E. & Salen, K. (2004). *Rules of play*. Cambridge, MA: MIT Press.

REFERENCES: GAMES

2K Boston/2K Australia (2007) Bioshock

BioWare (2003) Knights of the Old Republic

Blizzard Entertainment (2005) World of Warcraft

CCP Games (2003) Eve Online.

eGenesis (2003) A Tale in the Desert

Intelligent Systems (2007) Wario Ware: Smooth Moves

Introversion Software (2006) Defcon

Ion Storm (2000) Deus Ex

Konami (1999) Dance Dance Revolution.

Ledone, D (2006) Super Columbine Massacre RPG

Lionhead Studios (2005) Fable

Newsgaming.com (2003) September 12th

Origin Systems (1985) Ultima IV

Rockstar North (2004) Grand Theft Auto: San Andreas

Rockstar North (2002) Grand Theft Auto: Vice City

Rockstar North (2003) Manhunt

Team Ico (2006) Shadow of the Colossus

Valve Software (2000) Counter-Strike

This work was previously published in International Journal of Gaming and Computer-Mediated Simulations, Volume 1, Issue 3, edited by Richard E. Ferdig, pp. 1-13, copyright 2009 by IGI Publishing (an imprint of IGI Global).

Chapter 4
Game Design and the Challenge–Avoiding, Self–Validator Player Type

Carrie Heeter
Michigan State University, USA

Brian Magerko
Georgia Tech University, USA

Ben Medler
Georgia Tech University, USA

Joe Fitzgerald
Michigan State University, USA

ABSTRACT

Achiever and Explorer player types are well known in MMOs and educational games. Players who enjoy being a winner, but dislike hard challenges ("Self-Validators") are a heretofore ignored but commonly occurring player type. Self-Validators worry about and are distressed by failing. They can simply avoid playing overly difficult games for entertainment. But in a required learning game, Self-Validators' excessive worry about failing can interfere with learning. The authors consider whether and how eight very different modern games accommodate Explorers, Achievers, and Self-Validators and discuss implications for entertainment and learning game design and research. Seven of eight diverse games analyzed primarily served either the Explorer or Achiever player type. Self-Validators were partially accommodated in some Achiever-oriented games, through user-selectable difficulty. Design with all three types in mind would encourage inclusion of features that enable players to optimize their preferred style of play.

INTRODUCTION

Players who play a particular game purely by choice presumably do so because they derive satisfaction from playing that game. Individual gamers differ in which games they choose to play, how often, when, and for how long (Dawson, Craig, Taylor & Toombs, 2007). Individuals' preferred games and genres are probably associated with their enjoyment of the achievement

DOI: 10.4018/978-1-60960-565-0.ch004

and exploration pleasures provided by those games and genres. Many genres tend to be more closely associated with one or the other of those motivations. Achievement is the central paradigm in genres such as First-Person Shooters (FPSs), Fighting, Racing, Sports, and Action. Other genres such as Adventure, Strategy, RPG, Puzzle, and Simulation probably appeal more to Explorers because they interweave imagination, curiosity, and customization.

As digital games for entertainment expand to new audiences and playing games with a purpose beyond entertainment become required rather than voluntary, perspectives on player types must also grow. Players who play a game because they are required to (as is the case with games for the classroom or training games) or because they should (for example, physical or cognitive exercise games) are rarely afforded a choice of genre, or of which game to play, or even whether or not to play. Games for which play is required serve reluctant as well as eager players.

Achievers and *Explorers* are player types found in MMOs and educational games (Bartle, 2006; Heeter & Winn, 2008). Achievers are motivated by extrinsic rewards such as leveling up and earning high scores. Explorers are motivated by intrinsic factors such as curiosity, role play, and learning. Educational research on mindset and motivation reveal two distinctly different mechanisms of extrinsic motivation (Dweck, 2006; Lepper & Henderlong, 2000). Performance-approach learners are bored by easy tasks. They enjoy the thrill of mastering hard challenges and welcome good grades and teacher approval as just rewards (Elliot & Church, 1997). Performance-avoidance learners are anxious about failing. When performance-avoidance students perform graded tasks, they aspire to prove themselves, to validate their worth rather than aspiring to learn. They prefer easy challenges where success is likely over harder challenges where they might fail.

In this article we propose that Self-Validators are a heretofore ignored, but commonly occur-ring player type. We consider whether and how eight very different modern games accommodate Explorers, Achievers, and Self-Validators and discuss implications for entertainment and learning game design.

MOTIVATION AND LEARNING

Extrinsic Motivation and Learning

Formal education tends to be structured to use the threat of poor grades to motivate homework and learning. At the beginning of a semester or school year, teachers describe how standardized grades will be fairly assigned. Students are expected to do what is necessary to "pass" or better yet, to excel on the exams and other kinds of performances. Report cards document standardized achievement, informing students and parents about the learner's performance. In the context of this kind of achievement-focused education, learning scientists have looked at the impact of achievement orientation on learning. Achievement or goal orientation refers to how individuals perceive and respond to achievement situations (Dweck & Leggett, 1988). People who have a high achievement motivation enjoy challenges much more than those with a low achievement motivation (Lee, Sheldon, & Turban, 2003).

Elliot and Church (1997) considered two quite different reasons individuals might have for pursuing extrinsic, performance goals such as grades. Performance-approach goals are linked to displaying competence and earning a favorable judgment. Performance-avoidance goals focus on trying to avoid failure. Elliot and Church found positive outcomes for performance-approach goals including positive emotions and absorption in the given task. Performance-avoidance prompted efforts to escape potential consequences of failure and was associated with anxiety. Performance-avoidance interfered with mental focus, blocking the individual's ability to concentrate and become absorbed in an activity. The performance-approach goals approach enhanced mental focus.

Dweck (2006) made similar observations. She studied how people approach or avoid challenge in a school context. She found that about 42% of students have what she calls a growth, or Mastery mindset. These people believe that intelligence is malleable; that they are capable of improving if they try. Another 42% holds a Fixed or helpless mindset. They believe that intelligence is fixed at birth and cannot improve. They avoid situations that they cannot easily do well at. Failure undermines their confidence and if they fail, they become depressed and ineffective. (The remaining 16% could not be classified as either Fixed or Mastery mindset.) Having a Fixed mindset can undo a natural love of learning. In contrast, effort and learning make mastery-motivated students feel good about their intelligence; easy tasks waste their time rather than raising their self-esteem. Dweck describes the conundrum of the Fixed mindset. "If you're in a Fixed mindset, both positive and negative labels can mess with your mind. When you're given a positive label, you're afraid of losing it. When you're given a negative label, you're afraid of deserving it" (Dweck, 2006, pp. 75-76).

Mangels worked with Dweck and other colleagues to measure brain activation among individuals with a Fixed and Mastery mindset (Mangels, Butterfield, Lamb, Good, & Dweck, 2006). Participants completed a pretest that allowed researchers to classify them as one or the other mindset. They answered a series of knowledge questions, and were given feedback about whether their answers were right or wrong and what the right answer was. Brain scans revealed people with a Mastery mindset paid close attention to what the right answer was. Those with a Fixed mindset showed activation of the limbic, or emotional system, but paid much less attention to learning the right answer. In other words, Fixed mindset people focused on their own emotional response to being told they were right or wrong,

whereas Mastery mindset people paid most attention to learning new information.

Fixed mindset, performance-avoidance individuals are likely to experience anxiety when faced with achievement situations. Those with a Fixed mindset might be considered Self-Validators because when called upon to perform on a test at school or in a game, they worry about how others might perceive them if they fail. This concern may motivate studying, but this preoccupation with appearing to be successful can also interfere with performance and learning.

Having a Fixed mindset is considered dysfunctional for learning because it focuses learners on performance instead of mastery. Educators who are aware of the research look for ways to ease learners out of a Fixed mindset and into a Mastery mindset. They also craft feedback to focus on ways the learner can improve, rather than on labeling the person a success or failure (Dweck, 2006; Lepper & Henderlong, 2000).

INTRINSIC MOTIVATION AND LEARNING

Intrinsic goals internal to the act of learning can motivate learning, such as the pleasure of mastering a new topic, prior personal experiences related to the subject matter, or the sense of expertise as knowledge grows. Experimental schools such as Montessori nurture intrinsic motivation to drive learning. Rather than structuring a learning progression through standardized curriculum and standardized grades, Montessori tries to instill an internal sense of purpose. They avoid setting learners up to compete for the highest grade in the class. According to Montessori president Tim Seldin, "Students learn not to be afraid of making mistakes; they come to see them as natural steps in the learning process" (Seldin, 2008, p. 2).

Beswick (1971, 1974) found that intrinsically motivated individuals need time to explore. He explains that intrinsically motivated individuals "tend [to] be more aware of a wide range of phenomena, while giving careful attention to complexities, inconsistencies, novel events and unexpected possibilities. They need time and freedom to make choices, to gather and process information..." (Beswick, 2007, p.1).

MOTIVATION, PLAY STYLE AND GAMES

Player types were initially studied in the realm of commercial games. Intrinsic explorers and extrinsic achievers consistently show up in these studies, but Self-Validators have either not been studied (perhaps because they were not playing the games) or else they have not been noticed. Richard Bartle was one of first researchers to observe players inside Multi-User Dungeon (MUD) games (Bartle, 2006) in order to create a set of player types. Based on personal observations of game players he classified players into four categories: *Achievers*, who strive for prestige in the game by leveling up and winning and *Explorers*, who seek to understand the game's environment. Two other types were unique to multiplayer games: *Socializers*, who interact with other players and *Killers*, who interfere with other players' experiences (e.g., killing new users, etc.).

Nick Yee's Daedalus Project surveyed thousands of massively multiplayer online (MMO) game players and asked what motivated them to play MMO games (Yee, 2006; 2008). Although the surveys are based on self-reported responses, the resulting information found many confirmations and some contrasts with Bartle's original player types. Yee also discovered that these dimensions were not necessarily mutually exclusive. Statistically, the factors were not orthogonal. Players were not necessarily either achievement or exploration oriented but might also be motivated by both kinds of goals.

Yee's (2008) analysis of MMO play motivation based on player surveys identified three motivation domains: achievement, social, and immersion. Subcategories within Yee's *Achievement* construct included Advancement (progress, power accumulation, and status), Mechanics (numbers optimization, templating, and analysis), and Competition (challenging others, provocation, and domination). *Immersion* included Discovery (exploration, lore, finding hidden things), Role-Playing (story line, character history, roles, fantasy), Customization (appearances, accessories, style, color scheme), and Escapism (relax, escape from real life, avoiding real-life problems). Like Bartle, Yee also found a *Social* motivation included Socializing (casual chat, helping others, making friends), Relationship (personal, self-disclosure, find and give support), and Teamwork (collaboration, groups, group achievement).

Neither Bartle's nor Yee's description of Achievement include Self-Validation. Self-Validators, like Achievers, are motivated by extrinsic rewards. Like their mastery-oriented counterparts, Self-Validator players seek prestige and like to win. However, Self-Validators particularly dislike losing, so much so they would prefer an easy victory to a challenge where the probability of failing is high. Perhaps such were not interested in playing the MMOs these researchers studied. Or perhaps they did not discuss their fear of failure.

Self-Validators and Other Player Types in Serious Games

Learning games and other serious games tend to be single player. They lack the social dimension found in multiplayer games. Even within the more narrow range of available interactions in a single player learning game, researchers have observed systematic variations in play styles. Heeter and Winn (2008) proposed learning game play styles based on speed of play and problem-solving success. Adopting Ko's (2002) random-guesser and problem solver player types, successful problem-solvers were classified as either *Achievers* or *Explorers*. Achievers played quickly, paying attention to what was necessary to succeed and hurrying to complete the game. Explorers took their time playing, checking out necessary as well as extra in-game content. Random-guessers who played quickly and made many mistakes were considered *Careless* players. Random-guessers who played slowly yet made many mistakes were labeled *Lost*. Players classified as Careless and Lost probably includes many Self-Validators. These players did not seem to make any effort to play well. Failing without trying to succeed might be less devastating to a Self-Validator than trying hard and risking failure.

Heeter, Winn, Winn, and Bozoki (2008) found empirical evidence of Self-Validator play behavior in a memory game. When players were given complete control over the difficulty level, about 4 out of 10 opted for easy victories over and over again, never advancing to more challenging play. The easy victory players averaged higher performance (93% perfect scores) than their challenge-seeking counterparts (82% perfect scores). Self-Validator players adjusted the amount of challenge they faced to consistently earn high scores, while challenge-seeking Achiever players opted to forego near-perfect scores to strive for more difficult memory goals. Self-Validator is a dysfunctional play style for cognitive exercise games. To receive cognitive benefits, players need to stretch a little beyond what is already comfortable and easy (Mahncke et al., 2006). Limiting play to easy brain game challenges minimizes the games' benefits.

Game Design and Intrinsic and Extrinsic Motivation

Learning research has shown that under some circumstances, extrinsic and intrinsic motivations can coexist. In a review of 25 years of research on intrinsic versus extrinsic motivation, Lepper and Henderlong (2000) conclude that offering extrinsic rewards reduces intrinsic motivation, particularly if the extrinsic rewards are unrelated to the learning task. However, extrinsic rewards can complement intrinsic motivation when the rewards provide information about competence (such as offering encouraging feedback about positive aspects of player performance or suggesting ways to improve), but rewards undermine intrinsic motivation when they serve only to assign status (such as grades or points).

Game designers who want to accommodate both Achievers and Explorers can try to include something for everyone, but sometimes Achievers' and Explorers' needs are incompatible, forcing design choices that privilege one or the other form of preferred play. For example, Squire and Steinkuehler (2006) describe tensions between players with opposing goals when they posted feature requests about how to improve Star Wars Galaxy. Players with power-leveling, achievement goals wanted more pre-set story and clearly stated, fairly enforced standards for advancement. Players with a role play goal valued emergent play and freedom to invent their characters and actions.

Self-Validators and Achievers share an interest in extrinsic rewards, but are very different in their tolerance for failure. The mantra "easy to learn, hard to master" describes one of the holy grails of game design (Playyoo, 2008). This tenet could serve Self-Validators well and yet also satisfy Achievers. Much of the time, though, game designs to satisfy Self-Validators' desire for easy victory are incompatible with Achievers' desire to try to overcome impossible odds.

Methods

We were curious about how well today's games are designed to serve Achievers, Self-Validators, and Explorers. Do games tend to specialize in a single player type? Are Self-Validators' needs accommodated? Eight games available in single player mode (shown in Table 1) were chosen to represent a range of genres and to include a mix of games likely to appeal to intrinsically and extrinsically motivated players. Genres covered

Table 1. Games, their genre and well-served player types

Game	Genre	Player Motivation
Bioshock	FPS	**Ⓐ** Ⓢ Ⓔ
Guitar Hero	play along	**Ⓐ** Ⓢ Ⓔ
Keep It In Mind	brain game	Ⓐ Ⓢ Ⓔ
Puzzle Quest	puzzle/RPG	Ⓐ Ⓢ Ⓔ
Animal Crossing	virtual life	**Ⓐ** Ⓢ Ⓔ
Budget Hero	budget simulation	Ⓐ Ⓢ Ⓔ
FlOw	sensory experience	Ⓐ Ⓢ Ⓔ
Play The News	current events	Ⓐ Ⓢ Ⓔ

include first person shooters (FPS), play along, brain games, puzzle/role play games (RPG), virtual life, sensory experience, current events, and budget simulation. Four of the games (Bioshock, Guitar Hero, Keep It In Mind and Puzzle Quest) offer extrinsic rewards to the player. The other four games (Animal Crossing, Budget Hero, FlOw, and Play the News) mainly offer intrinsic rewards. Each of the four co-authors analyzed two games. A second coauthor reviewed and edited their analysis.

We provide a short synopsis of each game and its main mechanics. We discuss which player types are served by the game mechanics and conclude by envisioning specific additions or subtractions that might make the game more appealing for each player type. At the beginning of each game section, beneath the game title, a figure graphical summarizes how much each game promotes or focuses on the three player types (A = Achiever,

S = Self-Validator, and E = Explorer). A black circle means that player type is highly focused upon by the game. A half black half white circle means the player type is somewhat focused upon and the white circle means the game focuses very little on that player type.

RESULTS

Individual Game Analyses

Animal Crossing: Wild World (DS)

Animal Crossing: Wild World (DS) is a life/garden simulation game. The player takes charge of an embodied character in a small, contained game

world. The player is given a home and then has to earn money to pay back a mortgage by planting trees, fishing, searching for treasure, talking with NPCs, creating clothing, buying and selling items, and so forth. There is no ending; the game continues for as long as the player plays.

Animal Crossing contains intrinsically motivated gameplay. The game has very few goals to achieve, leaving players to create their own goals. Explorers can enjoy playing at their own pace while discovering how the world works. When players discover how to perform certain actions the game opens up related rewards. For example, learning to fish allows players to collect all available fish. Self-Validators can easily achieve the game's main goal of paying off a mortgage while facing minimal challenge. Achievers are likely to find the lack of clear goals and hard challenges uninteresting.

Animal Crossing could be adapted to please Achievers by providing more overt goals, increasing the difficulty level, and allowing NPCs to compete with players. Providing a series of goals (such as you must pay off half your mortgage within a week) would allow Achievers to experience continuous progression. Self-Validators would enjoy less stressful goals than Achievers, but would benefit from more recognition of their accomplishments. Unlike Achievers, Self-Validators would enjoy subtle hints given by the game's NPCs to improve their performance. The game already provides myriad discovery activities for Explorers.

Bioshock

Bioshock is an FPS that incorporates RPG game mechanics. The story takes place in a huge underwater city where the player gets caught up in a civil war. Players must fight their way through multiple levels using different types of weapons to win the game. Standard firearms with genetic modifiers give players unique powers (such as the ability to create fire). Players must figure out effective way to use these weapons alone or in combination to progress through the game.

Bioshock mostly offers extrinsically motivated play. The main point is to gather weapons and complete levels as quickly and efficiently as possible. An Explorer may enjoy the storyline (told through in-game journal entries) and learning how to upgrade weapons; however, these features of the game primarily exist to help the player progress through each level. The game continuously rewards Achievers for progressing. Bioshock's dynamic difficulty system presents all players with ever tougher challenges. This ideally suits Achievers, but may turn away Self-Validators who take more pleasure in success than in challenge.

Adapting Bioshock for Explorers would call for less of an exclusive focus on combat and more emphasis on storyline. Explorers would enjoy more choice as to when, where and whether to enter combat. Other mechanisms to victory such as out-smarting rather than out-fighting enemies could also broaden appeal. The preferences of Achievers and Self-Validators are incompatible. Curbing the difficulty of the game and quickly offering help might please Self-Validators, but would alienate Achievers.

Budget Hero

Budget Hero challenges players to set a new budget for the U.S. government. The player chooses which departmental policies to fund, such as the military or educational policies, as well as which tax plans to use. Players lay out their spending plans by choosing policy cards which equate to spending or cutting funding of specific policies. Players then submit the budget and see simulated results of their budget over the next two decades. The game provides extra information on each policy card to aid their decision and to allow the player to search through archived player budgets to see how their choices compare to other players' based on everyone's demographics.

This small serious game teaches provides few extrinsic rewards. Explorers would enjoy Budget Hero because of its rich, abundant information. Each time a policy card is selected the user may read the card's summary, pros and cons, or the impact a certain policy will have on the country. When a policy card is added to a player's budget, the effects that the policy has on the budget are shown, giving the player a clear picture of how each policy affects their budget. The game is very forgiving. Players can change their minds as often as they want before submitting a final budget. Self-Validators will enjoy the instant feedback; however both Self-Validators and Achievers will be bored by the lack of extrinsic rewards.

Achievers would need more goals and constraints if Budget Hero were modified to serve them. Anonymous budgets could be replaced by nicknames and leader boards, allowing players to be recognized for their achievements. Awards could be given, such as an award for building a balanced budget with the fewest cards. Adding extra constraints that affect how the player builds their budget, such as declaring that the military spending must be cut in half, could provide extra challenges. Self-Validators share the desire for more goals and recognition, but not for harder goals. Self-Validators (because it would help them succeed) and Explorers (because they are curious) would both enjoy more information on how policy cards interact with one another.

Flow

In Flow, the player is a free-floating, free-flowing creature in the abyss of a fluid and deep space. The goal of the game is to eat and evolve by devouring smaller entities to help your creature become larger and more complex. The game contains an embedded dynamic difficulty system which gives the player intuitively customized gameplay based on their skill. Play occurs at the player's own pace. Players can customize the appearance of their organism.

Flow is Explorer oriented because of the immersion of the game. The main extrinsic reward is evolution. Players evolve when they eat other organisms. Each evolutionary step changes the game play because the organism is different. Players wander each level discovering new creatures to eat and battle. The adaptive difficulty allows Self-Validators to progress through the game at a challenge level they are comfortable with. However, battling does not accrue reward points or awards which both Self-Validators and Achievers like to receive. Players can set their own goals such as trying to unlock all of the evolutionary forms or speeding through the levels as fast as they can. Because there are few performance metrics, Achievers and Self-Validators have no way to measure their success.

Adapting Flow to Achievers by adding points, distinct levels, boss battles, and rewards would transform the game into a traditional arcade game and would potentially drive away Explorers. Constraints such as a health bar or timer would also increase Achiever enjoyment. Self-Validators would need a more helpful version of the player interface, perhaps including a map showing them the locations of other creatures. Making larger creatures easier to kill or allow players to replay levels would also help Self-Validators. Explorers could be allowed to switch evolutionary form freely or even to combine evolutionary forms.

Guitar Hero

In Guitar Hero the player is a guitarist in a rock band who plays songs on a special guitar-like peripheral device. Playing through a list of increasingly difficult songs earns the title of "Rock God." Songs are played by pressing down multiple buttons to simulate guitar finger positions while hitting another button in rhythm with the song to simulate strumming guitar strings. Difficulty settings alter the complexity and tempo of the music. Players play alone or against one another. Successful play unlocks extra songs, characters, or guitar models.

Playing Guitar Hero is all about earning points and unlocking content. Players earn points for each note played correctly and gain bonuses for a succession of correct notes. Achievers enjoy the rewards and challenges that Guitar Hero offers and Self-Validators probably like being able to play through most of the songs on the difficulty setting of their choosing. Explorers will find the game unsatisfying because of the very linear and repetitive play that is required.

When adapting for Explorers, players would need more freedom to move about the game, especially within songs. Taking away the point-oriented mechanics in the songs would allow other mechanics to be implemented such as song recording, improvisation, and practice modes. Explorers also may enjoy the chance to learn about the songs that they play (such as the history of the song writers or the cultural relevance of the song). Self-Validators may need practice modes and the ability to slow down songs or to forgive more mistakes. The negative feedback that accompanies mistakes could also be removed for both Self-Validators and Explorers, taking away the audience meter and booing which can force a song to end in failure.

Keep it in Mind

Keep it in Mind is a short term memory game. Players select the category of items with wish to remember (numbers, letters, words, patterns, objects) and the difficulty level. The player is initially shown two items from their selected category and is asked to remember them, in the order shown. When trying to remember the items in a round the player is then shown 8 items for easy rounds and 16 items for medium and hard rounds which include the items they are trying to remember. The player picks out the items they remember. After each round players have the option of repeating the current number of items, advancing to try to remember one more item, or starting over at 2 items.

Of the 8 games, Keep it in Mind is the most oriented to Self-Validators because of it combines extrinsic rewards and complete player control over the challenge level. Achievers and Self-Validators can both enjoy the frequent extrinsic rewards of genius percent (accuracy) and speed that are shown after every challenge. Achievers can choose advanced difficulty level and work to remember all 7 items. Self-Validators can stick with challenges they succeed at easily. Explorers' needs are met only by being able to try a variety of cognitive domains and subcategories of items to remember.

Keep it in Mind could adapt to Explorers by allowing more customization and player generation of content. Players could add their own set of items to remember or allow them to mix and match sets of items to play with. For Achievers the game could include more awards and goals during gameplay.

Play the News

Play the News players become more informed about issues of the day. A player selects an issue to play, for example election coverage or regional skirmishes, and is presented with background information about the issues. Once players have examined the background information they are asked a question about the outcome of that issue. They are asked what outcome they believe *should* happen and they are asked to predict what outcome *will* happen. Each player is ranked as to how whether the player's "should" votes match the votes of other players (popular opinion). The game keeps statistics on player prediction accuracy. (This cannot be tabulated until the issue is resolved in real life, usually one to a few weeks after game play.) Players can also generate content in the form of creating their own games (based around a current event) and by writing or responding to other players' comments about the news.

The game oriented to Explorers. Play the News requires players to understand the ideas behind each issue they are presented with in order to do well in the game. Thus, being able to predict the outcomes with a high accuracy is a by-product of learning about the issues being presented. Explorers likely enjoy generating games and discussing the issues with other players. The game does include extrinsic rewards in the form of badges and awards such as Predictor of the Week or Streak (correctly predicting 3 issues in a row). Achievers may end up playing every issue in order to level up and become known winner. Self-Validators will be deterred by having their performance be public. They will not enjoy being wrong so they will probably stick to issues that they know a lot about.

Play the News could be adapted to appeal more to Self-Validators by allowing players the option of hiding their prediction accuracy. This would allow those players to give out information when they feel comfortable doing so. For Achievers, adding gambling style mechanics to the game could add more risk, for instance letting players state how sure they are about their answer or letting players vote without seeing any information.

Puzzle Quest: Challenge of the Warlords (DS)

Puzzle Quest is a RPG/puzzle game that takes place in a fantasy world. Players choose a class (profession) and must improve their skill statistics throughout the game in order to succeed at harder challenges as the story progresses. Players' skills are enhanced by items players can purchase and magic spells players can learn. All fighting and research is performed using a Bejeweled-style gameplay where players competitively match gems on a game-board to receive related points. The puzzles are one shot endeavors: the player either wins or loses. They earn money and experience points for each puzzle based on their success.

As is common in RPG games, Puzzle Quest is strongly oriented to extrinsic rewards for a wide variety of player actions. All battles eventually reward players with money or general experience points. Achievers will enjoy continually harder challenges. Self-Validators may not enjoy the game because rewarding success with a harder challenge is not their idea of a good reward. Explorers may enjoy the game much more than Self-Validators since they will get pleasure from the storyline, the many items and spells, and the ability to create their own items. Since Explorers by nature will explore and learn about what the game provides they will be better at solving challenges than Self-Validators who are not as curious.

Since Self-Validators have the roughest time playing Puzzle Quest the game could adapt to this player type by providing tailored help. For example, Self-Validators would benefit from practice turns in battle where they can see how their next move or spell will affect their enemy. The game could also list items and spells that the player has not seen yet along with hints about how to acquire the ones they need. Battles would also need to be rewarded by more than just money and experience; items and spells given automatically after battle could equip Self-Validators face future challenges. To appeal more to Explorers, Puzzle Quest could add new game mechanics (such as managing a cities or trading) so long as those mechanics do not hinder the progress of achievement-oriented players.

ACROSS GAME SYNTHESIS

Design for Individual Player Types

There are commonalities between the games that we have analyzed above that can lead us to make general prescriptions for games designed for each of the three player types. Each player type affords different design decisions and examples of what can be provided for each player type include:

Achievers need an increasing set of challenges and strict goals to follow. This includes: building dynamic difficulty systems, having specific points in the game that are extremely challenging, and performance metrics that rank players. Achievers should also be provided with goal-specific and unique constraints to overcome, and should be rewarded as they complete those goals.

Self-Validators need easier challenges where the game adapts to the skills players like to use most and rewards players implicitly as they make progress through the game. Self-Validators also need forgiving games, ones that give them gameplay hints, allow practice sessions, avoid negative feedback and enable them to hide bad performances.

Explorers do not necessarily need challenge, but if challenge is included it should revolve around in-depth game content. This can include more storyline information and greater number of mechanic choices. Explorers also enjoy having the means to test hypotheses and study the game-world through customization and free access to more game content.

Table 1 shows the complete set of games and how well each currently serves Achievers, Self-Validators, and Explorers.

Considering the games we have analyzed, games tend to primarily serve either the Explorer or Achiever player type. Focusing on one of these player types (e.g., Explorers) often means that a game serves the opposite player type (e.g., Achievers) less well. In terms of how well games serve the three player types, we tend to see either  or else .

Self-Validators are often supported to some extent within each game, through user-selectable difficulty settings and other challenge monitoring adaptive features. However, not every game we analyzed supported our player types in this order. Puzzle Quest, Keep it in Mind, and Play the News either focused on the Self-Validator type as their main player type or as their weakest type.

Overlap between Player Types

In addition to understanding how each game serves one or another player, developers also can consider how these player types connect to one another. In the subsequent sections these connections and the mutual traits of each player type pair are discussed.

Achievers and Explorers

Both of these player types enjoy learning as much as they can about a game, just for different reasons. Achievers learn as much as they can about a game to help them achieve more. If that learning does not connect back to achievement, Achievers will lose interest. Explorers learn as much as they can about a game because they are curious and like learning. A pure Explorer (one who is not also an Achiever) has no need for goals or achievement in a game. Puzzle Quest, an RPG, serves Achievers and Explorers by giving them a large content set and many goals to reach or explore. This leaves Self-Validators lost because they are faced with a game that has enormous depth, which the player must dive into in order to succeed, without sufficient help.

Achievers and Self-Validators

These two player types have extrinsic motivations in common. They both work towards rewards and judgments of their performance. They are also similar because Achievers, while they wish to perform as best as they can, have to start somewhere, usually at the challenge level that Self-Validators enjoy. Therefore, games like Bioshock and Guitar Hero can provide a spectrum of difficulty where both player types can enjoy playing the game. This can alienate Explorers because they have to play through the same redundant challenges as the other two player types which restrain them from exploring.

Explorers and Self-Validators

Since Self-Validators do not like extreme challenges (unless they succeed) and Explorers like to explore content at their choosing, games that provide easier means of progression through the game can work for both player types. Also, Explorers like to study and play with the mechanics provided within games, including customization. This feature also helps Self-Validators to set the difficulty of the game's challenges to a level that is comfortable. This leaves Achievers unfulfilled because players can progress through the game and earn rewards without any significant skill or mastery. It is not a fair competition when the

same goals are made easier for players who want them to be easy.

Must Players Be A Single Type?

As we already discussed, motivation research on learning and game research on play style show that extrinsic and intrinsic rewards are not necessarily mutually exclusive (Lepper & Henderlong, 2000; Yee, 2008). Among the four co-authors of this manuscript, one is a pure Explorer and the other three are self-described Achiever-Explorers. In different games and at different times when playing the same game a player may orient more towards one primary type. Self-Validator and Achiever motivations are the least likely to coexist. It would be contradictory for a player to prefer easy successes and hard challenges.

Changing How Players Play

Finally, another way that games may use player types is to introduce ways to change a player's motivation into a different one. The most logical instance of this would be to subtly nudge a Self-Validator into being more of an Achiever. Dweck's (2006) research has shown than mindsets can be changed. Since Self-Validators focus on whether they are being judged favorably or unfavorably rather than on whether they are learning, an adaptive system might be designed to nudge them to focus more on mastery. This could include giving them hints throughout the game about how learning from failure can greatly increases players' chances of future success. Focusing players' attention more on nuanced strategies and context and giving feedback that helps players improve could move them towards playing as an Achiever rather than a Self-Validator. Also, enabling them to review their progress and to replay content would improve understanding and encourage them try new ideas and techniques.

DISCUSSION

Implications for Learning and Other Serious Game Design

Games for learning are more likely to be played by Self-Validators than are games for entertainment because players are often forced to play and because success in the game tends to be linked to sensitive constructs such as intelligence, ability, and real world advancement. Unlike entertainment games in which a player's performance can be private, the teacher or supervisor may monitor in-game achievement. All of these factors encourage potentially susceptible players to adopt a Self-Validator approach. The Self-Validator Fixed mindset interferes with classroom learning and with learning in games. Rather than "lowering the stakes" and offering easy challenges, learning game designers may instead want to dampen the sting of failure. This can be done by careful attention to the tone and content of player feedback for both success and failure. Feedback that focuses on player performance (for example, in Budget Hero, "you completed the Health and Wellness and the Competitive Advantage budget badges, but did not complete the Energy Independence badge") rather than feedback that evaluates the player (for example, in Budget Hero, "you're almost a budget hero") can help nudge Self-Validators towards a mastery orientation.

Games and learning scholar James Gee writes that "good computer and video games are complex, challenging, and long; they can take 50 or more hours to finish" (Gee, 2007, p. 45). Gee points out that failing is part of playing a video game. Failure in video games "allow[s] players to take risks and try out hypotheses…" (p. 153). In fact, failing is a key mechanism in games by which players learn and improve. Self-Validator seems to be a dysfunctional player type for learning games. Gee's celebration of the gamer ethic of learning from failure works well for Achievers but not for Self-Validators. Similarly, the benefits from

cognitive games can best be realized if the player can be enticed into taking on hard challenges.

Thus, game designers want to discourage players adopting a Self-Validator play style, without driving players away. Careful crafting of feedback might help nudge players into an Achiever style. If players are seriously concerned about their cognitive health, the feedback can be quite prescriptive. Here is a hypothetical example of feedback designed to entice Self-Validators to play like Achievers. "You correctly remembered 3 items (quartz, tiger eye, and granite) and missed two (azurite and jade). Trying hard challenges helps keep brains healthy. Repeat the 5 item challenge and earn two-for-one points or go back to the easier challenge of 4 items." Serious games can also add content and depth to interest Explorers and to encourage players to experience intrinsic rewards from playing and learning.

Implications for Game Design

A main take away from this work is that it is likely helpful for designers to be aware of the commonalities and differences between (as well as simply the existence of) the discussed player types. While it is not an exhaustive review of all player motivations (e.g., social or physical health goals are not taken into account), it does offer a clear picture of the kinds of game mechanics in various game genres that map to these player types.

This illumination can be put to use in two different ways. The first is simply to help designers and producers make a more informed decision on how to make games for target audiences. Further research needs to be done on exploring the distribution of these player types in different populations (e.g., what percentage of 18-25 year old males are Achievers?); however, having a clearer idea of the motivations of a target audience can influence the design process for a given game. Inversely, understanding how a game's design relates to the motivations of different audiences can help a team understand which audiences are likely to play it.

The second use of this work is in the application of our knowledge of player types to the intelligent adaptation of games. As described by Magerko (2008), games have the potential to be intelligently adapted based on models of the player interacting with it. Designers do not have to necessarily build incredibly large or complex games that have something for everyone (e.g., World of Warcraft arguably has game features for most player types) in order to target multiple player types. The deconstruction of multiple games done earlier in the article illustrates of how games have multiple possible versions of the core game idea that can appeal to multiple types of players. Therefore, games have the potential to be designed as flexible media experiences that adapt based on the type of player interacting with it. For example, if an Explorer is playing Guitar Hero, then it may alter the gameplay to incorporate the kinds of recommendations we make above (e.g., including music history content to explore about the songs in the game). This adaptive approach to games has the potential to provide a powerfully individualized experience to game players. Our current work on designing games that provide this kind of adaptivity is described in Magerko, Heeter, Medler, and Fitzgerald (2008).

REFERENCES

Bartle, R. (1990). *Interactive multi-user computer games.* MUSE Ltd, British Telecom, December.

Bartle, R. (2006). Hearts, clubs, diamonds, spades: Players who suit MUDs. In Salen, K., & Zimmerman, E. (Eds.), *The game design reader* (pp. 754–787). Cambridge, MA: MIT Press.

Casual Games Market Report. (2007). *All about casual.* Retrieved April 11, 2009, from Casual Connect web site: http://www.casualconnect.org/newscontent/11-2007/CasualGamesMarketReport2007_Summary.pdf

Dawson, C. R., Cragg, A., Taylor, C., & Toombs, B. (2007). *Video games: Research to improve understanding of what players enjoy about video games, and to explain their preferences for particular games. British Board of Film Classification.* BBFC.

Dweck, C. (2000). *Self-theories: Their role in motivation, personality, and development.* Philadelphia, PA: Taylor & Francis.

Dweck, C. (2006). *Mindset: The new psychology of success.* New York: Random House.

Dweck, C. S., & Leggett, E. L. (1988). A social-cognitive approach to motivation and personality. *Psychological Review, 95,* 256–273. doi:10.1037/0033-295X.95.2.256

Elliot, E. S., & Church, M. A. (1997). A hierarchal model of approach and avoidance achievement motivation. *Journal of Personality and Social Psychology, 72,* 218–232. doi:10.1037/0022-3514.72.1.218

Gee, J. (2007). *Good video games + good learning: Collected essays on video games, language, and learning.* New York: Peter Lang.

Heeter, C., & Winn, B. (2008). Implications of gender, player type and learning strategies for the design of games for learning. In Kafai, Y., Heeter, C., Denner, J., & Sun, J. (Eds.), *Beyond Barbie and Mortal Kombat: New perspectives on gender and gaming.* Cambridge, MA: MIT Press.

Heeter, C., Winn, B., Winn, J., & Bozoki, A. (2008, October). The challenge of challenge: Avoiding and embracing difficulty in a memory game. *Meaningful Play Conference.* East Lansing, Michigan.

Ko, S. (2002). An empirical analysis of children's thinking and learning in a computer game context. *Educational Psychology, 22*(2), 219–233. doi:10.1080/01443410120115274

Lazzaro, N. (2007). The 4 most important emotions of game design. *Game Developers Conference*. San Francisco.

Lee, F. K., Sheldon, K. M., & Turban, D. B. (2003). Personality and the goal striving process: The influence of achievement goal patterns, goal level, and mental focus on performance and enjoyment. *The Journal of Applied Psychology, 88*, 256–265. doi:10.1037/0021-9010.88.2.256

Lepper, M. R., Aspinwall, L. G., Mumme, D. L., & Chabay, R. W. (1990). Self-perception and social perception processes in tutoring: Subtle social control strategies of expert tutors. In J. Olson & M. P. Zanna (Eds.), *Self inference processes: The Sixth Ontario Symposium in Social Psychology* (pp. 217-237). Hillsdale, NJ: Erlbaum.

Lepper, M. R., & Henderlong, J. (2000). Turning "play" into "work" and "work" into "play": 25 years of research on intrinsic versus extrinsic motivation. In Sansone, C., & Harackiewicz, J. M. (Eds.), *Intrinsic and extrinsic motivation: The search for optimal motivation and performance* (pp. 257–307). San Diego: Academic Press. doi:10.1016/B978-012619070-0/50032-5

Magerko, B. (2008). Adaptation in digital games. Entertainment Computing Column. *IEEE Computer Magazine, 41*(6), 87–89.

Magerko, B., Heeter, C., Medler, B., & Fitzgerald, J. (2008). Intelligent adaptation of digital game-based learning. In *Proceedings of the FuturePlay Conference*, Toronto.

Mahncke, H. (2006, August 15). Memory enhancement in healthy older adults using a brain plasticity-based training program: A randomized, controlled study. *Proceedings of the National Academy of Sciences of the United States of America, 103*(33). doi:10.1073/pnas.0605194103

Mangels, J. A., Butterfield, B., Lamb, J., Good, C. D., & Dweck, C. S. (2006). Why do beliefs about intelligence influence learning success? A social-cognitive-neuroscience model. *Social Cognitive and Affective Neuroscience, 1*, 75–86. doi:10.1093/scan/nsl013

Playyoo (2008). *Snacking on casual games*. Retrieved April 11, 2009, from Playyoo Blog: http://blog.playyoo.com/tags/casual-games/

PopCap Games. (2006). *Study: Women choose "casual" videogames over TV; 100 Million+ women now play regularly, for different reasons than men*. Retrieved April 11, 2009, from Popcap Games web site: http://www.popcap.com/press/release.php?gid=2006-10-02

Seldin, T. (2008). *Montessori 101: Some basic information that every Montessori parent should know*. Retrieved April 11, 2009, from Montessori web site: http://www.montessori.org/sitefiles/Montessori_101_nonprintable.pdf

Squire, K., & Steinkuehler, C. (2006). Generating CyberCulture/s: The case of Star Wars Galaxies. In Gibbs, D., & Krause, K. (Eds.), *Cyberlines2: Languages and cultures of the Internet* (2nd ed.). Albert Park, Australia: James Nicholas Publishers.

Yee, N. (2007). Motivations of play in online games. *Journal of CyberPsychology and Behavior, 9*, 772–775. doi:10.1089/cpb.2006.9.772

Yee, N. (2008). Maps of digital desires: Exploring the topography of gender and play in online games. In Kafai, Y., Heeter, C., Denner, J., & Sun, J. (Eds.), *Beyond Barbie and Mortal Kombat: New perspectives in gender and gaming*. Cambridge, MA: MIT Press.

This work was previously published in International Journal of Gaming and Computer-Mediated Simulations, Volume 1, Issue 3, edited by Richard E. Ferdig, pp. 53-67, copyright 2009 by IGI Publishing (an imprint of IGI Global).

Chapter 5
Using Recommendation Systems to Adapt Gameplay

Ben Medler
Georgia Institute of Technology, USA

ABSTRACT

Recommendation systems are key components in many Web applications (Amazon, Netflix, eHarmony). Each system gathers user input, such as the products they buy, and searches for patterns in order to determine user preferences and tastes. These preferences are then used to recommend other content that a user may enjoy. Games on the other hand are often designed with a one-size-fits-all approach not taking player preferences into account. However there is a growing interest in both the games industry and game research communities to begin incorporating systems that can adapt, or alter how the game functions, to specific players. This article examines how Web application recommendation systems compare to current games that adapt their gameplay to specific players. The comparison shows that current games do not use recommendation methods that are data intensive or collaborative when adapting to players. Design suggestions are offered within this manuscript for how game developers can benefit from incorporating the lesser used recommendation methods.

INTRODUCTION

Games are often designed with a one-size-fits-all approach. Each player will get the same experience within the game regardless of their personal playing style. Developers attempt to design games in this way so that a game will reach as many players in their target audience as possible. The demographics that make up these markets however are varied (Herrmann, 2007). Additionally, as the number of online players grows (Herrmann, 2007) developers will need ways to precisely target their current player markets along with new potential markets becoming available. Developers could create niche games that focus on specific groups of players or they could broaden the appeal of a game by leveraging features that adapt game play to better suit a particular player's needs. Players who are familiar with personalized content delivered online, via recommendation systems, will come to expect games that mold, or adapt, to their preferences and tastes. This manuscript argues that designing games that adapt to specific players could provide more challenging and engaging experiences for those players. A first step towards building adaptive games is to understand how recommendation systems provide personalized content to users.

Recommendation systems filter user input information in order to provide users with suitable content based on their preferences and tastes (Chen, Han, Wang, Zhou, Xu, & Zang, 2007). This is done by first collecting input information, for instance a user's rating scores for a list of movies on a movie recommendation website. The system then filters that information by making correlations within the data using different filtering methods and searching for patterns between the data and the system's users (Adomavicius & Tuzhilin, 2005; Segaran, 2007; Vozalis & Margaritis, 2003). The system then determines which patterns are the most relevant, for instance if a user ranks action movies higher than movies in other genres this creates a pattern showing that the user most likely enjoys action movies. These patterns are then used to deliver the final recommendation to each user (a user that enjoys action movies will be recommended more action movies).

Adaptive systems operate in a similar fashion as recommendation systems. In an adaptive game, adaptation occurs when a game modifies the player's character, non-player characters, or the game's environment/statistics based on player information the game gathers (Bailey & Katchabaw, 2005; Charles, Kerr, McNeill, McAlister, Black, Kücklich, 2005). Thus instead of a system that recommends related items, an adaptive game will alter the gameplay or game content, in order to fit the preferences of each player. Some current games already offer adaptive features that manipulate gameplay based on the player's skill level (Miller, 2004). There also exists a growing

field of researchers that are building games that model player goals and traits in order to adapt to that particular player (Magerko & Laird, 2003; Thue, Bulitko, Spetch, & Wasylishen, 2007; Togelius, De Nardi, & Lucas, 2007).

This article will examine how examples of recommendation systems work within the web domain and how the techniques used by those systems can help produce games that incorporate similar techniques for adaptive purposes. Beginning with a theoretical framework the author will examine why recommendation and adaption techniques are valid practices for producing games. Next, an overview of how recommendation systems work is provided and is compared to other current, game-related, adaptive and recommendation systems. Finally, after determining the missing techniques not employed by adaptive games, when compared to recommendation systems, design suggestions are made in order to relate current examples of recommendation techniques can be used to enhance gameplay.

THEORETICAL FRAMEWORK

While developer motivations for producing games that reach a wider audience are financial, if players do not enjoy playing games that adapt to their preferences then the players will choose not to purchase the game. Beyond financial reasons, there are also pedagogical reasons for adaptive games. Serious games, or games used for educational purposes, that can adapt to specific students could provide personalized learning experiences for each student. How do we know that adaptive games will produce experiences that players will want to play and potentially help those players that are using games as learning tools?

Players play games for different reasons (Lazzaro, 2008; Sherry, Lucas, Greenberg, & Lachlan, 2006; Yee, 2007). In theory, having an adaptive game that can cater to a user's specific reasons for playing will provide a better experience for the player than a game that has static gameplay. One of these reasons for playing is facing challenges, meaning that players wish to improve their skills by facing new challenges (Lazzaro, 2008; Sherry et al., 2006), such as discovering new information, customizing or become a better team worker (Yee, 2007). Games inherently have conflicts or sets of challenges that players must overcome (Salen & Zimmerman, 2003) and the reason why players want to face challenges within games can be related to how people learn as they face new challenges.

Lee Vygotsky's "Zone of Proximal Development" (Vygotsky, 1978) posits that students learn best when they are challenged at the fringes of their abilities, yet may need a more knowledgeable peer or teacher at times to guide their learning. The "Zone of Proximal Development" is determined by how much help a student needs verses how much they can achieve by themselves. This is similar to the concept of scaffolding (Instructional scaffolding, 2007) where students are given initial support and is slowly taken away as they master the material. Scaffolding has been used in other adaptive learning systems, called intelligent tutoring systems, that monitor a learner's progress, aiding the learner when needed (Anderson, Corbett, Koedinger, & Pelletier, 1995). Treating games as learning environments, and following the concepts of scaffolding, an adaptive game system can observe how a player is performing in a game and act accordingly. Understanding how well a player is performing in the game can be used to gauge the challenge level a player should face in the game.

James Gee, following Vygotsky's work, outlined a series of learning principles that he believes characterize great video games (Gee, 2007). These features, not coincidentally, also characterize great pedagogy. Five of these principles are relevant to adaptive systems: achievement, practice, ongoing learning, "regime of competence" and probing. The first principle, Achievement, provides learners with rewards and incentives to continue to push forward. The Practice and Probing principles

give learners safe environments where they can continually test their skills without the fear of being judged. Finally the Ongoing Learning and "Regime of Competence" principles explain how games continually challenge learners and allow them to become a master of a skill set, just like the "Zone of Proximal Development" states. All of the principles share one thing in common: they are dependent on a learner's skill level. Determining a learner's skill level is similar to determining their tastes or preferences in order to provide adapt gameplay and, as discussed later, how recommendation techniques can help in the adaption process. Additionally the probing principle is an example of how a player's performance can be monitored. As players continually probe the game their actions can be recorded and used to adjust the game's content accordingly, which parallels how a recommendation system works.

In addition to pedagogy principles, adaptive games can deliver challenging experiences for entertainment purposes. However, not all players wish to continually face challenges and may want to play games for relaxation or to escape reality (Sherry et al., 2006; Yee, 2007). Adaptive games, for entertainment purposes, should be built to take these factors into account by monitoring how much of a challenge is needed to engage a player. Csikszentmihalyi's flow theory explains that an individual is in a "flow" state, or an engaged state, when they are experiencing a situation that is equal to their skill level (Csikszentmihalyi, 1991). This means that the activity they are performing is not so hard that they become frustrated but not too easy where they become bored. Similar to Gee's and Vygotsky's theories, flow theory looks at bringing a player to the edge of their competency level and continually challenging that level. Flow theory can also be used to keep users in a state that they find engaging and enjoyable without having to continually push them with new challenges. Adaptive games can use flow theory to determine whether or not a player wants to increase their proficiency in the game and can continue to provide for that player's desires.

Achieving a challenging experience is similar to achieving a challenging learning environment given the theories stated in this section. Also, understanding how to provide a challenging experience can be used to create a less challenging, yet engaging, experience if it is deemed necessary. In order to create these challenging or engaging experiences a game must monitor and make assumptions about the player of the game, adapting to their preferences. While recommendation systems do not traditionally challenge users, this manuscript argues that recommendation systems can help adaptive games determine player preferences and help produce challenging and engaging environments for players.

RECOMMENDATION SYSTEMS

Recommendation systems gather information from a specific set of information, filter the information (meaning finding useful patterns), and then output relevant results to users or the system's designers. These systems can be classified into three types of approaches: Content-based, Collaborative and a Hybrid approach (Adomavicius & Tuzhilin, 2005).

- **Content-based recommendations:** The user will be recommended items similar to the ones the user preferred in the past.
- **Collaborative recommendations:** The user will be recommended items that people with similar tastes and preferences liked in the past.
- **Hybrid approaches:** These methods combine collaborative and content-based methods.

Content-based approaches take an item-based and user-centric attitude while filtering. This means the output a user receives will be based

heavily on the connections that exist between the items and themselves. An example of this is when Google Ad Sense determines the frequency of words on a Web page and delivers ads based on the most common words. In this case the user is the Web page and the items being recommended are the ads. Conversely, collaborative filtering takes a population-based approach to finding recommendations (both in terms of item population and user population). Looking at large population groups, collaborative approaches find patterns among the connections between an entire group of users and item. These definitions are over generalizations of both content-based and collaborative systems but explain the principles of how each approach relies on different connection information that exists between users and items.

When a system has a low population a content-based approach performs better, since they find connections between a single user and items (Segaran, 2007). Once a large number of users have contributed enough data to a system the collaborative approaches become much more useful (Segaran, 2007). Combining content and collaborative systems into a hybrid system can help alleviate the differences that exist between the two approaches (Adomavicius & Tuzhilin, 2005). For instance, a hybrid approaches is to perform a content-based filter when the system's user population is low, and then performing a collaborative filter as the population grows (Vozalis & Margaritis, 2003). The content-based and collaborative systems never touch one another, in this case, but greater integration of these two types of systems is possible (Adomavicius & Tuzhilin, 2005).

Input, Filter, Output

The three phases of a recommendation system: input, filtering, and output rely heavily on how a system sets up the connections between the system's users and items. These connections exist as three different types: User to User, Item to Item, and User to Item. These connections allow a recommendation system's filter to deliver outputs based on the connection patterns found. This subsection will review each of these three phases and state how they compare and contrast to adaptive games.

Input

A recommendation system and adaptive game information connections begin with the collecting of initial input data, for instance the movie recommendation system needs movie information (genre, actors, and critic ratings) and user information (demographics, user ratings, and user actions). These information areas can be sorted into four categories:

- **User Demographics:** Contains any personal user information: age, gender, occupation, or user relation information such as a user's friends.
- **User Opinions:** The user's explicitly stated preferences about items or users. User rankings, user created categories, and user reviews would all fit into this category. Setting a game to easy, medium or hard is a small example of a player opinion found in games.
- **User Actions:** Actions that a user performs while using the system. These actions are generally implicit actions, not specifically asked to be performed, since the explicit actions that users can perform fit in the demographic or opinion categories. Examples of implicit actions include how users navigate a Web sites or what music a user has in their playlist. For games, how a player navigates the game's world or which quests they complete are implicit actions.
- **Content Data:** Any information that is used to describe items or content. Again, a movie recommendation system will describe a movie by its genre, the actors that star in

the movie, when and where the movie was shot, and so forth. In games describing the properties of a race track or player items are examples that compose the game's content data.

There are three things to focus on when relating recommendation systems to adaptive games, given these categories of information input. First, content data and demographics work the same in both kinds of systems; both follow generalized information templates that define users or content. Yet few games have begun collecting user-generated information, while user-generated content Web sites (YouTube.com) and demographic / profile Web sites (Facebook.com, Myspace.com) allow users to contribute their own information for recommendation purposes. Second, user opinions are not often found in games but are important in recommendation systems for delivering output. Third, both recommendation and adaptive systems obtain user actions and process them in real-time (or as close to real-time as possible). Recommendation systems usually process output on-demand or single instances but adaptive games need to produce output in real-time and continuously. However, looking at ways that games can use single instance recommendation and faster ways to output recommendations continuously may expand how adaptive games operate. How adaptive games, and recommendation systems, decide what recommendations to deliver to their users is by searching the connections that exist between the four categories of data above and applying filters.

Filter

Filtering is the heart and soul of any recommendation system. The search algorithms and the type of connections they search make up a system's filter, the process that will finally deliver the recommendation output. For example, a movie filter can recommend movies based on a user's movie rankings and which movie genres they enjoy, each of which could be searched through separately or in various combinations. The different kinds of filter algorithms are too numerous to explain in detail within this manuscript. Instead a general overview of algorithm approaches and their different search techniques will be discussed.

There are two main types of filters: memory-based and model-based. Filters that are memory-based, meaning they have access to the input data (Vozalis & Margaritis, 2003), will use two types of connection or data comparisons: popularity and proximity. Popularity entails looking at how much weight (i.e., importance) is given to connections or data that occurs between items and users. Some examples include: Google Ad Sense which looks for frequency of keywords within a document in order to display ads, a ranking Web site like Amazon uses explicit user ranking scores to find item popularity among users, and eHarmony.com connects users with potential dating partners who share common interests. Proximity comparisons look at how close data or connections occur between one another. One example is how Last.fm, a socially-drive music Web site, takes each user's music playlists and determines how often different recording artists are found together within the same playlist. Using these two types of comparisons similarities between users and items are able to be determined based on the initial input data that is provided to a recommendation system.

Model-based approaches to filtering use methods to predict a user's preferences instead of reviewing the entire input dataset for every recommendation calculation (Vozalis & Margaritis, 2003). These filters will use the initial input data to train themselves to create a user model of each user, meaning each user is represented in a logical way (like an equation). Once these models are created a system can make prediction how a user will act, such as how they will rank an item. Examples of model-based approaches include using Bayesian networks and Monte Carlo algo-

rithm methods (Adomavicius & Tuzhilin, 2005; Vozalis & Margaritis, 2003). These model-based approaches have high overhead costs when they first compute the user models but these models provide recommendations faster than memory-based filters after they are created but do not have access to the most up-to-date information after created.

Games already make extensive use of model-based approaches when it comes to adapting to players because they can produce faster results once a model is formed (Magerko & Laird, 2003; Thue et al., 2007). However, memory-based approaches, which use large datasets of input data, have not been implemented for adaptive gameplay purposes. These two approaches to filtering data will be discussed in the context of games in the next section.

Output

Each recommendation system's output is based on the patterns that the system's filters found when searching through, or creating a model from, the input data. These final recommendations can include item recommendations, user relationship recommendations, popularity rankings for items or users, etc. Different filters will affect what kinds of recommendation sets are available for output. A content-based approach will give recommendations based on similarities between items a user has previously ranked, while collaboration systems will compare multiple users to one another and provide recommendations based on their collective input.

One thing that differentiates a recommendation system from an adaptive game is that recommendation systems typically produce single instances of output and do not have to worry about ongoing interactivity. Adaptive games, on the other hand, can make use of their output to perform ongoing system behavior changes such as affecting the game's storyline or altering the game's difficulty level. This means that adaptive game output can have repercussions well beyond the current state of the game or have to consistently create new output in order to keep up with the interactivity of the game.

GAME-RELATED RECOMMENDATION AND ADAPTIVE SYSTEMS

Recommendation systems and adaptive games have been shown to have similarities but there are also differences:

1. Adaptive games are often used to challenge users whereas recommendation systems help users.
2. Adaptive games rely on implicitly gathering user actions to adapt games and do not obtrusively ask for user opinions, demographics and user-generated content, whereas recommendation systems gather data from each category.
3. Adaptive games face a greater technological challenge because they gather, filter, and react to user data in real time; whereas recommendation systems operate with less time pressure and less input.

This section will look at current examples of recommendation and adaptive systems that are related to games in order to explore these differences further. These examples are split into two groups: systems that exist outside of gameplay (non-real-time) and systems that function as real-time adaptive game systems. As will be shown, the example systems that occur outside of gameplay take on the role of traditional recommendation systems while the in game examples will take an adaptive approach, making use of model-based filters to produce continuous output.

Recommender Systems Related to Gaming

Game review Web sites and game matchmaking systems both use recommendations. While not connected to any physical game, rating and review Web sites allow players to rate games and receive recommendations about which games may be worth purchasing. These Web sites take a collaborative approach to recommendation and use a memory-based filter to deliver a popular vote for games to the website's users. These Web sites do not create recommendations in real-time but will provide some insight as to how memory-based filtering can be utilized for adaptive game design

Matchmaking systems, which pair unrelated players together before they play a game, typically use collaborative approach as well but will build models of their players instead. The TrueSkill (TrueSkill (TM), 2007) system employed by Xbox Live match players based on their skill level creating an evenly matched game which offers players a better experience. While acting like a recommendation system, TrueSkill function as an adaptive system by challenging players, recording data implicitly and roughly works in real time. Operating outside of games in that manner, however, limits matchmaking systems from ultimately affecting gameplay, unlike adaptive systems that exist inside of games.

Adaptive Games

Adaptive Difficulty Level Systems

Most games allow a player to choose a difficulty level at the beginning of the game. This choice is set on a single linear scale from easy to hard. A few games get rid of this choice and instead use dynamic difficulty by adjusting the difficulty level throughout the game. One way to achieve this is by using techniques like rubberbanding (Rubberband, 2008) which affects the strength of each player throughout the game. A system using rubberbanding makes it hard for players to fall behind or get too far ahead in the game. For example, the game Mario Kart, a racing game, uses rubberbanding by giving special items to the players that are lagging behind in the race. Rubberbanding is an example of a collaborative system using a simple model-based filter, based on each player's current position, to determine how much help or hindrance each player receives.

For multiplayer competitive environments (e.g., sports or racing), with two or more players, rubberbanding can be used effectively. Single player games must use a player's performance based upon difficulty assumptions of the gameplay itself in order to create a competitive environment. Max Payne, a first-person shooter (FPS), is an example of a single player game where a player's information: health, accuracy, and number of kills, is recorded and used to adjust the game's difficulty. These records are compared against difficulty thresholds that are used to judge how well a user is playing the game (e.g., the player's accuracy was perfect in the last level so the game's difficulty will rise). This is another instance of a model-based approach within a content-oriented system where the player's most recent performance is used to determine the player's overall skill level (the model) for the next phase of the game (the content). This is supposed to create a flow situation where the user is constantly being challenged based on their skill level but never overwhelmed (Csikszentmihalyi, 1991).

Player Modeling

Researchers are working on building adaptive systems that use player types (Bartle, 1996, 2003; Yee, 2007) as a means to model players and alter gameplay accordingly (Magerko & Laird, 2003; Thue et al., 2007; Togelius et al., 2007). Three systems will be discussed in this section and each take a slightly different approach to gathering player data and creating internal player models. These player modeling systems are similar to

content recommend systems using model-based approaches because they gather input from a single user and use their actions to form an internal prediction model of the player.

The Interactive Drama Architecture (IDA) was built to use a player model to help restrain the player from breaking the bounds of a game's story (Magerko & Laird, 2003). Interactive Drama is the concept of adapting a story to facilitate the preferences of a player, generally being achieved by using artificial intelligence (AI) to analyze a player's actions. IDA contains an AI Director agent which records the player's actions as they advance through the story. When the Director thinks the player is about to affect the story in a negative way (e.g., kill a main character, leave the playing area, or stall the story) proper actions can be taken in order to keep the story flowing (causing a distraction or providing a subtle hint) and moving forward.

A similar approach can be found in the PASSAGE system (Thue et al., 2007). Built on top of the Never Winter Nights engine, Aurora (BioWare, 2002-2008), the PASSAGE system also records a player's actions throughout a role-playing game (RPG). These actions affect different traits about a player that help determine what type of player is playing the game. There are five traits that a player is scored on: Fighter, Method-Actor, Storyteller, Tactician, or Power Gamer. Traits then determine what kind of quests the system will recommend and present to the player. For example, a player that chooses to always fight to finish a quest will be given future quests that focus mainly on fighting.

Last, a system built by (Togelius et al., 2007) adapts racetracks within a racing game. Each time a player completes a race a new track is procedurally generated based on the skill level of the player. The authors of this system found that optimizing tracks based on the player's skill were boring to players but that tracks were enjoyable when they were slightly harder than the player's skill level. As long as the player continues to play within the system it is able to create better track recommendations based on that player's skill level.

It should be noted that these systems do not allow players to affect their player model directly. Users of recommendation systems feel that the system works better when they have more control and wish the system to merely augment their experience, not completely take over (McDonald, 2003). It has been suggested that players be given a more explicit means of providing data in games as an additional way of gathering user input for adaptive purposes (Charles et al., 2005).

RECOMMENDING ADAPTIVE GAMEPLAY

Figure 1 graphs Web-based recommendation and game adaptation systems based on each system's approach and filtering methods. The graph shows that while both types of systems take different approaches, content, collaborative or both, Web-based systems focus on memory-based filters while game systems focus on model-based filters. This phenomenon occurs of the differences between adaptive games and recommendation systems: games need to produce challenges, games need to adapt in real-time and games do not collect memory intensive information.

Games need to produce extremely fast interaction results to provide real-time actions and challenges. Models will allow a system to avoid consistent checking and rechecking of input data, which would occur using memory-based models. Yet model creation incurs high overhead costs. Current entertainment games get around this fact by implementing limited modeling algorithms. For instance, the TrueSkill system and dynamic difficulty systems will produce player models only at specific points during the game or after its conclusion, and will only create collaborative models using small groups of players. Additionally models that continuously update themselves (i.e., the rubberbanding model) use simplistic

information that can be quickly processed, such as race position, and do not use make use of memory intensive information. However, player modeling systems that are currently being researched have begun to go beyond these simplistic modeling functions to allow for more information to be gathered.

Web-based recommendation systems using memory-based systems are efficient in their own way. Connections between items and users can be easily computed and stored by employing databases to keep computation time down. While real-time computing is not as necessary for Web-sites they do need access to accurate information, which is why memory-based filters are preferred. Under these circumstances Web-based systems can relay recommendations back to the user that are up-to-date. Finally, the rare use of models for Web-based systems may be due to the fact that models run the risk of over generalizing users and with most Web-based systems containing thousands, if not millions of users, this could limit recommendation results.

While these two mediums, games and Web-based systems, may have different goals in mind that does not mean they cannot learn from one another. Looking at games specifically, the notion of using memory-based filters seems to be nonexistent (although game review Web sites use memory-based filters their goals are the same as other Web-based recommendation systems, not games). Additionally entertainment games only make use of simple model-based approaches that deal with data from either a single player or a small group of players. Recent academic work has looked at expanding these models for single player use but multiplayer games could use model-based filters that work with larger player populations. Reviewing ways that adaptive games can use explicitly gathered information (e.g., player opinions) with memory-based filters and create models from larger populations may prove useful for creating adaptive games.

Games Using Memory-Based Filters

Memory-based filters use large datasets that are collected over an extended period of time and contain the latest player and game information. These datasets could include information from the four information areas that recommendation systems gather. Examples of how games can use these information areas include examples that are already used by Web-based recommendation systems: ranking content, profile matching, and tracking user actions.

Ranking Game Content

Ranking systems are the most common form of recommendation systems (Adomavicius & Tuzhilin, 2005). Users rank items with a fixed number scale (1 to 5, 0 to 10, etc.) and are combined to give overall scores. Games rarely allow players to express their opinions in such a fashion but could use ranking systems as a way to adapt games. First, ranking a game's difficulty level would help dynamic difficulty algorithms adjust the challenges presented to the player.

Second, players could rank game content. Ranking the difficulty, storytelling, or aesthetics of things such as levels or quests in a game would allow those scores to be used to recommend other game content to players. The game Spore already allows players to rank player-generated content (Shaw, 2008) and will download content for the player automatically. This ranking procedure could even be integrated into the games story where various non-player characters (NPC) within a game could ask the player for their ranking scores while staying in character.

Profile Matching

Profile matching occurs on a number of different Web sites and is used for: social networking (Facebook.com), dating (eHarmony.com) and information sharing (Last.fm). These Web sites ask users to contribute demographic or content information so they may match the users together based on the data provided. This is in contrast to game related matchmaking systems previously mentioned which only care about implicit player information. Combining the two approaches will be useful for both gameplay and for socializing.

Inside of games, matchmaking could be combined with other game features for bring players together. World of Warcraft (WoW) allows users to announce when they wish to group (i.e., collaborate) with other players yet does not match players together based on skill level or any other criteria. Building in a matchmaking system into WoW would mean players spend less time looking for other players and would allow players with similarities to play together. This matching could also be extended outside of the game where developers could offer social networking opportunities to players. Players could create profile, rank their favorite content, role-play as their game characters and give them a place to connect with other players. Furthermore, player profiles could be made global and used by multiple games, which would help game portals or content delivery systems (Web sites or programs that allow players to access many games, for example Valve's Steam system (Valve Corporation, 2007)). These profiles would extend beyond any one particular game, becoming similar to online social networking profiles (e.g., Facebook and Myspace).

Action Tracking

Statistics tracking of player actions allow developers to review how players are playing their game and find any faults that may exist (Ludwig, 2007). Current commercial games do record actions for gameplay purposes, while some build extensive statistics tracking systems such as Steams statistics system (Valve Corporation, 2007). Action recording is used to gather information including: how long a game took to complete, which in-game characters are the most popular, or where players die the most often in the game. This information could be used as information for an adaptive system that could automatically change the gameplay. If the game has recorded that 80% of time players die in a certain area then the system could adapt to give a nonskilled player an easier time in that area. Other examples include the games Dungeon Siege, which changes a player's character based on what items or skills they use frequently as they play the game, and Oblivion, where a player's behavior in the game's tutorial is used to suggest which role the player should choose for rest of the game.

Games Using Model-Based Filters

The second way that games can utilize recommendation system functions is to gather data from a larger player population. Games that use model-based filter are usually limited to single players or smaller populations, in the case of rubberbanding, matchmaking, or the adaptive game systems being built by researchers. Yet, model-based filters could connect player data together and form generalized player models using a game's entire population space.

StumbleUpon.com will group users together who have similar profile data and action patterns. These groups act as models for the users of the groups. Games could use a grouping approach to create multiple player models that would be used to categorize players. Once a player model is created from a group of player's information it could be uploaded online and then be applied to other connected players who exhibit similar gameplay behavior. In cooperative multiplayer games player models could also be used to match players with other players of the same or complimentary models or, alternatively, players with conflicting models could also be matched together for competitive games.

Thinking big, player modeling could be used to create games that contain vastly different game-

play experiences based on each player's model. Imagine if one player likes to play real-time strategy (RTS) games and another likes games from the first person shooter (FPS) genre, they would have separate player models and have to play separate games. Games such as Natural Selection or Savage get around this fact by having different game mechanics available to different players where one player gets to player an RTS while the rest play an FPS. A player who likes to fight could receive more battle statistics or special moves that cause more damage, while a player who likes to trade could receive better trading options or economic features. Player modeling could shift gameplay completely based on the analysis of how a player plays a game.

CONCLUSION

This article has described how recommendation and adaptive systems monitor users in order to understand and aid each user individually. Recommendation systems monitor users to help the system filter information that will be used to output relevant recommendations, specific to that user. Adaptive games also monitor players to output recommendations but these recommendations create a challenging or engaging experience in the game for each player. Since both recommendation systems and adaptive games monitor users and filter information they employ similar methods and techniques.

Those methods and techniques follow an input, filter, and output to produce relevant recommendations to users or players. Recommendation systems begin by collecting data in these four categories: user demographics, user opinions, user actions, and content data. Connections exist between these categories and recommendation systems can be content-based (i.e., focuses on single user connections), collaborative (i.e., uses entire user population connections) or a combination. Filters within these systems can take a memory-based (slower and accurate) or model-based (faster and generalizes) approach when searching for connections to finally output as recommendations or to adapt a game.

While adaptive games and recommendation systems use similar techniques they contrast in their goals which has caused different characteristics in currently available systems. Games need to provide output that is in real-time and continuous. This means adaptive games usually make use of model-based filters in order to make recommendations quickly as to how the game should progress. Since memory-based filters are not used by games, player information (opinions, demographics and actions), are not stored long-term and player actions are gathered implicitly as to speed up the information gathering process. Meaning a game's model-based filter must (a) process simple information or (b) gather information in small intervals throughout the game which is discarded once a new model is formed. Additionally, to order to provide continuous output, model-based filters only model single players or a small group of players at once within current games.

What this article has shown is that while model-based approaches have been achieved and do provide challenging experiences for players, adaptive games have yet to seriously employ memory-based and complex collaborative model-based filters. Reviewing how these approaches are being handled by Web-based systems new design suggestions for how they may be incorporated into games were discussed. These include: ranking game content, allowing player profiles, tracking player actions, and relating entire player populations together. Given that adaptive gameplay and recommendation systems follow the same principles, exploring these design suggestions will lead to new approaches for creating adaptive gameplay.

REFERENCES

Adomavicius, G. & Tuzhilin, A. (2005). Toward the next generation of recommender systems: A survey of the state-of-the-art and possible extensions. *Knowledge and Data Engineering, IEEE Transactions on, 17*(6), 734-749.

Anderson, C., Corbett, A., Koedinger, K., & Pelletier, R. (1995). Cognitive tutors: Lessons learn. *The Journal of Learning Sciences, 4*(2), 167-195.

Bailey, C. & Katchabaw, M. (2005). An experimental testbed to enable auto-dynamic difficulty in modern video games. In *Proceedings of the 2005 GameOn North America Conference* (pp. 18-22). Montreal, Canada.

Bartle, R. (1996). Hearts, clubs, diamonds, spades: Players who suit MUDs. *Journal of MUD Research, 1*(1).

Bartle, R. (2003). *Designing virtual worlds.* New Riders Games.

BioWare (2002-2008). *For builders - Aurora neverwinter toolset.* Retrieved April 11, 2009, from http://nwn.bioware.com/builders/

Blizzard Entertainment (2008). *New interface preview: Looking for group.* Retrieved April 11, 2009, from http://www.worldofwarcraft.com/burningcrusade/townhall/lookingforgroup.html

Charles, D., Kerr, A., McNeill, M., McAlister, M., Black, M., Kücklich, J., Moore, A., & Stringer, K. (2005). Player-centered game design: Player modelling and adaptive digital games. In *Proceedings of the Digital Games Research Conference* (pp 285-298). Vancouver, Canada.

Chen, T., Han, W.-L., Wang, H.-D., Zhou, Y.-X., Xu, B., & Zang, B.-Y. (2007). Content recommendation systems based on private user profile. *International Conference on Machine Learning and Cybernetics, 4,* 2112–2118.

Csikszentmihalyi, M. (1991). *Flow: The psychology of optimal experience.* Harper Perennial.

Gee, J. (2007). *What video games have to teach us about learning and literacy.* Palgrave Macmillian.

Herrmann, J. (2007). Got gamers? Video games: An engaging brand experience (Electronic Version). *Neilsen, Consumer Insight.* Retrieved April 11, 2009, from http://www.nielsen.com/consumer_insight/issue2/ci_story1.html

Instructional scaffolding. (2007, July 13). *Wikipedia, The Free Encyclopedia.* Retrieved April 11, 2009, from http://en.wikipedia.org/w/index.php?title=Instructional_scaffolding&oldid=144464722

Lazzaro, N. (2007). *The 4 most important emotions of game design.* Presented at the Game Developers Conference, San Francisco, CA.

Ludwig, J. (2007). *Flogging: Data collection on the high seas.* Presented at the Austin Game Developers Conference, Austin, TX.

Magerko, B. & Laird, J. E. (2003). *Building an interactive drama architecture.* Paper presented at the International Conference on Technologies for Interactive Digital Storytelling and Entertainment, Darmstadt, Germany.

McDonald, D. (2003). Recommending collaboration with social networks: a comparative evaluation. In *Proceedings of the Conference on Human Factors in Computing* (pp. 593-600). New York: ACM Press.

Miller, S. (2004). *Auto-dynamic difficulty.* Retrieved April 11, 2009, from http://dukenukem.typepad.com/game_matters/2004/01/autoadjusting_g.html

Pardo, R. (2008). *Rules of engagement: Blizzard's approach to multiplayer game design.* Presented at the Game Developers Conference, San Francisco, CA.

Rubberband, A. I. (2008, March 2). *Wikipedia, The Free Encyclopedia.* Retrieved April 11, 2009, from http://en.wikipedia.org/w/index.php?title=Rubberband_AI&oldid=188500815

Salen, K. & Zimmerman E. (2003). *Rules of play: Game design fundamentals.* MIT Press.

Segaran, T. (2007). *Programming collective intelligence: Building smart Web 2.0 applications.* Sebastopol, CA: O'Reilly Media.

Sherry, J., Lucas, K., Greenberg, B., & Lachlan, K. (2006). Video game uses and gratifications as predictors of use and game preference. In P. Vorderer & J. Bryant (Eds.), *Playing video games* (pp. 213-224). Mahwah, NJ: Lawrence Erlbaum Associates.

Shaw, C. (2008). Pollinating the Universe: User-generated content in SPORE. Presented at the Game Developers Conference, San Francisco, CA.

Thue, D., Bulitko, V., Spetch, M., & Wasylishen, E. (2007). *Interactive storytelling: A player modelling approach.* Paper presented at the Artificial Intelligence and Interactive Digital Entertainment conference, Stanford, CA.

Togelius, J., De Nardi, R., & Lucas, S. (2007). *Towards automatic personalized content creation in racing games.* Paper presented at the IEEE Symposium on Computational Intelligence and Games, Honolulu, HI.

TrueSkill (TM). (2007). *Microsoft research.* Retrieved April 11, 2009, from http://research.microsoft.com/mlp/apg/Details.aspx

Valve Corporation. (2007). *Steam & game stats.* Retrieved April 11, 2009, from http://www.steampowered.com/v/index.php?area=stats

Vozalis, E. & Margaritis, K. G. (2003). *Analysis of recommender systems' algorithms.* Paper presented at the Hellenic European Conference on Computer Mathematics & its Applications, Athens, Greece.

Vygotsky, L. (1978). *Mind in society: The development of higher psychological processes.* Harvard University Press.

Yee, N. (2003-2006). *The daedalus project.* Retrieved April 11, 2009, from http://www.nickyee.com/daedalus

Yee, N. (2007). Motivations of play in online games. *Journal of Cyber Psychology and Behavior, 9,* 772-775.

This work was previously published in International Journal of Gaming and Computer-Mediated Simulations, Volume 1, Issue 3, edited by Richard E. Ferdig, pp. 68-80, copyright 2009 by IGI Publishing (an imprint of IGI Global).

Chapter 6
Leveraging Open Source Technology in 3D Game Engine Development

Tim Stowell
Utah State University, USA

Jon Scoresby
Utah State University, USA

K. Chad Coats
Utah State University, USA

Michael Capell
Utah State University, USA

Brett Shelton
Utah State University, USA

ABSTRACT

Market 3D engines have all the capabilities needed for developing full-featured 3D simulation and game environments. However, for those in education and small-business, it remains a formidable task to acquire the resources needed to purchase or create a development platform with cutting-edge capabilities. Leveraging existing and open-source software libraries can greatly enhance the main application development, freeing developers to focus more on the application concept itself rather than the needed supporting pieces. This chapter explores the nuances of successfully mixing core code with these third-party libraries in creating a fully functioning development environment. Many steps with accompanying checks-and-balances are involved in creating a game engine, including making choices of what libraries to use, and integrating the core code with third-party libraries. By offering insights into our open source driven process, we help inform the understanding of how game engines may be generated for other educational and small-budget projects.

DOI: 10.4018/978-1-60960-565-0.ch006

INTRODUCTION

Market 3D engines have all the capabilities that one would need to build full-featured 3D environments. Those that develop these market 3D engines often invest vast resources of money and people and, therefore, market 3D engines cost a significant amount to license. Educational institutions rarely have the funds to purchase a current top-of-the-line engine, choosing instead to research alternate avenues. These avenues focus mainly on current open source engines or older engines that could be purchased for a lower price (Cruz, 2006). These engines would not support many current development needs, or were too dated to use for cutting edge applications. Choosing instead to create a 3D engine from scratch allows the flexibility to customize functionality and development structure.

Our group teamed up with the Institute of Emergency Services and Homeland Security (IESHS) to develop software they could use in their training. Generally, our task is to build an incident command training simulation for firefighters. The simulation has been generated as a multiuser first-person perspective training program. Even though the simulation is designed for multiple user participation, the training is meant for the incident commander of that emergency situation. Currently the training will take place in the IESHS computer lab, but future development will allow this training to be expanded to firefighters to participate in the simulation via the Internet. The simulation is partitioned into two primary roles, a facilitator and client user. The *facilitator* starts and records the simulation whereas the *client* is meant for the individual firefighters participating in the simulation. The facilitator can also load previously recorded scenarios for learning. Part of the development is to expand this training to EMT, police officers, and other emergency personnel. To encompass all of these areas, we use the moniker Hazard Emergency & Accident Training (HEAT) to describe

the needs of our game engine. As described by Shelton at al. (2010), the HEAT engine aims to be a full-featured 3D training environment that includes single-player and multi-player scenarios, interactive menus triggered by key events, and support for specific instructional attributes such as automated assessment and replay. As such, it requires a number of pieces that many 3D game engines also share, including:

- 3D graphical capabilities
- VOIP (Voice Over Internet Protocol)
- Sound and physics

Developing software for any one of the above components is a large task in and of itself. To save time and money, it is often desirable to use "off-the-shelf" software components that already include the needed functionality. However, there are many issues to consider when making the choice to use available libraries because of potential issues that may exist within open code (Shelton, et al., 2010). For the HEAT engine, we used the following process when building necessary functionality of high-end systems, with each point to be described in more detail throughout the paper:

1. Perform background research into the library functionality
2. Make choices based on that research
3. Start developing core code (code developed in-house for the main project, not relying on off-the-shelf components)
4. Begin an iterative process of integration of core-code with 3rd party libraries

We next discuss the process we used for searching and deciding on what open source libraries to use to develop the 3D engine. Reading the forum discussion boards helped in making decisions—what has worked for others, and which library code to avoid (see Figure 1). It is difficult to contrast our particular open source approach with existing ones. There may be documentation available that discusses how to build 3D game engines, but there are few if any that discuss how to mix and match open source libraries for 3D engine development. Most companies keep their processes a closely-guarded trade secret; therefore, we must learn from forums, discussion boards, and through implementing scientific method. We emphasize throughout the paper the focus on *open source* techniques and shared information, which can be generally considered different than the development processes used within large, in-house development teams.

BACKGROUND RESEARCH INTO THE LIBRARIES

There are extremely large numbers of software projects available on the Internet; one only has to browse the popular site sourceforge.net to get a feel for vast amount of code that developers have made available. The Internet contains multiple software libraries of almost every type imaginable, and most are just a click away. For HEAT, we primarily used Google searches based on topics of interest. When searching for libraries and reading web sites of interest, there were several factors necessary to prioritize including licenses, costs, community, quality and support, and platform.

License

Most libraries that we found were protected under some version of copyright license, which can have an effect on one's application. The GNU GPL (Gnu's Non-UNIX General Public License) allows the use of a library for most any purpose, but does include the very strict and limiting requirement that the core code utilizing the component must also fall under the GPL (GNU Project GPL, 2008). The

Figure 1. A list of some of the forums and mailing lists that were used to find the libraries needed for our game engine

Forum:	Sub-forums used:
Gamedev.net http://www.gamedev.net/community/forums	Game Programming, General Programming, Graphics Programming & Theory, and Site-Wide Searches.
Ogre 3D http://www.ogre3d.org/phpBB2	Help, Artists & Content Creators, Google Summer Of Code, and General Searches.
Ogre 3D Add-ons http://www.ogre3d.org/addonforums	NxOgre (*Ogre wrapper for Ageia Physics*), PCZ SceneManager (*Portal Connected Zone Manager, used for scene management*), QuickGUI (*GUI library*), OgreNewt (*Ogre wrapper for Newton Physics*), and General Searches.
CEGUI (GUI library) http://www.cegui.org.uk/phpBB2/index.php	Beginners Help, Advanced Help, General Discussion, and General Searches.
Devmaster.net forums http://www.devmaster.net/forums	General Development, and General Searches.
Nvidia PhysX developer.nvidia.com/forums/index.php? showforum=16	PhysX SDK 2.7 and 2.8, PhysX Tools, PhysX Features.
Networked Physics http://gafferongames.wordpress.com/game-physics/networked-physics	Discussion Board (*trs79 in the comments section is Tim Stowell*).
WxWidgets (UI library) http://wxforum.shadonet.com	C++ Development and General Searches.
Newton Game Dynamics (physics library) http://www.newtondynamics.com/forum	General Development and General Searches.
Mailing Lists: Sweng-gamedev (http://lists.midnightryder.com/listinfo.cgi/sweng-gamedev-midnightryder.com) General Game Development Info & LUA (http://www.lua.org/lua-l.html)	

GPL license states that the code must be explicitly open source, and therefore prohibits users from creating closed proprietary software. For HEAT, this licensing was too restrictive. If HEAT had a GPL license, we would have had to make the entire codebase publicly available to anyone that we distributed HEAT to, thus we chose to avoid libraries with this license when possible.

The GNU LGPL (Lesser General Public License) was a more attractive option for HEAT (GNU Project LGPL, 2008). Software libraries utilized as dynamically loadable libraries (like .dll files under Windows) do not require that the core code fall under the same license, as long as the linkage is dynamic and not static. In other words, we can distribute our core HEAT.exe file and not have to release its source code, as long as the libraries it uses are .dll files on the same computer. When static linking a library, that library becomes an internal part of HEAT.exe without any .dll present. The only situation that we would have to release any source code is if we were to make any changes to the particular .dll in question. Users of the LGPL encourage use of their libraries by those that would make improvements because they are forced to release those changes to the public, so everyone benefits from the improvements.

There are a wide variety of other license types, like the Berkeley Software Distribution (BSD) license (Berkley Software, 2008) and Mozilla Public License (Mozilla Foundation, 2008). Many of these licenses allow static linkage without forcing that license onto the core code. For HEAT, we only used libraries that either allowed liberal static linkage or dynamic linkage through .dll files, so GPL libraries were not utilized.

Cost and Feature Set

Because we work in a government sponsored non-profit educational institution, our funding depends largely upon grants we are awarded. The size and nature of the grant determines how much money we receive and how that money can be allocated. Because our budget is modest for HEAT, we were mostly interested in either free or inexpensive libraries. Most all of the free libraries that we integrated are open source, which means we then become part of the unique "open" culture. One of the very positive aspects of the open source community is the synergy and global collaboration within that group. Developers from many different parts of the world will volunteer their time to make improvements to existing software and add completely new components of their own. Google even sponsors a "Summer of Code" project where they choose Open Source projects and pay students to develop (Google, 2008). The Object-Oriented Rendering Engine, Ogre3D participated in the Summer of Code and one person contributed a new shadow technique to the Ogre3D library (Streeting, 2009). It is an altruistic experience—a very rewarding feeling to contribute back to open source communities. We participated by answering several Ogre3D forum members' questions with regard to skeletal rag doll setups. We also contributed a new solution for ray casting with a custom projection matrix (Stowell, 2006). Later in this paper we discuss the Ogre3D library in more detail.

License fees are not the only costs to consider then implementation of third-party libraries. Development resources necessary when integrating third party libraries also need to be considered. For example, when researching audio libraries, we considered the commercial library FMOD and the free library OpenAL. FMOD was free for non-commercial use and had considerable functionality already "built-in" while OpenAL required more work to integrate. The FMOD API had functions that would handle recording of voice data while OpenAL has no such pre-built functions. The developers would need to create the code that sets up the microphone and encodes the sound data, among other tasks. Sometimes the license fee costs could be quite small in comparison to the time-related costs of implementing the needed functionality ourselves.

Community

However, there can be negative repercussions to relying on open source code. Recently we learned that the lead developer of a GUI project we were using for HEAT, CEGUI, abruptly left the forums without explanation. Other community members were anxious to keep the project from dying, but no one seemed capable of accepting the new leadership role. As a result, we were forced to find a different solution for our GUI, although in the second year of development the leader did return. It was for this reason and the fact that CEGUI did better meet our needs that we re-adopted it, although with some trepidation.

Another drawback to using open source code is that the lead developers of the project typically do not put in X feature or Y request as they are not "for hire" and are not being paid. We could not expect any commissioned help from them or expect them to implement what we wanted. In the open source forums if users attempt such requests they are almost always met with a response like "you have the source code, implement it yourself!". The developers work on their own schedules and have their own agendas, so it was up to us to implement what we needed, without waiting for it to magically appear.

Quality and Support

Despite the limited budget for HEAT, we wanted to ensure that the libraries, while mostly free, were still high quality. At the same time, due to the large numbers of competing libraries for the same purpose (i.e., many different graphics and audio libraries etc.), it was important to gauge the quality of the library and pick the best one. One way we monitored a quality standard was to track how many times a particular library was mentioned on different sites, and how often it

was recommended as a solution to a particular problem in forums.

Because many of the libraries we used are free, the support for the engine was limited to public forums or mailing lists. After further research, some libraries that first appeared interesting were later revealed to be troublesome. The time spent to look deeply into the functionality of each library costs valuable time. We looked at the "page last modified" link at the bottom of web pages, and the dates of postings in the forums (if any) to see how recent the library pages supported user activity. Good documentation was another important factor in choosing which library to use.

Target Platform

In addition to the above concerns, we accounted for compatibility issues of the platforms for each of the third-party libraries. The libraries needed to support several platforms from the start, such as our development machines and those meeting our estimates of the hardware and software for the eventual completed HEAT environment. In addition, we did not want to limit our potential audience for the project. Incorporating libraries into the HEAT environment that could be compiled for a broad range of both hardware and software would enable us to deliver versions of the environment tailored to those platforms without integrating yet another library for each new system. We could not invest the time in development to design our own. Libraries that were already designed with such considerations were more appealing (Shelton, et al., 2010).

Several libraries we looked at were structured as "wrappers". Ogre3D wrapped DirectX and OpenGL, and wxWidgets wrapped underlying Win32 code, Linux X windows code, and Mac OS UI code. By forcing operating system-specific code to adhere to detailed interfaces, the libraries presented a single Application Programmers Interface (API) for all the supported platforms. The API would enable us to exploit the functionality the libraries provided without having to consider the underlying code.

As a simple example, consider the following:

```
void windows_doSomething()
{
    windows-specific code
}
void linux_doSomething()
{
  linux-specific code
}
void library_doSomething()
{
   if(using_windows)
    windows_doSomething()
   else if(using_linux)
linux_doSomething()
}
```

We chose libraries that were open in this way, rather than requiring one specific OS or other functionality; however, at times we opted to use OS specific code if it better suited our purposes. For example we used native Win32 code to create the window for runtime HEAT. We found it simpler than trying to use a wrapper library like WxWidgets or Microsoft Foundation Classes. One potential drawback with choosing platform independent libraries over dependent libraries is performance. That is, it is often the case that libraries built to work within a specific platform may be customized to work best for a particular use, which is not fully realized in a platform independent approach.

An additional consideration is the availability of adding script bindings for the library. Integrating a scripting language into the engine would help to manipulate objects from third-party libraries, offering a desirable ability to control and manage those objects from the outside, rather than having to supply a full wrapper within HEAT. If the library already had bindings for a particular language, choosing that scripting language for our engine would automatically create that control. For example, if the rendering library, physics library, and graphic interface library all have bindings available for Python, we could integrate Python into our engine and use that language to create object-manipulation scripts. Alternatively, we have to write a wrapper within HEAT for all objects that use the features of the rendering, physics and graphic interface libraries.

Ease of use is another very important factor when choosing libraries. Early in the project we experimented with creating the windows for the HEAT editor in the Win32 API, which involved an amount of low level programming. For example, the logic to center a child window when a parent window is resized had to be programmed from scratch. Centering functionality is often taken for granted when using modern desktop applications. It would take a lot of time to develop what is usually considered simple functionality for our GUI. Instead, we chose to use higher-level libraries like WxWidgets for the HEAT editor. WxWidgets already contains code to handle centering, resizing and repositioning for windows. Even though WxWidgets is potentially slower in terms of performance, its ease of use made it preferable to the lower level Win32 API.

MAKING CHOICES BASED ON RESEARCH

Researching, choosing and assessing best-fit arguments of open source code is an iterative process, and the choices we make are not necessarily set in stone. Our initial research for HEAT led us to some important conclusions that allowed our application to gain momentum. For graphics, we chose the Object Oriented Graphics Engine (Ogre) 3D library (Milne & Rowe, 2005). Ogre can be used with OpenGL or Direct X, which made it an attractive cross-platform option. Ogre implements standard 3D functionality, provides a nice shader network, and has a scene graph. Ogre was mentioned many times as a good graphics library throughout the Internet discussions and forums. We also researched a 3D engine database on devmaster.net where Ogre was rated as #1 (Streeting, 2007). We found the Ogre forums to be very helpful and quick when answering our posted questions.

There were other popular graphics engines that had similar functionality as Ogre, for example, *Open Scene Graph* (OSG, 2008); however, it does not have built-in skeletal animation support, which Ogre does. Also, Ogre has a nice binary format for its model files called *.mesh*. Model files can also be stored in .xml format for easier editing. Ogre also has a clean API, and is designed to be a generic rendering solution which makes it more readily adaptable for a wider variety of purposes.

As a limitation, Ogre is not a "game engine," but rather strictly a rendering library. We learned that there is a significant difference between the two. A rendering library is for the most part strictly for presenting the visual aspect of a simulation. A full game engine contains not only the visual component, but also contains at least the following:

- An audio library for sound effects
- Input functionality to handle keyboard, mouse, joystick, etc. inputs
- Networking capability
- Collision detection, i.e., physics library

It is a time-consuming process to integrate all of the game engine functionality into HEAT, even when using existing libraries whose purpose it is to fulfill these needs (see Figure 2).

Other libraries we researched purported to be fully-functioning "game engines." *Panda 3D* claims to be such an engine, but the graphics examples on the website did not look as impressive as Ogre (Carnegie Mellon, 2006). Also, the

Figure 2. A list of some of the libraries we researched and their purposes. Any of these libraries on their own would not fulfill our needs for a full game engine, but without any of them we would be missing a crucial piece of functionality

Library	Purpose	Drawbacks
Raknet	Networking	Networking libraries allow information to be shared between computers on the same network, or even over the Internet.
Enet	Networking	
OpenSceneGraph	Graphics	Rendering libraries only deal with drawing pixels to the screen.
Ogre 3D	Graphics	
Open Input System (OIS)	Input & Window Creation	Input code deals with reading mouse movement, clicking buttons, etc. and keyboard presses. This code also creates the window HEAT runs in.
Native Win32 Code Message Loop	Input & Window Creation	
Microsoft Foundation Classes (MFC)	Input & Window Creation	
Newton Game Dynamics	Physics (Collision Detection)	Physics libraries deal with collision detection, which prevents objects from passing through other objects. It also deals with simulating real-world forces like gravity, cloth, friction, fluid, etc.
Ageia/Nvidia PhysX	Physics (Collision Detection, Fluids, etc.)	
QuickGUI	Graphical User Interface (GUI)	A GUI library draws "widgets" the user can interact with, i.e. buttons, labels, scroll bars, textual input boxes, etc.
CEGUI	Graphical User Interface (GUI)	
OpenAL	Audio	An audio library handles playing background music, sound effects, and also handles recording of voice data for things like Voice Over Internet Protocol (VOIP).
FMod	Audio	

user base was smaller, and after inquiring on Panda forums, we discovered it did not contain any inherent robust scene culling mechanisms. Other game engines we researched were not free, but still somewhat inexpensive (see Figure 3). Most of these engines seemed to lack features or elements we desired such as easy integration of programmable shaders, robust scene management, good community reviews, active community support, and impressive examples of end products.

For physics libraries, we chose the *Ageia PhysX* library, which has subsequently become the Nvidia PhysX library (Nvidia, 2009). This is a proprietary but free physics library used by many large commercial games and titles, including the *Unreal 3* engine(Epic Software, 2008). We were attracted to this library due to its support for a Physics Processing Unit (PPU) add-in card that makes realistic real-time fluid possible. Initially, we chose an open source library called *Newton Game Dynamics*, but we had trouble getting the gravity to feel right for the characters in the game (Newton, 2008). For example, when a character jumped it would float down to the earth. In retrospect, this may have been more of an issue of

scale of models than the library itself, but Ageia also offered a built-in character controller, which is a simple bounding volume and movement library that easily moves the character across terrain. The built-in character controller also keeps players in the scene from going through solid objects. Newton did not have any such built-in functionality, and the forums were littered with posts by developers attempting to figure out an effective and simple way to do it. Figure 4 shows the libraries we ultimately used for HEAT.

WRITING CORE CODE/CREATING 3D MODELS AND ART ASSETS

House Model

3D models and their structure are very important to the success of the HEAT simulation. In the initial scenario of emergency response training, there is one main house model that has interiors that player(s) can go inside and explore. Initially, this house was modeled in the open source 3D modeling program *Blender* (Blender, 2009). However,

Figure 3. A list of some commercial inexpensive engines

Engine:	Link	Price	Drawbacks
Unity	*http://unity3d.com*	$199–$1499	Authoring could only be done on a Mac. Our lab was all PC based.
Trinigy Vision	*http://www.trinigy.net*	(under non-disclosure agreement)	At the time, didn't support networking natively. This may not be the case anymore.
Multiverse	*http://www.multiverse.net*	10% of revenue or up-front fee	Too immature at the time. When we started HEAT, it was still in beta testing stages.
Torque Game Engine	*http://www.garagegames.com*	$749	No general shader support.
Torque Game Engine Advanced/ Torque Shader Engine	*http://www.garagegames.com*	$1495	Hadn't been released when first starting HEAT.
TrueVision 3D SDK	*http://www.truevision3d.com*	$150	Did not test.
C4 Engine	*http://www.terathon.com/c4engine*	$350–varies according to type of use	Did not test.
3D Game Studio	*http://www.3dgamestudio.com*	$199	Did not test.

Figure 4. Libraries ultimately used for HEAT, with associated licenses. The links between libraries are shown via solid arrows. The dashed gray arrows represent dependencies. The .dll libraries must have all dependencies explicitly linked when the .dll file is built

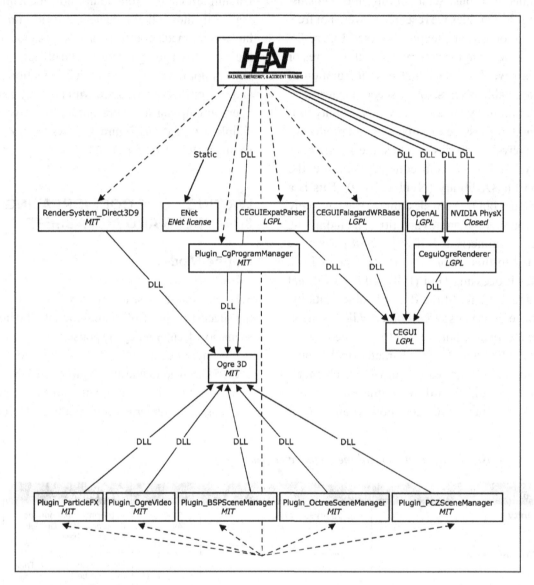

when the time came to export this model into the .mesh format which Ogre uses, we experienced a number of problems. While the house looked good as an offline software render, the game engine was a lot pickier. These points are further described below.

Triangle Count

Offline renders that do not need to produce images in real time (i.e., at least 30 times per second) can work with very large triangle counts because a "render" can be initiated and then left to process for many hours. However, in a real-time environment the more triangles there are the more work the GPU must perform to render the objects as the player moves around in the virtual environment. Initially the house modeled in Blender used approximately 70,000 triangles. The total triangle count in the scene with the house and other models was approximately 73,000 triangles. When shadows were added to the simulation, the frame rate was forced considerably slower. Additionally, when attempting to "spray" fluid inside of the house, the frame rate suffered even more. We initially attributed this performance degradation to the high number of triangles. Judicious triangle management proved to be a wise investment of time. For example, in the original house layout a large number of polygons were used in rendering the hand rails for the stairs. In the improved model, the rails were greatly simplified without much visual change, which allowed us to use those polygons in other areas, enriching the visual aspects of the environment overall.

Reduction Methods Necessary?

In an attempt to prevent the slowdown with the rendering and physics, we considered more efficient scene management schemes. Ogre3D natively supports simple frustum culling, which means that if the bounding box of an object is not at all visible within the camera's frustum (i.e., the part of the world that the camera "sees") then that object is not sent to the graphics card for rendering. We also considered implementing occlusion culling. Frustum culling alone will not prevent occluded objects, such as a plant behind a wall, from getting drawn, even when the viewer cannot see it. Occlusion culling will not send occluded objects to the graphics card for processing. Another type of scene management is portal culling. This works well for house environments, where each room is a separate entity and the doorways between rooms are portals. If you can see through a portal, then the room it is connected to is also drawn. An Ogre community member was working on a portal culling scene management plug-in but

could not give a definite date as to completion. In the interim, we found another scene management plug-in by following the personal link of an Ogre community member he listed in the Ogre forums as part of a discussion on the subject (Volca, 2007). This scene manager plug-in was built for another purpose, but there was some code for screen-space portal management. We began experiments with the portal portion of this code in HEAT, showing a visual display of the portal as a screen space rectangle that also was clipped against the camera frustum. After posting on the Ogre forums, we learned that the creator of the work-in-progress portal scene manager used his prototype by splitting up interior rooms and exporting each room as a totally separate, self-contained model. So, we modified the HEAT house model using the 3D application *Maya* (Autodesk Software, 2006). We grouped rooms by splitting all geometry that belonged to a certain room into a separate object and then assigning it to a layer to make it easier to determine the room's visibility. In the end, even though all the rooms were separate objects, we opted not to use portal-based scene management due to lack of time for a proper implementation.

In addition to portal scene management, we had to consider spatial partitioning structures. These are data trees that split up the environment's triangles into data structures that accelerate the testing of whether given triangles should be rendered. Examples of these include Binary Space Partition (BSP) trees (Wade, 1998), Octrees (Suter, 1999), and K-Dimensional (KD) trees (ReedBeta, 2008). We found a certain type of binary data tree, called an adaptive binary data tree, described in the gamedev.net forum (Lombard, 2002a). We could not find any formal white papers written describing this method, and all implementation details had to be gleaned by searching the forums. However, one author created a program demonstrating Adaptive Binary Trees (ABT) for publication in the book More OpenGL Game Programming (Villagrana, 2007). We found that Villagrana's website offers free downloads of the code, which we compiled in order to observe the results first-hand. An ABT works by recursively subdividing Axis Aligned Bounding Boxes (AABB's) that contain equal amounts of triangles to improve frustum culling efficiency (Lombard, 2002b).

The implementation of ABT's seemed fairly complex, and we hesitated to implement it, wondering if it was a good solution to our performance problems. We posted some questions on the gamedev.net forums, and received some very helpful responses. Eventually it came to light that we had seriously underestimated the potential calculation power of modern graphics cards. The creator of ABT's replied to our post and mentioned that ABT's were designed for scenes consisting of hundreds of thousands to millions of triangles. For 70,000 triangle models such as the house model for HEAT, it would be far faster to use a "brute force" approach and simply send all triangles to the GPU. Brute force, in the case of our system, means that instead of trying to send visible triangles to the GPU we are actually sending or forcing all 70,000 at once to be rendered by the GPU. This method was wasteful but effective. Even triangles that are occluded behind walls (and therefore invisible) to the viewer would be rendered without adversely affecting the speed of the render.

By the time we made this discovery, we had already spent considerable time making each room of the house a separate object. Fortuitously, this method provided us with a beneficial result. As part of the training simulation, there is a facilitator whose role is to watch the actions and positions of the "players." For teaching purposes, the facilitator can keep track of actions, and time of which those actions are taken. We understood that having separate rooms would still be beneficial for HEAT because it would now be possible for the facilitator to track what room the player was currently in at any given point and time, as well as the sequence of rooms they chose to enter. Separate rooms allow the facilitator to observe

and record the location of each player for later instructional review.

Physics Interaction

One of the main elements of the HEAT simulation is the use of real-time fluid. We needed participants to have the ability to spray fluids (e.g., water to put out the fire) on any surface at any given time. During incident command training, it is important to follow specific steps to ensure effective communications and strategies in chaotic situations. If players wasted time by spraying water in places without fire they would not succeed in containing the incident with the least amount of damage. To this end, we began to make the exterior of the house one continuous solid mesh. Originally the house model was not continuous, that is, certain portions of the roof were not connected via triangles to other portions of the roof, they were modeled separately and then stacked on top. As mentioned earlier in this paper, creating the house in this manner made for fine off-line renders, but was unacceptable for physics purposes in the simulation. In order for the physics library to calculate collisions of fluids against the house geometry, the triangles comprising the house model must be created and converted to a suitable format by the physics system (called "cooking" the geometry). In order for optimal management, the vertices of the triangles should not be duplicated, but rather stored once in a master list passed to the physics code. If two triangles shared a vertex, they should both reference the single vertex. Otherwise, the physics library would not know if two vertices in the list were in the same position in 3D space, complicating the hardware performance problems (Ageia PhysX, 2007a).

Interestingly enough, the Ogre .mesh Maya exporter has an option to export vertex normals (Bisco, 2008). A normal is the normalized vector that is perpendicular to the triangle. The normal defines the direction the triangle is facing (Alexandrov, 2007). To this point we had been leaving that option "checked" upon export but we suspected this option might be causing problems. The house model by nature has many hard edges. In order for the graphics hardware to render two triangles that have a hard edge, each vertex shared by the triangles must have its own normal. This effectively doubles the amount of vertices in the model. While duplicate vertices are needed for the visual rendering of the model, it only confuses the physics system (see Figure 5). If each vertex only has a single normal, it will be the average of the normals of all triangles sharing that vertex and give the appearance of softer edges.

The Ogre Exporter for Maya was exporting 24 vertices, rather than the eight we were expecting. This caused the HEAT engine code to submit many duplicate triangles to be cooked for physics, since the positional information is duplicated three times for each vertex (once for each normal). A "workaround" for this is to export the model once without vertex normals. A one-time export will create a .mesh file with a single vertex entry per vertex, eliminating the redundancy as seen in Figure 6.

Visual Considerations

We used several techniques in Maya to accomplish keeping the number of triangles as low as possible when working on the house. First, it was very helpful to turn on the display of triangles without actually creating them, since quads (quadrilateral, a 4-sided polygon) are generally easier to use. Due to the nature of quadrilateral geometry, we occasionally inadvertently created non-planar geometry. Non-planar geometry was a problem, since when the model is converted to triangles and the normals hardened, unintended creases will be seen in the geometry. Maya has an option to highlight non-planar faces. We used the non-planar face option to make apparent the cases when moving a vertex created a non-planar face. We found some very helpful free *Mel* scripts

Figure 5. A cube with hard edges, multiple normals at each vertex required

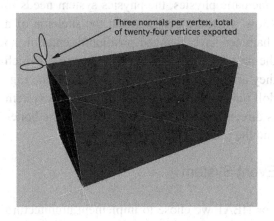

Figure 6. A cube with single averaged normal at each vertex, yielding softer edges due to interpolation across normals (a). Shown without wireframe (b)

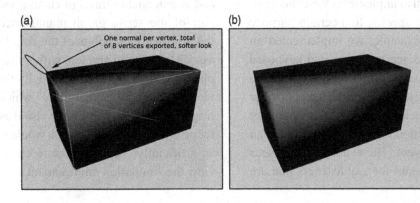

online that allowed us to fix non-planar faces as part of a cleanup stage (Roberts, 2007). We also found it very useful to delete any non-necessary edges or vertices, as Maya would automatically create triangle edges as needed.

Core Engine Architecture

The HEAT simulation involves many "objects" at any given time. An object can refer to a wide variety of items within the environment including items one can see (an axe, fireman, fire truck, etc.) as well as potentially invisible items such as a sound emitter. The architecture of the engine describes how the simulation objects are tracked, how each object is notified of important events within the simulation, and how each object can interact with other objects. For example, with kinematic physics, the physics system needs to know when the bones within the skeleton of a character have changed position/orientation so the physics actors can match the bone to which they are assigned. At other times when the rag-doll functionality is enabled, the physics system is directly responsible for controlling the bones and the relationship is reversed.

Event System

For HEAT we chose to implement architecture similar in scope to what is described in Game Coding Complete with an event manager that registers "listeners" for specific events (McShaffrey, 2003). This architecture also implements the concept of controllers that are specific to a certain purpose and context. For example, we implemented an editor controller to accept mouse and keyboard inputs in the context of editing objects within the world. When an object is selected, the controller triggers an "object selected event." When dragging an object to reposition it, the controller sends an "object moved" event. The event manager sees these events and looks for any listeners that are registered for that event. When the manager finds a listener that is registered, it notifies the listener.

The concept of differing controllers is important because when participants are using the simulation, they have no need for editing the environment. Instead, we eliminate the editing controller and place in the environment a simulation controller. A simulation controller takes mouse and keyboard inputs during the playing of the simulation, which sends events like "player moved" when the directional keys are pressed and "view changed" when moving the mouse, rather than the "dragged events" described in the previous paragraph. In addition to global-level events like processing mouse and keyboard inputs, we also implemented a similar event system on an object level used to handle events triggered by specific components. For example, each object that has a 3D position in space fires events for when that position has changed. Event firing is used to synchronize the positions used by each of the audio, physics and rendering systems.

The architecture also separates the simulation into three distinct systems—a system adapter, an engine, and a game manager. The system adapter handles receiving input from the operating system and translates that information into an engine-compatible format. The engine handles top-level event management, subsystem updating and processing, and the primary loop for the game manager, the event system, and the subsystems (see Figure 7). The game manager controls the scene graph, supplies the game logic, and is extendable through custom view classes. Part of the scene graph management includes the different viewpoints of the simulation, often associated with characters within the simulation plus a "god's eye view." Typically the character views include a "human view" which would be responsible for managing the visual aspect of the scene, and an "AI view" which would include how an artificially controlled game character might view the simulation environment.

Figure 7. Event flow through the system

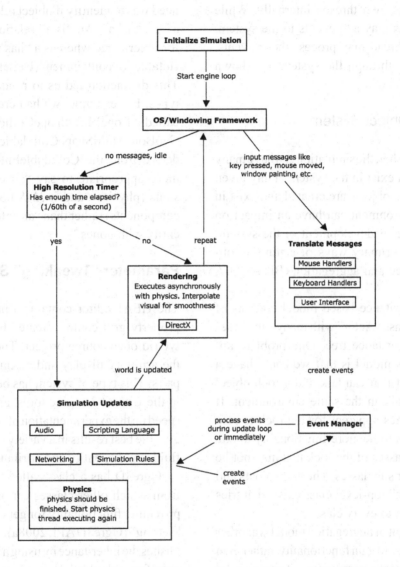

This separation of concepts resonates with our project in several ways. Initially with HEAT, we had used Ogre SceneNodes as position holders for the objects. This notion was conceptually in error since the Ogre SceneNodes should only be used as transforms for the visual pixels rendered to the screen. It is best to have a second set of coordinates to represent the game objects themselves (Junker, 2007).

Using events in a multithreaded setup would have been difficult, since an application using the engine could theoretically send an event at the same time as the rendering thread, creating the need for locking the event queue or some other synchronization method. We worried about performance issues due to synchronization methods because some systems would send many events hundreds of times per second. Eventually, we decided it would be most beneficial to implement a single simulation thread, even though each subsystem may manage its own threads internally. While multiple threads may add events to the system, only a single thread may process those events. Events flowing through the system are shown in Figure 7.

Simulation Object System

As described earlier, the simulation can have many objects that can exist in the system at any given time. How these objects are created and exist in the virtual environment can have an impact on the overall ease of development of the system. We found two primary ways of setting-up objects: inheritance and aggregation (Bilas, 2007, Wilson, 2007;).

A pure inheritance based model consists of one top-level class "Actor" with many subclasses and a deep inheritance tree. One problem apparent with this model is that we could have a character object that can talk and a rock object that does not talk in the same environment. If the need becomes apparent for the rock to also speak, there has to be more functionality to one of the parent classes of the rock that may not be needed by other subclasses. The code bloats and one "monolithic" top-level class exists that tries to be everything to every class.

A containment or aggregation model is another option. For a class to gain functionality, rather than have it inherit from a parent class, it contains the functional class as a member. For example, for a rock to talk, the rock class might have a talk object as one of its members. The advantage of this system is that one can build functionality ala-carte, by hand picking what components any given object may have. An object-level event system beneficially affects the entire design of the system, in that it allows components to communicate via events, which makes it possible to reuse components in a variety of situations. In other words, an object is the sum of its components.

Our research indicated that our fundamental need was to identify if object relationships are "is a" or "has a". An "is a" relationship is suitable for inheritance whereas a "has a" relationship is suitable for containment (Deitel & Deitel, 2001). This distinction led us to re-analyze our object types. For example, we had created two classes called "BoneMultiShapeCollidableEntity" and "NoBoneMultiShapeCollidableEntity" that both derive from the CollidableEntity class. It was more appropriate to say "an entity *HAS* collisions (physics), and it *HAS* bones" (hence two components) rather than "an entity *IS* a collidable entity with bones."

Parameter "Tweaking" System

The HEAT editor contains a property sheet, or property grid control created by the wxPropertyGrid open source project. The grid allows for the arbitrary display and editing of name/value pairs. This type of system has been implemented in the *Unreal 3* engine tools, and would greatly speed up the experimentation of what numbers will give the best results in a variety of areas including fluid, smoke, entity and attributes.

Ogre3D has a class called "StringInterface" from which other classes can inherit properties providing functionality for generic "getting" and "setting" (Ogre3D API, 2008a). The class accomplishes the inheritance by using a ParamCommand class from which other classes can inherit, providing both a set function and get function that take strings. Passing all values as strings simplifies the class interfaces, albeit at some performance cost because the setting and getting functions must convert from string to the intended format, such as a float. Choosing an object-built-from-components idea as described earlier, the parameter grid can display components as top-level categories with the members of those components as attributes to edit (see Figure 8). Editing fluid parameters are especially helpful with a property grid, as there

Figure 8. A property window screen capture of the editable parameters for the firefighter

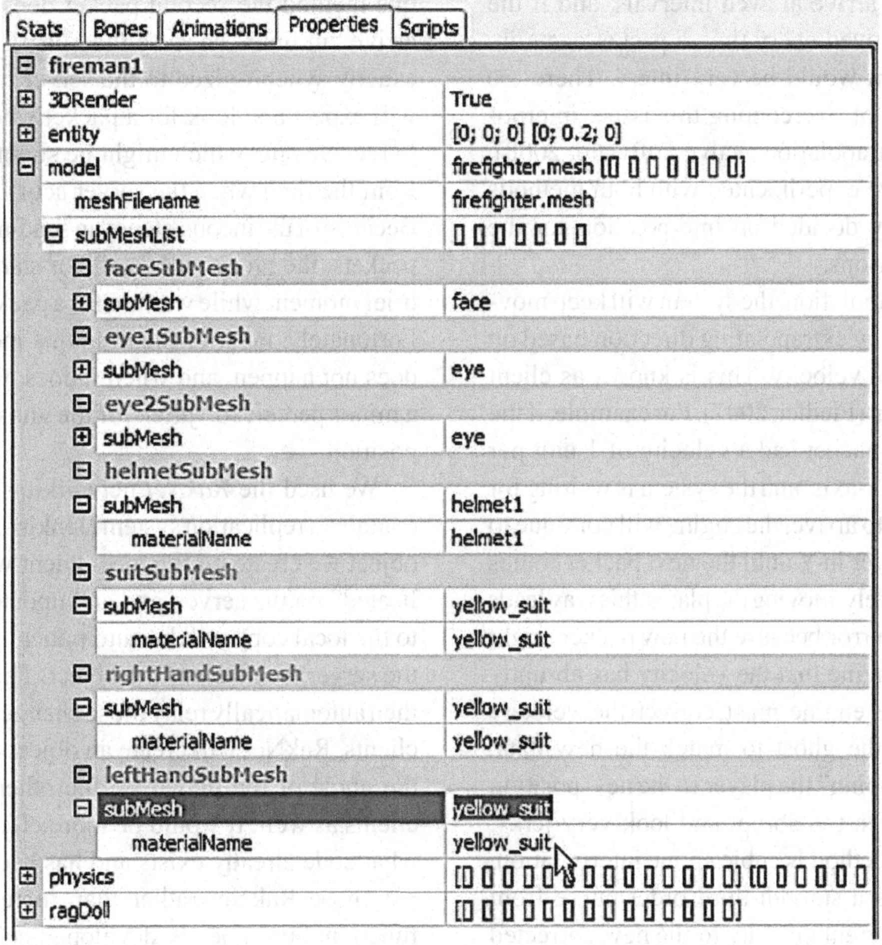

Stats	Bones	Animations	**Properties**	Scripts

⊟ fireman1	
⊞ 3DRender	True
⊞ entity	[0; 0; 0] [0; 0.2; 0]
⊟ model	firefighter.mesh [[] [] [] [] [] [] []]
meshFilename	firefighter.mesh
⊟ subMeshList	[] [] [] [] [] [] []
⊟ faceSubMesh	
⊞ subMesh	face
⊟ eye1SubMesh	
⊞ subMesh	eye
⊟ eye2SubMesh	
⊞ subMesh	eye
⊟ helmetSubMesh	
⊟ subMesh	helmet1
materialName	helmet1
⊟ suitSubMesh	
⊟ subMesh	yellow_suit
materialName	yellow_suit
⊟ rightHandSubMesh	
⊟ subMesh	yellow_suit
materialName	yellow_suit
⊟ leftHandSubMesh	
⊟ subMesh	yellow_suit
materialName	yellow_suit
⊞ physics	[[] [] [] [] [] [] [] [] [] [] [] [] [] []] [[] [] [] [] [] []]
⊞ ragDoll	[[] [] [] [] [] [] [] [] [] [] [] [] []]

are many different values and settings for fluids, each of which is very sensitive to changes.

Eventually, we abandoned the parameter editor along with its tweaking system, mostly due to other changes in the design of the engine and how well the parts worked together. Instead, we developed a custom data language (a subset of XML) that is used in a similar way. The custom data language allows each component within an object to save its current state to a generic binary form, which can then be used for other purposes. Currently, the generic form is used to load object settings from a file, or save them to a file. However, the form could also be used as a generic way to implement parameter tweaking within a new editor.

Networking

Networking ability is important for HEAT because the training environment requires the accommodation of multiple participants working together. Implementing an effective networking scheme has many well-known issues to overcome. One of these issues is packet latency. When a player moves, his position is sent to the server that records it and in turn sends that new move to every other connected client. Other clients will have a visual representation, or "ghost" of that player on their screens. A problem lies with the packets that may not arrive at even intervals, and if the ghost only moved every time a packet came in, the movement would be very jittery. There are two methods of overcoming this issue, interpolation and extrapolation (Valve Software, 2008). For HEAT, we experimented with both methods but ultimately decided on interpolation for the following reasons.

With extrapolation, the system will keep moving the ghost by extrapolating direction based on its last known velocity. This is known as client side prediction (Fiedler, 2007). For example, if the last received packet had a velocity of 1 unit per second in the Y-axis, and the system is waiting for a new packet to arrive, the engine will continue to move the player in Y until the next packet comes in. Unfortunately, moving the player this way leads to prediction error because the new packet might inform the engine that the velocity has abruptly changed. The engine must correct the velocity and path of the ghost to match the new data. Simply "snapping" the player to the new position would be much too abrupt and look very jerky. A smoother method is cubic spline interpolation, which creates a smooth third order curve from the ghost's current velocity to the new corrected velocity. In HEAT we implemented cubic spline interpolation with good results, except for when the ghost stopped moving. When the remote client stopped moving, the ghost would keep moving, and then have to curve back around resulting in a consistent "overshoot" of the player, which eventually became visually unacceptable.

Interpolation works by "double buffering" packets, meaning the engine does not begin to move a ghost until it has received and queued at least two packets. The engine moves the ghost toward the position in the first packet, and by the time it has reached that position, it immediately has the second packet to move toward. As long as the engine can stay at least one packet ahead, it will always have a correct position to move towards and there is no need for correc-

tive action. When experimenting in HEAT using this method the second packet does not always arrive "in time" because the client's time is not exactly synchronized to the server time. Clients will expect and look for a packet when it is time to receive one, which might be slightly different from the time when the server actually sent one. Because of the inconsistency in sending/receiving packets, the ghost will "stall" or stand still for a brief moment while waiting for a packet to arrive. Fortunately, most of the time this inconsistency does not happen, and when it does, there is only a minor perceived "jitter" of the ghost's physical position.

We used the *RakNet* networking library that contains a replication system (Jenkins, 2008). Any object we create on the local client will be "replicated" on the server, and any updates we make to the local copy will be automatically relayed to the server's version of the object. The server can then automatically relay those changes to all other clients. RakNet will create an object to represent the ghost of the player on the other connected clients as well. It would be more effective to use what code already exists and has been tested, so we chose RakNet rather than to replicate that functionality in newly developed code. Another benefit to the RakNet system is that if a player takes an object, that object will disappear from that player's environment, and the replication system will remove that object from the views of all the other connected clients. It is helpful functionality to maintain consistency of the environment between different networked players. RakNet was a good choice, but we eventually moved to the lower-level Enet networking library because RakNet started to exhibit random freezes when trying to load our data (Salzman, 2008).

Third Person Camera System

In the game *Star Wars Jedi Knight*, Jedi Outcast has a very useful crosshair that in essence is an extension of the player's vision (LucasArts

Entertainment Company, 2002). For example, the crosshair will change colors and pulsate if the player is looking at something with special attributes. For HEAT, we also wanted some way for players to identify that they could pick up an object or determine other functionality. The crosshair, normally an open circle, would change to a closed fist if the player were "looking" at a "take-able" object. By "looking" he would have the crosshair sighted over the object.

Another feature of the Star Wars game we found intriguing was when the player moved his mouse quickly in any direction, the crosshair would first move, then the view would smoothly pan towards that view, much the same way a walking person first moves their line-of-sight before changing directions. To accomplish this in HEAT, we used functionality of the Ogre Quaternion class that generates a new quaternion that orients itself towards a vector. We used an exponentially smoothed moving average to make the rotation less and smoother the closer the orientation gets to its vector goal (Fiedler, 2007). This discovery came by accident as we were experimenting with code from an Ogre wiki site and left in a line of code that technically did not belong. As it happens, we found a nice solution for moving a character following line-of-sight (Petkovesk, 2007). In the original implementation, the player was meant to

rotate at a constant rate to a destination orientation via linear interpolation. Inadvertently we made the rate not constant, i.e., the player rotated slower as it approached the destination orientation. An alternative would have been to use cubic interpolation instead of linear, but the math would have been more difficult that way.

We observed in the Star Wars game and in Quake 3 that if a wall emerged between the player and the camera behind his head, that the camera would move forward until it was not occluded anymore. We decided that since collidable geometry was modeled using the physics library, we could use the raycast functionality to test if the camera was occluded by something between it and the back of the player (Ageia PhysX, 2007b). We used the distance returned by the raycast to know how far to move the camera forward. We also moved the camera depending on how close the player was to a wall so the camera was not directly behind the player's head, as seen Figure 9 (Quake Engine, 2007).

HEAT Editor Issues

To address the development of the building-block pieces that go into the functionality of the engine (e.g., 3D graphical capabilities, VOIP, sound and physics), creating a 3D development editor was

Figure 9. Head being obscured (a). Camera adjusted so the head is not obscured (b)

(a)

(b)

necessary. We named our 3D engine development editor HEAT-ed (editor) seen in Figure 10.

This editor allows us the opportunity to import 3D models of characters and environments into the game engine rendered and viewed as it would be in the HEAT application itself. Here, resizing and polygon checking could be accomplished, as well as assigning physics boundaries to the mesh structure. Previewing and tweaking in the editor saved time and effort for development rather than using external software programs.

When building functionality into the HEAT editor, some unexpected issues arose. For example, we wanted the ability to add physics boundaries to objects, as well as manipulate the size of the boundary shape and position. Adding

physics boundaries required that we have some way to visualize the physics shape, since the shape is purely a mathematical property as far as the physics is concerned. We opted to manually draw a wireframe capsule, cube, or sphere with all of the parameters of the physics library. This capsule gave us something to be able to "click" on and select for editing.

Another issue that arose was if the physics was dynamic and thereby affected by gravity, it might be causing an object in our virtual environment to be rolling all over the ground, and the user would have to "chase" after it just to select it again. The solution we used was that when the user clicks on an object, gravity turns off and the object stays in place. "Disallowing" gravity to edit an object

Figure 10. A screen capture of the HEAT-ed interface

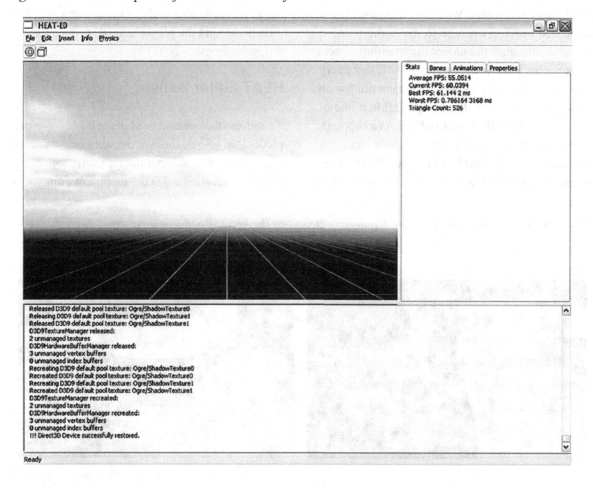

allows the user to edit the physics shape. When the user de-selects the object, the gravity turns back on, and the physics will cause the object it is affecting to begin to drop, roll, or whatever it would do in the virtual environment as dictated by its shape and position. An alternative might be to have a global "on and off" button that turns all physics on and off (Mohamed, 2006).

Similar to many 3D modeling programs like Maya or 3D Studio Max, we wanted some manipulator tools to interact with objects in the environment. These tools include a trackball-style rotation widget, a translate widget, and scale widget. We were not sure how to create the rotator ourselves due to the complex spherical clicking and dragging, so we researched the Open Inventor library that provided many different types of manipulators. Integrating this library proved to be a difficult effort (Silicon Graphics, 2008).

First, we needed to find a way to draw the *Open Inventor* widgets. Open Inventor is designed to work with pure OpenGL, and already contains code to prepare the vertices for rendering, much like Ogre. It will only render its manipulators if the engine is using the Open Inventor library. Because we are not using Open Inventor, we needed a way to capture those triangles and render them using Ogre instead. Open Inventor has a triangle callback function that is called for every triangle it processes. We captured that callback and passed the triangles to Ogre instead. We could not use a file-based geometry format because Open Inventor used its own type, and some of the shapes are hard coded as data in the code. The easiest solution was to let Open Inventor get and process the triangles however it wanted, then to catch them for our rendering choices.

We also had to capture mouse clicks and pass them to Open Inventor to recognize if a manipulator was selected or dragged. Open Inventor uses a different default projection matrix than that of Ogre. This issue was apparent when Ogre would draw the rotator widget, and an attempt to click one of the rotator bands was initiated. Because the

Open Inventor system used a different projection matrix, internally the system would not recognize that the rotator was selected, even though the user would see in Ogre that they were clicking on it. An offset existed of about half an inch from the visual manipulator to the invisible internal Open Inventor representation.

Open Inventor did not provide a way to override its projection matrix, but Ogre did, so to solve the issue we set the Ogre projection matrix to match the Open Inventor one (see Figure 11). In addition to a generic rotation and translate/scale manipulator, Open Inventor also had several light manipulators with handles for Ogre lights in the scene. We later removed the dependency on Open Inventor and opted to create our own translation, scale, and rotation widgets.

Solution File and Multiple Projects in Visual C++

Initially we tried to include many of the third-party open source libraries as projects within the HEAT solution of Microsoft Visual C++. This option held numerous advantages, including being able to ensure that each library was compiled to the correct C runtime library, and easy dependency linking via the Visual Studio project dependency dialog. However, doing so also introduced additional clutter to the workspace. Some of the libraries we used did not provide source code, or it was provided via make files and not with Visual Studio solution files, so there was no consistent way to include all third-party libraries in the solution. We decided to remove most of the projects and instead compile each one to its own .lib file for linking. Initially, we created a directory structure similar to that described in *Game Coding Complete* (McShaffrey, 2003).

As the structure evolved, we decided to separate all third-party libraries from the main engine development to assist in project management. In its current structure, third-party libraries are built individually as defined by the library vendors, and

Figure 11. The visual physics shape on the breathing apparatus (a). A screen capture showing object manipulators in HEAT (b)

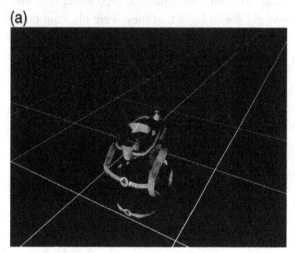

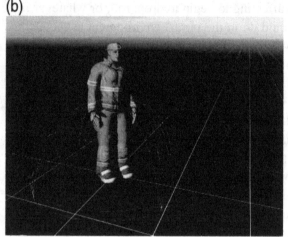

their binaries and source are all stored in a special "extern" directory, which is accessible to the main engine solution (see Figure 12). This structure allows the engine and all other projects to use all features of the libraries, including the ability to debug inside the third-party library, without having to clutter the solution with projects that are rarely, if ever, modified.

The structure also makes it easier to manage any changes made to the open source libraries. Incorporating a new library follows a specific procedure that is described below.

1. A library is built according to the system established by its vendor. The version is noted in the file *Versions.txt* and any custom changes made to the library such as build settings or open source code modifications are noted in the file *Modifications.txt*.
2. The library header files are copied to *Extern\ Include* which enables the incorporation of all third-party libraries by including a single directory in the build settings.
3. The library source files are copied to *Extern\ Source\<library_name>*. Even though the

source code is not strictly necessary, it is included for debugging purposes.

4. The library outputs (.lib, .dll, and various debugging files) are copied to *Extern\<Platform_Name>*. All libraries are placed in the same directory for ease of use, similar to the header files in step 2.

Multi-Threading Issues

We implemented the HEAT editor with two threads, one to run the GUI and handle the windows message pump, and one to run the rendering. This implementation held the advantage that if a "file open" dialog was open, the rendering thread would continue to render the environment regardless of what the GUI was doing. However, we encountered many issues trying to make the implementation system work effectively. If the Ogre thread wanted to communicate back to the GUI thread, it required that the Ogre thread post a custom message in a thread safe queue via wxWidgets (Smart, 2008). This procedure added another layer of complication. For example, if a user clicked on a physics shape in the environment,

Figure 12. The directory structure was very useful for accessing the source code and other files

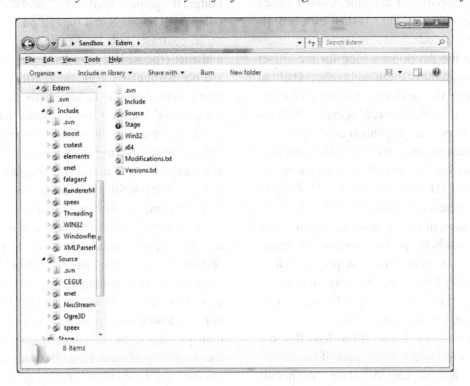

the engine would have to send a custom message to the GUI thread, and from there the GUI would pass the message to the property grid member that would then dissect the message for parameters and populate the parameter grid. The protocol is followed under a Windows OS because the thread that created the window is the only thread that is allowed to modify it (wxWidgets Book, 2007). If both Ogre and the GUI were on the same thread, then Ogre could directly populate the property grid itself without the need for a custom message.

Another issue that arose was handling window resize events. A participant can resize the window—a command handled by the GUI thread. The problem is that the Ogre thread could attempt to render a scene at that same moment, and when the GUI thread decides to call Ogre->resize() the application would abnormally end because Ogre was already busy rendering. To overcome this handling issue, we had the GUI thread post a resize

message that the Ogre thread could read when it was not rendering, and then call *resize* on itself.

After realizing that we would have to synchronize events for objects, we opted to keep Ogre and the GUI on the same thread. The decision made coding much easier, and resizing the window was a smoother process. We decided that multi-threading for our engine did not justify the problems it created.

ITERATIVE INTEGRATION PROCESS OF THIRD-PARTY LIBRARIES WITH CORECODE

Our open source development process seems to differ in some ways from that of the commercial engines. First, while commercial programmers and open sources alike have plenty of problems to solve, the commercial developers tend to try to solve problems themselves versus seeking out third-party support. For example, *Unreal 3* uses Ageia/Nvidia physics, but has their own proprietary rendering code.

Reading the developer's blog for the Offset engine details some of the thought process behind implementing the rendering system and other engine aspects. In each case, McGrath (2004) appears to be the primary implementer of ideas, even though he sometimes is privy to things like new video cards from Nvidia (2009). John Carmack, co-founder of ID Software and the Quake and Doom franchises, detailed some of his development processes, in particular about how to solve a geometry visibility problem so that the engine would not slow down when the player walked into a geometry heavy area. He writes of thinking how to solve this issue in the middle of the night while lying in bed (Abrash, 2000).

Because we knew that we did not have the time or resources to build every aspect of the HEAT engine ourselves, we considered from the beginning about what libraries existed to potentially solve our problems, and coded with integration of those libraries in mind. Considering the new integration of a third-party library, we created a design that exposes the features of that library to the engine without creating duplicate access and management to the objects supplied by that library. There is also a need to have working results early in the development process. The design should try to be extendable so that core features can be implemented immediately and other, less-used features may be integrated as needed.

Another aspect in which we differ is that commercial developers have the luxury of doggedly pursuing a problem until it is solved. There are several accounts of this difference. The intended audience of gamers is fairly particular and will judge harshly any game that they feel does not meet their expectations. In the above example of Carmack's visibility problem, he had to solve that or else gamers would not have been able to have a smooth gameplay experience. This would have frustrated them and they would not have

bought the game, which would have damaged the company's business and reputation.

In contrast, with HEAT we have a different audience (focused on emergency personnel) who are not particularly concerned with having the best graphics nor the fastest performance. Also, we are working on a much smaller budget and timeline; we cannot necessarily perfect any one option before moving to the next. Commercial companies have to make compromises as well, but differing priorities can lead to vastly different kinds of compromises and amounts.

Yet another difference between our process and that of commercial engines is related to openness. Commercial engines tend to be highly proprietary, not revealing much if anything about their development processes and often requiring non-disclosure agreements before even allowing their product to be sampled. We inquired as to the possibility of working with some commercial engines and were either bluntly told no, or were given a weak commitment that later fell through. In contrast, with an open source development approach we had access to resources and help, and we felt we could contribute at least some of our development back to the community without the need for total secrecy. John Carmack is kind of an anomaly, a juxtaposition of openness in an otherwise commercial environment. People like him are crucial in helping smaller projects learn about 3D engine development.

In the following sub-sections we will discuss our integration experience with various libraries used to meet our needs for collision detection, VOIP, user interfaces, serialization, and particle systems.

Collision Detection

Integration of 3rd party libraries is an iterative process. The attempts at initial integration often prove to be incorrect or need a significant amount of tweaking to get right. In HEAT we need robust collision detection, something exclusively handled by the physics library. In early development stages, we did not have a human firefighter model, so we used a ninja model packaged with the Ogre library. We practiced setting collision capsule shapes on the arms, legs, and torso of the model, and then dropped physics cubes onto the ninja. When the ninja was animated, we had to get the world space position and orientation and apply that to the physics collision shape so it would match the arm, leg, and all parts of the character appropriately.

Initially we based this position on a built-in feature of Ogre that allows one to "attach" objects to bones (Ogre3D API, 2008b). We attached the visual representation of the physics capsule to the bone and use that to obtain the position and orientation information since Ogre would move the capsule in-sync with the bones. This tight coupling of the positional information with Ogre was not the most effective way to handle movement updates because it was assumed that the capsule would always be visible (which is only true in development or debug mode). Also, if another skeletal animation library were ever used instead of Ogre, it would be much harder to exchange libraries. It would manifest as sloppy coding.

Later, we found code on the Ogre forums that described a way of obtaining the position and orientation of just the bone without needing to attach any objects to the bone. The method consists of performing the correct calculations of multiplying quaternions to get a relative rotation from the bind pose, as well as a world position (Spacedude, 2007). This way we could obtain the information we needed properly which eliminated the need to have a visual representation of the physics shapes. For simple physics objects, we implemented an auto-generation feature that creates the collision for the object at the cost of runtime performance. This method is likely not desirable under circumstances where a simulation is underperforming, but it does allow for quick turnaround of new art assets, allowing them to be placed and used in-engine during testing.

VOIP

For HEAT, Voice Over Internet Protocol (VOIP) capability was needed so that participants could speak to each other over the existing game network, allowing interaction from remote participants. The networking library provided examples with two audio libraries used for microphone input and speaker output, *PortAudio* (Bencina, 2008) and *FMOD* (Firelight Technologies, 2008). PortAudio was free, but did not provide much in the way of game-type sound functionality, such as 3D positional sound or *SoundBlaster Hardware* accelerated sound effects (Creative Technology, 2008). FMOD was the other extreme; it wrapped all the low-level sound functionality into a nice library; however it was prohibitively expensive for our project. We then decided to use the *OpenAL* sound library (Creative Labs, 2008). OpenAL does not provide as much high-level code, but it does have 3D sound positioning and other attractive functionality.

We began by copying the RakNet code for the FMOD example and attempted to modify it for use with OpenAL. The modifications needed proved to be challenging because OpenAL requires a double-buffer in the incoming sound to result in a smooth streaming flow of microphone input, something the RakNet examples failed to illustrate. Initially we did not double buffer the sound and the voice input incorporated pops and delays. There were examples of streaming .wav files in the OpenAL API distribution that we tried to modify for voice input, but our attempts met with little success. Finally after much Internet searching, we discovered code to run a suite of tests against the OpenAL library to ensure its functionality, maintained by the OpenAL developers. This suite of tests was only available on the *Subversion* website svn://connect.creativelabs.com/OpenAL, not the public API download, which is partially why we had such difficulty in finding it. The test code had a portion that demonstrated streaming voice input, and used it with the RakNet sample to successfully enable VOIP capability.

Due to the complexity of using OpenAL, we ultimately emailed the FMOD developers and they gave us permission to use FMOD for free because of the non-commercial nature of HEAT.

GUI System

We originally opted to use Crazy Eddie's GUI System (CEGUI) because it was considered the "official" Ogre GUI system (Turner, 2008). As we began to work with CEGUI, we found it a large library requiring many external dependencies. When we integrated it we employed the "stock" textures created by others. One problem arose when we attempted to direct one of our graphic artists in how to prepare the custom HEAT art for the buttons, list boxes, etc. With CEGUI, the interface art involved creating one single texture filled with the different button icons for the different states (i.e., an "over" state, "down" state, and so on) and then specifying box coordinates for each piece of that single texture. The button state information was entered into an xml file along with other xml files to create the GUI layout. We felt this process was overly complicated in that it takes significant time for a project with numerous GUI functions. Because the project leader for CEGUI had quit the development, and coupled with its complexity, we were led to evaluate other GUI options. Although in the end we went back to CEGUI, we searched the Ogre forums and discovered that community members were creating their own small GUI systems, which opened up many new possibilities.

An HTML-Based GUI

One forum member utilized the Mozilla browser library in a novel manner and rendered it into the 3D Ogre window, effectively allowing us to write a GUI in HTML and render it in Ogre (Ajs15822, 2007). We evaluated this option and decided that it

was not the best for our needs because of our wish to integrate the GUI with direct render-to-texture operations. The operations are needed to render the mini-view ports of other participants in the simulation. In addition, these view ports needed to be scrollable within a scroll box.

Ogre Overlay-Based GUI System

The rest of the solutions suggested in the Ogre forums involved using the Ogre overlay system. Ogre supports simple 2D overlays that can have a texture or text within them. We found several libraries that used vector-based imagery rather than pixel based bitmaps. We felt using vector-based imagery was too complex for our immediate needs and so chose to use regular bitmap images.

The overlay system allows the creation of separate .png files for each button state, and the use of Ogre .material scripts to specify what texture should be used for each state. This was a quicker and easier option than preparing images for CEGUI. Two of the community overlay-based projects seemed to standout as most advantageous, *QuickGUI* (KungFooMasta, 2008) and *BetaGUI* (BetaJaen, 2006). *QuickGUI* was more complex but complete, with *BetaGUI* being simpler and less complete. To complicate matters, another community member had modified BetaGUI and made it more functional. This version was known as *Bullet-BetaGUI* and was the recommended version by many forum members (Kuarnes, 2008). Ultimately, we started with the codebase of Bullet-BetaGUI and added parts of QuickGUI to it to complement it, all while molding the system to fit the guidelines presented in *Game Coding Complete* (McShaffrey, 2003).

We integrated the GUI system into the HEAT editor so that our developers can visually position widgets like buttons and edit parts of them. This system allows us to position the GUI elements in real time without having to recompile for every change. CEGUI used a scripted system based on an xml file to allow description of the layout of screen elements without having to recompile the code every time a reposition is needed. The scripted system is very time saving. However, HEAT uses a custom saving format with the Boost Serialization library, which can output xml files or binary files (Ramey, 2004). We did not have to worry about the scripted aspect—it was handled by the library.

Serialization Library Experiences

One lesson we learned with HEAT was that it is normally best to not hack or recode existing library code even when it seems like the right option. For example, we opted to use the Boost Serialization library. This library assumes that all objects will be newly created via placement on the heap. We could allow this placement easily enough for our HEAT objects, but Ogre creates most of its important objects via class factories. Developers never use the new operator with class factories, even though the factory returns a pointer to the newly created object. Initially we tried to modify the serialization library to take a pointer to an already created object as a parameter. After numerous crashes and debugging attempts, we could not get the library to cooperate. In the end, we compensated by using another property of the serialization library to first create the object ourselves, although it requires an extra step beyond directly using the library.

The physics system was similar in that we use "create" functions to return pointers to things like actors and character controllers. The physics provide the opportunity to use custom memory allocators, such that the allocator is called anytime a system tries to create a new object via "new." In this way, we could still create something like a character controller via the physics factory function, and then pass that pointer into the allocator. When the serialization library attempts to create a new object, the allocator gives it the address of the object we previously created rather than allocating new space. Later, we developed our

own serialization system in the form of a custom data language, which replaced the need for Boost Serialization altogether.

Integrating Particles into the System

Many 3D simulations and games feature visual effects such as fire, smoke, and water (Chiba, Muraoka, Takahashi & Miura, 2006). Given the nature of the simulations the HEAT environment was designed to render, our goal was to make these effects so the user can directly interact with them while maintaining high visual quality. Toward this goal our implementation relies heavily on the use of particle systems (Reeves, 1983). Among several considered techniques we chose to implement our visualization based on that taken by Nvidia in the popular GPU Gems series that renders each particle as a billboard and applies a frame of a flame animation to it as a texture (Fernando, 2004). The same technique, seen in Figure 13, was used to render smoke in the environment (Kipfer, Segal & Westermann, 2004; Nguyen, 2004).

In addition to the rendering of the effects, we also needed a way to simulate their behavior in response to a changing simulated environment. Initially, we accomplished the simulated behavior by using the particle simulation engine provided by the graphics SDK. Because of the limitations inherent in this approach, we redesigned the component to take advantage of the capabilities offered by the physics library, which, contrary to the often used Navier-Stokes computational model for fluids, implemented and optimized the Smoothed Particle Hydrodynamics approach (Harris, 2004).

As previously mentioned, integrating the animated billboard approach into our chosen graphics engine proved to be challenging. Although Ogre has functionality similar to our stated choice of technique, a full implementation required delving into the SDK and, roughly, "hacking" the third-party source code to achieve our goal. Even with these modifications, we were left with the problem

Figure 13. Smoke in a kitchen, rendered in the HEAT engine

of allowing the user to interact with the flames and smoke, and vice-versa. The physics engine we employed would handle this functionality, but because of an update feedback problem with regard to collisions, it was unfeasible to continue using that technique. Instead, we chose then to use the particle simulation capabilities of the physics library. In doing so, we bypassed the feedback problem mentioned before, but were left with the problem of how to display the simulated systems. The add-on libraries available for Ogre nearly solved the problem, but proved to be too limited for our intended use. We have since undertaken the task to implement the particle display functionality in our core code.

Migration Application Independencies

As we were building HEAT, we wanted to keep open the possibility of using the engine for other educational applications like language learning, physics education, etc. At this time we are still waiting on grants to use the engine for other purposes, but we already see ways in which to make the process easier with other engine implementations. For example, we want to find a more streamlined "pipeline" of getting art assets like models and textures into the environment. We have looked at using the Collada format as an interchange 3D XML model format and then converting that to an Ogre .mesh file (Khronos Group, 2008). We have looked at a scripted code and data build system, with code being standard C and C++ source code and data being textures and models in various forms (Jensen, 2008). One can program a build system that can transform 3D models from Collada XML into the Ogre .mesh equivalent, and can compress textures in uncompressed formats (like .psd, .tiff) into graphics card-friendly compressed formats like .dds (Microsoft Developer Network, 2009). The very same build system can automatically compile and link source code into the final executable. Automating some of these tedious development processes can give a consistent and error-free method of not only creating the executable, but also creating optimized forms of art assets.

In contrast, as we developed HEAT, we just exported to the Ogre .mesh directly from Maya, which tended to force all artists to conform to Maya. Also, our lead artist had to manually track which image files had been converted to .dds files. Freeing team members from such restrictions can lead to a more productive workflow and give them more time to focus on project specific goals in any given context.

CONCLUSION AND IMPLICATIONS

The process of developing our own 3D engine has been an illuminating experience by revealing what is needed to make a game engine successful. Our practice has been to pay attention to each individual detail during development, a methodology that should continue to serve us well as we enhance the engine by creating new scenarios for our existing application. Diligence is necessary to keep abreast of updates to discussions, enhancements to open libraries, and nuances presented by other developers placed on the Internet. This care will enable HEAT to make use of components shared by many 3D game engines—cutting-edge 3D graphics, VOIP, sound, and physics. Keeping up on the differences between VOIP libraries led to choosing the one that worked the best for our needs at the time. Some libraries may be the "newest" for what we are attempting, however, in some cases during implementation it is possible that the "newest" library may not work with other libraries we have already implemented. There is a need to remain flexible.

Building HEAT has taught us important implications in creating a 3D engine from scratch. A list of suggested practices when using open source libraries to develop 3D game engines includes:

- There is an active support community for any library you choose to adopt.
- Make sure the library has clear documentation (such as in Doxygen format).
- Try to see if the library has been used in any finished titles, or at least has some real-world impressive demos or samples of its work.

- Be prepared to learn (sometimes long into development) that certain libraries may not give the performance or benefits originally hoped for. Be open to switching to another open source library if time allows or even to a closed source solution if it is better in meeting the needs of the project. The end result should drive library selection.
- Try to use libraries that are mature enough to be stable. We learned that the QuickGUI library, while enticing at first due to its simplicity, ended up being too young and simple to meet our needs and we had to switch to the more full-featured CEGUI.
- Make sure that all libraries/components chosen can work together, and make sure to have an idea of how much/what "glue code" will need to be written in-house.
- Decide if the licensing scheme of the particular library is compatible with your project's goals, i.e. if you do not want to make the source code open, do not use any libraries with a GPL license.
- Setup a plan of how to link with each library (see Figure 4), i.e., which should remain as .dlls and which will be statically linked. (This choice is also constrained by the licensing of the particular library as well).
- Make sure to have some kind of organized build plan for how to compile all the libraries and what output directories to use, etc. For HEAT, we used Microsoft Visual Studio 2005/2008 and had a single solution containing all the open source 3rd party libraries.
- If using libraries that are allowing high-level access to underlying low-level functionality, be sure to understand the low-level process to use the high-level library efficiently. For example, the Ogre3D library wraps DirectX as the lower-level

API. We learned that we had to group triangles into large "batches" or groups to get good rendering speeds. We could not just expect Ogre3D to compensate if we tried to use it inefficiently.

The development and success of the HEAT engine would not be where it is without the use of open source materials. They are integral to our process of researching what libraries give us needed functionality, developing core code and integrating the two successfully within the engine. The dependency upon these materials has its drawbacks, but a huge benefit of using the open source materials is that most developers want their code to be implemented by others. Open source developers are often willing to help with implementation by answering questions posted in developer forums. Though it requires troubleshooting, the use of open source components has allowed us to develop the engine within our available budget (Shelton, et al., 2010).

Offering our experience of using open libraries to build a virtual 3D game engine should enhance the body of knowledge to give others insight into building new, exciting, and powerful software.

Because the lack of resources is one of the largest barriers to break into game and simulation development, a project like that of HEAT may be the answer for others to gain entry into the world of gaming development. While some commercial developers are fairly open about their design production processes, commercial engines by and large guard their development process very closely, and it will be up to open projects like HEAT to aid others in developing their own projects. The trend even for commercial companies may be shifting to more adoption of third-party libraries. *Unreal 3* seems to be partnering with more and more third-party commercial institutions, like Illuminate Labs for their rendering lightmap baking and Scaleform GFx for Flash GUI integration. So it appears that even the trading companies are realizing the potential benefit to using third-party code. For those with limited budgets and for development within education, we expect our experience to contribute to the open source efforts in building cutting edge technology.

ACKNOWLEDGMENT

The authors wish to thank Jeff Maxfield, Dennis Goudy, James Hunter, Greg Rynders, Gary Noll, Hugh Connor, Devon Bartlett, Dave Smellie, and Alan Hashimoto for their subject matter expertise and support.

REFERENCES

Abrash, M. (2000). *Inside Quake: Visible-surface determination*. GameDev.net. Retrieved February 10, 2008, from http://www.gamedev.net/reference/articles/article981.asp

Ageia Phys, X. SDK documentation. (2007a). *Collision detection, meshes, cooking.* [Electronic version]. Mountain View, CA: Ageia.

Ageia Phys, X. SDK documentation. (2007b). *Lesson 305–Raycast report*. Mountain View, CA: Ageia.

Ajs15822 (forum name). (2007, May 24). *Navi.* Retrieved from http://www.ogre3d.org/forums/viewtopic.php?t=32384

Alexandrov, O. (2007). *Surface normal*. Retrieved March 4, 2008, from http://en.wikipedia.org/wiki/Surface_normal

Autodesk Software. (2006). *Autodesk Maya*. Retrieved January 20, 2009, from http://usa.autodesk.com/adsk/servlet/index?id=7635018&siteID=123112

Bencina, R. (2008). *Portable cross-platform audio API*. Retrieved January 20, 2009, from http://www.portaudio.com/

Berkley Software. (2008). *BSD license definition.* Retrieved January 20, 2009, from http://www.linfo.org/bsdlicense.html

BetaJaen (forum name). (2006, November 7). *BetaGUI: BetaGUI 2.5 update - Style system added.* Retrieved from http://www.ogre3d.org/forums/viewtopic.php?f=11&t=25853&start=275

Bilas, S. (2007). *A data-driven game object system.* [Electronic version]. Retrieved from http://www.drizzle.com/~scottb/gdc/game-objects.ppt

Bisco. (2008). *Tools.* Retrieved January 20, 2009, from http://www.ogre3d.org/index.php?option=com_content&task=view&id=413&Itemid=133

Blender. (2009). *Blender.* Retrieved January 15, 2009, from http://www.blender.org/

Carnegie Mellon Entertainment Technology Center. (2006). *Welcome to Panda3D!* Retrieved January 20, 2009, from http://panda3d.org/

Chiba, N., Muraoka, K., Takahashi, H., & Miura, M. (2006, October). Two-dimensional visual simulation of flames, smoke and the spread of fire. *The Journal of Visualization and Computer Animation, 5*(1), 37–53. doi:10.1002/vis.4340050104

Creative Labs. (2008). *OpenAL.* Retrieved January 20, 2009, from http://connect.creativelabs.com/openal/default.aspx

Creative Technology. (2008). *Sound blaster.* Retrieved January 20, 2009, from http://www.soundblaster.com/

Cruz, D., Wieland, T., & Ziegler, A. (2006). Evaluation criteria for free/open source software products based on project analysis. *Software Process Improvement and Practice, 11*(2), 107–122. doi:10.1002/spip.257

Deitel, H., & Deitel, P. (2001). *C++ how to program* (3rd ed.). New Jersey: Upper Saddle River.

Epic Software. (2008). *Unreal technology.* Retrieved January 20, 2009, from http://www.unrealtechnology.com/

Fernando, R. (2004). *GPU gems: Programming techniques, tips, and tricks for real-time graphics.* Canada: Addison-Wesley Professional.

Fiedler, G. (2007). *Clients approximate server physics locally.* Retrieved January 20, 2009, from. http://www.gaffer.org/game-physics/networked-physics/

Firelight Technologies. (2008). *FMOD music and sound effects system.* Retrieved January 20, 2009, from http://www.fmod.org/

Google. (2008). *Google summer of code.* Retrieved January 20, 2009, from http://code.google.com/soc/2008

Harris, M. (2004). *Fast fluid dynamics simulation on the GPU* (pp. 637–655). GPU Gems. Addison Wesley.

Jenkins, K. (2008). *Jenkins software.* Retrieved January 20, 2009, from http://www.jenkinssoftware.com/

Jensen, S. (2008). *JamPlus.* Retrieved January 20, 2009, from http://redmine.jamplex.org/projects/show/jamplus

Junker, G. (Xavier, forum name). (2007, January 31). *Movable object listener.* Retrieved from http://www.ogre3d.org/phpBB2/viewtopic.php?=&p=200435

Khronos Group. (2008). *Collada—3D asset exchange schema.* Retrieved January 20, 2009, from http://www.khronos.org/collada/

Kipfer, P., Segal, M., & Westermann, R. (2004). Uberflow: A GPU-based particle engine. *Proceedings of the ACM SIGGRAPH/Eurographics Conference Workshop on Graphics Hardware* (pp. 115–122).

Kuarnes, T. (2008). *Ogre bullet forum index*. Retrieved January 20, 2009, from http://www.ogre3d.org/addonforums/viewforum.php?f=12&start=0

KungFooMasta (forum name). (2008). *QuickGUI forum index*. Retrieved January 20, 2009, from. http://www.ogre3d.org/addonforums/viewforum.php?f=13

Lombard, Y. (2002a, November 11). Combining octrees and BSP trees... is it possible? Retrieved from http://www.gamedev.net/community/forums/topic.asp?topic_id=123169

Lombard, Y. (2002b, November 14). Combining Octrees and BSP trees... is it possible? Retrieved from http://www.gamedev.net/community/forums/topic.asp?topic_id=123169

LucasArts Entertainment Company (2002). *Jedi knight II: Jedi outcast* [CD-ROM].

McGrath, S. (2004). *Developer's blog: September 8th, 2004 – Post processing framework, HDR pipeline*. Project Offset. Retrieved September, 2007, from http://www.projectoffset.com/blog.php?id=15

McShaffrey, M. (2003). *Game events and scripting languages. Game coding complete* (2nd ed.). Scottsdale, AZ: Paraglyph Press Inc.

Microsoft Developer Network. (2009). *DDS*. Retrieved January 20, 2009, from http://msdn.microsoft.com/en-us/library/bb943990(VS.85).aspx

Milne, I., & Rowe, G. (2005). Interpreting computer code in a computer-based learning system for novice programmers. *Software, Practice & Experience*, *35*(15), 1477–1493. doi:10.1002/spe.680

Mohamed, M. (2006, April). *Stop your physics simulation*. Retrieved November 3, 2007, from http://reality.artificialstudios.com/twiki/bin/view/Main/RigidActors

Mozilla Foundation. (2008). *Mozilla code licensing*. Retrieved January 20, 2009, from http://www.mozilla.org/MPL/

Newton. (2008). *Newton game dynamics*. Retrieved January 20, 2009, from http://www.newtondynamics.com/index.html

Nguyen, H. (2004). *Fire in the "Vulcan" demo* (pp. 87–105). GPU Gems. Addison Wesley.

Nvidia. (2009). *NVIDIA PhysX*. Retrieved January 20, 2009, from http://www.nvidia.com/object/nvidia_physx.html

Ogre3D API. (2008a). *Ogre: String interface class reference*. Retrieved January 20, 2009, from http://www.ogre3d.org/docs/api/html/classOgre_1_1StringInterface.html

Ogre3D API. (2008b). *Ogre: Entity class reference*. Retrieved January 20, 2009, from http://www.ogre3d.org/docs/api/html/classOgre_1_1Entity.html

OSG. (2008). *Welcome to the OpenSceneGraph website*. Retrieved January 20, 2009, from http://www.openscenegraph.org/projects/osg

Petkovsek, C. (2007). *Quaternion and rotation primer*. Retrieved January 15, 2007, from http://www.ogre3d.org/wiki/index.php/Quaternion_and_Rotation_Primer

Project, G. N. U. (2008a). *GNU general public license*. Retrieved January 20, 2009, from http://www.gnu.org/copyleft/gpl.html

Project, G. N. U. (2008b). *GNU lesser general public license*. Retrieved January 20, 2009, from. http://www.gnu.org/licenses/lgpl.html

Quake Engine. (2007). *id software*. [Electronic version]. http://www.idsoftware.com/games-/quake/quake3-teamarena/

Ramey, R. (2004). *Serialization overview*. Retrieved January 20, 2009, from http://www.boost.org/doc/libs/1_37_0/libs/serialization/doc/index.html

ReedBeta. (2008). *Kd-trees*. Retrieved January 20, 2009, from. http://en.wikipedia.org/wiki/Kd-tree

Reeves, R. (1983, April). Particle systems—A technique for modeling a class of fuzzy objects. *ACM Transactions on Graphics, 2*(2), 91–108. doi:10.1145/357318.357320

Roberts, N. (2007). *Naughty's MEL scripts, modeling scripts*. Retrieved September 1, 2007, from http://www.naughtynathan.supanet.com/data/mel.htm

Salzman, L. (2008). *Enet*. Retrieved January 20, 2009, from http://enet.bespin.org/

Shelton, B. E., Stowell, T., Scoresby, J., Alvarez, M., Capell, M., & Coats, C. (2010). A Frankenstein approach to open-source: The construction of a 3D game engine as meaningful educational process. *IEEE Transactions on Learning Technologies, 3*(2). http://doi.ieeecomputersociety.org/10.1109/TLT.2010.3

Silicon Graphics. (2008). *Open inventor*. Retrieved January 20, 2009, from http://oss.sgi.com/projects/inventor/

Smart, J. (2008). *What is wxWidgets?* Retrieved January 20, 2009, from http://www.wxwidgets.org/

SpaceDude (forum name). (2007, March 31). *Ragdolls*. Retrieved from http://www.ogre3d.org/phpBB2addons/viewtopic.php?t=3949&highlight=ragdoll

Stowell, T. (trs79, forum name). (2006, November 6). *Custom projection matrix changes RaySceneQuery?* Retrieved from http://www.ogre3d.org/forums/viewtopic.php?f=2&t=25673

Streeting, S. (2007). *DevMaster.net. 3D engines database, Ogre 3D*. Retrieved August 1, 2006, from http://www.devmaster.net/engines/engine_details.php?id=2

Streeting, S. (2009). *What is Ogre?* Retrieved January 20, 2009, from http://www.ogre3d.org/index.php?option=com_content&task=view&id=19&Itemid=105

Suter, J. (1999). *Introduction to octrees*. Retrieved January 20, 2009, from http://www.flipcode.com/archives/Introduction_To_Octrees.shtml

Turner, P. (CrazyEddie, forum name). (2008). *Welcome to crazy Eddie's GUI system*. Retrieved January 20, 2009, from http://www.cegui.org.uk/wiki/index.php/Main_Page

Valve Software. (2008). *Source multiplayer networking*. Retrieved January 20, 2009, from http://developer.valvesoftware.com/wiki/Source_Multiplayer_Networking

Villagrana, J. (2007). *Downloads*. ABT. Retrieved April 10, 2007, from. http://www.3dgloom.net/html/downloads.html

Volca (forum name). (2007). *CVS code repository*. Retrieved April 3, 2007, from http://opde.cvs.sourceforge.net/opde/opde/src/

Wade, B. (1998). *BSP tree frequently asked questions* (FAQ). Retrieved January 20, 2009, from http://www.gamedev.net/reference/articles/article657.asp

Wilson, K. (2007). *Game object structure: Inheritance vs. aggregation*. Retrieved July 18, 2007, from http://gamearchitect.net/Articles/GameObjects1.html

wxWidgets. (2007). *wxWidgets book*. Retrieved August 1, 2006, from http://www.wxWidgets.org

Section 2
Learning Outcomes of Games and Simulations

Chapter 7
Promoting Civic Thinking through Epistemic Game Play

Elizabeth A. S. Bagley
University of Wisconsin-Madison

David Williamson Shaffer
University of Wisconsin-Madison

ABSTRACT

A growing body of research suggests that computer games can help players learn to integrate knowledge and skills with values in complex domains of real-world problem solving (P. C. Adams, 1998; Barab et al., 2001; Gee, 2003; Shaffer et al., 2005; Starr, 1994). In particular, research suggests that epistemic games—games where players think and act like real world professionals—can link knowledge, skills, and values into professional ways of thinking (Shaffer, 2006). Here, we look at how a ten hour version of the epistemic game Urban Science developed civic thinking in young people as they learned about urban ecology by role-playing as urban planners redesigning a city. Specifically, we ask whether and how overcoming authentic obstacles from the profession of urban planning in the virtual world of a role playing game can link civic values with the knowledge and skills young people need to solve complex social and ecological problems. Our results from coded pre- and post-interviews show that players learned to think of cities as complex systems, learned about skills that planners use to enact change in these systems, and perhaps most important, learned the value of serving the public in that process. Two aspects of the game, tool-as-obstacle and stakeholders-as-obstacle, contributed to the development of players' civic thinking. Thus, our results suggest that games like Urban Science may help young people— and thus help all of us—identify and address the many civic, economic, and environmental challenges in an increasingly complex, and increasingly urban, world.

INTRODUCTION

I personally believe...that U.S. Americans are unable to do so because...uh, some... people, out there in our nation, don't have maps.

—2007 Miss Teen South Carolina, when asked why a fifth of Americans cannot find the United States on a world map.

DOI: 10.4018/978-1-60960-565-0.ch007

Today, half of the world's population—some 3.3 billion people—live in cities. By 2030, the urban population will exceed 5 billion. (United Nations Population Fund, 2007, p. 1) As the United Nations Population Fund suggests, "their future, the future of cities in developing countries, the future of humanity itself, all depend very much on decisions made now in preparation for this growth." Thus, understanding and engaging with the complex interrelationships of cities is a fundamental form of citizenship in the 21st Century.

Unfortunately, as a geographic literacy study suggests, "young people in the United States...are unprepared for an increasingly global future...Far too many lack even the most basic skills for... understanding the relationships among people and places that provide critical context for world events" (The National Geographic Education Foundation, 2006, p. 7). One-fifth of Americans cannot even locate the United States on a world map—a statistic that led a Miss Teen USA contestant to suggest that geographic illiteracy is so pervasive because "U.S. Americans... don't have maps." (R. Adams, 2007)

But the problem is not that U.S. Americans lack maps. Nor is it even that young people cannot locate the United States on a world map, depressing though that may be. Rather, the problem is that our public understanding of what it means to be geographically literate equates geographic thinking with the ability to locate places on a map. Questions like this focus solely on *knowledge*: bits of information disconnected from any meaningful context.

Of course civic thinking does require knowledge of social, economic, and ecological—and, yes, geographic—information. But as Ehrlich (2000) argues, civic thinking means more than just recall of isolated facts. Solving civic problems requires putting knowledge in the context of real world skills and in the service of civic values that create a democratic republic (2000). Developing civic thinking requires learning opportunities where the use of knowledge and skills are guided by civic, social, and ecological values.

A growing body of research suggests that computer games can help players learn to integrate knowledge and skills with values in complex domains of real-world problem solving (P. C. Adams, 1998; Barab et al., 2001; Gee, 2003; Shaffer et al., 2005; Starr, 1994). In particular, research suggests that *epistemic games*—games where players think and act like real world professionals—can link knowledge, skills, and values into professional ways of thinking (Shaffer, 2006). To establish these links, epistemic games present players with the same meaningful obstacles that professionals-in-training face and give players a chance to reflect on those obstacles with more experienced mentors.

Here, we look at how the epistemic game Urban Science develops civic thinking in young people as they learn about urban ecology by role-playing as urban planners redesigning a city. Specifically, we ask whether and how overcoming authentic obstacles from the profession of urban planning in the virtual world of a role playing game can link civic values with the knowledge and skills young people need to solve complex social and ecological problems—and thus be a powerful context for learning civic thinking.

THEORY

Ehrlich (2000) argues that civic education has two distinct, but related, parts: civic engagement and civic thinking. For Ehrlich, *civic engagement* consists of "individual and collective actions designed to identify and address issues of public concern" (2000, p. xxvi). Activities that impact and strengthen the community—such as volunteering at a soup kitchen or picking up trash on Earth Day—are important components of civic education. But, according to Ehrlich, the *civic thinking* that develops from such activities is what creates a long-term commitment to civic engagement. Civic thinking prepares people to participate in their communities (Ehrlich, 2000).

For Ehrlich, civic thinking is composed of three separate, but interrelated elements: knowledge, skills, and values, or as he describes it, "mutually interdependent sets of knowledge, virtues, and skills" (2000, p. xxvi). *Knowledge* of civic thinking, in this sense, includes understanding the institutions and the processes that drive civic, political, and economic decisions in the body politic—including understanding how a community operates, the problems it faces, and the richness of its diversity (p. xxx).

Ehrlich writes that the *skills* of civic thinking are essential for applying this knowledge to solve civic problems (p. xxvii). Civic skills include: communicating clearly, orally and in writing; collecting, organizing, and analyzing information; thinking critically and justifying positions with reasoned arguments; seeing issues from the perspectives of others; and collaborating with others. However, civic knowledge and skills are incomplete without the core *value* of civic thinking: willingness to listen to and take seriously the ideas of others. (p. xxvi)

This conception of civic education in terms of knowledge, skills, and values is reflected in the National Assessment Governing Board's Civics Framework (2006). The civics framework consists of three components that guide its curriculum benchmarks: knowledge, intellectual and participatory skills, and civic dispositions:

Civic skills involve the use of knowledge to think and act effectively and in a reasoned manner in response to the challenges of life in a constitutional democracy. Civic dispositions include the dispositions to become an independent member of society; respect individual worth and human dignity; assume the personal, political, and economic responsibilities of a citizen, participate in civic affairs in an informed, thoughtful, and effective manner; and promote the healthy functioning of American constitutional democracy. (2006, p. xi)

As Ehrlich points out, however, civic education is not merely about learning a list of knowledge, skills and values:

Such a listing may imply that the elements involved have precise definitions and parameters that might be gained through a single course or even reading a few books. (2000, p. xxvi)

Instead, he argues that civic education needs to integrate these different domains of understanding into a coherent vision of responsible civic action.

In this paper, we look at how a particular kind of computer game can help players develop and integrate the knowledge, skills, and values of civic thinking.

Games and Learning

A growing body of research suggests that computer games can promote learning (P. C. Adams, 1998; Barab et al., 2001; Gee, 2003; Shaffer et al., 2005; Starr, 1994). In the popular commercial game SimCity, for example, players can learn about civic issues by designing and running a city. In the game, they have to manage issues such as an increasing population, environmental changes, urban and economic development, crime, and transportation. Players raise or lower taxes, build and destroy schools, hospitals, power plants and other civic infrastructure, and rezone and reshape their virtual city.

Gaber (2007), Adams (1998), and Teague and Teague (1995) have shown that SimCity provides a dynamic decision-making environment in which students can understand urban geography and community planning concepts by thinking about cities as ecological and social systems. For example, Gaber argues that students playing SimCity in his college course, learned "about the multi-dimensional 'systems' understanding of cities and the interconnected aspect of planning decisions" (p. 119).

But while SimCity can help players think about complex systems, there are also significant limitations in using this game to encourage civic thinking. As Beckett and Shaffer (2005) discuss, SimCity models the whole city whereas people typically experience cities and their impacts locally. In addition, time in SimCity is compressed. Civilizations can develop from small hamlets to empires in a matter of minutes or hours, covering hundreds of years in the blink of an eye. Finally, and perhaps most importantly, decisions in real cities are made through a complex process of political deliberation. In SimCity, players exercise God-like power. The sims who live in the city are free to come and go, but they have no voice in the fate of their city. SimCity provides a fictionalized process of urban growth, in which the lives of citizens are glossed over by the scale of the model, the scope of the timeframe, and the despotic powers of the players.

Professional Practices of Planners

Like players of SimCity, urban planners have to think about cities as complex systems. But rather than working as virtual urban despots like in SimCity, real urban planners use professional skills to serve the public interest.

Barton & Tsourou (2000) argue that planners view a city as a living, breathing organism, the health of which is closely linked to that of its citizens. Planners work with the complex, interrelated components inherent in urban systems, and in this sense, SimCity reflects some of the knowledge professional planners have. But as Ehrlich argues (2000), knowledge is just one component of civic thinking. Here we examine how urban planners, unlike SimCity players, use particular civic skills and values to solve complex problems in urban systems.

A professional planner develops skills to "manage the planning process itself, involve a wide range of people in making decisions, understand the social and environmental impact of planning decisions on communities, and function as a mediator or facilitator when community interests conflict" (American Planning Association, 2010). As Friedmann (1987) suggests, planning links "scientific and technical knowledge to actions in the public domain" (p. 61).

Planners use their professional skills to manage an urban system that involves people, their opinions, and their life experiences. Planning-related decisions are made daily through a complex, often politically charged process involving the interests of multiple stakeholders (Nedovic-Budic, 2000). Thus, a core value of planning is to:

involve all affected parties in important planning decisions; help communities to develop their own vision of the future, preparing plans responsive to shared community objectives; analyze qualitative and quantitative information to suggest possible solutions to complex problems; evaluate the cost-effectiveness of proposed projects and plans; and present recommendations to public officials and citizen groups in a comprehensive and understandable way. (Association of Collegiate Schools of Planning, 2009, p.8)

In other words, though Herwig and Paar (2002) argue that the urban planning profession can be interpreted as a complex strategic game, the profession of planning is markedly different from SimCity. Professional planners think about cities as systems, but also have specific professional skills that they use to serve the public interest. Upon leaving the virtual world of SimCity, players find few roles for aspiring urban despots in the urban planning community of their own cities. On the other hand, a game modeled on the professional practices of planners might create an environment in which players could learn to connect civic knowledge with real-world civic skills and values.

Professional Obstacles

Shaffer (2006a) argues that becoming a professional, such as an urban planner, involves developing the epistemic frame—the ways of knowing, of deciding what is worth knowing, and of adding to the collective body of knowledge and understanding—of a particular community of practice. For example, the epistemic frame of planning involves thinking about cities as systems and using professional skills to serve the public interest.

Epistemic games are role playing games that help young people learn the knowledge, skills, and values of a profession by simulating professional training. By playing, for example, a well-designed game based on the training of real urban planners—rather than on a fictionalized process of urban growth and development—young people can begin to engage in the complex compromises and decision making processes that shape their social and physical realities.

Professional training, including the training of urban planners, is characterized by a professional practicum—a training environment that allows a novice to do things he or she would do as a professional and discuss the outcomes with peers and mentors (Schon, 1987; Shaffer, 2006b). For example, in a planning practicum, novices are hired by organizations to complete a planning project. They visit the site in question, meet with stakeholders, use geographic information system (GIS) models to weigh tradeoffs, create preference surveys and final plans, and present their findings (Shaffer, 2006b). During the practicum, novices meet with their instructor for advice and feedback, and collaborate closely with peers.

In other words, in a practicum, novices encounter the kinds of challenges and obstacles that are faced by trained professionals—but they do so in a supervised setting with the help of expert mentors. Learning takes place in a practicum when a novice encounters these professional obstacles while trying to accomplish a meaningful goal (Shaffer, 2006b). The obstacles, in effect, push back on the intentions of the players, forcing them to use particular kinds of knowledge, skills and values to solve a problem or take an action. The basic structure of a practicum is thus a set of professional obstacles, combined with forms of feedback relevant to the ways of thinking and working of a particular profession. This experience lets a novice act—and thus to learn to think—as a particular kind of professional.

Urban planners do not use the term 'obstacles' when referring to stakeholders since they do not see stakeholders as obstacles to overcome, but rather as people with whom and for whom they work. However, in this paper we refer to stakeholders as obstacles with the understanding that obstacles drive learning, and thus help players learn to value the public interest. According to Dewey (1934), learning—and specifically learning by doing—is characterized by trying to do something, making mistakes, and then figuring out how to fix them. The kind of learning that involves overcoming obstacles is the foundation of all learning by doing (Dewey, 1934). As a result, players learn to see stakeholders not as obstacles by encountering and overcoming them first as obstacles. Thus, seeing stakeholders as a problem helps players see them as part of the solution.

In previous work, Beckett and Shaffer (2005) constructed an epistemic game modeled on an urban planning practicum. It incorporated professional obstacles that addressed two components of civic thinking: knowledge of systems thinking and skills for enacting real world processes. The interactive geographic information system (GIS), MadMod, modeled the complex relationships between land use zoning decisions and important social and ecological factors, such as the number of jobs and housing units. To solve problems using MadMod, players had to think of the city as a complex system and understand the social and environmental impact of planning decisions on the community. In this sense, the GIS model itself was the professional planning obstacle: a *tool-as-*

obstacle which required players to use planning knowledge and skills to succeed in the game.

Beckett and Shaffer's study showed that players of the game gained a deeper understanding of the domain of ecology and of their city as an ecological system. Players made frequent reference to urban planning practices when explaining their thinking about ecological interconnectedness. In short, the game helped players think like planners (Beckett & Shaffer, 2005).

Here, we extend that work through the epistemic game Urban Science. In developing Urban Science, we hypothesized that building additional professional obstacles into Beckett and Shaffer's original game would preserve the knowledge and skill gains and further improve players' civic thinking abilities. Specifically, we hypothesized that by incorporating virtual stakeholders and their feedback into the game, players would begin to think about a core value of the planning profession and component of civic thinking: the value of serving the public interest.

In this paper we examine Urban Science and ask: (1) Did the Urban Science epistemic game help players develop urban planning knowledge, skills, and values? (2) Did the professional obstacles, specifically the stakeholders, help players develop this civic thinking?

METHODS

Urban Science Game

Game play in Urban Science was modeled on an ethnographic study of a graduate-level planning practicum, Urban and Regional Planning 912, at the University of Wisconsin-Madison (Bagley, 2010). As described above, this capstone practicum helped novice planners develop the epistemic frame of urban planning through a series of mentored activities. The practicum included:

- a site visit, where novice planners learned about the features of the planning challenge from first-hand observations and meetings with stakeholders
- preference surveys, where novice planners prepared alternative plans using GIS software to elicit feedback from stakeholders about features of the neighborhood they wanted preserved
- staff meetings, where teams of novice planners discussed information gathered and proposed planning solutions
- drafting of a final plan, where teams decided on and constructed a proposed plan using GIS software
- proposal preparation, where teams developed a presentation that explained and justified their proposed plan
- final proposal, where teams presented their proposals to relevant stakeholders.

Game play in Urban Science adapted these activities to be played by a group of twelve middle school students during two weekend days. Table 1 provides a summary of the relationship between a planning practicum and the Urban Science game.

The game began with a cut scene, in which a local expert planner charged the players with redesigning State Street, a popular pedestrian thoroughfare in Madison, Wisconsin: "We need a plan," he said, "that incorporates the various visions of a sustainable State Street into one comprehensive plan. The plan should create an economically vibrant, distinctive district that reflects the cultural heritage of the area."

Players acted as planning liaisons for one of four stakeholder groups concerned with the development of State Street:

- Business Council
- People for Greenspace
- Urban League
- Cultural Preservation Organization

Table 1. Urban science activity structure

Planning practice	Day 1	Urban Science Activity
Cut Scene	10:30	Staff meeting:Introduce problem through visit from expert planner(s)
	10:45	
Site visit	11:00	Visit virtual person 1 on State Street, take pictures, record impressions in digital voice recorder
	11:15	Visit virtual person 2 on State Street, take pictures, record impressions in digital voice recorder
	11:30	Visit virtual person 3 on State Street, take pictures, record impressions in digital voice recorder
	11:45	Lunch
	12:00	
	12:15	Debrief from site visit. Discuss stakeholder issues and introduce idea of thresholds
	12:30	
Preference survey	12:45	Model creating alternative scenario probes for stakeholders
	1:00	Begin working on 3 plans for one stakeholder by deciding what issues each plan will address
	1:15	Make zoning changes to create one plan for team's stakeholder
	1:30	Model the feedback the probes elicited from stakeholders
	1:45	Discuss the results from the current plans and suggest changes
	2:00	Make changes to model
	2:15	Submit plans to stakeholders for feedback
Staff meeting	2:30	Model understanding the stakeholder feedback and presentation of process
	2:45	Write a summary of the stakeholder's preferences for team presentation
	3:00	
	3:15	Team meeting to compare stakeholder feedback with whole group (jigsaw)
	3:30	
	Day 2	
Draft plan	9:30	Welcome back/staff meeting. Model incorporating numerous stakeholders into plans
	9:45	Begin working on final plan in teams. Discuss ways to craft the final plan to please all stakeholders
	10:00	Make zoning changes to incorporate all stakeholders' needs
	10:15	Teams report progress
	10:30	Incorporate changes discussed in team meeting and finalize plan
	10:45	
Proposal preparation	11:00	Model writing justifications
	11:15	Write justification statements
	11:30	Finish final plan as a team
	11:45	Lunch
	12:00	
	12:15	Model final presentation
	12:30	Prepare for final presentation
	12:45	
	1:00	Organize speaker order and practice
	1:15	
Final proposal	1:30	Final presentations with client
	1:45	
	2:00	

In teams, players conducted a site visit of State Street with digital cameras and handheld global positioning system (GPS) units. While on the site visit, stakeholders' pictures and text characterizing their visions for the future of the community appeared on the handheld GPS units at pre-determined locations. For example, when players came to the one small park on State Street, they "met" Maya, a member of People for Greenspace, who said:

Hey, I'm Maya, and I'm a member of People for Greenspace. We're committed to improving the natural beauty of State Street by creating parks. Too much congestion and back-to-back buildings make for a crowded and unhealthy city environment. Cities need natural areas to support birds, trees, and plants, and people are happier when they have access to natural places—now and in the future. There are other advantages of greenspace, such as cleaner water, cleaner air and more wildlife! This is the only park on all six blocks of State Street. We definitely need more!

Players recorded the virtual stakeholders' opinions in their planning notebooks, and returned to the computer lab to incorporate their findings into a custom-designed interactive GIS model, iPlan (Figure 1).

In iPlan, players could change zoning designations for the parcels, units of land held by a single owner, on State Street. Zoning codes included "Arts and Humanities", "Local Retail Store", "National Chain Store", "Greenspace", "Parking Garage", and a variety of options for housing above the retail establishments (Figure 2). Each zoning code was represented on the map in a unique color:

The iPlan model also included graphs representing social and economic indicators important to State Street:

- Crime
- Cultural index
- Greenspace
- Housing
- Jobs
- Parking
- Trash
- Total sales

Figure 1. An image of the iPlan interface. Zoning changes were dynamically reflected in graphs representing indicators such as crime, cultural index, greenspace, housing, jobs, parking, trash, and total sales

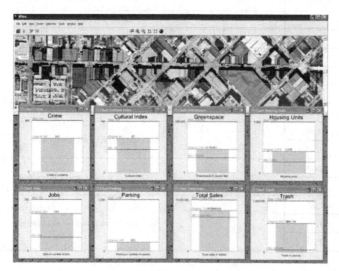

As players made changes in the zoning of parcels, the graphs dynamically updated, showing the projected impact of the zoning changes on the social and economic conditions of the neighborhood. For example, if players chose to rezone a large arts complex as a surface lot to increase parking, not only would the cultural index decrease, but jobs and total sales would also suffer. Any single change to the physical representation of State Street resulted in changes in the eight indicator values: crime, cultural index, greenspace, housing, jobs, parking, trash, and total sales.

Using iPlan, in other words, players saw a physical representation of State Street, the land use allocations for the street, and the consequences of their zoning changes (Figure 3).

Using iPlan, players worked in their stakeholder teams to construct preference surveys. As in the planning practicum, preference surveys in Urban Science were a set of possible planning alternatives designed to elicit information about the desires and hopes that stakeholders had for

their neighborhood. Specifically, players in Urban Science developed and used preference surveys to try to determine the minimum or "threshold" values that would lead stakeholders to support (or reject) a proposal. For example, players may have used a preference survey to determine how many additional housing units were needed in a plan to gain the support of the Urban League—or how many additional square feet of parks were needed for the support of the People for Greenspace.

Once completed, players submitted their preference surveys to their stakeholder group. The virtual stakeholders responded to the preference surveys through short dialogue based on the specific indicator levels, delivered in the form of a printed report from a focus group. For example, one player working with the Urban League received the following feedback from a stakeholder named Ed:

"I've looked at your plan and there's really no way that it's going to work for us. There just isn't enough housing on the street! With so few places to live, landlords will be able to raise rents as much as they want, and there will be even less affordable housing. I'm sorry, but this is unacceptable."

Next, players held a staff meeting in their planning teams to summarize the feedback they received. Each planning team presented their findings to the group as a whole, and new planning teams (with one player from each stakeholder planning team) were formed to draft a final plan.

Each team worked to create a final plan using iPlan that could incorporate the needs of all of the stakeholder groups. When plans were complete, each team prepared a presentation of their findings and recommendations, which was delivered to a local planner acting as a representative of the city council.

Figure 2. Zoning codes used by players to change land use designations of State Street's parcels

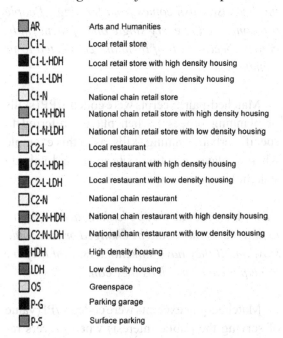

☐	AR	Arts and Humanities
☐	C1-L	Local retail store
■	C1-L-HDH	Local retail store with high density housing
■	C1-L-LDH	Local retail store with low density housing
☐	C1-N	National chain retail store
☐	C1-N-HDH	National chain retail store with high density housing
☐	C1-N-LDH	National chain retail store with low density housing
☐	C2-L	Local restaurant
■	C2-L-HDH	Local restaurant with high density housing
■	C2-L-LDH	Local restaurant with low density housing
☐	C2-N	National chain restaurant
☐	C2-N-HDH	National chain restaurant with high density housing
☐	C2-N-LDH	National chain restaurant with low density housing
■	HDH	High density housing
■	LDH	Low density housing
☐	OS	Greenspace
■	P-G	Parking garage
■	P-S	Surface parking

Figure 3. An image of the iPlan interface. Players created preference surveys and final plans by choosing the zoning codes of parcels and aligning their zoning choices with indicator values

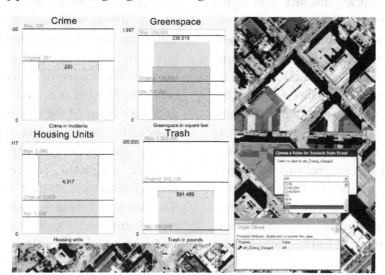

DATA COLLECTION AND ANALYSIS

In April 2006, twelve middle school aged players (eight females, four males) recruited from 4-H clubs, Girl Scout troops, and home school networks in southwestern Wisconsin played a 10-hour version of Urban Science. Players had no prior experience with urban planning.

We conducted an hour-long interview with each player before and after the game. In the interviews, players answered open-ended questions about science, technology, and urban planning. During post-interviews, we also asked questions about the game and players' experiences during game activities.

Pre- and post-interviews from the game were transcribed and recorded. Transcriptions were segmented into units representing one complete answer to a question, and included any follow-up questions or clarifications between the player and the interviewer. A single rater coded excerpts for elements of an urban planning epistemic frame, the interrelated set of skills, knowledge, values, identity and epistemology of the profession. Paired t-tests were used to compare interview responses between pre- and post-interviews.

Coding

Matched-pair excerpts were coded K/CS (knowledge of cities as systems) when they mentioned interconnections inherent in cities.

"...To get to a job, you need transportation... Transportation and trash are connected to housing because trash comes from housing...People are connected to every single one of them [indicators] because all of them are connected to us somehow..."

Matched-pair excerpts were coded S/PP (skills of planning process) when players referred to specific urban planning skills, as in this example where a player mentions site visits and helping stakeholders:

"They go to the site they're looking at and like try to find things that could be changed or that could stay, and if they have stakeholders, that they try to help them as much as they can."

Matched-pair excerpts were coded V/PI (value of serving the public interest) when players referred to particular norms of good urban planning practice. In this excerpt, for example, the player used norms of the urban planning practice to explain why State Street looks the way it does:

"...When they were building State Street...the urban planners were compromising between... trying to plan how the community and groups like that would want it planned..."

Excerpts from questions asked only in the post-interview were coded SO (stakeholders as obstacles) when players referred to the difficulties of responding to stakeholders' needs.

"It was definitely a hard feeling to like think that you've got to please, you want to please everyone, but you can't please everyone because it's just really hard..."

RESULTS

We present our results in two sections. First, we look at the knowledge, skills, and values of planning that players developed in Urban Science. Then we examine the role of stakeholders in this development.

Knowledge

Matched-pair questions from pre-interviews were coded for K/CS (knowledge of cities as systems) significantly more in post-interviews than in pre-interviews (mean pre = 0.17, mean post = 2.33; $p<0.05$, Figure 2).

Before the game, only two of the players could define ecology; seven could do so after the game. For example, before the game, one player defined ecology as planning or sculpting a place:

"Well okay, that's to do with something; the planning of something involving, I don't know...City scaping."

In the post-interview, the same player described ecology in terms of a complex system:

"Ecology, well my view of the...word has changed since yesterday to today...I guess it's the interconnectivity in a complex system. I mean I guess like if you change one thing, it's going to change another thing in some way, and everything is all related."

Skills

Matched-pair questions from pre-interviews were coded for S/PP (skills of the planning process) significantly more in post-interviews than in pre-interviews (mean pre = 0.58, mean post = 1.5; $p<0.05$, Figure 2).

When asked before the game what an urban planner does, one player said an urban planner "plans an urban environment." After the game, the same player said:

"Well first you need to talk to the general public to see what they want...Talk to your stakeholders who actually own the stuff, and begin to plan stuff, find your problems, work up compromises with your stakeholders, talk to the general public again about what you work out with your compromises...Have the general public vote on 4 or 5 plans. Whichever plan is used, you go back and debug it with your stakeholders again, and then you publish your plan, and then you start demolishing stuff that needs to be demolished and start building back up...Talk to our stakeholders, make a plan, talk to our stakeholders again, go back to the general group, go back and take one person from each group, and make a finalized plan."

In other words, after the game this player was able to talk about the specific skills planners use to make decisions.

Values

Matched-pair questions from pre-interviews were coded for V/PI (value of serving the public interest) significantly more in post-interviews than in pre-interviews (mean pre=0.92, mean post=1.9; p<0.05, Figure 2).

For example, during the pre-interview, when asked what planners need to know, one player focused his answer on the location of businesses, but not on the people involved in the process:

"I think they need to know what type of businesses...would be best for whatever spot...I don't know; to have like auto body shop like built right next to like a car part shop instead of way across town..."

In the post-interview, the same player recognized the importance of listening to and acting on the ideas of people involved in the planning process and explicitly talked about serving the public interest.

"...I think [planners] need to know how to be able to listen to everybody and incorporate everyone's ideas to the best of their abilities, and if they can't do that, then be able to justify like fairly."

Similar to previous work conducted in this area of research, in Urban Science players learned about systems thinking and real world processes. However, in Urban Science, players also engaged with the core planning value of serving the public interest and learned civic thinking as a result

Game Features Contributing to Value Creation: Interacting with Stakeholders

In this section we look at the role of stakeholders in the development of planning values in Urban Science. First we examine data from the post-interviews on stakeholders as obstacles at two key points in the game. Then we describe the experiences of one player during the game, illustrating the role that tool and stakeholders played in the development of planning knowledge, skills, and values.

Stakeholders as Obstacles

During the post-interviews, 11 out of 12 responses from players were coded for SO (stakeholder as obstacle) when talking about feedback they received from virtual stakeholders in the preference survey. For example, one player discussed

Figure 4. Changes in knowledge, skills, and values for 12 Urban Science players

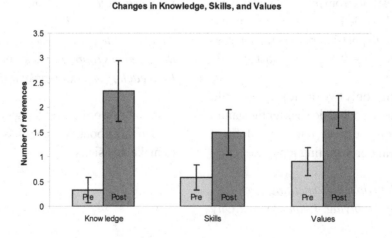

the challenge of meeting stakeholders' conflicting requests with a single plan:

"It's really hard to get the, what all the stakeholders wanted, and you, like whenever you put in a parking garage or a building, you also affected the things of some other thing, like if you put a parking garage in, the greenspace would go down and you wouldn't want the greenspace to go down..."

Similarly, 9 of 12 responses from players were coded SO when asked about their experiences making the final plan. For example, one player said:

"I thought [making the final plan] was sort of hard because we had to make everyone's like idea fit in, and that was sort of hard to have everyone like put their ideas together because some people had really wide like wants and stuff, so that was sort of hard..."

In other words, players saw pleasing stakeholders as a challenge in the planning process in the game.

Sara's Story

To see how planning values were developed through game play with virtual stakeholders, we now draw on data from the post-interview questions about the game to look at the experiences of one player, whom we will call Sara.

Like all of the players, Sara started the game by going on a site visit which she thought was "fun", and she thought that "practically everything was interesting." On the site visit, Sara encountered stakeholders as an obstacle when she heard from the virtual People for Greenspace stakeholder group and realized that the range of civic indicators that stakeholders would accept could be very narrow. The stakeholders, she said "helped me learn that it's hard to please everybody because

some people have big ranges, some people have small ranges."

After hearing the People for Greenspace's desires, Sara encountered the tools as obstacle when she used iPlan to change zoning designations and create a preference survey and final plan. She said she learned "a lot" from using iPlan. Specifically, she said that she learned "how when you change something, a rate [indicator value] might go down or up in another one. They are all somehow connected...It was like crime was connected with trash, and trash was connected with housing, and it was all connected."

After creating a planning alternative, Sara submitted her preference survey to her stakeholder group for feedback. "It was good," she thought, "because then I started understanding a bit more like how to deal with it and how like what I should do because I didn't know exactly how we were supposed to balance it out, and once I got the feedback, I actually learned from it, like learned some of the things like how to balance it, and I also learned that it's really hard to please everyone. It's really, really hard."

After receiving the stakeholders' feedback, Sara worked with a new team to create a final plan that could meet the needs of all of the stakeholders. In the process of creating a final plan, both the tool and stakeholders became obstacles. Sara found trying to satisfy all of the stakeholders "kind of stressful because you would find out like you thought that you had it but then you would look onto the [preference survey] and say, oh my gosh, I forgot this person didn't want so much, so you would have to go back and change it all." Once Sara and her planning team were able to satisfy the stakeholders, it "felt good." Sara said: "It was fun trying to [satisfy them]...since it was so hard."

Sara and her team presented their final plan to a local planning expert. Sara told us that she "usually doesn't like standing in front of a lot of people, but [presenting] was fun, especially since I wasn't alone because I feel more excited when I'm alone and I have to be speaking every single thing."

Sara's experience presents a picture of how Urban Science proceeded for one player. While using iPlan to construct the preference survey and final plan, Sara struggled with the tool as an obstacle and learned about the interconnectedness of the urban system and the skill of enacting real world processes. When she received feedback on her preference survey and worked to create a comprehensive final plan, Sara encountered the stakeholders as an obstacle and learned that meeting the diverse needs of stakeholders is difficult—but also that trying to serve the public interest is satisfying and motivating.

DISCUSSION

Today, civic thinking and community participation are more important than ever. As Ehrlich (2000) argues, solving complex civic problems requires putting knowledge in the context of real world skills, and in the service of civic values, rather than merely recalling isolated facts or locating countries on a map.

The results presented here show that Urban Science gave players a chance to engage with exactly these kinds of complex civic problems. In Urban Science, players learned to think of cities as complex systems. They learned about skills that planners use to enact change in these systems. And perhaps most important, they learned the value of serving the public in that process.

Two aspects of game contributed to the development of players' civic thinking. First, as had been shown by Beckett and Shaffer (2005), players developed civic *knowledge and skills* through their work with the *tool-as-obstacle*. The geographic information system in the game modeled the complex relationships between land use decisions and important social and ecological tradeoffs in the city. The obstacles to action that the GIS model presented were thus concepts and

processes urban planning professionals routinely use. As a result, as Shaffer (2006b) suggests, in overcoming these obstacles in pursuit of a meaningful goal—in this case, creating a comprehensive plan for civic redevelopment—players came to see the city as a complex system and understand how planners make changes in it.

In a similar way, the data here suggest that players developed the professional *value* of serving the public interest by working with *stakeholders-as-obstacle*. Though urban planners do not see stakeholders as obstacles, in this paper we referred to stakeholders-as-obstacle with the understanding that obstacles drive learning, and thus, help players learn to value the public interest. In the game, virtual stakeholders presented conflicting responses to proposed zoning changes that were difficult—and in many cases impossible—to resolve. The virtual stakeholders modeled the complex relationships between people and land use decisions in the city. The obstacles to action that the stakeholders presented were resolved only using a key value of urban planning: serving the public interest. As a result, in working with stakeholders in pursuit of a meaningful goal, players linked civic knowledge and skills with civic values. In other words, players learned to see stakeholders not as obstacles by encountering and overcoming them first as obstacles. Thus, seeing stakeholders as a problem helped players see them as part of the solution.

The results presented here have several limitations. First, this preliminary study only describes what a small number of students did while participating in 10 hours of the Urban Science epistemic game. As a result, this work provides insufficient grounds for making strong causal claims. Follow-up work is already underway, and we look forward to establishing more broad claims in future papers (Shaffer, et al., 2009).

Another clear limitation is in the profession of urban planning itself. As one planning scholar remarked, "Urban planning is a mile wide, inch deep profession. We know a little about a lot of things." (D. Marcoullier, personal communication, 2005) However, our goal in creating Urban Science was not to capture every aspect of the planning profession in exhaustive detail. Rather, we presented players with a specific view of the profession modeled on an ethnographic study of one planning practicum. Thus, this design represents only one way that planners approach and solve problems within their profession.

During this iteration of Urban Science, all of the planning consultants were game researchers with limited urban planning experience. The planning consultants were minimally trained and were in the same place as the players at all times. The planning consultant to player ratio (1:3 in this case) is not a ratio that can be duplicated in most traditional school settings. Follow-up work is currently testing remote mentoring using an internal chat program with a 1:12 mentor: player ratio (Chesler, et al., 2010).

Despite these limitations, however, the results here suggest several implications for the larger community of people interested in games and game development.

First, educational game designers might use these results to consider when and how including pro-social non-player-characters (NPCs) can develop pro-social values through game play. In the specific context of Urban Science, the NPC stakeholders provided pro-social obstacles that led to the development of professional values and civic thinking.

This success, in turn, suggests that further research needs to be done on the role of pro-social NPCs and the conditions under which they contribute to the development of players' values. Here we have explored one specific hypothesis: that NPCs modeled on real-world roles in professional training can recreate the effects of real-world training through game play. However, more work clearly remains in determining the impact (and limits) of that process.

Finally—and perhaps most directly, these results suggest that teachers may be able to use games that link knowledge and skills with values via professional obstacles to develop civic thinking. Games like Urban Science may help young people—and thus help all of us—identify and address the many civic, economic, and environmental challenges in an increasingly complex, and increasingly urban, world.

ACKNOWLEDGMENT

The authors would like to thank the colleagues and sponsors who have contributed to this work, particularly Gina Navoa Svarovsky, David Hatfield, Padraig Nash, Aran Nulty, Kelly Beckett, Justin Bagley, and the staffs of the University of Wisconsin-Madison Department of Educational Psychology and the Wisconsin Center for Educational Research. The research reported in this paper was supported in part by a grant from the Macarthur Foundation, a National Science Foundation Faculty Early Career Development Award (REC-0347000), a Spencer Foundation/ National Academy of Education Postdoctoral Fellowship, a grant from the Wisconsin Alumni Research Foundation, the Academic Advanced Distributed Learning CoLaboratory, and by the Wisconsin Center for Education Research, School of Education, University of Wisconsin-Madison. Any opinions, findings, or conclusions expressed in this paper are those of the author(s) and do not necessarily reflect the views of the funding agencies or cooperating institutions.

REFERENCES

Adams, P. C. (1998). Teaching and learning with SimCity 2000. *The Journal of Geography*, *97*(2), 47–55. doi:10.1080/00221349808978827

Adams, R. (2007, August 27). Now, where is America anyway? *Guardian*. Retrieved September 26, 2010, from http://blogs.guardian.co.uk/news/archives/2007/08/27/now_where_is_america_anyway.html

American Planning Association. (2010). *What is Planning?* Retrieved September 26, 2010, from http://www.planning.org/aboutplanning/whatis-planning.htm#2

Association of Collegiate Schools of Planning. (2009). *Career Guide*. Retrieved September 26, 2010, from http://www.acsp.org/sites/default/files/ACSP_2009_FINAL_Book[1].pdf

Bagley, E. (2010). *Epistemography of an Urban and Regional Planning Practicum: Appropriation in the Face of Resistance* (WCER Working Paper 2010-8). Madison: University of Wisconsin-Madison, Wisconsin Center for Education Research.

Barab, S. A., Hay, K. E., Barnett, M. G., & Squire, K. (2001). Constructing virtual worlds: Tracing the historical development of learner practices/understandings. *Cognition and Instruction, 19*(1), 47–94. doi:10.1207/S1532690XCI1901_2

Barton, H., & Tsourou, C. (2000). *Healthy urban planning: A WHO guide to planning for people*. Oxford: Taylor & Francis.

Beckett, K. L., & Shaffer, D. W. (2005). Augmented by reality: The pedagogical praxis of urban planning as a pathway to ecological thinking. *Journal of Educational Computing Research, 33*(1), 31–52. doi:10.2190/D5YQ-MMW6-V0FR-RNJQ

Chesler, N., Bagley, E., & Shaffer, D. W. (2010). *Professional Practice Simulations for Engaging, Educating, and Assessing Undergraduate Engineers*. Paper presented at the International Conference of Learning Sciences Engineering Workshop, Chicago, IL.

Dewey, J. (1934/1958). *Art as experience*. New York: Capricorn Books.

Ehrlich, T. (2000). *Civic Responsibility and Higher Education*. Phoenix: American Council on Education and The Oryx Press.

Friedmann, J. (1987). *Planning in the public domain: From knowledge to action*. Princeton, NJ: Princeton University Press.

Gaber, J. (2007). Simulating Planning: SimCity as a Pedagogical Tool. *Journal of Planning Education and Research, 27*, 113–121. doi:10.1177/0739456X07305791

Gee, J. P. (2003). *What video games have to teach us about learning and literacy*. New York: Palgrave Macmillan.

Herwig, A., & Paar, P. (2002). Game Engines: Tools for Landscape Visualization and Planning? *Trends in GIS and Virtualization in Environmental Planning and Design*, 161-172.

National Assessment Governing Board. (2006). *Civics Framework for the 2006 National Assessment of Educational Progress. NAEP Civics Project*. Washington, D.C.: National Assessment Governing Board.

Nedovic-Budic, Z. (2000). Geographic Information Science Implications for Urban and Regional Planning. *URISA Journal, 12*(2).

Schon, D. (1987). *Educating the reflective practitioner: Toward a new design for teaching and learning in the professions*. San Francisco: Jossey-Bass.

Shaffer, D. W. (2006a). Epistemic frames for epistemic games. *Computers & Education, 46*(3), 223–234. doi:10.1016/j.compedu.2005.11.003

Shaffer, D. W. (2006b). *How computer games help children learn*. New York: Palgrave MacMillan. doi:10.1057/9780230601994

Shaffer, D. W., Hatfield, D., Svarovsky, G. N., Nash, P., Nulty, A., Bagley, E., et al. (2009). Epistemic Network Analysis: A prototype for 21st Century assessment of learning. *International Journal of Learning and Media*, *1*(2), 33–53. doi:10.1162/ijlm.2009.0013

Shaffer, D. W., Squire, K., Halverson, R., & Gee, J. P. (2005). Video Games and the Future of Learning. *Phi Delta Kappan*, *87*(2), 104–111.

Starr, P. (1994). Seductions of sim: Policy as a simulation game. *The American Prospect*, *5*(17), 19–29.

Teague, M. G., & Teague, G. V. (1995). Planning with computers: A social studies simulation. *Learning and Leading with Technology*, *23*, 20–25.

The National Geographic Education Foundation. (2006). *National Geographic-Roper Public Affairs 2006 Geographic Literacy Study*. New York, NY: National Geographic Society. Retrieved September 26, 2010, from http://www.national-geographic.com/roper2006/findings.html

United Nations Population Fund. (2007). *State of the World Population 2007: United Nations Population Fund*. Retrieved September 26, 2010, from http://www.unfpa.org/swp/2007/english/introduction.html

Chapter 8

Learning as Becoming:
Values, Identity, and Performance in the Enaction of Citizenship Education through Game Play

Yam San Chee
Nanyang Technological University, Singapore

Swee Kin Loke
University of Otago, New Zealand

Ek Ming Tan
Nanyang Technological University, Singapore

ABSTRACT

In this chapter, we share a model of game-based learning for use in the context of classroom learning in school. The model is based on the dialectic interaction between game play and dialogic engagement with peers and teacher on one hand and a developmental trajectory of competence-through-performance on the other. It is instantiated in the context of a learning program related to citizenship education using the computer game Space Station Leonis. We argue for the importance of values in all learning, based upon a theory of becoming citizens that is founded on process philosophy. We relate values to dispositions as articulated manifestations of values and describe how the Leonis learning program helps to achieve dispositional shifts befitting citizenship education in a globalized and multi-cultural world.

INTRODUCTION

Educators face an increasingly difficult challenge in nurturing students who will develop to become civic-minded, active, and productive citizens. Effective citizenship education is particularly vital today due to the forces of globalization and multiculturalism that impact the lives of citizens worldwide (Banks, 2008). As societies become more cosmopolitan (Appiah, 2007), better understanding between nations and cultures is urgently needed in order to avoid ideological, racial, and cultural conflicts.

DOI: 10.4018/978-1-60960-565-0.ch008

In the context of schools, citizenship education is the usual means through which students' values, dispositions, beliefs, and attitudes are nurtured to realize the goals of active rather than passive citizenship. According to Selwyn (2002), passive citizenship is the product of an education that seeks to develop knowledge, understandings, and behaviors of citizenship, while active citizenship augments the passive model with an ability to critique, debate, and propose alternative models of the structures and processes of democracy.

Effective education for becoming citizens does not consist merely of being told what one ought to do and to be. Neither does it primarily revolve around learning *about* the birth of a nation and its consequent development. Rather, effective citizenship education needs to focus on students' *being* and *becoming*: on how they understand themselves as persons—their identity and being—and on their developmental trajectories of becoming, projected into the future.

In this chapter, we report on a pedagogical innovation involving the use of a computer game, *Space Station Leonis*, to foster values and dispositions that, we hope, will help lead to beliefs, attitudes, and actions that are more inclusive, thoughtful, and critically considered. We argue for the centrality of values in all human knowing. We also adopt a process worldview in framing our theoretical approach to understanding and to influencing the developmental trajectory of human learning. Key to this process perspective is the element of experience that arises out of "that which is lived" (Mesle, 2008, p.43). This perspective, grounded in process philosophy (Rescher, 2000; Whitehead, 1978), avoids the dualism of Descartes: namely, that minds think and do not exist in space, while bodies do not think and exist in space. Instead, it posits that in as much as we cannot understand ourselves (including our minds) without understanding the world of which we are a part, neither can we understand the world without understanding ourselves as a part of it (Bateson, 1979; Mesle, 2008).

In the next section of this chapter, we make the argument that values are central to all human knowing, and we make the connection between values and values education. We then locate the importance of values within the broader context of the metaphysics of process philosophy. Next, we describe the background and context of the research study that revolves around the Leonis learning program, comprising the use of the computer game *Space Station Leonis*, associated curriculum materials, and classroom activity structures and participation frameworks. We then focus on our survey data of student dispositions gathered from a pre-test and post-test survey instrument. We present the data analysis and results on dispositional shifts arising from participation in the Leonis learning program, then discuss our findings and conclude the chapter.

CENTALITY OF VALUES

There is widespread belief, especially amongst laypersons, that facts and values are fundamentally separate from and independent of each other. Given the influence of modernism and the advent of the physical sciences, "facts" are seen as "real," "objective," and "proven," and hence are universal. "Facts" are esteemed above "values," which are often viewed as "fuzzy," "subjective," and "unprovable." Consequently, it is common to find many schoolteachers, students, and parents esteeming factual learning as a concrete accomplishment on the part of students while according values education second place, treating it as something desirable but less important. This difference in valuation is reflected, for example, in the different number of curricular hours committed to "hard" subjects such as science and mathematics compared to "soft" subjects such as civics, citizenship education, and literature. The situation is exacerbated in schools by the teaching of subjects, such as science and mathematics, in a manner that strongly assumes, or implies, that the "facts" of these subjects are completely objective and value-free.

The idea that facts are independent of values is a myth. This notion of the independence of axiology, the study of values, from ontology, the study of the things that are, that is, the separation of value and fact, is completely rejected by Whitehead in particular (Leue, 2005) and by process philosophy in general. As Putnam (2002) indicates, understanding how normative judgments are presupposed in all reasoning is important in all of life. Hence, we find that the construction of theory in science is driven by the value of parsimony. The construction of theory in mathematics is driven by the value of elegance. Reasoning about epistemology is significantly influenced by the values of consistency, coherence, applicability, and adequacy (Mesle, 2008). And as Ferré (1996) argues,

our values precede our theories in real life and lead us in their construction (or approval). Even in the sciences, we have become aware of the degree to which expectations, including such factors as hopes and career commitments, influence what we notice within the total range of the presented data. Attention is selective. We should expect, therefore, that our values will have a role in suggesting possible fruitful lines of thought. In addition, these values will play a decisive role in influencing us on how long to hang on to a theory, model, or worldview threatened by problems (p.14).

Thus, values are inseparable from all our thinking and all our being. Indeed, they are inseparable from all our professional practices.

Values are equally important in the domain of citizenship education. In fact, they are vital. They directly influence the kind of person that one seeks to become, based on a vision of the kind of projected social environment one views as being preferred. Values undergird the dispositions of individuals, leading them to act, and to prefer to act, in certain ways rather than others. In this sense, values are instrumental: if there is a desirable goal, they motivate and activate the means to reach it.

From the perspective of process philosophy, Rescher (2008) argues that the processes and patterns of process that characterize us personally— our doings and undergoings, either individually or patterned into talents, skills, capabilities, traits, dispositions, habits, inclinations, and tendencies to action and inaction—are what characteristically define a person as the individual that he or she is. Character is shaped by dispositions that, when translated into action, manifest as repeated decisions that become habits of mind and purpose. The self that has these habits is known in the flow of experiences, decisions, and actions that are taken by the individual (Mesle, 2008).

Once we conceptualize the core "self" of a person as a unified manifold of actual and potential process—of action and capacities, tendencies, and dispositions to action (both physical and psychical)—then we secure a concept of personhood that renders the self or ego experientially accessible, based on the understanding that experiencing is simply constitutive of such processes.

The Ministry of Education, Singapore, has articulated a set of desired outcomes of education (Singapore Ministry of Education, 2008). It states that, "Education is about nurturing the whole child . . . The foundation of a person is his *values*. From these spring his outlook on life and his goals in life" (italics added). Specific outcomes desired of post-secondary and tertiary education students include the following:

- be morally upright, be culturally rooted yet understanding and respecting differences, be responsible to family, community, and country
- believe in principles of multi-racialism and meritocracy, appreciate the national constraints but see the opportunities

- be willing to strive, take pride in work, value working with others
- be able to think, reason, and deal confidently with the future, have courage and conviction in facing adversity
- think global, but be rooted to Singapore

It should be evident that the stated outcomes are strongly oriented to *being* certain kinds of people. But, as we shall see in the next section, being is more appropriately approached from the perspective of *becoming* from a process point of view. Much has been written about civics, moral education, and citizenship education within the Singapore school system. For example, Chew (1998) argues that civics and moral education takes the form of citizenship training in schools that aims to "transmit" national values for economic and political socialization. Tan and Chew (2004) argue that civics and moral education is more a matter of training students to "absorb" pragmatic values deemed important for Singapore to achieve social cohesion and economic success, rather than moral education as the development of intrinsic commitment to and habituation in the practice of values defended on autonomous moral considerations. While the critique of a highly pragmatic approach to educational philosophy in Singapore may be well known, two issues are particularly noteworthy. The first issue is the clear suggestion that the pragmatic agenda overrides the interest of an authentic moral education. The second issue is that the authors adopt the language of human information processing ("transmit," "absorb") in making their arguments.

We choose to adopt a developmental and process-oriented approach to learning and eschew the assumptions of objectivist, transmissive learning. In the next section of the chapter, therefore, we briefly outline the process approach to learning that focuses on learning as becoming (Semetsky, 2006).

THE PROCESS APPROACH AND BECOMING

Process philosophy is a longstanding tradition that emphasizes becoming and changing over static Being. It is characterized by an attempt to reconcile the diverse intuitions—ethical, religious, scientific, and aesthetic—found in human experience into a coherent holistic scheme (Hustwit, 2007). From the perspective of process philosophy, the world is ultimately composed not of "things" but of events and processes. As explained by Mesle (2008), "[e]verything that is actual becomes and perishes. Becoming is the ultimate fact underlying all others" (p. 79). Furthermore, "[t]he universe is a vast web or field of microevents" (p. 95). Citing Whitehead (1978), he states that "the actual world is a process, and the process is the becoming of actual entities" (p. 22).

The philosophy of Being rather than Becoming has, however, dominated Western thought. Plato established the primacy of Being when he argued that this world of change is merely a shadow copy of a realm of unchanging forms (Mesle, 2008). Since the time of Aristotle, Western metaphysics has consequently had a marked bias in favor of things or substances rather than processes (Rescher, 2008).

While substance metaphysics and modern science have posited that the world is made up of material objects, Whitehead (1978), however, argues that "organism" is a better term for things that exist. Whereas matter is self-sustaining, externally related, valueless, passive, and without an intrinsic principle of motion, organisms are interdependent, internally and externally related, value-laden, active, and intrinsically active. Consistent with the latter perspective, Edelman (1992) shows in his Darwin III simulation of a simple autonomous agent that the agent never achieves a stable repertoire of behavior without the encoding of value.

Process philosophers, like modern physicists, reject the Newtonian view that time and space exist as a fixed background or framework separate from the events that happen within them, as if time and space form a bottle around us that would still exist even if all events disappeared. Time simply is the passage—the becoming and perishing—of events (Mesle, 2008). At the microlevel, what is usually deemed a physical thing, a stable perduring object, is itself no more than a statistical pattern—a stability wave in a surging sea of process. The so-called enduring "things" that we are so well acquainted with come about through the emergence of stabilities in statistical fluctuations. Thus, processes are not the machinations of stable things; rather, things are the stability-patterns of variable processes (Rescher, 2008).

According to Whitehead (1978), "*how* an actual entity *becomes* constitutes what that actual entity *is*; . . . Its 'being' is constituted by its 'becoming.' This is the 'principle of process.'" (p. 23). Each actual entity begins with an "initial aim:" the causal force of the past, combined with "God's presentation" of the relevant possibilities and a "lure" toward some possibility rather than others. This is what we have referred to as "dispositions" above: a tendency to act in a certain way based on certain value. The aim at tomorrow's needs, representing an instrumental orientation toward the future, is often what creates satisfaction in the present. Anticipation of satisfaction for tomorrow's achievement feels good today (Mesle, 2008).

Ferré (1996) argues that,

[w]hat needs to be remembered is that experience is not neutral. It is not a sensory mirror of a value-free world of mere objects. Experience is instead shot through with intuitions of value, both intrinsic and instrumental. We find data of experience inseparable from interests and aversions, hopes and fears, joys and pains, sorrows, satisfactions, and obligations. Normal experience is full of vague intuitions of importance, drawing our attention toward some features rather than others. Such intuitions change with added experience; they are corrigible and educable (p. 13).

Whitehead's philosophy, referred to as a "philosophy of organism," is a philosophy of universal life . . . Values are essential to this notion of existence and to the understanding of it (Leue, 2005). To cite Whitehead (1926, p. 100):

Value is inherent in actuality itself. To be an actual entity is to have a self-interest. This self-interest is a feeling of self-valuation; it is an emotional tone. The value of other things, not one's self, is the derivative value of elements contributing to this ultimate self-interest. This self-interest is the interest of what one's existence, as in that epochal occasion, comes to. It is the ultimate enjoyment of being actual.

Thus, actuality is linked to a value reaction of selection and rejection, approach and withdrawal, liking and disliking. Value is necessary to every physical thing in order for it to exist because it can be a separate thing and have a definite character only by reacting selectively to its causal antecedents. Otherwise, all things would be alike, and there would be no definite character (Leue, 2005). Values are thus essential in the becoming of a citizen. They undergird dispositions, the tendencies to act in certain ways that are preferred. We refrain, therefore, from essentializing persons as (fixed) objects with variable attributes. Instead, we view persons as ongoing process: always in the process of becoming and always constituted in and by the flow of the experiences of life.

THE LEONIS LEARNING PROGRAM

The Leonis learning program is a school-based pedagogical innovation for citizenship education. The program comprises the computer game, *Space Station Leonis*, together with associated curriculum materials, learning processes, formative assessments, and a summative assessment. The program has been designed to provide students with an augmented learning space that incorporates dyad-based game playing, Wiki-driven peer discussion and reflection, and class-based dialogic engagement on critical issues related to citizenship education in the Singapore education context. It comprises nine lessons of two hours per lesson.

The game *Space Station Leonis* was designed and developed by the Learning Sciences Lab of the National Institute of Education, Nanyang Technological University, Singapore. It is a hybrid game that consists of four episodes of role-playing and three episodes of simulation game play. Role-playing both opens and closes the entire game, with students playing the role of the default protagonist. For episodes 2 and 3, students can choose between two available characters. The game is a single-player game. It was developed for personal computers running the Windows operating system.

The game is a futuristic sci-fi adventure. Set in the context of the 23rd century, the inhabitants of Earth have colonized the Moon and other planets, including Mars. Leonis is a space station that orbits the Earth. Its inhabitants include emigrants from Earth, the Moon colonies, as well as Mars. Lacking natural resources, its long-term survival

is somewhat precarious. Cooperation between the multi-ethnic and multi-faction inhabitants of Leonis is vital if Leonis is to be sustained and is to prosper. The context described is actually an allegory of Singapore, with its limited natural resources and its multi-ethnic, multi-racial population. It serves as a microcosm within which all the key issues related to citizenship education can be explored in the classroom, based on the conceptual framework described later.

To provide readers with a feel of the game, Figures 1 and 2 illustrate playing the game in role-playing mode.

Figure 1 depicts the situation where the protagonist, Radha (the woman shown on the right who comes from the Moon colonies), discusses with her friends, Alan and Charlie (also from the Moon colonies), about the Leonis government's directive that, at a forthcoming national parade, Leonis inhabitants who emigrated from the Moon colonies should be prohibited from wearing their national costume. This directive was motivated by fear of inadvertently promoting an undesirable association between the Lunar national costume

Figure 1. Screen snapshot illustrating game-based learning in role playing mode

Figure 2. Screen snapshot illustrating a decision point during role playing

and identification with a terrorist group, the Lunar Liberation Front.

Figure 2 shows Radha faced with a decision point in the game: should she (1) respect (and accept) the government's wishes, or (2) participate in a petition against the government's directive so that she and her friends can wear the Lunar national costume at the parade? Decision points like these in the role-playing segments of the game were deliberately designed to throw up ideological tensions related to values so as to create a context within which sensitive issues related to differences arising from race, religion, other beliefs, and so on, could be surfaced and addressed in a constructive and non-threatening way. Through role play, students participate in projective embodiment of the protagonist character in the 3D game space and act vicariously through their on-screen avatar. This design allows students to act in the first person, and to learn by making decisions and having to live with the consequences thereof. A high level of personal agency is thereby realized, helping to make the experience of game play emotionally engaging and the learning experience impactful.

In contrast, Figure 3 illustrates game play in simulation mode. Here, students assume the role of the president of the space station. They have to learn to manage the economy and "affairs of state" of the space station (including foreign relations and terrorist attacks) so as to sustain and seek the long-term survival and prosperity of the station's inhabitants. The screen snapshot shows, in particular, the development of the economy and social infrastructure of the space station. These include the provision of housing and education, as well as medical and defense needs.

The conceptual framework for the Leonis learning program is shown in Figure 4. It is grounded in the key theoretical idea of learning as becoming. Game-based learning is conceived of in terms of a dialectical interplay between recurrent cycles of game play that are coupled with whole-class dialogic activity (Bakhtin, 1981; Sidorkin, 1999). Over time, a trajectory of developmental learning is achieved through participatory appropriation (Rogoff, 1993) in the lifeworld of the students. From the viewpoint of learning design, we instantiate a generalized model of game-based learning that includes two parts: (1) the play–dialog dialectic that involves immersive game play and stepping out of and back from the game space into the classroom space to engage

Figure 3. Screen snapshot of Space Station Leonis game play in simulation mode

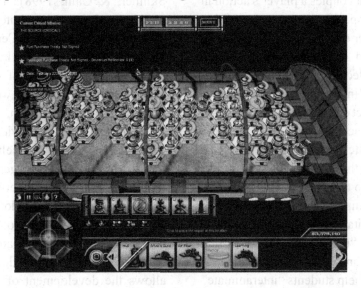

in multi-voiced dialogic exchanges, facilitated by the teacher, in the spirit of heteroglossia (Bakhtin, 1981), and (2) the competence-through-performance trajectory that entails the development of self-identity through participatory appropriation of skills, knowledge, identity, values, and epistemology (Shaffer, 2006) that constitute the continuing flow of becoming in the lifeworld of students.

As depicted in Figure 4, game play takes place in the material world realized through the digital representation of the game. Students project themselves (Gee, 2007) into the immersive game world—projective identity (Type 1)—and thereby engage in an embodied, embedded, and experiential form of learning (Chee, 2007). Importantly, this is a form of first-person learning, where personal agency can be exercised to drive learning and where students are able to act upon choices of their own making. Learning interaction is transactional in the sense articulated by Dewey and pragmatist philosophers. That is, a player's action in the game world is always a trans-action

Figure 4. Conceptual framework of the Leonis learning program

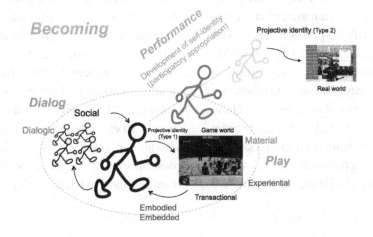

(or cross-action) that couples a player's action in the world with the specific consequence of that action that the player experiences as "feedback" in and from the world. As game play time is action time rather than reflection time, students are required to "pull back" into a dialogic learning space where they can reflect on their actions in the game and on the consequences that ensued. At the same time, they participate in critical and reflective dialog with peers on the value-laden issues deliberately designed into the game (as illustrated by the role playing example above). This entire dialogic process is facilitated by a teacher whose role is not to promote a "right answer"—given that there are no "right answers" in value-laden issues—but rather to help students "interanimate" the utterances of one another (Bakhtin, 1981). Through this process, students crystallize their ideas on issues and take personal positions on key themes related to citizenship as the ideas contributed to the public discourse space vigorously "rub up against each other." The overarching pedagogical objective is to have students become more critically aware of, and then to develop, their own set of values so that preferred dispositions— the tendencies to act in certain ways rather than others—can be nurtured. We speak here of "preferred" dispositions rather than, say, "positive" dispositions because we wish to avoid imposing our personal value judgments on the students. We prefer instead that they be given the personal "space" and discretion to decide on their personal values, but always in a manner that allows them to be able to justify the position they choose to adopt on an issue and always with full understanding that they must be completely willing to accept the consequences of whatever (inherently value-laden) actions they choose to take. These learning activities are situated within the broader context of helping students with the process of becoming: constructing themselves and developing their self-identity (Holland, Lachicotte, Jr.,

Skinner, & Cain, 1998). This developmental learning trajectory constitutes a performance of the self (Carlson, 2004). Central to the idea of performance is engagement in patterned behavior: the doing and re-doing of certain identifiable activities, such as the way we present ourselves in everyday life (Goffman, 1959). However, a ritualized pattern of behavior constitutes a performance only if there is a self-consciousness, on the part of the person or agent, of the doing and re-doing of a pattern of activity. This self-consciousness gives rise to a double consciousness: a person's self awareness of an actual behavior being enacted that is compared with an ideal intended behavior. Thus, a double consciousness allows the development of reflexivity and the ability of a student to hold her own actions and behaviors up to personal scrutiny and interrogation. This reflexive interrogatory capacity allows the student to renegotiate the status quo. As performance, learners can reconstruct and redefine the kind of person they wish to be. This process is ongoing, and it constitutes the person's trajectory of learning.

Through performance, it is theorized that students construct their personal identity. It must be borne in mind, however, that identity, as construed here, is always in the making and never becomes an eternal fixture. Assessment of learning outcomes, in a program such as Leonis, can never be conclusive, as the real test of the effectiveness of the program will only become manifest, and then only partially, by what students say and do later on in life; for example, how they participate in civic life or respond to a terrorist attack subsequent to their participation in the learning program. This prospective behavior is shown as "Projective identity (Type 2)" in Figure 4. An extended explication of the theoretical model is contained in Chee (2010b). Additional descriptions of the game and its design rationale can be found in Chee (2007).

THE RESEARCH STUDY

The study reported here focuses on students' dispositional changes arising from participation in the Leonis learning program. We describe a classroom intervention study, conducted from August to September 2008, at a government funded, neighborhood secondary school. As explained previously, the focus on self-reported dispositions is based on the perspective that dispositions are tendencies to act in fairly stable and habitual ways, based on values. Ultimately, the learning program seeks to inculcate "preferred" values based on critical self-awareness of issues, while not taking a dogmatic stance on any particular issue.

Based on the foregoing, we detail findings derived from a comparison between pre-test and post-test responses that students offered to a set of questions eliciting the extent to which they agreed with statements relating to six themes associated with citizenship education in Singapore, namely, (1) cooperation with others, (2) empathy for others, (3) embracing racial diversity, (4) belief in racial equity, (5) sense of self-responsibility, and (6) civic consciousness and active citizenship.

Subjects

The subjects in this study comprised 42 students of mixed gender in a government secondary school (33% boys and 67% girls). On average, students were 15 years old. This class of students was selected by the Head of Department of Social Studies to participate in the learning program on the basis that they comprised one of the better classes in the 15-year-old cohort of students in the school.

Materials

As part of the Leonis learning program, students played the computer game *Space Station Leonis*. They also used a Wiki, with a template prepared in advance for each class lesson, to document the key actions they took while playing the game and to document the associated reasons they had for taking the said actions. Data from the Wiki was used to guide formative assessment. Engagement in the dialogic segment of each lesson was often contextualized by recent newspaper reports dealing with issues pertinent to the particular lesson; for example, "import" of foreign talent into the Singapore workforce, riots in China, and the war in Iraq.

Students were also asked to design and create an end-of-program campaign artifact (for example, a flyer, poster, or podcast) that they would use to advocate a certain position on a contentious issue. For instance, students could try to advocate racial harmony through policies to develop a shared Singapore identity, an attempt to homogenize the different races by "stirring" into a common melting pot, or they could seek to achieve racial harmony by encouraging races (factions in the context of Leonis) to preserve their distinct practices and customs, a policy that seeks to achieve harmony by preserving diversity and respecting difference. (Interestingly, in Singapore, both policies are pursued simultaneously.)

As part of the evaluation of changes in disposition arising from the Leonis learning program, an instrument was designed to elicit student responses to statements related to the six themes mentioned above.

Procedure

The Leonis learning program was carried out as a required complementary component of the secondary three curriculum on social studies. Lessons took place once a week, on average. The students' regular social studies teacher led in the implementation of the program. She was provided with two sessions of professional development prior to the commencement of the program. Assessment derived from the program constituted

50% of students' subject mark for social studies for term 4 of the school year.

The pre-test instrument on students' dispositions was administered about a week prior to the commencement of the program. Students were asked to respond to 17 statements by choosing the extent to which they disagreed or agreed with them. The scale comprised six descriptors, namely strongly disagree, disagree, partly disagree, partly agree, agree, and strongly agree. To avoid systematicity in the tendency of the "preferred" response always being on the same end of the scale, seven questions, randomly selected, were restated so that the "preferred'" response required disagreement with the statement instead. Several students were also interviewed, some as a group and others individually.

The post-test was conducted during the week in which the program ended. As a precaution against the phenomenon known as the "response shift bias" (Howard, 1980; Rockwell & Kohn, 1989), students were asked, in the post-test, to also provide a retrospective pre-test rating. The adoption of this device has the advantages of (1) ensuring that pre- and post-test ratings are done on an "internally consistent" intra-individual scale, and (2) avoiding potential ceiling effects that can arise from students initially over-rating themselves positively. The motivation for the said strategy rests in the recognition that the research intervention, as an *intervention*, is in itself a source of perturbation that can, and usually does, lead students to modify their putative intra-individual scale. Executing the post-test in the manner described has the benefit of explicitly recognizing the potential impact of the intervention on changing each student's intra-individual scale response. More importantly, it allows us, as researchers, to assess whether, and, if so, to what extent, there is a systematic effect with respect to such putative scale shifts.

DATA ANALYSIS

To evaluate the students' change in dispositions over the course of the research intervention, a paired samples *t*-test was performed comparing their post-test response with their retrospective pre-test response. The analysis was performed using the statistical package SPSS. Student responses were coded with the numbers 1 to 6, corresponding to the disagreement–agreement scale. In performing the statistical analysis, reverse data coding was executed in respect of statements that required disagreement as a preferred outcome; hence, stronger disagreement on such questions were coded with a larger numeric score. The data sample size was 42. Each variable was found to have a normal distribution.

RESULTS

Table 1 summarizes the results of the paired-sample *t*-tests. Reverse coded statements are shown in italics. We shall present the results according to the six themes of citizenship education referred to above. Overall, they show that changes in students' dispositions were significant, with the exception of item (3), and with the changes being marginally significant ($p < .10$) for items (11) and (13).

The first theme, cooperation with others, is represented by item (1) only: "problems between people are best handled by working together to find a solution." The difference between pre and post-test was significant ($p < .001$), with a medium effect size (Becker, 2000).

The next set of dispositional items, relating to the theme "empathy for others" comprises items (2), (3), (5), and (11). Item (2), "I think about how my decisions will affect other people," was significant ($p < .001$), with a large effect size. However, item (3), "I sometimes find it difficult to see things from another person's point of view," showed no significant change ($p = .314$) due to

Table 1. Summary table of paired-samples t-tests on 17 dispositional statements related to citizenship education

Item No.	Statement	n	Pre-test mean	Post test mean	t statistic	p (one-tailed)	Cohen's d
1.	Problems between people are best handled by working together to find a solution.	42	4.86	5.43	5.27	.000**	0.78††
2.	I think about how my decisions will affect other people.	42	4.43	5.31	7.11	.000**	1.07†††
3.	*I sometimes find it difficult to see things from another person's point of view.*	42	3.10	3.02	-0.49	.314	n/a
4.	Singapore is a better country because people from many different cultures live here.	42	4.69	5.12	4.71	.000**	0.62††
5.	*Other people's problems don't bother me.*	42	3.76	4.14	2.72	.005**	0.29†
6.	*I base my decisions on what I think is fair and unfair.*	42	2.24	2.00	-1.82	.039*	-0.23†
7.	No matter how angry someone makes me, I am still responsible for my own actions.	42	4.90	5.48	4.81	.000**	0.68††
8.	All people should have equal chances to get a good education in Singapore.	42	5.54	5.86	3.12	.002**	0.58††
9.	People should be judged for what they do, not where they are from.	42	5.33	5.67	3.32	.001**	0.45†
10.	*Pollution is not a problem that is important to me.*	42	4.12	4.55	2.95	.003**	0.30†
11.	*The poverty of others is not a problem that is important to me.*	42	3.90	4.14	1.53	.067	n/a
12.	As teenagers, my friends and I should find ways to help others in the community.	42	4.19	4.90	5.75	.000**	0.67††
13.	*I don't care what's happening in politics.*	42	3.21	3.45	1.57	.062	n/a
14.	As teenagers, my friends and I have a responsibility to do what we can to protect the environment.	42	4.50	5.02	4.22	.000**	0.58††
15.	I feel that I can make a difference in my community.	42	3.86	4.57	5.55	.000**	0.68††
16.	People should discuss social and political problems that affect the future of Singapore.	42	4.50	5.10	4.50	.000**	0.61††
17.	*The world would be a better place if people were free to do what was best for themselves.*	42	2.88	3.40	2.75	.005**	0.31†

** p<.01; *p<.05
††† large effect size; †† medium effect size; † small effect size

the relatively large standard deviation of means. Item (5), "Other people's problems don't bother me," was significant (*p* = .005), with a small effect size, and item (11), "The poverty of others is not a problem that is important to me," was marginally significant (*p* = .067). Items (3), (5), and (11) were reverse coded items.

The third theme, embracing racial diversity, is reflected in item (4): "Singapore is a better country because people from many different cultures live here." This item was statistically significant (*p* < .001), with a medium effect size.

The fourth theme, belief in racial equity, consists of item (6), (8), and (9). Item (6), "I base my decisions on what I think is fair and unfair," is a reverse coded item that showed a statistically significant change (*p* = .039) with a small effect size, but in the direction opposite to what was "preferred." Item (8), "All people should have equal chances to get a good education in Singapore," showed a statistically significant difference (p = .002) with a medium effect size. Item (9), "People should be judged for what they do, not where they are from," showed a statistically significant difference (p = .001) with a small effect size.

The fifth theme, sense of self-responsibility, comprises one item: item (7). This item, "No matter how angry someone makes me, I am still responsible for my own actions," was statistically significant (p < .001), with a medium effect size.

Finally, theme six, civic consciousness and active citizenship, consisted of seven items: (10), (12), (13), (14), (15), (16), and (17). Item (10), "Pollution is not a problem that is important to me," showed a statistically significant change (p = .003) with a small effect size. Item (12), "As teenagers, my friends and I should find ways to help others in the community," was also statistically significant (p < .001), with a medium effect size. Item (13), "I don't care what's happening in politics," was marginally significant (p = .062). Item (14), "As teenagers, my friends and I have a responsibility to do what we can to protect the environment," showed a statistically significant difference (p < .001), with a medium effect size.

Item (15), "I feel that I can make a difference in my community," showed a statistically significant difference (p < .001) with a medium effect size. Similarly, item (16), "People should discuss social and political problems that affect the future of Singapore," showed a statistically significant difference (p < .001) with a medium effect size.

Finally, item (17), "The world would be a better place if people were free to do what was best for themselves," showed a statistically significant difference (p = .005) with a small effect size. This item was reverse coded.

DISCUSSION

The results above indicate that, overall, the Leonis learning program, when enacted according to the principles embodied in the conceptual framework

of Figure 4, can contribute to shaping students' (imputed) values, as manifested in dispositional statements, in educationally "preferred" directions.

The theme of instilling cooperation with others was an explicit consideration in designing some of the role-playing segments of the game. Player decisions at important junctures of the game helped students to explore the circumstances under which group interests need to be prioritized over self-interest. In one particular episode, students played the role of the protagonist Mei Ling who, along with other residents, was trapped in the ruins of Sector Two of the space station with the oxygen supply fast diminishing. The needs of other residents seeking to escape to Sector One, including elderly residents, is made "emotionally real" to the students through the stark choices that they are required to make in the course of game play. The results strongly suggest that this game design was effective as students showed a statistically significant shift in disposition toward valuing working together to find solutions, with a medium effect size.

The second theme, focusing on encouraging empathy for others, showed mixed outcomes. Disposition (2), relating to thinking about how one's decisions affect other people, is noteworthy for its statistical significance and especially its large effect size (*Cohen's d* = 1.07). This outcome is particularly satisfying because the design of the decisions that students had to make while playing the game was oriented directly at having students learn to be sensitive to the impact of their own decisions in the game on other characters in the game. Thus, there was an occasion where the player, as the protagonist Stahl, had to decide whether to (1) inform the leader of the invading Martian forces, who had shown himself to be very friendly, about a planned meeting of the resistance movement, or (2) to keep quiet about it. The design of these decisions play upon the tensions of trusting others versus being discreet about matters whose import may as yet be unclear.

The finding on item (5), which was reverse coded, shows a shift in the "preferred" direction of appropriating a disposition of concern related to the problems of others and recognizing that no person is an island unto herself or himself in a multi-ethnic and multi-cultural world. Item (11) is an instantiation of a particular problem faced by others, namely, poverty. This item was marginally significant statistically, and it suggests some development of empathy for those who are less well off materially.

The result on item (3), related to seeing things from other people's point of view, was not significant. This item may have been problematic because the experience of game play could have pulled students in opposite directions. On one hand, as a reverse coded item, we expected students to more strongly disagree with the statement at the close of the research intervention compared to the beginning; that is, they would find it less difficult to see from another person's point of view. However, the game design also sought to instill a tolerance for diversity and hence the acceptance of multiple points of view. This tension may have accounted for the non-significant finding.

The third theme, comprising one item on racial diversity, was statistically significant with a medium effect size. This outcome can be attributed to the design of the game, which sought to instill the cultural value of multiracialism found in Singapore. By design, inhabitants of the space station were all immigrants from other planetary locales (e.g., Earth, moon, and Mars). In order not to have to address issues of race directly—as this is always a potentially sensitive political issue in Singapore—factions were used as a surrogate for race, to embrace all the entities that would hold symbolic value for any particular community. The need for mutual respect and peaceful co-existence was emphasized in the game episodes.

Like the theme above, the fourth theme, racial equity, is also a cornerstone of Singapore's National Education agenda. Item (8) focuses on the agenda of equal access to education for all,

regardless of race. On this item, we see that students empathized with this sentiment. Their disposition shifted in favor of equal access with a medium effect size. Item (9) sought to encourage students to judge people on the basis of their actions rather than from their country of origin. On this item, students showed a positive dispositional shift with a small effect size.

The dispositional change related to item (6), concerning basing one's decisions on what one thinks is fair or unfair, was significant, but in the direction opposite to that "preferred." A previous study with another group of students (Chee et al., 2008) found a similar result. We have come to believe that this unexpected outcome is the result of a problematic wording of the item. As a reverse coded item, the intention was that students would move away from self-centric thinking and begin to appreciate the need to consider the thinking of others as well in problem solving situations; that is, the focus of the item was on the phrase "what I think." It appears that many students interpreted the item primarily in terms of the words "fair and unfair" instead, leading them to stronger agreement with the statement rather than disagreement (before reverse coding). In view of this outcome, we plan to rephrase this item in future work.

The fifth theme, focusing on self-responsibility, consisted of one item that highlighted self-control and responsibility for one's own actions. The dispositional change here was statistically significant with a medium effect size. We attribute this change directly to the game design. A key objective was to help students grasp the fact that while they were free to choose any of the options the game presented to them, they would have to learn to accept the consequences of their choice. In the episode where the protagonist Mei Ling was travelling with a band of people and trying to escape from Sector Two of the space station that had suffered a power failure with the consequence that the amount of oxygen in the atmosphere was rapidly diminishing, she had to put up with her pesky young brother, Ken, who was throwing a tantrum because he had lost his toy along the way. Critical decision points during this episode allowed the students playing the game to deal with Ken in ways that would either help or hinder progress in the group's trek to safety. By the choices that students made, they learned the importance of seeing beyond the trials of the moment and to appreciate the bigger picture of what was at stake and the role their own choices played in the sequence of unfolding events.

The sixth theme, civic consciousness and active citizenship, comprised seven items. Items (10) and (14), related to pollution and protection of the environment, were significant. In the simulation segment of the game, students had to decide where to locate factories relative to human dwellings. They also had to consider the importance of ecological balance in developing the economic infrastructure of the space station, as failure to do so would incur both economic and social costs. We believe that episodes such as these sensitized students to the issues tapped into by these items.

Students in Singapore are well known for their political apathy. We were therefore very pleased that there was a shift of marginal statistical significance away from this attitude, as manifested by their responses to item (13). While this shift may not quite constitute an embracing of active citizenship, it is nevertheless a promising step in the preferred direction. On a related note, students learned to recognize the need to discuss and negotiate the political future of Singapore (item 16), a dispositional shift that is of considerable local importance.

The positive dispositional shifts with medium effect size reflected in items (12) and (15) are particularly satisfying. They demonstrate that, through learning with the Leonis program, students developed a belief in their ability to make a difference as well as a sense of obligation and responsibility toward the social and political future of Singapore. Item (17) reinforces the general orientation toward placing the interests of the community above the interests of oneself.

To summarize, the findings above clearly suggest that a game-based learning program, comprising student game play that is complemented with dialogic learning, can be efficacious in helping students develop desirable dispositions related to *becoming* citizens. We emphasize that our pedagogical goal is not the learning of facts and skills from the game but, rather, the fostering of values and dispositions appropriate to citizenship education through learning *with* the game and with one another (including the teacher). This approach targets the authentic learning objectives of education as the *becoming* of a certain type of person through the development of values, personal identity, and epistemology, in addition to knowledge and skills. Based on this approach, knowledge and skills are no longer simply elements that are the target of instruction. Rather, we argue that what is entailed is an entirely new onto-epistemology (Barad, 2003) that is based on values, identity, and performance: the VIP onto-epistemology (Chee 2010a). The approach of process philosophy, with its orientation toward *becoming*, provides the foundation for the design of a learning program in these terms.

More generally, in our ongoing work in this field, we have found it productive to think of human learning in terms of the general framework for researching human learning depicted in Figure 5. This framework is appropriated from Collen (2003) and modified to suit our research purpose. In the original framework, the philsophical basis for human systems inquiry comprises three fundamental ideas from Greek philsophy: *ontos*, *logos*, and *praxis*. Together, they yield a praxiology for human inquiry. *Ontos*, or ontology, is the study of human being, human existence, and of what is. *Logos*, referring to epistemology, is the study of human knowing, what can be known, and what constitutes human knowledge. *Praxis*, or praxiology, is the study of action, the practices of human beings, and of what we (as humans) do. To understand human learning authentically and in all its rich complexity, we deem it vital that learning be studied in the context of humans engaged in situated action, including participation in speech acts and discursive practices that accompany everyday actions (Austin, 1975; Clancey, 1997; Dewey, 1938; Gergen, 1999). In taking this position, we explicitly reject learning outcomes where students can only talk *about* citizenship, without the ability to engage in the practice of citizenship. The framework in Figure 5 emphasizes that human *knowing* is inseparable from human *doing* and human *being*. The components of the framework are necessarily embedded within a background context of axiology, the study of human values because knowing, doing, and being are inherently value-laden activities (Ferré, 1996, 1998; Putnam, 2002). Humans make basic value distinctions related to all processes and outcomes of learning. These distinctions guide their learning actions toward outcomes that create positive value.

As a program of learning innovation, our research experience with the Leonis program and the associated research findings have implications for educational policy, research, and teaching and learning practice. From a policy perspective, our work suggests a viable, alternative approach to citizenship education that can provide the traction

policy makers and school administrators seek in principle but so often fail to achieve in practice. This situation is prevalent in Singapore where the objectives related to the "O" level social studies curriculum include a distinct set of components dealing with the development of students' values and attitudes (e.g., students will respect and value diverse perspectives and cultural and historical backgrounds of people; students will work toward peaceful relationships). Such learning goals are usually lost when translated into practice because official examinations only assess the other two easily assessable components of the curriculum that concern (1) knowledge and understanding, and (2) skills and processes. Our research suggests that a more holistic evaluation of student learning is not only desirable but also possible.

From a research perspective, our work highlights the critical importance of approaching student learning in a broader and more authentic manner, recognizing that impactful learning transforms students in lasting, developmentally oriented ways. Such learning increases students' capacity for meaningful and desirable performance in the real world, in ways that have high social

Figure 5. A general framework for undertaking research on human learning

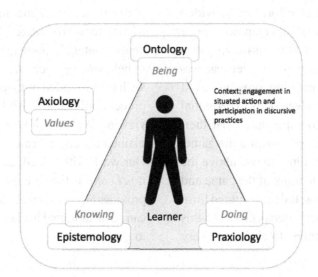

capital. Our grounding on process philosophy helps us to cast the educational agenda in a radically different light, placing emphasis on innovation, creativity, and personal growth that can arise when students, as empowered agents of learning, strive toward the construction of a "better tomorrow." In respect of the pedagogical design of game-based learning, our work reiterates the importance of careful learning design that achieves alignment between the design of in-game experiences and the de-sired outcomes of learning. It also highlights the importance of designing the learning environment to include a dialogic space within which students' ideas can interact as the students engage in a collaborative process of group meaning making. Thus, students do not simply learn *from* technology, but rather learn *with* technology and with one another.

Finally, from the perspective of teaching and learning practice, we emphasize that innovation implies change, and preparation for change, in respect of both teachers and students, is vital to the success of any program of learning innovation. Teachers need to "buy in" to the innovation not only "with their head" but also "with their heart." The challenge faced by teachers is quite daunting as adopting a learning innovation usually entails taking a big step into the unknown. Scaffolding the process for teachers is thus a vital component of the research effort. We provided teachers with professional development prior to the commencement of the classroom intervention. Our approach was to first let teachers experience the Leonis learning program as if they were students themselves. This experiential approach helped them to appreciate what their students would encounter when using the game. It also helped them, over time, to rise above the game itself and to begin to think of the game and complementary dialog as a student-centered form of learning from a teacher's perspective. To this end, we tried, as researchers, to always be very

sensitive to teachers' feedback and operational concerns, such as the time required to enact the learning program (given limited curriculum time) and the modes of assessment to apply. Overall, we positioned our interaction with the teacher as a collaborative endeavor and as taking a journey together. This positioning made us partners in a common endeavor and helped to develop the trust and rapport needed for the innovation program to succeed. In this way, learning was inescapably experiential for the teacher as well as for us, as researchers. With regard to students, it should be noted that student expectations must be carefully managed prior to, as well as during, the course of the implementation of the learning program. Game-based learning makes both new and greater demands on students compared to what they are accustomed to in class: being told about things as they sit passively listening. Getting student "buy in" is equally important to getting "buy in" from teachers for the program to succeed.

CONCLUSION

In this chapter, we have articulated a model of game-based learning that recognizes the importance of play, dialog, and the development of self in the process of learning as becoming through performance. Recognizing that the competencies needed for active citizenship do not reside in students' content knowledge but, rather, in the need to help students become certain kinds of people, we have grounded our work on the foundation of process philosophy. We have argued in favor of viewing learning in terms of *becoming* and explained the critical role of values to this process. Our work with the educational game *Space Station Leonis* in the domain of citizenship education provides an exemplar of how game-based learning can be instantiated in classroom learning contexts to good effect.

ACKNOWLEDGMENT

The work reported in this chapter was funded by a Learning Sciences Lab research grant, number R8019.735.NG03. In a project of this scope and diversity, a multidisciplinary team is indispensable. We wish to acknowledge the contributions of all team members: Nathanael Ng, Liu Yi, Loi Hui Min, Yuan Tao, Eric Chan, Eric Salim, Henry Kang, Chen Jieyang, Rave Tan, Ahmed Hilmy, and Kenneth Lim.

REFERENCES

Appiah, K. A. (2007). *Cosmopolitanism: Ethics in a world of strangers*. London, UK: Penguin Books.

Austin, J. L. (1975). *How to do things with words* (2nd ed.). Cambridge, MA: MIT Press.

Bakhtin, M. M. (1981). *The dialogic imagination: Four essays*. Austin, TX: University of Texas Press.

Banks, J. A. (2008). Diversity, group identity, and citizenship education in a global age. *Educational Researcher*, *37*(3), 129–139. doi:10.3102/0013189X08317501

Barad, K. (2003). Posthumanist performativity: Toward an understanding of how matter comes to matter. *Signs: Journal of Women in Culture and Society*, *28*(3), 801–831. doi:10.1086/345321

Bateson, G. (1979). *Mind and nature: A necessary unity*. New York, NY: Bantam Books.

Becker, L. (2000). *Effect size*. Retrieved December 9, 2008, from http://web.uccs.edu/lbecker/Psy590/es.htm

Carlson, M. (2004). *Performance: A critical introduction*. New York, NY: Routledge.

Chee, Y. S. (2007). Embodiment, embeddedness, and experience: Game-based learning and the construction of identity. *Research and Practice in Technology Enhanced Learning*, *2*(1), 3–30. doi:10.1142/S1793206807000282

Chee, Y. S. (2010a). Possession, profession, and performance: Epistemological considerations for effective game-based learning . In Cai, Y. (Ed.), *Interactive and digital media for education in virtual learning environments* (pp. 7–24). New York, NY: Nova Science Publishers.

Chee, Y. S. (2010b). *Learning as becoming through performance, play, and dialog, and performance: A model of game-based learning with the game Legends of Alkhimia*. Manuscript submitted for publication.

Chew, O. A. J. (1998). Civics and moral education in Singapore: Lessons for citizenship education? *Journal of Moral Education*, *27*(4), 505–524. doi:10.1080/0305724980270405

Clancey, W. J. (1997). *Situated cognition: On human knowledge and computer representations*. New York, NY: Cambridge University Press.

Collen, A. (2003). *Systemic change through praxis and inquiry*. New Brunswick, NJ: Transaction Publishers.

Dewey, J. (1938). *Experience and education*. New York, NY: Macmillan.

Edelman, G. M. (1992). *Bright air, brilliant fire: On the matter of the mind*. New York, NY: Basic Books.

Ferré, F. (1996). *Being and value: Toward a constructive postmodern metaphysics*. New York, NY: SUNY Press.

Ferré, F. (1998). *Knowing and value: Toward a constructive postmodern epistemology*. New York, NY: SUNY Press.

Gee, J. P. (2007). *What video games have to teach us about learning and literacy* (rev. and updated ed.). New York, NY: Palgrave Macmillan.

Gergen, K. J. (1999). *An invitation to social construction.* London, UK: Sage.

Goffman, E. (1959). *The presentation of self in everyday life.* New York, NY: Anchor Books.

Holland, D., Lachicotte, W. Jr, Skinner, D., & Cain, C. (1998). *Identity and agency in cultural worlds.* Cambridge, MA: Harvard University Press.

Howard, G. S. (1980). Response shift bias: A problem in evaluating interventions with pre/post self-reports. *Evaluation Review, 4*(1), 93–106. doi:10.1177/0193841X8000400105

Hustwit, J. R. (2007). Process philosophy. *The Internet Encyclopaedia of Philosophy.* Retrieved November 18, 2008, from http://www. iep.utm. edu/p/processp.htm

Leue, W. H. (2005). *Metaphysical foundations for a theory of value in the philosophy of Alfred North Whitehead.* Ashfield, MA: Down-to-Earth Books.

Mesle, C. R. (2008). *Process-relational philosophy: An introduction to Alfred North Whitehead.* West Conshohocken, PA: Temple Foundation Press.

Putnam, H. (2002). *The collapse of the fact/value dichotomy.* Cambridge, MA: Harvard University Press.

Rescher, N. (2000). *Process philosophy: A survey of basic issues.* Pittsburgh, PA: University of Pittsburgh Press.

Rescher, N. (2008). Process philosophy. *Stanford Encyclopaedia of Philosophy.* Retrieved November 4, 2008, from http://plato.stanford.edu/entries/process-philosophy/

Rockwell, S. K., & Kohn, H. (1989). Post then pre evaluation. *Journal of Extension, 27*(2), 19–21.

Rogoff, B. (1993). Children's guided participation and participatory appropriation in sociocultural activity . In Wozniak, R. H., & Fischer, K. W. (Eds.), *Development in context: Acting and thinking in specific environments* (pp. 121–153). Hillsdale, NJ: Lawrence Erlbaum.

Selwyn, N. (2002). *Literature review in citizenship, technology and learning* (Report No. 3). Bristol, UK: Futurelab.

Semetsky, I. (2006). *Deleuze, education, and becoming.* Rotterdam, The Netherlands: Sense Publishers.

Shaffer, D. W. (2006). *How computer games help children learn.* New York, NY: Palgrave Macmillan. doi:10.1057/9780230601994

Sidorkin, A. M. (1999). *Beyond discourse: Education, the self, and dialogue.* New York, NY: SUNY Press.

Singapore Ministry of Education. (2008). *Desired outcomes of education.* Retrieved November 27, 2008, from http://www.moe.gov.sg/education/desired-outcomes/

Tan, T. W., & Chew, L. C. (2004). Moral and citizenship education as statecraft in Singapore: A curriculum critique. *Journal of Moral Education, 33*(4), 597–606. doi:10.1080/0305724042000315644

Whitehead, A. N. (1926). *Religion in the making.* New York, NY: Macmillan.

Whitehead, A. N. (1978). *Process and reality: An essay in cosmology* (Corrected ed.). New York, NY: Free Press.

Chapter 9
Rule of Engagement:
The Presence of a Co-Player Does Not Hinder Gamers' Focus

B. J. Gajadhar
Eindhoven University of Technology, The Netherlands

Y. A. W. deKort
Eindhoven University of Technology, The Netherlands

W. A. IJsselsteijn
Eindhoven University of Technology, The Netherlands

ABSTRACT

This chapter presents an empirical study of social setting as a determinant of player involvement in competitive play. We conceptualize player experience as roughly comprising of components of involvement and enjoyment. Involvement relates to the attentional pull of games encompassing feelings of immersion, engagement, and flow. Enjoyment taps into the fun and frustration of playing. A few recent studies indicate that co-players boost player enjoyment, yet the effect on involvement is still largely unknown. In line with enjoyment, involvement could increase with the sociality of settings. On the other hand, the presence of others provides a potential distracter and threat to involvement in games. Results of an experiment where social setting was manipulated within groups indicated that players' involvement remains constant or even increases with mediated or co-located co-players compared to solitary play. Hence, co-players do not break the spell of a game, but become part of the magic circle.

INTRODUCTION

Digital gaming has become extremely popular across North America, Europe, Australia and Asia (Tan & Jansz, 2008). Simultaneously, digital gaming has also become a more and more social activity. There has been a strong shift from solo-play to multi-play options, and the widespread penetration of the Internet now allows for social play without the restriction of co-players having to be in the same room. As a result, digital games are increasingly played together with

DOI: 10.4018/978-1-60960-565-0.ch009

other people, who indisputably become part of the player experience (Nielsen, 2005). However, this fact has not been considered in most of the player experience literature (Goldstein, 2007; de Kort & IJsselsteijn, 2008).

There are numerous reasons why the experience of playing with others differs from playing alone, many of which have their roots in the fundamental human need for affiliation, our need to belong (Baumeister & Leary, 1995). Playing together implies interaction with another person, and perhaps even a relationship, be it weak or strong, temporary or lasting. This alone makes the event meaningful. In addition, the presence of others may induce social facilitation, evaluation apprehension, and increased self-awareness, which impact on performance and affect (e.g., Cottrell, 1972; Carver & Scheier, 1981). Affective states are affected by observable affective states of others through mechanisms of empathy and emotional contagion (Hatfield, Cacioppo, & Rapson, 1992), which may induce strong feelings of affiliation (e.g., Chartrand & Bargh, 1999). Moreover, sharing experiences with others and recognizing similarities in terms of interest or affect induces affinity and interpersonal attraction (Moreland & Zajonc, 1982) and engenders an even stronger feeling of belonging (Raghunathan & Corfman, 2006). On the other hand, with the presence of others comes also the potential for pride or shame over performance, and impression management mechanisms to save face in the case of potentially negative perceptions of one's personality or capacities. Although this is clearly not a comprehensive overview of psychological processes that explain why social settings influence experience, it does illustrate that game experience cannot be restricted to the interaction between the game and the player alone.

Incorporating all these social processes and the way they impact on experience into player experience models is no mean feat, yet this does not free us from the need to consider the importance of social context in digital play. This impact is likely to vary with varying play settings such as solo-play, online play and multi-play, with interpersonal familiarity, and with players' awareness of and potential to communicate with the other player(s). Recently, de Kort and IJsselsteijn (2008) introduced a framework considering how social processes become significant when games are played with others, and how they impact on game experience. Based on theoretical considerations, they argue that the degree to which other people play a significant role in player experience is shaped by characteristics of the social, physical and media setting. These characteristics shape the affordances for players to communicate and to monitor each other, and create a setting for co-player reinforcement. For instance room layout, furniture, and screen arrangements determine viewing lines between players in co-located settings, whereas the availability of additional communication channels such as chat functionality or an audio connection determine possibilities for meta-communication during game play. De Kort and IJsselsteijn furthermore argue that the influence of these affordances on player experience is mediated by players' awareness of and involvement with their co-player, in other words their experienced level of social presence.

In line with this view we prefer the term *player experience* to *game experience*. It indicates the experience not only as a result of playing the game, but also as a result of playing it with others and in a particular context. Player experience is a broad term, which can be roughly subdivided into player enjoyment and player involvement. Enjoyment relates to the amount of pleasure or displeasure a player experiences, and involvement is defined as the attentional pull of the game encompassing feelings of immersion, engagement and flow.

Recently, Gajadhar, de Kort & IJsselsteijn (2008a) empirically demonstrated the effects of social context on player enjoyment, and its mediation via social presence. The results indicated that presence of co-players significantly adds to the fun, challenge, and perceived competence in a game and therefore influences player enjoyment. Results of social effects on player involvement on the other hand have not been tested empirically yet. Some have suggested that others present may distract players from the game and potentially break their concentration (e.g., Sweetser & Wyeth, 2005), yet the popularity of social play appears to contradict this. This paper therefore focuses on experiential components describing a player's involvement when a co-player is either absent, co-present online, or sitting next to them during digital game play.

Player Involvement

Immersion, engagement, and flow appear to lie at the heart of player experience, yet today the field still has not established consensus on the definitions of these and related terms. In this paper we use the term *player involvement* as a generic name to denote the umbrella construct under which concepts are placed which describe a player's focus and interest during digital play. Unfortunately, as yet researchers use different names for overlapping experiences, and identical names for clearly different phenomena. We will briefly review the most relevant literature below.

Immersion is a metaphorical term originating from the experience of being submerged in water. In digital gaming it connotes the feeling of being surrounded by another reality, the reality of the game itself. Ermi and Mäyrä (2005) discuss a model for immersion in games which includes three components: sensory immersion - based on the audiovisual qualities of games -, imaginative immersion which is based on the fantasy of the game and identification with the game character, and challenge-based immersion - based on skills addressed in the game. We define immersion as the experience of being surrounded by the game as a result from the absorbing power of the game's audio, video, and narrative. In this sense the third component of Ermi and Mäyrä's model, challenge-based immersion, appears to fit better

under the second component of game involvement we propose: engagement.

We define *engagement* as the state of absorption in a game, where players appear cut off from the real world, forget everything around them and are deeply involved in the medium, mainly through the cognitive challenges posed to them. Brown and Cairns (2004) defined a model of game involvement containing three levels: engagement, engrossment, and total immersion. They propose that the level of engagement players experience during the game strongly depends on the effort they put into the game, or are willing to put into it.

Flow is also prominent in discussions of gameplay and game experience. We adopted the definition of flow from Csikszentmihalyi (1975; 1988) who studied the enjoyment derived from various sports and leisure activities. He stated that flow is the optimal experience where one is performing at best, is alert, is in effortless control and where one's sense of time is altered and sense of self is lost. There are no tangible rewards one gets from flow; however it is such a pleasant experience that people are willing to reach and maintain the state for its own sake (Csikszentmihalyi & Csikszentmihalyi, 1988). Although flow theory was not developed as an explanation of media enjoyment, the association between flow and digital games has been made frequently in the past decade (e.g. McKenna & Lee, 1995; Sweetser & Wyeth, 2005). The flow experience differs from engagement in the sense that flow is considered only to emerge when the players' skills and the games' challenges are optimally balanced.

The three concepts described above – immersion, engagement, and flow – are obviously related and show some overlap in terms of their phenomenology. Yet they do have their own typicalities and connotations with game characteristics. For instance, engagement relates to appealing personal challenges in the game, immersion to the richness and qualities of graphics, sounds, or narrative, and flow to the exact matching of challenges and skills ('optimal performance').

Besides these conceptual considerations, empirical findings confirm the multidimensionality of player involvement. In a large-scale empirical exploration of in-game player experiences (Game Experience Questionnaire; IJsselsteijn, de Kort & Poels, in preparation) seven reliable components of player experience emerged in factor analyses: Positive affect, competence, challenge, frustration, boredom, flow, and immersion. At least three of these reflect player involvement: 'immersion', 'boredom' (the antonym of engagement), and 'flow'. Yet the question of how these constructs relate to the social context of gaming has not been addressed before.

Player Experience Models

To date, even though some authors acknowledge the role of social elements in gaming, co-players and spectators are only marginally included in most player experience models (e.g. Sweetser & Wyeth, 2005; Ermi & Mäyra, 2005). As an exception, Calleja's (2007) model does explicitly acknowledge a social component, related to the consequences of one's performance, i.e., failing vs. succeeding, being visible to others in online play. Yet all current game experience models are insufficient for describing social processes such as shared enjoyment (Vallius, Manninen, & Kujanpää, 2006), or social anxiety and choking (Kimble & Rezabek, 1992), and for explaining social effects such as the increased challenge in competition (Vorderer, Hartmann & Klimmt, 2003). The general view in player involvement literature is that social interactions during play may have a negative influence on the focus players need to play games. Sweetser and Wyeth (2005) argue that during game play other people provide players a link to the real world, potentially interrupting flow or immersion and pulling attention away from the game. Their view can be supported by the work of Baron (1986), who argues that others can be seen as a source of distraction and consequently may interfere with information

processing which ultimately will influence our performance and experience. After all, in essence these phenomena describe situations in which all attention is directed at the game, and from this perspective co-players can be considered a distraction. However, no empirical results were found in literature that supported this theory. In contrast, a few studies contradict the argument of interrupting involvement by indicating that social interaction is the number one motivation for digital gaming (e.g. Nielsen, 2005; Jansz & Martens, 2005). Perhaps this apparent contrast explains why most scientists have been hesitant to adopt social components in their player experience models. Since writings on this matter have mostly been conceptual or theoretical, empirical findings on the influence of the presence of co-players on player involvement are recommended in future studies.

We argue that player experience can only be understood fully when the player's social context is also accounted for. To do so, we approach digital gaming with social presence theory. Social presence is defined as *the sense of being with another* (Biocca, Harms, & Burgoon, 2003). The concept has mainly been applied in respect to communication technology, but was recently introduced in digital gaming research by de Kort, IJsselsteijn, & Poels (2007). In a preliminary study, Gajadhar et al. (2008b) showed that players' reported level of social presence varied, depending on whether they played against a computer agent (virtual other), a mediated other (online), or a co-located other, and whether they played against a stranger or a friend. Other empirical work had also indicated that the nature of a competitive situation is influenced by familiarity of the opponent and influences player experience (Ravaja, Saari, Turpeinen, Laarni, Slaminen, & Kivikangas, 2006; Ravaja, 2009).

In a subsequent study (2008a) Gajadhar et al. showed that competitive play in a richer social setting brings significantly more player enjoyment, i.e. more positive affect, competence and challenge. This effect was mediated by social presence. Although not addressed in that article, player involvement components were also measured in this particular study, in addition to components of player enjoyment. In the current chapter, results concerning player involvement are analysed and discussed, to test whether the player's focus was undermined by the presence of co-players whilst enjoyment clearly increased.

METHOD

Experimental design

To address the research question a mixed groups design was employed. Co-player Presence was manipulated as a within groups factor (Virtual Co-Player vs. Mediated Co-Player vs. Co-located Co-Player). These three conditions represent very common and increasingly socially rich play configurations. The second factor – Player Performance (Winner vs. Loser) - was created post-hoc for each play session, based on players' scores in the experiment. Player experience was measured with a combination of self-report measures after each session.

Participants

Eighty-six Dutch graduate and post graduate students (59 males), aged between 16 and 34 (M_{age} = 22.4; SD_{age} = 3.5), participated in the experiment. However, since participants played in dyads, and dyadic data are non-independent (Kenny, Kashy & Cook, 2006), only half of the data was actually used for the current analyses (the data of all players '1'). Therefore the actual sample size was 42 participants (27 males; 26 friends). Participants were recruited from a participant database via email, or approached during breaks in seminars at the university. All participants had played digital games before, a substantial number of them indicated they played them regularly.

Apparatus

The game *WoodPong* by Resinari (2005) was used in the experiments, displayed on a 17" monitor. This arcade-like game has simple controls and is thus easy to learn and has a short learning curve. Furthermore, the game has a non-violent character which prevents biased preferences in gender. Also it offers a clear outcome of winner and loser, which was necessary to include the effects of player performance in player experience. WoodPong was derived from tennis: the player has to return the approaching ball and hit it towards the other player by controlling the bat (see Figure 1). The music and side effects within the game were played via a headphone which players wore in all conditions and were identical for both competing players.

Experimental Manipulations and Procedure

The experiment was conducted in the PsyLab at the Eindhoven University of Technology, consisting of eight separate participant booths. Participants were welcomed in pairs by the experimenter, entered the lab together, were asked to fill in a consent form and were led to believe that the purpose of the study concerned the effect of latency on player experience in digital games. For each experimental condition, participants were redirected to another booth where the social context was alternated: in the *virtual co-player* setting participants were told that they played against the computer (in separate rooms), although in fact they played against their partner (see below). In the *mediated co-player* setting the pairs played online against each other (in separate booths), and in the *co-located co-player* setting they played against each other in the same booth, on the same console (see Figure 2).

Based on the results of a pilot study (Gajadhar et al., 2008b) it was decided not to have participants play against the computer in the virtual co-player setting for two reasons (as also discussed

Figure 1. Interface of WoodPong where both slices of the same color are simultaneously controlled by the keyboard; the game stops when one of the players has 6 points.

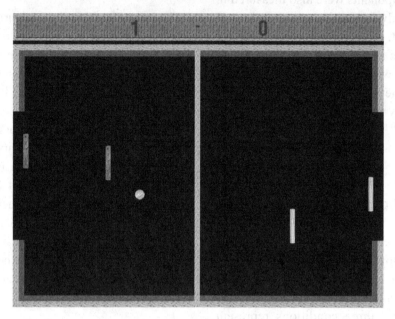

in Gajadhar et al., 2008a). First, the design provided a confound as results revealed that all players lost their game against the AI. Second, in case there would be an effect of co-player presence, it would be impossible to attribute this to either the social meanings and affordances of the setting or - alternatively - to the fact that computers play with fixed algorithms and thus differently than humans. Instead, in the current experiment the

virtual and the mediated co-player settings were in fact identical, except for the fact that players *thought* their co-players were AI instead of human. To make this difference more convincing, a visible cable was connected between the two computers in the mediated setting. However in the virtual setting, cables which connected both computers were unnoticeable. As a result, in all experimental conditions participants played

Figure 2. (a) Setting in virtual and mediated co-playing. (b) Setting in co-located co-playing. Note that in all settings each participant actually played against the same competitor.

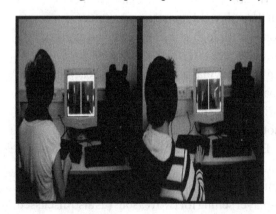 

against the same (human) competitor which prevented any confounds by differences in difficulty level. The only difference between the settings was in their social meaning and richness, which increased from virtual to mediated to co-located play.

In each condition, three sets of *WoodPong* were played. A set was started by the experimenter via a wireless keyboard, and ended automatically after one of the participants won six points. After three sets a winner was noted, and the request to fill in a questionnaire appeared on both participants' displays (always filled in, in separate rooms). The order of settings was randomly assigned per couple. Lastly, they were debriefed, paid and thanked for their participation. The experiment lasted 30 minutes; participants received a standard compensation of €5,-.

Measurement Instruments

After each condition, participants completed a set of self-report measures in which they rated their experiences during the game. The combined questionnaire probed three categories of experiences: social presence, player enjoyment and player involvement. Results relating to the second category - enjoyment - are addressed in a separate publication (Gajadhar et al., 2008a) and will not be reported here.

Three subscales from the Social Presence in Gaming Questionnaire (SPGQ) (de Kort et al., 2007) were administered to verify the manipulation of social presence in the three play configurations under study. *SPGQ-Psychological Involvement Empathy* tries to measure the experience of positive feelings with questions such as "*I empathized with the other*". *SPGQ-Behavioral Engagement* approaches the feelings that one's actions depend on one's co-player's actions in the game, and vice versa, with items such as "*what the other did affected what I did*". Because two items from the *SPGQ-Psychological Involvement Negative Feelings* appeared to have been ambigu-

ous to participants, only the item "*I felt jealousy towards the other*" was used to study the negative feelings; the other items were excluded from analyses. Table 1 shows the internal consistencies of the SPGQ-components per setting.

Player involvement was measured with three scales from the GEQ. GEQ-Immersion was probed with items such as '*it was aesthetically pleasing*'. Engagement was probed with the GEQ-Boredom and the GEQ-Flow scales. GEQ-Boredom measures negative affect, in particular related to feeling bored and distracted during the game. In other words it is a reversed engagement scale with questions such as "*I found it tiresome*". The GEQ-Flow scale measures the degree of absorption and the experience of being cut off from the real world, with items such as "*I lost track of time*". Since it was felt that the GEQ-Flow scale did not perfectly target the *optimal* experience as described by Csikszentmihalyi (1975; 1988), a Revised-Flow scale was constructed with 4 items such as "*for a moment it felt as if I succeeded in all my actions*", and "*sometimes it felt as if my fingers were pushing the buttons automatically*". As involvement potentially also relates to the willingness to learn and refine skills for a better performance, a Performance Improvement Drive scale was constructed, consisting of 3 items such as "*I wanted to become better in the game*", and "*I wanted to be a natural at playing the game*". Reliabilities of these scales were satisfactory to excellent (see Table 2).

The combined questionnaire included 55 items. Participants could respond on 5-point unipolar scales, ranging from 1 (not at all) to 5 (extremely),

Table 1. Schematic overview of the Cronbach's Alpha for the social presence components

	SPGQ-PIE.	SPGQ-BE.
Virtual	.66	.90
Mediated	.77	.91
Co-located	.78	.85

to indicate the intensity of the described experience. Additionally, all in-game scores were logged to determine whether players had won or lost (post-hoc constructed Player Performance factor).

RESULTS

Mixed Model Analysis was performed on each of the self-report scales of player involvement with Co-Player Presence and Player Performance as fixed factors; participant numbered was entered as random factor. First the social presence manipulation check is reported, after which the effects on the dependent variables are analyzed.

Social Presence Manipulation Check

Social presence was measured with 3 scales from the SPGQ: Psychological Involvement Empathy (SPGQ-PIE), Behavioral Engagement (SPGQ-BE), and Jealousy (SPGQ-Jealousy). Table 3 shows the bivariate correlations between the components; modest significant correlations emerged between SPGQ-PIE and the other two social presence components.

Linear Mixed Model Analyses (repeated measures) were performed for each component of the SPGQ with Co-Player Presence as a within groups factor and Player Performance as between groups factor; participant number was included as random factor. As intended, results showed significant differences for Co-Player Presence on all social presence scales (see Table 4).

Virtual co-play scored lowest on all social presence scales ($M_{BE} = 2.5$ (0.2); $M_{PIE} = 1.3$ (0.1); $M_{Jea} = 1.0$ (0.1)). Co-located co-play scored highest ($M_{BE} = 3.1$ (0.1); $M_{PIE} = 3.0$ (0.1) ; $M_{Jea} = 1.7$ (0.2)), and mediated co-play scored in between ($M_{BE} = 2.8$ (0.2); $M_{PIE} = 1.9$ (0.1); $M_{Jea} = 1.5$ (0.1)) for all social presence subscales. Contrast analyses showed that scores increased significantly

Table 4. Schematic overview of the results of Co-Player Presence on the social presence components

	SPGQ-PIE	SPGQ-BE	SPGQ-Jeal.
F-statistic	4.55	0.42	10.67
p-value	.001	.001	.001
R-squared	.73	.28	.33
Denominator df.	82.5	79.7	77.2
Numerator df.	2	2	2

Note: Adjusted R-Squared are reported since LMMA does not provide the R-Squared based on the Sum of Squares; the adjusted R-squared (based on variance of residuals) can also have negative values.

Table 2. Schematic overview of the Cronbach's Alpha for the player involvement related components

	GEQ-Bor.	GEQ-Flow	GEQ-Immer.	Rev-Flow	PID
Virtual	.77	.87	.68	.63	.83
Mediated	.90	.92	.69	.70	.73
Co-located	.66	.93	.74	.70	.81

Table 3. Schematic overview of the Pearson correlations between the social presence components

	SPGQ-PIE	SPGQ-BE	SPGQ-Jeal.
SPGQ-PIE	1	.35**	.35**
SPGQ-BE	.35**	1	.15(*)
SPGQ-Jeal.	.35**	.15(*)	1

08; **$p<.001$

with each subsequent category for all scales (p=.03); except for SPGQ-BE between virtual and mediated co-play, the difference here only approaches significance (p=.08). Figure 3a presents the scores of the social presence indicators.

Furthermore, SPGQ-Jealousy revealed a significant main effect of Player Performance ($F(1,108.3) = 15.93$; p<.001, R^2=.16) and a significant interaction effect between Player Performance and Co-Player Presence ($F(2,103.2)=4.08$; p=.02, R^2=.16). Losers (M=1.8 (0.1)) experienced more jealousy towards their co-players than winners ($M = 1.1$ (0.1)), and the increase for each subsequent category of Co-Player Presence was larger for losers than for winners (see Figure 3b).

Player Involvement

As part of player experience, player involvement was measured with 5 scales: GEQ-Immersion, GEQ-Flow, GEQ-Boredom, Revised-Flow, and Performance Improvement Drive. Table 5 shows the bivariate correlations between the components; significant correlations emerged between almost all components.

Linear Mixed Model Analyses (repeated measures) were performed for each component of player involvement with Co-Player Presence as a within groups factor and Player Performance as between groups factors. Analyses revealed significant main effects of Co-Player Presence on

Figure 3. (a) Social Presence as a function of Co-Player Presence; (b) SPGQ-Jealousy for winners and losers as a function of Co-Player Presence (1 = not at all, 5 = extremely; SE indicated in graph).

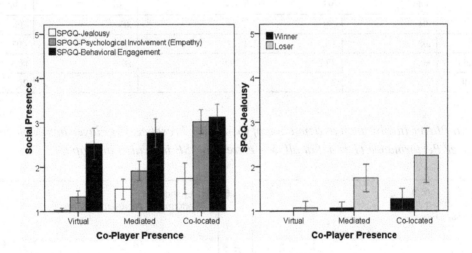

Table 5. Schematic overview of the Pearson correlations between the player involvement related components

	GEQ-Bor.	GEQ-Imm.	GEQ-Flow	Rev- Flow	PID
GEQ-Bor.	1	-.19*	-.19*	.07	-.28**
GEQ-Imm.	-.19*	1	.49**	.36**	.26**
GEQ-Flow	-.19*	.49**	1	.34**	.42**
Rev-Flow	.07	.36**	.34**	1	.19*
PID	-.28**	.26**	.42**	.19*	1

*p<.05; **p<.001

GEQ-Boredom, GEQ-Immersion, and Revised-Flow; see Table 6.

As is shown in Figure 4a, three subscales show modest, yet significant differences for the three levels of Co-Player Presence. Subsequent contrast analyses show that boredom was significantly higher in virtual co-play (M = 1.6 (0.1)) than in mediated (M = 1.4 (0.1); p=.04) and co-located (M = 1.4 (0.1); p=.02) co-play. Furthermore, immersion is significantly higher for co-located play (M = 2.1 (0.1)) than for mediated (M = 1.8 (0.1); p=.02) and virtual (M = 1.9 (0.1); p=.02) co-play. Similarly, contrast analyses show that Revised-Flow is significantly higher for co-located (M = 2.7 (0.1)) than for virtual co-play (M = 2.4 (0.1); p=.01); the contrast between mediated (M = 2.5 (0.1)) and co-located co-play approached significance (p=.08).

Findings of Player Performance showed significant main effects on Revised-Flow ($F(1,117.1)$ = 12.38, p<.001, R^2=.16) and Performance Improvement Drive ($F(1,114.9)$ = 3.80, p=.05, R^2=.02), see Figure 4b. Winners (M = 2.8 (0.1)) reported more flow than losers (M = 2.3 (0.1)). In contrast, winners (M = 3.3 (0.1)) reported a

Table 6. Schematic overview of the results of Co-Player Presence on the player involvement related components

	GEQ-Bor.	GEQ-Flow	GEQ-Imm.	Rev-Flow	PID
F-statistic	3.46	.96	3.33	3.86	1.36
p-value	**.04**	.39	**.04**	**.03**	.26
R-squared	.05	-.07	.17	.15	-.07
Denominator df	80.5	79.7	79.9	80.6	80.8
Numerator df	2	2	2	2	2

Figure 4. (a) Player Involvement as a function of Co-Player Presence, (b) Player Involvement as a function of Player Performance (1 = not at all, 5 = extremely; SE indicated in graph).

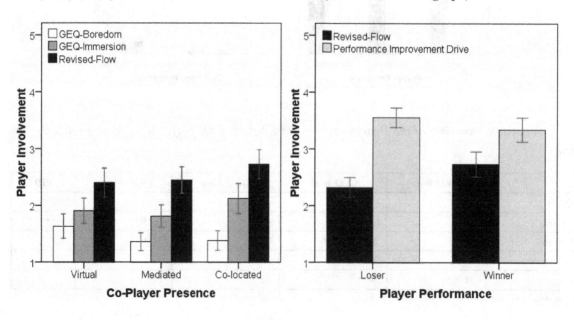

lower drive to improve their performance than losers ($M = 3.6$ (0.1)).

Mediation Analyses

The results on player experience indicated significant effects of Co-Player Presence on three player involvement scales; the analyses on the SPGQ scales had already indicated that social presence increased from the virtual to the co-located setting. To test whether these effects of Co-Player Presence on player involvement were mediated by the subjective sense of social presence of the co-player, the Linear Mixed Model Analyses on the player involvement scales were repeated with SPGQ-PIE, SPGQ-BE and SPGQ-Jealousy (i.e. Social Presence) as covariates. In the case of mediation, the covariate(s) should become significant, and the effects of Co-Player Presence on player involvement should disappear (Baron & Kenny, 1986).

The main effects in Co-Player Presence on the involvement related scales disappeared or were reduced due to the inclusion of the SPGQ-Jealousy scale as a covariate (see Table 7). Only for GEQ-Immersion, the effect of Co-Player Presence approached significance. SPGQ-Jealousy became highly significant after the mediation analyses with GEQ-Boredom ($p=.01$), GEQ-Immersion ($p<.001$), and Revised-Flow ($p<.001$).

These results confirm that social presence mediates the effects of Co-Player Presence on player involvement. An additional Sobel test (1982; 1986) was performed to check for any Type 1 and Type 2 errors based on a bootstrapping procedure (Preacher & Hayes, 2004). Again these results confirmed mediation, as the Sobel test revealed that mediation by SPGQ-Jealousy was significant for GEQ-Boredom ($z = 2.14$, $p=.03$), GEQ-Immersion ($z = 2.34$, $p=.02$), and Revised-Flow ($z = 2.01$, $p=.04$). These findings indicate

that indeed the differences between the three settings of Co-Player Presence are fully accounted for by the subjective sense of social presence, in particular of the jealousy subscale for involvement related scales.

DISCUSSION

To test whether co-players influence player involvement, we performed an empirical study exploring the effect of co-player presence on player experience in a competitive setting. Furthermore, differences in winning vs. losing were accounted for, as previous work had indicated that these factors influence player experience as well. In contrast to what some scholars have suggested in the literature (e.g., Sweetser & Wyeth, 2005) the current study showed that the presence of co-players does not present a threat to game involvement. The results indicated that although it was hypothesized that others might interrupt a player's attention to the game, players' involvement and engagement in WoodPong was not reduced by others' presence. In fact, some indicators of involvement even showed modest improvements with more social settings.

Table 7. Schematic overview of the results for the mediation analysis with social presence for the player involvement related components

	GEQ-Bor.	GEQ-Imm.	Rev-Flow
F-statistic	1.58	2.93	.30
p-value	.21	.06	.74
R-squared	-.06	.13	-.06
Denominator df	89.7	78.5	83.8
Numerator df	2	2	2
SPGQ-PIE	-	-	-
SPGQ-BE	-	-	-
SPGQ-Jeal.	*	**	**

*$p<.05$; **$p<.001$

Manipulation of Social Setting

A manipulation check indicated that social presence increased for each subsequent setting; in virtual co-play settings co-player presence was experienced the least and in co-located co-play social presence experience was strongest, with intermediate scores for the mediated co-play setting. This was reflected in all social presence subscales: psychological involvement, behavioral engagement and jealousy. We can therefore conclude that the manipulation in social presence was successful: in the mediated and even more so in the co-located co-play setting, players were more aware of each other, felt more connected to each other, and their in-game actions depended more on the other.

Player Involvement

In spite of their increased awareness of the other player, players' involvement in the game was not reduced in the two (human) co-play settings. On the contrary, players even scored higher levels of imaginative immersion and flow (revised-flow scale), and reported less boredom; the other scales (GEQ-flow and performance improvement drive) showed no differences and were insensitive to varying social settings. Immersion and flow were higher in the co-located setting than the other two settings. This indicates that "the story of the game" (which in WoodPong is nothing more than the chronological course of the scores) was experienced as more involving when both competitors could see and hear each other. Co-located play also enabled discussions of in-game moments, potentially drawing both players into the game even more. The level of flow players experienced did not drop as Sweetser and Wyeth (2005) hypothesized. If anything, gamers came closer to Csikszentmihalyi's (1975; 1988) optimal experience, in spite of their increased awareness of the other, residing in 'the real world'. Apparently the presence of the other player does not

break the spell of the game, or prevent them from entering 'the zone'. The boredom players experienced was higher in the virtual play setting than in both social settings. Perhaps competing with a non-human entity was perceived as less meaningful or challenging than competing with a virtual opponent. Considering the low scores on boredom overall, it can be concluded that the whole activity of playing digital games generally was engaging.

Mediation analyses revealed that the increase in involvement also could be attributed to the subjective sense of social presence induced in the settings. These outcomes support the view that social presence is a good discriminator for social play settings. Interestingly, results from the analyses on enjoyment scales are somehow different with those on involvement related scales (see Gajadhar et al., 2008a). First of all, for player enjoyment related scales, the empathy component of social presence mediated the effects of the co-player manipulation. Digital play got more enjoyable as the sense of being with and feeling empathy towards the co-player increased. However, for player involvement the jealousy component of the social presence scale emerged as mediator of co-player manipulations. Players seemed to get more focused in the activity as the presence of the human opponent became more succinct and elicited stronger feelings of rivalry. These empirical findings support findings from Gajadhar and colleagues (2009a) in that digital gaming with others is a mix of experiencing social fun and social competition. Second, the effects on player involvement scales were substantially smaller than those reported for enjoyment, especially for positive affect. We speculate that this distinction can result from differences in the type of cues that are signaled to display enjoyment in co-located settings. Observations during a pilot study (Gajadhar, de Kort & IJsselsteijn, 2009b), suggest that enjoyment is often signaled by both verbal (e.g., laughing, talking) and nonverbal (e.g., smiling, hand gestures) cues, while involvement is only signaled by nonverbal cues (e.g., leaning forward towards screen, eyes on screen) that are harder to detect for co-players in digital gaming. After all, players look towards the screen during games rather than towards each other (Gajadhar et al., 2009b). The current study was not designed to investigate verbal and non-verbal cues and their role in increasing social presence. In a follow-up study we will explore such cues in greater depth across different co-play settings.

Players' performance impacted two indicators of involvement. Flow (revised-flow scale) was higher among winning participants, whereas their drive towards performance improvement was lower. Since this factor was created post-hoc (winning or losing was not manipulated but measured), the causality remains unclear. It does however seem likely that those players who lost focused on the fact that they wanted to become better at playing, whereas those who won felt more in control and on top of the situation. The findings do indicate that these indicators tap into different experiences.

Limitations

The results presented here are based on the experiences in one specific digital game. This particular game belongs to the class of classic arcade games, and is a very early example of games in the sports genre. Choosing a game from a different genre – such as First Person Shooter (FPS), adventure, role playing - most likely would have influenced our results based on other features such as a higher level of violence, the ability to play with more than 2 co-players, or a captivating and highly immersive narrative. Also, we have only considered competitive playing modes. Experiences of social presence may well differ for collaborative playing modes and as a result influence player experience differently. However, results in the current empirical study are supported by earlier findings in a survey study, in which a range of game genres and playing modes were considered

(IJsselsteijn et al., in preparation). We therefore expect that our results may be influenced by differences in genres and roles of the co-player, however not in a way that will violate our main conclusions. Nevertheless, we have conducted additional studies that employ a different game than WoodPong, and provide findings for competitive and collaborative play modes as well (Gajadhar et al., 2009b; Gajadhar, 2010).

In addition, we have found that jealousy mediates feelings of involvement. However, in contrast to the other components of social presence, jealousy consisted of a single item since other items – that were not exclusively targeting negative feelings – were excluded. We acknowledge the concern for discussing these results of jealousy and aim in future studies to include more items that measure jealousy (or better; that measure negative feelings).

CONCLUSION

The aim of our research was to understand the influence of social context on player experience, in particular on experience components related to involvement or the attentional pull of the game. Earlier analyses had demonstrated that player enjoyment - a second class of player experiences - increased with increasing social richness of the play setting. Moreover, this effect was mediated by the players' experienced social presence, in other words, their awareness of and connectedness to the other (Gajadhar et al., 2008a). In the present analyses we investigated whether similar effects would occur for players' involvement in games.

To our best knowledge, writings on this matter have mostly been conceptual or theoretical. Some speculated that other persons present would, as any other external stimuli, negatively affect a player's concentration on and engagement in a game. On the other hand, others reflected on the popularity of multi-player games and the positive effects of co-players on game enjoyment and conjectured similar paths for player involvement. These contradictions perhaps explain why scholars have been hesitant to adopt social components in their player experience models.

From our results we can conclude that player involvement is not necessarily impaired by others present. If anything, co-players contributed to the players' involvement in the game. The measurements of social presence furthermore indicate that players did not forget or ignore their competitors: they became more aware of them and felt more connected to them. These findings imply that co-players in fact become part of the game or game world and should not be considered external distracters.

The effects of social setting on player involvement do differ from those on player enjoyment. For this latter class of experiences, effects of social setting were stronger and mediated by more positive feelings that induce social presence. We argue that models of player experience that do not take the social play setting into account are clearly incomplete. Furthermore, we propose that different relationships exist between this variable and two related, yet different classes of player experience: involvement and enjoyment. These classes therefore deserve different positions in such a model.

ACKNOWLEDGMENT

The author thanks Martin Boschman for the assistance with the laboratory setups. Support from the European Games@Large and FUGA project is gratefully acknowledged.

REFERENCES

Baumeister, R. F., & Leary, M. R. (1995). The need to belong: Desire for interpersonal attachments as a fundamental human motivation. *Psychological Bulletin, 117*(3), 497–529. doi:10.1037/0033-2909.117.3.497

Biocca, F., Harms, C., & Burgoon, J. K. (2003). Criteria for a theory and measure of social presence. *Presence (Cambridge, Mass.), 12*(5), 456–480. doi:10.1162/105474603322761270

Brown, E., & Cairns, P. (2004). *A grounded investigation of game immersion*. ACM CHI 2004, (pp. 1297-1300). Retrieved November 11, 2008, from http://complexworld.pbwiki.com/f/Brown+and+Cairns+(2004).pdf

Calleja, G. (2007). Digital game involvement: A conceptual model. *Games and Culture, 2*, 236–260. doi:10.1177/1555412007306206

Carver, C. S., & Scheier, M. F. (1981). The self attention-induced feedback loop and social facilitation. *Journal of Experimental Social Psychology, 17*, 545–568. doi:10.1016/0022-1031(81)90039-1

Chartrand, T. L., & Bargh, J. A. (1999). The chameleon effect: The perception-behavior link and social interaction. *Journal of Personality and Social Psychology, 76*(6), 893–910. doi:10.1037/0022-3514.76.6.893

Cottrell, N. B. (1972). Social facilitation. In McClintock, C. G. (Ed.), *Experimental social psychology* (pp. 185–235). New York, NY: Holt, Rinehart & Winston.

Csikszentmihalyi, I., & Csikszentmihalyi, M. (1988). *Optimal experience: Psychological studies of flow in consciousness*. New York, NY: Cambridge University Press.

Csikszentmihalyi, M. (1975). *Beyond boredom and anxiety*. San Francisco, CA: Jossey-Bass.

de Kort, Y. A. W., & IJsselsteijn, W. A. (2008). People, places and play: A research framework for digital game experience in a socio-spatial context. *ACM Computers in Entertainment, 6*(2), Article No. 18.

de Kort, Y. A. W., IJsselsteijn, W. A., & Poels, K. (2007). Digital games as social presence technology: Development of the social presence questionnaire (SPGQ). *Proceedings of Presence 2007 Conference*, October 25-27, Barcelona.

Ermi, L., & Mäyrä, F. (2005). Fundamental components of the gameplay experience: Analysing immersion. In S. de Castell & J. Jenson (Eds.), *Changing views: Worlds in play* (pp. 15-27). Retrieved November 11, 2008, from http://www.uta.fi/~tlilma/gameplay_experience.pdf

Gajadhar, B. J. (2010). *See no rival, hear no rival.* Presented at the 4th meeting of the Flemish Chapter of the Digital Game Research Association (Ghent, Belgium, June 4th 2010). Abstract in proceedings.

Gajadhar, B. J., de Kort, Y. A. W., & IJsselsteijn, W. A. (2008a). Shared fun is doubled fun: Player enjoyment as a function of social setting. In Markopoulos, P., de Ruyter, B., IJsselsteijn, W., & Rowland, D. (Eds.), *Fun and games* (pp. 106–117). New York, NY: Springer. doi:10.1007/978-3-540-88322-7_11

Gajadhar, B. J., de Kort, Y. A. W., & IJsselsteijn, W. A. (2008b). *Influence of social setting on player experience of digital games*. Works in progress paper CHI'08 Extended Abstracts, April 5-10, Florence, Italy. (ACM 978-1-60558-012-8/08/04).

Gajadhar, B. J., de Kort, Y. A. W., & IJsselsteijn, W. A. (2009b). See no rival, hear no rival: The role of social cues in digital game settings. *Proceedings of CHI Nederland 2009*, (pp. 25-31). June 11, Leiden, the Netherlands.

Gajadhar, B. J., de Kort, Y. A. W., IJsselsteijn, W. A., & Poels, K. (2009a). Where everybody knows your game: The appeal and function of game cafés in Western Europe. *Proceedings of ACE 2009*, (pp. 28-35). October 29-31, Athens, Greece.

Goldstein, J. (2007). Games and society: The engine of digital lifestyle. *Proceedings of ISFE Expert 2007 Conference*, (pp 24–28). June 26&27, Brussels.

Hatfield, E., Cacioppo, J. T., & Rapson, R. L. (1992). Primitive emotional contagion. In Clark, M. S. (Ed.), *Emotion and social behavior* (pp. 151–177). Thousand Oaks, CA: Sage.

IJsselsteijn, W. A., de Kort, Y. A. W. & Poels, K. (forthcoming). *The game experience questionnaire: Development of a self-report measure to assess the psychological impact of digital games.*

Jansz, J., & Martens, L. (2005). Gaming at a LAN event: The social context of playing video games. *New Media & Society, 7*, 333–355. doi:10.1177/1461444805052280

Kenny, D. A., Kashy, D. A., & Cook, W. L. (2006). *Dyadic data analysis*. New York, NY: Guilford Press.

Kimble, C. R., & Rezabek, J. (1992). Playing games before an audience: Social facilitation or choking. *Social Behavior and Personality: An International Journal, 20*(2), 115–120. doi:10.2224/sbp.1992.20.2.115

Lim, S., & Reeves, B. (2006). *Responses to interactive game characters controlled by a computer versus other players*. International Communication Association Conference, San Francisco, CA, USA.

McKenna, K., & Lee, S. (1995). *A love affair with MUDs: Flow and social interaction in multi-user dungeons*. International Communication Association Conference, Chicago, IL, USA. Retrieved June 6th, 2008, from http://fragment.nl/mirror/various/McKenna_et_al.nd.A_love_affair_with_muds.html

Moreland, R. L., & Zajonc, R. B. (1982). Exposure effects in person perception: Familiarity, similarity and attraction. *Journal of Experimental Social Psychology, 18*, 395–415. doi:10.1016/0022-1031(82)90062-2

Nielsen Interactive Entertainment. (2005). *Video gamers in Europe - 2005. Research Report Prepared for the Interactive Software Federation of Europe*. ISFE.

Poels, K., de Kort, Y. A. W., & IJsselsteijn, W. A. (2007). It is always a lot of fun! Exploring dimensions of digital game experience using focus group methodology. *Proceedings of Futureplay 2007 Conference*, (pp. 83-89). Toronto, Canada.

Preacher, K. J., & Hayes, A. F. (2004). SPSS and SAS procedures for estimating indirect effects in simple mediation models. *Behavior Research Methods, Instruments, & Computers, 36*(4), 717–731. doi:10.3758/BF03206553

Raghunathan, R., & Corfman, K. (2006). Is happiness shared doubled and sadness shared halved? Social influence on enjoyment of hedonic experiences. *JMR, Journal of Marketing Research, 43*(August), 386–394. doi:10.1509/jmkr.43.3.386

Ravaja, N. (2009). The psychophysiology of digital gaming: The effect of a non co-located opponent. *Media Psychology, 12*, 268–294. doi:10.1080/15213260903052240

Ravaja, N., Saari, T., Turpeinen, M., Laarni, J., Slaminen, M., & Kivikangas, M. (2006). Spatial presence and emotions during video game playing: Does it matter with whom you play? *Presence (Cambridge, Mass.), 15*, 381–392. doi:10.1162/pres.15.4.381

Resinari, R. (2007). *WoodPong*. DoubleR Software.

Sobel, M. E. (1982). Asymptotic confidence intervals for indirect effects in structural equation models. In Leinhardt, S. (Ed.), *Sociological methodology* (pp. 290–312). Washington, DC: American Sociological Association.

Sobel, M. E. (1986). Some new results on indirect effects and their standard errors in covariance structure models. In Tuma, N. (Ed.), *Sociological methodology* (pp. 159–186). Washington, DC: American Sociological Association.

Sweetser, P., & Wyeth, P. (2005). GameFlow: A model for evaluating player enjoyment in games. *ACM Computers in Entertainment, 3*, Article 3A.

Tan, E. S., & Jansz, J. (2008). The game experience. In Schifferstein, H. N., & Hekkert, P. P. (Eds.), *Product experience*. San Diego, CA: Elsevier. doi:10.1016/B978-008045089-6.50026-5

Vallius, L., Manninen, T., & Kujanpää, T. (2006). Sharing experiences - Co-experiencing three experimental collaborative computer games. *Proceedings of Futureplay 2006 Conference*, London, Ontario, Canada.

Vorderer, P., Hartmann, T., & Klimmt, C. (2003). Explaining the enjoyment of playing video games: The role of competition. In *Proceedings of 2nd International Conference on Entertainment Computing, ICEC 2003*, ACM Digital Library.

Zajonc, R. B. (1980). Compresence. In Paulus, P. B. (Ed.), *Psychology of group influence* (pp. 35–60). Hillsdale, NJ: Erlbaum.

Chapter 10
Game–Based Representations as Cues for Collaboration and Learning

Matthew J. Sharritt
University of Hawai'i at Manoa, USA

Daniel D. Suthers
University of Hawai'i at Manoa, USA

ABSTRACT

Literature suggests that games can support learning in schools by enabling creative problem solving, allowing dynamic resource allocation, providing a motivating, immersive activity, and supporting explorations of identity. A descriptive, inductive study was carried out to identify how high school students make use of the video game interface and its representations. Results demonstrate that specific cues direct attention, helping to focus efforts on new or underutilized game tasks. In addition, consistent and well-organized visualizations encourage learning and collaboration among students by providing shared referential resources and scaffolding coordinated sequences of problem solving acts during gameplay. Conversely, when affordances are inconsistently represented, students' focus can shift from problem solving at the goal level (game strategy, etc.) to problem solving at the game interface level (which is frustrating their goals). In general, the design of game representations and behaviors can help guide or hinder student learning.

INTRODUCTION

Squire (2005) suggests that games provide a rich learning context, in which gamer strategizing and the management of complex problems can foster creative thinking skills and demonstrate to players how their decisions have dynamic outcomes. According to Squire (2005), "it seems the important question is not can games be used to support learning, but how" (p. 1). In this chapter, we provide a description of how high school students make use of video game interfaces while engaged in playing commercial video games in a school setting (*Civilization IV, RollerCoaster Tycoon 3*, and *Making History: The Calm & the Storm*). This study focused on ways that the designed

DOI: 10.4018/978-1-60960-565-0.ch010

visualizations and behaviors of game interfaces guide player activity and collaboration, creating opportunities for learning; and how those player interactions in turn influence player activity to support learning. Concepts from previous work on representational guidance (Suthers, 2001; Suthers & Hundhausen, 2003) were applied to video game interfaces to provide a description of how students collaboratively made use of the game interface for learning. A qualitative, inductive case study drawing on ethnomethodology (Garfinkel, 1967; Koschmann, Stahl & Zemel, 2005) and grounded theory (Glaser & Strauss, 1967; Charmaz, 2006) was conducted to provide a descriptive analysis of the acts through which participants used the video game interface to support learning and collaboration in an educational setting. Results revealed patterns in collaborative activity among students, and revealed ways in which the video game representations guided student learning and collaboration.

This article begins with a brief discussion of the analytic and methodological foundations of the work. Then the study context and data collection methods are described. The remainder of the chapter identifies several findings and provides examples of the data on which these findings were based

BACKGROUND

Research on gaming and education is diverse, examining for example: the adoption (or lack thereof) and impact of games in the classroom (Annetta et al., 2006; Sandford, Ulicsak, Facer & Rudd, 2006; Squire, 2005), the educational value of specific games (Murray, Mokros, & Rubin, 1998), gender and gaming (Cassell & Jenkings, 1998), social behavior in massively multiplayer games (Ducheneaut, Yee, Nickell & Moore, 2006; Nardi & Harris, 2006; Sherlock, 2007), embodied interaction in games as virtual environments (Moore, Ducheneaut & Nickell, 2007), design frameworks

(Winn, 2008), and evaluation frameworks (Sharritt, 2010c). Gee (2003) and Shaffer & Gee (2006) provide comprehensive yet accessible accounts of the learning potential of games. The present research views games from a different perspective, taking a close examination of the relationship between the designed features of games and the behavior of collaborating gamers. The approach is inspired originally by Collins & Ferguson's (1993) concept of "epistemic forms" that guide different inquiry practices, and was developed further by Suthers (Suthers, 2001; Suthers & Hundhausen, 2003) into the concept of "representational guidance." Apart from this theoretical motivation, the present work remained deliberately open on what constitutes a learning episode, adopting methods that allow for emergence of understanding what is happening in game play. We summarize these theoretical and methodological influences below.

Theoretical Motivations

The fundamental concept of representational guidance is that the perceived affordances of a representational tool will influence the actions considered and taken by users of that tool. Affordances are potentials for action that reside in the *relationship* between an actor (in this study, students) and an object (elements of the video game interface and peers). It follows that the same object might offer different affordances for different actors. As described in Heeter (2000), "A child might scan a kitchen and notice playthings and treats, a non-cook might notice possibilities for eating quickly -- a microwave, refrigerator, and bag of potato chips, while a chef would see myriad tools and ingredients". Originally, affordances were described as potentials for action by an animal in its environment, as part of an ecological theory of perception (Gibson, 1977, 1979). Later, the concept was adapted by the field of human-computer interaction, which focused primarily on *perceived* affordances (Norman, 1988).

Perceived affordances provide a useful perspective on how game features can influence activity within the game. Suthers (2001) outlined two major sources of influence: the constraints and salience provided by action-affording representations in a software environment. First, the environment constrains the expressive acts that are possible, as the representational notation offers a (deliberately) limited set of objects and potential actions (Stenning & Oberlander, 1995). Similarly, games might guide action by providing a constrained set of action potentials. Second, representational artifacts constructed in a visual notation make particular aspects and interpretations of the represented information prominent, possibly while hiding others (Larkin & Simon, 1987; Sharritt, 2010a). Similarly, games might aid gamers by making certain aspects of the game state salient. In addition, as Oliver and Pelletier (2005) point out, "it may be important to consider how representational cues can be used to indicate to the player that distinct objects are of the same type (obey the same game rules) so that they will be able to transfer strategies learnt for one class of object to other related instances" (p. 12).

Suthers & Hundhausen (2003) were interested in how representational guidance might apply to collaborative activity, and identified three ways in which representations influence collaboration beyond their effects on individuals (later expanded to seven influences by Suthers, 2006). First, when two persons need to decide how to act jointly on an environment, the visible potentials for action (perceived affordances) may influence the options that are considered and negotiated: there are *negotiation potentials*. Second, representations that result from participants' negotiation and coordinated action hold meanings for those participants that may not be apparent to others not involved in their production. These meanings may be invoked by reference (e.g., by deixis or pointing) to appropriate elements of the representation: they are private *referential resources*. Third, the orientation of each participation towards the current environ-

ment (e.g., their physical orientation or their locus of activity) provides clues to the other participants concerning that actor's attentional and intentional state: the representations support *implicit awareness*. Suthers and Hundhausen (2003) compared differences in collaborative discourse between participants using software tools supporting the same task but through different notations (text, graph, and matrix-based). Their results demonstrate "that the type of representations that learners use in collaborative investigations will impact the focus of their discourse" (Suthers & Hundhausen, 2003, p. 202). Similarly, the designed visual and behavioral features of games, particularly the ways in which they make affordances and game state visible, can influence the interaction between gamers. The present study examines how video games can mediate the collaborative interactions of students, and how particular kinds of collaborative interactions are promoted by the game affordances.

Methodological Influences

Although the study was initiated under the theoretical orientation just discussed, it was conducted in a manner to be open to discovery of what students do with games and indeed, what constitutes learning with games. Ethnomethodological principles (Garfinkel, 1967; Sharritt, 2010b) inspired this open-ended, bottom-up approach of the study. Our analysis integrated methods of ethnomethodology and grounded theory (a method of constructing hypotheses from data) in order to identify patterns in the data and to generalize other situations (Glaser & Strauss, 1967; Charmaz, 2006).

Clayman and Maynard (1995) describe the ethnomethodological perspective as examining "the nature and origins of social order" by rejecting top-down theories that "attempt to explain social order in terms of cultural or social structural phenomena which are conceived as standing outside of the flow of events in everyday life" (p. 2). Ethnomethodology takes a "thoroughly 'bottom-up' approach" and "seeks to recover social organization as an emergent achievement that results from the concerted efforts of societal members acting within local situations." (Clayman & Maynard, 1995, p. 2). Koschmann, Stahl, and Zemel (2005) present an updated and concise application of Garfinkel's policies for the purpose of video analysis. In this study, several of these policies influenced our method and data analysis. For instance, a-priori definitions of learning were avoided in order to follow the ethnomethodological principle of *relevance*, which requires that explanatory constructs be relevant to (or compatible with) participants' own accounts of their activity, rather than imposed by the analyst. The policies of *contingently-achieved accomplishment* and *indexicality* describe how the process of ongoing activity by group members are contextually embedded. Actions are sequential and are both context-building and context-shaped, serving to construct social order. Data analysis (of videotaped student game play, and described in detail in the method section) was influenced by this principle as it suggested that analysis should shed light on how group members build context and accomplish learning through their activity (Koschmann, Zemel, et al., 2005).

Grounded theory is a sociological method that concerns itself with the "discovery of theory from data" that is not "based on a preconceived theoretical framework" (Glaser & Strauss, 1967, p. 45). This idea is referred to as *emergence*, as theories emerge from the data. Glaser and Strauss describe grounded theory as a "general method of comparative analysis" (p. 1). The researcher makes constant comparisons of ideas while studying the data: looking for themes or "theoretical categories" and constantly reevaluating those categories (taking advantage of replication to test those ideas). A major premise of grounded theory is that the human brain is a superb pattern recognizer and hence a useful analytic instrument for detecting regularities. Repeated review of data reveals regularities that might not

be apparent at first, including regularities that would be missed if investigation were limited to coding criteria determined in advance (an option that is also discouraged by ethnomethodology's principle of relevance). For the purposes of this study, grounded theory provided a methodological framework to bridge between ethnomethodology (which resists generalization) and our desire to seek inductive generalizations.

Method

Three video games were selected for study and are discussed below. Games were played collaboratively by dyads (two students) using a single computer. For each of the games, two dyads situated side by side played the game (four students playing each game; two per computer). Each student played only one of the games. Students played their respective game over four study periods of approximately 50 minutes each in a school setting. A complete video record was made of the game play, with a video camera filming each dyad and their computer screen. The logic of the study is the inverse of an experiment: rather than holding all but one variable constant to see what co-varies with that variable, the study allows many variables to change (the games and the participants) to identify what stays constant (recurring patterns of behavior) that can be postulated as inductive generalizations.

School and Student Selection

Teachers at two high schools assisted the researcher in identifying male and female students with various levels of gaming experience. Students were chosen based on their willingness to participate and the willingness of their parents. Different students were chosen to play different games: *RollerCoaster Tycoon 3* involved students from a related business course (Advanced Marketing), while *Making History* and *Civilization IV* involved teachers and students who had taken corresponding history classes. Both student assent and parent consent were obtained.

The design of the study involved four students per game, playing in pairs. Literature suggests that group phenomena require three or more participants (Wiley & Jensen, 2006). Additionally, learning may also result from between-dyad as well as within-dyad interaction (similar to what occurs in classrooms). While it is difficult to seat two students per computer, the choice was made to videotape gameplay in dyads in order to elicit both collaborative and competitive behaviors among students, and to record the increased verbosity of students who are engaged in an activity together. As described in Linn & Burbules (1991), collaborative play can result in situations where students must verbalize and discuss their beliefs, which can lead to more frequent challenges by peers and teachers. This interaction can in turn lead to learning through cognitive dissonance (Festinger, 1957), socio-cognitive conflict (Doise & Mungy, 1984), or other mechanisms of collaborative learning (Dillenbourg, Baker, Blayne & O'Malley, 1996; Sharritt, 2010c; Slavin, 1990). Collaborative play can also lead to a significant increase in physiological arousal as well as a sense of presence and identification in non-violent games (Lim & Lee, 2007). In this study, two dyads were used so that between-dyad collaboration could be recorded (similar to what might occur upon implementation of games into curricula when classrooms of students are involved).

In order to avoid classroom disruption and coordination problems, participating teachers were consulted as to when it was most convenient for their students to participate in the research. In all cases, students were asked to participate during a study period that corresponded to a time period that their teacher was not scheduled to teach a class. This helped avoid disruptions to the teacher's scheduling of topics and information presentation, as well as coordination problems caused by attempting to move all of their students into a computer lab to play a game.

Game Selection

Preference was given to games containing quality graphics, gameplay and control, with a well-designed and understandable game interface that would be expected in most contemporary games and contained a blend of entertainment and educational content on subjects that were highly correlated with subjects of formal schooling. Games were sought that involved moderate levels of strategy development to encourage immersion and collaborative game play. Games with low computer hardware requirements were sought, since schools are unlikely to have the latest processors and 3D video hardware. Games containing low levels of violence, foul language, or sexually themed content were chosen (ESRB rating of 'E' for everyone, age 10+). Based on these criteria, the games in Figure 1 were chosen.

Three games were strategically chosen in order to generalize among differing game subjects and types. Both *RollerCoaster Tycoon 3* and *Civilization IV* are COTS (Commercial-off-the-shelf games, created by large game corporations), while *Making History: The Calm & the Storm* was developed for educational use. Both *Making History* and *Civilization IV* are historically-based games (*Making History* focuses on World War II, while *Civilization IV* focuses on world history), and can be applied in world history or 20th century history classes. In contrast, *RollerCoaster Tycoon 3* is applicable to business courses such as Economics or Marketing since it enables the creation of products and services, and the managing of finances (such as balancing supply and demand). Additionally, the three games varied in complexity, with *Civilization IV* being the most complex game of the three. This allowed generalizations to be made across COTS and games designed for educational use, between games of varying complexity, and between subjects (history vs. business) during analysis.

Figure 1. List of games chosen for study

Game:	Brief Description:	Game web site:
RollerCoaster Tycoon 3 (Atari) ESRB rating: E (Everyone)	Game player can build a virtual theme park; building rides and managing attractions within the park	http://www.rollercoaster tycoon.com
Making History: The Calm & the Storm (Muzzy Lane) ESRB rating: E (Everyone)	Game player takes the role of a country in World War II and can play scenarios from that country; managing resources, etc.	http://making-history.com /products/mh
Sid Meier's Civilization IV (2K Games) ESRB rating: E 10+ (Everyone 10 and up)	Game player can play an ancient civilization (Greeks, Romans, etc) and make dynamic decisions affecting their success compared to other civilizations	http://www.2kgames.com /civ4/

Data Gathering and Procedure

As displayed in Figure 2, the primary data-gathering tool was a widescreen video camera to partially capture the heads and gestures of participants as well as the computer screen. Clip-on microphones were wired into the left and right channels of the video camera for quality audio recording of dialogue. The configuration in Figure 2 was replicated for each of the two dyads in each gaming session.

Each of the three games mentioned were played over the course of four full school periods. Average class periods were approximately 45-50 minutes, providing a total of approximately three hours of gameplay per dyad (each dyad playing one game). Over the course of the four days, the majority of student dyads finished their games or chose to restart from the beginning each day; however, one of the dyads playing *Civilization IV* played the same scenario throughout (saved their game and continued the next day).

Analysis

The videos were imported into the Transana™ system. Transana enables remote access to a shared analytic database (the authors were not co-located). Transana supports Jeffersonian transcript notation,

a notational system developed in the Conversation Analysis community for the annotation of transcripts to convey differences in intonation or speed, pauses, overlapping speech, and non-verbal behavior (Jefferson, 1984). Analysis followed a hybrid qualitative research strategy that was initially data driven and inductive, but then brought in theory for specific purposes (described further in Sharritt, 2010b). The study adopted methods from grounded theory (described previously) to identify and abstract patterns in the data.

Data analysis was conducted in two phases. *Phase I* of analysis identified learning episodes, and then identified patterns among these episodes through the constant comparison and iterative sampling of episodes (Charmaz, 2006). In order to remain open to potential forms of learning through gaming, learning was defined as "a change in behavior as a result of experience". Results of Phase I are described in Sharritt (2008), which discusses the particular properties of learning episodes uncovered by this open-ended stance to learning. Specifically, learning episodes occurred at different granularities, including short episodes, identifiable sequences of short episodes, and gradual trends over time. Learning appeared at several levels: learning the physical computer interface, learning to use the game interface (including icons, objects, etc., and their corre-

Figure 2. Data gathering of collaborative gameplay

sponding functionality), and learning advanced strategies required to win the game. Although there was a progression through the levels of learning, with more emphasis on the lower levels early in gameplay, all three levels appeared through gameplay (i.e., strategy was exhibited from the beginning). However, advanced strategies were typically on a larger scale, and examined what was being accomplished as a whole during game play (such as motivations to play). Finally, learning often appeared to be triggered by social peers or by particular game features. *Phase II* of analysis, results of which are partially described in this chapter (other results in Sharritt, 2010a; Sharritt, 2010c), examined patterns of interaction (Jordan & Henderson, 1995) and the sequential use of affordances for each instance of learning (the same set analyzed in Phase I). Iteration through focused coding helped in sorting and saturating theoretical categories to create hypotheses based on patterns in the video.

Significant data reduction was required since approximately 24 hours of video were gathered. The videos contained many instances of learn-

ing since students were constantly exhibiting behavior changes through game play. Learning episodes that exhibited recurring patterns were selected by repeatedly reviewing the video data (see prior discussion of grounded theory). The most frequently occurring patterns of behavior change were tagged by the first author, and reviewed by the second author before episodes were selected by consensus for further analysis. Approximately 100 clips qualified, averaging a few minutes each. This process of selection of the most frequently occurring learning patterns possibly biases and limits the scope of findings, but was necessary in order to perform a deep, descriptive investigation of the learning episodes.

Results

We begin by describing how game cues can suggest and lead to the pursuit of related action, as game player activity was often influenced by game messages, which resulted in a corresponding goal selection. Following, social affordances are described as a means by which players can

Figure 3. Avatar interaction in Civilization IV

reference in-game objects, aiding them in goal selection. Next, game behaviors and rules which can limit available action potentials at each step are described, thus providing salience and easing appropriation by game players. Consistent rules in behavior allowed students to focus on game play and strategies, rather than focusing on memorizing particular sequences of action. Consistent organization, visualizations, and behaviors also assist learning by creating the affordance of discussion among peers, as in-game objects can be easily referenced by peers.

Game Cues Triggering Related Actions

Game representations can often suggest and lead to the pursuit of related action by student dyads. An example is found in *Civilization IV*. Diplomacy

with other civilizations is a key aspect that needs to be mastered in *Civilization IV*. Often, the game's computer-run civilizations will address the game players. At first, this often surprises the game players, as they are intently focused on their own civilization and then they are interrupted from what they are doing. Diplomatic interactions take the form of a large pop-up that fills the screen with the avatar of another civilization, as shown in Figure 3.

The Greek civilization's avatar, named 'Alexander', has a classic 'Greek' appearance, with features such as a bronze chest plate and a building in the background resembling the Parthenon. The character is animated and his body language corresponds to his mood (for instance, if bad relations exist, he will appear angry), as shown in Figure 3. Following is this group's first interaction with avatars during the first day of game play:

L: ((Presses 'Enter' on keyboard))

R: ↑What?↑ ((Trader window pops up))

L: 'I am (unclear speech)' ((Reading from pop up window of a leader who has something to say))
He's Greek.

R: He's gonna declare war against us. ((Laughs))

L: ((Laughs)) Oh.

R: We should probably –

L: We should probably go start building an army. ((Uses a shortcut on the keyboard))

The first interaction with a computer avatar shows the dyad reacting to the pop-up in the game. After realizing that other civilizations exist, the suggestion to build an army (and build up defenses) was offered as a future course of action. This is an example of a game cue triggering action. Another example (not illustrated here) is *Civilization IV*'s flashing of the icon of a suggested activity, which we have seen influence student behavior.

The Social Affordance of Collaborative Gaming and persistent Game Objects

Persistent game representations aided discussion and action in both intra-dyadic and inter-dyadic interaction, as they were an unchanging referential resource that students could assume were present in the other pair's screen. Consider the following example, which occurred very early in the first day of one group's play. While game players often initially focus on exploring the game interface, players also form initial strategies and goals. In the following example, at least two factors are in play: first, students made use of the peer dyad for feedback and follow their example; second, they seem to form an early strategy potentially based

on an activity that they assumed they should be fulfilling (possibly they feel they should start wars because they are playing a World War II game). Little direction was given to students as to *why* they were playing the game. Perhaps an involved teacher and curriculum integration would assist in developing early strategies; however, in this study, students developed game strategies on their own. Therefore, those strategies were influenced more by game presentation and feedback. Being presented with a game about World War II, students may have chosen their initial strategies based on their assumption that their activity should be warfare. This presentation may have led them away from other very important game goals such as managing the diplomatic and economic aspects of their country. The following transcript highlights the development of initial strategies by following the example of a peer dyad:

Peer 1: Declare war <on>

Peer 2: Do it (0.5) ha ha declare war.

L: ((Scrolling through map))

Peer 1: OK, we're declaring war on uh (0.5) on Britain here. >READY AND, GO!< We just declared war.

L: How did you [declare war?]

R: [↑How did you declare↑ war?]

Both students appeared interested in the peer dyad's progress and aware of what the other dyad was communicating and doing. Awareness of other games' activities is an affordance of collaborative game play. The dyad responded by questioning the peer dyad. The peer dyad was used as an information source, as a means of checking their own progress, and as an example of potential action (in this case, the dyad copied the peer dyad's strategy). The following transcript illustrates how

Figure 4. Diplomacy menu in Making History: The Calm & the Storm

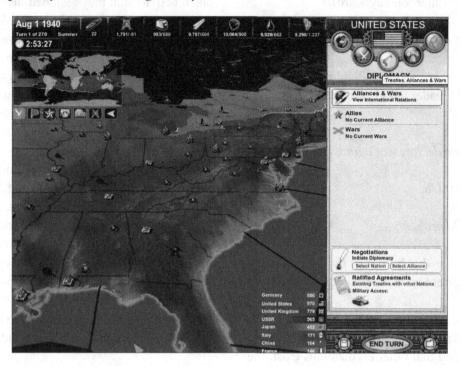

the peer dyad responded with information about how they accomplished declaring war:

Peer 2: No idea.

Peer 1: I don't know, we just clicked [International] =

L: Here you can try. ((Mouse control traded from L to R))

Peer 2: [Click the] middle button with like the piece of paper

L: ((Followed the direction of the peer dyad; clicked on the Diplomacy (middle) button))

Peer 1: = and it gave us the ability to go to war at the very bottom.

Following peer direction, the dyad found the 'Diplomacy' icon in the upper-right portion of the screen (Figure 4). Under the country name (the nation that the dyad was commanding), are five icons. These five icons represent the game's major areas of focus and are persistent icons (they remain there on every screen). Therefore, these icons are a resource for discussion among peers (as shown above). Figure 4 shows the 'Diplomacy' menu:

After gathering information from the peer dyad about how to declare war, the dyad began executing the borrowed strategy:

L: We don't have any °current wars°. ((Reading from Diplomacy Screen)) Oh, let's make some negotiations.

R: Select uh. (.5) Who should we select? ((Clicked on 'Select Nation'))

L: Let's get ↓uhh↓

R: Bhutan? ((Laughs))

L: ((List of countries came up for the dyad to choose from)) *Let's get (.) Germany.*

R: ((The dyad selects Germany, which brings up a new menu of diplomatic options with Germany))

((Mouses over 'Diplomatic Relations' buttons))

The representations provided by the game, as well as the terminology presented by the game, create opportunities for discussion and influence strategic choices (such as when one reads of 'current wars', or suggests 'let's make some negotiations'). By offering lists of "current alliances" and "current wars" as well as "initiate diplomacy", the game interface suggests that these are things one might want to have or do.

The dyad successfully found the diplomacy menu with the help of the peer dyad through the discussion of a persistent resource, leading them to explore diplomatic options. Exploration of the menu continued, looking at options for peace treaties, alliances, and eventually declaring war:

L: *<Propose> (0.5) Should ((Laughs)) we declare war against them?*

R: ((Scrolls over 'Declare War' in the 'Diplomatic' menu choices))

L: *>NO NO, CHINA, CHINA< China, cuz they (.5) we need their oil.*

R: *Where the hell is China?* ((Clicks on 'X' button to return to previous screen))

((Clicks 'Select Nation', then clicks China)) *(1.0) So like, declare war against [China?] ((Laughs))*

((Clicked on 'Declare War' button))

L: *[Yeah I] don't know why. ((Laughs))*

R: *Cuz we need their oil. ((Laughs))*

L: ((Confirmed war against China))

Negotiation occurred, changing the strategy to declare war on China. After clicking 'Select Nation', a list of countries appears in the game. Selection of a nation will change the right side of the screen from the 'Diplomacy' screen to a screen focusing on diplomatic action with only that nation. The dyad selected China and then clicked 'Declare War'.

One of the students decided that China was a good choice for war, justifying his choice of China because of their large supply of oil. While it is unclear where he obtained this information (the game does not present this information), his reasoning for declaring war seems clear: the conquest of countries with oil. Coincidentally, the dyad was playing as the United States, and the dyad invoked a diplomatic strategy recently used by the United States (going to war for control of an oil-producing region).

In the above episode, the information passed between dyads focused on a persistent icon in the game, a property that made it easily discussed among peer dyads. When asking the peer dyad how to declare war, the peer dyad did not respond with a description of the items on the sub-menu under diplomacy (such as 'Select Nation' under 'Negotiations', then picking a country, then clicking 'Declare War'). The peer dyad felt it was sufficient to communicate the first step of choosing the 'Diplomacy' icon (it is more easily discussed as a persistent resource), followed by a summary of what to do ("it gave us the option to go to war at the very bottom"), allowing the peer dyad to figure out the rest of the procedure.

Reducing Affordance, Cognitive Offloading

Game representations can assist in learning to achieve goals. For example, a sequence of actions is required when building rides in *RollerCoaster Tycoon 3*. Each step in the process automatically displays new game representations. Specifically, when building a ride in *RollerCoaster Tycoon 3*, the following process occurs: selecting a ride will automatically begin the procedure of placing the ride; placing the ride will automatically begin the procedure of placing entrances; and placing the entrance will automatically begin the procedure of placing the exit. The design of this forced sequence eased the cognitive load of student game players in building predesigned rides, as they were not required to memorize procedures. Similar to Nielsen's Heuristics (Nielsen, 1994), the game constrains potential actions in ways that improve players' ability to achieve the task. This is a form of "scaffolding" (Collins, Brown & Newman, 1989).

The following sequence of episodes highlights the development of a strategy to make money in *RollerCoaster Tycoon 3*. High school students from a class in advanced marketing played the game. It was apparent from the beginning that students understood their role: to manage a theme park and make it profitable. All of the participants had either played or heard of the game prior to the study. Game players focused on feedback from the game in developing a strategy of building rides and setting prices. The game feedback appeared to be well understood by game players and served the game players well in developing their strategy.

The first episode included some negotiation between students on what rides to build, how to customize them, and how to set the ride price.

L: ↑*Let's just do um*↑ *(.5) [let's do] ((*Pulls up the ride list choices menu))

R: [Water?]

L: ↑*No. Let's do some uh*↑-

R: *Thrill rides, Junior Rides? ((*Reading options from 'Rides' menu))

L: ((*Clicked on 'Junior Rides')) Yeah that's fine. Well there's only the one so*

R: *The Merry-Go-Round ((*Laughs))

L: *Yeah so we'll do that one like [here] ((*Clicks on Merry-Go-Round))

Some negotiation between the dyad occurred in the selection of a ride to build. Water rides, thrill rides, and junior rides are all different categories of rides to build in the theme park. They are represented by the first three icons on the ride sub-menu located on the left side of the screen. The first level of menus (icons) are persistent in *RollerCoaster Tycoon 3*, making them a persistent resource and potential for action; where the second level (sub-menu) of icons appears after clicking on a first-level icon, as seen in Figure 5.

The dyad decided to make a 'Junior Ride' and then selected a 'Merry-Go-Round' from a list of rides that appeared.

Following ride selection, the dyad looked for an area to place the ride. In *RollerCoaster Tycoon 3*, after selecting a ride to build, the ride turns red when placement conflicts with other items on the map (or when not enough money exists), and turns blue when placement is satisfactory. When an object being placed is colored red, clicking the mouse will not result in placement, as placement is not possible. However, if the object is colored blue, clicking the mouse will place the object in the current location, as shown in Figure 6.

Immediately following ride placement, the game prompts for placement of ride entrances and exits, following the red and blue labeling. Attempting to place the entrance in an open location is allowed; however, the entrance will turn red if one attempts to place it over the top of one of the adjacent footpaths (a conflict exists as something is already built in that space).

As can be observed in the figures, each click will result in new menu visualizations popping up on the screen, creating an affordance for their exploration, discussion, and use. Selection of a ride results in the ride appearing in a blue container in the bottom left side of the screen (more ride op-

Figure 5. Ride menu in RollerCoaster Tycoon 3

Figure 6. Proper placement of a ride in RollerCoaster Tycoon 3

tions). After being placed, the ride appeared in the bottom-right corner of the screen (surrounded by icons for ride options), immediately followed by the appearance of a new box during entrance and exit placement (options for the ride entrance and exits). The affordance of sufficient object placement, signified by the blue and red (acceptable vs. unacceptable placement) appeared to be well understood by the students. Following, the dyad placed their ride and its entrance and exit booths:

((Places the Merry-Go-Round in a clearing))

R: [Yeah]

L: Is that cool?

R: Yeah that's good.

L: <And>

R: A path. (.5) What's that? Oh the booth to get in. ((Ride entrance for the Merry-Go-Round appears))

L: ((Placed entrance to get into ride)) °Yeah.°

L: ((Placed ride exit))

R: Exit booth and entering booth. Perfect.

L: ((Clicked on 'Paths'))

((Successfully connected the path from the entrance / exit to the main path)) Cool.

At this point, the ride has been built and an entrance and exit have been placed. The dyad successfully connected the ride's entrance and exit to an adjacent footpath so customers could get to and from the ride. The process of placement appeared to be well understood.

As shown in Figure 7, ride placement will create a ride menu in the lower-right corner of the screen. In the above figure, this appears as a picture of the ride, surrounded by icons that can customize the ride. The game seems to place this object on the screen in order to encourage ride customization. Selecting a ride later in the game (clicking on any ride) will result in a similar representation appearing in the lower-right corner of the screen, with options for customization appearing. This can prompt their exploration, discussion, and use (as revealed in the transcripts). With the ride selected, some of the ride options (icons) are explored by the dyad in the ride menu:

R: [Is there any]

L: [Go on the Merry-Go-Round] Yeah I think people are getting on.

R: [What are] all these things mean? ((Points to the ride options)) Can we change them?

Figure 7. Customizing a ride's colors in RollerCoaster Tycoon 3

L: ((Scrolls over the ride options))

((An explanation of each ride icon appears while scrolling over each icon))

R: *'Test Results, open' Make sure it's open.*

L: *'Not assessed yet.'* ((Reading ride status. Not yet assessed because it hasn't been tested))

R: *Go to.*

L: °*Vehicles.*° ((Clicked on the 'Colors' icon for the vehicles of the ride. A selection of colors popped up))

R: *All the colors of the ride. Oh that's cool.* ((Clicked on the 'Colors' icon))

((Changed the colors of the vehicles))

L: °*That's good.*°

Similar to that displayed in Figure 7, the dyad edited some of the ride's options, accomplished through a blue box extending from the ride menu.

After customizing the colors of the Merry-Go-Round, the dyad looked at other ride options in the ride menu; similarly shown in the lower-right corner of Figure 7.

R: *Go to this one.* ((Point to the 'green flag')) *[Click extension]*

L: *['Guest Thoughts'] none.* ((Scrolls over the ride options))

((Clicked on 'Guest Thoughts' icon))

R: *Make sure it's open.*

L: ((Continues to scroll over ride options menu)) '*Maintenance*'. ((Reads from the pop up of the icon he just scrolled over))

R: *Go the flag*

L: ((Clicks on the flag and changes it to green)) *[It is open.]*

R: *[Then hit] the green. There. Yeah see now it's open.*

By default, new rides are closed for business and students need to click the green flag in order to open them. After exploring ride icons, the dyad opened it for business. The icon that looks like a green flag (see Figure 7) controls whether the ride is open or closed.

By making all new rides closed by default, game players are required to explore and use the ride menu to open the ride. This design decision forces the attention of game players on (and encourages exploration of) the ride menu and requires its use. In the above transcript, attention is drawn to all of the various ride options under the ride menu, which is noted by verbalization of ride icons while exploring and determining their purpose (such as guest thoughts, color options, test results, etc.). Ultimately, this helps the game players quickly learn the game interface, and awareness of potential actions for the rides helps keep them focused on theme park design concerns (in contrast to an example to be presented later).

Continuing the above episode, more icons were explored and the dyad moved on to build other rides. Once the ride is open for business, attention shifted to building more rides relatively quickly:

L: *Have we tested it?* ((Clicks on 'Test Results' icon))

R: *'Excitement Rating'. Low.*

L: °*Whatever. It's all good. I don't care as long as people go on it.*°

R: ↓*Oh we got a visitor.*↑

L: Let's build more <u>rides.</u> ((Clicks on 'Rides' icon on left side menu))

The shift of attention to building more rides reinforced the dyad's goal of making money. More rides in the park will translate into more dollars being spent by visitors in the theme park. Making a profit on existing rides allows the building of more rides in the future as well. Following, the dyad explores ride options after opening up the ride for business:

R: 'Finances', 'Maintenance' ((Reading from pop up window))

L: ((Scrolling over the ride option icons))

R: What's this?

L: ((Clicks on 'Test Results' icon))

R: How about this one? ((Points to the 'Colors' icon for the ride)) (.5) °No that's not it.°

L: ((Clicks on 'Finances')) ↓Admission price is going up.↑ ((Moves cursor over to 'price', raises price))

R: ((Laughs))

L: How much money do you want it to go up? ↑Because there's a lot of people coming.↓

R: Make it like 2 dollars. ((Laughs)) More?

L: ↑<u>Suckers.</u>↑ ((Raises the price on the ride))

R: We have to go see if they come in or not.

L: Uh oh they're stopping. ((Laughs))

R: ((Laughs)) Oh they're going in.

Above, the dyad discovered a 'Finances' icon, which allowed them to set the price of the ride. The 'Finances' icon was the only icon that they utilized out of all the icons explored. Perhaps, after initially exploring ride options, the 'Finances' icon is the only icon (and affordance) needed to support their game strategy. In line with making money, the dyad raised the price of the ride, attempting to maximize profits. Rather than reading customer thoughts, the dyad watched people approaching the ride to see whether they continued to get on the ride (game feedback displays customers either entering the ride or turning away, due to high cost or other problems). This confirms to the dyad that their strategy of raising the ride price was successful, because customers continued to pay to get on the ride.

Consistency in Representation Design and Behavior

In the episode just reviewed, students' discourse focused largely on their design goals, with intermittent consideration of the game interface elements as instrumental means to these goals. In contrast, the following episode illustrates a recurring problem in which a representational inconsistency leads students to shift their focus entirely from domain concerns to problem-solving the game interface, thereby losing opportunities for learning in the domain. In *RollerCoaster Tycoon 3*, there is an inconsistency: one can quickly access default designs for some ride types by clicking on their picture, while clicking the picture of roller coasters will instead invoke a complex custom roller coaster building process. For instance, as shown previously in Figure 7, one can select a 'Merry-Go-Round' by clicking the picture of it. Clicking the picture of the Merry-Go-Round selects the ride, and placement of the ride begins, as displayed earlier in Figure 6.

This process is the same for both 'Junior Rides' and 'Thrill Rides'. However, selecting the picture of a roller coaster will cause the custom coaster

Figure 8. Roller coaster selection in RollerCoaster Tycoon 3

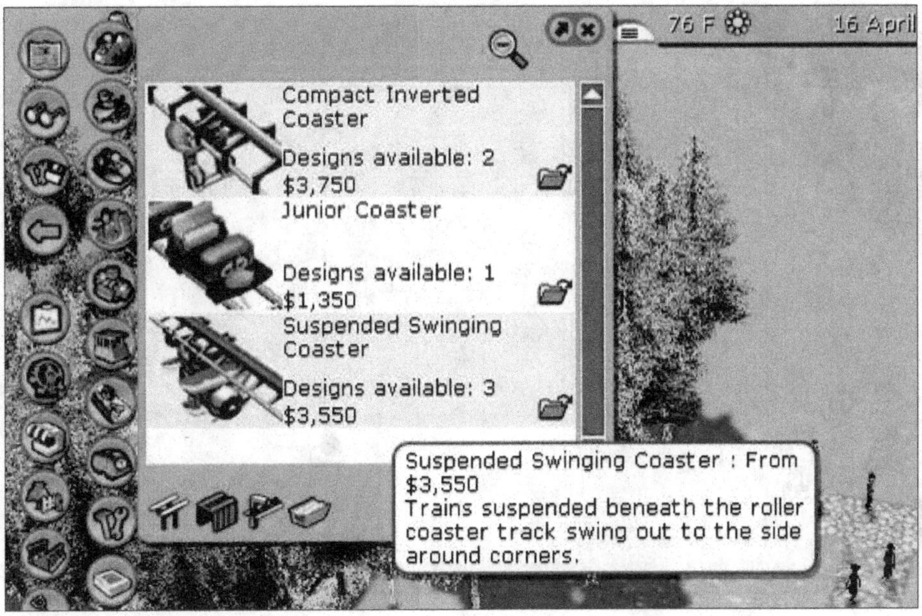

design menu to appear, as shown in Figure 8 and Figure 9.

Clicking a picture of a roller coaster will launch custom roller coaster creation, where the gamer must choose each section of the track, piece-by-piece, as shown in Figure 9.

The conversation of students in the following transcript is initially focused entirely on what kind of ride to build. But when roller coasters are selected, they were surprised that they had to build the coasters one piece at a time:

L: ↑What rides you wanna do?↓ ((Scrolled through the rides they can create))

R: Do a thrill one.

L: Let's do a rollercoaster. ((Partner's request ignored)) ((Clicks on 'Rollercoaster' icon))

R: ↑Yeah that's what↓ °I meant.°

L: Which one you wanna do?

R: Suspended swinging roller.

L: ((Scrolls over roller coaster options))

((Clicks on a different roller coaster))

R: Ok do that one.

L: ((Zooms out from ride))

R: We should do it towards. Oh, we actually build it?

L: Yeah.

R: Oh God.

It seems that the dyad expected pre-made designs to be available. However, pre-made roller coaster designs are available in the game: when selecting the roller coaster to build, one can click on the little yellow folder icon, which will bring up pre-made roller coaster designs of that type.

Figure 9. Construction of a custom roller coaster in RollerCoaster Tycoon 3

This can be seen in Figure 10 and Figure 11, respectively.

Clicking the folder icon in Figure 10 will display the screen shown in Figure 11.

Selecting a track from the list, then clicking the green 'check' icon allows placement, a behavior similar to other types of rides. Figure 12 displays placement of the ride:

The students missed the small yellow folder icon next to the roller coaster pictures (in the roller coaster selection menu), and the dyad proceeded to build a custom roller coaster. Notice how participant R is still trying to address domain design concerns, but L, who must operate the mouse, is becoming absorbed in the operation of the design tool:

L: ((Clicked around the grounds of the park in an empty area))

L: ((Clicks on the one piece that he already placed and nothing happens))

((Clicks a different piece to build- from the building menu))

((A game prompt appears stating that the two pieces they are trying to join will not connect together)) Never mind. ((Continues to click on different pieces to connect to their original piece already placed on the park grounds))

R: How do we go up? We should make it really really high.

L: ((The new piece chosen works))

((They continue to click and build pieces in a circular pattern, higher and higher))

R: Oh that's how? ((Laughs)) Oh my <u>God</u>.

R: ↑Okay, go straight across, then dip down.↓

L: ((Clicks on a new piece that is straight))

R: Yeah, do straight, and then go. ((Laughs))

Figure 10. Accessing pre-designed roller coasters in RollerCoaster Tycoon 3

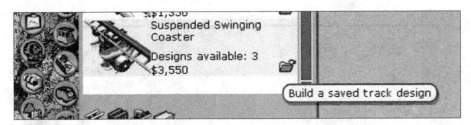

Figure 11. Pre-designed roller coaster selection in RollerCoaster Tycoon 3

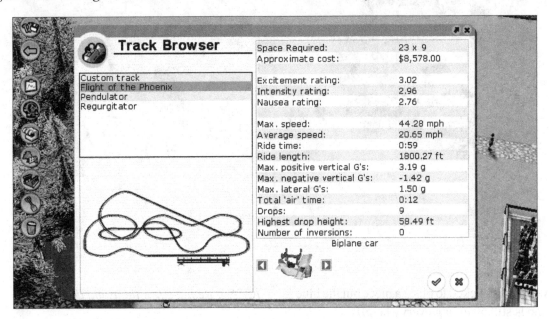

((Prompt comes up saying that the two pieces do not connect))

L: ((Clicks on another piece to build))

((Another prompt comes up telling them that the piece chosen will not connect))

R: You know people are gonna get sick on this ride.

L: Yes ma'am.

L: That's my goal. ((Clicks on a different piece to build))

((Moved cursor to the ride being built))

Negotiation of the appearance of the roller coaster continued between students. After some time attempting to design the custom roller coaster, the dyad struggled to complete the ride. At this point, discussion of design concerns has been derailed, and both students are focused on figuring out how to get the tool to work:

((An outline of where the piece would go started swinging everywhere without L doing anything))

R: °What?° (.5) What happened to the top? ((Points to the top of the ride they are building))

Figure 12. Placement of a roller coaster design in RollerCoaster Tycoon 3

L: No idea. ((Clicked to place a piece but the blue outline is still swinging everywhere))

R: What's going on?

L: ((Clicks on another piece to place))

((A prompt comes up stating that it cannot connect to the other track piece already placed))

((Continues to click on different pieces))

((The same prompt pops up saying that it cannot connect the pieces))

R: Maybe you can't do anymore.

L: ↑Probably out of money.↑ ((Laughs))

R: °No, we have five thousand dollars.°

L: ((Closes building ride menu))

Research shows that regular incremental reward is an important principle of game design for sustaining motivation (Ducheneaut et al., 2006; Sharritt, 2010a; Winn, 2008). The present case has failed on this principle. After some struggle of completing the roller coaster, the dyad gives up and moves to another task:

L: ↑OK this one is not working out for us. ((Clicked on the 'Delete Object' icon instead)) So let's go↓ °work on this ride.° >Should we just delete this ride?<

R: Yeah. [It's gonna cost more.]

L: *[And work on it later?] Yeah. No.* ((Clicked on single trash to delete ride))

((The ride is not deleting))

L: *Ok you guys, lets uh...*

R: *Time to delete.*

Following the abandonment of the custom roller coaster, the dyad attempted to delete the partially built ride, but struggled to use the 'delete' icons in the game: even their goal of abandoning their goal is frustrated!

L: ((Clicking around the ride trying to delete it)) *Yeah, lets delete this man.* ((Clicked on the double trash can to delete more space))

((Prompts keep coming up saying that they cannot delete the ride))

L: ((Deleting ride pieces one at a time)) *What? Why can't we delete it? Delete! OK. I guess we just have to work on it then.*

R: *Let's put some food places in there, so that people are hungry.* ((Points to food stands menu))

L: *No, well no, we gotta work on our ride, dude.* ((Clicked on 'Rides' menu again))

((Choose to build a ride from scratch))

((Build menu popped up for new ride to be built))

After manually removing some of the sections of the track, but unable to remove the ride completely, the dyad abandoned the task and began working on a new ride. The affordance of pre-designed coasters can be easily missed. The game does not draw attention to the folder icons after several missed attempts: the dyad missed the icons for the duration of their game play, over several

days. It is not enough to have an affordance: the affordance must be represented in a manner that makes it salient.

The sequence of actions to build other rides in the game (clicking its picture, and then placing it) would lead game players to think they had executed the proper sequence of actions to build roller coasters. For the other two types of rides (thrill rides and junior rides), clicking the icon will go immediately to placing the entire ride, not pieces of the ride. Based on four days of building custom roller coasters, the dyad appeared to believe that the only way to build roller coasters in the game was to do it manually, piece by piece. The inconsistency in affordances led the students to think that this was the only way to build a ride. Missing the pre-designed coasters drastically altered the nature of the dyad's game play, shifting their focus from game-domain design concerns to game-interface debugging. While experts might enjoy custom roller coaster design, novices (such as the students) struggled to figure it out, and much time was spent (and much of their profits were wasted) unsuccessfully creating custom roller coasters.

DISCUSSION AND CONCLUSION

The results showed how game cues can suggest and lead to the pursuit of action. Often game messages resulted in a corresponding goal selection. Consistency in game behaviors and visualizations was vital, as was a scaffolding game interface. Inconsistent behaviors, such as those encountered by game players of *RollerCoaster Tycoon 3* while attempting to build a roller coaster, could lead students away from solving problems and achieving goals in the game, thereby transferring efforts to debugging the user interface instead of incrementally achieving game goals. Additionally, the design of in-game visualizations, including their placement, layout, and persistence on the interface can have associated impacts in the way their related features are appropriated during game play.

Feedback Mechanisms Assisting Goal Formations

Results revealed how the feedback from in-game features and behaviors could trigger new strategy development by game players. Cues may come from a game's ability to detect user behavior, a game message or pop-up, or from user interaction with game objects. Feedback mechanisms triggered learning by prompting students to take up new tasks during game play. The design of in-game triggers is important, as they may serve in cueing game players to pursue related tasks that encourage learning. Feedback channels can also serve to reduce uncertainty and increase a game's ability to present a scaffolding interface, thus aiding in gamer interpretations and corresponding informed activity.

Cognitive Offloading and Scaffolding game Interfaces

Game representations can assist game players to learn procedures to achieve their goals. For example, when building rides in *RollerCoaster Tycoon 3*, a sequence of actions is afforded by the game. Each step in the process automatically displays new game representations, with a limited set of potential actions that can be performed at each step in the process. Specifically, building a ride in *RollerCoaster Tycoon 3* results in the following process: selecting a ride will automatically begin the procedure of placing the ride; placing the ride will automatically begin the procedure of placing the entrance; and placing the entrance will automatically begin the procedure of placing the exit. By requiring that each step in the process of building a ride is successively launched following the previous step's completion, the potential for novice game players to become lost, confused,

or distracted (and cause an error) is significantly reduced during the ride building process.

The game design of game features, such as the behavior sequence mentioned above has several effects on game play. First, they reduce the cognitive load of game players, as they are not required to memorize the sequence of actions required through the process as a whole. Because each step in the process automatically is followed by the next required step in the process, game players are able to skillfully build rides without memorized knowledge of the process required. A second effect of consistent game features on game play is their ability to provide an affordance for discussion among peers through their persistent representation or behavior. Collaborative discussion and negotiation can rely on the consistent game behavior (or visualization), making it easily referenced during communication, or more efficiently described (as in the example in *Making History: The Calm & the Storm*, as a complex procedure of declaring war is communicated by its first step). Finally, consistent game behavior can ease appropriation by limiting affordances, presenting a limited number of choices that are relevant to that step of the process. By incorporating scaffolding into the game interface, more attention can be placed on problem solving the goals within the game rather than troubleshooting specific operations within the game interface.

FUTURE WORK

Ongoing analyses could address the motivation of students in the learning episodes selected in this study. For example, the exploration of failure during game play can reveal how students respond to different types of failure. Our own early findings suggest that there were patterns in how different students experience failure, and this in turn influenced their motivation to play and the learning that occurred.

Additional work could examine the communication and collaborative activity that occurred in this study among students within the dyads, between the dyads, and between students and teachers. Analyses of within-dyad communication could be analyzed to reveal the extent to which students maintain a joint conception of the problem (Teasley & Roschelle, 1993) and the sequential processes or "members' methods" (Garfinkel, 1967) by which participants make use of game affordances. Between-dyad communication could be examined to reveal how student dyads exhibit both competitive and collaborative behavior while helping each other play and strategize throughout game play. Our initial analysis has revealed a developing set of social norms during student interactions with peers and teachers, which in turn affected student game play and learning.

Further research addressing the role of the teacher will be required. While this study was completed in an educational setting (high schools), it occurred during school study periods where the teacher had limited presence. Additionally, teachers were not familiar enough with the games used to guide their students effectively. More research needs to examine actual implementations within school curriculums to observe the capacity and role served by the teacher in the learning process.

ACKNOWLEDGMENT

The first author would like to thank his dissertation chair, the second author, for all the vital capacities in which he has served. The participation and interest in the research of both teachers and students at Wheaton-Warrenville South High School and Naperville Central High School made this study possible and was much appreciated as well. In addition, the three video games[2] used in the study were chosen due to their excellent presentation and potential for learning. Much was learned from the analysis of these games and the cumulative effort and hard work of those involved in their design was evident.

REFERENCES

Annetta, L. A., Murray, M. R., Laird, S. G., Bohr, S. C., & Park, J. C. (2006). Serious games: Incorporating video games in the classroom. *EDUCAUSE Quarterly, 29*(3), 16–22.

Cassell, J., & Jenkins, H. (Eds.). (1998). *From Barbie to Mortal Kombat: Gender and computer games*. Cambridge, MA: MIT Press.

Charmaz, K. (2006). *Constructing grounded theory: A practical guide through qualitative analysis*. Thousand Oaks, CA: Sage Publications.

Clayman, S., & Maynard, D. (1995). Ethnomethodology and conversation analysis. In ten Have, P., & Psathas, G. (Eds.), *Situated order: Studies in the social organization of talk and embodied activities* (pp. 1–30). Washington, DC: University Press of America.

Collins, A., Brown, J. S., & Newman, S. E. (1989). Cognitive apprenticeship: Teaching the crafts of reading, writing, and mathematics. In Resnick, L. B. (Ed.), *Knowing, learning and instruction: Essays in honor of Robert Glaser* (pp. 453–494). Hillsdale, NJ: Lawrence Erlbaum Associates.

Collins, A., & Ferguson, W. (1993). Epistemic forms and epistemic games: Structures and strategies to guide inquiry. *Educational Psychologist, 28*(1), 25–42. doi:10.1207/s15326985ep2801_3

Dillenbourg, P., Baker, M., Blayne, A., & O'Malley, C. (1996). The evolution of research on collaborative learning. In Spada, H., & Reimann, P. (Eds.), *Learning in humans and machine: Towards an interdisciplinary learning science* (pp. 189–211). Oxford, UK: Elsevier.

Doise, W., & Mugny, G. (1984). *The social development of the intellect- International series in experimental social psychology* (*Vol. 10*). Pergamon Press.

Ducheneaut, N., Yee, N., Nickell, E., & Moore, R. J. (2006). Alone together? Exploring the social dynamics of massively multiplayer online games. In R. Grinter, T. Rodden, P. Aoki, E. Cutrell, R. Jeffries, & G. Olson, (Eds.), *Proceedings of the SIGCHI Conference on Human Factors in Computing Systems*, (pp. 407-416). Montreal, Quebec, Canada, April 22 - 27, 2006. New York, NY: ACM.

Festinger, L. (1957). *A theory of cognitive dissonance*. Stanford: CA Stanford: University Press.

Garfinkel, H. (1967). *Studies in ethnomethodology*. Malden, MA: Blackwell Publishing.

Gee, J. P. (2003). *What video games have to teach us about learning and literacy*. New York, NY: Palgrave Macmillan.

Gibson, J. (1977). The theory of affordances. In Shaw, R., & Bransford, J. (Eds.), *Perceiving, acting, and knowing*. Hillsdale, NJ: Lawrence Erlbaum Associates.

Gibson, J. (1979). *The ecological approach to visual perception*. New Jersey, USA: Lawrence Erlbaum Associates.

Glaser, B., & Strauss, A. (1967). *Discovery of grounded theory: Strategies for qualitative research*. Piscataway, NJ: Transaction Publishers.

Heeter, C. (2000). Interactivity in the context of designed experiences. *Journal of Interactive Advertising, 1*(1). Retrieved September 30, 2008, from http://www.jiad.org/article2

Jefferson, G. (1984). Transcript notation. In Heritage, J. (Ed.), *Structures of social interaction*. New York, NY: Cambridge University Press.

Jordan, B., & Henderson, A. (1995). Interaction analysis: Foundations and practice. *Journal of the Learning Sciences, 4*(1), 39–103. doi:10.1207/s15327809jls0401_2

Koschmann, T., Stahl, G., & Zemel, A. (2005). The video analyst's manifesto (or the implications of Garfinkel's policies for studying practice within design-based research). In Derry, S., & Pea, R. (Eds.), *Video research in the learning sciences*. Mahwah, NJ: Lawrence Erlbaum Associates.

Koschmann, T., Zemel, A., Conlee-Stevens, M., Young, N., Robbs, J., & Barnardt, A. (2005). How do people learn? In Bromme, R., Hesse, F. W., & Spada, H. (Eds.), *Barriers and biases in computer-mediated knowledge communication and how they may be overcome*. Dordrecht, The Netherlands: Springer. doi:10.1007/0-387-24319-4_12

Larkin, J. H., & Simon, H. A. (1987). Why a diagram is (sometimes) worth ten thousand words. *Cognitive Science, 11*, 65–99. doi:10.1111/j.1551-6708.1987.tb00863.x

Lim, S., & Lee, J. R. (2007). *Effects of coplaying on arousal and emotional responses in videogame play*. International Communication Association Conference. San Francisco.

Linn, M. C., & Burbules, N. C. (1991). Construction of knowledge and group learning. In Tobin, K. G. (Ed.), *The practice of constructivism in science education* (pp. 91–119). Washington, DC: AAAS Press.

Moore, R. J., Ducheneaut, N., & Nickell, E. (2007). Doing virtually nothing: Awareness and accountability in massively multiplayer online worlds. *Computer Supported Cooperative Work, 16*, 265–305. doi:10.1007/s10606-006-9021-4

Murray, M., Mokros, J., & Rubin, A. (1998). Where's the math in computer games? *Hands On, 21*(2), 8–11.

Nardi, B., & Harris, J. (2006). *Strangers and friends: Collaborative play in World of Warcraft*. 20th Anniversary Conference on Computer Supported Cooperative Work (pp. 149-158). New York, NY: ACM.

Nielsen, J. (1994). Heuristic evaluation. In Nielsen, J., & Mack, R. L. (Eds.), *Usability inspection methods*. New York, NY: John Wiley & Sons.

Norman, D. A. (1988). *The design of everyday things*. New York, NY: Doubleday.

Oliver, M., & Pelletier, C. (2005). *The things we learned on Liberty Island: Designing games to help people become competent game players*. DiGRA 2005: the Digital Games Research Association's 2nd International Conference, Changing Views: Worlds in Play, Vancouver, British Columbia, Canada, June 16-20.

Sandford, R., Ulicsak, M., Facer, K., & Rudd, T. (2006). *Teaching with games: Using commercial off-the-shelf computer games in formal education*. Harbourside, United Kingdom: Futurelab.

Shaffer, D. W., & Gee, J. P. (2006). *How computer games help children learn*. New York, NY: Palgrave Macmillan. doi:10.1057/9780230601994

Sharritt, M. J. (2008). Forms of learning in collaborative game play. *Research and Practice in Technology Enhanced Learning*, 3(2), 97–138. doi:10.1142/S1793206808000471

Sharritt, M. J. (2010a). Designing game affordances to promote learning and engagement. *Cognitive Technology Journal, 14*(2)-*15*(1), 43-57.

Sharritt, M. J. (2010b). An open-ended, emergent approach for studying serious games. In Annetta, L., & Bronack, S. (Eds.), *Serious educational game assessment*. Rotterdam, The Netherlands: Sense Publishers.

Sharritt, M. J. (2010c). Evaluating video game design and interactivity. In Van Eck, R. (Ed.), *Interdisciplinary models and tools for serious games: Emerging concepts and future directions*. Hershey, PA: IGI Global. doi:10.4018/978-1-61520-719-0.ch008

Sherlock, L. M. 2007. When social networking meets online games: the activity system of grouping in World of Warcraft. In *Proceedings of the 25th Annual ACM international Conference on Design of Communication*, (pp. 14-20). El Paso, Texas, USA, October 22 - 24, 2007. New York, NY: ACM.

Slavin, R. (1990). An introduction to cooperative learning. In Slavin, R. E. (Ed.), *Cooperative learning: Theory research and practice* (2nd ed., pp. 1–46). Boston, MA: Allyn and Bacon.

Squire, K. (2005). Changing the game: What happens when video games enter the classroom? *Innovate, 1*(6).

Stenning, K., & Oberlander, J. (1995). A cognitive theory of graphical and linguistic reasoning: Logic and implementation. *Cognitive Science, 19*(1), 97–140. doi:10.1207/s15516709cog1901_3

Suthers, D. D. (2001). Towards a systematic study of representational guidance for collaborative learning discourse. *Journal of Universal Computer Science, 7*(3), 254–277.

Suthers, D. D. (2006). Technology affordances for intersubjective meaning-making: A research agenda for CSCL. *International Journal of Computer-Supported Collaborative Learning, 1*(2), 315–337. doi:10.1007/s11412-006-9660-y

Suthers, D. D., & Hundhausen, C. (2003). An empirical study of the effects of representational guidance on collaborative learning. *Journal of the Learning Sciences, 12*(2), 183–218. doi:10.1207/S15327809JLS1202_2

Teasley, S. D., & Roschelle, J. (1993). Constructing a joint problem space: The computer as a tool for sharing knowledge. In Lajoie, S. P., & Derry, S. J. (Eds.), *Computers as cognitive tools* (pp. 229–258). Hillsdale, NJ: Lawrence Erlbaum Associates.

Transana. (2008). *Jefferson transcript notation.* Retrieved January 9, 2008, from http://www.transana.org/support/OnlineHelp/Team1/transcriptnotation1.html

Wiley, J., & Jensen, M. (2006). When three heads are better than two. *Proceedings of the Annual Conference of the Cognitive Science Society.* Retrieved April 18, 2007, from http://litd.psch.uic.edu/personal/jwiley/Wiley_Jensen_06.pdf

Winn, B. (2008). The design, play, and experience framework. In Ferdig, R. (Ed.), *Handbook of research on effective electronic gaming in education.* Hershey, PA: IGI Global. doi:10.4018/9781599048086.ch058

ENDNOTES

[1] "When another leader makes you an offer, you must choose to refuse or accept the offer. If you accept, the trade occurs immediately. If you decline, the other leader may ask you to make a counter-offer, may end diplomacy, or may declare war on you." (*Civilization IV* Manual, p. 101)

[2] The following three video games were purchased by the researcher for use in this study:

*Roller Coaster Tycoon 3 (*http://www.atari.com/rollercoastertycoon*)* © 2004 Atari Interactive, Inc. All rights reserved.

*Making History: The Calm & the Storm (*http://www.making-history.com/edu*)* © 2007 Muzzy Lane Software. All rights reserved.

*Sid Meier's Civilization IV (2K Games) (*http://www.2kgames.com/civ4*)* © 2005 Take-Two Interactive Software and its subsidiaries. All rights reserved.

Chapter 11
Designing Learning Activities for Sustained Engagement:
Four Social Learning Theories Coded and Folded into Principals for Instructional Design through Phenomenological Interview and Discourse Analysis

Brock Dubbels
University of Minnesota, USA

ABSTRACT

The experience of a successful adolescent learner will be described from the student's perspective about learning the video game Dance Dance Revolution (DDR) through selected passages from a phenomenological interview. The question driving this investigation is, "Why did she sustain engagement in learning?" The importance of this question came out of the need for background on how to create an afterschool program that was to use DDR as an after school activity that might engage adolescents and tweens to become more physically active and reduce the risk of adult obesity, and to increase bone density for these developing young people through playing the game over time. The difficulty of creating this program was the risk that the students would not sustain engagement in the activity, and we would not have a viable sample for the bone density adolescent obesity study. Implications of this study include understanding the potential construction of learning environments that motivate and sustain engagement in learning and the importance of identity construction for teachers to motivate and engage their students. In addition to the analysis of sustained engagement through the four socio- and cultural-cognitive theories, four major principals were extracted from the operationalized themes into a framework for instructional design techniques and theory for engaging learners for game design, training, and in classroom learning.

DOI: 10.4018/978-1-60960-565-0.ch011

INTRODUCTION

This article seeks to understand what engages young people in learning, and what sustains their interest to continue. It explores the elements that inform the lived experience of a chosen play activity and the possible social learning theories that might inform it. Four theories were chosen and operationalized for coding the transcript of the phenomenological interview because of their focus on motivation, social learning, and identity construction: Communities of Practice (Wenger, 1998), Affinity Groups (Gee, 2001), Social Interdependence (Johnson & Johnson, 1994, 2009), and Self-Determination theory (Deci & Ryan, 2002).

All of these theories seek to explain the motivation behind learning as socially constructed and distributed phenomena; all seek to describe the process of identity construction as an impetus for situated learning. The assumption in this study was that it is through the process of identity construction that engagement is sustained and supported through the process of group affiliation and is distributed through apprenticeship, modeling, group interaction, interdependence, and situated in space.

Identity Construction Rituals and Rites of Passage

Traditionally, communities gather to provide ceremony for initiation and status transition for such things as the celebration of status change, where a child becomes an adult, and initiation, where single people become married couple. Although there may be many more transitions and rituals in today's society because of the great variety of cultural subgroups (i.e., churches, car clubs, self-help groups like Alcoholic Anonymous, and hobby groups like The Peoples' Revolutionary Knitting Circle, etc.), many of these groups traditionally necessitated face-to-face interaction. But with the Internet and today's computing power, these relations can be mediated digitally through portals like Facebook, Xbox Live, *Second Life*, and other social networking tools—as well as expert systems that provide feedback based on performance, such as a video games like Dance Dance Revolution (DDR).

The DDR game club might be represented as a ritual rite of passage to understand how and why people build identities around their play, and sustain engagement to ultimately develop expertise. Central to the rite of passage is the initiation ritual (Van Gennep, 1960), where new roles and status are conferred through public performance where play (Geertz, 1973), the subjunctive mood (Turner, 1969), situates the activity, so that rules, roles, and consequences are suspended and participants can explore new identities, associated activities, and their semiotic domains and thus develop new status.

With this in mind, well-designed video games and their fan bases may represent and express new forms of the rite of passage and initiation ritual. Like a rite of passage, games are structured activities that are valued by certain cultural subgroups, depend on play as a subjunctive mood, represent expert systems that resemble apprenticeship activities, and involve performance initiation. The subjunctive mood observed in games and ritual are said to decontextualize the action and provide a suspension of rules, roles, and consequences found in ordinary life to allow for the exploration of new identities, rules, roles, actions, and social affiliations and status in a safe space. Games can do this well.

The ritual and process of identity construction may be an organizing principle in understanding motivation and engagement. The four social learning theories presented for discourse analysis seek to provide the impetus for motivation and engagement and how to structure it, and rely upon aspects of identity construction; these theories do not present themselves as descriptions of the identity construction process. Each theory has a different focus and seeks to describe aspects of identity and focus on an element that informs identity construction: Community (Wenger, 1998), Activity (Gee, 2001), how individuals interact with each other (Johnson & Johnson, 1994, 1999), and needs of the individual (Deci & Ryan, 2002). For the purposes of this study, these theories were operationalized to provide insight for designing instructional environments that will motivate and sustain the engagement of the learner.

Purpose of the Study

This interview was to inform design features to develop a program for pre-adolescent exercise with DDR for the study of obesity reduction and increasing bone density. The study was also intended to get a sense of why a young woman sustained engagement with DDR over 3 years to develop expertise, and how educators might replicate that kind of commitment to learning and practice. This study may be especially pertinent to designing instructional contexts, exergaming, and structuring interaction and professional development.

Background of the Study

Health care professionals have observed an increase in levels of childhood obesity. This increase has been attributed in large part to physical inactivity. Physical inactivity can lead to obesity and poor cardiovascular health, and it can also have negative effects on bone health. Bones function to support a mechanical load (a force exerted by body weight, muscle, growth, or activity). Bone is constantly formed and reabsorbed throughout life in a generally balanced way. However, in a three- to four-year window during puberty, bone formation is accelerated. In that period, as much bone material is deposited as will be lost during a person's entire adult life. During these pivotal years of bone development, physical activity is important for optimizing bone health, as it has been shown to reduce the incidence of fractures later in life.

Because it is difficult to motivate children to participate in the type of cardiovascular activities that adults engage in (running, cycling, aerobics), new strategies must be developed, and these may demand elements that motivate the learner to sustain engagement over a longer period of time in order to promote and sustain life habits for physical conditioning.

Dance Dance Revolution is not Your Typical Video Game

DDR is a game that you set up with mats, a TV, a game console and a game disk, and up to four people can play simultaneously (Figure 1). To play DDR, a participant responds to a series of directional arrows (see Figure 2), displayed on a video or TV screen to perform choreographed dance steps or hops synchronized to music. Song tempo and degree of difficulty increase as the player

Figure 1. Dance Dance Revolution set up

Figure 2. Screen shot and description of DDR

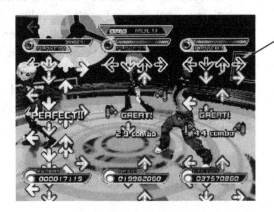

The arrows moving up the screen from the bottom need to match the arrows at the top. When they match, you need to step on the corresponding arrow on the mat. Good players do this in time to the music showing their rhythm & flow—maybe doing spins and hand slaps on the mat.

In this instance, the next move would involve the bottom arrow and the right arrow being stepped upon simultaneously.

successfully progresses in the game. Because of the game's popularity and its cardiovascular exercise and jumping (bone-building) components, it could represent an appealing model for reducing physical inactivity in children.

DDR may be a possible solution to increasing activity and mechanical load because of the amount of jumping activity, but the young person must be motivated to start, and engagement must be sustained for the activity to produce valid and reliable measures of obesity and bone density.

The issue under investigation was how to help young people start an activity and sustain it; the simple answer to this was, seemingly, to make it fun—to make it a high-interest activity—but many toys, games, and activities are often tried once and then put aside. What came out of the interview was:

- the importance of aligning the outcomes with a desirable activity,
- autonomy-supporting environments,

- the importance of group and environment to the construction of status and identity that makes belonging to a group desirable along with the sustenance of a common activity,
- the importance of status and relation for reinforcement,
- the centrality of group performance,
- the role of play as a subjunctive mood and portal to engagement,
- and again, the importance of identity construction for transformation to instantiate sustained engagement conveyed through affiliation, apprenticeship, positive interdependence, and expertise. The big idea here is that perception leads to transformation.

Interview-ee/Informant

To explore this, we recruited Ellen as a DDR expert and possible employee to lead an after-school program at one of our sites at the Minneapolis Public Schools. We posted a hiring description for

DDR experts and had a number of responses. One respondent, Charles, shared that he had a lot of friends who were really good at DDR, and Ellen was listed as one of those people. Ellen came into the lab to show us her DDR play, and we were impressed with her expertise.

What was interesting about Ellen was that she was not from a subversive or reactionary subculture. Ellen is part of one of the least studied cultural subgroup in schools (Buckingham, 2007)—an urban, middle-class teen that is successful in school, is respectful to teachers, has a part-time job, plays varsity soccer, in traveling band, is part of the International Baccalaureate Program, and has a satisfying home life.

These elements of her identity were surprising. We usually assume that video game players are a disenfranchised fringe group at school who do not engage with the typical academic fare. Ellen was able to balance not only her academics and music instruction, work a part-time job, but also play sports and have friendships. These elements of balance were enticing and we wanted to know how she was doing it so that we might try and replicate not only the physical health benefits in our bone density study, but also some of the psycho-social and affective elements necessary for sustaining engagement (Chapman, 2003). She seemed like a great role model for creating a curriculum that would rely heavily on identity development and she was an intriguing informant to help us understand how play identities might lead to work habits that help form healthy minds and bodies.

Methodology and Review of Literature

The question driving this investigation is, "Why did she sustain engagement in learning?"

According to Chapman (2003), engagement is more than behavioral time on task. When looking to measure growth or change, or even to understand whether a learner has truly engaged, an educator should also look for evidence of commitment and positive attitudes related to the activity and subject matter.

- Engagement is not just doing the work, it is a connection and an affinity to an activity supported from the affective domains (Chapman, 2003).
- Skinner and Belmont (1993, p. 572) report that engaged learners show sustained behavioral involvement in learning activities accompanied by a positive emotional tone, select tasks at the border of their competencies, initiate action when given the opportunity, and exert intense effort and concentration.
- Pintrich and De Groot (1990) see engagement as having observable cognitive components that can be seen or elicited through exploring the learner's use of strategy, metacognition, and self-regulatory behavior to monitor and guide the learning processes.

These attributes do not appear in an activity because a student is told that it is good for them, and that they should commit to their betterment. Least likely is that they do an activity because we threaten, or just because we want them to.

A student must make a choice to commit to an activity and have that commitment reaffirmed over time to sustain engagement. True engagement in an activity is in some sense transformative and resembles identity construction, in that it changes who one is through cognitive, affective, and behavioral elements. It seems likely that without positive reinforcement (Skinner, 1938) the behavior may result in extinction and the game becomes another resident on the island of misfit toys. We look at social learning theories to explore issues of sustaining engagement through socially distributed reinforcement.

DDR is considered a high interest activity for many young people, and it does have a reward system that gives real-time feedback on performance with rewards for successful play. But, without aligning those rewards and achievement with social capital, they lack meaning and status, and the reinforcement system remains a token economy (Ferster & Skinner, 1957) whose tokens are unredeemable except as social capital.

The work of Buckingham on identity development may provide some insight for connecting identity with purpose, motivation, and sustained engagement. Buckingham (2008, p. 3) states that

Identity is developed by the individual, but it has to be recognized and confirmed by others. Adolescence is also a period in which young people negotiate their separation from their family, and develop independent social competence (for example, through participation in "cliques" and larger "crowds" of peers, who exert different kinds of influence).

Identity and status were traditionally conferred through rites of passage, and there may have been many culturally-specific instances of these rites for different groups and related activities. Video games may represent a new wrinkle in the way that we enact and view rites of passage. They may offer a form of guided, ritualized behavior for identity construction and group affiliation as an autonomy-supporting environment (Ryan & Deci, 1999), Affinity Group (Gee, 2001), Social Interdependence (Johnson & Johnson, 1994, 1999) or Community of Practice (Wenger, 1998).

A rite of passage does not need to resemble the tribal practices that led to vision quests, ritual markings, or exodus. A rite of passage may be organized in three forms: the process of separation, transition, and integration, (Van Gennep, 1960), but all three of these rites may also be presented as single rite (Barnard & Spencer, 1996). What was important for Van Gennep was the idea of Liminality, or the threshold. The threshold in an initiation represents a portal—a representative movement from the status of one social space to another, where ritualistically, the individual or group makes a transition by passing through a metaphorical or literal portal to represent a change in social status and position.

In the context of Liminality, the activity space may be far removed from reality, and roles, rules, tools, values, and status may be situated in the flux of play as if a hybrid or interstitial space (Turner, 1969). This concept of the threshold and liminality seems to validate Geertz (1973) and his description of the "Center Bet" in describing the ritual of Balinese Cockfighting and Benthams' concept of Deep Play. According to Turner (1969), there may be many rites of passage in a person's life through sub-cultural affiliation (Cock Fighting, DDR, First Job) where identity and entitlement are inculcated through desire to become a respected and acknowledged group member, where the individual can share in and contribute to group activity, participate in group spaces, and publicly renew and further their status.

For Wenger (1998), identity is central to human learning; identity construction and learning are distributed through community and relations; learning is socially constructed; and motivation is based on a desire for sharing and participatory culture. The work of Wenger shares many attributes with Gee's work, but the focus for Wenger was on socially distributed cognition and learning as social participation. Earlier work (Lave & Wenger, 1991) explored the role of learning in apprenticeship, where newcomers would enter into a space where learning was situated and contextualized, and goals and purpose were evident due to entering the space. One entered the space to gain apprenticeship and attempt to acquire and learn the sociocultural practices of the community. Thus, the individual is drawn to the group and begins to engage and learn by finding their role in a distributed, networked, cultural-cognitive process with the purpose of the individual as an active participant in the practices of a social community and become an acknowledged member with skills, knowledge, and the requisite values.

This participation leads to the construction of his/her identity through these communities. From this understanding develops the concept of the Community of Practice: a group of individuals participating in communal activity, creating their shared identity through engaging in and contributing to the practices of their communities.

The difficulty with this theory is that group membership is hard to define. A person may want to be part of group and claim group membership, but not have the identifiable characteristics that define the membership.

Since identity is conferred from others, there are factors that can identify a person as a group member and as having identity markings. For Gee (2001), the activity is primary and provides the motivation and engagement, the source of group membership and the identity markings; for Gee the community and relations are ancillary and stem from the interaction related to the activity. He states that these communities and spaces are hard to identify without knowing exactly why people are there. Whether a person actually claims group membership or is acknowledged can be difficult.

For Gee, whether group membership is acknowledged—claimed or not—attributes can still be observed. The role of Gee's work is central to operationalizing identity and group membership through offering observable sociocultural markers that come from semiotic domains central to the activity as evidence of group membership.

A semiotic domain recruits one or more modalities (e.g., oral or written language, images, equations, symbols, sounds, gestures, graphs, artifacts, and so forth) to communicate distinctive types of messages. By the word "fluent" I mean that the learner achieves some degree of mastery, not just rote knowledge... Semiotic domains are, of course, human creations. As such, each and every one of them is associated with a group of people who have differentially mastered the domain, but who share norms, values, and knowledge about what constitutes degrees of mastery in the domain and

what sorts of people are, more or less, "insiders" or "outsiders." Such a group of people share a set of practices, a set of common goals or endeavors, and a set of values and norms, however much each of the individuals in the group may also have their own individual styles and goals, as well as other affiliations. Gee (2001, p. 2)

This work allows for certain attributes of group membership to be observable rather than subjective. A young person may have grown up participating in an activity with parents and young friends, but during the puberty years, may reject that affiliation based upon new goals for group membership and status. A new group may be more desirable than a current group, and the young person may cast off markings that identify them with the old group such as a hat from a uniform, ways of speaking, values, etc. This does not mean that markings of prior group membership with parents, family, and childhood affiliations are not still observable—an accent or mannerism may indicate origins or influence. For Gee (2001), it is the activities and the group practices that provide evidence of social learning and group membership from semiotic domains, and it is activity that is central to identity construction.

For Deci and Ryan (2002), the focus comes from work on motivation with a focus on Autonomy, possibly built from early work by White (1959), where organisms have an innate need to experience competence and agency and experience joy and pleasure with the new behaviors when they assert competence over the environment—what White called effectance motivation.

For Deci and Ryan, motivation is based on the degree that an activity or value has been internalized, and this is based upon the degree to which the behavior has meaning within the context of the arena of performance.

In order to sustain engagement for Deci and Ryan, motivation must be internalized—the external contingency must be "swallowed whole." The learner identifies the value of the new behavior

Figure 3.

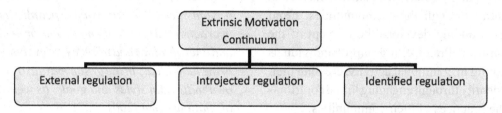

with other values that are part of the self. This process of engagement is the transformation of an extrinsic motive, one that is reinforced from outside the learner's values, into an activity that is assimilated and internalized by the learner as an intrinsic value that becomes part of their personal identity. This process involves constructing values aligned with the group and environment, and thus assimilates behavioral norms that were originally external as part of a new identity. Based on the degree of control exerted by external factors, levels of extrinsic motivation can be aligned along a continuum. (Figure 3)

- External regulation: doing something for the sake of achieving a reward or avoiding a punishment.
- Introjected regulation: partial internalization of extrinsic motives.
- Identified regulation: doing an activity because the individual identifies with the values and accepts it as his own.

Identified regulation is autonomous and not merely controlled by external factors. It is motivation for an activity that has been integrated as part of the learner's values, and refers to identification with the values and meanings of the activity to the extent that it becomes fully internalized and autonomous (Ryan & Deci, 2000).

Social Interdependence describes what informs students' goal attainments (Johnson & Johnson, 1994, 1999). According to Johnson and Johnson (1999)

Students' learning goals may be structured to promote cooperative, competitive, or individualistic efforts. In contrast to cooperative situations, competitive situations are ones in which students work against each other to achieve a goal that only one or a few can attain. In competition there is a negative interdependence among goal achievements; students perceive that they can obtain their goals if, and only if, the other students in the class fail to obtain their goals

In cooperative situations, students work with Positive Interdependence, where group members perceive that they are linked with each other, and that the success of each member is linked to the success of the others.

Twelve themes from these theories of identity construction, ritual and rites of passage, engagement, motivation, and social learning were taken to code the interview transcript to inform analysis and make decisions on what factors might be important for the construction our after-school program for tracking design efficacy and measure performance.

Themes for Coding

Of these twelve themes, there seemed to be four major themes, and the rest seemed to be interdependent sub-levels that were common across all of the theories. With this in mind, the major themes are:

- Play as Subjunctive Mood
- Activity Space

Table 1. Themes for coding

Play Subjunctive Mood	Activity Space	Desirable Social Grouping
Ritual Rites of Passage Initiation, separation, integration	Positive Interdependence	Belonging/ Relatedness
Desirable Activity	Identified regulation	Apprenticeship
Affective Commitment	Autonomy/ Competence	Cognitive Theories of Action

- Desirable Social Grouping, and
- Desirable Activity.

These themes were the most common descriptions of "why" when Ellen described her DDR play. These three themes also represent an aggregation of each theory, but with emphasis on activity, space, and groups, as well as the mood that needed to be present in those themes to be attractive.

Data Collection

The phenomenological interview methodology (van Manen, 1997) was used to try to elicit responses beyond descriptions of rationale to gather "thick descriptions" (Geertz, 1973) of affective, social, corporeal, and cognitive behaviors behind the activity and experience of playing DDR. And, also to encourage descriptions that were thick enough that the researcher might be able to identify instances of learning and engagement situated and distributed across networks of time and space, mediated through shared activity, and perhaps to see if there were evidence indicating what elements in the identity construction process inform motivation and engagement.

Data Analysis

The critical discourse methods as espoused by Gee (1999) and Fairclough (2003) not only provide methodologies that are fundamental to qualitative analysis, but are also fundamental to the study of "the scaffolding of human affiliation within cultures and social groups and institutions," Gee

(1999, p. 1) and "how do existing societies provide people with the possibilities and resources for rich and fulfilling lives," Fairclough (2003, p. 202). It was for this reason that these methods were used to explore and code the phenomenological interview transcript. Although a sample of one participant is not very robust for generalization, it provided a starting point for more focused theory testing, as well as to provide insights for us as designers, theorists, and education practitioners.

Interview

This first excerpt from the interview begins to describe the motivation to learn to play Dance Dance Revolution. Ellen and I met on a nice spring day in the Whittier neighborhood near the Minneapolis Institute of Arts at a coffee shop called Spy House. When I asked her about her experience of playing DDR, she said:

The first time I ever played Dance Dance Revolution was with my friends Tyler and Ben. They had it at Devon's house and everyone was playing this game. Really, I wanted to hang out with them, I wanted to participate and so that's when I started learning. Then it was after playing with those guys for so long that I really started to enjoy the game. I actually didn't have a play station before that, so I went out and bought a play station just so I could play DDR, yeah... yeah, I didn't want to be left out of it. Games are fun and I just wanted to spend time with my friends and this is something that they were all doing.

The basis for Ellen's learning was Belonging/Relatedness to a Desirable Group. This idea of relatedness and Belonging were fundamental in her development of skills and collection of resources to develop as a player. However, she did not have the feeling of connectedness until she was really able to engage in the activity as a participating member—Autonomy/Competence. This indicated introjected regulation, and Identified Regulation seems to require the performance and seems to require some external indication of having internalized the values of the group that are expressed through public performance in the group and a commitment to practice that showed her effort toward group success as an indication of Positive Interdependence.

Surprisingly, the activity was not initially a Desirable Activity, "I wanted to participate and so that's when I started learning." After some time participating, she found enjoyment along with her sense of Belonging to a Desirable Group. This phenomenon suggests precedence of Belonging to a Desirable Group for Ellen over engaging in a Desirable Activity, and also suggests that an individual can develop interest in activity that might not have been initially motivating due to a desire to belong. Speculatively, there may be some indication for the importance of Play as a Subjunctive Mood for developing affinity for an activity. It was clear that she had already identified with the people, but, based on the next excerpt, she had not identified or been identified with the activity. The descriptions she offers indicate that the activities need to be playful and not so serious, and that the activity should offer success for assured status. There must be an entry point for a public performance, and perhaps since this game was new, she could enter without the loss of status that would come from being new and unskilled while the skilled players watched her and perhaps lost interest in her performance, and possibly in her.

I was excited because this was something I could participate in. I've played Halo and I'm not that good at it and everyone was starting out on this for the first time, so I thought I could be one of those good people at it and get respect from people. I was really excited. They have this huge TV at Devon's house and everyone's around you. I was kind of nervous too because you have to do this in front of people. Well, we were all kind of sitting on the couch watching the men and I was like I want to try it. I mean, some of them were interested in seeing me probably because they knew I never played before and they made me where I was probably going to fail, but then I actually really wanted to do it, so I was like, I want to do it next! I thought I was going to be better at the game than I thought I was because I'm thinking, oh these guys they don't have any coordination. This'll be easy for me. I'm kind of in shape, so I was thinking it would be pretty easy and then I do some of these songs and I was like oh, I need to go down a level! I thought I caught on fairly quickly.

What was clear from this passage was the importance of the activity and her feeling that she could be successful participating and "be one of those good people at it and get respect from people." There are several parts to this that are especially interesting:

1. Belief in her ability to succeed was essential in her willingness to perform publicly. Research on adolescents' engagement in literacy, for example, has found that adolescent perceptions of their competence and ability to succeed may be a more important predictor of whether they will engage, than their past performance. (Alvermann, 2001; Anderman et al., 2001; Bean, 2000; Guthrie & Wigfield, 2000). Studies of adolescents have also found that they prefer to perform where they know they will have success

(Csikzentmihaly, Rathunde, & Whalen, 1996).

2. The fear of performing in front of the group with Autonomy/Competence, but that since people were just starting out, she might have a chance to be good at it and to be respected. This may have played an even larger role because she was one of the girls who watch from the sofa, not one of "the men" who play the games and perform.

3. The importance of the Activity Space and its affordances as well as the possible change in atmosphere with this new game, where there may have been more emphasis on Play as the Subjunctive Mood.

4. The role of Belonging/Relatedness seemed to be an important component in her participating in the activity and her feeling of becoming an acknowledged group member. The structure of the activity, according to the next excerpt indicated that DDR, as compared to other games, offered more of an Apprenticeship situation, where others were willing to teach and share; raising the level of success and fun through Positive Interdependence.

This makes a case for the importance of Affective Commitment, Belonging, and Competence, as well as a Cognitive Theory of Action. Although these seem to be sublevels of Desirable Activity and Desirable Group, that inform and reinforce action, they are important factors that indicate engagement and are likely fundamental to its sustenance, and also seem to indicate a form of reinforcement as socially distributed affect and cognition.

Ellen had created a Cognitive Theory of Action and knew that it was essential for her to perform to be acknowledged and claim membership—another indication of Chapman's (2003) description of engagement, and evidence of Identifiable Regulation. To claim Belonging to this Desirable Social Group, she realized whether implicitly or not, that she needed to participate through performance (Autonomy/Competence) to Belong. This supports Deci and Ryan's position that Autonomy, Belonging, and Competence are basic needs that underlie motivation and engagement and satisfy Skinner and Belmont's (1993) assertion of affective involvement. What is central to these needs are the Activity Space where these young people could interact as a community through the game; the subjunctive mood of play that may have allowed for the desirability and beliefs in success; and the game itself, which seems to be structured to promote Positive Interdependence and can create Identified Regulation through structuring relations through space and activity.

Ellen had already aligned her values internally as Introjected Regulation, but she had not found an opportunity with a Desirable Activity where she might have success in the Activity Space and feel confident that she would succeed and enjoy the activity, "I could be one of those good people at it and get respect from people."

Halo and *Counterstrike* she described as work (Sutton-Smith, 1997), which has consequences for failure—the desirable group may have been much more advanced in their performance in *Halo* and *Counterstrike*, and perhaps took playing the game much more seriously and raised the stakes of the performance.

Games and play are often about choices without life-threatening consequences, but that does not mean that games are not taken seriously. They can be performance tests (Autonomy/ Competence) and Ritual/Rites of Passage that allow for the development and affirmation of a place within a group, establishment of pecking orders, and through this, community status and entitlement; it is possible that the experience of being positioned to perform and possibly fail was some sort of initiation, a form of deep play (Geertz, 1973).

This act of bettering oneself in public can be risky situation—and it really must occur in public for a person to be seen as Competent/Autonomous and as an acknowledged group member (Belonging). This Ritualistic phenomenon was described by Geertz as the "Center Bet" in "Deep Play," (1973) and based on Ellen's description, it may be that as competence and expertise evolve, the play gets more serious and the stakes and status of the performance (Ritual) change, the fear of failure increases with the perceived change in subjunctive mood from play to work ethos.

The Performance/Initiation

Previously, Ellen may have wanted to be part of the group, but Ellen stated that the games they were playing did not provide her with much interest to play, even though she wanted to belong to the group and participate in their space. Because of this, she may not have been considered as part of the group, but maybe more of a tourist or poser because belonging seemed contingent on being able to "do."

I have a lot of friends who play Counterstrike and a lot of... almost every guy I know plays Halo. You can enjoy watching those games. I don't enjoy it as much. Like I said, it's just way more serious. They get more serious. Well, it's like everyone is more quiet and focused, like they really get into trying to hunt these people down and kill them before they are hunted down and killed. DDR, you are playing against someone but then with Halo and Counterstrike you're against all these people and you have to be, like, watching your back all the time. Even the people watching, they zone out and just watch it. For me it's not as fun. As for DDR, it's more like people jumping around and are less serious, but it's still a lot of fun.

Prior to Ellen's embrace of the game, she was a groupie. She could talk about how Devon did, but not about her own experience. This came, in part, as being recognized as a player by her community, but it was also a confidence that came of public performance (Autonomy/ Competence); sustaining engagement with the practice; and

working hard to develop status and identity related to the group and the activity and the freedoms and responsibilities that accompany them.

So, what followed was me just trying to find where I could go to play. Then I kind of got eventually frustrated with it—well, not frustrated, but I wanted to play more, so I decided to buy it for myself. Yeah. You play by yourself to get better to play with other people. I mean, it's always fun to play by yourself and unlock new songs and things like that. I got it for Christmas from my parents, so I didn't have to buy it, but I had to persuade them and make sure they got me what I wanted. They didn't really understand but they felt okay about it because it wasn't something violent or anything like that. Then I was, like, look what I can do! They watched me. They thought it was kind of interesting. This was with my family on Christmas. Then my uncles and my little cousin, who was maybe like seven, they all got really interested by it. So my fifty-year-old uncles are trying it and they're getting really excited. My little cousin, she's getting excited too. She doesn't even really understand what's happening on the screen but she's like jumping around on the pad.

In the DDR trial, Ellen was tested to see how she would respond to public failure: she could have quit and gone home, or she could have laughed it off and found the fun in learning and worked towards acceptance. Ellen found that there were others who were beginners that she could improve with, and more experienced players who were actually helpful and willing (Apprenticeship/ Positive Interdependence) to teach. She, also, found that there is no substitute for experience, and that in order to become a part of the group, she had to go through the rites of practice and public initiation. According to Van Gennep (1960) this ritualized process is common to many societies where an individual passes from one stage of life to another, and it can involve separation from childhood environment, transition, and incorporation with new status. For Turner (1969), this game may not be as monumental as rites celebrating marriage or death, but it still represents a moment of social transition and eventual change in status. The importance of this is the public acknowledgement of Competence. This seems to be essential to identity construction and acceptance as a member of a group through the activity that is structured in a way that resembles positive interdependence, and may be the reinforcement for sustaining engagement.

It was through the activity that Ellen was conferred status and identity as member not only by her new friends, but through her family and the community, that had the power to convey her status and acceptance. She became a "gamer girl." This conferred new identity and acceptance allowed her to become that gamer beyond her normal relations and to extend her community network and develop new relations and status:

Because we shared this thing, so it would be, like, oh, so whose house are we going togo to tonight to play DDR? Okay. Well, my friend Devon, his house was the main DDR house just because he had a great room for it and everything. And his parents didn't really care how much noise we made or how late we stayed there, so his house is generally the DDR house. Tyler, who was my friend prior, we would get together and practice a lot. Michael, he bought DDR around the time that I did and we were basically kind of on the same level, and I got to know him better that way just by spending time with all these people. Nick, all these other guys, I had kind of known beforehand, but now we spent all this time together. So, it was basically we all met at Devon's house and that's what we would do for weekend-after-weekend-after weekend.

If we can draw from these Activity Spaces and domains and inspire the learner to feel a connection and affinity to traditional academic fare like engineering, literature, mathematics, and so forth as Desirable Activities, we may provide a portal to embracing academic learning. The challenge seems to be embedding the learning outcomes in a high-interest activity with a reinforcement network to sustain the activity and continue to validate the identity.

As Ellen's ability with the game progressed, she was being recognized as a DDR "gamer girl," and this conferred upon her a new identity and status. She began to find new connections through familiar school activities. Her familiar conversations changed to unexpected connections in school and at her job; as more people learned about her new status as a gamer girl, the more she began to meet others with an interest in DDR and to connect with the gamer culture. She had begun to move beyond her former status as an International Baccalaureate student (Academic), varsity soccer player (Jock/Athlete), Band Member (Musician/band geek) into a more generalized, pop-culture status, where she was seen as not so serious and more approachable. It may have been important to Ellen to branch out and change people's perceptions. Perception seems to be essential to transformation. We can work to create an identity, but it must still be acknowledged to have status. This may have been her first activity that was run by her contemporaries—autonomous and not overseen by adults.

Perhaps all her work in academics, sports, and band had made her appear to be too serious, and easily influenced by adults—a follower. She may have also felt constrained by all of her commitments and wanted to break out to meet new, fun people, "Really, I wanted to hang out with them... games are fun." The proposition that might follow as if a syllogism is that: Gamers are fun, and I want to be fun too.

It is only conjecture and anecdotal, and she did not abandon her commitment to band, sports, or academics—she graduated with an International Baccalaureate diploma—but as can be imagined, all her work in those areas may have made it important to her to find friends who had interests beyond her everyday world, and that being a gamer would allow her to step away from conversations about the team, assignments, practicing certain pieces of music, and set her apart. Playing the game and being part of that community allowed her the ability to decontextualize and detach from work and become perceived as fun.

Developing these relations may be more than fun; it may be an apprenticeship to develop a coping tool. The importance of play, according to Vygotsky (1978), is decontextualization, where an individual can gain gratification and pleasure even in the midst of unresolved issues and larger, and time- consuming projects. The role of pretense and imagination can bring about pleasure and gratification in the face of uncontrollable circumstances; this can provide some relief through affective reward and pleasure. Perhaps the gaming provided an opportunity to decompress and laugh in the midst of all that responsibility and preparation. But, it was seemingly more than that. It was also a way to connect and extend her status by initiating new players and drawing on the interest and social capital, for example, in a hotel room on a band trip—another autonomy supporting activity space where the identity could be reinforced with status from new participants.

Yeah, it was a school band trip. So, a lot of us went and it turned out that a wholebunch of people knew what DDR was. It was interesting to see them play. Tyler and I, we kind of felt cool because our group that we had played with had progressed better than these other people that we were seeing play. They were like, oh man, this kid is so good and we play with him all the time. Tyler and I played against these people. Yeah, we beat them pretty bad.

In this instance, the game activity did extend beyond the familiar Activity Spaces like Devon's basement; it even seemed to provide an activity that would make others see her as representative of a Desirable Group. The game and her new status seem to have supplanted the importance of being part of the gamer group in Devon's basement. The activity became a means for extending her friend identity reinforcement network as an Affinity Group (Gee, 2001), where people affiliate because of an affinity for an activity, maybe to be part of the fun—to play. As the activity began to change for the group members, relationships started to change, and the emphasis on the game, itself, diminished.

Well, a lot of the guys that I started playing it with, they moved on to other games because that's what they do. They focus in on something for a really long time and then they'll find something else will be just released and everybody else will just be playing that, so they'll jump into that. Then there was always the people who have it, like Tyler and I, who will still play it. We didn't get bored with it; it's just then there were other things. No. I don't play it as much as I do anymore and my friendships through that have become different. I mean, we're all still friends. DDR was just like this common thing that we had to, like, start us talking and then after that we talked about normal things. I became pretty good friends with a lot of people. I dated one of the guys that I met for awhile. I don't know, it wasn't, like, any different than like you meet people playing for a sports team. You have something in common and that's what you're coming together to do, and then you talk about other stuff because we're not just focused on DDR. Well, at my work it's kind of similar too. We're all stuck working together and so then we get talking. Soccer and sports a lot. Any kind of group that you all come together and you have something to talk about and then we just eventually expand on that and that's how we became friends.

The DDR game did facilitate relationships in ways that other games and activities did not, but in the end, the initial motivation may need to come from a purpose that only the individual can develop. But, play can facilitate this and may make the entrance to a group, the practice, and eventual mastery of knowledge, activity space, and activity more likely to be enticing, and possibly provide for sustained engagement and eventual mastery. This makes a case for Play as a Subjunctive Mood and the importance of Positive Interdependence.

Playgroups, and the activities that support them, provide a common ground for interaction. There is definitely a pecking order that comes from demonstrable competence and evidence of knowledge from the semiotic domains from the game. Games are built upon play, pretense, and decontextualization, but once these activities no longer provide pleasure and gratification, the activity may quickly end and the relationships and spaces that contextualize and support them may change in the way that Ellen's DDR group cooled off: "and my friendships though have become different. I mean, we're all still friends."

Games are structured forms of play, Dubbels (2008) that provide rules and roles that are defined to help members to decontextualize from the ordinary world where they have responsibility, deadlines, and environments that they cannot control. These same rules and roles also help them to know their status in the game, share common, spontaneous, and authentic experience without going too deeply into personal motives, negative feelings, and Freudian melt-downs. Corsaro (1985) called this play group phenomenon the Actors Dilemma. According to Corsaro, the Freudian meltdown, or over-sharing, is one of the most common causes of playgroup breakup. Perhaps play is the coping mechanism that allows for detachment and the ability to constructively work on what can be changed and separating out that which cannot be changed. Game roles may also allow for exploration of other peoples' values and experience in a safe space without getting too deep or real, which represents an opportunity to try on and project different emotions, and build comfort and trust through a common experience.

In terms of identity construction, the game may take a form of a Ritual/ Rite of Passage:

The Activity Space is no longer like the ordinary world. The rules and roles in a game are different and even changed for the sake of experimentation with social norms. Interpersonal boundaries can be tested without endangering status and relationships—it is a trial, a testing. As with Ritual/ Rites of Passage, when Play acts as the Subjunctive Mood, different parts of person can emerge and people can try on different personae without recrimination, because they are only playing.

CONCLUSION

In answering the original question, "Why did she sustain engagement?" it became evident that her motivation to sustain engagement over time changed. She was attracted to the activity because she wanted to be friends with the kids who hung out at Devon's basement—she wanted to be an acknowledged member of the group, not part of the fan club. To do this she had to perform and risk ridicule and a possible reduction in status. Geertz (1973) described this spatially in that the further away one is from the "Center Bet," or the central public performance, the lower your status and importance to the main event and performers.

To be part of this group, she needed to perform, but she was hesitant to try because the games being played did not mesh with her sense of play and fun. Perhaps because the play of these group members with these games (*Halo, Counterstrike*) was already too far advanced for them to tolerate a "newb" (new player) at the controller, and might create a break-down of the activity. In this case, the challenge is learning how to improve performance through the activity of playing better players than oneself.

Ellen decided that it might be better not impose her learning during prime-time play and risk the ridicule or contempt of poor performance. The lesson seems to be readying oneself to play in the "Center Bet," which she did with DDR. If one is not contributing to the play, learning, and/or status of the group, perhaps spectators understand their place on the periphery, and that perception is the key to transformation, and this is mediated through play as subjunctive mood.

This ability to detach and decontextualize through play can be a very valuable trait when dealing with pressures of studying for exams, working, and other responsibilities that cannot offer immediate gratification. This inability to decontextualize and detach is one of the central behaviors inherent in Play Deprivation (Brown, 1999), a diagnosis used to make sense of the incredible violence of Charles Whitmore and his shooting spree from the bell tower at Texas A&M University. It was found that Whitmore was raised in a very rigid environment where he was not allowed friends or play. He experienced a life that looked very successful on the surface. But, in 1966 he committed what was the largest mass murder in the history of the USA. According to the National Institute for Play (1), Brown, who was a psychiatrist at Baylor College of Medicine at the time, collected behavioral data for a team of expert researchers, appointed by the Texas governor, to understand what led to Whitmore's mass murder. What was found through interview, diary, and reconstructing is that Whitmore had been under extreme, unrelenting, stress. After many unsuccessful efforts to resolve the stress, he ultimately succumbed to a sense of powerlessness; he felt no option was left other than the homicidal-suicidal... Whitman had been raised in a tyrannical, abusive household. From birth through age 18, Whitman's natural playfulness had been systematically and dramatically suppressed by an overbearing father. A lifelong lack of play deprived him of opportunities to view life with optimism, test alternatives, or learn the social skills that, as part of spontaneous play, prepare individuals to cope with life stress. The committee concluded that lack of play was a key factor in Whitman's homicidal actions – if he had experienced regular moments of spontaneous play during his life, they believed he would have

developed the skill, flexibility, and strength to cope with the stressful situations without violence.

Brown continued exploring Play Deprivation as a construct and found similar patterns in other violent offenders, and even traffic deaths related to aggression and chemical issues. The role of play cannot be underestimated for its ability to decontextualize and reframe experience. Play therapy currently is a treatment in child psychology for helping children talk about and understand forces beyond their control.

RELEVANCE OF ANALYSIS

The utility of this analysis comes from these recalled phenomena as a pattern for planning instruction and understanding why people learn. We learn to become. We create and engage to gain new experience and entitlement and gain status without danger in our social network, as well as to learn from others, whether it is a workplace competency, gaining social skills, or as a means of adapting to stress.

The role of Play as a Subjunctive Mood in these Activity Spaces and Desirable Groups may be the organizing principle that makes these groups and activities desirable as part of identity construction, as well as the means for identity construction and reinforcement to sustain engagement. For a person to facilitate and construct an identity, they may need to play, just as children play as doctors, firefighters, teachers, mothers, and even animals and dinosaurs in games. It is through pretense that we are able to imagine and create cognitive theories of action and circumstance, and it is through play that we develop this capacity.

If we want to sustain engagement, we need to help students develop the capacity for Identified Regulation, where they may turn their play into meaningful performance when asked to perform in activities that begin to resemble rites of initiation and deep play. This process creates a subtle transition where the initial play activity becomes serious and is approached with the focus of work. Like what Ellen experienced watching advanced players of *Halo* and *Counterstrike*, and eventually what she experienced in practicing in addition to school, homework, and lessons, to prepare for DDR at Devon's.

Implications and Lessons for Designing Instructional Environments

This transcript from Ellen's experience makes a case for developing instructional environments that allow for playful, autonomous group interaction structured as a game to allow for play in much the same way that ritual demands play. The group and space "Re–Place" and the rite offers "Re-Creation."

The use of play as the basis for designing instruction should not be underestimated. Often we forget that play is our natural approach to learning. When working with very young people, such as infants, toddlers, and small children, we align instruction with their interests, and allow objects to help direct inquiry. It is through the use of toys and exaggerated actions and emphasis in modeling target behavior that we allow for failure to be an inherent and necessary part of learning. The hesitation many educators express with this approach is that we have much to do, and little time to do it. It begins to sound like the white rabbit in Alice's Adventures in Wonderland running worriedly and anxiously "we're late, we're late!"

Stress pressure and anxiety are a natural part of learning, just as play is a natural part of learning, however, fear and threat scenarios are not often great motivators, in addition, fear and stress eventually take their toll on the body, mind, and spirit. Play may be the correct context for sustaining engagement and creating the initial portal for engaging learners in focused approaches to work and delay of immediate gratification for the kind of rewards that rigor and sacrifice deliver.

I have used these principles on several occasions to explore games and play as effective methods for aligning content and process with resistant and reluctant learners. I have used it to create games for reading instruction, literature instruction, engineering, mathematics, leadership, and organizational change. To demonstrate how this can be done, I created a game called *Dry Dock* to teach engineering that I will use to demonstrate the four major instructional design principles for play.

Principle 1: Play as a Subjunctive Mode

Engineering can be a very fun class, but the curriculum I was supposed to teach was very un-fun. In fact the curriculum was the source of the dys*fun*ction. I was being asked to start class by presenting standards, why the standards were important, and tell the students why they were learning what they were learning. I found that this was much more for the benefit of observers evaluating the quality of my teaching than it was to motivate and engage the students.

I use standards, and I feel it is important to share the larger scheme of things behind activities and what they might be preparing for, but I do it with Play as the Subjunctive Mood. The first thing I did was to quit thinking that these kids would commit to a curriculum just because it was posted up on the wall. It is not enough to tell students how they are going to fulfill standards and a rubric.

For most, fear of failure was not an issue. Many of them were accustomed to it. They had checked out as an act of integrity, and in doing so, had found that they could dictate terms to teachers because of their disruptive behavior. Although my departure from the scripted curriculum of having students redesign coffee mugs and the "do it or fail" curriculum did not always sit well with the administrators; it did result in engagement from my students (who did not drink coffee).

I told the students that we were going to be having a boat race, and that I would be bringing in my wading pool from home, and that we would be making sail boats out of Styrofoam to race across the pool. I structured all of the engineering, statistics, and technical writing so that they were embodied in the task, and that through experience, they could discover them. What was essential in this case was not so much joining a desirable group, but in participating in a desirable activity where their group could interact in the activity space semi-independently, and that the task was one where they believed that they would have early and instant success.

In addition to this, I also tried an experiment where I used a different approach to creation of subjunctive mood in the activity: Work as subjunctive mood: I told the students that we were really behind in our work and that we would have to work hard and be rigorous in our approach to these boats. I stressed that it was incumbent upon us to learn terms like resistance, surface area, momentum, and force and apply them into our hull designs. I was talking, but they were ignoring me, tuning me out. When I asked them what they were supposed to do, many of them did not know, and many of them expressed that they did not care.

To test this I introduced the activity where Play was the subjunctive mood: I told the class that we had a fun activity where we were going to be building boats and that we were going to have four kinds of races: speed, weight bearing, stability, and general purpose. I told them that I was going to be showing them examples of boat hulls and that they should play with them a bit to decide what style of boat they were going to make for the races they were going to participate in. I found that kids had listened, knew what to do, and really wanted to start. All of the same principles and terms were still present in the unit, but they now had permission to be playful and perhaps fail. Play implies failure, recovery and experimentation. Many of the kids made crazy boats that would never work, but they were fairly successful in using the terms to justify their design for each race. It is not always what you do,

or whom you do it with—it is how you do it, and that you do it at all.

Principle 2: Desirable Activities

One of the key issues in creating sustained engagement and identified regulation is in creating activities that align with the goals and purposes of the learner, or exposing the learner to something they think is really cool and they want to do. Making boats was not what many teens would consider a "cool" activity, but it did hold attraction for them when I showed them the tools, the materials, and gave a brief overview of what they would have to do. Getting kids to engage may just be a matter of creating some fun, and showing that they can have early and instant success; that they can work with some autonomy in a space where there is wiggle room for them to be expressive; and that they can make adjustments if they make mistakes. There must be time allowed to go deeply into learning to allow for the student to commit to the *expression of self* into their work. This might mean going off task and making red sails even though it has nothing to do with learning the Bernoulli Effect, the competition, or the embedded learning outcomes.

The opportunity to make aesthetic and seemingly inconsequential changes allowed them investment in the activity through personal expression and to eventually invest in a cognitive theory of the activity, and also allow for a belief in their future success. Add to this the opportunity to work cooperatively and learn from the work of other class members—some call this copying, I call it modeling and apprenticeship—then they can make a start (often full of errors and mistakes) and adjust for excellence as they work with others and begin to better understand the project/activity. In this way we enable the spontaneous neutral experience that can be useful for beginning the learning process and also building relationships and belonging, and autonomy and competence through the activity.

The key to this principle is in embedding the learning in the activity so that learners can discover the learning principles in the process of the activity through performance and reflection, where they compare what they have done with the work of others, and the instructor can provide encouragement to scaffold further development— this is an apprenticeship model with roles, rules, and positive interdependence. Oddly, this is often also the process of inquiry, discovery, and failure recovery, although time consuming, is often the process through which scientific principles were discovered before they were concentrated into abstractions in textbooks for memorization and testing-- they were tripped over by the scientists and then operationalized into methodology. This can be done when we think of instruction as games and learning as structured forms of play. Some important elements for designing instruction as play are offered in this framework of play for instructional design modified from Dubbels' (2008) Taxonomy of Play:

- Cognitive Theories of Action: we capture the imagination and build cognitive theories of action through imagery/ visualization (mental modeling).
  - A key word for the instruction should be "IMAGINE".

This first category in the taxonomy provides a basis for testing comprehension. It is important to be able to create mental model and theory of the action. The key attributes are visualization and imaginatively creating mental models and segmenting process and attributes for indexing in memory. If learners index and visualize well, they will likely have fine grain memory of the experience to draw upon for future use. Thus, creating these mental images is very important for creating the motivation to engage, belief in future success, and a cognitive theory of action.

- Desirable Groups: provide roles and identities they can try on and play with and offer the ability to change roles and play with the identities.
  - A key word for instruction should be "TOGETHER"

Working with others: A great draw because it allows for interaction. Many students need to be able to copy other students until they are able to IMAGINE and create a cognitive theory of action. Some learners do not learn well from instructors. They need to watch another learner translate the experience. Through this, they not only learn how to start the assignment, but also how to create a cognitive theory of action on which they can improvise and express themselves through and commit to the activity. I cannot tell you how many times I have seen resistant learners get into a groove and not want to stop the project once they finally get started!

- Roles: In the case of the boat project, they became Naval Architects and Marine Engineers; just learning about what these folks do as a profession, and, that these professions exist opened a lot of student eyes and created schema for the semiotic domains of each role. They also had Learning and Functional roles (see Appendix B).
- Structuring group work: The creation of roles in cooperative learning as Johnson and Johnson suggest (1994) is very powerful and also what we see in early childhood play, as well as more advanced game experience for video games, teaching empathy, and modeling interaction for professional development. In structuring the work through roles, each group member has role specific tasks. One can play Return to Castle Wolfenstein or look at game-specific roles (character classes) in Appendix A and Appendix B, and imagine how these roles would culminate in teamwork for a

mission. Each character class has several unique abilities and these come with different learning roles and functional roles.

- ○ Identity / Semiotic Domains/ Epistemic Frames: Provide rules, roles, values, language, actions, and tools associated with the roles and identities (semiotic domains) that they can work with, and act on that which is inherent to the task, where the performance is the assessment. The role of the Naval Architect is to design a marine vessel for specific activities. The elements that define this role are the tools, activities, language, values, and outcomes associated with the role, and ultimately, the boat floats or it doesn't. This embodiment is informative assessment, where the action provides immediate feedback through complete or partial mastery, or failure and the role provides for measure of progress and schema development based on knowledge of the semiotic domains.
- ○ Create choices and branching decision network: It is important here that the learners explain their cognitive theories of action and are asked to utilize and explain the identity tool box to support their choices and why they did what they did, and what might be next.
- ○ Contingency/Probability: This comes about when we consider the possible contingencies that might come from an action through prediction and hypothesis testing. Examples of this are resource management; awareness of likelihood of an action based on knowledge of the game and instructional environment, and attempted quantification and probability of failure or success.

This structure for instructional design comes from A Taxonomy for Play and is aligned with a scale for levels of cognitive theories of action in Dubbels (2008). This triarchical model, the third leg being reading comprehension, has been the basis for a number of successful curriculum units as well as digital games, allowing for direct linkage to learning and comprehension metrics and is also available at http://www.vgalt.com.

Principle 3: Spaces

Spaces are where we can offer activity, autonomy, interaction, and relationships. By creating spaces where learners can self-govern to an extent, we make them desirable, especially if there are desirable tools and resources as affordances. What I did with the boat unit was to create a rite of passage to get from one learning space to another. The students were told that to use the tools and start on their hull designs, that they had to use the hull examples and sketch a hull design, and then explain why and how the hull would perform well in specific race conditions (speed, weight-bearing, stability, general purpose)—then they were to go and test their design and hypotheses.

I was able to create different work spaces by offering tools and independent construction of their boats with a number of hot-wire cutting tools (for the Styrofoam) if they were able to sketch and explain their design based upon the hull exemplars and key vocabulary I had postered around the classroom walls; this was also where I had placed the wading pool for the races, and where students could make test runs of their constructed boats.

In a sense, I had created a threshold or Liminality into my classroom space, much like a game allows one to level up, or passing a rank elevates a soldier. It was a rite of passage of one space to another. The new space allowing more autonomy and less controlled interaction through a verbal examination and demonstration of applied knowledge and competence—a knowledge act (Dubbels, 2008).

Principal 4: Desirable Groups

This was mentioned in the Desirable Activities, but this deserves its own principal. The role of Desirable Groups was primary for Ellen as a motivator for her to become a DDR expert. What makes it especially relevant is the role of socially desirable groups and the influence they hold in conferring identity, the entitlement, and status that go with it. The role of groups cannot be underestimated for identity construction and the rituals that convey it. If Wenger (1998) is correct, and identity is central to human learning, and as Buckingham states, that identity is developed by the individual, but must be recognized and conferred through community through some type of performance or ritual, then the structuring of ritualized activities for status and competency construction may be immensely important for not only creating engaging activities, but to sustain them and make them life habits.

The studies operationalized in this analysis provide several key features, that when brought together provide a very powerful tool kit for instructional design:

- Communities of practice, which represent the established pathway into community, status, and entitlement. This model aids in our understanding of the distribution of knowledge through webs and networks of sharing, modeling, and instruction through status, identity, community ritual, and affiliation

- Affinity Groups, which explicate the importance of the activity in conveying group membership and status through evidence from the semiotic domains, which are signs, signals, and markings acquired and bestowed through experience in communities of practice and apprenticeship experiences.

- Self-Determination Theory provides the elements that lead to internalization of these activities, values, language, rela-

tions, and spaces for the actualization and internalized regulation of motivation and engagement into activities and habits that provide a source of satisfaction beyond the external, or extrinsic rewards that into activity that is self-satisfying and self-fulfilling for enjoyment and effectance, so that engagement is sustained and informs the individual's identity and status.

- Social Interdependence and Cooperative Learning, which provide insights into how to structure learning contexts and positive interdependence for learning, relations, and alignment of identity with valued cultural norms through Instructional design.

These are all brought together with the awareness that play may be the foundation for the construction and development of these descriptions—a portal to work, where we learn that play is the initiation, as well as the rite—and through ritualized behavior, activity, and representation, with allowance for learning and failure recovery we grow, evolve, and make meaning through mental models and prediction-- and thus innovation and deep seated cognitive theories of action due to the inherent process of reflection and do-overs in play and games to heighten public performance and status.

Play seems to be the subjunctive mood that mediates entry into work and competence, and possibly to expertise. As play becomes more competitive through more complex cooperation and trust, play and learning deepens into effort, application, and work.

In addition, play is the foundation for ritual and representation, and central to creating the context and subjunctive mood for performance that supports apprenticeship, culture, and social learning. Play is fundamentally important for building life habits such as fitness, reading, and even simple things such as manners and cooperative behavior. In his treatise on play, *Homo Ludens*, Johan Huizinga (1938) posited that play was the basis of culture, and Lewis Mumford (1945) reasserted this in his treatise *The Myth of the Machine*—stating that it was it was imitation (mimesis), role play, the creation of miniature environments, and the symbolic fields of play where every function of life were modeled as a game to develop competency and advance what was known and yet to be known.

Dubbels (2008), in the spirit of Vygotsky, (1978), furthered this by stating that play and representation are the factory of our conceptual abilities, and if play involves the creation of abstractions and models of the world, then sharing play necessitates complex communication as well as a means for innovation and production, and perhaps the basis for cognitive theories of action, mental models, hypothesis creation, and ultimately comprehension.

With play central to our approach, we may find that motivation and engagement increase with little need for threat because of the inherent pleasure of learning without the dangers of repercussion or loss of status through failure. Failure is an inherent part of play, but a gentle entry with play and the promise of early and instant success (as in sail painting) can provide the portal to more profound success through failure recovery, modification, continuous improvement, and iterative design. In a game, there is often a loser, and in order to get better, we assume that we must fail to get better, as we must seek better players and more difficult conditions to improve, develop, and even transform.

Games are structured forms of play (Dubbels, 2008) that can provide the portal to complex social and cultural cognitive enhancement and progression. They represent new forms of ritual and safe contexts for contest and accomplishment through challenging apprenticeships in expert systems, where an expert might not have been available in the past. Games may be the new rite of passage and rituals, or as Vygotsky (1978) called toys "pivots," where a banana can become a phone in a child's play, where play is a transitional stage that is the beginning of separating the meaning of an object from literal to figurative. Games may be an elaborate pivot for accomplishment, status, and entitlement through modern day social and cultural networks in virtual and real space, and these may be the elements that motivate and sustain engagement and provide real answers for designing learning contexts and sustaining engagement and creating the kinds of identities that engender habits of lifelong learning and activity.

REFERENCES

Alvermann, D. E., Moon, J. S., & Hagood, M. C. (1999). *Popular culture in the classroom: Teaching and researching critical media literacy*. Newark, DE: International Reading Association.

Barnard, A., & Spencer, J. (Eds.). (2002). *Encyclopedia of social and cultural anthropology*. New York, NY: Routledge.

Bentham, J. (1882). *The theory of legislation*. London, UK: Trubner.

Brown, S. (1999). Play as an organizing principal: Clinical evidence and personal observations. In Beckoff, M., & Byers, J. A. (Eds.), *Animal play: Evolutionary, comparative and ecological perspectives* (pp. 247–248). Cambridge, UK: Cambridge University Press.

Buckingham, D. (Ed.). (2008). *Youth, identity, and digital media*. Cambridge, MA: MIT Press.

Chapman, E. (2003). Alternative approaches to assessing student engagement rates. *Practical Assessment, Research and Evaluation, 8*(13). Retrieved May 11, 2009, from http://PAREonline.net/getvn.asp?v=8&n=13

Corsaro, W. (1985). *Friendship and peer culture in the early years*. Norwood, NJ: Abex.

Csikszentmihaly, M., Rathunde, K., & Whalen, S. (1996). *Talented teenagers: The roots of success and failure*. New York, NY: Cambridge University Press.

Deci, E. L. (1985). *Intrinsic motivation and self-determination in human behavior*. New York, NY: Plenum Press.

Deci, E. L., & Ryan, R. M. (2002). *Handbook of self-determination research*. Rochester, NY: University of Rochester Press.

Dubbels, B. R. (2008). Video games, reading, and transmedial comprehension. In Ferdig, R. E. (Ed.), *Handbook of research on effective electronic gaming in education* (pp. 251–276). Hershey, PA: Information Science Reference. doi:10.4018/9781599048086.ch015

Fairclough, N. (2003). *Analysing discourse*. New York, NY: Routledge.

Ferster, C. B., & Skinner, B. F. (1957). *Schedules of reinforcement*. New York, NY: Appleton-Century-Crofts. doi:10.1037/10627-000

Freebody, P. (1992). A socio-cultural approach: Resourcing four roles as a literacy learner. In Watson, A., & Badenhop, A. (Eds.), *Prevention of reading failure* (pp. 48–60). Sydney, Australia: Ashton-Scholastic.

Freebody, P., & Luke, A. (1990). Literacies programs: Debates and demands in cultural context. *Australian Journal of TESOL*, *5*(7), 7–16.

Gee, J. P. (1996). *Social linguistics and literacies, ideology in discourses*. Bristol, PA: Taylor & Francis.

Gee, J. P. (2005). Semiotic social spaces and affinity spaces: From The Age of Mythology to today's schools. In Barton, D., & Tusting, K. (Eds.), *Beyond communities of practice* (pp. 214–232). New York, NY: Cambridge University Press. doi:10.1017/CBO9780511610554.012

Gee, J. P. (2007). *Good video games + good learning*. New York, NY: Peter Lang Publishing.

Geertz, C. (1973). Deep play: Notes on a Balinese cockfight. In Geertz, C. (Ed.), *The interpretation of cultures: Selected essays*. New York, NY: Basic Books.

Huizinga, J. (1938). *Homo Ludens: A study of the play element in culture*. Boston, MA: Beacon Press.

Johnson, D., & Johnson, R. (2009). *What is cooperative learning?* Retrieved May 11, 2009, from http://www.co-operation.org/pages/cl.html

Johnson, R. T., & Johnson, D. W. (1994). An overview of cooperative learning. In Thousand, J., Villa, A., & Nevin, A. (Eds.), *Creativity and collaborative learning*. Baltimore, MD: Brookes Press.

Lave, J., & Wenger, E. (1991). *Situated learning: Legitimate peripheral participation: Learning in doing: Social, cognitive and computational perspectives*. Cambridge, UK: Cambridge University Press.

Mumford, L. (1945). *The myth of the machine: Technics and human development*. New York, NY: Harcourt, Brace, & World.

National Institute for Play. (2009). *Play deprived life - Devastating result*. Retrieved April 16, 2009, from http://nifplay.org/whitman.html

Pintrich, P. R., & De Groot, E. V. (1990). Motivational self-regulated learning components of classroom academic performance. *Journal of Educational Psychology*, *82*, 33–40. doi:10.1037/0022-0663.82.1.33

Shaffer, D. W. (2006). Epistemic frames for epistemic games. *Computers & Education*, *46*(3), 223–234. doi:10.1016/j.compedu.2005.11.003

Skinner, E. A., & Belmont, M. J. (1993). Motivation in the classroom: Reciprocal effects of teacher behavior and student engagement across the school year. *Journal of Educational Psychology, 85*(4), 571–581. doi:10.1037/0022-0663.85.4.571

Sutton-Smith, B. (1997). *The ambiguity of play*. Boston, MA: Harvard University Press.

Van Manen, M. (1997). *Researching lived experience*. London, Ontario, Canada: Althouse Press.

Vygotsky, L. S. (1978). *Mind in society: The development of higher psychological processes* (Cole, M., John-Steiner, V., Scribner, S., & Souberman, E. (Trans. Eds.)). Cambridge, MA: Harvard University Press.

Wenger, E. (1998). *Communities of practice: Learning, meaning, and identity*. Cambridge, UK: Cambridge University Press.

APPENDIX A. CHARACTER CLASSES

Typical character classes and game roles from a video game can be used as a model for designing classroom instruction for learning roles (see Appendix B also). In this case from the game *Return to Castle Wolfenstein*. Each character class has different skills and fit what Shaffer (2006) calls an Epistemic Frame: the ways of knowing, of deciding what is worth knowing, and of adding to the collective body of knowledge and understanding of a community of practice, where by playing the medic and learning the opportunities and constraints, one begins to create a cognitive framework, or schema for a content domain of identity, knowledge, competence, language, values, and activity. Roles like these can be structured into instruction, just as they are reinforced in communities of practice and the hegemony of social practice and institution.

From Wikipedia:

Soldier: The soldier is the only class that can use heavy weapons. They are: mortar, portable machine gun (MG42), flamethrower, and bazooka/Panzerfaust. On the No-Quarter mod the Venom machine-gun and the BAR (Allies) or StG44 (Axis) have been added as well. Leveling up gives the Soldier benefits such as the ability to run with heavy weapons (instead of being slowed down).

Medic: The medic has the unique ability to drop health packs, as well as revive fallen players with a syringe. They also regenerate health at a constant rate, and have a higher base health than any other class, which makes them the most common class for close-in combat. When a player has achieved skill level 4 in medic, they get Self Adrenaline, which enables them to sprint for, longer and take less damage for a certain amount of time. Some of the medics act as Rambo Medics. Their emphasis is on killing rather than healing or reviving.

Engineer: The engineer is the only class which comes equipped with pliers, which can be used to repair vehicles, to arm/defuse (dynamite or land mines), or to construct (command posts, machine-gun nests, and barriers). As most missions require some amount of construction and/or blowing up of the enemy's construction to win the objective, and as defusing dynamite can be very useful, engineers are often invaluable, and one of the most commonly chosen classes. The engineer is also the only class capable of using rifle muzzle grenades.

Field ops: The field ops is a support class which has the ability to drop ammo packs for other players, as well as call air strikes (by throwing a colored smoke-grenade at the target) and artillery strikes (by looking through the binoculars and choosing where they want the artillery support fired). This class has low initial health, but makes up for having an unlimited supply of ammunition.

Covert ops: The covert ops is the only class which can use the scoped FG42 automatic rifle, the silenced Sten submachine gun (or MP-34 on some Mods), and a silenced, scoped rifle (M1 Garand for Allies, K43 Mauser for Axis). The covert ops has the ability to wear a fallen enemy soldier's clothes to go about disguised, throw smoke-grenades to reduce visibility temporarily, and place and remotely detonate explosive satchels. By looking through a pair of binoculars, the covert ops can spot enemy landmines, bringing them up on their team-map. The covert ops also show enemy soldiers on the team-map. Medic, Engineer, This creates a fluid transition to the next category.

APPENDIX B. LEARNING AND FUNCTIONAL ROLES FOR DESIGNING STRUCTURED INTERACTION AND POSITIVE INTERDEPENDENCE

Functional Roles–Adopted from http://www.myread.org/organisation.htm

ENCOURAGER AND COP

Reads instructions and directs participation
Read the instructions
Call for speakers
Organize turn-taking
Call for votes
Count votes
State agreed position

ENCOURAGER and SPY

Summarizes findings and trades ideas with other groups
Check up on other groups
Trade ideas with other groups
*Allowed to leave your place when directed by the teacher

ENCOURAGER and SCRIBE

Writes and reports groups ideas; is not a gatekeeper.
Record all ideas
Don't block
Seek clarification

ENCOURAGER and STORE KEEPER

Locates, collects and distributes resources including informational resources like web pages and encyclopedia entries

Get all the materials for the entire group
Collect worksheets from the teacher
Sharpen pencils
Tidy up
*Allowed to leave your place without teacher permission

LEARNING ROLE for LITERACY

Freebody (1992) and Freebody and Luke (1990) identify the roles literate people take on that can be used in a classroom for activities that involve reading or the study of literacies that involves narratives and cultural phenomenon.

CODE BREAKER

How Do I Crack this Code?

What words are interesting, difficult or tricky? How did you work them out?
What words have unusual spelling?
What words have the same sound or letter pattern or number of syllables?
What words have the same base word or prefix or suffix?
What words mean the same (synonyms)?
What smaller word can you find in this word to help you work it out?
What words are tricky to pronounce?
How is this word used in this context?
What different reading strategies did you use to decode this text?
Are the pictures close ups, mid or long shots?
Are the pictures high angle or low angle?
Were there any word pictures, eg similes and metaphors? How did you work them out?

USER

What Do I Do with this Text?

What sort of text is this? (Information, story/narrative) How do you know?
Is it fact or opinion? How do you know?
How can you find information in this text?
How did the author start this text? Did it suit its purpose?
Who would read a text like this? Why?
If you wrote a text like this what words and phrases would you use?
How is the language the same/ different from other similar texts you have read?
Could the text help solve a real life problem?
If you were going to put this text on a web page, how would it be different to the print version?
What is the purpose of this text?
Could you use these ideas in a poem, story, play, advertisement, report, brochure or poster?
How would the language, structure and change?

PARTICIPANT (EXPERT)

What Does This Text Mean to Me?

Does the text remind you of something that has happened to you or to someone else you know?
What does the title/cover suggest that the text is about?
What might happen next? What words or phrases give you this idea?
What are the characters thinking and feeling? How do you know?
What message is the author presenting?
What are the main ideas presented?
What do the pictures (graphs, diagrams, tables, captions, illustrations) tell us?
Do they fit in with the text and do they provide more information?
What did you feel as you read this part?
Describe or draw a picture of a character, event or scene from the text.

ANALYST (INVESTIGATOR)

What Does This Text Do to Me?

Is the text fair?
What would the text be like if the main characters were girls rather than boys and vice versa?
Consider different race and cultural backgrounds too.
How would the text be different if told from another point of view?
How would the text be different if told in another time or place, eg 1900 or 2100?
Why do you think the author chose this title?
Think about why the author chose particular words and phrases.
Are there stereotypes in the text?
Who does the text favor or represent?
Who does the text reject or silence?
How does this text claim authority? (Consider language, structure and content)
Who is allowed to speak? Who is quoted?

Section 3
New Theoretical Considerations of Games and Simulations

Chapter 12
Computational Literacy in Online Games:
The Social Life of Mods

Constance Steinkuehler
University of Wisconsin-Madison, USA

Barbara Z. Johnson,
University of Minnesota-Duluth, USA

ABSTRACT

Modding communities are particularly ripe environments for rethinking what it means to be IT literate in the contemporary world. Mods are, as we argue, computational literacy artifacts, exemplifying not merely computer literacy but also the ability to understand and use computational models and processes to conceptualize and solve problems. In this article, we describe modding practice in the context of the best-selling computer game to date: World of Warcraft. By analyzing such activities as a form of computational literacy practice "in the wild," we demonstrate how modding illustrates what it means to be technically literate in the contemporary participatory sociotechnical world. Based on our analysis, we argue for reconsideration of computer literacy as computational literacy, authorship as collaborative and negotiated rather than individually achieved, and digital media literacy practice as one involving design and production, not merely passive or critical consumption.

INTRODUCTION

There is a great digital divide between schools and the contemporary world beyond them. Despite extended efforts of the last decade to integrate technologies into schools, the ways in which computers and other digital media are used outside the classroom contrasts sharply with how they are used within it. Within schools, information technology (IT) is still frequently taught as a decontextualized base of knowledge and skills (such as *keyboarding*)—computer science, for example, reduced to nothing more than computer programming (Denning, 2004)—rather than as a goal-driven practice in authentic contexts where the outcomes might actually count. When integrated into subject matter, where students might have a better opportunity to experience technology as a powerful means toward various ends, it is often implemented in unreflective ways with little attention paid to designing students' experiences with the technology itself and not just with the content it is seen to (more or less transparently) mediate. In schools, "problems are assigned and understood by everyone as thinly veiled occasions to exercise tool knowledge or skills rather than as reasons for the existence of the tools" (diSessa, 2000, p. 40) in the first place. As educators, we have the deceiving luxury of acting as if computer literacy were some individual trait when, everywhere beyond the school, computer literacy *practice* is necessarily, increasingly social, distributed, and collaborative (Barron, 2004; Bell, 2005). In classrooms, technology is single media not multimedia, focused on content delivery not content creation and exchange (International Society for Technology in Education, 2007) with students positioned as passive recipients rather than active, critical participants in the production pipeline.

From this perspective, schools are one of the last remaining bastions of the old transmission model of technology and learning in the contemporary age of *participatory media* (Jenkins, 2006; Papert, 2007). Participatory media—such as blogs, Wikis, social bookmarking and networking sites, and mashups—are many-to-many media where both production and dissemination is distributed across an entire network of people (also see Web 2.0 discussions, O'Reilly, 2005). Today's adolescents and young adults are growing up in an age where participatory (rather than broadcast) environments are increasingly the norm: "Some 57% of online teens create content for the internet. That amounts to half of all teens ages 12-17, or about 12 million youth" (Lenhardt & Madden, 2005). Thus, while schools vigorously maintain the asymmetry between content provider (teachers and textbooks) and consumer (student), the con-

temporary world outside the school increasingly challenges such distinctions, in part, through the demand for and use of increasingly interactive media. This is all part of what some now call the *professional-amateur (or Pro-Am) revolution*:

The twentieth century was shaped by the rise of professionals... From education, science and medicine, to banking, business and sports, formerly amateur activities became more organized, and knowledge and procedures were codified and regulated.... But in the last two decades a new breed of amateur has emerged: the Pro-Am, amateurs who work to professional standards... The Pro-Ams are knowledgeable, educated, committed and networked, by new technology. The twentieth century was shaped by large hierarchical organisations with professionals at the top. Pro-Ams are creating new, distributed organizational models that will be innovative, adaptive and low-cost. (Leadbeater & Miller, 2004, p. 12)

Our current educational approaches to IT literacy do not prepare students for civic participation in such spaces—by a long shot (Jenkins, Purushotma, Clinton, Weigel, & Robison, 2006).

But if contemporary classrooms are not the right model of education in the contemporary age of participatory, Pro-Am culture, what is? One reasonable candidate for investigation is the informal learning communities that develop organically around popular interactive media out "in the wild" (Hutchins, 1995). One such example is the emergent communities found in massively multiplayer online games (MMOs). MMOs are virtual 3D gaming environments in which players, through their online digital character or *avatar*, are able to play not only with the computer software environment and characters but also with other human players. They are, in effect, persistent virtual social and material worlds in which players engage in collaborative or competitive activities (Steinkuehler, 2006a, 2006b) or, more minimally, individual activity in a populated social context (Ducheneaut, Yee, Nickell, & Moore, 2006). MMOs function as naturally occurring, self-sustaining, indigenous online communities of learning and practice, and the constellation of intellectual practices that constitute gameplay in such spaces—socially/materially distributed forms of cognition, collaborative problem solving, digital media literacy practices, scientific inquiry, reciprocal apprenticeship, and so forth—are all hallmark characteristics of participatory cultures more generally. Thus, their study can tell us something important about how such participatory, Pro-Am communities form and function in the everyday world. In this article, we focus on one such intellectual practice in particular: *modding*.

Game *mods* (short for modifications) are derivations of a given, professionally released (typically, computer) game title (Moshirnia, 2006; Nieborg, 2005). They either augment the content of the original, commercially released game (partial conversion mods) or exist as entirely new games created out of the original game engine (total conversion mods). Game companies vary in terms of their willingness and ability to support modding communities based on their commercial titles, with some companies providing modding tools and documentation with the original software to support such endeavors and other companies attempting to legally stop all such activities on the basis of purported intellectual property issues. For developers and fans alike, however, modding is oftentimes viewed as a means to increase replayability of and interest in a given title. The mod *Counter-Strike*, for example, continues to be the most widely played online first-person shooter in the world, besting Valve Software's *Half-Life*, the game it was originally based upon (Doug Lombardi, marketing director at Valve Software, quoted in ScuttleMonkey, 2007).

Modding communities are particularly ripe environments for rethinking what it means to be IT literate in the contemporary world. Mods are, we argue, computational literacy artifacts (cf. diSessa, 2000), exemplifying not merely com-

puter literacy (such as the ability to burn digital files to a CD)—the set of skills often emphasized in technology related programs in schools—but rather the ability to understand and use computational models and processes to conceptualize and solve a given problem. In this article, we describe modding practice in the context of the best-selling computer game to date: the MMO *World of Warcraft* (WoW*)*. By analyzing such activities as a form of computational literacy practice "in the wild," we demonstrate how modding illustrates what it means to be technically literate in the contemporary participatory sociotechnical world. Using online forum data, design documents, and interviews, we then detail the social life of two distinct WoW mods—one that closely emulates professional practice in the open source community, and one that illustrates what protoforms of such practices might be—in order to suggest one potential learning trajectory marked by a shift from consumption to production in the context of gameplay. Based on this analysis, we argue for a reconsideration of computer literacy as computational literacy, authorship as collaborative and negotiated rather than individually achieved, and digital media literacy practice as one involving design and production, not merely passive or critical consumption.

(RE)CONCEPTUALIZING IT LITERACY FOR THE CONTEMPORARY WORLD

Computational literacy refers to ability to interpret and express ideas through computational means (diSessa, 2000; Fernaeus, Aderklou, & Tholander, 2004; Veeragoudar Harrell & Abrahamson, 2007). At root, it is computer science, but not in the reduced sense of merely "computer programming" as typically emphasized in schools. Rather, computational literacy entails the fundamental principles and practices of computer science as a discipline and practice whose "fundamental principles are in design and in the mechanics of computation, communication, coordination, recollection, and automation…. [and] four core practices are programming, engineering of systems, modeling, and innovating" (Denning, 2004, p. 16). Here, the emphasis is on systems-oriented design and engineering, not merely the implementation of a given algorithm (i.e., step-by-step explicit procedures) via some particular programming language:

Computational thinking is using abstraction and decomposition when attacking a large complex task or designing a large complex system. It is separation of concerns. It is choosing an appropriate representation for a problem or modeling the relevant aspects of a problem to make it tractable. It is using invariants to describe a system's behavior succinctly and declaratively. It is having the confidence we can safely use, modify, and influence a large complex system without understanding its every detail. It is modularizing something in anticipation of multiple users or prefetching and caching in anticipation of future use. (Wing, 2006, p.33)

Programming in a conventional language (e.g., C, Fortran, or Java) alone is neither necessary nor sufficient to computational literacy so defined. One the one hand, some spreadsheet operations and advanced HTML programming for Web pages, for example, can entail the very same practices and understandings (National Academy of Science, 1999). On the other hand, rigid translation of a mathematical function into code with no design or understanding of the problem that it is intended to solve in the first place is to computational literacy as reading without comprehension is to print.

Such skills are fundamental for everyone, not just for computer scientists. Computer programming may be easily outsourced to the lowest bidder, but computational literacy is increasingly a crucial part of how we get on with the business of our everyday professional and personal lives.

We live in an information society where computers are an increasingly ubiquitous part of all aspects of our day-to-day. Computational models (such as those produced by Microsoft or Google) shape the publication, distribution, and access to information. In order to genuinely participate as citizens in the increasingly digital world, we must understand how such computational models work, in both general conceptual terms and in their specific implementations. The National Academy of Science (1999) states, "Universal knowledge of these principles is fundamental to an information society. To apply and exploit information processing technology that creates, manipulates, searches, and displays information, the population must be able to think algorithmically" (3.1.2. ¶3). This bar is too low. If we take creative production (and therefore design) into equal account, as we argue we should, then we need computational literacy, not just algorithmic thinking.

In a world increasingly defined by participatory media and the rise of vital Pro-Am communities, computational literacy serves as part of the very foundation on which the shift from passive consumption to active production of knowledge rests. It underlies the massive collective problem-solving behaviors found in corners of the Pro-Am world such as astronomy (Leadbeater & Miller, 2004), alternate reality games such as *I Love Bees* (McGonigal, in press), and other collective intelligence (Levy, 1999) projects such as those conducted by MIT's Center for Collective Intelligence. If predictions are correct and mass collaboration does indeed become one of the core features of the workplace and marketplace of the future (Malone, 2004; Malone, Laubacher, & Morton, 2003; Tapscott & Williams, 2006), then computational literacy—the ability to interpret and express oneself via computational models—will only become more and more crucial to participation in the global community. Our days of reliance on "high tech scribes" (Fisher, 2005) are over; citizenship in today's digital community requires the ability to read and write using computational media.

RESEARCHING COMPUTATIONAL LITERACY IN THE WILD: THE CASE OF MODDING

If computational literacy is a crucial form of IT fluency that should be emphasized for 21st century citizenry in the global networked world, then modding communities such as those found in WoW fandom are particularly useful sites for study as they tell us something important about the production, dissemination, and consumption of computational artifacts in informal (nondesigned or required) settings. In WoW, mods take the form of so-called user interface (UI) *add ons*—essentially, patches to the game software that change the user interface in some way—that are created by and for the community of players themselves. For example, some mods change the visual appearance of the interface or add additional *hot key* functions for the player's ease of use. Others collect and process performance data of the individual, generating charts and graphs that display one's performance, say, in a given group activity compared to other participants. Still others enhance specific in-game features such as the chat system, guild management, resource finding, or in-game maps.

Modding began early in the history of WoW with the developers (Blizzard) encouraging the practice, providing the basic infrastructure necessary for such work such as source code and artwork for the interface, documentation on the form and function of the code (Lua, a scripting language much like Python), and an online forum to enable the design, development, and debugging of the community's creations—in effect, the "knowledge sharing structures within that community which facilitate the modding process" (Moshirnia, 2006, p. 122).

As tools, such mods "carry traces of the funda-mental values and goals of the community. They accomplish the jobs that define and justify the very existence of the community [and] are badges of membership" (diSessa, 2000, p. 39). Two years after the game's original release, some mods have become so central to the game-playing community that many in-game groups (guilds) no longer allow their members to engage in collaborative activities such as large-group raids without them (Taylor, 2006). In some cases, highly effective and popular mods have even been incorporated by the game company directly into the official software itself. Mods that reach such levels of prominence and saturation across the community become part of the architecture of the game itself, either informally (through norm and law) or formally (through the game's literal code). In effect, they function as hubs in the sociotechnical network, calibrating the gameplay of others in tangible ways. The sheer number of downloads of various WoW mods illustrates this point: At last check, the number of downloads for *Titan Panel* (an interface enhancement mod) was over eight million; for *Auctioneer* (discussed later on), over 3.5 million; even Alamo (a nonfunctional albeit funny mod that builds on a longstanding joke in the WoW druid community), had, at last check, over 1,600 downloads. Compared to the average number of readers for an academic journal article (i.e., five), such audience sizes are indeed impressive.

Are such large numbers of downloads the exception or the rule? As Figure 1 illustrates, while some mods do reach widespread saturation across the WoW player base with downloads far into the millions, the majority of mods remain on a much smaller scale with less that ten thousand downloads on average. The curve here is a familiar one: a version of the classic power law or "long tail" (Anderson, 2006) graph that characterizes other online *markets* (such as Amazon or general blog readership) where products that are in low demand collectively make up a market share that rivals or exceeds the handful of blockbusters. In

Figure 1. Number of WoW mods by number of downloads on curse-gaming.com, the most popular mod distribution site to date. The top six mod distribution sites show the same "long tail" pattern.

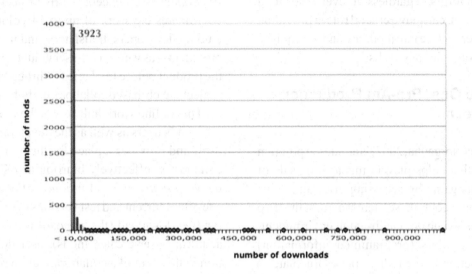

other words, while some mods reach levels of production and market saturation that parallel large scale, professional software practice, modding on the smaller, more *inde* scale of the Pro-Am spectrum collectively rivals them in distribution and perhaps even influence.

Examination of the culture of WoW modding shows interesting patterns as well, thoroughly debunking the popular stereotype of the sole genius creator working in solitude in his bedroom or basement. In practice, modding is not a solitary activity. Loosely organized development metacommunities (for example, *Ace* or *Titan*), actively facilitate new developers' entry into the modding world through their publicly available tutorials, code libraries, forums, and guidelines, As such, they function as informal apprenticeship communities similar to the service and repair community documented by Brown and Duguid (2002). As one informant noted, "With few exceptions, the community is absolutely wonderful. Authors are more than willing to share their knowledge, and we all have good laughs in #wowi-lounge on irc.freenode.net" (M. Orlando, personal communication, June 22, 2007).

Throughout such communities, the line between author and user/consumer is consistently blurred with users actively encouraged on mod distribution and development Web sites to download test versions, submit enhancement requests, discuss relative merits of features or code versions, and even upload suggested program versions of their own in an informal joint application development environment (Scacchi, 2001). At these rich intersections, authors and users wrestle with issues fundamental to computational literacy such as how to represent and express information accurately and efficiently, how to decompose a complex problem into manageable tasks, and how to define and automate routine functions. In so doing, WoW mod developers use a wide range of development cycles and team structures in order to accomplish their design goals, ranging from those that closely emulate professional practice to others that illustrate protoforms of such practices. In what follows, we detail two illustrative and contrasting cases: the first, an example of high-end mod production that emulates professional open source software development; the second, a smaller scale, more amateur form of production that nonetheless presages the first. Our basic claim is that both forms, regardless of level of seeming sophistication, can play a crucial role in providing game players entrée into modding and its requisite computational literacy skills.

Example One: Pro-Am Production of Auctioneer

Auctioneer (Norganna, 2007) is an add-on program for WoW that helps players manage the sale of items in the game by accessing price and value information about these items across the two major sales venues in the in-game environment: the game vendors (programmed information) and the auction house (where prices fluctuate as players buy and sell items). *Auctioneer* does this by aggregating server data on the virtual items currently on auction; this, in turn, allows the user to identify bargains on the market by determining price trends on a given item and then comparing current prices to that trend. With this tool, players are then able to use the auction house in a fashion similar to the stock market—essentially, "playing the market" by purchasing under-priced items at the auction house in order to turn around and sell them for a profit at the market norm. The mod collects, organizes, and displays complex information for every in-game item on auction, including basic statistics (such as mean, median, range) on the given item's previous and going prices, what the items can be used for, and who uses it. Since every player participates in the in-game economy at some level (if only by the sheer fact that killing in-game monsters generates virtual goods and currency), *Auctioneer* has a clear use for any WoW player regardless of character type; as a result, it has an exceptionally large user base with millions of downloads to its credit. It is consistently rated among the "top picks" on the most popular mod distribution sites and is a frequently recommended UI add-on on game-related discussion forums and within social networks such as guilds.

As stated previously, the practice of modding is not a solitary activity but a communal one, and *Auctioneer* is no exception. Its project manager coordinates the work of up to 14 volunteers including developers, translators, and user support providers—as well as end-user volunteers who test the product before final release through use of the project's Web-based collaborative hub (see Figure 2). This online work hub serves the needs of the program's users as well as the development team itself and provides a place for the two groups to collaborate, effectively blurring any strong line between *consumer* and *producer*. For users, the site offers current and test versions of the program for free download (the standard mechanism for acquiring user-created mods), user documentation in the form of a collaboratively written Wiki text, and news about the mod such as the release dates of new updates, fixed bugs, and so forth. For developers, the site provides space for managing bugs, production milestones, planned enhancements, and versions of the mod's code through the Tracker and Source sections of the Web site. The two groups interact through the online chat and forum tools where users can ask for support, make recommendations, and even post suggested code segments of their own for incorporation into subsequent versions of the mod itself. Users are encouraged to take advantage of the team's own bug tracking software directly, further blurring the line between consumer and producer as is characteristic of open-source software development. Compare this process, for example with Linux, one of the most widely known open-source development products to date: In both, the production team maintains control of the official version of the program while welcoming contributions from its user base (Weber, 2004).

With its relatively permeable boundaries, the *Auctioneer* development team is an example of informal *joint application development*—an emerging model of open-source development in which systems are developed incrementally and in collaboration between globally distributed end

Figure 2. The main page of Auctioneer's online development hub (located at http://auctioneeraddon. com), providing access to tools for the production team, documentation for the mod's userbase, and space for collaboration and communication between the two parties.

users and software developers using online tools (Scacchi, 2001). Users test each release, report bugs, and suggest features using the team's tracking tools. These in turn are slated for release milestones that are publicly viewable and discussed using the team's online forums. Thus, *consumers* are loosely integrated into the development team with the use of online knowledge sharing tools and therefore have an impact on the product they use, while the official *developers* make the best use of their skills and talent in designing and maintaining the program itself. On both ends, you find, in essence, the ability to *read* and *write* through computational means.

Example Two: Protoform Production of Quark

Auctioneer is an example of a high end, large scale mod that lies at one end of the continuum not only in terms of number of downloads but also in terms of the Pro-Am spectrum; as Figure

1 shows, however, most mods are on a more modest scale. An example of such is *Quartz* (Nymbia, 2007), a lightweight, highly configurable add-on that helps the player closely monitor the amount of time required by various activities (typically, spell casts) within the game. Like *Auctioneer,* *Quartz* has utility for nearly any WoW player; unlike Auctioneer, however, *Quartz* is a relatively new program (first released in June 2007) whose early examination can give us clues about how a particular computational artifact begins and evolves over time.

Quartz' production team is, at first glance, the simplest of all types: a single person. However, as Moshirnia (2006) found in his study of first-person shooter (FPS) mod communities, here the solo mod author is tied to larger, informal communities via mod discussion forums where mod enthusiasts exchange information, knowledge and skills:

The modding forum serves as group dynamics on the cyber stage. Video game players consider themselves to be part of a group, which gives players access to a cadre of like-minded friends (Moskal, 2004). Members regularly examine each others' game replays and share knowledge, skills, and constructive abilities. When an individual creates an especially creative or impressive mod, she demonstrates that she has skills that can aid other members. Adding skilled modders to the game forum increases the diversity of available mods and the richness of the game playing experience. To that end, trainers tutor new users and answer questions on game mechanics and programming. In this situation, all members of the community have powerful incentives to teach techniques to new members of the forum while experimenting in order to discover new knowledge. (p. 126)

In the case of *Quartz*, the mod is part of the large community that has formed around Ace (McLemore, 2007), a set of standardized tools designed to facilitate the development of WoW mods (see Figure 3). *Ace* not only provides a discussion forum but also serves as an incubator for smaller scale developers, providing many of

the tools that larger mods with more professional looking programming teams rely upon such as version control and bug-tracking databases. Thus, the small team or solo author is introduced to commonly accepted programming practices such as modularity, reusability, bug tracking, and version control early on in their evolution. Through Ace, mod developers are connected with other developers as well as end users such that designs become subject to peer commentary and review via either the discussion forum or a special white board reserved for the suggestion of new mod ideas. Making beta versions of one's mod available is established practice, allowing end-user volunteers and other developers to assist in finding and reporting errors—a process that ultimately leads to an improved next iteration before official public release.

As part of a modular system, *Quartz* fits the reusable components model of software development (Scacchi, 2001) as a type of open-source program development. *Quartz*, for that matter

Figure 3. The main page for Quartz at Ace's Web site (http://www.wowace.com/wiki/Quartz). Links on the left provide access to tools available to all developers; links on the right provide access to online where the mod author can interact with end-users of the mod or other developers.

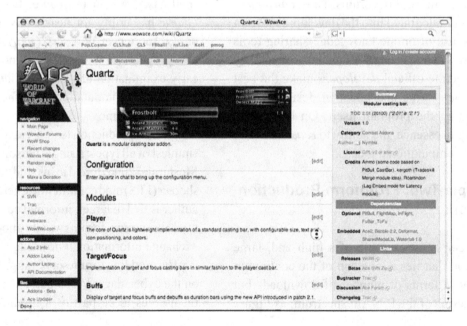

all mods that make use of frameworks and libraries such as the *Ace* and *Titan Panel* families of mods, are good examples of modularization as a powerful computational skill that allows entry into programming for new comers and reduces the work load of officially recognized professionals. If *Quartz* were to expand (for example, translated into different languages, as is the *Auctioneer* mod), such modularization, coupled with the availability of a community knit together by the various collaboration and tracking tools available at Ace, could enable a team to grow and expand beyond the single original author (as the history of many mods has demonstrated). Regardless of the potential for future possible expansions of Quark's core development team, however, it has already earned itself an active user-community following who make suggestions for improvements and extensions to the mod as currently designed, with nearly 500 forum posts made within the first few weeks of its release and over 4,000 downloads of the tool itself.

From Consumption to Production

In the last section we detailed the production process for two example mods: one developed by a well-organized, distributed team of near professionals under an informal joint application development model, the other developed by a single individual within a collaborative context following the reusable components model. While the complexity and sophistication of the production process of the two vary, both represent important computational literacy practices "in the wild." We argue that the latter represents a prototype of the former—if not in literal practice (with one practice evolving into the other on the individual level) then at least in terms of the computational literacy skills they represent. Smaller, more modest WoW mods represent requisite component skills required by the larger, more complex ones. Said another way, if the goal of a given activity were to enable participation in the development

of software of the caliber of the more advanced and prestigious mods (such as *Auctioneer*), then ample experience with a well ordered set of the more modest—yet still well conceived and well implemented—mods would be the ideal form of preparation.

Based on our data thus far, a potential learning trajectory emerges, one that runs a course from mod consumption to mod production and, from there, to increasingly complex (and ostensibly professional) forms: mod *users* become mod *critics* become mod *adapters* become mod *producers* in their own right. While all modders we have interviewed to date report an interest in computational media that predates playing WoW, many also report that they got their start in modding as users, not coders per se. The following interview excerpt illustrates:

... my most-popular mods grew out of wanting improved versions of other mods—Group Buttons from Guon's Health Warning... Discord Action Bars from BibToolbars (wanted to be able to set the number of buttons per bar and configure the appearance of buttons...), Discord Unit Frames from just about every unit frame mod (none of them were ever satisfying so I decided to make one where the user defines everything). One mod I could never find was a simple report that tells you how much money you have on each character and the total amount you have among all your characters. ... So I resolved to write such a mod and my first mod, Total Gold, was born... I've done almost nothing but mod in-game since March. I've found it to be a lot more fun for me than actually playing... (Lozareth, personal communication, November 2005)

Thus, it is quite plausible that participation in MMO gameplay evolves into the use of WoW mods, which in turn provides entrée into mod critique and then production itself—for some. An important next research question to ask, then, is for whom and under what conditions. Issues of equity become more pressing when one considers the real world payoffs for participation in the practices detailed here. When asked if modding has payoffs outside of the game, our interviewees consistently respond that it does. Bryan McLemore, the head of *Ace* WoW mods (see Figure 3), is a case in point. In his own words, "It already has [real world payoffs]. It's helped me land what could be considered my dream job, being a web developer after doing retail management for years." (B. McLemore, personal communication, June 22, 2007). Another talks about a recent book deal he landed for a co-authored book on writing WoW mods, pointing out the very "real financial and professional rewards involved" (M. Orlando, personal communication, June 22, 2007).

CONCLUSION AND IMPLICATIONS

In this article, we have argued for a reconsideration of computer literacy as computational literacy—an ability to understand and express oneself using computational media. If one looks at how computational literacy works out "in the wild," we find some fairly obvious trends. Authorship is collaborative and negotiated—not just among participants at a given stage in the production pipeline but among so-called *end users* as well. Even in the case of a single author computational artifact, development crucially entails a community of others who constrain and enable the work through, in these cases, online work hubs that function as many-to-many media where both production and dissemination is distributed across an entire network of people. This pattern is hardly a novel one; it characterizes participatory, Pro-Am culture (also referred to as Web 2.0) more generally. We have argued that this is, in fact, part of the very reason that modding should be of particular interest to educators of so-called *computing* and *IT skills*. Modding gives us an interesting model for how we might think about redesigning *computer literacy* activities in classrooms to better reflect

contemporary needs and demands. In making this argument, we second diSessa (2000), who states:

I believe computational media and associated new literacies may be exactly the infrastructural change that can support converting schools, particularly mathematics and science classes, into vital communities of tool building and sharing. The new genre of software I have in mind is a set of open, reconfigurable, repurposeable tools for student tasks, tasks that are more like design and student research than conventional activities such as exercises and short problem solving. (p. 41)

Such findings have implication not only for educators in IT-related fields but also for researchers in education more broadly. First, it suggests that we should consider teaching computational literacy for a broad audience and not just computer science for computer science majors or IT as a remedial or beginners course. Current computer-related courses reduce the topic to basics such as keyboarding and relegate any authoring work to more advanced courses designed for intended majors. There is a genuine need for courses that cover ground between these two by focusing on the production of meaningful computational artifacts without the need for advanced proficiency in reading and writing computer code. Second, this work also suggests that such computational literacy practices should be taught as collaborative activities that are goal-driven. In practice, this means that the creation of computational solutions should be a social production, graded as such, with metacommunities of practice fostered and encouraged such that student performance is scaffolded by access not just to tools but to communities using them as well. The days of the lone student working on computer code in isolation are outdated; what we need are assignments that allow students permission to build code-based solutions to problems they choose (goals) and access to each other throughout the process of solving them (collaboration). Third and finally, this work also suggests that one strategy for closing the digital divide between classrooms and the world beyond them is to take seriously the contemporary shift toward participatory media and Pro-Am culture though studies of how such informal settings function. Studies of intellectual communities of practice beyond those we contrive within schools themselves tell us something important about the production, dissemination, and consumption of computational artifacts "in the wild." Such research can form the foundation of intentional learning activities designed to prepare students for the contemporary world.

REFERENCES

Anderson, C. (2006). *The long tail: Why the future of business is selling less of more*. New York: Hyperion.

Barron, B. (2004). Learning ecologies for technological fluency: Gender and experience differences. *Journal of Educational Computing Research, 31*(1), 1-36.

Bell, P. (2005, October 23-24). *Reflections on the cognitive and social foundations of information and communication technology fluency*. Paper prepared for the National Academy of Sciences Workshop on CIT Fluency & High School Graduation Outcomes, Washington DC.

Brown, J. S., & Duguid, P. (2002). *The social life of information*. Boston: Harvard Business School.

Denning, P. J. (2004). The field of programmers myth. *Communications of the ACM, 47*(7), 15-20.

diSessa, A. (2000). *Changing minds: Computers, learning, and literacy*. Cambridge MA: MIT Press.

Ducheneaut, N., Yee, N., Nickell, E., & Moore, R. J. (2006). Alone together? Exploring the social dynamics of massively multiplayer games. In *Conference Proceedings on Human Factors in Computing Systems* (CHI2006) (pp. 407-416). Montreal, QC, Canada.

Fernaeus, Y., Aderklou, C., & Tholander, J. (2004). Computational literacy at work: Children's construction of digital material. In *Proceedings of CELDA*, Lisbon, Portugal.

Fischer, G. (2005) Computational literacy and fluency: Being independent of high-tech scribes. In J. Engel, R. Vogel, & S. Wessolowski (Eds.), *Strukturieren - Modellieren - Kommunizieren. Leitbild mathematischer und informatischer Aktivitäten* (pp 217-230). Franzbecker, Hildesheimhttp.

Hutchins, E. (1995). *Cognition in the wild*. Cambridge MA: MIT Press.

International Society for Technology in Education. (2007). Introduction: All children must be ready for a different world. *National Educational Technology Standards (NETS)*. Retrieved June 2, 2007, from http://cnets.iste.org/intro2.html

Jenkins, H. (2006). *Convergence culture: Where old and new media collide*. New York: University Press.

Jenkins, H., Purushotma, R., Clinton, K., Weigel, M., & Robison, A. (2006). *Confronting the challenges of participatory culture: Media education for the 21st century*. Chicago IL: The MacArthur Foundation. Retrieved June 1, 2007, from http://www.digitallearning.macfound.org

Leadbeater, C., & Miller, P. (2004). *The pro-am revolution: How enthusiasts are changing our economy and society. Demos*. Retrieved June 1, 2007, from http://www.demos.co.uk/publications/proameconomy

Lenhardt, A., & Madden, M. (2005). *Teen content creators and consumers*. Washington DC: Pew Internet & American Life Project. Retrieved from http://www.pewInternet.org/PPF/r/166/report_display.asp

Levy, P. (1999). *Collective intelligence: Mankind's emerging world in cyberspace.* (R. Bononno, Trans.). Cambridge, MA: Perseus Books.

Malone, T. W. (2004). *The future of work: How the new order of business will shape your organization, your management style and your life.* Cambridge, MA: Harvard Business School Press.

Malone, T. W., Laubacher, R., & Morton, M. S. (Eds.). (2003). *Inventing the organizations of the 21st century.* Cambridge, MA: MIT Press.

McGonigal, J. E. (in press). Why I love bees: A case study in collective intelligence gaming. In K. Salen (Ed.), *Ecologies of play.* Chicago: The MacArthur Foundation.

McLemore, B. (2007, May 25). *Ace: World of Warcraft.* Retrieved June 24, 2007, from http://www.wowace.com/

Moshirnia, A. V. (2006, November 29-December 1). An analysis of knowledge sharing structures within modification culture. In *Proceedings of the Fourth IASTED International Conference on Knowledge Sharing and Collaborative Engineering*, St. Thomas, U.S. Virgin Islands.

Moskal, B. (2004). Evaluating the effectiveness of a new instructional approach. In *Proceedings of 25th SIGSCE technical symposium on computer science education* (pp. 75-79) New York: ACM Press.

National Academy of Science. (1999). *Being fluent with information technology.* Washington DC: National Academy Press.

Nieborg, D. B. (2005, January 11-12). *Am I mod or not? An analysis of first person shooter modification culture.* Paper presented at the Creative Gamers Seminar: Exploring Participatory Culture in Gaming, Finland.

Norganna. (2007). Auctioneer (Version 4.0) [computer software].

Nymbia. (2007). Quartz (Version 1.0) [computer software].

O'Reilly, T. (2005, September 30). *What is Web 2.0: Design patterns and business models for the next generation of software.* Retrieved June 1, 2007, from on http://www.oreillynet.com/pub/a/oreilly/tim/news/2005/09/30/what-is-web-20.html

Papert, S. (2007). *Technology in schools: To support the system or render it obsolete?* Retrieved June 5, 2007, from: http://www.mff.org/edtech/article.taf?_function=detail&Content_uid1=106

Scacchi, W. (2001). Process models in software engineering. In J. J. Marciniak (Ed.), *Encyclopedia of software engineering* (2nd ed.). New York: John Wiley and Sons.

ScuttleMonkey. (2007, May 16). *User created content is key for new games. Slashdot.* Retrieved June 1, 2007, from http://games.slashdot.org/article.pl?sid=07/05/16/1955246&from=rss

Steinkuehler, C. (2006a). The mangle of play. *Games & Culture, 1*(3), 1-14.

Steinkuehler, C. A. (2006b). Massively multiplayer online videogaming as participation in a Discourse. *Mind, Culture, & Activity, 13*(1), 38-52.

Tapscott, D., & Williams, A. D. (2006). *Wikinomics: How mass collaboration changes everything.* New York: Portfolio.

Taylor, T. L. (2006). Does WoW change everything? How a PvP server, multinational player base, and surveillance mod scene caused me pause. *Games & Culture, 1*(4), 318-337.

Veeragoudar Harrell, S., & Abrahamson, D. (2007, July 16-21). Computational literacy and mathematics learning in a virtual world: Identity, embodiment, and empowered media engagement. In C. Chinn, G. Erkens, & S. Puntambekar (Eds.), *Proceedings of he Biennial Conference on Computers Supported Collaborative Learning*, New Brunswick, NJ.

Weber, S. (2004). *The success of open source.* Cambridge, MA: Harvard University Press.

Wing, J. M. (2006). Computational thinking. *Communications of the ACM, 49*(3), 33-35.

Chapter 13
What Players Like about Video Games:
Prediction of Video Game Playing through Quality Perceptions and Player Types

René Weber
University of California Santa Barbara, USA

Patrick Shaw
Scientifically Proven Entertainment, USA

ABSTRACT

Video game developers make multimillion dollar decisions based on hunches, personal experience, and iteration. A theoretical model of video game player behavior – how one chooses, plays, and evaluate games – can provide an important framework for these decisions. According to social cognitive theory, one's behavior can be understood as the result of expected outcomes resulting from direct and observational learning processes. Video game players use symbolic representations (quality perceptions) of their direct and observed experiences with video games to build expectations of whether playing a specific video game will satisfy their needs. A series of in-depth interviews and a subsequent survey with students of a large mid-western university was conducted to enumerate groups of similar players (player types), and video game quality perceptions. Both concepts were used to provide empirical evidence for a model to predict video game playing. Results show that, in prediction models, the best player types are those that include player type-specific quality perceptions.

INTRODUCTION

Video games[1] continue to grow in popularity. In 1998, Video games generated 4.8 billion dollars in sales. By 2009, sales grew to 10.5 billion dollars (Entertainment Software Association,

2008, 2010). This 119% increase is even more remarkable in light of sluggish global economy in many other sectors. And this growth doesn't cover pirated, subscription based, and online games. People who have grown up with games are called the "gaming generation" (Beck & Wade, 2004). Games are a growing, cultural force to be reckoned with. What is it about video games that

DOI: 10.4018/978-1-60960-565-0.ch013

make them so popular? Why do certain people play certain games and enjoy playing them? What is important to players when they chose to play a video game for entertainment? How can game developers understand their "audience" better to create better games?

Traditionally, media scholars have addressed these important questions with various theories and models of media use and media enjoyment. Those theories and models span from explorative media-user types (e.g. Espe & Seiwert, 1986), the uses and gratification paradigm (Rosengreen, 1974; Palmgreen, Wenner, & Rosengreen, 1985), selective exposure theory (Zillmann & Bryant, 1985), to general theories of human happiness, balance, and well-being such as flow theory (Csikszentmihalyi, 1990; Sherry, 2004) or self-determination theory (Ryan & Deci, 2000). Meanwhile, all these perspectives have been applied to video game play.

For example, Bartle (1996, 2004) created a player-type model for MUDs ("multi-user dungeons", a primitive precursor to modern online games) in which players with similar motivations were observed to behave similarly in the game. He found four principle types of players: achievers, explorers, socializers, and killers. Players within each of these groups are characterized by distinct behaviors and game playing motivations. Based on a large online survey, Yee (2006) updated Bartle's work and identified a five factor model of MMORPGs (Massively Multi-user Online Role-Playing Games, graphical descendants of MUDs) play motivations. People seem to play MMORPGs because they want to achieve goals, build relationships to others, become immersed in a virtual world that can be manipulated and used to escape the real-world.

Sherry, Lucas, Greenberg, and Lachlan (2006) constructed a uses and gratifications model of player motivation to predict video game preference and use. In its original version, the uses and gratification paradigms posits that basic needs, individual differences, and contextual societal factors combine to result in a variety of perceived problems and motivations to which gratifications are sought from media (here video games) leading to differential patterns of media use (cf. Palmgreen, Wenner, & Rosengreen, 1985; Rosengreen, 1974). Guided by this assumption Sherry et al. (2005) found arousal, challenge, competition, diversion, fantasy and social interaction as the most relevant motivational dimensions of video game playing. These findings mirrored the results of early uses and gratifications based video game studies (cf. Selnow, 1984; Wigand, Borstelmann, & Boster, 1985).

Other recent uses and gratifications studies (cf. Griffiths, 1991; Phillips, Rolls, Rouse, & Griffiths, 1995; Vorderer, Hartmann, & Klimmt, 2003) added more general video game play motivations such as "to pass time", "to avoid doing other things", and "to cheer oneself up", which correspond to the notion that video games (and entertainment media in general) are primarily used to regulate emotions as suggested by selective exposure theory and Zillmann & Bryant's (1985) affect-dependent theory of stimulus arrangement (see also Zillmann, 1988). This theory assumes that (1) people are motivated to minimize exposure to negative, aversive stimuli and to maximize positive, pleasurable stimuli, and (2) that we learn through prior experience to associate media content with emotional outcomes. In simple terms, we watch enjoyable television programs, read entertaining books, use the internet for entertainment, and play fun video games when we know it makes us feel good and we can successfully manage our moods by using media. Following this rationale, Bryant and Davis (2006) demonstrate that all four sub-processes of selective exposure theory, i.e. excitatory homeostasis, intervention potential, message-behavioral affinity, and hedonic valence can be observed when people play video games and thus it may be justified to assume that video games are particularly potent mood managers (see also Grodal, 2000).

Similarly, the assumption that an individual's desire to manage their moods by using entertaining media such as video games, can be well integrated into more general theories of human happiness, well-being, and human motivation such as flow theory (Csikszentmihalyi, 1990) and self-determination theory (Ryan & Deci, 2000). Applying flow theoretical assumptions to video game play (cf. Sherry, 2004), exposure to video games is an intrinsically rewarding experience in which video game players try to achieve a highly engaging and enjoyable flow state. One of the essential prerequisites for attaining a flow state is a balance between the challenges offered by a video game and a player's skills which is optimized by most video games through inbuilt "skill levels" or other adaptive features.

Likewise, self-determination theory applied to video game play (Vorderer, Steen, & Chan, 2006; Ryan, Rigby, & Przybylski, 2006; Tamborini, Bowman, Eden, Grizzard & Ogan, in press) posits that people play video games because they ideally satisfy basic psychological needs for autonomy (i.e. when activities are done for interest or personal value), competence (i.e. when activities are a challenge and provide a feeling of effectance), and relatedness (i.e. when a person feels connected to others). According to Ryan, Rigby, and Przybylski's (2006) study, those factors account for the psychological attractiveness or "pull" of games, and this even regardless of specific genre or individual differences.

While each of the outlined theories highlights specific aspects of the question why do people play video games or what makes video games attractive for people, there is obviously considerable overlap. In addition, it is well-known that most of the mentioned theories assume that individuals can accurately report their own needs and motivations for media use or playing video games when asked. However, needs and motivations are complex psychological constructs. It is a common observation that video game players usually do not think of their video games and their playing

behavior in terms of psychological constructs and have difficulties when being forced to describe playing motivations without prompt. Simply talking to players or visiting one of the countless discussion groups or video game blogs (e.g. see http://www.gamespot.com) reveals that video game players mostly talk about game features and the game experience when explaining (or justifying) why they play a certain game or why a video game is "cool", "a great game" (i.e. a high-quality game), or "just fun to play". Accordingly, video game professionals need to think about specific video game features and players' perceptions of those features. Imagine that a media scholar is consulted by a video game developer and is asked "what makes our video game great so that players are motivated to play the game and have fun?"[2] This media scholar would answer, for example, "you have to make sure that your game addresses your players' need for autonomy, competence, and relatedness". While this is certainly true based on scientific evidence, the question is how does these complex psychological constructs help a video game developer to modify or adjust a video game's design? Still, this developer has to rely on gut feeling and is forced to make multimillion dollar decisions based on hunches and guesses about what game features might satisfy the needs of video game players.

A more thorough understanding of how players relate to various game characteristics will also contribute to improvements of video game effects research. Weber, Bates and Behr (2010), for example, argue that video game interactivity and players' perceptions of interactivity moderate video game effects. Knowing the particular features that contribute to (perceived) video game interactivity will allow researchers to propose and test more specific effects hypotheses. For example, hypotheses that investigate the impact of various customization features on the identification potential of video game characters (cf. Lewis, Weber & Bowman, 2008). Past research has shown (cf. Lucas & Sherry, 2004) that there are considerable individual differences among players when studying game playing motivations and video game preferences. Furthermore, many of those differences are of biological nature (Sherry, 2001). Most of the outlined theories do not explicitly account for those differences when defining player types or playing motivations and most empirical studies have simply overlooked biological factors.

Hence, what is needed is a model to predict video game playing that is (1) grounded in a solid theory of human behavior, (2) captures not only motivational aspects of video game playing but also biological-individual differences, and (3) provides an operational basis for video game professionals and media scholars who are interested in a-posteriori predictions of video game preference and use. We assert that Bandura's general social cognitive theory (1986) and Bandura's social cognitive theory of mass communication (2001) provide a useful theoretical frame for such a model.

Social Cognitive Theory Based Model of Video Game Playing

Social cognitive theory (SCT) (Bandura, 1986) is a general theory of human behavior. SCT has been applied to mass media in order to understand the psychological mechanisms through which symbolic communication influences human thought, affect, and behavior (Bandura, 2001). LaRose and Eastin (2004) suggested a social cognitive perspective of media uses and gratifications and adopted the theory's premises to explain and predict internet use. Similarly to LaRose and Eastin, we follow SCT's basic assumption that behavior is an observable act and is determined by expected outcomes moderated by personal, social, or environmental factors.

Expected outcomes are formed by direct or vicarious experiences. We learn through our prior experiences to associate media use with emotional (e.g. happiness) and cognitive (e.g. knowledge) outcomes, i.e. we learn to use video games because

they seemed to offer the reward we were looking for in the past. However, not only "learning by doing" is an effective method to engage in new activities, but also "learning by observing". SCT assumes that "virtually all behavioral, cognitive, and affective learning from direct experience can be achieved vicariously by observing people's actions and its consequences for them" (Bandura, 2001, p. 126). Given that most video game play is socially motivated and increasingly embedded in a social context (Williams, 2006) it seems obvious that emotional and cognitive outcomes of video game play are also learned by observation. Thus, video game play can be considered as overt behavior and is determined by expected outcomes as a result of own and vicarious experiences. Further, SCT suggests that personal and vicarious experiences, or direct and observational learning, are governed by four sub-processes: (1) attentional processes, (2) retention processes, (3) production processes, and (4) motivational processes. At a glance, people need to select aspects of an experience or observed event, they have to symbolically code and remember the experience, they have to translate a symbolic representation into an appropriate action, and they have to link an appropriate action to an incentive for an action in order to execute a learned behavior. All four sub-processes depend on a dynamic and reciprocal interaction among a variety of environmental, personal (including biological factors such as temperaments), and behavioral variables, which is the reason for the extreme complexity of any exhaustive SCT based behavioral model.

It is not a goal of this investigation to provide an exhaustive SCT model of video game play but rather to seek for a theoretical link between motivations of playing video games and operational video game features. Thus, we focus now on concrete retention, production, and motivational processes as these processes are of particular interest for an operational and SCT inspired player type model of video game play.

According to SCT, outcome expectations are guided by six basic types of incentives for human behavior: status, social, monetary, enjoyable activity, novel sensory, and self-reactive incentives (Bandura, 1986, pp. 232 f.). We choose to sub-divide the social and status incentives based on whether the incentive is targeted at one's self, others, or the game to better reflect our own observations of why people play games. For example, for the status incentive, one may try to get a good score as source of personal pride, to beat one's friends, or to simply master the game itself.

In addition to incentives, people can also regulate their actions and mood. This self-regulation has four parts: self-monitoring, judgment, self-reactive incentives, and self-efficacy. Self-monitoring is the capacity to be aware of one's self and actions. Generally, this self awareness is used to evaluate the outcomes of behaviors – what is my state and what am I doing that may be affecting that state? However, one may engage in activities that suspend self-monitoring to pass the time or partially to escape from a stressful situation. Judgment is an evaluation of behavior compared to personal and social standards. That is, I may choose not to play *Barbie Horse Adventures: Wild Horse Rescue* because, being a male academic in his thirties, that would be viewed as "unusual" or "weird" by social standards. Self-reactive incentives are psychological motivations for maintaining personal or social standards. Again, we choose to sub-divide this incentive to reflect that in immersive games the player is part of a fictional world that has its own fictional standards. For example, in a role-playing game, the one may want to play a character whose personal and cultural norms are different from their own. This is different from someone who seeks experiences that deliberately reflect their own normative values.

Finally, self-efficacy[3] (cf. Bandura, 1997) is the belief in one's ability to successfully complete an action. In video games, self-efficacy takes three forms. One, if the player has difficulty using the game controller or understanding the interface, then the player would be less confident in his or her ability to play the game. Two, if the game is too hard, then the player will become frustrated and stop playing. Finally, the player needs to feel that they can accomplish their goals within the game world. For example, if a player feels strongly about exploring a distant mountain range within an open ended sandbox style game, but the game does not allow the player do so, the player may feel discouraged from playing the game in general.

Both behavioral incentives within motivational and self-regulation processes within production processes interact with environmental (e.g. social context), behavioral (e.g. habits), and personal variables (e.g. personality, gender, temperament). Furthermore, retention processes are characterized by symbolic representation of direct or observed experiences. "It is with symbols that people process and transform transient experiences into cognitive models that serve as guides for judgment and action. "Through symbols people give meaning, form, and continuity to their experiences" (Bandura, 2001, p. 122). People digest experiences into symbols that are used to create schema for future judgments and actions. As people experience video games either by directly playing or observing others play, they construct symbols to describe their experience. Some of these symbols represent intrinsic qualities of the game itself. These particular symbols to the games themselves can be referred to as "quality perceptions", and provide the operational link missing from other player types of video game play.

For example, when a player is asked about his/her playing experience or what he/she has observed when his/her peers played the game, a realistic answer could be "...the game was amazing. It was like in the real world. Characters and the environment reacted as I would expect it in real-life. I love to play this game". In fact, this answer stems from one of our research participants. Note that we did not encounter statements like "... the game was amazing. I wanted to immerse in a game-world that is like the real-world (or I saw others who played because they wanted to become immersed in a game-world that is like the real-world). As the game allowed me to experience this immersion I love to play this game". Thus, symbols – or game quality perceptions – are used by people to guide future behavior. By using quality perceptions, people plan a course of action and evaluate an expected outcome. If game quality perceptions match with self-regulation – an important prerequisite for the production of a behavior – and with behavioral incentives, which motivate to execute a behavior, then playing a particular video game and describing the experience positively becomes more likely.

Thus, with this investigation we are exploring the symbolic representation of video game playing, i.e. we are exploring common video game quality perceptions. To our knowledge, the enumeration of operational video game quality perceptions in this paper, which is based on empirical data, is the first one provided in a scholarly journal.

Further, we are using self-regulation, theoretically derived behavioral incentives (based on SCT), and person-individual differences to define player types such that players within a player type are maximal homogeneous and players that differ in player-type are maximal heterogeneous regarding self-efficacy, behavioral incentives, and other personal variables. We know from SCT, that one has to consider the dynamic and reciprocal interactions of numerous personal, behavioral, and environmental variables within each learning-sub-process in order to predict a behavior (see above). For the sake of simplicity and feasibility, however, we focus our empirical investigation to interactions with personal variables only, knowing that the accuracy of player types might be different when considering the full complexity of social cognitive processes (i.e. considering a specific social environment, habits, etc.). As explicitly mentioned in Bandura's SCT (1986, p. 153), but rarely included in empirical studies, we consider biologically rooted temperaments (Windle, 1986, 1992) when defining player-types.

Temperaments are defined as "biologically rooted individual differences in behavior tendencies that are present early in life and are relatively stable across various kinds of situations and over the course of time" (Bates, 1989, p.4; see also Sherry 2001). Temperaments are assumed to be inherited and as such are explained by individual differences in neurological function and plasticity. In addition, temperaments are expressed behaviorally and are based on observational studies of infants and children rather than on self-report data of adults (as most of the uses and gratification dimensions are for example). Sherry (2001) has shown that temperament was a consistent and causal factor in forming television use motivations. Particularly potent predictors of television use were negative mood, low task orientation, and behavioral rigidity. We believe that when outcome expectations are accompanied by incentives for human behavior then those incentives should reciprocally interact with biologically rooted individual difference behavior variables as stated by SCT. For example, novel sensory incentives within SCT include the search/need for novel information and are similar to information seeking gratifications within the uses and gratification perspective of media attendance. It can be assumed that incentives provided by novel information interact with an individual temperament of approach-withdrawal, which is defined as an individual's positive (approach) or negative (withdrawal) nature of initial responses to new stimuli (cf. Thomas & Chess, 1977). By including biologically rooted individual difference behavior variables and combining them with theoretically derived incentives for human behavior, we expect more reliable and more valid player type categorizations than prompted self-reports on a-posteriori justifications of playing behavior can provide. To our knowledge, this study is the first that considers interactions among SCT based incentives for human behavior with biologically rooted individual difference behavior variables to define player types and predict video game playing.

HYPOTHESES

Given the theoretical framework above, we hypothesize that if "it is with symbols that people process and transform transient experiences into cognitive models that serve as guides for judgment and action", then we should expect that quality perceptions of video games should predict video game playing. Thus:

H1: Quality perceptions of video games predict video game playing.

If player types are based on the concept of video game self-regulation as prerequisite for the production of a behavior, on behavioral incentives that motivate to execute a behavior, and on biologically rooted individual difference behavior variables, then these player types should predict video game playing. Thus:

H2: Player types predict video game playing

Further, if (a) video game playing can be considered as overt behavior and is determined by expected outcomes as a result of direct and observational learning processes; and (b) according to SCT, learning processes include dynamic and reciprocal interactions among a variety of environmental, personal, behavioral variables; then (c) on a simplified level, we should see that symbolic representations of video game playing (quality perceptions) in interaction with player types, or player types specific quality perceptions, should provide the most accurate models to predict video game playing. Thus:

H3: Quality perceptions moderated by player types, or player types specific quality perceptions, predict video game playing better than player types or qualities alone.

Finally, if we find support for H1, H2, and H3, then of course it will become interesting how

different symbolic representations of video game playing are weighted within given player types. Thus, in the form of a research question we ask:

R1: Which of the identified video game quality perceptions are most important for a specific player type?

By answering this research question we follow our call that a model is needed that provides an operational basis for both video game professionals and media scholars who are interested in a-posteriori predictions of video game preference and use.

METHOD

To our knowledge, no study has been published yet in a scholarly journal that looked into symbolic representations, i.e. quality perceptions, of video games. Thus, in a first pre-study (study 1) we explored video game qualities that experienced video game players value by means of in-depth interviews. The goal of study 1 was to generate a comprehensive list of video game quality perceptions. In a subsequent second study (study 2) we conducted a standardized online survey. The goal of study 2 was to optimize the list of video game quality perceptions, to define and analyze our SCT based player types, and to test whether we can find empirical support for our hypotheses and research question as described above.

Participants

For study 1, interview participants were recruited via theoretical sampling (Glaser & Strauss, 1967; Draucker, Martsolf, Ross, & Rusk, 2007) in order to maximize the theoretical space of video game players. Based on prior research on video game playing motivations (see above), the most important dimensions for exploring the theoretical space of video game quality perceptions were determined to be gender and game play experience, forming four cells (experienced male, experienced female, inexperienced/casual male, inexperienced/casual female players). Participants from each cell were recruited and interviewed until no new quality perceptions were discovered. After we conducted focused, in-depth interviews with a total of 15 participants (3 experienced males, 3 experienced females, 3 inexperienced/casual male, and 6 inexperienced/casual female players) we observed convergence and saturation of our participant's responses. The last 2 participants of each cell did not add any new quality perceptions that were not mentioned by the other participants.

For study 2 data were collected from a purposive sample of 422 students in six communication classes at a large Midwestern university who received extra credit for their participation. On average, participants were 21 years old (SD = 2.2) and played about 3 hours video games per week (SD = 1.1). 265 of the 422 students (62.8%) were women, 157 (37.2%) were men. 40.7% of the sample played at least 1-2 times per week video games, 27.1% at least 3-4 times, 15.5% at least 5-6 times, and 10.2% played video games every day. 59.3%, however, played video games 2-3 times a month or less. Students who did not play video games at all were filtered out and were not part of the sample.

Measures & Procedures Study 1

For study 1 we first reviewed a series of leading gaming magazines (e.g. *GamePro*; *Electronic Gaming Monthly*; *Nintendo Power*; *Game Informer*) as well as various video game discussion groups and video game blogs (e.g. http://www.gamespot.com; http://www.metacritic.com/games/), and produced a preliminary list of potential quality indicators based on how players describe video games they have played. This list was used to create a two part focused, in-depth interview.

In the first part, the interview asked a series of open ended questions about participants' video game play experience (e.g. "when was the first time you ever played a video game?"; "do you prefer to play video games with friends or by yourself?")[4]. In the second half, again with open ended questions, the interviewer explored the participants playing experience further, using the preliminary list of quality perceptions as a guide, but not as prompts.

Two experienced video game players (graduate students) were trained as interviewers and advised to interfere with the participants' answers as little as possible. The in-depth interviews took place in small classrooms and lasted between 1.5 and 2.5 hours. All participants consented to the study prior to collecting any data and were compensated with class credit. The interviews were taped and the audio from the interviews was content analyzed to refine the preliminary list of quality perceptions. This refined list of quality perceptions was then used for study 2.

Measures & Procedures Study 2

In study 2 an online survey was conducted using the Web Surveyor 4.1 software. The survey was divided into four major sections (see Figure 1)[5]:

The survey began with several basic demographic questions such as age and gender. In addition, respondents were asked about their general game play behaviors (e.g. playing frequency), game play experience, and genre preferences. Questions were adapted from a comprehensive BBC survey of video gamers (Pratchett: & Harris, 2005).

The second part of the survey asked the respondents to think about a specific, recent experience with playing a video game. Respondents were asked to provide the video games' title and genre, how often (eight point rating scale reaching from "every day" to "less than once a month") and how long (weekly playing time in minutes) they usually play the specified game, and an overall opinion

Figure 1. A simplified overview of the survey

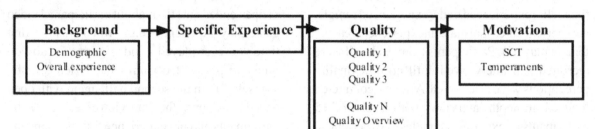

of the game. Frequency and duration of playing the specific game served as dependent variable (video game playing) in our analyses. At the end of part two, the respondents were then provided with an open ended question to describe their game experience in their own words.

The third section dealt with the player's evaluation of the various video game quality perceptions (resulting from study 1) within their recent experience. As quality perceptions build on each other and can be both general and specific, we organized related quality perceptions hierarchically into first and second tier quality perceptions (see Table A1 in the appendix). For most of the first tier quality groups, a simple filter question was used in case that quality group was missing from the game. The following groups were considered to be universal to all video games and did not have a general filter question: controls, game world, graphics, replayability, and socializing (see Table A1). The structure of the questions within each quality perception group is visualized in Figure 2.

During the interviews it was noted that respondents understood the second tier quality perceptions better than the first tier ones. Asking second tier questions first helped the respondents to understand and evaluate the more general, first tier quality perceptions better. Thus, in the survey as well, the second tier questions were asked first. For example, within the "music" group, the respondent was first asked questions about whether the game used licensed, recognizable music or

original, unique music and how originality in music influenced the experience. Afterwards, the respondent is asked how the music in general influenced the game experience. Within the first tier quality perception groups, the tier two quality questions were preceded by filter questions as well. For example, although many video games have music, most do not have licensed music and asking respondents about licensed music would not have made sense.

For each second tier quality perception, respondents were asked to indicate their agreement to a series of questions, such as "In my recent game experience, the unique *game world elements* were well done". Participants responded using a six point scale reaching from "strongly disagree" to "strongly agree". After answering the second tier questions, participants answered a series of questions for the first tier quality perceptions. Again, participants were asked to agree with a series of questions using the same six point scale as for the second tier quality perceptions. For example, "In my recent game experience, the graphics made the game more believable". Finally, after evaluating each group separately, the respondents were then asked to compare the different first tier qualities against each other.

The final survey section dealt with the psychological constructs described in the introduction of this paper. For the six basic types of incentives for human behavior (status, social, monetary, enjoyable activity, novel sensory, and self-reactive in-

Figure 2. The structure for questions within each group of game quality perceptions. The respondent is first presented with questions from the second tier. Although this format is more complicated for the respondent, it aides the respondent in understanding the more general, tier one questions.

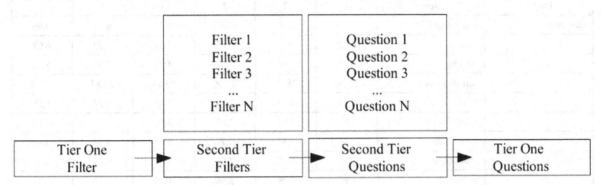

centives) as well as for the concept of self-efficacy, three items for each dimension were created and pre-tested. For example for the dimension "novel sensory" we used the items (1) "I seek new experiences"; (2) "I want things to remain the same"; (3) I want to do something that I've never done before. For the concept of self-efficacy we used the following three items: (1) "I prefer doing things that I know I can accomplish"; (2) "I get really frustrated if I can't figure out what to do"; (3) "I feel comfortable when I believe I am in control of a situation". The temperament measures are based on Windle's (1992) revised dimensions of temperament survey (DOTS-R) with the dimensions flexibility, activity, quality of mood, rhythmicity, task persistence, approach-withdrawal. For all scales we obtained scale reliabilities of 0.85 and above (Cronbach's alpha). Identical to the quality perceptions questions we used a six point scale reaching from "strongly disagree" to "strongly agree" for the participants' responses.

Study participants were provided with a link to an online survey presented in undergraduate classes and by email. At the first page of the online survey, participants consented to the study. Respondents were then asked how often they played video games. Respondents who did not play video games more than once a month were excluded from the survey because they lacked the experience to adequately respond to survey questions. The online survey lasted between 35 minutes and one hour. All study participants were compensated with class credit.

RESULTS

The focused interviews produced a substantial hierarchy of video game quality perceptions. From our interviews we identified thirteen top tier quality perceptions and 47 second tier quality perceptions. An organized list of first and second tier quality perceptions can be found in Table A1 (see appendix).

While some quality perceptions were taken directly from the interviews, others were inferred. For example, one interviewee reported that Patrick Stewart's voice acting was important to her experience of playing *The Elder Scrolls IV: Oblivion*. She had enjoyed Patrick Stewart's work in other media (building a symbol from direct experience) and deliberately played the game to hear his performance (using the symbol to guide her future behavior). We initially classified this as a "recognizable voice actor" sub-dimension of the pre-established "spoken dialog" quality perception. Logically, we extended this "recognizable" concept to other dimensions such as music and

Table 1. Discriminant analysis – classification function coefficients for items and player types

| Factor | Item | Player Type | | | | | |
		1	2	3	4	5	6
Incentive	Enjoyment	9.09	10.36	10.83	8.77	9.74	9.66
	Monetary	6.52	6.30	5.83	7.08	6.79	6.69
	Novelty	6.47	3.62	4.97	4.92	5.54	5.70
	Self-Reactive	22.96	25.88	24.06	23.04	22.87	23.34
	Social Game	4.94	2.65	2.24	3.55	3.22	1.58
	Social Other	2.88	1.02	4.65	0.54	4.42	4.17
	Status Game	0.08	0.82	-2.86	0.00	-1.86	-1.05
	Status Other	3.81	5.07	2.62	4.52	4.75	2.75
	Status Self	1.83	0.99	2.36	-0.40	2.23	1.74
Self-Regulation	Self-Efficacy	3.66	4.33	4.65	2.83	4.20	2.75
	Self-Monitor	11.42	10.52	11.67	11.33	11.28	11.91
	Social Judge	4.63	7.89	6.64	4.66	6.25	4.25
Temperament	Activity	11.92	13.08	11.31	12.20	11.39	11.20
	Approach	-2.13	-0.57	-3.42	-3.22	-2.43	-2.51
	Flexibility	5.30	3.49	3.41	5.87	4.58	5.43
	Mood Quality	0.54	-0.16	1.02	-0.62	0.00	-0.41
	Persistence	3.61	5.72	4.46	4.32	4.64	5.12
	Rythmicity	6.63	8.13	7.99	6.99	7.39	6.87
(constant)		-213.38	-235.48	-213.26	-179.27	-217.96	-195.70

sound effects. When we considered the "recognizable" sub-dimension for characters, we agreed that real-world recognizable characters are important in games such as *Madden* or *Smackdown*. We also realized that in other cases, it is the recognizable fictional characters that are important. For example, part of the attraction of the *Smash Brothers* franchise is its impressive roster of fictional characters from Nintendo games. We realized that we needed to further sub-divide "recognizable" into "real-world" and "fictional" subcategories. Hence, direct interview responses and inferred deductions were important to the final list of game quality perceptions.

In our subsequent survey study (study 2) most of the resulting first and second tier quality perceptions showed small significant correlations with overall game experience.[6] Comparing the first tier quality perceptions, controls ($r = 0.15$, $p < 0.05$), game characters ($r = 0.23$, $p < 0.01$), music ($r = 0.16$, $p < 0.05$), replayability ($r = 0.24$, $p < 0.01$), sound effects ($r = 0.19$, $p < 0.01$), socializing ($r = 0.19$, $p < 0.05$), and game world ($r = 0.18$, $p < 0.01$) had a significant relationship with overall experience.

We performed an explorative, hierarchical cluster analysis (Ward algorithm) on our participants' responses to the incentive, self-regulation, and temperament items in study 2. Based on the cluster analysis' dendrogram (i.e. a visualization of the increase in error variance after cluster combination), we identified six clusters as optimal solution – each cluster representing one of six player types. We then used a linear discriminant analysis to determine the significance of these player types. Using the six player types, the

Table 2. Player type item means

Factor	Item	Player Type					
		1	4	2	3	5	6
Incentive	Enjoyment	5.28	5.07	5.16	4.38	5.21	4.66
	Social-Game	4.98	4.25	5.28	3.65	5.36	4.86
	Status-Other	4.98	5.16	4.81	3.68	5.10	4.64
	Novelty	4.89	3.94	4.27	3.79	4.55	4.63
	Self-Reactive	4.42	3.87	2.79	3.48	3.45	2.53
	Social-Other	4.39	4.93	2.64	3.67	3.50	2.98
	Status-Self	4.01	4.14	4.08	3.72	3.93	4.04
	Status-Game	3.99	5.09	3.28	3.83	4.58	3.17
	Monetary	3.93	4.06	3.86	3.68	4.37	3.67
Self-Regulation	Self-Efficacy	4.67	4.97	4.88	3.95	4.86	3.88
	Social-Judge	3.38	4.86	4.25	3.11	4.31	3.08
	Self-Monitoring	3.37	3.19	3.71	3.44	3.46	3.86
Temperament	Mood Quality	5.13	4.56	5.11	3.94	5.07	4.79
	Approach	4.25	4.46	3.69	3.35	4.13	3.91
	Flexibility	4.01	2.75	3.38	3.52	3.69	4.14
	Activity	4.01	4.36	3.79	3.68	3.76	3.45
	Persistence	3.34	4.26	3.30	3.33	3.58	3.59
	Rythmicity	2.97	4.43	3.28	3.33	3.22	3.18

discriminant analysis yielded five canonical functions which were all significant (Wilks Lamba = 0.037, p < 0.01). These functions define a matrix of classification coefficients for each item and player type (see Table 1).

These coefficients represent how important each item is to classify a respondent into a player type. To assign a participant to a player type, one would calculate the sum of item scores multiplied by their corresponding player type's item weight. The higher the resulting score, the more closely the participant matched the player type. The participant was assigned to the player type that had the highest player type score based on the participant's responses. These coefficient weights classified 88.3% of the original sample into the correct player type.

Player types are best described in plain English by comparing their average ratings for each item.

Overall, many player types rated enjoyment and improving one's self very highly (status – self), and both mood quality and approachability highly (see Table 2).

Competing against others, socializing with others and activity were important among some of the player types. Nearly all player types ranked socializing with game characters and rythmicity very low. Given the means in Table 2, we interpreted our player types as follows: [7]

Player Type 1 – "Hedonist": These players are characterized by strong enjoyment incentives, novelty, self-improvement, and approachability. Hedonists have a somewhat strong desire for control in their lives, but rank low in terms of self-awareness of their actions and regulating their actions based on what other people think.

Player Type 2 – "Competitors": Competitors ranked self-improvement, competition with others, positive mood and approachability highly, while ranking novelty, socializing with game characters, and flexibility lowly. Competitors also had high scores for self-efficacy and social judgment. This blend of factors paints a picture of a competitive player who enjoys playing by the rules.

Player Type 3 – "Organizers": Similar to Socializers and Team Players (see below), Organizers are very social and reported high levels of self-improvement, mood, and approachability. Unlike Socializers and Team Players, Organizers are very active. They also ranked their self-regulation items (self efficacy, judgment, self-awareness) highly. In general, they were not particularly persistent or flexible, nor are they interested in playing games for competition. This paints a picture of someone who likes to organize events and expects everyone to show up on time.

Player Type 4 – "Rebel": Similar to the competitors, rebels are very interested in competing with others. However, they are highly flexible and particularly inclined to care about what people think of them (low social judgment), and rate lowly in approachability, persistence, and rythmicity. This player type seems to be more someone who is willing to win using any means necessary.

Player Type 5 "Team player": Similar to Organizers and Socializers (see below), Team Players are very social and ranked self-improvement, mood, and approachability highly. Similar to Organizers, Team Players ranked self-efficacy and social judgment highly. Unlike Organizers, Team players are more interested in playing against others, are less active, and ranked self-monitoring lower. Team players seem to be players who like gathering for games, but seem to be more relaxed than Organizers.

Player Type 6 – "Socializer": Similar to Organizers and Team Players, Socializers are very social and ranked self-improvement, mood, and approachability highly. Unlike Organizers and Team Players, Socializers are very flexible, like

novel sensory experiences, and rated their self-regulation items lowly. Socializers also seem to be not interested in competition with the game or other people. Socializers are best described as people who enjoy gaming primarily as a means of engaging in new experiences with others.

We then tested our three hypotheses with three regression based path models using the quality perceptions in Table A1 (see appendix) as independent variable, our identified player types as both independent and moderator variable, and video game playing (frequency and duration) as dependent variable. Figure 3 visualizes our results:

As our analyses in figure 3 demonstrate, both quality perceptions and player type predict video game playing as stated in hypothesis one and two. quality perceptions alone explain 9%, player type alone 7%, and quality perceptions and player type together as independent variables explain 14% of the variance in self-reported video game playing. However, by considering the player types as moderator variable, i.e. by using player type specific quality perceptions as predictors, the model's accuracy increased to 27% explained variance. As we consider these results as support for our three hypotheses with small to medium effect sizes we think it is worthwhile to further investigate our research question R1, i.e. to analyze which of the identified video game quality perceptions are most important for a specific player type.

Within the first tier quality perceptions, seven of the sixteen dimensions had significant correlations with at least one player type. In contrast, all lower tier quality perception that could be analyzed for each player type correlated significantly with at least one player type. Table A2 and A3 in the appendix list all quality perceptions that were analyzed and produced results. quality perceptions beta coefficients in bold are statistically significant ($p < 0.05$). A demonstrative interpretation of these results can be found in the discussion section.

Figure 3. Test of hypotheses H1, H2, and H3. Player type specific quality perceptions predict video game playing best.

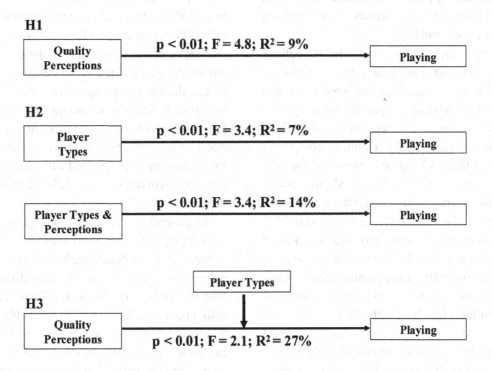

DISCUSSION

Two studies have been conducted and reported in this paper. Study 1 was a series of interviews with game players that encouraged them to discuss prior video game experiences. The interviewees rarely discussed abstract, academic notions of psychological or physiological behavior incentives. Rather, they discussed their reactions to specific elements – "that game was fun because the graphics were cool!" The interviewees had encoded elements of their experience into symbols that they used to guide future behavior. In order to enumerate symbolic representations or game quality perceptions, we iteratively interviewed individuals whom we thought represented a wide range of game experience: both male and female players, and hardcore and casual gamers. All groups contributed to our quality list although the

hardcore players were more articulate in providing the lower tier qualities.

Our analysis of quality perceptions' relationship with overall game experience not only provided information on what quality perceptions are important, but also reflected on the quality of the list. All of the lower tiered qualities that could be analyzed for all player types were important to at least one player type (see Table A3 in the appendix). This can be interpreted in two ways: First that our respondents in study 2 were similar to our interviewees in study 1, and second, that the identified quality perceptions can be generalized to a larger population.

We believe that the generated list of video game quality perceptions in this paper is the most comprehensive list available at this time. However, we recognize that our list (nor any list) could be exhaustive of every possible game feature. Although our list may not cover all quality perceptions for all types of games, game developers can use the results and methodology from study 2 to evaluate game quality perceptions not included in our study.

Among models of player behavior, we believe our model is unique because it directly links behavioral factors (incentives, self-regulation, and biological variables) to specific game quality perceptions. Some of our incentive factors parallel factors in other models. For example, comparing Bartle's (1986) motivation factors and motivational processes in SCT, the social motivations can be considered as identical. Bartle's achievement and exploration factors correspond to SCT incentives of status and novelty. Bartle's "killer" player type is driven by power and infamy, and can thus be understood as a combination of status and social incentives as well as low social judgment and high levels of self-efficacy. Although the importance of self-regulation and biological factors has been studied in other media (e.g. Sherry, 2001), they have been neglected in video games so far. Incorporating these additional factors makes a more robust model of player behavior, and one that is more useful to game developers.

Quality perceptions and player types individually predicted video game playing with a small to medium effect size (R^2=9% and R^2=7%, respectively). It may seem obvious that if players like a game as operationalized with our identified quality perceptions (i.e. game's features), then they should tend to play the game more. However, if our study had not shown any relationship (or main effects), then we would have been forced to conclude that there was something wrong with our quality perceptions and player type classification. Furthermore, the affirmative result also supports part of our theoretical model: quality perceptions as symbolic representations serve as guides for judgment and action. Most importantly, however, we showed that player types and quality perceptions combined, i.e. quality perceptions moderated by our player types, create the best prediction of video game playing by a significant margin. Our

model explains 27% of the variance in video game playing, which corresponds to a correlation of about 0.52 and as such indicates a strong effect. The clear support for our three hypotheses provides empirical evidence for the assertion that our model gives video game designers a means of classifying groups of players and enumerating specific features including their importance for players within a player type. In our research question we explored how the various game quality perceptions are weighted within the identified player types in respect to how players experienced their game play.

In general, player types and game qualities were highly effective in predicting overall game experience. In tendency, the lower tiered qualities were more important to the overall experience than the first tier qualities (see Table A2 and A3 in the appendix). This trend was probably partially due to the more nebulous nature of the broader categories. It may also be due to the fact that our hierarchical organization of qualities may have been too rigid or not match participant's own logical grouping. For example, many of our first tier qualities had a customization sub-dimension and some players may have valued customization over everything else. Because of this, these players may have liked character customization but were indifferent to other character dimensions. Their second tier quality (character customization) would have stood out, whereas the first tier quality (character) may have been weak. Because differences between player types become stronger with more refined qualities, game developers may need to carefully examine their design and determine whether a given quality may need to be further sub-divided and evaluated for a given player type.

However, given our list of quality perceptions and player types, the question is: How does a game designer use this information to say develop a game for a Hedonist player type? Referring to Table A3 in the appendix as demonstration, quality perceptions values listed in bold are statistically significant ($p < 0.05$), that is, not due to pure chance. Larger numbers are more important to a player type. Comparing voice acting for example, an original voice actor (0.81) is more important to the experience than someone famous (0.16) in this example. Thus, for a game that – based on market research or other sources – is assumed to appeal most to Hedonists, a game designer can say with confidence that the precious game budget is better spent elsewhere than for hiring Hollywood actors. Hence, Table A3 serves as a guide to game developers who might otherwise be forced to make decisions by the seat of their pants. At the same time, Table A2 and A3 in the appendix provide an operational answer to our raised research question, i.e. they inform which of the identified video game quality perceptions are most important for specific player types.

The player types described here are produced through cluster analysis of survey data. Questions in this survey were based on different theoretical assumptions (mainly social cognitive theory and theories of temperament). As stated, these resulting player types had statistically significant associations with specific quality perceptions, validating the model's application for video game designers. However, we are not overly happy with the ambiguity of the identified player types themselves. Interpreting the quantitative statistics to construct a qualitative description of each player type was particularly challenging. We believe that this ambiguity may be due to the complexity of behavioral and temperament factors considered. In particular, the sub-division of SCT factors was interesting but probably too ambitious for an initial foray into an already complex model. As an initial study into the association between behavioral factors, player types, and quality perceptions, it may have been more prudent to build a foundation study with fewer dimensions that produced a clearer picture of the individual player types.

There is no empirical study without limitations: A clear limitation of our study is that our participants were all undergraduate students from a large mid-western university. It is possible that our survey failed to capture additional player types that may be present in other, more diverse populations. In addition, our respondents also choose to participate. People who choose not to participate may form one or more different player types. Similarly, our model explicitly states that players have learned what game qualities match their incentives. This learning process takes place in a particular social and cultural environment. Although there is some diversity in an undergraduate class, it may not be enough to generalize to other distinct population groups. It would be interesting to replicate our empirical strategy in representative samples of video game players and to compare the findings.

Participants were also asked to evaluate a recent game experience. Overall, one would expect that participants are usually playing games they like. This may have produced a halo effect where the participants may have overstated their evaluation of individual features because they liked the game overall. A future study could present participants with a random selection of popular games to rate. Alternately, a study could ask participants to play a game chosen by the researcher and evaluate its qualities versus overall experience.

Finally, we have no knowledge how the environment affected the experience. For example, was the player trying to play a story intensive RPG while her roommate was blasting music? The playing environment can have a profound affect on the player's experience and this is not accounted for in our study.

Ultimately, game developers need to know whether a game designed to conform to a player type's important game quality perceptions is "more fun" and preferred over other games. Although our studies demonstrate that player types and quality perceptions are useful in explaining and predicting past behavior, further research is required to determine whether our model can be used to guide a game developer to produce better and more successful video games.

REFERENCES

Bandura, A. (1986). *Social foundations of thought and action: A social cognitive theory*. Englewood Cliffs, NJ: Prentice Hall.

Bandura, A. (1997). *Self-efficacy: The exercise of control*. New York, NY: W.H. Freeman.

Bandura, A. (2001). Social cognitive theory of mass communications. In Bryant, J., & Zillmann, D. (Eds.), *Media effects: Advances in theory and research* (2nd ed., pp. 121–153). Hillsdale, NJ: Lawrence Erlbaum.

Bartle, R. A. (1996). *Hearts, clubs, diamonds, spades: Players who suit MUDs*. Retrieved April 7, 2008, from http://mud.co.uk/richard/hcds.htm

Bartle, R. A. (2004). *Designing virtual worlds*. Berkeley, CA: New Riders.

Bates, J. E. (1989). Concepts and measures of temperament. In Kohnstamm, G. A., Bates, J. E., & Rothbart, M. K. (Eds.), *Temperament in childhood* (pp. 3–26). New York, NY: John Wiley & Sons.

Beck, J. C., & Wade, M. (2004). *Got game: How the gamer generation is reshaping business forever*. Boston, MA: Harvard Press.

Bryant, J., & Davis, J. (2006). Selective exposure to video games. In Vorderer, P., & Bryant, J. (Eds.), *Playing video games - Motives, responses, and consequences* (pp. 181–194). Mahwah, NJ: Lawrence Erlbaum.

Csikszentmihalyi, M. (1990). *Flow: The psychology of optimal experience*. New York, NY: Harper and Row.

Draucker, C. B., Martsolf, D. S., Ross, R., & Rusk, T. B. (2007). Theoretical sampling and category development in grounded theory. *Qualitative Health Research*, *17*, 1137–1148. doi:10.1177/1049732307308450

Entertainment Software Association. (2008). *The essential facts about the computer and video game industry*. Retrieved April 6, 2008, from http://www.theesa.com/facts/ sales_genre_data.php

Entertainment Software Association. (2010). *Video games in the 21st century*. Retrieved September 3, 2010, from http://www.theesa.com/facts/pdfs/VideoGames21stCentury_2010.pdf

Espe, H., & Seiwert, M. (1986). European television-viewer types: A six-nation classification by programme interests. *European Journal of Communication*, *1*(3), 301–325. doi:10.1177/0267323186001003004

Glaser, B., & Strauss, A. (1967). *The discovery of grounded theory*. Chicago, IL: Aldine.

Griffiths, M. D. (1991). Are computer games bad for children? *The Psychologist: Bulletin of the British Psychological Society*, *6*, 401–407.

Grodal, T. (2000). Video games and the pleasure of control. In Zillmann, D., & Vorderer, P. (Eds.), *Media entertainment: The psychology of its appeal* (pp. 197–212). Mahwah, NJ: Lawrence Erlbaum Associates.

LaRose, R., & Eastin, M. S. (2004). A social cognitive theory of Internet uses and gratifications: Toward a new model of media attendance. *Journal of Broadcasting & Electronic Media*, *48*(3), 358–377. doi:10.1207/s15506878jobem4803_2

Lewis, M. L., Weber, R., & Bowman, N. D. (2008). They may be pixels, but they're my pixels: Developing a metric of character attachment in role-playing video games. *Cyberpsychology & Behavior*, *11*(4), 515–518. doi:10.1089/cpb.2007.0137

Lucas, K., & Sherry, J. L. (2004). Sex differences in video game play: A communication-based explanation. *Communication Research*, *31*(5), 499–523. doi:10.1177/0093650204267930

Palmgreen, P. C., Wenner, L. A., & Rosengreen, K. E. (1985). Uses and gratification research: The past ten years. In Rosengreen, K. E., Wenner, L. A., & Palmgreen, P. C. (Eds.), *Uses and gratifications research: Current perspectives* (pp. 11–37). Beverly Hills, CA: Sage.

Phillips, C. A., Rolls, S., Rouse, A., & Griffiths, M. D. (1995). Home video game playing in schoolchildren: A study of incidence and patterns of play. *Journal of Adolescence, 18*, 687–691. doi:10.1006/jado.1995.1049

Pratchett, R., & Harris, D. (2005). *Gamers in the UK. Digital play, digital lifestyles*. London, UK: BBC Audience Research.

Rosengreen, K. E. (1974). Uses and gratifications: A paradigm outlined. In Blumler, J. G., & Katz, E. (Eds.), *The uses of mass communications: Current perspectives of gratification research* (pp. 269–286). Beverly Hills, CA: Sage.

Ryan, R. M., & Deci, E. L. (2000). Self-determination theory and the facilitation of intrinsic motivation, social development, and well-being. *The American Psychologist, 55*, 68–78. doi:10.1037/0003-066X.55.1.68

Ryan, R. M., Rigby, C. S., & Przybylski, A. (2006). The motivational pull of video games: A self-determination theory approach. *Motivation and Emotion, 30*(4), 347–363. doi:10.1007/s11031-006-9051-8

Selnow, G. W. (1984). Playing videogames: The electronic friend. *The Journal of Communication, 34*(2), 148–156. doi:10.1111/j.1460-2466.1984.tb02166.x

Sherry, J. L. (2001). Toward an etiology of media use motivations: The role of temperament in media use. *Communication Monographs, 68*(3), 274–288. doi:10.1080/03637750128065

Sherry, J. L. (2004). Flow and media enjoyment. *Communication Theory, 14*(4), 328–347. doi:10.1111/j.1468-2885.2004.tb00318.x

Sherry, J. L., Lucas, K., Greenberg, B., & Lachlan, K. (2006). Video game uses and gratifications as predictors of use and game preference. In Vorderer, P., & Bryant, J. (Eds.), *Playing video games - Motives, responses, and consequences* (pp. 213–224). Mahwah, NJ: Lawrence Erlbaum.

Tamborini, R., Bowman, N. D., Eden, A., Grizzard, M., & Ogan, A. (in press). Defining media enjoyment as the satisfaction of intrinsic needs. *The Journal of Communication*.

Thomas, A., & Chess, S. (1977). *Temperament and development*. New York, NY: Brunner & Mazel.

Vorderer, P., Hartmann, T., & Klimmt, C. (2003). Explaining the enjoyment of playing video games: The role of competition. In D. Marinelli (Ed.), *Proceedings of the 2nd International Conference on Entertainment Computing (ICEC 2003), Pittsburgh* (pp. 1–8). New York, NY: ACM.

Vorderer, P., Steen, F. F., & Chan, E. (2006). Motivation. In Bryant, J., & Vorderer, P. (Eds.), *Psychology of entertainment* (pp. 3–17). Mahwah, NJ: Lawrence Erlbaum Associates.

Weber, R., Bates, C., & Behr, K.-M. (2010). *Developing a metric of interactivity in video games*. Paper presented at the 96th Annual Convention of the National Communication Association November 14 -17, 2010, San Francisco.

Wigand, R. T., Borstelmann, S. E., & Boster, F. J. (1985). Electronic leisure: Video game usage and the communication climate of video arcades. *Communication Yearbook, 9*, 275–293.

Williams, D. (2006). A brief social history of game play. In Vorderer, P., & Bryant, J. (Eds.), *Playing video games - Motives, responses, and consequences* (pp. 197–212). Mahwah, NJ: Lawrence Erlbaum.

Windle, M. (1992). Revised dimensions of temperament survey (DOTS-R): Simultaneous group confirmatory factor analysis for adolescent gender groups. *Psychological Assessment, 4*, 228–234. doi:10.1037/1040-3590.4.2.228

Windle, M., & Lerner, R. M. (1986). Reassessing the dimensions of individuality across the life span: The revised dimensions of temperament survey (DOTS-R). *Journal of Adolescent Research, 1*, 213–230. doi:10.1177/074355488612007

Yee, N. (2006). The demographics, motivations and derived experiences of users of massively multi-user online graphical environments. *Presence (Cambridge, Mass.), 15*(3), 309–329. doi:10.1162/pres.15.3.309

Zillmann, D. (1988). Mood management: Using entertainment to full advantage. In Donohue, L., Sypher, H. E., & Higgins, E. T. (Eds.), *Communication, social cognition and affect* (pp. 147–171). Hillsdale, NJ: Lawrence Erlbaum Associates.

Zillmann, D., & Bryant, J. (1985). Affect, mood, and emotion as determinant of selective exposure. In Zillmann, D., & Bryant, J. (Eds.), *Selective exposure to communication (pp. 157-*190). Hillsdale, NJ: Lawrence Erlbaum Associates.

ENDNOTES

[1] We use the label "video games" as collective term for both computer games and console games. The terms video games, electronic games, and digital games are considered as synonyms.

[2] This actually happens quite frequently and large video games corporations such as Electronic Arts even host workshops for media scholars on a regular basis to ask and focus on this important question.

[3] Within SCT, self-efficacy is not part of self-regulation, but a separate concept. However, self-efficacy has a similar effect on behavior as self-regulation factors. For clarity, we group it with the other self-regulation factors.

[4] The complete interview guide is available upon request. Please send an email to the first author at renew@comm.ucsb.edu.

[5] The complete survey is available upon request. Please send an email to the first author at renew@comm.ucsb.edu.

[6] Overall game experiences was measured with three items: (a) "Overall, the game was of good quality"; (b) "I really liked the game I played"; (c) I really enjoyed the game I played (all scales from (1) strongly disagree to (6) strongly agree).

[7] In general, we compared means within a player type, rather than between player types to avoid any systematic bias within a given player type.

APPENDIX

Table A1. Hierarchical schema of video game quality perceptions

First Tier	Second Tier	Description
Player Controlled Characters		Characters that the player had direct control over in the game world. This may include vehicles or other non-humanoid entities the player experiences the game action through
	Number	The number of characters the player can control at a given time
	Customization	The capacity to change the character's appearance, abilities, occupation, etc.
	Non-fictional	One or more of the characters is based on a person from real life
	Fictional	One or more of the characters is based on a character from another fictional medium.
	Original	One or more the characters is unique and not based on a real person or a fictional character from another medium.
Game Controlled Characters		Characters that the player have no direct control over in the game world. This may include vehicles or other non-humanoid entities the player experiences the game action through.
	Number	The number of characters the player can control at a given time
	Customization	The capacity to change the character's appearance, abilities, occupation, etc.
	Non-fictional	One or more of the characters is based on a person from real life
First Tier Indictor	Second Tier Indicator	Description
Game Controlled Characters cont.	Fictional	One or more of the characters is based on a character from another fictional medium.
	Original	One or more the characters is unique and not based on a real person or a fictional character from another medium.
Game Response		The game's artificial intelligence. This describes how well the game reacts and functions in the game world.
Spoken Dialog		Spoken dialog that is part of the game experience.
	Recognizable Voice Actor	One or more of the voice actors is known to the player from a source outside the game.
	Recognizable Character Voice	One or more of the characters are known to the player from a source outside the game.
	Unique Voice	One or more the voices is completely new to the player.
Sound		Non-musical sound with the game, including diegetic and interface sounds.
	Recognizable	Sound effects that deliberately imitated sound effects from another source
	Unique	Sound effects that do not sound like sound effects from another game or other media.
	Unique usage	Sounds that are used in a novel or surprising way.
	Customization	The ability to create or add sound effects
	Control	The ability to adjust the sound effect volume in the game
First Tier Indictor	Second Tier Indicator	Description

continued on the following page

First Tier	Second Tier	Description
Music		Musical sound with the game.
	Recognizable	Music that deliberately imitates music from another source.
	Unique	Music that does not sound like music from another source.
	Unique usage	Music that is used in a novel or surprising way
	Customization	The ability to create or add sound effects
	Control	The ability to adjust the music volume in the game.
Game World		A game's time, place, and theme.
	Non-fictional	Specific game world elements that were deliberately borrowed by real life.
	Fictional	Specific game world elements that were deliberately borrowed from another fictional source.
	Original	Specific game world elements that were intentionally different from elements from real life or from fictional sources
	Customization	The ability to change or alter the game world in a substantial way.
First Tier Indictor	Second Tier Indicator	Description
Graphics		The visual elements of the game.
	Recognizable	Graphics that deliberately imitate graphics from another source.
	Unique usage	Graphics that were used in a novel or surprising way.
	Style	Graphics that have a distinct style
	Customization	The capacity to adjust the level of graphic quality.
Controls		The means that the player uses to interact with the game.
	Customization	The capacity to change the game's control scheme.
Questionable Content		Content that is considered by certain groups to objectionable. This is not necessarily a negative factor. Some may play a game such as *Grand Theft Auto* IV because of its questionable content.
	Violence	Violence
	Sexual themes	Sexual themes
	Adult Language	Adult Language
	Adult Themes	Adult Themes
	Controlled Substances	Controlled Substances
	Customization	Capacity to change the amount of questionable content
Socializing		Socialization (or lack of) with other players
Story		Telling of events within the game. Narrative.
First Tier Indictor	Second Tier Indicator	Description
Replayability		General motivation to play the game over and over.
	Nostalgia	Replaying a certain part of the game
	Character	Play as different character or characters
	Endings	Pursuing alternate goals within the game
	Goals	Pursuing alternate goals within the game
	Mods	Capacity to add or change the game's content

Table A2. Standardized coefficient beta weights of first tier video game quality perceptions as rated by individual player types (values in bold are significant at p < 0.05)

First Tier Quality Perceptions	1	2	3	4	5	6
Controls	-0.09	0.61	-0.22	1.00	-0.11	0.54
Game Characters	-0.03	0.67	0.38	-0.06	-0.02	0.05
Game World	-0.01	0.31	0.07	0.93	0.08	0.58
Music	**0.34**	**0.90**	-0.09	1.78	0.02	-0.29
Player Characters	0.11	0.18	-0.09	0.96	-0.03	**0.49**
Questionable Content	-0.22	-0.11	0.07	-1.33	-0.02	0.00
Replayability (addictive gameplay)	0.05	-0.27	0.07	-2.32	0.01	-0.47
Replayability (characters)	0.16	-0.01	0.40	-0.64	0.13	-0.28
Replayability (goals)	**0.37**	-0.10	0.05	1.71	-0.10	0.03
Replayability (mods)	0.11	0.32	-0.1	-0.59	0.08	0.06
Replayability (story)	-0.09	-0.18	-0.31	-0.51	0.04	**-0.52**
Social (Playing Alone)	0.13	-0.21	0.07	-0.42	0.01	0.44
Social (Playing with Others)	0.19	-0.37	-0.23	-0.78	**0.27**	-0.20
Sound	-0.09	-0.35	0.33	-0.12	**0.42**	0.48
Spoken Dialog	0.02	-0.67	0.15	0.79	0.03	-0.13
Story	0.14	0.40	-0.15	-0.39	**-0.08**	-0.11

Table A3. Standardized coefficient beta weights of second tier video game quality perceptions as rated by individual player types (values in bold are significant at p < 0.05; missing cells are due to insufficient respondents who experienced the quality perception – e.g. not all games feature characters).

Second Tier Quality Perceptions	1	2	3	4	5	6
Player character: number of characters	**0.18**	..	0.17	.	**0.1**	0.05
Player character: customize Species/Race	0.08	..	0.11	..	0.01	0.19
Player character: customize physical shape	0.09	..	-0.08	..	0.02	..
Player character: customize attributes	0.00	..	-0.20	..	-0.06	-0.11
Player character: customize clothing	-0.03	..	-0.09	..	-0.01	-0.06
Player character: customize hair style	**-0.18**	..	0.21	..	**-0.24**	..
Player character: customize equipment	0.11	..	0.17	..	**0.25**	0.18
Player character: customize culture	**-0.15**	..	..	..	**-0.14**	
Player character: customize character class	0.06	..	-0.65	..	0.02	..
Player character: customize occupation	0.09	..	0.32	..	**0.23**	..
Player character: customize personality	0.15	..	..	..	**0.22**	0.14
Player character: customize powers / abilities	0.01	..	0.21	..	-0.02	0.06
Second Tier Quality Perceptions	1	2	3	4	5	6
Player characters: familiar in real life	0.00	..	0.35	..	0.16	0.17
Player character: familiar as fictional character	0.07	..	0.04	..	0.22	-0.01
Player characters: original	0.22	..	0.44	..	0.24	0.04

continued on the following page

Second Tier Quality Perceptions	1	2	3	4	5	6
Player character: attachment	0.55	..	0.41	..	0.65	..
Game characters: customize species/race	..	..	..	..	**0.22**	-0.12
Game characters: customize physical shape	..	..	..	..	**-0.44**	..
Game characters: customize attributes	0.10	..	..	..	-0.10	..
Game characters: customize clothing	..	..	**0.25**	..	**0.54**	..
Game Characters: customize hair style	..	..	..	..	-0.05	..
Game characters: customize equipment	**0.15**	..	..	..	**0.39**	**-0.49**
Game character: customize culture	..	..	..	..	**0.32**	..
Game character: customize character class	..	..	..	..	**-0.3**	..
Game character: customize occupation	..	..	..	0.46	**-0.13**	**0.54**
Second Tier Quality Perceptions	1	2	3	4	5	6
Game characters customize personality	0.07	..	**-0.17**	-0.13	**-0.20**	**0.54**
Game characters: customize powers / abilities	**-0.09**	..	..	..	**-0.14**	-0.09
Game characters: familiar in real life	**0.12**	..	-0.08	..	**0.12**	..
Game characters: familiar as fictional character	**0.10**	..	**0.13**	-0.16	-0.05	-0.05
Game characters: original	**0.25**	..	**0.18**	0.10	**0.30**	0.08
Game characters	**0.76**	..	**0.81**	0.63	**0.67**	**0.67**
Familiar voice actor performance	**0.16**	**0.46**	**0.32**	0.29	**0.23**	0.08
Familiar character's performance	0.094	0.198	**0.18**	**0.44**	**0.27**	**0.25**
Original voices	**0.81**	**0.67**	**0.64**	0.30	**0.80**	**0.72**
Familiar sounds	**0.23**	**0.24**	**0.38**	0.51	**0.33**	**0.13**
Original	**0.75**	**0.88**	**0.62**	0.67	**0.74**	**0.78**
Original sound usage	-0.04	-0.07	**-0.09**	-0.01	**-0.05**	-0.03
Second Tier Quality Perceptions	1	2	3	4	5	6
Sound creation	..	0.04	..	-0.31	**0.08**	-0.05
Sound volume control	**0.11**	0.00	**0.1**	0.19	**0.12**	0.09
Familiar music	**0.47**	**0.88**	**0.38**	0.89	**0.65**	**0.44**
Original music	**0.57**	**0.56**	**0.69**	1.55	**0.62**	**0.76**
Original music usage	**-0.12**	**-0.30**	**-0.10**	-0.99	**-0.17**	**-0.31**
Music creation	..	**-0.15**	**-0.20**	-0.74	**-0.00**	..
Music volume control	**0.151**	**-0.13**	0.03	-0.26	**0.187**	0.15
Familiar game world elements	**0.58**	**0.59**	**0.58**	0.66	**0.65**	**0.57**
Original game world elements	**0.32**	**0.41**	**0.32**	0.55	**0.45**	**0.56**
Changing the game world elements	**0.06**	-0.07	0.06	-0.22	**0.09**	-0.02

Chapter 14
The Play of Persuasion:
Why "Serious" Isn't the Opposite of Fun

Nicholas Fortugno
Rebel Monkey, USA

ABSTRACT

Game designer Nick Fortungno's keynote speech at the Meaningful Play conference talked about the conundrum of whether serious games can or even should be fun. Fortugno looks back at historical works of popular culture that exerted transformative effects on society. He examines three current persuasive games and offers his thoughts on what it will take for a game to achieve societal transformation.

Before I begin, let me make some preliminary points. First of all, this talk is about games that aim to persuade. That's what I happen to be interested in and what I'll be exploring today. The talk is specifically focused on a category of serious games designed to pass a message on to the user. The second thing you'll notice is that "serious" in the title is in quotes. I only do that because I am trying to be clever. I do sit in the camp of people who dislike the term "serious games" for reasons you'll see in a moment. But given that the other industries I work in are also misnamed "casual games" which an average player plays for an equal amount as a hardcore game, and "big games" because the first game that was made in the field had the word "big" in the title—I'm not overly bothered by the fact that the serious genre is labeled incorrectly.

I'm co-founder of Rebel Monkey, based in New York. We're working on a casual MMO, more about which will be revealed in early 2009. I've been a game designer for several years. My most famous piece of work is Diner Dash. It's a totally entertainment based game; in fact most of my work has been in non-serious games. In Diner Dash, you wait tables. It's a time management game. But I have also worked on serious games, notably Ayiti: The Cost of Life, a serious game I designed at GameLab in which you manage a family of Haitians and attempt to get their collective level of education up as you struggle against the conditions of poverty in Haiti. The point of the game is to teach a lesson about how education differs in a developing country from in the United States.

But I also teach game design courses and this talk was inspired by my class. I teach a class at Parsons' called Game Design 1, the purpose of which is to introduce students to the basic ideas of game design. It's a studio class where students make board games and card games. This semester I went through a typical lesson that I use in my class and it had an interesting result. To understand where I am going with this, you should know that Parsons has a new program called PETLAB, a lab for game design and game development. Its purpose is tied closely to games for change. Its mission is to explore games that are capable of making social change.

In Game Design 1, the very first lesson in the very first class is to have the students generate a list of games. We use that list of games to try to derive a definition of games that we can use throughout the semester. This fall I asked the class to name some games. We came up with a list (Scrabble, Mario Brothers, God of War, Poker, Tag, Midnight Club, Halo, Legend of Zelda, Pac-Mac, Football, Shadow of the Colossus, Ikaruga, Persona 3, Double Dragon, etc.) and, as usual, it was varied and the games represented a large spectrum. I like to let the brainstorming go on for a while to generate as big and diverse a list as possible so that we can go on to identify aspects that are elemental and essential. When the list is large enough, I ask, what do these games have in common? Just think about it for a second, using the list above. And over the years that I've taught, I've found (just like anyone who has taught for some time) that the answers tend to gravitate around certain wells, and I can predict that certain responses are going to emerge. Every game on the list has rules, goals, and players; a game is a system that has objectives players try to reach; there are constraints on achieving those objectives that form the rules of the game: there's agency in the game. Often students will mention

challenge or competition. Here too the goal is to generate lots of ideas.

But there's an obvious commonality that nobody ever gets at first, something that takes some prodding to elicit. Eventually, after enough prodding, the class says, "FUN!!!" The presumption is that all games attempt to be fun. This is what happens normally. But this year when I asked that question—what's that one more obvious thing, and the answer came "fun" I then asked the question: Do games have to be fun? About a third of the class said no. That's never happened to me before. It was a bit of a shock to me, as someone who comes to games originally and primarily from an entertainment perspective, the idea that you would start a class in games and say that games don't have to be fun. The class argued about it for about 20 minutes before I had them move on. This exchange tells me something about the direction games are moving.

Do games need to be fun? In traditional game design, this is a ridiculous question. Fun is a deep principle of traditional game design. When I work as a game designer, fun is the barometer of success in development. You'll be sitting around the room with a bunch of designers. You'll have made a prototype, you'll look at the prototype, and the question is: is it fun? If the answer is no, you go back to the drawing board. So the idea that a game doesn't have to be fun is unsettling to traditional game designers. I think it is part of the reason there is resistance in traditional game design to serious games in general. Once you lose the fun barometer, as a designer you're floating out in the middle of nowhere.

The "games don't have to be fun" perspective in the classroom came particularly from students who were interested in and being trained in serious games. When they thought about fun, they thought about entertainment, which they considered frivolous. Games about serious issues shouldn't be frivolous, by their assessment, so they should be instead something else. They had a deep resistance to using the word FUN. The other words they came up with were COMPELLING and ENGAGING. In fact, the fight in class was really about whether we could use the word "engaging" instead of the word "fun." I think that's because words such as "engaging" are more SERIOUS.

Are games about issues and fun necessarily mutually exclusive? Obviously fun might not be the kind of reaction designers want if they are making a game about the genocide of Darfur. Should that game be fun? Clearly the genocide in Darfur is not fun, and it is not necessarily something you ever want to make light of in the context of trying to get people to take action on it. So do we even want to approach fun at all? Games could pursue a host of other emotions. We could try to design game that pursues emotions different than what we feel playing Chess or soccer or poker or Halo or Diner Dash. If we are going in the direction of these non-traditional game emotions, regardless of the message, is fun necessarily still a design goal?

Games are not the first entertainment medium that has been used to try to push social messages or try to convince someone of something. To answer the question of games and social issues, I decided to see what we can learn from how other media have approached serious issues. When another medium is trying to convince us of something, how do they do it? Being someone who comes from a literature background, my head immediately went to two different things.

The first is 19th century Pop. When one thinks back to works of fiction that actually influenced American history, there is one huge inescapable example: *Uncle Tom's Cabin*. It was written in 1852 by Harriet Beecher Stowe. It was the best-selling novel of the 19th century, selling over 1.5 million copies around the world. (The Bible is the only book that sold more in that period.) Regarding Stowe, Abraham Lincoln famously said "so this is the little lady who made this big war."

In its time, was seen by the public as at least a contributor if not a primary motivator of activity that lead to the greatest conflict on American soil. It was written in response to the Fugitive Slave Act. A very, very quick retelling of the plot… there is a slave holding plantation. There are two slaves on it (Tom and Eliza, the main characters). The slave holder is in debt and has to sell slaves. He wants to sell Tom and Eliza's baby. Eliza runs away with the baby. Tom stays, which creates a little foil structure). The story is basically about Tom's descent to a noble death at the hands of merciless slave holders as he is passed around the slavery system in the South, and Eliza's escape to Canada after being reunited with the father of her child and finding freedom. The message behind the story is a clear abolitionist message. Stowe saw herself as an abolitionist and saw the project as abolition. To that end it was an incredibly powerful argument because if you study the history of abolitionism, abolitionism pre-existed Stowe, reaching back to the very early days of the United States. The idea that Stowe was working in an abolitionist message that already existed is particularly interesting. It took the creation of *Uncle Tom's Cabin* to really galvanize the issue to the point where it couldn't possibly be ignored.

What interests me about *Uncle Tom's Cabin* in particular is not just its message, but also how the book is written. When you look at the book in the context of its period, it doesn't stand out in exactly the way we might expect. In what is probably the most famous scene of the book, Eliza carries her child across the frozen Ohio River as the river flows are breaking down, being chased by people who have been tasked to retrieve her. Obviously, the reference to the Fugitive Slave Act is extremely clear. Here are lines of text from that scene: "The huge green fragment of ice on which she alighted pitched and creaked as her weight came on it but she stayed there not a moment. With wild cries and desperate energy she leaped to another and still another cake stumbling leaping slipping, springing upwards again Her shoes are gone her stockings cut from her feet while blood marked every step but she saw nothing, felt nothing, till dimly as in a dream she saw the Ohio side and a man helping her up the bank" (Stowe, 1900, pp.94-85).

This is an action scene in the book. There are dogs chasing her; there are men shouting; she is jumping from ice flow to ice flow; she is diving across the river. This is a melodramatic action scene. And in fact, if you read literary criticism of *Uncle Tom's Cabin*, both from its time and contemporarily, there are many people who don't like the book as a work of literature. There are many people who think it's just a sentimentalist novel. The curious thing is that, in some sense, it is just a sentimentalist novel. The sentimentalism novel movement in literature was very strong in the 19th century. There were many, many successful 19th century sentimentalist novels, except they didn't have anything to do with slavery. Two examples are *Charlotte Temple* by Susanna Rowson and *The Wide Wide World* by Susan Warner, which would have been the most successful novel of the 19th century if *Uncle Tom's Cabin* had not come out. If you look at the plots of these books, and you compare them to the plot of Eliza in *Uncle Tom's Cabin*, they are extremely similar. They are all about a young woman who is pure, who is ruined by circumstance, and either succumbs to vice and is destroyed or endures suffering and succeeds.

While *Uncle Tom's Cabin* is pushing what was at the time an extremely controversial message, and was pushing a story largely about equal rights, the message was masked in a melodramatic popular form. Many people point out today there are issues of representation of race in *Uncle Tom's Cabin* and it's not a totally pleasant book. It is offensive in certain ways about the depiction of race and the stereotypes it portrays. But the book does push a radical message of abolitionism and it does so in a purely, purely popular way, using a form that audience knew, using a methodology the audience was totally familiar with. In a sense *Uncle Tom* is exactly like the things that came before it. *Uncle Tom's Cabin* does not innovate at the level of its writing. It fits exactly into the tradition of several books of its period.

Let's take this to the modern day and consider another example in the fiction of our time. Telenovelas are short run soap operas. They began in Brasil, Mexico, and Cuba. It's a form that took root in Latin and South America and now it's everywhere (including the Philippines, China, Russia, the United States, and Germany).

Miguel Sebido in the 1970s looked at this emerging form and saw an opportunity to use it in a different way. This form was already extremely popular in many countries. Telenovelas are like soap operas, but without the U.S. restrictions on propriety. That means they can be more sexy, and I guess objectify women more. Sebido's jump was to realize we could take this storytelling form and use it to educate people about social issues. (He had already worked in political theater.) He became involved in the design of telenovelas that taught social messages. One specific example was to build a story around issues of parenting in Mexico: issues about raising children, birth control, whether to have a child or not have a child, and if the dad is going to run away or stay with the family. By designing a soap opera story like that, he could inject into the conversations issues of parenting and get people in the country who were watching and talking about the show to talk about issues of parenting. The success of this led to other educational telenovelas that cover a variety of topics such as AIDS, literacy, women's rights, and social class that are being distributed around the world right now. There have been social issues telenovelas designed for India, China, and Southeast Asia, particularly around issues such as AIDS, designed to push AIDS education around the world. *Miranda de Mujer* is an example of this kind of telenovela, where the main character's best friend got AIDS and then died.

What's interesting about this is a telenovela is a soap opera, and the storyline of a soap opera is filled with melodramatic trash. It's thick with bizarre turns and deus ex machina and crushing movement. I can't think of a soap opera that was considered a serious form in terms of criticism –

it's always seen as a form of pop culture. Soap operas don't aspire to be anything more than pop culture, and they are wildly successful. Even in telenovelas that deal with social issues, there is still a ton of sex and melodrama. Even when we're talking about AIDS or family values, there are still people sleeping with each other and weird family politics. And it's certainly not to say that social issue telenovelas dominate the telenovelas market. The telenovelas market continues to plow out formulaic pieces of melodrama. But because that form has success, a message can be slipped into it that will be consumed by the same audience.

We can point to myriad other examples of social issues in pop culture, both successful and unsuccessful. There have been other books, such as *The Jungle* (exploring food production), movies such as *Erin Brockovich* (about corporate malfeasance), shows such as *Will and* Grace (about homosexuality), or songs about voting rights like *Mosh* by Eminem (made specifically for the 2004 election to encourage young people to vote). It's controversial but there's some evidence that *Mosh* succeeded in persuading young voters, although it did not succeed in not getting Bush elected. And of course there's *Captain Planet*, a cartoon about global warming and environmental issues.

What does all of this mean for games? The lesson here is that people will watch a message delivered using the expected formulas found in favorite genres. A quick caveat: I am certainly not advocating against systems of games or directions of games that are more controversial, that are pushing at the boundaries of things we already know, or that are pursuing emotions that deviate from formulas we already know. I think all of that exploration is absolutely essential to the development of games. In fact, my work as a game designer has been in innovative game design and I intend to continue to innovate because I think it is not just artistically valuable to me as a creator but I think worthwhile to the whole industry. But my point is that if your main goal is to distribute

a message, and a game is your vehicle for that message, you should recognize that games are a part of our culture and the formula for games culturally is strongly entrenched. There are people who play them and play them and play them. Those players have definite expectations of what games are supposed to be like.

So, if you want to send a message through a game, MAKE IT A GAME. We're not trying to dodge the basic nature of games by making it about a social issue. We come to the game because we recognize it as a pop medium that is capable of connecting with people well. Then why don't we just treat social issue games as games and make them fun? After all that's what the audience is looking for. If I am coming to a sentimentalist novel, I am coming to read sentimental melodrama. I want action and melodrama and thwarted romance, and I guess the slightly sadistic thrill of watching a young girl suffer. That's what I'm looking for, so give that to me. If I come to a telenovela, I want intrigue, and family politics, repressed and open sexuality. So give me that. And then I'll eat your message about AIDS and literacy too.

We should recognize that at this point there is no *Uncle Tom's Cabin* for games. You've probably heard similar laments in other contexts. There's no Citizen Kane for games; there's no Hamlet for games. I really don't like that "Citizen Kane" complaint because it set a weird standard. There have been games that are really awesome games. And I would argue that there have been many games that ludologically are as awesome as Hamlet. Nonetheless, we can plainly say that there has been no game that has shaped culture anywhere close to the extent culture was shaped by the two pop examples I gave. That's a bar we can look at. When the president of the United States shakes the hand of a game designer and says "so you are the little designer who started this big…" hopefully not war, (I may have painted myself into a corner there)—when we have that moment, that's when we know games have achieved that prize in terms of their persuasiveness.

Still, there are games that do persuade. What I want to do for the remainder of this talk is to focus on three examples. They are all similar in the sense that they were made to deliver a message. They all subscribe to the persuasive game theory that Ian Bogost promotes in his book, *Persuasive Games*. All of these games are pursuing messages and games that pursue messages use common methodologies regardless of the message.

I want to look at 3 persuasive games and see how they work as games. I will unabashedly start with an art game because I am a flag waving member of the games as art camp, if only just to be able to make more games as art and not be questioned about it. My art game example is a typical one, *Shadow of the Colossus*. I would argue that *Shadow of the Colossus* is attempting to hit an emotional space that games don't normally approach, which is tragedy. It uses straight up traditional tragedy. There is a character with hubris, who acts in hubris, makes mistakes, and ruins things in the surrounding world. This tragedy is expressed at a number of levels but the most local level of the tragedy is the fighting of the colossus

You are tasked with killing colossi because a woman whom you love is dead and you are trying to bring her back to life. A god-like being in a temple tells you that if you kill these colossi, there is a chance that your lover could be brought back to life. You ride out through vast wastelands of nothing where you might see a lizard or a bird or once I saw a turtle. You come to a field where there's a colossus. Some of the colossi will hunt you as soon as you show up. They will try to stomp you. But there are other colossi, particularly the flying colossi, that generally don't care about you at all. All three of the flying colossi either remain seated where they happen to be sitting when you arrive, or they fly around in the sky and totally ignore you until you start shooting arrows at them, drive them to the ground, jump on them, climb on their body, stab them repeatedly until they start spewing black ichyra over everything and kill them. When you kill them, the end of each colos-

sus defeat is the same. You hear a melodramatic track of orchestral music as the colossus in slow motion crashes to the ground and falls like a limp doll. It's sad, or at least it's intended to be sad.

In the case of the flying colossi, it's particularly troubling. At the end of the game there is a flying colossus that has air sacks and it will literally just fly around forever. It will never do anything to you. I won't spoil the puzzle of it but you don't kill it the first time you bring it down. When you finish fighting it, it just goes right back up into the sky again and spins around in circles until you bring it down again. The point of this is it would just keep flying around in circles and not hurt anyone; even you and you just wounded it. It doesn't care. It just goes back to what it was doing. You really have to go out of your way to kill it.

The interesting thing is that this is coupled with a very traditional kind of boss mechanic. To kill the colossus, I have to solve a puzzle, and depending on the colossus I am killing, I have to solve a complicated jumping puzzle, or I have to figure out the colossus's weakness, or I have to figure out a path along the colossus's climbable parts to get someplace. This mechanic of exploration and puzzle solving goes back a long way, found all the way back in the boss fights at the ends of dungeons in *The Legend of Zelda* – it's all about this sort of clever puzzle solving mechanic. At that level, it's simply, straightforwardly, a game about killing bosses. That's something gamers are familiar with. If you have a discussion with gamers about *Shadow of the Colossus*, there's a lot of talk about which one is their favorite and there are people who like the jumping puzzles and people who hate the jumping puzzles, but like the colossi where you have to be clever enough to figure out a weakness. The game doesn't try to push away from the mechanic that makes a game like this compelling for people, even though it's aiming at a totally different direction. In fact, the killing of a colossus is fun because the puzzle solving around the killing of a colossus is fun.

So I have fun killing the colossi. If I didn't, I wouldn't play the game. If I felt miserable the whole time as I was climbing up the monster, it would be difficult to motivate me to do it. But because the mechanic is basically familiar to me and because it taps into some of these basic game desires, this is something I want to solve, and I move forward into it. While each creature's death is a tragedy, but the killing of each creature is a puzzle. The puzzle is fun and that pushes me forward in the tragic narrative. What's so brilliant about this game is that the very struggle that I have to go through to kill a colossus and the cognitive dissonance that it generates after you have to try 15, 16, 20 times to get the colossus to stand over the geyser at the right time at the right angle so you can shoot an arrow into its foot. After the struggle you go through, the reward is supposed to be fun. The reward you are going for is the sense of triumphant accomplishment. This is one of the most typical, standard emotions of a single player game. But it is this reward moment that the game then harnesses into a tragic direction. It doesn't cease to be a game even though it is tragic. It uses the emotions and mechanics of the game to push forward the tragedy.

What about a serious game? My favorite serious game to date is called *Peacemaker*. It was created by Impact Games out of Carnegie Melon. The idea is that you play through the Palestinian-Israeli conflict. You can choose to play through it as either the Prime Minister of Israel or the President of Palestine or you can let the game assign a random position. Your goal is to make peace, and the way you make peace is to get the approval meters of the various sides high enough that you pass a certain threshold for both of them simultaneously. You do this by taking actions, such as giving speeches to different people; making negotiations with the other side, increasing military power, and so forth. It's a turn-based game and every action you take affects the approval meters of the various constituencies, from your nation and the world. What's interesting

about the game is that when you pick an action, the actions the Palestinians like are often actions the Israeli's don't like. So when I move one bar in one direction, the other bar will often go in the opposite direction. It's very hard to maneuver so the other bar doesn't go down. The game is about plate balancing as the stakes get higher and higher and the actions get more dramatic. Throughout the game, random things happen like bombs going off or mass protests that you have to respond to, making the plate balancing more difficult.

The reason I like *Peacemaker* so much is that at the heart of it is this game of balancing the approval meters. There are actions that push you in one direction or another and they are pretty intuitive. For example, as the Israeli leader you can set up new settlements in the West Bank, which after playing the game for about 10 minutes you realize would be a horrible idea, because all of the Palestinians will immediately hate you. So there are actions that are not very effective in the short run or maybe only effective in very specific ways. You are constantly trying to massage the balance and take actions to move towards peace. You are constantly trying to guess what you're supposed to do. You are slowly trying to figure out what the climate of the two countries is. You leave the game with is a profound appreciation of how hard this problem is to solve.

Peacemaker's message is the difficulty of achieving peace between Israel and Palestine. But the game play is about balancing approval meters by selecting actions. The longer I play the game the less attention I pay to the specific narrative. This is something Jesper Juul talks about in detail in his book *Half-Real*. As I get better at playing, I pay less and less attention to narrative events, but it doesn't matter because the system of the game remains tied to the message. The game itself is compelling, but the act of balancing the approval meter is in fact the lesson of the game – the difficulty of keeping everyone happy when sides are strong, mutually exclusive positions. *Peacemaker* clearly isn't *Uncle Tom's Cabin*. But it uses the mechanics of play to point towards your goal. The player just keeps eating the message.

I want to end with a propaganda game: the McDonalds game. I don't consider this an incredibly good game, but I think it's an interesting game to talk about. You are tasked with running the McDonald's Empire. (I should point out it is not sponsored by McDonalds.) Your attention is divided between four mini-games activities: growing the food you need, managing the cows, running the butcher shop, and running the restaurant. The game is from the alert state genre—something goes wrong and you have to focus on that game and click on that screen to resolve the problem. I don't think the game is super compelling. There's not a lot of choice in the game – a cow gets sick, and you click on the cow to kill it.

What is interesting is the attempt to take a management sim game and apply it to McDonalds. The game puts you in cross purposes – you are trying to maximize the goals of the game, to make as much money as possible for McDonalds, but in the process you're doing horrible things to animals and the environment. You rip up rainforests and plant crops that destroy the soil, feed cows parts of other cows, and rip off customers You willfully do this over and over again in your quest to make money. This is a mechanic a lot of games use quite effectively. Another game that does this is the *Redistricting Game*, where you are tasked with redistricting congressional districts. You pick a side and you have to try to maximize the district distribution for your candidate, but in the process you subvert democracy lethally.

This is a methodology of game propaganda. You have a statement you want to make. You have

game play that allows you to push on that system. You force the player to experience the message you want to experience by engaging with the system. In the *McDonald's Game*, the core play is a management sim about different aspects of the industry or process. The player's goal is to maximize profit, by doing disgusting things.

There is a long tradition of political art following popular media. I would argue it's that side, the pop side, of the equation that's done the most to get awareness of issues out into the public sphere. The pop art side has really pushed things. Of course, not all games should be popular culture. Not all message games should strive to recreate existing mechanics with political messages. Persuasive games can pursue all types of effects. I encourage designers to go out and purse more innovative models. But if your sole point is to deliver a message, then you should look hard at what game players do and focus on that as your design principle. If you're working to try to attract players, look at what players like to play. In that sense, serious games can, and should, be fun too.

ACKNOWLEDGMENT

Keynote Speech delivered at Meaningful Play, East Lansing, October 2008.

REFERENCES

Stowe, H. B. (1900). *Uncle Tom's Cabin, or, Life Among the Lowly*. H. Altemus.

This work was previously published in International Journal of Gaming and Computer-Mediated Simulations, Volume 1, Issue 3, edited by Richard E. Ferdig, pp. 81-88 copyright 2009 by IGI Publishing (an imprint of IGI Global).

Chapter 15
Researching and Developing Serious Games as Interactive Learning Instructions

Christian Sebastian Loh
Southern Illinois University-Carbondale, USA

ABSTRACT

As serious games gain momentum in the academic arena, no doubt more educators and instructional technologists will begin considering the possibility of making their own games for instruction. As developers of instructional resources, instructional technologists need to steer clear of producing more 'video' games, and instead, developing more 'serious' games that incorporate both learning and assessment. The research community needs to learn from tested processes and best practices to avoid repeating old mistakes. The model for serious game making presented in this article has been used successfully for the creation of an award winning project, and will now be shared for the benefits of fellow researchers, educators, and instructional technologists.

INTRODUCTION

Games and education have had a long-standing partnership for a large part of the known human history. Botturi and Loh (2009) showed that the ancient Greek used only one word, *ludus*, to mean both *school* and *game*, as learning and playing

games were once considered to be the same. School teachers of that time were referred to as *magister ludi* (literally, game masters) because they were experts who drew upon the principles of game playing for the training and instruction of their pupils. Based on this *game-is-education* perspective, the use of digital video games for serious learning can hardly be called revolutionary. Hence, when nearly all (99% of boys and 97%

DOI: 10.4018/978-1-60960-565-0.ch015

of girls) teenagers report playing video games regularly as a preferred pastime (Lenhart, Kahne, Middaugh, Macgill, Evans, & Vitak, 2008), many educators acknowledged this to be the key to the hearts and minds of the digital native generation (Miller, 2008).

The video game industry had always stayed on the cutting edge by pushing for advancement in digital (graphic) technology. When coupled with the passion among game developers to out-do one another, this has given rise to an industry that is relentless in its pursuit for products with ever-escalating production qualities. Compared to just a few years ago, not only are players able to perform a lot more actions within a game environment; the shelf-lives of commercial, off-the-shelf (COTS) games are constantly diminishing, being given over to newer games to fuel tomorrow's technology. This means that many well-known computer games (such as *The Oregon Trail*, *Math Blaster*, and *Reader Rabbit*) were not only outdated, but would cease to work on the newest computers. Even the abundant 2D-animation (Flash) games found on educational websites would pale in comparison to what the industry offers today.

Since the debut of 3rd generation game consoles (such as PS3 and Xbox 360), today's game engines can easily simulate real-world physical laws (such as gravity and inertia), and produce realistic lighting and water effects in games. As faster computer processors and online streaming technology continue to provide support for better game effects, immersive online play, and massive multiplayer virtual worlds; the knowledge gap between the gaming industry and outsiders to the industry (such as educators and researchers) will continue to widen. There was little reason to conclude non-professional game developers could ever create games at the industry production quality. Why then, should educators and instructional technologists care about making video games?

HISTORY OF GAME MODIFICATION (MODDING)

The watershed came in the form of a military training game, called *Marine Doom* (1998), created for the purpose of training soldiers in teamwork and decision making skills when live training time and opportunities were limited during peaceful times. Instead of creating the video game from scratch, the U.S. Marine (in-house) development team decided to modify (or, *mod*) a COTS game, *Doom* (1992), to take advantage of the game mechanics and resources already present in the game engine, as well as to reduce production cost and time. This game *mod*ification process—whereby a COTS game's own engine is re-used to create a "home-brew" (and very much playable) game—has come to be known as *modding* among the gamers. Since then, the U.S. Marine Corps have gone on to create other military game modules (or *mods*), including the highly successful *America's Army*, with over 26 versions released since its debut in 2002. Gamers have easy access to thousands of game *mods* (made from a plethora of COTS games) that were distributed through repositories and websites created just for mod enthusiasts—for example, the Vault Network (http://vault.ign.com), and the Game Mod Database (http://www.moddb.com).

Instead of producing a full-fledged video game, it would be far more likely for educators, researchers, and trainers to develop prototypic games for the demonstration of educational concepts, research frameworks/methodologies, or training procedures. As such, game modding would prove to be most appropriate and invaluable in reducing development cost and time while attaining industry production quality in the artifact produced. Because a game mod would be of a similar feel and quality to the original COTS game used to create it, learners would be motivated by the medium and willing to learn the new training tool. Similarly, research projects using mod of well-known COTS games could benefit from easier recruitment of human subject participants and reduce the need for (re-)training.

Increasingly more game developers have chosen to give away game development kits (GDKs) along with the sale of their games; a move which is sure to encourage more modding projects. Priced at US$20–50 per game, these GDK/game bundles are a small price to pay, when compared with commercial-grade game engines (e.g., *Unreal*), which could cost up to several hundreds of thousand dollars per seat of license. Examples of GDK/game bundles include the *Crysis Mod SDK* for *Crysis*, the *Electron Toolkit* for *Neverwinter Nights 2*, and *Hammer Editor* for *Half-Life 2*. Several of these tools have also been uses in the creation of educational projects, research test-beds, and workplace training. Notable projects in this arena include *HistoriCanada: The New World* (a *Civilization III* mod) by Bitcasters (completed in 2008), and *Revolution* (a *Neverwinter Night* mod) by Education Arcade (completed in 2004). Some educators have come to regard game mods as computational literacy artifacts (Steinkuehler & Johnson, 2009); hence, students who engaged in modding must possess high standards in computational and literacy skills.

THE RISE OF SERIOUS GAMES

The success of video games as an educational and recruitment tool (e.g., *America's Army*) (Bounds, 2007) has prompted renewed interest among educators and researcher to re-examine digital games for raising literacy (Gee, 2003), as well as for supporting research and instruction (Ferdig, 2008; Miller, 2008). The mounting interest eventually translated into the Serious Games Summit 2004, marking the beginning of a new sub-industry known as *serious games* (Sawyer, 2005). The term was chosen to encompass any type of digital game and game-like application (including simulations and virtual worlds) that had been specifically designed for serious learning or training purposes. Even though the serious games industry began as a niche market targeting human performance improvement and personnel training, it has attracted the attention of several industries, including the military, healthcare, business, government, and educational sectors. As one study (Hewitt, 2008) revealed, out of 70% of major U.S. corporations that were already using interactive software for human performance improvement, many had expressed interest in digital game-based training.

SERIOUS GAMES AS INTERACTIVE LEARNING INSTRUCTION

Unfortunately, the last joint effort between game developers and instructional designers to create (revenue generating) educational video games was less than successful. As the fateful name suggested, those early *edutainment* titles were half-baked attempts at doing *edu*-cation and enter-*tainment* concurrently; thus, resulting in a large collection of *boring* games (Hopson, 2006; Prensky, 2005; van Eck, 2007). Since history has revealed that the notion of creating educational games simply by mixing learning materials with "gaming activities" was wishful thinking, serious games developers have exercised much caution in what they produced. They chose to focus on discovery (or exploratory) learning, which dealt more with critical thinking and problem solving skills, than trying to sensationalize fanciful gaming activities, such as shooting objects, navigating pathways, or *twitching* (i.e., pressing quick combination of button in set order).

Unlike the edutainment titles which were available for sale through nation supply chains, such as WalMart and BestBuy, most serious games chose *not* to compete with COTS game titles. Instead, these serious games were either distributed at no cost through special educational downloads (Amarelo, 2008; Federation of American Scientists, 2006), or through direct marketing to

Figure 1. A game log in plain-text format

```
Alice (Fordlindon, 7 armies, 3 lost) attacked Bob (Harlindon, 1 armies, 1 lost),
conquering it. 4 armies advanced.
Alice (Harlindon, 4 armies, 3 lost) attacked Bob (The Shire, 13 armies, 0 lost),
failing to conquer...
Bob.....
```

specific target industries (e.g., fire fighting, police enforcement, and disaster response). Examples of serious games include: *Immune Attack* (high school and college immunology, by the Federation of American Scientists), *Flame-Sim* (fire fighting, by Flame-Sim, LLC.), and *Tactical Iraqi* (foreign language acquisition, by Alelo, Inc.).

Assessment of Learning

Readers may question what advantages serious games have over edutainment, if it is to become successful. Having interviewed experts from the industry, Michael and Chen (2006) suggested that the *assessment of learning* is the key element in making serious games better than edutainment. Because "data-driven assessments of learning" have become the foremost issue on the minds of many trainers and educators today (Mandinach & Honey, 2008), the inclusion of assessment components in serious games would allow instructors and trainers access to game-related statistics (that were otherwise unavailable) for the creation of performance improvement and Return of Investment (ROI) indices.

Depending on the training industry, these game-related data may be tailored to include any pertinent information; for example, amount of time taken to complete a task, total number of cases solved and percentage of tasks/missions accomplished. In most cases, a *screen-dump* (where mission-related achievement scores are shown just *once*, on screen, at the end of a game mission) may be sufficient for self-evaluation by the players. In other cases, a game *log* file may

be necessary to provide more permanent data for evaluation by instructors. Figure 1 shows an example of a (primitive) game log in plain text format; Figure 2 shows a more comprehensive game log in tag-enclosed XML format.

Besides game logs, military training games and simulators must further support the feature of After-Action Reports (AAR)—essentially a form of graphical game log, detailing a variety of statistics indicating how much rank and experience a unit gained during a simulated operation. Although AARs could also be found in COTS games like *Call of Duty IV* and *Tom Clancy's EndWar*, they were included mostly for the sake of military gameplay authenticity and served no training purpose beyond the game. Unlike their game counterpart, real AAR from live-training sessions (e.g., a flight simulator with 3-axis tilt) could include biofeedback data collected during *test flights*. Such biofeedback data has been useful to predict soldiers' performance and the likelihood of adverse physiological reactions (e.g., gravity-induced loss of consciousness during a flight) in future, real life operations. Since the assessment of learning (and performance), as well as data visualizations, are salient features that set serious games well above edutainment. It is important to design these features into future serious games, and not to regard them as *optional* features—to be added only as an afterthought.

Media Comparison Research

In many educational sectors where scientific methods of research were upheld—including Medi-

Figure 2. A sample objective hierarchy map depicting the information trails of game events within a role-playing serious game

```
<?xml version="1.0"?>
<game>
<maptype>Africa</maptype>
<timeleft>12hrs 16min 20sec</timeleft>
<round>3</round>
<players>
<starting>8</starting>
<surviving>4</surviving>
<teams>4</teams>
<player>
<name>trey</name>
<rank>New Recruit</rank>
<team>3</team>
<cards>4</cards>
<armies>20</armies>
...
<event>
<type>deploy</type>
<from>NA</from>
<to>Sparta</to>
<armies>3</armies>
<defender>NA</defender>
</event>
<event>
<type>attack</type>
<from>Sparta</from>
<to>Yarmen</to>
...
```

cal/Pharmaceutical studies, Learning Science, Agricultural Education, Science, and Computer Science Education—the research design would typically call for a comparison between treatment and control groups. Researchers would test for the effects of an intervention by comparing the recipient group with a control group that did not receive the treatment. The rationale for this design being: should the intervention (e.g., a new drug in a clinical research) prove effective for the condition (e.g., cancer), a measureable change (positive or negative) would be detectable in the treatment group, and would not be present in the control group (i.e., use of placebo, or no intervention). If no statistically significant difference between the intervention and control groups could be found, then the intervention was regarded as having no effect (ineffective) for the recipient group under the circumstances.

For this type of research design to be applied in digital game-based instruction, researchers must make the assumption that the educational interventions (or technology used) were similar in effects to chemical/biochemical/pharmaceutical used in agriculture/medical/clinical interventions, respectively. If technology or technology-based instruction was the *magic pill*, then the correct control condition (to counter the treatment condition) would be no pills, or placebos. In the case of serious game learning, a treatment group would naturally be playing serious games, and a control group would be receiving teacher-only instruction.

A Flawed Assumption

However, since the 1980s, these types of treatment/control studies—more commonly known as *media comparison studies* in educational and instructional technology circles—have long been criticized as flawed based on many inherent theoretical and design problems (Locke, Moore, & Burton, 2001; Thompson, Simonson, & Hargrave, 1992). Although the comparison design was a proven method in many scientific fields, they were deemed to be an "inappropriate research design for measuring the effectiveness of instructional technology" (Lockee, Burton, & Cross, 1999, p. 33). Researchers who conduct media comparison studies have overlooked inherent factors found only in human learning, including learner characteristics, media attributes, instructional strategies, and influence of teachers, that were not present in plant growth, biochemical pathways, or human physiology. Technology (such as serious games) in and of itself could not affect learning, it was the technology-mediated instruction that would affect learning in the learners (Haertel & Means, 2003).

Since the research question of comparing instructional media/method to 'direct instruction' (as control condition) was inherently confounded, any discussion of the invalidated research findings would become meaningless. This explains why media comparison studies (such as the case study above) would commonly yield *no (statistically) significant effect* findings, which could be doubly damaging. Firstly, policy-makers might interpret the findings to mean the intervention was ineffective for learning since there was no measureable effect (and such were the criticisms put forward by pundits). Secondly, researchers were led about on a wild-goose chase, as they tried to improve upon the (poor) experiment believing in the presence of a Type II (false-negative) error—when it was the research design that was flawed.

To illustrate the problems and flawed arguments commonly found in this type of research, a media comparison study is presented in Table 1 to serve as a case study. The case was taken from a true research study conducted in 2009 in a rural high school in the United States. Details were withheld/ altered to protect the identity of the researcher and the institution.

Just As Effective?

History revealed that media comparison studies tended to be conducted when researchers tried to justify (or prove) the effectiveness of a new instructional technology to stakeholders, by comparing it against traditional classroom instruction (or, direct instruction). Some researchers have argued for the *no significant difference* findings to mean the two media under comparison were *just as effective*, in order to circumvent the problem of having no strong reason to recommend a change in the instructional media (Locke et al., 2001). They have, in effect, failed to recognize that these findings were indicative of a poorly designed and confounded study.

As history tends to repeat itself, another wave of media comparison studies is currently underway; no doubt being conducted by serious games researchers who were overly eager to prove the superiority of serious games over traditional teaching. As evidenced in the above case study, having made the first mistake of "media comparison," the researcher had gone on to comment about the discovery of a *significant* interaction effect among group and ethnicity even when such findings make little sense: Why would race affect game playing? Frequently, unexpected interaction effects were detected in media comparison studies due to the presence of the confounding factors. However, instead of recognizing the unexpected findings to point to potential flaw in the research design, many researchers went on to commit a second mistake by trying to explain away the unexpected effect as a valid finding and even to recommend "further studies" in that direction. Researchers conducting

Table 1. Example of a media comparison study

Rationale: Because of the infancy of research on digital game-based learning, little is known about how to effectively design effective situated learning environments. This study adopts a design-based research approach to investigate the effects of digital game based learning based on gender, ethnicity, and socio-economic status of students.

Research Method: A total of 250 students (10th grade) from a rural high school participated in this study. Students were randomly assigned to one of the twenty classes. Out of the twenty classes, ten (with 150 students) were randomly assigned to the **Treatment condition** (playing a digital online game: name withheld) and ten classes (with 100 students) were assigned to receive the **Control condition** (direct instruction).

There were 125 males and 125 females (comprised of 20 African American, 4 Asian American, 170 Caucasian, 1 Hispanic, and 55 Native American students). A total of 134 students received free or reduced lunch, 1 English language learner (ELL), and 15 special education students.

Procedures: A set of pretest and post-test with parallel test items were developed by the researchers and a mathematics teacher to determine the effects of digital game play with MMOG on mathematics achievement. The pretests and post-tests were administered to students from both the treatment and control groups, prior and after the 5-month long implementation period.

The first part of the instruments included a background survey to determine student involvement in digital game play, the types of games played, the amount of time spent playing games daily, and what a game must have to keep one engaged. The second part of the instruments included 20 multiple choice test items constructed from released 10th grade math and Algebra II state test items and from sample test items from the state department of education's website. The structure of the math test was similar to the state's high-stakes tests, the 10th grade criterion-referenced test (CRT) and the Algebra II end-of-instruction (EOI) test.

Findings: A 2 (treatment, control) X 2 (male, female) X 3 (Caucasian, Native American, Other) X 2 (F/R, non-F/R) ANCOVA was conducted to examine the interactions of treatment/control groups, gender, ethnicity, and socio-economic status of students. The dependent variable was posttest results and the covariant was pretest results.

While **no significant main effects** in mathematics achievement were found within group, gender, and socio-economic status. There was a significant interaction among group and ethnicity. $F(2, 191) = 3.14$, $p = 0.045$, $\eta^2 = 0.03$.

Interpretation: Results suggested that while students' gender or social class did not have hypothesized impact, students' ethnicity may impact their learning outcomes with educational games. Our findings suggest that it may be very difficult to reach certain ethnic groups, such as the Native American population in our study, with digital game-based learning. Therefore, we recommend that in designing and implementing digital game-based learning environments educators have to consider cultural issues. We also recommend further studies in this area to identify why, for some ethnic groups, digital game-based learning may not be a viable educational alternative in the classroom.

further studies based on such poor advice would eventually arrived at even more bizarre results with no hope of finding any evidence pointing to the good of the technological intervention. In order to advance the field, serious game researchers must abandon media comparison research immediately, and recognize digital games as a new kind of instructional media, which must be evaluated through new research methodologies (see Haertel & Means, 2003). In the words of Hastings and Tracey (2004, p. 28), "After 22 years, it is time to reframe the original debate to ask, not *if*, but *how* media affects learning. We agree that media comparison studies are inherently flawed and support the argument that we must identify research designs that will provide answers to this question in significantly less time."

Better Serious Games Research

The many problems associated with "media comparison" studies should not preclude researchers from using the empirical research experiment involving intervention/control conditions as a research design. Those who must use a control condition in their experiments only need to be careful so as to not fall into the same trap. For example, the following four designs *all* made use of empirical research methodology. Three of these methods (A-C) involved comparing a learning method (i.e., game-based learning) against a controlled condition. The last method (D) was a whole new way of looking at designing serious game research: by turning the entire game into one big assessment. (Unlike typical media comparison studies, the research measurement employed by Methods A-C did not directly compare technology against traditional instruction by teachers (i.e., control), and hence, they were considered to be *meaningful* comparisons.)

A. **Compatible comparisons**—by designing two similar games (A and B) with different instructional strategies (say, individual learning vs. social learning) and having all 250 students randomly assigned to play either game A, or game B. In this manner, the two games would be compatible with each other and the differences in achievement could be safely attributed to the difference in instructional strategies.

B. **Repeated-Measure Studies**—allow all 250 students to participate in the intervention, and repeatedly test them (say, monthly) throughout the intervention period in regular intervals. Because participants in a repeated-measure study became their own control, there is no need for an isolated control group. Moreover, this approach also eradicated the possible ethical/fairness concern as to why only some students were being exposed to a beneficial (or harmful) intervention.

C. **Improved Repeated-Measure Study**—by temporarily removing the intervention in the middle of the (5-month long) treatment period. The rationale for this removal was to verify if the achievement of the participants was truly attributed to the intervention. The expected outcome would be for the achievement to plateau or declined during the absence of intervention. If student achievement score rose despite the removal of the intervention, then the "learning" must come from another source.

D. **Designing the Game as Assessment**—one of the criticisms of the video game designers from the industry was that teachers made games boring by testing the students after they played the games. The students might also come to resent the game sessions as nothing more than disguised lessons. Hence,

a fourth (but much better) approach would be to design the entire game as an assessment, in which the students' actions and behaviors would be used as indicators of their understanding in the topics or subjects being studies. (Further explanations are given in point *No. 6: Interactive Learning Instruction Design* in the section below.)

ALL GAMES ARE "NOT" EQUAL

Besides the pitfalls of media comparison studies, critics should avoid applying one label on all game studies as if all games are created equal. Instead of examining the instructional contents and contexts found in various genres of games, and how the design and presentation of instruction and information might affect learning outcomes; many pundits chose to intermix findings of research using pen-and-paper games, board games, text-based computer games—such as Multi-User Dungeons (MUD) and MUD Object Oriented (MOO) from the 1990s, and edutainment from before 2005—essentially treating all games as equal. Using a counter argument similar to the approach by the proponents of media comparison studies, they concluded that serious games were *just as ineffective* as all other forms of games for instruction (cf., Clark, 2007; Kirschner, Sweller, & Clark, 2006). Readers should recognize that this was no different to the error committed by the other group of researchers who claimed that instructions using technology were *just as effective* as traditional teaching when findings showed no statistically significant differences between the two.

First, many of these earlier studies were media comparison studies that should have been invalidated, and not be included in any meta-analysis study. Secondly, critics who interpreted no significant differences finding to mean *just as ineffective* were equally guilty as their counterparts who claimed the instructional media to be just as effective. Thirdly, intermixing findings from research studies using board games, video games, and MMOGs, are like comparing apples, lettuce, and beef. The exercise is meaningless because it is simply another form of media comparison.

Unless researchers can look beyond the quagmire of media comparison studies, they will be dragged into this meaningless debate. It is far more useful to research appropriate methodologies for measuring the assessment of learning, and just as important to understand what kind of learning is possible with serious games. It is only to be expected that critics who do not grow up with video games (Prensky, 2007) will continue to distrust the technology and arrive at a conclusion contrary to that of the digital-natives (e.g., Barab, Thomas, Dodge, Carteaux, & Tuzun, 2005; Parker, Becker, & Sawyer, 2008). Last but not least, game developers who are trying to make a quick profit with serious games need to realize any attempt to pass off poorly designed video games—albeit with high entertainment values but lacking the means to instruct and assess learning—as serious games are likely to hurt the industry during this critical growth period. Instead, serious game publishers should seek to work with selected experts who were interested in creating exemplary serious games that will take the field to the next level.

Developing Serious Games as Interactive Learning Instructions

In the near future, instructional technologists might assume the role of designers of interactive learning instructions (Squire, 2003) and be tasked with designing/developing prototypes of learning games/mods using newly developed game design toolkits. Because such mods would be just as playable as COTS games (but much smaller in scope), they can be used as research platforms for data collection, for the testing of new instructional paradigms, or for soliciting '*buy-in*' (Castillo & Novak, 2008) from clients, stakeholders, game publishers, and funding agencies for the support

needed to fully produce the *interactive learning instruction*, or serious game.

Instead of delegating the design of serious games to game developers, instructional technologists need to learn from experts from other fields, such as the cognition and learning sciences, and the game design industry. They would also need new design processes and development models that could integrate interactive learning instructions and assessment of learning into one package. Collaboration with others might even produce new authoring tools for serious game making, as dedicated serious game authoring tools would be invaluable to instructional technologists to ease them over the initial steep learning curve. This idea is not new, as attested by Wikipedia's page on "video game making software." Instructional technologists with game modding/development experience should share their working models and the lessons learned readily with the community, to make up for the knowledge gap found in the literature at this moment.

Besides the abovementioned research and design issues that needed to be addressed, another problem faced by many instructional designers and technologists is the lack of a development model for serious games (as interactive learning instructions). Without a proper model to anchor the development work, designers must resort to trial and error and may end up with a well-designed game that is too expensive to build; or worse, run out of budget in mid-stream and end up with an unusable game. The following sections present a viable (and tested) development model based on a real serious game project (Loh & Byun, 2009). The below model was distilled from the original process and should prove useful as a launch pad for other developers of interactive learning instructions.

[*Note:* The following 10-step development model was presented as a viable guide for instructional technologists. As it would be highly unlikely for instructional technologists to be called to produce a full-fledge game-for-profit, the following guide may be used for the development of smaller serious game and game mods, such as prototypes for product demonstrations, classroom instructions, and research studies.]

10-Steps Instructional Development Model

A total of 10 distinct steps are described in the game modding/development process (Figure 3). Serious game development components that are not found in video game development are distinguished using

asterisk (*) marks. The game development cycle for the original project (i.e., *Saving Adryanee*) took less than four months for completion. Only the *Aurora Toolkit/Neverwinter Nights* bundle was used in the creation of the serious game mod. Subsequently, a screen capturing program named *Camtasia* was used (in conjunction with *Microsoft PowerPoint*) to create an endgame movie, which displayed a scrolling credit listing the names of the four-member development team and their affiliated higher institution.

Figure 3. A serious game development model

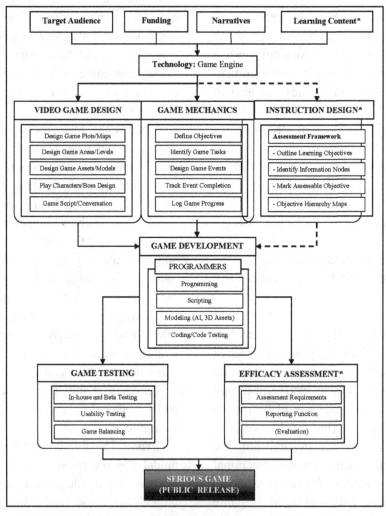

* *Essential Serious Game Components* (without which, this would be a Video Game Development process)

1. DETERMINING TARGET AUDIENCE AND LEARNING CONTENT *

The first step in any development project should rightly be a full analysis of the Learning Contents and the Target Audience. Instructional technologists understand this to be a very important step in the instructional design process because without a proper understanding of the audience's needs, the instructional media (learning contents) created may miss the mark completely. Special characteristics of the learner can also affect how the game or instruction is to be designed. For example, male players may prefer more *high-impact* actions, whereas female players tend to favor problem solving, emotional exchanges, and unexpected plot twists.

2. DETERMINING THE AMOUNT OF FUNDING AND TIME AVAILABLE

The amount of funding and time allocated can also affect the outcome of the game project. Serious game designers must consider these two factors carefully, particularly when the project involves tax-payers' money or federal funding. Besides reporting the usual research findings, it will be well for researchers to report the amount of money and time spent, in order for the community to gain a better sense of the cost vs. benefit ratio of the project. Instructional technologists need to be more pragmatic about serious game development because they tend to be measured in months and years, not weeks. Sufficient time must be allocated (along with enough buffers) to ensure the project will proceed as planned. For example, *Immune Attack*, a full-fledged game took 3 years to complete. Since game modding projects are much smaller in scope, they may be completed within a much shorter time frame.

3. WRITING GAME NARRATIVES

Finding a suitable story or writing an original game narrative can easily be the most difficult task in the game development process. When time is of the essence, it will be wise to settle on a storyline as quickly as possible. Since prototype games are not usually made to earn a profit, but are created for demonstration or for research, the narrative can easily take second place. A short and simple, but believable narrative is much more effective than an elaborated story. Some unique or memorable event should be planned within the first fifteen minutes to grab the player's attention and to draw them into the story. Game narratives have one other important purpose: they serve as acting scripts, listing all the props and characters needed to stage the game story. Should a designer be hit with a mental block, one can always hire professional game writers (Despain, 2008) to lend a helping hand.

4. SELECTING THE GDK/GAME BUNDLE

The GDK/game bundle should ideally be selected only after the decisions of the target audience, learning content, amount of funding/time, and game narratives have been finalized. This will help ensure an unbiased choice for the best development platform. However, because it can take much time and efforts to learn a GDK and to become familiar with its use, some professional development houses have chosen to place Step 4 above Steps 1–3. This flip-flop in the sequence of decision may, at times, result in a phenomenon known within the game industry as *sequelitis*—games produced by one production house becoming less and less original (i.e., as if they are mere sequels of one game). On the contrary, some game publishers argue that sequelitis can, in fact, be a benefit. As the development team becomes more familiar with a particular GDK through frequent use, the production time will speed up and the time saved can be channeled into other projects. Moreover, there are many examples of game sequels that are just as successful as the original title, because they have remained true to the winning formula, particularly, evergreen series such as *Castlevania*, *The Legend of Zelda*, and *Final Fantasy*.

Instructional technologists need to bear in mind that the choice of the GDK/game bundle will frequently impact the look and feel, as well as the plot of a game. Because GDKs have been custom-made to produce a particular genre of game, such as First Person Shooter (FPS) or Role Playing Game (RPG), it will be difficult to use an FPS-oriented GDK to create an RPG, and vice versa. This explains why the U.S. Marines chose *Doom* (an FPS game) when they wanted to create a training game (another FPS) for the soldiers.

If budget is not a concern, project managers may choose from any of the following to maintain full control of the development environment: (1) licensing a commercial game engine, (2) farming out the game development project, or (3) commissioning the creation of a new proprietary GDK. These will naturally be very expensive approaches: Option 1 can cost several hundred thousand dollars per license; Option 2, a couple million dollars; and Option 3, several million dollars.

In a game modification project, instructional technologists must learn to work within the monetary and time constraints, and be contented with the finite resources provided by the GDK/game bundle. Hence, game modules may only cost the company a few hundred dollars (minus salaries of developers). Depending on the approaches chosen and the amount of a priori planning and design efforts put in, it is possible to create a serious game without the need for a big budget.

5. VIDEO GAME DESIGN AND GAME MECHANICS

Once all preparations (Steps 1–4) have been completed, it is time to create an early prototype to test out the look (design) and the feel (mechanics) of the proposed game. This tends to be a very long drawn-out process for those working in the COTS game industry. The process will usually begin with the production of concept arts by a graphic designer/artist to create the design for the proposed game world. It may include level (map) design, bosses, all the props needed for the game, and both player and non-player characters (PCs/NPCs). Once the artist's impressions have been approved, a modeler or texturer will then create all the models as conceptualized by the graphic designer. A mock-up game (ranging from pen-and-paper to computerized stick figures version) will be created to test if the proposed game mechanics will work smoothly; answering questions such as: How will a city wall that takes three game cycles to complete affect the game play? What will happen if the completion of city wall takes just two game cycles, or four?

Because the game mechanics can ultimately affect the feel of the game, it is important to take time to balance all the game objects (i.e., weapons against vulnerability) to prevent tipping the scale unfairly. This turns out to be a very easy step for game modification; since most of the game resources and game mechanics are already provided for by the GDK, there is nothing much to do, except for minor tweaking of object properties, such as textures and colors.

6. INTERACTIVE LEARNING INSTRUCTION DESIGN*

[*Note:* This is a unique step for serious game development.] Because an assessment component is the defining factor for serious games (Chen &

Michael, 2005), instructional technologists must learn to identify "game-appropriate learning/ training objectives" from game narratives. They will need help from the subject matter experts as to the metrics to be used as evidence of learning in relation to the player's performance within the game. The planning must be done a priori for proper assessment of learning, and will need to be integrated at this point (before Step 7).

If this step is omitted, the resulting serious game may still be useful for instruction, but only as an instructional tool. However, its value as a research tool will be diminished, because it will be very difficult to differentiate what a player really *learned* from the game. Did players learn the intended learning contents, or simply how to beat the game? No doubt many researchers will be tempted to employ multivariate testing methods (such as pretest/post-test) to ascertain the effects of serious game on learner performance. Although a pretest/post-test method can certainly measure the effects of *game playing* as a whole, it will be impossible to determine if the changes in performance are affected by the *game playing*, or the *learning contents* within the game. A better research design would be repeated measure of the effects of the learning contents using a series of pretest/post-test over a period of time (1 to 2 months) to rule out any signal interference (such as learning from another external source).

Moreover, the above method will not be able to measure for the effects of *individual learning tasks* within a game. Since a serious game can contain any number of learning objectives, it will be important for researchers to breakdown the game-based learning by tasks and by objectives. Hence, an *integrated assessment framework* (such as the one described in the next section) will be necessary to magnify the granularity of the research method, and allow for the measurement of the effects of *individual learning objectives* within serious games.

AN INTEGRATED ASSESSMENT FRAMEWORK *

In order to facilitate data-driven assessment—what Mandinach and Honey (2008) referred to as "linking data to learning"—with serious games, some kind of data collection process must occur during a game play session in order to allow for a player's performance data to be collected. An integrated assessment framework will be invaluable to serious games used for research purposes. However, the literature has very little to say about an established assessment framework or software infrastructure that is targeted at data collection in serious games.

Loh and colleagues (Loh, 2006; Loh, Anantachai, Byun, & Lenox, 2007) have argued for the need of a software framework to facilitate automated data collection within virtual environments, and has subsequently presented a conceptual framework known as *Information Trails* (Loh, 2008). Conceptually, the Information Trails is a series of agent-detectable markings left by moving agents within an information ecology. Operationally, the assessment framework would facilitate virtual tracking of objects within information ecology, including that of serious games and multiuser virtual environments. Once a virtual object (such as player avatar) became traceable, the decision-making processes of its agent (the person behind the avatar)—reflected in the object's actions and behaviors—could then be used as evidence for assessment and analysis of the learners' performance.

The following steps are necessary for the creation of a serious game with Information Trails:

1. Starting with desire learning outcomes, create a game narrative that would incorporate as many learning objectives as possible.
2. Segregate game events from the narratives into player-dependent and player independent events—in this case, player-independent events would be plot-related events that

Figure 4. A sample objective hierarchy map depicting the Information Trails of game events within a role-playing serious game

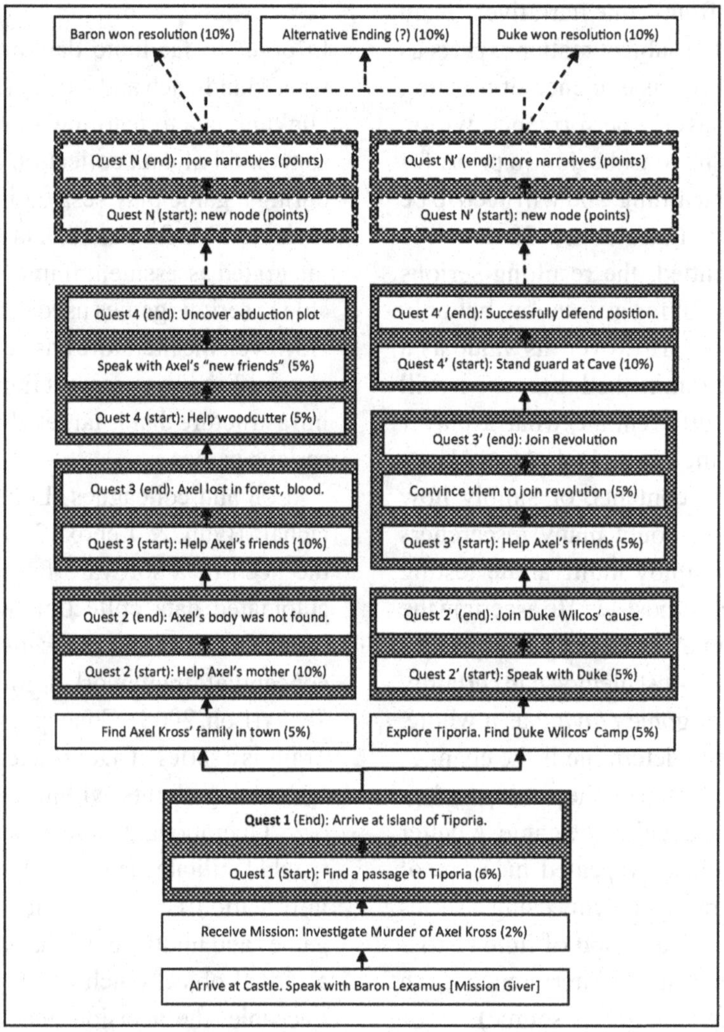

will occur regardless of what players choose to do in the game.

3. List and match desired learning objectives to player-dependent events.

4. Breakdown *all* game events by hierarchy (into main and sub-objectives), and create an *Objective Hierarchy Map* (OHM) (Berg et al., 1999) for the game. (An example of an OHM is shown in Figure 4.)

5. Identify *Information Nodes* within the game narrative where:

a. Player-independent events occurred (from Step 2), and

b. Player-dependent events occurred (i.e., identified the Mission-start and -end points)

6. *Hook* event-tracers into place (to record actions and behaviors of players) at *all* Information Nodes, and send the data collected to a data store.

7. Access the data store and re-assemble events traced into Information Tails.

8. Perform assessment of learning analysis of players based on their performance and behaviors in the game, using appropriate data mining techniques and/or visualization tools.

Additional programming help may be needed to help create an appropriate Application Programming Interface (API) to facilitate crosstalk between external data stores and function calls within the game environment.

7. THE GAME DEVELOPMENT CYCLE

Should this be a COTS game development project, the GDK will be assembled at this point. Programmers will be working on software functions such as Artificial Intelligence (AI), collision detection and network balancing to be included in the GDK, while game developers will have first-hand use of the GDK to materialize the game world. The development process used to put together both the GDK and the game world will need to happen in tandem, a process known as *co-evolution* among electronic engineers.

A Level Designer may assume the role of Team Manager and to ensure the game development cycle will move forward. All game assets will be placed in accordance with the preapproved game design document. Voice artists and musicians may be hired to record voiceover for NPCs and background music for the game, if necessary. Depending on how much time is still available, the game design cycle may be repeated up to a couple of times, or until both the design team and the game publisher can come to an agreement for sign-off. As the months roll by, the onus will be on the Level Designer to conduct game testing, draw the development cycle to a close, and adhere to the public release date.

Besides leading a serious game development team, instructional technologists must also be prepared to take on a serious game (prototype) all by themselves, especially during an economy downturn when additional personnel are hard to come by. Even though it may sound preposterous, many graduate students who need to create a game towards completing their Master or PhD degree have demonstrated that it is possible to create a game by oneself, when given enough motivation.

Putting all the pieces together in a game mod project is really quite enjoyable because it is the heart of the game modding process. Since the GDK already contains all (or most) of the necessary resources for making a game mod, instructional technologists need only to learn the toolkit and then piece together land mass, buildings, creature spawn points, background music, and conversations between PCs and NPCs, before they proceed to test-run the whole assembly.

8. BETA TESTING AND USABILITY TESTING

Like many other software development processes, game development also includes a testing phase (about 4–6 weeks) to ensure production quality. During this period, groups of independent players may be recruited to test-play the pre-released game with the intention to find and eliminate software bugs before public release. Some major game publishers may undertake additional usability testing to ascertain if any segment of the game needs further tweaking or balancing. It is also common to conduct focus group interviews to solicit direct feedback from test-players.

Since testing can further delay the timeline for game release, there will come a point in time when the public release date must be adhered to. It is then up to the Level Designer to determine if last minute adjustment must be done before giving the final approval for the game to make its public debut. (This final step is akin to the final director cut in film making.) In the case of game modification, beta and usability testing are usually less of an issue because the game publishers would have already conducted these tests prior to the release if the GDK/game bundle.

9. PUBLIC RELEASE

In the game industry, the end of the game development project is usually marked by the pressing of the master/gold CD of the finished game. Once the gold CD is released for mass production, the development team will generally be dismissed or reassigned to work on other game projects. If severe problems are discovered after the point of sale, the problems will usually be taken care of via patch releases.

Educators may be surprised to learn that few game publishers are interested in taking steps to improve a game after point of sales. In an instructional development environment, a created artifact (instructional resource) is usually subjected to several rounds of evaluation and improvement, and may be re-used year after year to maximize investment. There is hardly any incentive for game publishers to revise a published game to make it run better.

From a game publisher's point of view, the game has already been evaluated (through beta and usability testing). Moreover, game buyers understand that the game is sold *as is*. Publishers who care about their reputations and their customers may offer to patch a broken game after release, but not much more. In very rare cases, a couple of the original programmers may be kept on a part-time payroll to provide after-sale support for a game. To date, Bioware, Inc. is the only game development house that has chosen to support *Neverwinter Nights* for an unprecedented 6 years. It is premature to speculate whether the serious games industry will choose to provide sustained support for their games, or go the route of commercial game publishers.

10. EFFICACY ASSESSMENT *

Efficacy is a term used in the medical and pharmaceutical fields to measure if a particular medical intervention is able to produce a clinically measurable effect. *Efficacy assessment* is, therefore, an evaluation to judge if an intervention is "effective for the intended use" (Albrecht, 1997). Many educators believe that serious games have the potentials to turn the education process around by motivating students to learn as they play. However, the lack of efficacy assessment research in serious games has prompted critics to question its worth in the supposed education reform (Clark, 2007). Lacking clear empirical data, it will be impossible to calculate the cost-benefit ratio of serious games, meaning its effectiveness will always remain suspect.

The persistent use of media comparison studies by researchers to measure the effectiveness of serious games will only yield more no significant difference findings. Researchers and game developers must push for an *integrated assessment framework* that will allow for in situ data collection. Once individual learning objectives can be accurately measured, researchers must go on to improved the research methodologies to better analyze the data collected, and go on to model learner behavior and measure the efficacy of serious games.

CONCLUSION

During his keynote speech during the 2008 Annual Conference for the Association for Educational and Communication Technology (AECT), James Gee gave several examples to support his claim that *modding* is fast becoming the method of thinking and learning for the new generation of students. Furthermore, modding has also been proven useful for building teamwork (Antti, Tuula, & Marja, 2007) and collaboration (Hämäläinen, Manninen, Järvelä, & Häkkinen, 2006) among both young adults (e.g., Berger, 2006; Szafron et al., 2005) and school children (BBC, 2004; Wyeld, Leavy, Carroll, Gibbons, Ledwich, & Hills, 2007), in the learning of language and story-writing skills (Robertson & Good, 2005), and other social skills, such as logical thinking, communication, negotiation, public speaking (Loh & Byun, 2008), and even computer programming (Becker & Parker, 2005). Game making activities have also been successfully implemented to help at-risk children to read and write better (Peppler & Kafai, 2007), for after-school programs, student computer clubs, and by the public library to raise literacy (Gilbert, 2009). Although there are many reasons to use serious games, virtually nothing has been published about the actual cost involved in serious game development. This is an unfortunate oversight on the part of academia to focus their discussions on research findings only, when the cost of developing instructional materials (in this case, serious games) often become the sole determining factor for its adoption.

In summary, researchers need to apply appropriate learning theories when designing serious games, steer clear of media comparison studies, avoid intermixing older problematic game research findings with the new, and be on the constant look out for new methodologies that will yield conclusive empirical findings about the efficacy of serious games—possibly through new data mining and data visualization techniques. Sharing and learning from one another is not just a noble academic idea, but an essential 21st century skill to advance the increasingly global economy and society. To advance serious games as a viable instructional option in the arena of interactive learning, much work and collaboration need to occur. Game designers and developers (including game modders) need to share insights, experience, methodologies, metrics, practical lessons learned, and visionary perspectives to help craft the new paradigm for effective serious game-based learning. Researchers and educators need to achieve rigors and standards in both

research and development—by avoiding media comparison research and improving instructional developing models, before moving on to assess and evaluate the efficacy of learning that results from these new instructional media.

REFERENCES

Albrecht, R. (1997, May 28). *General considerations for clinical studies... from protocol to results*. Retrieved Aug 20, 2008, from http://www.fda.gov/cder/present/genconra/sld009.htm

Amarelo, M. (2008, May 22). *Fixing the education digital disconnect one video game at a time–FAS launches immune attack*. Retrieved May 28, 2008, from http://www.fas.org/press/news/2008/may_ialaunch.html

Antti, K., Tuula, N., & Marja, K. (2007, September 24-28). *Team structure in the development of game-based learning Environments*. Paper presented at DiGRA 2007, Tokyo, Japan. Retrieved May 20, 2008, from http://www.digra.org/dl/db/07344.35576.pdf

Barab, S., Thomas, M., Dodge, T., Carteaux, R., & Tuzun, H. (2005). Making learning fun: Quest Atlantis, a game without guns. *Educational Technology Research and Development, 53*(1), 86–107. doi:10.1007/BF02504859doi:10.1007/BF02504859

BBC. (2004, August 11). Video games "good for children". *BBC News*. Retrieved April 30, 2008, from http://news.bbc.co.uk/go/pr/fr/-/1/hi/scotland/3553352.stm

Becker, K., & Parker, J. R. (2005, Oct 13-15). *All I ever needed to know about programming, I learned from re-writing classic arcade games*. Paper presented at the Future Play: The International Conference on the Future of Game Design and Technology, East Lansing, MI.

Berg, J., Bradshaw, B., Carbone, J., Chojnacky, C., Conroy, S., Cleaves, D., et al. (1999). *Decision protocol 2.0*. Washington, DC: USDA Forest Service.

Berger, A. (2006, January 31). Neverwinter nights in the classroom. *University of Minnesota News*. Retrieved April 30, 2008, from http://www1.umn.edu/umnnews/Feature_Stories/22Neverwinter_Nights22_in_the_classroom.html

Botturi, L., & Loh, C. S. (2009). Once upon a game: Rediscovering the roots of games in education. In C. Miller (Ed.), *Games: Their purpose and potential in education* (pp. 1-22). New York: Springer Publishing Company.

Bounds, J. (2007, April 6). Game on! *Dallas Business Journal*. Retrieved February 2, 2009, from http://dallas.bizjournals.com/dallas/stories/2007/04/09/focus1.html

Castillo, T., & Novak, J. (2008). *Game level design*. Clifton Park, NY: Delmar Cengage Learning.

Chen, S., & Michael, D. (2005). Proof of learning: Assessment in serious games. *Gamasutra*. Retrieved from http://www.gamasutra.com/features/20051019/chen_01.shtml

Clark, R. E. (2007, May-June). Point of view: Learning from serious games? *Educational Technology*, *47*, 56–59.

Despain, W. (Ed.). (2008). *Professional techniques for video game writing*. Wellesley, MA: A. K. Peters, Ltd.

Federation of American Scientists. (2006). *Summit on Educational Games 2006: Harnessing the power of video games for learning*. Washington, DC: Author.

Ferdig, R. E. (Ed.). (2008). *Handbook of research on effective electronic gaming in education*. Hershey, PA: Information Science Reference.

Gee, J. P. (2003). *What video games have to teach us about learning and literacy* (2nd ed.). New York: Palgrave Macmillan.

Gilbert, B. (2009, March 5). *American library association goes gaming*. Retrieved March 9, 2009, from http://www.joystiq.com/2009/03/05/american-library-association-goes-gaming

Haertel, G. D., & Means, B. (Eds.). (2003). *Evaluating education technology: Effective research designs for improving learning*. New York: Teachers College Press.

Hämäläinen, R., Manninen, T., Järvelä, S., & Häkkinen, P. (2006). Learning to collaborate: Designing collaboration in a 3-D game environment. *The Internet and Higher Education*, *9*(1), 47–61. doi:10.1016/j.iheduc.2005.12.004doi:10.1016/j.iheduc.2005.12.004

Hastings, N. B., & Tracey, M. W. (2004). Does media affect learning: Where are we now? *TechTrends*, *49*(2), 28–30. doi:10.1007/BF02773968doi:10.1007/BF02773968

Hewitt, D. (2008, June 23). *Use of video game technology in the workplace increasing*. Retrieved Oct 20, 2008, from http://www.theesa.com/newsroom/release_detail.asp?releaseID=24

Hopson, J. (2006). We're not listening: An open letter to academic game researchers. *Gamasutra*. Retrieved from http://www.gamasutra.com/features/20061110/hopson_01.shtml

Kirschner, P. A., Sweller, J., & Clark, R. E. (2006). Why minimal guidance during instruction does not work: An analysis of the failure of constructivist, discovery, problem-based, experiential, and inquiry-based teaching. *Educational Psychologist*, *41*(2), 75–86. doi:10.1207/s15326985ep4102_1doi:10.1207/s15326985ep4102_1

Lenhart, A., Kahne, J., Middaugh, E., Macgill, A. R., Evans, C., & Vitak, J. (2008). *Teens, video games and civics: Teens' gaming experiences are diverse and include significant social interaction and civic engagement*. Washington, DC: Pew Internet & American Life Project.

Locke, B., Moore, M., & Burton, J. (2001). Old concerns with new distance education research. *EDUCAUSE Quarterly, 24*(2), 60–62.

Lockee, B. B., Burton, J. K., & Cross, L. H. (1999). No comparison: Distance education finds a new use for 'No significant difference.'. *Educational Technology Research and Development, 47*(3), 33–42. doi:10.1007/BF02299632doi:10.1007/BF02299632

Loh, C. S., & Byun, J. H. (2009). Modding neverwinter nights into serious games. In D. Gibson & Y. K. Baek (Eds.), *Digital simulations for improving education: Learning through artificial teaching environments* (pp. 408-426). Hershey, PA: Information Science Reference.

Loh, C. S. (2006). *Tracking an avatar: Designing data collection into online games*. Paper presented at the annual conference of the Association for Educational Communications and Technology (AECT 2006), Dallas, TX.

Loh, C. S. (2008). Designing online games assessment as "Information Trails." In V. Sugumaran (Ed.), *Intelligent information technologies: Concepts, methodologies, tools, and applications* (Vol. 1, pp. 553-574). Hershey, PA: Information Science Reference.

Loh, C. S., Anantachai, A., Byun, J., & Lenox, J. (2007, November 21-23). *Assessing what players learned in serious games: In situ data collection, information trails, and quantitative analysis*. Paper presented at the Computer Games: AI, Animation, Mobile, Educational & Serious Games (CGAMES 2007), Louisville, KY.

Mandinach, E. B., & Honey, M. (2008). *Data-driven school improvement: Linking data and learning*. New York: Teachers College Press.

Michael, D., & Chen, S. (2006). *Serious games: Games that educate, train, and inform*. Boston: Thomson Course technology PTR.

Miller, C. T. (Ed.). (2008). *Games: Purpose and potential in education* (1st ed.). New York: Springer Science+Business Media, LLC.

Parker, J. R., Becker, K., & Sawyer, B. (2008, January/February). Re-reconsidering research on learning from media: Comments on Richard E. Clark's point of view column on serious games. *Educational Technology, 48*, 39–43.

Peppler, K. A., & Kafai, Y. B. (2007, September 24-28). *What videogame making can teach us about literacy and learning: Alternative pathways into participatory culture*. Paper presented at DiGRA 2007, Tokyo, Japan. Retrieved May 20, 2008, from http://www.digra.org/dl/db/07311.33576.pdf

Prensky, M. (2005). *Engage me or enrage me: What today's learners demand*. Retrieved July 25, 2005, from http://www.marcprensky.com/writing/Prensky-Engage_Me_or_Enrage_Me.pdf

Prensky, M. (2007). *Digital game-based learning*. St. Paul, MN: Paragon House Publishers.

Robertson, J., & Good, J. (2005). Story creation in virtual game worlds. *Communications of the ACM, 48*(1), 61–65. doi:10.1145/1039539.1039571doi:10.1145/1039539.1039571

Sawyer, B. (2005). The state of serious games. *Gamasutra*. Retrieved from http://www.gamasutra.com/features/20051024/sawyer_01.shtml

Squire, K. (2003). Video games in education. *International Journal of Intelligent Games & Simulation, 2*(1).

Steinkuehler, C., & Johnson, B. Z. (2009). Computational literacy in online games: The social life of mods. *International Journal of Gaming and Computer-Mediated Simulations, 1*(1), 53–65.

Szafron, D., Carbonaro, M., Cutumisu, M., Gillis, S., McNaughton, M., Onuczko, C., et al. (2005). Writing interactive stories in the classroom. *Interactive Multimedia Electronic Journal of Computer-Enhanced Learning, 7*(1).

Thompson, A. D., Simonson, M. R., & Hargrave, C. P. (1992). *Educational technology: A review of the research*. Washington, DC: Association for Educational Communications and Technology.

van Eck, R. (2007). Building intelligent learning games. In D. Gibson, C. Aldrich, & M. Prensky (Eds.), *Games and simulation in online learning: Research and development frameworks*. Hershey, PA: Idea Group, Inc.

Wyeld, T. G., Leavy, B., Carroll, J., Gibbons, C., Ledwich, B., & Hills, J. (2007, September 24-28). *The ethics of indigenous storytelling: Using the torque game engine to support Australian Aboriginal cultural heritage*. Paper presented at DiGRA 2007, Tokyo, Japan. Retrieved April 30, 2007, from http://www.digra.org/dl/db/07312.11188.pdf

Section 4
Creating and Living in Virtual Worlds

Chapter 16
Visual Analyses of the Creation of Avatars

Erik W. Black
University of Florida, USA

Richard E. Ferdig
University of Florida, USA

Joseph C. DiPietro
University of Florida, USA

Feng Liu
University of Florida, USA

Baird Whalen
University of Florida, USA

ABSTRACT

Video games are becoming more popular; there has been a particular rise in interest and use of massively multiplayer online role-playing games (MMORPGs). These games utilize avatar creation; avatars can be seen as the technological instantiation of the real person in the virtual world. Little research has been conducted on avatar creation. Although it is has been anecdotally postulated that you can be anything you want online, there is a dearth of research on what happens when participants are told to create avatars, particularly avatars within given contexts. In this study, we used the Second Life avatar creation tool to examine what would happen when participants were told to create avatars as heroes, villains, their ideal self, and their actual self. Data analyses reveal that characters often refuse to change permanent aspects of their features, instead modifying only temporal aspects. This research has provided support for the quantitative review of avatar characteristics as predictors of vignette groupings.

INTRODUCTION

Video games have emerged as a mainstream form of entertainment in today's popular culture. One popular form of gaming is the MMORPG that allows hundreds of gamers to interact in real time. Millions of gamers now participate in these evolving virtual worlds simultaneously over the Internet. The number of active MMORPG player subscriptions worldwide doubled between July 2004 and June 2005 to a 500-million player base (Chen, Huang & Lei, 2006). Research by Griffiths, Davies, and Chappell (2003) indicate that the majority of MMORPG players are male (approximately 85%), over 60% of players were older than 19 years and players possessed a wide variety of education.

MMORPGs are generally thematically oriented, representing genres ranging from science fiction to knights-of-the-round-table fantasy. Players interact with the game and other players through an interface which usually consists of a viewing screen that allows for control of the player's character and several rows of buttons that allow players to perform game-related actions such as casting a spell or utilizing a special ability. Communication between players is facilitated by typing text in a chat box located within the interface (Ducheneaut, Yee, Nickell, & Moore, 2006).

In order for a player to interact within the gaming environment, a character must be created. This character represents the physical representation of the self in virtual environments. Known as avatars, they have become icons that represent much more than the physical in-game features of the character. The avatar has become an in-game alternative self (Castronova, 2003). The avatar represents an evolution of the alternative identity, an evolution that began with authors creating pen names under which to write works and proceeding to the creative user names adopted by Web forum members. "Broadly defined, '*avatar*' encompasses not only complex beings created for use in a shared virtual reality but any visual representation of a user in an online community" (Hemp, 2006, p. 50).

Through the experience of interacting in a virtual environment, the avatar's appearance can develop. Gamers can purchase or earn clothing or equipment that personalizes the avatar's appearance, tailoring the look and characteristics of their online persona. While *avatars'* anonymity is part of their appeal, many gamers take substantial efforts to tailor their avatars to aspects of their identity. "You can be whoever you want to be. You can completely redefine yourself if you want. You can be the opposite sex. You can be more talkative. You can be less talkative. Whatever" (Turkle, 1995, p. 184). The avatar and its role in the psychology of its owner runs parallel to the concept of the possible self: the cognitive manifestation of enduring goals, aspirations, motives, fears and threats (Markus & Nurius, 1986). As such the analysis of the avatar can provide a window into the individual, granting the opportunity to explore what is typically not revealed.

The act of *being* online means you can create whatever character you want, unfortunately, we know very little about what people decide to create when given the opportunity. More importantly, we know even less about what they decide to create when given a context or scenario for creation. Previous research by Kafai, Fields, and Cook (2007a, 2007b) studied avatar development by adolescents in an online community. Research by Bruckman (1993) illustrated the complexities of gender exploration and identity in text-based multi-user dungeons (MUDs). Kolko (1999) described the rhetorical process of avatar creation, Yee (2008) focused his analysis on the characteristics of World of Warcraft avatars, and research by Baylor, Rosenberg-Kima, and Plant (2006) has evaluated avatar task efficacy based upon aspects of their appearance. Because an online game generally provides the scenario or context through which a player constructs a character, studying avatar development within a given context or scenario is essential.

Avatar research is important because the manner in which people represent themselves has a lot to do with the building of a community of practice (Wenger, 1998), regardless of whether that community of practice is a business, a school, or an informal learning environment. A better understanding of character avatars thus helps us explore the underlying psychology that the avatar represents to the user. The research discussed in this article focuses on the construction of the avatar by undergraduate students. Students were given specific vignettes to read, these vignettes were reflective of gaming scenarios, prior to the construction of their avatars. Four specific questions guided the visual analysis of the finished avatars:

1. How do undergraduate students at a large southeastern university design *hero* avatars created through the *Second Life* character creation engine?

2. How do undergraduate students at a large southeastern university design *villain* avatars created through the *Second Life* character creation engine?

3. How do undergraduate students at a large southeastern university design *ideal self* avatars created through the *Second Life* character creation engine?

4. How do undergraduate students at a large southeastern university design *actual self* avatars created through the *Second Life* character creation engine?

METHOD

Subjects

Subjects consisted of 102 undergraduate students of which 13 were male and 89 female. All participants were enrolled in face-to-face, educational technology classes as part of a teacher education program at a research institution in the Southeastern United States. The disparate male to female ratio was anticipated and is indicative of the gender make-up seen in undergraduate teacher education classes. The vast majority of participants were white (96), six participants were African American. Although no direct analysis of previous gaming experience was conducted, the majority of subjects indicated that they had no previous experience with *Second Life* (Linden Research, Inc., 2003) and did not consider themselves recreational computer gamers.

Tools

Second Life (Linden Research, Inc., 2003) advertises over 5 million residents, defined as "a uniquely named avatar with the right to log into *Second Life*, trade Linden Dollars and visit the Community pages." On average, approximately 25,000 unique residents log in daily. In addition, *Second Life* has a thriving economy, trading its own currency called the Linden. Within *Second Life,* users can create 3D artifacts, buildings, and social spaces for trade, interaction, and personal use. The ability to create items is only limited by the user's imagination and programming skill. In this research project, we used second life because of the ease in creating and evaluating avatars.

Second Life (Linden Research, Inc, 2003) is not an MMORPG in the purest sense. *Second Life* was utilized by the research team because it is free to download and play and it has a fairly complex character creation engine enabling a large amount of variability in avatar features.[1]

Vignettes

Four separate narrative vignettes were constructed to provide a background for avatar construction. These vignettes were based upon consistent player character themes found in video games and mythology (Campbell, 1949) and served as a guide for the construction of the avatar. Three vignettes situated the participant in one of the following thematic roles: the hero, the villain, or the ideal self. The forth vignette, the actual self, served as a control. Within the vignettes, mentions of parents, siblings, culture, or specific location were avoided in an effort to elicit a response without the subjects' preconceived notions of common thematic characteristics. The questions asked of the reader within each vignette were vague and open ended as to avoid influencing the traits of the character. The terms you and your hero/villain/ideal were intentionally chosen to reinforce the subject's personification of the character. All gender and age references were removed in an attempt to refrain from biasing the participants. See Table 1 for a summary of vignette narratives.

Data Collection

Upon entering the gaming lab, a digital photograph of each participant was taken. The participant was then randomly assigned to one of the four vignettes and provided this vignette to read. Participants received a brief set of instructions regarding the creation and customization of an avatar using the *Second Life* (Linden Research, Inc, 2003) character creation engine and were informed that there was no time limit to complete the task at hand. Participants were instructed that researchers could assist with technical concerns throughout the experience but could not offer direction or advice on aesthetic issues regarding the avatars. Once the participant indicated that

Table 1. Vignette narratives

Hero	You have lived your life with wonderful people. The members of your community have always been supportive and helpful. Yet, life is not the same as usual. With each passing day you get a sense of an impending change in your comfortable life. Nobody has said a thing, but they seem to intuitively know. The safety and confines of this familiar existence are coming to an end. The nature of your challenge is unknown. Even the most direct questioning produces no answers from anyone. You can tell they know something, but they insist on remaining silent. Who do you turn to? How will you know what to do? Why will they not help!? These questions rage in your mind. One day an answer begins to form in your troubled soul. Over the days you begin to understand the dilemma. The others cannot help you. You are the hero this day; the unknown challenge must be met and it will be your burden. It is time to venture forth on the journey. You will save the day. It is your destiny. How can you be this hero? Your task is to make your hero from the character creator provided.
Villain	You are the community outcast. The feeling has become part of your very being. A familiar separation, never understood, always outside looking in, your existence is marked by these thoughts. The furtive glances caught out of the corner of your eye. Their constant unjust suspicion hangs in the air. These people you will never know you. Your life is an unceasing struggle for fairness. The confrontation is on the horizon. They have no idea what you're capable of. You will show them. The time is now! You are this anti-hero. Your task is to make your anti-hero from the character creator provided.
Ideal	Mirror, mirror on the wall, I am the luckiest of all. Life is joyful, with safety and contentment your steadfast companions. Each day you arise and face the dawning new day. What joys will life bring this day? You are the ideal. Your task is to create your ideal self from the character creator provided.
Actual	You will be participating in an online course next semester. Use the character generator to build a visual representation of yourself that you will use to interact with other students in this course.

they were finished with the construction of their avatar, the participant notified a researcher and a picture of the avatar was recorded for analysis. Figures 1 and 2 provide examples of live people and the avatars they created.

Following the experiment, avatars and digital photographs were analyzed using 12 different categories. Those categories included: accessories, body type, clothing, eye color, gender-specific characteristics, general appearance, hair color, hair length, hairstyle, height, musculature, and skin tone. A complete description of each of the characteristics is provided in Table 2. The rubric used to score the characteristics is presented in Appendix A. Avatars and digital photographs were not matched initially in the analyses in order to

Figure 1. Live female participant and her created avatar (villain vignette)

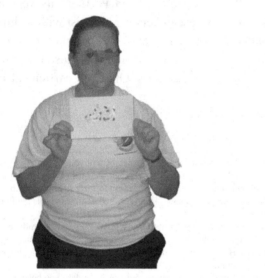 

Figure 2. Live female participant and her created avatar—this time a male avatar (villain vignette)

prevent biased judgments; each photo or avatar screenshot was analyzed separately.

These categories were selected by the research team as they were deemed to offer the opportunity for variability in both the participants and the avatars the participants would be developing

(Helmers, 2006). They represent only a small possibility of the entire range of subjective characteristics on which an analysis could have been conducted. However, these characteristics are akin to those factors a person may use to evaluate meeting someone for the very first time (Eagly, Ashmore, Maskhijani, & Longo, 1991).

Table 2. Categories of analysis

Accessories	Consisted of visible jewelry, piercings, tattoos, hats, hand bags, backpacks, and sweaters. The research team sought to capture an overall first impression of the subject. At some point or another, almost all individuals have observed passersby in public and immediately tried to categorize their level of accessories. Does the person have a nose ring? Are they wearing a necklace? Is there a dog in their purse? Is there any aspect of their level of accessories that tips societal norms as excessive? Considering accessorizing is such an important aspect of MMORPG's and *Second Life* in particular, establishing a baseline for comparison was initially deemed critical for analysis.
Body Type	Participants and avatars were evaluated on an ectomorph-mesomorph-endomorphic scale. In an attempt to use common knowledge terminology for this portion of the study, the research team opted to use ubiquitous categories for analysis of various body types. Naturally, some participants did not easily fit into one particular category. To compensate for this phenomenon, the research team placed ectomorphic (slim or petite body type) on one end of a 7-point Likert, mesomorphic (normal body type) in the middle, and endomorphic (large or overweight body type) at the other extreme. This allowed the research team to place each participant, as well as their avatars, into a definitive category for the study.
Clothing	Style of clothing was evaluated, specifically regarding the nature of dress, whether casual or formal. For example, a tuxedo or uniform could be observed as formal. Sweatpants or a ripped and wrinkled T-shirt would be deemed casual.
Eye Color	Eye Color: Participant and avatar eye color were observed.
Gender-Specific Characteristics	An evaluation of the emphasis placed on male or female sex specific characteristics (eg: breast size, make-up), ranked from under- to over-accentuated. The research team sought to investigate the role of displayed sexual traits in both the digital snapshots and avatar screenshots.
General Appearance	This category rated the overall appearance of the subjects, from slovenly to well-refined. A well-pressed and wrinkle free outfit would be considered well-refined. A categorization of slovenly could include the opposite: dirty, wrinkled, or an overall unkempt look.
Hair Color	Avatar and participant hair color were observed.
Hair Length	Hair Length was observed as short, medium, or long.
Hair Style	A measure of the intricacy of the avatar and participants hair style. Ornate hair could include multiple layers, the use of hair products, and basically was surmised by the time it would take to produce the look of the subject. The more time deemed, the more ornate the hair style was rated.
Height	A measure of the height of the avatar and participant.
Musculature	A measure of the visible musculature of the individual and avatar, ranked from frail to strong. The prototypical cartoon weakling comes to mind for the frail end of the likert scale, and a muscle-bound gargantuan for the strong side of the scale. Male and female characters were analyzed equally in the sense of comparing muscle mass versus body mass and apparent body structure.
Skin Tone	An evaluation of the participant and avatar's skin tone, from light to dark, was included in this study. *Second Life* does allow users to create a multitude of interesting, unnatural skin tones including, but not limited to, blue, green, and purple. In order to rate these tones for sake of this study, the research team used a simple color wheel to determine the variance of light or dark.

Analysis procedures were conducted by the research team, all of whom are male and white, except for one researcher from China. Analysis was conducted in a collaborative manner with all researchers present at all times. Through this method, consensus regarding scoring across the 12 categories could be achieved through discussion. The methodological underpinnings of the analysis were consistent with the work of Pink (2001a, 2001b, 2004), Grimshaw (2001), Emmison and Smith (2000), and Prosser and Schwartz (1998).

Upon completion of the analysis, scoring for each participant was recorded and analyzed using SPSS Statistical Analysis Software (Version 13) and SAS Business Intelligence and Analytics Software (Version 8). Descriptive statistics were generated with regards to each category of analysis. Dependant samples t-tests were also conducted for all factors, comparing avatars to their human creators across the 12 specific categories. In addition, a stepwise regression was conducted utilizing vignette type as a dependant variable and the categories as independent variables.

Results

Table 3 documents means and standard deviations for participants across 11 different categories divided by vignette. For example, Hero Live Accessories described the mean score of accessories observed from the live people that participated in the study and were part of the hero vignette. Hero Created Accessories described the mean score of accessories observed in the avatars created by those same individuals. It is important to note that of the 12 initial characteristics, height was removed during the evaluation process. Due to methodological short-sightedness, the research team failed to place a reference object in the background of the digital snapshots. Considering the centered and thigh-up focus of the picture, it was nigh impossible to accurately determine participant height. This category was complicated further when investigating avatars as fore- and

background items were the only true was to judge any sort of scale whatsoever.

Dependent t-tests were run to measure differences of individuals between their actual self and their created avatar. The t-tests were grouped by vignette narrative to examine creation anomalies when given specific contexts. For the hero vignette, significant differences were found for clothing (p<.01), eye color (p<.01), general appearance (p<.01), hairstyle (p<.01), and gender-specific characteristics (p<.01). This means that when given the opportunity to create a hero, participants created avatars that had the same accessories, body type, hair color, hair length, musculature, and skin tone as themselves. They made significant changes to their clothing (more formal), eye color (lighter), gender-specific characteristics (more pronounced), general appearance (more refined), and hairstyle (more ornate) (see Table 4).

For the villain vignette, significant differences were found for clothing (p<.01), general appearance (p<.05), and hairstyle (p<.01). This means that when given the opportunity to create a villain, participants created avatars that had the same accessories, body type, eye color, gender-specific characteristics, hair color, hair length, musculature, and skin tone as themselves. They made significant changes to their clothing (more formal), general appearance (more refined), and hairstyle (more ornate) (see Table 5).

A large number of significant differences were found when participants were asked to create their ideal self. Significant differences were found for accessories (p<.01), clothing (p<.01), eye color (p<.05), gender-specific characteristics (p<.01), general appearance (p<.01), hair length (p<.05), and hairstyle (p<.01). This means that when given the opportunity to create their ideal self, only their body type, hair color, musculature, and skin tone were kept the same. They made significant changes to their accessories (less adorned), clothing (more formal), eye color (lighter), gender-specific characteristics (more pronounced), general appearance

Table 3. Mean scores, N, and standard deviations of characteristics across groups

	Vignettes	Hero		Villain		Ideal		Actual		Total	
		Live	Created	Live	Created	Live	Created	Live	Created	Live	Created
Accessories	Mean	3.0000	2.5926	3.4483	3.1034	3.5161	1.4839	4.1739	1.8696	3.5091	2.2636
	N	27	27	29	29	31	31	23	23	110	110
	Std. Dev.	1.3587	2.3739	1.6385	2.4545	1.6098	1.2348	1.9224	1.7137	1.6576	2.0795
Body Type	Mean	3.9630	3.7778	4.0345	4.1379	4.2258	3.8000	4.2609	3.8696	4.1182	3.8991
	N	27	27	29	29	31	30	23	23	110	109
	Std. Dev.	1.1596	1.5771	1.2096	1.9035	1.5429	1.5403	1.0098	1.4239	1.2542	1.6156
Clothing	Mean	3.0741	4.6667	3.2069	4.3448	2.7097	4.1290	3.0000	3.8696	2.9909	4.2636
	N	27	27	29	29	31	31	23	23	110	110
	Std. Dev.	1.2987	1.2089	1.5208	1.4212	1.6772	1.0565	1.4460	.91970	1.4931	1.1938
Eye Color	Mean	4.1111	3.3704	3.8276	3.5172	3.8387	3.2903	3.7826	3.0000	3.8909	3.3091
	N	27	27	29	29	31	31	23	23	110	110
	Std. Dev.	1.5771	1.4974	1.3905	1.8826	1.5937	1.7549	1.5063	1.3484	1.5044	1.6409
Gender Specific	Mean	3.6296	5.4444	4.2069	4.5517	3.1935	5.2581	3.4783	4.8696	3.6273	5.0364
	N	27	27	29	29	31	31	23	23	110	110
	Std. Dev.	1.2137	.93370	1.1142	1.8242	1.3018	.92979	1.4731	1.0576	1.3123	1.2845
General Appearance	Mean	3.3333	4.8519	3.5862	4.4483	3.1290	4.2903	3.5217	4.2174	3.3818	4.4545
	N	27	27	29	29	31	31	23	23	110	110
	Std. Dev.	1.0000	.86397	1.2961	1.2702	1.2843	.73908	.99405	.42174	1.1651	.91508
Hair Color	Mean	4.8148	4.1481	4.6652	4.7586	4.9032	4.3871	4.7391	3.7391	4.7818	4.2909
	N	27	27	29	29	31	31	23	23	110	110
	Std. Dev.	1.2721	1.7030	1.1426	1.9394	1.4687	1.5637	1.4212	1.4528	1.3159	1.6991
Hair Length	Mean	4.3704	4.5185	4.2759	4.5862	4.0000	4.4839	4.0870	4.6957	4.1818	4.5636
	N	27	27	29	29	31	31	23	23	110	110
	Std. Dev.	1.1485	1.3118	1.0656	1.2106	1.0000	1.4112	.84816	.87567	1.0243	1.2231
Hair Style	Mean	3.3704	5.1481	3.1379	5.3103	3.1935	4.7097	3.0870	4.8696	3.2000	5.0091
	N	27	27	29	29	31	31	23	23	110	110
	Std. Dev.	1.4451	1.0991	1.4072	1.0725	1.5367	1.2164	1.4744	.75705	1.4514	1.0794
Musculature	Mean	4.1111	4.4074	3.9310	3.8276	3.9677	4.1935	4.1304	3.9130	4.0273	4.0909
	N	27	27	29	29	31	31	23	23	110	110
	Std. Dev.	.75107	1.7815	.96106	1.7942	.87498	1.5582	.69442	1.2399	.82905	1.6173
Skin Tone	Mean	3.5556	3.4815	3.6207	3.3103	3.8065	3.7097	3.7826	3.6957	3.6909	3.5455
	N	27	27	29	29	31	31	23	23	110	110
	Std. Dev.	1.0500	1.4510	.90292	1.6925	.83344	1.1603	1.2777	1.3629	1.0023	1.4183

(more refined), hair length (longer), and hairstyle (more ornate) (see Table 6).

The actual self was the fourth category and it was treated as somewhat of a control group. We wanted to find out what avatars people would create when given the opportunity to represent their actual self. In other words, how honest would they be? A large number of significant differences were found when participants were asked to create their ideal self. Significant differences were found for accessories (p<.01), clothing (p<.01), eye color (p<.05), gender-specific characteristics

Table 4. Dependent t-test for hero vignette

| HERO | Paired Differences | | | | | t | df | Sig. (2-tailed) |
| | Mean | Std. Deviation | Std. Error Mean | 95% Confidence Interval | | | | |
				Lower	Upper			
Accessories	0.40741	2.89906	0.55792	-0.73942	1.55424	0.730	26	0.472
Body Type	0.18519	1.96189	0.37757	-0.59091	0.96128	0.490	26	0.628
Clothing	-1.59259	2.00498	0.38586	-2.38574	-0.79945	-4.127	26	0.000*
Eye Color	0.74074	1.09519	0.21077	0.30750	1.17398	3.514	26	0.002*
Gender Specific Characteristics	-1.81481	1.41522	0.27236	-2.37466	-1.25497	-6.663	26	0.000*
General Appearance	-1.51852	1.55342	0.29896	-2.13303	-0.90401	-5.079	26	0.000*
Hair Color	0.66667	1.88108	0.36201	-0.07746	1.41080	1.842	26	0.077
Hair Length	-0.14815	1.53682	0.29576	-0.75609	0.45980	-0.501	26	0.621
Hair Style	-1.77778	1.55250	0.29878	-2.39193	-1.16363	-5.950	26	0.000*
Musculature	-0.29630	1.75005	0.33680	-0.98859	0.39600	-0.880	26	0.387
Skin Tone	0.07407	1.35663	0.26108	-0.46259	0.61074	0.284	26	0.779
p<.05								

Table 5. Dependent t-test for villain vignette

| Villain | Paired Differences | | | | | t | df | Sig. (2-tailed) |
| | Mean | Std. Deviation | Std. Error Mean | 95% Confidence Interval | | | | |
				Lower	Upper			
Accessories	0.34483	3.21021	0.59612	-0.87627	1.56592	0.578	28	0.568
Body Type	-0.10345	2.17691	0.40424	-0.93150	0.72460	-0.256	28	0.800
Clothing	-1.13793	1.84631	0.34285	-1.84023	-0.43563	-3.319	28	0.003*
Eye Color	0.31034	2.07198	0.38476	-0.47779	1.09848	0.807	28	0.427
Gender Specific Characteristics	-0.34483	2.56732	0.47674	-1.32138	0.63173	-0.723	28	0.475
General Appearance	-0.86207	1.76724	0.32817	-1.53429	-0.18985	-2.627	28	0.014*
Hair Color	-0.10345	2.00615	0.37253	-0.86655	0.65965	-0.278	28	0.783
Hair Length	-0.31034	1.25651	0.23333	-0.78830	0.16761	-1.330	28	0.194
Hair Style	-2.17241	1.53690	0.28540	-2.75702	-1.58781	-7.612	28	0.000*
Musculature	0.10345	1.77974	0.33049	-0.57353	0.78043	0.313	28	0.757
Skin Tone	0.31034	1.79490	0.33331	-0.37240	0.99309	0.931	28	0.360
p<.05								

(p<.01), general appearance (p<.01), hair color (p<.01), hair length (p<.05), and hairstyle (p<.01). This means that when given the opportunity to create their ideal self, only their body type, musculature, and skin tone were kept the same. They made significant changes to their accessories (less adorned), clothing (more formal), eye color (lighter), gender-specific characteristics

Table 6. Dependent t-test for ideal vignette

Ideal	Paired Differences					t	df	Sig. (2-tailed)
	Mean	Std. Deviation	Std. Error Mean	95% Confidence Interval				
				Lower	Upper			
Accessories	2.03226	2.31637	0.41603	1.18260	2.88191	4.885	30	0.000*
Body Type	0.43333	1.65432	0.30204	-0.18440	1.05107	1.435	29	0.162
Clothing	-1.41935	2.07805	0.37323	-2.18159	-0.65712	-3.803	30	0.001*
Eye Color	0.54839	1.45691	0.26167	0.01399	1.08279	2.096	30	0.045*
Gender Specific Characteristics	-2.06452	1.71144	0.30738	-2.69228	-1.43675	-6.716	30	0.000*
General Appearance	-1.16129	1.52964	0.27473	-1.72237	-0.60022	-4.227	30	0.000*
Hair Color	0.51613	1.65068	0.29647	-0.08934	1.12160	1.741	30	0.092
Hair Length	-0.48387	1.06053	0.19048	-0.87288	-0.09486	-2.540	30	0.016*
Hair Style	-1.51613	2.01446	0.36181	-2.25504	-0.77722	-4.190	30	0.000*
Musculature	-0.22581	1.49910	0.26925	-0.77568	0.32407	-0.839	30	0.408
Skin Tone	0.09677	1.22079	0.21926	-0.35101	0.54456	0.441	30	0.662

p<.05

Table 7. Dependent t-test for actual vignette

Actual	Paired Differences					t	df	Sig. (2-tailed)
	Mean	Std. Deviation	Std. Error Mean	95% Confidence Interval				
				Lower	Upper			
Accessories	2.30435	2.32447	0.48469	1.29917	3.30952	4.754	22	0.000*
Body Type	0.39130	1.49967	0.31270	-0.25720	1.03981	1.251	22	0.224
Clothing	-0.86957	1.48643	0.30994	-1.51235	-0.22678	-2.806	22	0.010*
Eye Color	0.78261	1.59421	0.33242	0.09322	1.47200	2.354	22	0.028*
Gender Specific Characteristics	-1.39130	1.37309	0.28631	-1.98507	-0.79754	-4.859	22	0.000*
General Appearance	-0.69565	1.01957	0.21260	-1.13655	-0.25476	-3.272	22	0.003*
Hair Color	1.00000	1.41421	0.29488	0.38845	1.61155	3.391	22	0.003*
Hair Length	-0.60870	1.26990	0.26479	-1.15784	-0.05955	-2.299	22	0.031*
Hair Style	-1.78261	1.34693	0.28086	-2.36507	-1.20015	-6.347	22	0.000*
Musculature	0.21739	1.31275	0.27373	-0.35029	0.78507	0.794	22	0.436
Skin Tone	0.08696	1.31125	0.27341	-0.48007	0.65398	0.318	22	0.753

p<.05

(more pronounced), general appearance (more refined), hair color (lighter), hair length (longer), and hairstyle (more ornate) (see Table 6).

A multinomial logistic regression procedure was also performed, utilizing vignettes as dependant variables (holding the actual vignette constant) and utilizing 11 of the 12 characteristics as independent variables. Mulitnomial logistic regression is a statistical regression procedure for use with categorical dependant variables. The limited number of characteristics utilized during the regression procedure was due to the methodologically unreliable procedures used to try to account for height, resulting in its exclusion.

The multinomial logistic regression procedure revealed a significant result in a test of the omnibus hypothesis ($X^2 = 49.2802$, p >.034), indicating that characteristics utilized as independent variables have corresponding regression coefficients that are not equal to 0. This indicates that one or more characteristics will provide an element of predictability to vignette classification through the review of avatar characteristics. Data derived from the multinomial logistic regression is presented in a log-odds (or logit) format, log-odds are a representation of proportion or probability. Table 8 illustrates the relationship between a 1 point increase in a parameter value relative to the average actual self avatar (this avatar vignette served as a control) and the corresponding change in logit. For example, an increase of 1 point on the clothing scale decreasing the probably that an individual would be categorized as a hero by 37%.

The multinomial regression provides evidence that it is possible to predict the vignette from which an avatar was derived based on an analysis of avatar characteristics. For example, the data indicates that a one unit increase in the clothing parameter, relative to the mean of the actual self avatar clothing parameter, will result in the increased likelihood that the avatar is a member of the ideal vignette. Conversely, a one unit increase in the hairstyle parameter, relative to the mean of the actual self avatar hairstyle parameter, will result in an increased likelihood that the avatar is a member of the villain vignette.

Table 8. Multinomial regression results

Parameter	Vignette		
	Hero	Villain	Ideal
Accessories	.04	.43	-.18
Body Type	.15	.59	.05
Clothing	-.37	-.08	.25
Eye Color	-.26	-.22	-.1
Gender Specific Characteristics	-.54	-.73	-.02
General Appearance	-.64	-.74	-.86
Hair Color	-.21	.38	.09
Hair Length	.17	.14	.01
Hair Style	-.001	.37	-.22
Musculature	-.22	-.38	-.23
Skin Tone	.29	.01	.21

DISCUSSION

Analysis reveals that the individuals who participated in this study and were given the hero or villain vignettes created avatars that were visually similar to themselves. Participants were not interviewed, but it could be that psychologically each of us can see ourselves as a hero or villain. Though analysis of data indicates that being put into a hero or villain vignette does not change who subjects think they are or how they represented themselves.

Compare that to the outcomes of the ideal self, which had almost all of the variables significantly different. Most people create a different self given the opportunity to create an ideal version. This was also true for the actual self narrative vignette. Given the opportunity to represent oneself actually had more people seemingly representing an ideal version of themselves. Again, this is not necessarily surprising; people want to represent their best features or the features they wish they had (e.g., longer hair, different color of eyes, etc.). This is only surprising in the context of people leaving their hero or villain characters relatively unchanged from their current self.

More importantly, perhaps, is that when analyzing the characteristics that held significant difference between subjects and the avatars they created, the majority of the characteristics changed were temporal. Temporal characteristics are those that can be easily changed in real life: clothing, hairstyle, and with the advent of color contact lenses, eye color. On the other hand, enduring characteristics are those that are not easily malleable: body type, skin tone, musculature, and gender-specific characteristics. This result was unexpected, as conventional wisdom supported with research by Turkle (1995) and Yee (2006), indicates that given the opportunity to become an anonymous denizen of an online world, one would adopt a liberated persona and the physical characteristics to match that persona. Tables 9 and 10 reveal the significant differences between live and created for the different vignettes. Table 9 highlights the temporal characteristics and Table 10 showcases enduring traits. Only gender-specific characteristics were significantly different. That could be due to the fact that modern surgery now allows enhancements of chest, lips, and other body features.

The results of regression provide the opportunity to begin to categorize the characteristics utilized in the analysis. The logit or log-odds adjustment associated with a one unit change in the musculature and general appearance parameters (relative to the mean of the musculature and general appearance parameters in the actual self avatar) is evidence that these two characteristics are powerful indicators useful in future ethnographic analysis. This indicated that the rubric used in this survey has merit and specific characteristics should be analyzed to determine predictive validity.

Two interesting questions emerged in this study related to gender and race; Do female participants create male avatars (and vice versa)? Do participants create avatars of a different race? It is impossible with this data to statistically answer these questions as 87% of the participants were

Table 9. Temporal characteristics

Characteristic	Hero	Villain	Ideal	Actual
Accessories			.000*	.000*
Clothing	.000*	.003*	.001*	.010*
Eye Color	.002*			.028*
General Appearance	.000*	.014*	.000*	.003*
Hair Color				.003*
Hair Length			.016*	.031*
Hair Style	.000*	.000*	.000*	.000*
*indicates significant difference (p <.05) between user and avatar				

Table 10. Enduring characteristics

Characteristic	Hero	Villain	Ideal	Actual
Body Type				
Gender Specific Characteristics	.000*		.000*	.000*
Musculature				
Skin Tone				
*indicates significant difference (p <.05) between user and avatar				

Table 11. Breakdown of gender and related avatars

		Actual	Created Female	Created Male
Hero	Females	24	21	3
	Males	3	1	2
Villian	Females	24	16	8
	Males	5	0	5
Ideal	Females	27	25	2
	Males	4	0	4
Actual	Females	22	21	1
	Males	1	0	1

female and 96% of all participants were white. This is an important question for future research. Although we cannot answer this question with any degree of certainty, it is interesting that the only category where females created male avatars (with some degree of certainty) was the villain vignette (see Table 11). It is also interesting that some participants put their ideal or actual avatar as a different gender.

There were some obvious limitations to this study. First, there were some character creation issues. Individuals did not have complete privacy during the construction of their avatar. The *Second Life* (Linden Research, Inc, 2003) character creation engine is highly complex; true mastery of the engine is not easily achieved in the time frame available to participants. In addition, a serious industry has emerged within *Second Life* providing highly detailed wares and goods that can be purchased in order to customize one's avatar. This industry thrives on the opportunity to take nondescript characters built by others and advance their look and feel. According to Yee (2004), discerning specifics about an individual's psyche by analyzing a single avatar might be challenging, but if given multiple avatars created over time, more could be revealed.

A second limitation is that photographs were taken of participants prior to the construction of their avatar; this process may have created a heightened sense of self-awareness within the subjects. Third, given that the analysis was conducted by a group consisting entirely of males, gender bias must be considered. This is in direct comparison to the fact that most of the participants were female. Future groupings could change the outcomes. Finally, the characteristics analyzed were all accorded an equal weighting in the final analysis. Subsequent discussions of methodology have focused on the allotment of differing weighs for specific characteristics.

A further limitation relates to the nature of *Second Life* as compared to traditional MMORPGs, *Lineage* or *Anarchy Online*. Within the structure of a traditional MMORPG, an avatars appearance tends to be heavily influenced by the race or class chosen by the play. *Second Life's* nontraditional structure creates the question as to whether this research is transferable to other genres.

CONCLUSION

Prior to the explosion of Internet usage and even more recently the advent of MMORPGs, people would represent themselves in a number of different ways that were tied in some fashion to an aspect of their reality. It could be their job, the car they drive, the clothes they wear, and so forth. The advent of online avatars for recreation, education, or professional use provides an opportunity to more deeply examine the virtual representation of the psychological self. Online participants now represent themselves very close or very far from the core of their being. News stories are filled with horrifying tales of middle-aged men pretending to be 13. However, these representations do not need to be negative. They can simply be an exploration of an ideal self.

Avatar research is critical to multiple fields of study. Educators, who are now using online learning as a major medium for instruction, need to comprehend what it means to build communities of learners around virtual representations of self. Game designers need to explore how people choose characteristics or how they present characteristics of different vignettes to gamers (e.g., for stimulation of interest, for gaming buy-in, etc.). Advertisers will undoubtedly be interested in the ways in which they can offer new products to avatars based on the way they have been created. Imagine telling a consumer products manufacturer that you could predict future customers based on the way they designed their avatars. Imagine telling psychologists you could predict future behavior by choices being made in avatar creation. Imagine telling educators you could help build multicultural lessons by forcing students to switch genders or races in online environments.

In summary, this research has provided evidence that there is predictive validity in some characteristics. However, participants refused to play within the freedom of changing enduring traits. Whether it was their newness to the environment or a trait of gamers in general, future research needs to continue to build a rubric by which we begin to understand the ways in which people represent themselves. The line has been repeated over and over—you can be a dog online. But, when and why would someone be a dog online?

REFERENCES

Baylor, A. L., Rosenberg-Kima, R. B., & Plant, E. A. (2006). *Interface agents as social models: The impact of appearance on females' attitude toward engineering. In Conference on Human Factors in Computing Systems (CHI 2006),* Montreal, Canada.

Campbell, J. (1949) *The hero with a thousand faces.* Princeton, NJ: Princeton University Press.

Castronova, E. (2003). *Theory of the avatar* [CE-Sifo Working Paper Series No. 863]. Retrieved from http://ssrn.com/abstract=385103

Chen, K., Huang, P., & Lei, C. (2006). Game traffic analysis: An MMORPG perspective. *Computer Networks, 50*(16), 3002-3023.

Ducheneaut, N., Yee, N., Nickell, E., & Moore, R. (2006). Building an MMO with mass appeal: A look at gameplay in World of Warcraft. *Games and Culture, 1,* 281-317.

Emmison, M., & Smith, P. (2000). *Researching the visual: Images, objects, contexts and interactions in social and cultural inquiry.* London: Sage.

Griffiths, M. D., Davies, M. N. O., & Chappell, D. (2003). Breaking the stereotype: The case of online gaming. *CyberPsychology and Behavior, 6,* 81-91.

Grimshaw, A. (2001). *The ethnographer's eye: Ways of seeing in anthropology.* New York: Cambridge University Press.

Helmers, M. H. (2006). *The elements of visual analysis.* New York: Pearson Longman.

Hemp, P. (2006) Avatar-based marketing. *Harvard Business Review, 84*(6), 48-57.

Jones, D. (2006). *I, avatar: Constructions of self and place in second life.* Retrieved from http://gnovis.georgetown.edu/searchResults.cfm?searchQuery=avatar

Kafai, Y., Fields, D. A., & Cook, M. S. (2007a). Your second selves: Resources, agency, and constraints in avatar designs and identity play in a tween virtual world. In *Situated Play, Digra 2007,* Tokyo.

Kafai, Y., Fields, D. A., & Cook, M. S. (2007b). Blacks deserve bodies too! Design and discussion about diversity and race in a tween online world. In *Situated Play, Digra 2007,* Tokyo.

Kolko, B. E. (1999). Representing bodies in virtual space: The rhetoric of avatar design. *Information Society, 15*(3), 177-186.

Lange, G., Lattemann, C., & Fetscherin, M. (2007). *Second life research statistics. Second Life Research Blog.* Retrieved August 3, 2007, from http://secondliferesearch.blogspot.com/2007/03/second-life-residents-statistics.html

Linden Research, Inc. (2003). *Second Life* [Windows, MAC OSX, Linux]. (played July 19, 2007). San Francisco: Linden Research Inc.

Markus, H., & Nurius, P. (1986). Possible selves. *American Psychologist, 41*(9), 954-969.

Ondrejka, C. (2004). Escaping the gilded cage: User created content and building the metaverse. *New York Law School Law Review, 49*(1) 81-101.

Pink, S. (2001a). *Doing visual ethnography: Images, media and representation in research.* London: Sage.

Pink, S. (2001b). More visualising, more methodologies: On video, reflexivity and qualitative research. *The Sociological Review, 49*(4), 586-599.

Pink, S. (2004). Conversing anthropologically. In S. Pink, L. Kürti, & A. I. Afonso (Eds.), *Working images: Visual research and representation in ethnography.* New York: Routledge.

Prosser, J., & Schwartz, D. (1998). Photographs within the sociological research process. In J. Prosser (Ed.), *Image-based research: A sourcebook for qualitative researchers.* Bristol, PA: Falmer Press.

Turkle, S. (1995). *Life on the screen: Identity in the age of the Internet.* New York: Simon & Schuster.

Yee, N. (2004). *Avatar: Use/conceptualization and looking glass self.* Retrieved from http://terranova. blogs.com/terra_nova/2004/01/the_avatar_and_. html

Yee, N. (2008). *Our virtual bodies, ourselves? The Deadalus project: The psychology of MMORPGs.* Retrieved from http://www.nickyee.com/daedalus/archives/001613.php

ENDNOTE

[1] Many Second Life (Linden Research, Inc, 2003) aficionados have created businesses or services that are offered for sale in the virtual world; entrepreneurs have created entire businesses and derive substantial income through virtual business. Educators are also dabbling in Second Life, combining it with Moodle (an open source learning management system) to create learning environments (e.g., http://www.sloodle.com).

This work was previously published in International Journal of Gaming and Computer-Mediated Simulations, Volume 1, Issue 1, edited by Richard E. Ferdig, pp. 90-107 copyright 2009 by IGI Publishing (an imprint of IGI Global).

APPENDIX A: CHARACTERISTIC RUBRIC

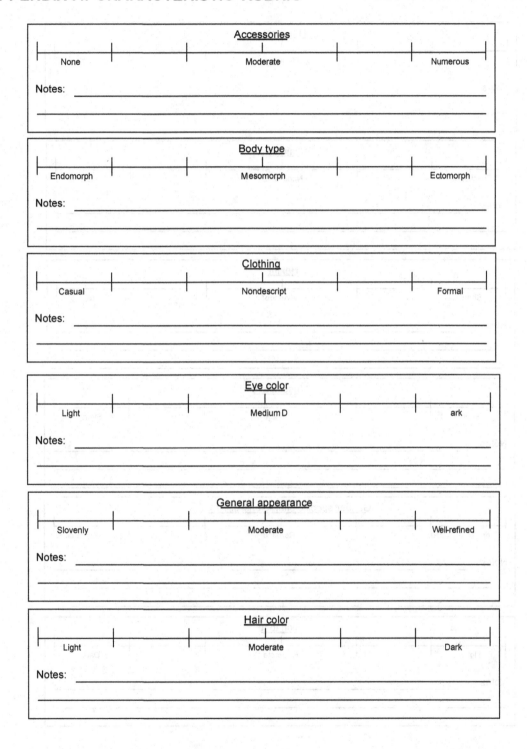

continued on following page

APPENDIX A: CONTINUED

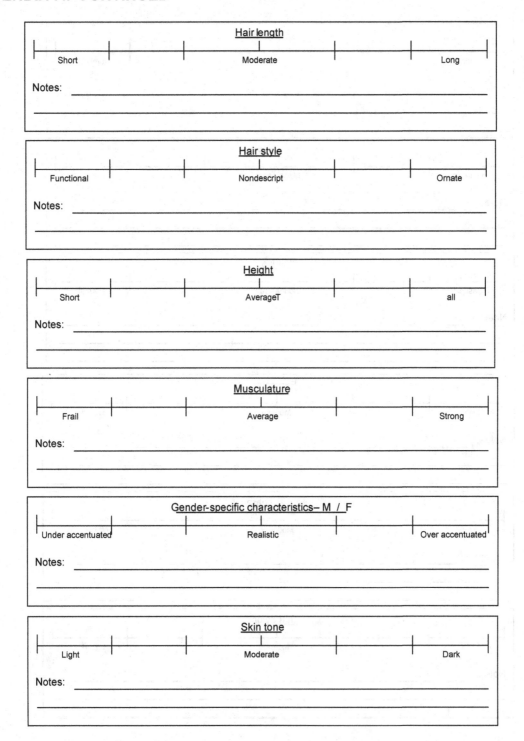

Hair length

Short   Moderate   Long

Notes: _____

_____

Hair style

Functional   Nondescript   Ornate

Notes: _____

_____

Height

Short   AverageT   all

Notes: _____

_____

Musculature

Frail   Average   Strong

Notes: _____

_____

Gender-specific characteristics– M / F

Under accentuated   Realistic   Over accentuated

Notes: _____

_____

Skin tone

Light   Moderate   Dark

Notes: _____

_____

Chapter 17
A Test of the Law of Demand in a Virtual World:
Exploring the Petri Dish Approach to Social Science

Edward Castronova
Indiana University, USA

Travis L. Ross
Indiana University, USA

Mark Bell
Indiana University, USA

James J. Cummings
Indiana University, USA

Matthew Falk
Indiana University, USA

ABSTRACT

We report results of an experiment on prices and demand in a fantasy-based virtual world. A virtual world is a persistent, synthetic, online environment that can be accessed by many users at the same time. Because most virtual worlds are built around a fantasy theme, complete with magic, monsters, and treasure, there is considerable skepticism that human behavior in such environments is in any way "normal." Our world, "Arden," was designed to test whether players in a typical fantasy environment were economically "normal." Specifically, we tested whether fantasy gamers conform to the Law of Demand, which states that increasing the price of a good, all else equal, will reduce the quantity demanded. We created two exactly equivalent worlds, and randomly assigned players to one or the other. The only difference in the two worlds was that the price of a single good, a health potion, was twice as high in the experimental world than in the control. We allowed players (N = 43) to enter and play the environment for a month.

DOI: 10.4018/978-1-60960-565-0.ch017

We found that players in the experimental condition purchased 43.1 percent fewer of the potions, implying a demand elasticity of -0.431. This finding is well within the range one expects for normal economic agents. We take this as evidence that the Law of Demand holds in fantasy environments, which suggests in turn that fantasy gamers may well be economically normal. If so, it may be worthwhile to conduct controlled economic and social experiments in virtual worlds at greater scales of both population (thousands of users) and time (many months).

INTRODUCTION: VIRTUAL WORLDS AS PETRI DISHES

Since 1997, there has been a rapid increase in deployment and use of virtual worlds: online computer-generated environments that can be accessed by thousands or even millions of people at the same time (Castronova, 2005). Each user explores the virtual world using an *avatar*, a human or human-like character that walks, talks, fights, and hugs, much as a real human does. While inhabiting her avatar, the user can chat with other people, play games, go on quests, or harvest virtual goods. The range of activities is determined by the designers and is typically vast since, unlike real-life people, an avatar can fly, turn into a fish, or become purple, just by changing the underlying computer code. With this kind of design flexibility, there are many possible applications for a virtual world beyond entertainment.

Until fairly recently the implementation of full-scale virtual worlds for research was limited due to cost and feasibility. Consider that World of Warcraft cost many millions of dollars to build and had teams of experienced individuals guiding the design and implementation. Obviously, a research team trying to recreate World of Warcraft has a herculean task ahead of them. However, post-dating the implementation of Arden a new possibility has arisen. The recent success of browser-based virtual worlds using Facebook and other social media platforms has made the development a virtual world for research and other serious applications a possibility for small teams with limited budgets (Ross & Cornell, 2010; Szell, Lambiotte, & Thurner, 2010).

In this paper, we consider a serious research application of virtual worlds: their use for controlled experiments. Several unique features argue for this kind of use. First, virtual worlds allow controlled experimentation at the level of an entire world. If desired, designers can fix the code so that two research environments are exactly the same, down to every leaf on every tree. Second, this technology allows truly vast research environments. If desired, a research team could create a world that covers hundreds of millions of square miles. Third, virtual worlds allow huge numbers of research subjects. Current commercial virtual worlds commonly have many millions of players. Fourth, virtual worlds allow a long time scale for research. Again, current commercial virtual worlds typically retain users for many years. One world, *Ultima Online*, has been in continuous existence since 1997. Finally, the people who engage with one another inside virtual worlds seem to constitute a genuine society. Casual observation reveals that, even at modest size, significant social relationships seem to develop. It appears, again to the casual observer, that friendships and reputations are forged and broken. Some individuals seem to acquire some kind of interpersonal or political power, while others are deemed "weak." Information networks seem to be active. Perhaps most surprising, virtual worlds seem to develop internal markets, in which players trade virtual items with one another at what appear to be stable and robust prices.

More careful observation of virtual worlds tends to confirm these suspicions. In a recent study, Chesney, Chuah and Hoffman (2009) conducted a series of classic experiments from experimental economics within the environment of Second Life. They found that, for the most part, the usual environment of a small-scale social science research lab can be replicated in a virtual environment. Almost all aspects of the usual experiment can be recreated virtually. The one exception to this finding was in the area of physical signals and cues, which of course are not transmitted by avatars (at least with current technology).

Results such as these raise the possibility that virtual experimental environments might be possible on an even greater scale. In an earlier paper, an effort was made to estimate the real-world productivity of characters in virtual worlds (Castronova, 2001). Real-world transactions of virtual currency for US dollars yielded a shadow price for the virtual currency. This in turn was used to translate virtual values into real values. By this kind of accounting, it appears that the gross level of economic transactions in virtual worlds has already grown into the billions of US dollars per annum (Castronova, 2007).

Similarly, anthropologists have said that they observe genuine cultural behavior in virtual worlds, as well as between them and the real world (Malaby, 2006); sociologists see genuine group formation (Jakobsson & Taylor, 2003); and legal scholars see the outlines of real-world law (Lastowka & Hunter, 2004).

With the exception of Chesney et al., all of these conclusions are based on direct observation. The method is that a reputable and careful scholar enters a virtual world, collects data (formally or informally) and then reports that the data seem to follow the same patterns in the virtual world as in the real world. No particular theory of behavior is tested. With the Chesney et al. study, the focus was on replicating the typical economics experiment lab, not society on a grand scale.

This leaves the real-world legitimacy of the large-scale behavior we see in virtual worlds in a state of doubt. Is the economy of such a game-world a real economy? It remains possible that, for most players, their participation in the virtual world is "just a game" and therefore any large-scale patterns are not analogs to real-world counterparts. Indeed, the stated object of participation in most virtual worlds is precisely that, to play a game, to behave in a way that is new, to experience things that are not possible in the real world. The mere fact that people trade things at certain prices, or inhabit this or that social role, need not imply that people are behaving according to our accepted economic and social theories. Perhaps when a man is an elf or an orc, he decides to buy high and sell low instead of the more sensible obverse pattern. Perhaps, when a woman play-acts a ship captain, she defers all decisions on the ship's course to the bilge crew, instead of making them herself. And why not? In a fantasy environment, it does not matter whether a person has enough money to "live" on, or whether a ship gets to a certain port "on time."

The previously cited observers of virtual worlds would counter with broad evidence that even in play-acting environments, human behavioral theories continue to hold water. The Stanford Prison Experiment and its follow-ups strongly suggest that people who are consciously play-acting a role nonetheless behave as if the role was real (Zimbardo, 2007). The fact that players of virtual worlds have committed murder and suicide over events within them certainly suggests that these events matter to those involved (though obviously not healthily so), despite the fact that the worlds are fanciful by design.[1]

This evidence is all indirect, however, and thus the question of whether virtual world behavior is "true" human behavior is open. Researchers in communications have tackled this question directly, however. Byron Reeves and Clifford Nass (1996) summarize a long series of brain experiments showing that people seem to treat media as real, apparently because of the simple fact that the brain evolved before media existed. More recently, Nick Yee and Jeremy Bailenson (2007) have coined the term "Proteus Effect" to describe the phenomenon of a person treating his or her virtual body as if it were a real body. In their studies, for example, people given a taller avatar in a virtual world act, in that world, more confidently. That is exactly the correlation we observe in the real world, namely, that height predicts social confidence. Yee and Bailenson demonstrate that this feature of the human evolutionary make-up translates directly into the virtual environment.

Yee and Bailenson's notion of a Proteus Effect can be studied in other contexts. Recent research seems to indicate that there is a Proteus Effect involving economic calculus. Using player data provided directly by Sony Online Entertainment, the makers of the virtual world Everquest 2, Castronova et al. (2009) found that the aggregate economic behavior of Everquest 2 was slightly more unstable than one would expect, but in general tended to follow the real world. In doing so, they also concluded that the implementation of the virtual world played a large role in the aggregate behavior. In other words, the design of the system had an influence on economic conditions.

Determining where virtual world behavior mimics real world behavior is quite important for methodological reasons. If virtual world behavior can be treated as a model of human behavior in general, this would allow a fresh approach to empirical social science. In the natural sciences, empirical work is based largely on a foundation of controlled experimentation. In the social sciences, controlled experiments can generally only be conducted on the most limited scale – a small number of people, over a small time period, for minor rewards. Yet the most pressing problems often involve large numbers of people in persistent environments. Researchers who have wrestled with this problem in the past have generally assumed that it would be impossible to conduct experiments that are truly macro-level and persistent. In the words of economist Robert Lucas, "The problem involved in convincing a collection of experimental subjects that they are in an infinite-horizon environment seems to me insurmountable" (1986, p. S421). Such a problem

may have been insurmountable in 1986, but virtual worlds provide a potential solution.

With virtual worlds, the experimental environment can be made to persist quite literally forever. Already, in commercial versions such as Blizzard Inc.'s *World of Warcraft,* we have millions of people, over the course of years, pursuing rewards of such value that they can even motivate some people to kill themselves or others. In such an environment, it would be possible to conduct controlled experiments at the macro level. Natural experiments that have already occurred seem to demonstrate the feasibility of this approach (Castronova, 2006).[2]

Such a method overcomes the difficulties faced by social researchers in establishing large-scale causation. In a typical regression analysis, one uses independent variables to attempt to isolate the direct relationship between the variable of interest and the dependent variable. However, even a lengthy list of independent variables is insufficient to completely isolate the effect of interest. Moreover, most regression analyses must make use of quite a bit more artillery – multiple equation systems, adjustment for unobserved variables, different functional forms, and so on. But none of this, of course, is sufficient to establish causation; it merely isolates the direct correlation between a specific independent variable and the dependent variable. This isolated relationship is then assessed for whether or not it is consistent with a casual theory. Contrast this complex and indirect method of inference with the far simpler method of controlled experimentation, on which the natural sciences are based. Place two equivalent Petri dishes on the counter. Insert the same yeast in each one. Expose one of the dishes to fire. Observe that the no yeast grows in the burned dish. Conclude: "Fire causes yeast to die." Causation is directly identified, in a method that is simple, replicable, and persuasive. This is the method that social science might be able to use, in place of regressions and classical statistical inference, if virtual worlds are found to induce behavior that generalizes to the real world.

Testing for general behavioral theory in virtual worlds is thus a necessary first step in exploring whether virtual worlds can serve as social science Petri dishes. The objective of the experiment reported in this paper was to conduct such a general behavioral test.

Our test focused on the Law of Demand, which holds that as the price of a good rises, all else equal, the quantity demanded of it will fall. There is perhaps no principle of human behavior more universally accepted in all of economic theory. We know of no introductory textbook that does not state the Law of Demand in its earliest, and foundational, chapters. Thus a test of the Law of Demand is indeed a stern one for virtual worlds. If the Law of Demand does not hold in a virtual world, we may as well conclude that virtual worlds generate no economic behavior of general interest.

Our test was simple: We created two virtual worlds that were exactly the same in all particulars save one: in one version of the world, the price of a single good was twice as high as in the other. We then assigned subjects randomly to the two worlds and observed how many items were purchased. The Law of Demand requires that, since, indeed, all else was absolutely equal in this experiment, the higher-priced good should have been purchased less frequently. But since our virtual world had monsters, treasure, and magic in it, and since the players took on the personae of elves, hobbits, and dwarves, perhaps there was no reason for anyone to pay attention to economic rationality. If not, the Law of Demand would be a clear casualty. Our experiment was designed to test whether this Law survived the translation from the real world into an environment of dungeons and dragons.

In the next section, we will describe the environment we created. Section 3 describes the experimental protocol. Section 4 presents results, and Section 5 offers a concluding discussion.

THE ENVIRONMENT: ARDEN

The virtual world supporting this experiment was named *Arden: The World of William Shakespeare*. Arden was built using the Aurora Toolkit, a virtual-world building software created by Bioware Inc. in support of its fantasy game *Neverwinter Nights*. The Aurora Toolkit allows the game designer to create a three-dimensional fantasy environment and populate it with non-player characters (NPCs), monsters, treasures, and quests. This environment can be hosted on a server and opened to traffic from the internet. People can then log in to the environment and choose a character (dwarven warrior, elven priestess, human thief, etc.). Using this character, they can then interact with whatever the play environment contains.

We created a world of 41 three-dimensional "zones," or play areas, 46 unique NPCs, 23 unique monsters, 25 special items, 111 conversation files (programs to handle interactions between a player and an NPC), and 204 custom scripts (programs to execute game functions). In addition, we used hundreds of the generic monsters, items, and objects available in the toolkit.[3]

The game was scripted using the Aurora Engine's scripting tool, which is similar to Java. For example there was one function in the code that would execute whenever a player opened an object labeled "Dropped Loot." On each such object was a local variable set to "High," "Medium," "Low, or "Wild," and depending on this variable, a certain number of gold pieces would be created within the object when it was opened. For example, a "low" item would generate "d12 + 4" gold pieces, meaning, a random integer between 1 and 12, inclusive, plus 4. Players in the world could walk their characters to the location of a Dropped Loot item and click on it. At this point the code would create gold pieces in the item, which the player could then take. The Dropped Loot item would then disappear for a time, reappearing later for a new player to come by and inspect. This in fact is how players obtained purchasing power: by harvesting gold pieces from the Dropped Loot items that appeared and disappeared from time to time. The Dropped Loot items were allocated so that every player would have a substantial, but not overwhelming, amount of purchasing power throughout the game.

The theme of our world was taken from William Shakespeare's *Richard III*. On entering the world, players were told (by a non-player character or NPC, named "Sergeant Bridgeford") that fires had broken out all over London and rioting had followed. They were then given a quest to help quell these riots, by order of King Richard III. Players then made their way across our virtual London, avoiding burning buildings as best they could while fending off attacks from mobs of thieves and looters. In the course of these attacks, they came across our Dropped Loot items and acquired the aforementioned gold pieces, the standard currency of the game. Upon reaching Newgate Prison, the epicenter of the riots, the players were told (again by an NPC) that they must go into the prison and kill the rebel leader, Rydderch ap Rhys. In doing so, they discovered certain information about the King's top advisor, William Tyrrel, revealing him to be quite unsavory. They also discovered evidence that the troubles in the city were directly linked to an outbreak of restless spirits in the Tower of London. The players then made their way to the Tower and battled the undead spirits until, in a big showdown deep within the Tower's crypts, they learned the truth about King Richard: that he is a tyrant and a murderer (as depicted in the play), who uses Tyrrel as his foul henchmen. Tyrrel's worst act: the murder of two young boys. Their ghosts then appeared to the players and pleaded that the players rebel against this evil King. Tyrrel himself then appeared and demanded that the players support law and order and kill these troublesome ghosts. Each player then chose whether to fight Tyrrel or the ghost-boys, thus placing themselves either on the side of the Lancastrians or the Yorkists in

the historical context of Shakespeare's play. This finished the game.

All told, a player might require 10 – 15 hours to complete this story; differences in hours played depend on player skills and tastes for exploration and pace. The environment included side quests and ancillary activities (social chatting with other players) that allowed players to vary the amount of time spent in the world. A player could enter the world at any time and exit it at any time; the world remained "switched on" around the clock, so that when the player returned, her character would be exactly where she left it. Players could experience the environment alone or as a group; a group could be formed in advance, by prior arrangement, or it could be random, as when several players happened to enter the same play zone at the same time. By design, a virtual world allows players to participate at whatever pace and in whatever way they wish, and this was the case in Arden.

As players made their way along, they encountered merchant NPCs, where they were able to use their cash to buy upgrades for their characters, such as stronger armor and sharper weapons. Each merchant offered hundreds of different items, at a wide variety of prices and features. The gold coin treasures were placed in the world so that a typical player going up to any merchant would always find many items that he could afford, as well as many that he could not afford. At the earliest levels, players would encounter enough Dropped Loot so as to acquire a minor endowment of 200 – 300 gold pieces fairly quickly. By the end of the game, a typical player might have 5,000 – 7,000 gold pieces. Of course, the items a player needs also grow more powerful, and more expensive, as the game progresses.

For example, among the most useful items in a game such as this are potions. By drinking a potion, a character could become invisible, gain increased armor, or learn the magical properties of an item. Health potions allow a character to restore her hitpoints, or HP. Hitpoints are a measure of the remaining stamina of a character during a battle. A character might start the fight with 20 HP. Each time the opponent makes a good blow, the character might lose 2, 5, or 10 of these HPs, reflecting the vigor required to fend the blow off. If an attack takes the character below 0 HP, she is considered defeated. "Defeat" here means not death, but rather being teleported back to a starting point of the zone. The character now has to fight through all the zone's monsters again in order to continue on with the game. Losing a fight is a setback in the player's progress.

A health potion helps during fights because it instantly cures HP. However, how much help it is depends on the character's level. A level 1 character might have 12 HP, meaning that a Potion of Cure Light Wounds, which heals up to 8 HP, can be quite useful. A level 10 character, however, might have more than 100 HP, and would typically be facing enemies that cause 15 or 20 HP of damage with each attack. For this character, a Potion of Cure Light Wounds has little use: the damage it cures is destroyed again in the time it takes to drink the potion. A Potion of Heal, which restores all HP, would be much better. Of course, Heal potions are many times more expensive than Cure Light Wounds potions. Thus, as a character levels from level 1 to level 10, her cash reserves increase, but so does the cost of operations.

In sum, the environment of Arden expressed most of the standards of fantasy virtual worlds. Players entered the world and navigated it as a kind of role-playing character; they received quests; they obtained treasure, magic items, powers, and spells; they encountered monsters and dungeons. Under all of this was a simple system by which players could obtain cash and buy items that would help them play. This underlying system of incomes and prices is something that the player could respond to in a "normal" way, that is, in the way economic theory predicts. Alternatively, because this is a fantasy environment in which no one really "dies," the economic calculus may be unimportant and economic behavior correspondingly off-kilter.

EXPERIMENTAL PROTOCOL

Research subjects were recruited from two undergraduate classes at Indiana University. Each participant received 20 points of course credit for playing the game and filling out a survey. Each student had to take a DVD with the game client on it, install it on their own computer, then create an account for online log-in.[4] The system requirements were such that not all students in the two classes had a suitable computer at home. Students who could not participate or elected not to participate were given an alternate assignment for equal credit. The final number of participants was 43.

When each participant was given login information, they received one of two IP addresses, one being "Arden A" and the other being "Arden B." These identities (version A or B) were not revealed to the subjects; the subjects were not informed that there was more than one research environment. Subjects were given one or the other IP addresses based on the last digit of their Social Security number. Numbers 0-4 were assigned to Arden A (22 subjects), while 5-9 were assigned to Arden B (21 subjects).

Arden A was the working game environment developed during the 12-month production phase of the project. Arden B was created the day before the experiment began. The Arden A environment was loaded into our game editor, and then it was given a new name, Arden B, using the "Save As" feature of the editor. In other words, Arden B was an exact copy, bit for bit, of Arden A.

After Arden B was created, we then edited it as follows. In Arden A, there were four merchants, located in the early stages of the game, who sold Potions of Cure Light Wounds, for 15 gold pieces each. Each merchant had a stock of 1,000 potions, which we assumed (correctly) would far exceed the maximum possible demand. After creating Arden B, we edited these four merchants so that the price of a Cure Light Wounds Potion was 30 gold pieces. No other changes were made.

Once Arden A and B were created, they were installed on an internet server and assigned IP addresses. At this point, subjects were told that the server was "live" and that they could log in at will. We kept the servers "on" for one month (specifically, 32 days). As it happened, all of the participants had made their way through the content of the game by the 27th day. Thus, in closing the server, we did not truncate the game experience for any of the players. Moreover, since the experimental intervention involved Potions of Cure Light Wounds – an item that is useful only to characters in the early levels (levels 1 – 6 or so) – we can be certain that all of our subjects experienced the content that was relevant to our experiment (the early content), well before the experiment was closed.

Subjects were given brief written instructions on how to play the game. These instructions included, among many other things, the information that healing potions could be used to restore hit points during combat. The game client also allowed subjects to play through a tutorial, in the course of which they were introduced to merchants, gold pieces, and the mechanics of buying and selling.

Subjects obtained gold pieces primarily through the Dropped Loot items, which were placed in the streets and tunnels throughout the game world, in places where they were not difficult to spot. Specifically, there were 114 treasure items in the "Low" category (giving anything from 5 gold pieces to 16 gold pieces), 139 in the "Medium" category (2 – 32 gold), 18 in the "High" category (4 – 64 gold), and 11 in the "Wild" category (8 – 160 gold). A subject who found each of these treasures would, on average, acquire 5,096 gold pieces. Additional funds could be obtained by doing extra quests to obtain up to 5 magic items, which could then be sold to merchants for prices ranging from 100 gold to more than 2,000 gold. Alternatively, players could keep those items and use them. Just how much gold a player obtained was therefore dependent on the extent to which he pursued treasure, as well as the luck of the die.

Unfortunately, due to the informational structure of our game-building software, we could not observe the gold accumulation of players. However, the amount of gold available seems sufficient to allow a typical player to purchase a number of Potions of Cure Light Wounds (whether priced at 15 gold or 30 gold).

In the course of the experiment, we discovered two bugs that had to be patched to allow two players to continue through the game. The bugs were of the nature of doors not opening even though the subject had the required key. Patching them required minor modification to the key-checking code. Both bugs occurred relatively late in the game content, and did not affect the health status or combat readiness of characters. Moreover, the bugs were exactly the same on both versions of Arden, and both were patched in exactly the same way. Thus it seems unlikely that the presence of these bugs had an impact on cross-world differences in purchases of Cure Light Wounds Potions.[5]

RESULTS

Table 1 compares the two subject groups on numerous demographic lines. It would appear that the random assignment protocol was successful in creating two similar populations for the two environments. That the sample is overwhelmingly male is a product of the classes from which the sample was drawn: one was a class in The Videogame Industry, the other in Multiplayer Game Design. It is typical that most enrolled students in these two classes are male.

The results of the experiment are summarized in Table 2. A reasonable number of potions were purchased in both worlds, 597 in the low-cost environment and 324 in the high-cost environment. Thus, it appears that the subjects found the potions to be useful in pursuing their goals within the game world.

It also appears to be the case that the subjects were respondent to price incentives, as the Law

Table 1. Experimental and Control Demographics

	Arden A (Control)	Arden B (Experiment)
Subjects	22	21
Age	22.7	22.1
Percent Male	87	93
Computer use hours[a]	34.9	29.2
Fathers with College[b]	50.0	58.8

[a] Computer use hours per week.

[b] Percent with fathers who have a college degree or more

Table 2. Experimental Results

	Arden A (Control)	Arden B (Experiment)
Subjects	22	21
Price of Potion	15 gold	30 gold
Potions Purchased	597	324
Potions Per Subject	27.14	15.43

of Demand suggests. Subjects in the low-cost world bought 27.14 potions on average, while those in the high-cost world bought only 15.43 Potions.

We judge this difference in potion consumption – a drop of almost half - to be substantively significant. However, because of a quirk in the game software that prevents us from calculating the sample variance of purchases, we are unable to conduct a full test of the statistical significance of the difference in means.[6] Nonetheless, we are able to determine that under reasonable assumptions about the variance, the difference in sample means is statistically significant.[7]

We can use the basic results to estimate the Elasticity of Demand, a general statistic used for comparisons in economic studies of consumer behavior. According to the data, doubling the price of potions from 15 gold to 30 gold reduced quantity demanded by 43.1 percent:

$$100x[1 - (15.43/27.14)] = 43.1$$

The formula for Elasticity of Demand is

ε = Percent Change in Quantity Demanded / Percent Change in Price

which in this case becomes

$$\varepsilon = -43.1/100 = -0.431$$

A demand elasticity of -0.431 is well within the range of normal demand elasticities, that is, demand elasticities that one usually sees in studies of the real world.[8] It thus appears that our research subjects' behavior did indeed conform to the Law of Demand.

DISCUSSION

We have provided evidence that fantasy game players respond normally to basic economic incentives. Despite being immersed in a synthetic fantasy environment, in which there was no real reason to follow the usual rules of social and economic conduct, the research subjects in this study nonetheless purchased fewer health potions when those potions were more expensive. We estimate that the elasticity of demand for health potions in our game was -0.431 – a thoroughly normal demand elasticity.

Numerous caveats must be applied to this finding. First, this experiment was not as controlled as is usual in the existing field of social science experimentation. In a typical laboratory experiment in economics, political science, game theory, or other fields, a similar number of subjects (20 – 50) spend several hours at once in a computer lab. Their communications are closely monitored and controlled. The information needed for their participation is presented in a strict protocol involving the reading of instructions and/or placement on a computer screen. Experimenters tightly restrict the narrative and contexts, to prevent subjects from inventing a "story" within which to place their decision-making. Whatever relationships, social or political or economic, there may be among the participants are either created by the experimenters or, if not, tightly controlled and sanitized by them for the duration of the test.

Our experiment, by contrast, did not occur in a lab. Communication was not controlled or observed. Instructions were provided in writing but no effort was made to ensure that subjects read the instructions or interpreted them in the same way. Most strikingly, our experiment embedded decision-making in a wild and detailed narrative, a rich context that was not only not sterile but fantastically different from the context of the real world. This was, of course, by design, in order to test whether such a thing made a difference in our theories of human behavior. We found in this case that it did not. We cannot conclude from this, however, that the narrative context will never make a difference. Rather, we are simply presenting evidence that one can give up the high levels of control that are possible in the laboratory, in order to achieve other advantages in terms of experimental scope in time and population. Nonetheless, the relative lack of experimental control, when compared to laboratory experiments, is a dimension along which studies like this can be legitimately criticized. In future work, protocols should be explored by which the communications of participants can be observed or regulated; and future experiments must determine where context matters and where it does not.

A second caveat might be that this finding is not as novel as we claim it to be. Numerous researchers have discovered that "normal" economic behavior occurs in many places where one might not expect it, such as POW camps (Radford, 1945), mental wards (Battalio et al., 1974; Battalio, Kagel, & Reynolds, 1977; Tarr, 1976) and among pigeons (Battalio, Kagel, Rachlin, & Green, 1981). Moreover, experimental economists have for a long time used linked computer networks to

do experiments and to teach students (Chesney, et al., 2009; Williams & Walker, 1993). Thus, our study only contributes the comparatively minor piece of information that one aspect of economically normal behavior – price sensitivity – occurs in online fantasy games. Some readers, familiar with these other studies, will find that to be unsurprising. However, we argue that the main question here is not about rationality per se, or about online networks per se, but rather about the effect of fantasy. It is not clear a priori whether, once gamers enter the fantasy zone, they become more like rational pigeons, or more like irrational pixies. Prior to embarking on this search, we encountered many skeptics, in many different fields, who argued that the fantasy context must invalidate most human behavioral theory. We have found evidence to the contrary. We feel this finding is relevant for numerous discussions, in numerous fields.

A third caveat worth noting is that our study was based on a few students, mostly male, at a large Midwestern university. It was not possible to observe the variance of purchases, and therefore tests of statistical significance were incomplete. Future work should take advantage of the flexibility of this technology and conduct virtual world experiments with many more people, from many more places, with better measurements. Some of this, of course, requires the relaxation of control, the subject of our first caveat. It would thus seem that there is a tradeoff between control and generality. Perhaps future methodological work could explicate this tradeoff and seek to reduce it. In any case, one great advantage of our protocol is that it is trivial to replicate. Future researchers could simply run the experiment with more subjects and better observational tools, to see whether our finding is unusual or not.[9]

Despite these clear limitations of the study, we argue that it is a reasonably solid first step in a promising new direction. There are major methodological advantages to addressing macro-scale social science questions using virtual world petri dishes. These advantages are shared with any experimental approach. We know, for example, that we have identified a change in quantity demanded – a movement along the demand curve - because of the experimental condition. The demand curve indicates the quantity demanded at a given price. It shows how the amount purchased should change as the price of the good changes, all else equal. In the real world, and with any kind of historical data, identifying movements along the demand curve is difficult. We observe a price change, and a change in the quantity sold, but we can never be sure that "all else" is truly "equal." On the contrary, with real-world data, we can be fairly confident that nothing else has remained fixed. Many other things have changed as well. The price of oranges rose, but something also probably happened to the price of grapefruits, the price of gasoline, and the incomes of people who drink juice for breakfast. Because of these other factors, we cannot be sure that the change in orange sales following a change in orange prices is truly a trace along the demand curve for oranges. Here, by contrast, we can be reasonably sure that we have identified a trace along the demand curve, because we can be reasonably sure that all else really is equal. The two worlds we have examined differed only in price. The populations of those worlds were apparently composed of very similar people, and nothing was done to one group that was not done to the other. Thus we can be reasonably confident that the demand elasticity of Potions in our world is actually -0.431 at the current market point.

This degree of confidence in identifying causality is one of the great advantages of the experimental method in general. Of particular interest here, however, is the possibility of conducting experiments on a much larger scale, both in terms of time and population. Game environments seem particularly attractive as forms of entertainment, and it has been observed that some game environments have millions of players for many years. Can these huge worlds be used to study human behavior on a vast scale? This study suggests

indeed that the presence of fantastical creatures and odd roles within these environments need not invalidate them as research sites. It may be true that players enter a game world only because they want to hunt dragons; but if they need health potions to do this, we can expect that the market for those potions will be, at base, a pretty normal market, with ordinary supply and demand curves and ordinary equilibrium conditions. This at least is the conclusion toward which the research in this paper points. Determining how far this kind of generality extends, however, is a task that should occupy the research agenda in this area for many years.

ACKNOWLEDGMENT

The work in this article was made possible by the members of the Arden Team at Indiana University. In a project of this scope and diversity a multi-disciplinary team is essential. Special thanks to all team members: Mark Carlton, Robert Cornell, Will Emigh, Michael Fatten, Paul LaFourest, Nathan Mishler, Justin Reynard, Sarah Robbins, Will Ryan, and Rory Starks. This research was also made possible by a grant from the MacArthur Foundation. Bioware, Inc., makers of the Neverwinter Nights videogame and the Aurora Toolkit, provided free software for use in the experiment.

REFERENCES

Balicer, R. (2007). Modeling infectious diseases dissemination through online role-playing games. *Epidemiology (Cambridge, Mass.)*, *18*(2), 260–261. doi:10.1097/01.ede.0000254692.80550.60

Battalio, R., Fisher, E. Jr, Kagel, J., Basmann, R., Winkler, R., & Krasner, L. (1974). An experimental investigation of consumer behavior in a controlled environment. *The Journal of Consumer Research*, *1*(2), 52–60. doi:10.1086/208591

Battalio, R., Kagel, J., Rachlin, H., & Green, L. (1981). Commodity-choice behavior with pigeons as subjects. *The Journal of Political Economy, 89*(1), 67–91. doi:10.1086/260950

Battalio, R., Kagel, J., & Reynolds, M. (1977). Income distributions in two experimental economies. *The Journal of Political Economy, 85*(6), 1259–1271. doi:10.1086/260636

Castronova, E. (2001). *Virtual worlds: A first-hand account of market and society on the cyberian frontier.* CESifo Working Paper No. 618.

Castronova, E. (2005). *Synthetic worlds: The business and culture of online games.* Chicago, IL: University of Chicago Press.

Castronova, E. (2006). On the research value of large games: Natural experiments in Norrath and Camelot. *Games and Culture, 1*(2), 163–186. doi:10.1177/1555412006286686

Castronova, E. (2007). *Exodus to the virtual world: How online fun is changing reality.* New York, NY: Palgrave/MacMillan.

Castronova, E., Williams, D., Shen, C., Ratan, R., Xiong, L., & Huang, Y. (2009). As real as real? Macroeconomic behavior in a large-scale virtual world. *New Media & Society, 11*(5), 685–707. doi:10.1177/1461444809105346

Chesney, T., Chuah, S., & Hoffmann, R. (2009). Virtual world experimentation: An exploratory study. *Journal of Economic Behavior & Organization, 72*(1), 618–635. doi:10.1016/j.jebo.2009.05.026

Jakobsson, M., & Taylor, T. (2003). The Sopranos meets EverQuest: Socialization processes in massively multi-user games. *FineArt Forum, 17*(8).

Lastowka, F., & Hunter, D. (2004). The laws of the virtual worlds. *California Law Review, 92*(1). doi:10.2307/3481444

Lofgren, E., & Fefferman, N. (2007). The untapped potential of virtual game worlds to shed light on real world epidemics. *The Lancet Infectious Diseases, 7*(9), 625–629. doi:10.1016/S1473-3099(07)70212-8

Lucas, R. E. (1986). The behavioral foundations of economic theory. *The Journal of Business, 59*(4), S401–S426.

Malaby, T. (2006). Parlaying value: Capital in and beyond virtual worlds. *Games and Culture, 1*(2), 141–162. doi:10.1177/1555412006286688

Radford, R. (1945). The economic organisation of a POW camp. *Economica, 12*(48), 189–201. doi:10.2307/2550133

Reeves, B., & Nass, C. (1996). *The media equation: How people treat computers, television, and new media like real people and places.* Cambridge, UK: Cambridge University Press.

Ross, T. L., & Cornell, R. D. (2010). *Towards an experimental methodology of virtual world research.* Paper presented at the 2010 Second International Conference on Games and Virtual Worlds for Serious Applications.

Szell, M., Lambiotte, R., & Thurner, S. (2010). Multirelational organization of large-scale social networks in an online world. *Proceedings of the National Academy of Sciences of the United States of America, 107*(31), 13636. doi:10.1073/pnas.1004008107

Tarr, D. (1976). Experiments in token economies: A review of the evidence relating to assumptions and implications of economic theory. *Southern Economic Journal, 43*(2), 1136–1143. doi:10.2307/1057338

Williams, A., & Walker, J. (1993). Computerized laboratory exercises for microeconomics education: Three applications motivated by experimental economics. *The Journal of Economic Education, 24*(4), 291–316. doi:10.2307/1183043

Yee, N., & Bailenson, J. (2007). The Proteus effect: The effect of transformed self representation on behavior. *Human Communication Research, 33*(3), 271–290. doi:10.1111/j.1468-2958.2007.00299.x

Zimbardo, P. (2007). *The Lucifer effect: Understanding how good people turn evil*. Random House Inc.

ENDNOTES

[1]   "Ill Hudson Man Took His Own Life After Long Hours On Web," Milwaukee Journal Sentinel, March 31, 2002. "'Game Theft' Led to Fatal Attack," BBC News, March 31, 2005.

[2]   An outbreak of "plague" in one virtual world was subjected to serious scrutiny by epidemiologists. See Balicer (2007) and Lofgren and Fefferman (2007).

[3]   A "Ring of Protection +1" is a generic item. Our "Hamlet's Ring" offered a magical effect of our own design, and was therefore a unique item. Similarly, a "Bear" is a generic monster, while our "Escaped Bear" had its own AI routines and was therefore a unique monster.

[4]   The usual network architecture of a virtual world, which we followed, is that users have a piece of "client" software on their home computers and they use this client to communicate with the main game server, hosted by the game's owners. The client is "dumb" in the sense that it knows nothing about the state of the virtual world; information about world state (location of characters, monster types and activities, location of treasure, quest states, etc.) is held secure at the central server. In our experiment, we hosted the world on our own server, and gave subjects client software that allowed them to log in to our server and experience the virtual world there.

[5]   Patching in virtual worlds is unavoidable. It is to expected that some bugs will be discovered only after the world has gone live. With the world being always "on," it will then be necessary to fix things "on the fly." This led us to an important lesson for virtual world experiments: An experimental protocol cannot reasonably require that there be no changes "on the fly" during an ongoing experiment; there will always be bugs, and they will need to be patched. Rather, researchers should always report patches so that readers can review whether the patch was relevant to the research findings.

[6]   To gather data, we placed a specific number of potions on potion merchants and then checked periodically how many were still there. The difference, we knew, must have been sold to players. However, this did not tell us who bought them. This is an example of a general problem with game-making software: the toolmakers give hardly any consideration to tools for data collection and analysis. It is very easy with contemporary tools to place a gnome in a cavern and have him interact in all kinds of ways with players. But it is almost impossible to get the gnome to record what he has done and write the information to a database in a way that makes sense for quantitative analysis. Our pre-research reviews of world-building toolkits indicated that the Aurora Toolkit had the best chance of allowing the data collection we would need. We made an intense effort, over several months, to modify the Aurora Toolkit so that it would report auction-based market purchases and sales out to a database. Unfortunately, we were not able to build a reliable system of markets and reporting within the 15-month time frame of our grant. In the interests of time, we then moved to a protocol of basic observation, manually counting what had been sold.

7   As indicated in note 6, the game did not allow us to record how many potions each user purchased. Thus, while we can calculate the average potions per user as total potions divided by total users, we cannot calculate the standard deviation of potions purchased across users (since that would require the purchases of individuals). Some measurement of the standard deviation would of course be required for Student's t. If we assume that the standard deviation is equal to one-half of the mean (ie, that the lower tail of the distribution of purchases just includes 0), Student's t is 3.4981, which yields statistical significance at significance levels well below 5%. After exploring several assumptions about this variance, our sense is that only a very high variance would yield statistical insignificance; the difference in means here is simply very large relative to the means themselves.

8   To make this more concrete: We would be very surprised at a positive demand elasticity, since that would directly violate the Law of Demand. We would also be surprised at anything very large in absolute value (above 50). A good with demand elasticity of -10 would be considered very elastic. Larger elasticities approach a condition known as "perfectly elastic demand." Similarly, an elasticity of 0 would be termed "perfectly inelastic demand." Both of these conditions are considered empirical rarities. The vast majority of real-world demand elasticity estimates that the lead author has seen in his career fall between -2.0 and -0.05. The experimental finding is in this range.

9   The experimental environment is available for free download at swi.indiana.edu. Follow the instructions there to run precisely the same experiment that we did.

Chapter 18
Virtual Worlds for Teaching:
A Comparison of Traditional Methods and Virtual Worlds for Science Instruction

Catherine Norton-Barker
Cornell University, USA

Margaret Corbit
Cornell University, USA

Richard Bernstein
Cornell University, USA

ABSTRACT

Immersive virtual worlds structured for education have the potential to engage students who do not respond well to traditional classroom activities. To test the appeal and usability of virtual environments in the classroom, four ninth grade science classes in a rural Upstate New York school were randomly assigned to learn an introductory genetics unit for three class periods in either an online, multi-user, virtual world computer environment or in a traditional classroom setting using lecture, worksheets, and model building. The groups were then reversed for a second three-day trial. Quizzes were given before, at midpoint, and at the end of the study. Both groups demonstrated significant knowledge gain of the genetics curriculum. This study demonstrates that self-directed learning can occur while exploring virtual world computer environments. The students were enthusiastic about using virtual worlds for education and indicated a strong preference for a variety of teaching methods, which suggests that offering mixed modalities may engage students who are otherwise uninterested in school.

INTRODUCTION

Motivating students in subjects such as mathematics and science remains challenging. Minorities and girls seem especially vulnerable to this phenomenon. They begin to lose interest in these subjects as early as middle school and ultimately become underrepresented in these career fields later in life (Clark, 1999). There appear to be very complex relationships among the motivational factors involved in this process. Dicintio & Gee (1999) found that at-risk students' academic motivation was strongly related to amount of control over decisions and choices they felt they had within

DOI: 10.4018/978-1-60960-565-0.ch018

the learning environment. This perceived control related to a decrease in boredom, confusion and desire to be doing something else. Unencumbered

Hidi & Harackiewicz (2000) suggest that engaging children in activities that interest them will naturally lead to goal-oriented behavior. They use the image of a child interested in baseball who practices swinging a bat thousands of times to perfect her swing to elucidate this point. The trick, they argue, is to engage children in a variety of activities, ideas and materials and let them find whatever aspects of a topic interest them personally. This will lead to the development of the students' personal mastery goals, which may be much more powerful motivators than any they receive from adults.

Deci et al (1991) review studies centered on the Self-Determination Theory of Motivation that provide evidence that classroom environments supportive of student autonomy (i.e., compared to those focused on controlling behavior) promote a higher level of intrinsic motivation, perceived competence and self-esteem. "When intrinsically motivated, people engage in activities that interest them, and they do so freely, with a full sense of volition and without the necessity of material rewards or constraints (p. 328). See also Deci & Ryan (1985).

Many adults have noted the intensity with which students play video games and wished these children would apply the same effort to their schoolwork. Educational researchers such as Gee (2005) offer suggestions for incorporating learning principles into video games in addition to content to maximize their educational potential. He states, "Challenge and learning are a large part of what makes good video games motivating and entertaining" (p. 34).

According to these authors, perceived control and interesting activities (such as video games) that also offer challenge are key factors to building self-motivated learning. It seems that numerous researchers have taken this advice to heart in the development of serious games for classroom. Chris

Dede's River City Project at Harvard University uses multi-user virtual environments with middle school students to enhance their motivation to learn science. This program is offered in addition to conventional classroom activities (Dede et al, 2005; Dede et al, 2004; Dede et al, 2003). In addition to being generally well-received by the students, the researchers have found that the program also improves attendance and reduces disruptive behavior (Dede et al, 2005).

Researchers at Indiana University (Barab, Gresalfi & Arici 2009) use virtual worlds to teach science content with the Quest Atlantis program. Cher et al (2006) conducted a study with fourth grade students in Singapore that demonstrated a significant amount of science learning with Quest Atlantis as measured on a pre and post test. And college students in an immersive virtual worlds condition significantly outperformed those using an electronic textbook on standardized test items (Barab, Goldstone & Zuiker, 2009).

Another study examined social knowledge construction and the development of "scientific habits of mind" (p. 530) in the popular online multi-user virtual world game environment World of Warcraft (Steinkuehler & Duncan, 2008). The authors illustrate how the nature of virtual worlds lends itself to scientific inquiry and problem solving within a social context, which provides further support for their potential for academic use.

There are also numerous articles offering guidance in designing and implementing virtual worlds to maximize the educational impact of these environments. Bellotti et al (2010) recommends creating realistic environments with a great deal of embedded information and activities students can discover on their own. De Freitas et al (2010) draw on experiences with adult learners in Second Life to introduce a four dimensional framework (i.e., Learner Specific, Pedagogical, Representative and Contextual) to design and evaluate educational experiences that apply to learners of all ages, across platforms. Warren et al (2009) take an in depth look at Quest Atlantis to offer advice on designing virtual worlds based on educational theory.

SciCentr, an outreach program at Cornell University in operation from 1999 to 2009, developed online, multi-user virtual worlds to engage middle and high school students in science, technology, engineering and mathematics (Corbit & Norton, 2007; Corbit et al, 2005; Corbit, 2005). SciCentr worked with fifteen school districts to support a variety of projects, ranging from virtual field trips to interactive exhibits to programs through which students created their own worlds. The SciCentr virtual world universe and associated programs moved to the Greater Southern Tier BOCES in 2009 under the new name EDUni-NY and continue to serve students in New York State today.

One creative program developed by SciCentr is a constructionist-based virtual science fair afterschool program, called SciFair, which began in 1998 in a rural upstate New York high school. In 2003, the teacher coaching this SciFair team developed virtual world classroom modules that align with the New York State Living Environment curriculum in his biology class, which later became the setting for this study.

In 2001, SciCentr received a SGER grant from the National Science Foundation to develop a prototype game world centered on transposons, or "jumping genes" and the genetic engineering of crop plants. The Jumping Genes world was designed by Cornell undergraduate students with guidance and oversight by SciCentr staff. The world is an archipelago of five islands, with a refuge in the sky above. The islands include an orientation space and four conceptual islands. Each island explores a different content focus - DNA basics, the mechanisms of nucleotide coding, the history and ethics of manipulating genes, and the impact of intracellular conditions on the potential for mutation. Each island features a different kind of game play. While funding for this prototype world ran out in 2005, work on the world and interest in using the completed portions as classroom modules continues. The Tree of Life island, featuring DNA basics, is the focus of this study.

As the SciCentr programs evolved, evaluation focused primarily on their motivational impact. Indeed, we found that SciCentr virtual world programs consistently receive high ratings from students enthusiastic to use the medium, regardless of the specific program or application (Corbit & Norton, 2007). This study provides an opportunity to test the hypothesis that students are able to learn science curriculum in a self-directed manner within a virtual environment with minimal direction from the teacher.

THE VIRTUAL WORLD ENVIRONMENT

Jumping Genes was built using the Active Worlds™ platform, which provides several key features for this project. In this environment, each user is represented by an avatar of their choice and can be identified by a unique citizen number and username. Users can explore, design and build virtual worlds together at the same time within a world. Users communicate with each other and with non-player-characters (NPCs) publicly through a chat interface and privately through a whisper feature. The building development system allows a variety of interactive features to be added to 3D objects. For example, users can be teleported to new locations as they interact with the virtual world and events can trigger pages to open in an integrated Web window.

The platform supports a mixture of two multi-user paradigms. Interactive elements can be synchronized for all users in some cases, where one user's actions affect everyone's experience; while in other cases interactions affect only an individual user. Both of these paradigms can be useful in designing different user experiences.

Active Worlds also provides an SDK (software development kit) with which developers can create applications, known as bots, that interact with the virtual world. Some bots take the form of NPCs capable of interacting in the same way as users - by moving an avatar, chatting, and building world content. Others are more hidden, behaving as interactive simulations by observing events and manipulating world contents in response to these events. Bots can also act as integrated components of the browser, bringing up web content, teleporting users, or sending system console chat messages. The back-end of these applications can include any functionality for processing and recording events and content, computing simulations, implementing games, or providing other interactive media.

Tree of Life Gameplay

On The Tree of Life island, players climb and explore a giant tree with a hollow core. They demonstrate their individual mastery of fundamental concepts in the mechanisms of nucleotide coding along the way. Once at the top, players in the final chamber must collaborate with others to escape through overgrown portals.

Students begin the experience by walking across the island toward the tree. As they walk, they can click two rotating sound objects that are loosely representative of speakers. This interaction brings up both voice recordings and a text-based Web page introduction, setting the scene for the challenge (Figure 1).

The students enter the tree and walk up the first level of a spiraling ramp. Walking into and through signs on the ramp brings up introductory Web pages about the basics of DNA coding (Figure 2). Students can also access the curriculum content by clicking on pieces of a DNA double helix model that runs up the middle of the tree (Figure 3). At the end of the first level, each student encounters an NPC Quizmaster that challenges them to demonstrate their knowledge of the material presented through series of multiple choice questions (Figure 4). The student must answer three out of five correctly to be teleported

Figure 1. The Tree of Life

Figure 2. Walking through signs triggers new content to appear in the Web window

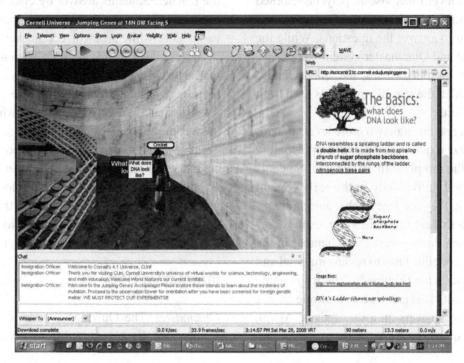

Figure 3. Looking up through the center of the Tree of Life

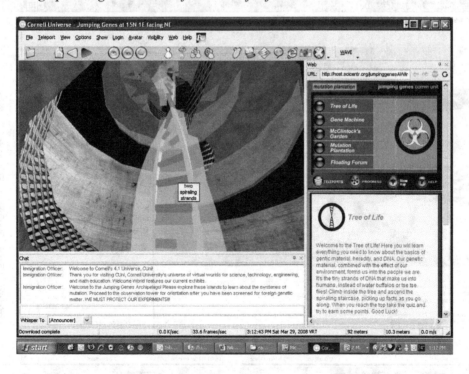

up to the next level, otherwise the player is returned to the beginning. Students can refer back to the Web content to answer the questions. While the Web content and Quizmaster system were original parts of Jumping Genes, the teacher chose and/or provided the specific questions used to fit his lesson plans.

Students rise through two more levels of content and quizzes covering subsequent topics before arriving at the top platform of the tree. Students are challenged individually in the early content levels. While they are free to chat among themselves, each student must answer questions correctly to reach the top. A domed chamber in the tree canopy contains links to review material and a group trivia game (Figure 5). The trivia game is a team event. This game posts multiple choice questions and answers on a set of signs. Again, the specific questions were chosen in advance by

the teacher. Students answer by clicking the appropriate sign - a correct answer increases the team score while an incorrect answer decreases it. Wrong answers by a single student hurt the whole group. Students will be most successful if they work together, but one can also choose not to participate and wait by the exit while others answer the questions. Once the team achieves six points, the gates open for a few seconds and players can escape to the outside platform.

Students who make it to the outside platform grab (i.e., click) a floating medallion that triggers an announcement of their success to the other players through the chat console (Figure 6).

Interactive Bots

Quizmaster. The Quizmasters are bots (NPCs) written in C. Each loads a different data file con-

Figure 4. Interacting with the first Quiz Master

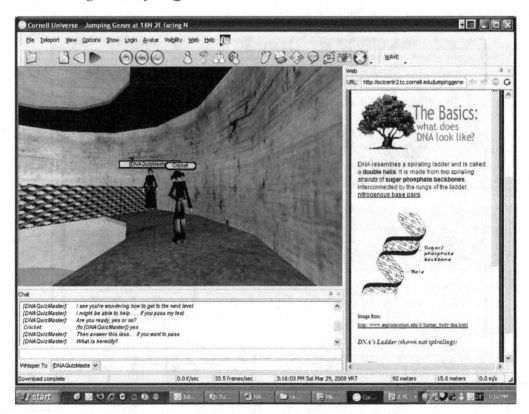

Figure 5. A group trivia game is the final challenge

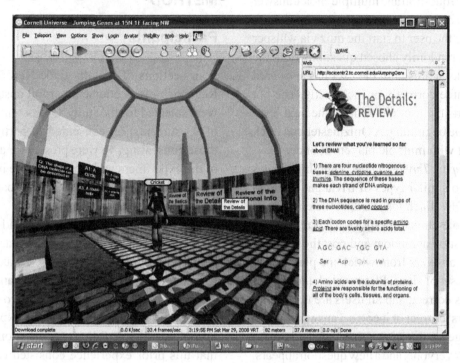

Figure 6. Clicking the blue and purple DNA medallion will signal to others that the student has mastered the challenge

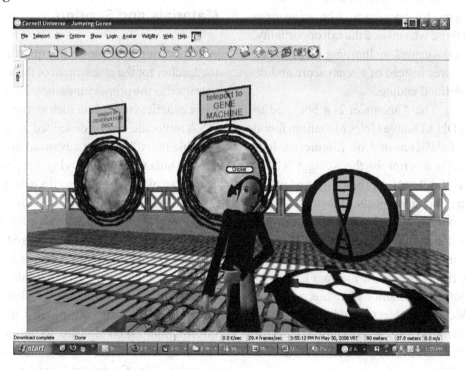

taining 12-16 question and multiple choice answer sets. The bot detects when a user enters its vicinity and prompts the user to start the quiz via whisper chat. It asks randomly chosen questions from the set and tracks scores until the user has answered a total of three correctly or incorrectly. The bot then teleports the user either up to the next level or back to the beginning. A Quizmaster can track and interact with multiple players at once.

GateKeeper Trivia Game. Jumping Genes contains two similar types of trivia games, both written in C++. Each loads a data file containing 10-20 multiple-choice questions. They repeatedly select a question at random and post the question and a set of answers from which the players can choose on a set of signs. Players click the answer they think is correct, and all users are notified of other players' correct or incorrect answers. When any player gets a question correct, that answer is indicated to everyone, and a new question appears. The GateKeeper version of the trivia game, which appears at the top of the Tree of Life, keeps only a group score, and briefly opens the exit gate for all users when the score reaches six points. It then restarts the game for new players who arrive in the area and for those who missed the exit opportunity. All other trivia games in Jumping Genes keep individual scores instead of a team score and do not have a defined ending.

Announcer. The Announcer is a bot used to monitor the DNA Double Helix Medallion found at the top of the Tree of Life (Figure 6). It is implemented as a script for the Xelagot X1 bot system. This script runs continuously, and monitors for users clicking objects. It then parses the interactive commands on the objects and extracts chat-related commands intended for it.

These commands can include the chat method (i.e., chat, whisper or console message), font settings and simple substitutions like username and time. The Medallion object includes a command that instructs the script to send a console message to all users that a given user grabbed the medallion and at what time.

METHOD

Participants

Four sections of a ninth grade New York State Regents biology course in a rural upstate school were selected for the study. Of a potential sample of 93 students, 69 consented to participate. Of those consenting, 46 were present for all six days of the experiment and were therefore included in the analysis. Thus, there was a 49.5% participation rate in the statistical sample.

There were 24 young women and 22 young men, ranging in age from 13 to 16 years. The students' reported ethnicities were Caucasian (65%), Mixed/Other (24%), American Indian (9%) and African American (2%). Seventy-two percent of the sample reported having prior experience in virtual worlds. A follow-up question revealed that this prior experience consisted exclusively of exposure in this same science course through an exploration of a virtual world designed by the teacher to introduce cell structures.

Materials and Scoring

A ten question multiple-choice quiz developed by the teacher for the assessment of the genetics unit was used as the primary measure. The quiz covers basic genetics curriculum such as, (question) "The DNA molecule can be described as a:" (answer) "double helix," to more advanced material.

The quiz was scored giving one point for each correct answer. This produced a measure that had a possible range of 0 to 10, with higher numbers indicating greater knowledge of introductory genetics. The quiz was administered before the first trial, at the midpoint between trial one and two and again after the second trial.

Surveys were administered along with the quizzes. The pre-survey solicited demographic information, asked students to define the terms "internet" and "virtual world" and contained three measures. The Computer Experience Inventory was developed by outreach evaluators at Cornell University. It contains ten 5-point Likert-type agreement items. This scale has a possible range from 10 to 50, with higher scores indicating more frequent computer use. The Modified CASS is a five item 5-point Likert-type measure of Computer Anxiety with a possible range of 5 to 25, with a higher score indicating greater computer anxiety. This measure was adapted from the Affective Items subscale of the Computer Attitude Scale for Secondary Students (CASS) (Jones & Clarke, 1994), as discussed in Smalley et al (2001). The full CASS totals 40 items, with three subscales. The affective subscale has 15 items, of which five were randomly chosen for this study in the interest of brevity. The Science Attitude Assessment, developed by independent evaluators at University of Washington through NSF funding for the development of the Jumping Genes virtual world, contains six 5-point Likert-type agreement items with a possible range of 6 to 30. A higher score indicates a more positive attitude about Science.

The mid-survey repeated the Modified CASS and the Science Attitude Assessment. Students were also asked to rate the experience of learning in the environment encountered in the first trial on a scale where 1 = poor and 5 = excellent and to indicate the extent to which the genetics unit was "easy" to learn, where a 1 = strongly disagree and a 5 = strongly agree.

The post-survey solicited a rating for the learning environment encountered in the second trial and to compare the traditional learning environment to the virtual world environment based on how easy it was to learn, how much fun it was to learn, and how much they felt they had learned. Students were also asked to indicate how well they could explain the Jumping Genes virtual world to others, whether they would recommend it to others, how interested they were in exploring the world, how interested they were in learning other subjects in a virtual world, how easy it was to navigate the virtual world, how often they felt lost and finally to indicate their ideal learning

experience from 100% traditional environment to 100% computer-based virtual world environment. All of these questions were ratings on 5-point Likert scales.

The multi-user virtual world used for the study was Jumping Genes, specifically the Tree of Life island. As discussed previously, this prototype game presents much of the genetics curriculum content for high school biology in New York State. The Tree of Life has the appeal of a trivia game, however the material becomes increasingly complex by level and can be quite challenging. This activity was designed to be a self-directed learning experience for the students. The students used worksheets to take notes about the genetics content they encountered as they progressed up the tree and worked in a completely self-directed manner. The teacher acted in an entirely supportive role, assisting with log-ins and answering any questions that arose.

Procedure

The four class sections were randomly assigned to one of two conditions for a three class period trial. One group learned an introductory genetics unit in a virtual world environment using a self-directed worksheet as a guide. The other learned through traditional methods: one day each of lecture, building models and completing in-class worksheets.

After the first trial, the groups were provided with the other mode of teaching for an additional three class periods so that all students received both learning modalities. This was done to ensure equity in the classroom, while simultaneously providing control groups. See Figure 7 for a graphical representation of the quasi-experimental crossover research design used.

Results

The students in the virtual world group demonstrated significant knowledge gain of the mate-

Figure 7. Research Design

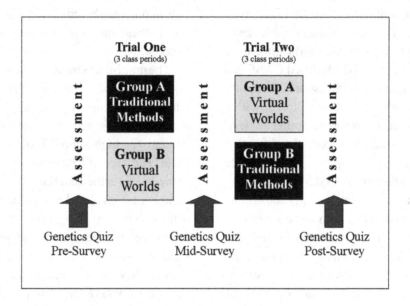

rial after the first trial (i.e., the mean grade rose from 2.17 to 6.13, $t(22) = -10.28$, $p < .001$). The traditional group also learned a significant amount of the material (i.e., mean grade rose from 2.65 to 8.17, $t(22) = -11.35$, $p < .001$). The groups achieved means of 7.30 and 8.83 in the post-quiz, respectively. See Figure 8.

Sex, ethnicity, computer anxiety, computer experience and science attitude did not appear to be significant factors in the analysis. This mirrors Dede et al's (2004) finding that gender and race do not seem to be predictors of learning success in educational virtual environments.

Figure 8. Quiz Means by Condition

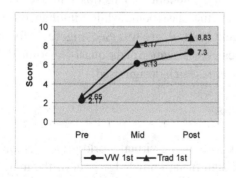

Modality Ratings Comparison

The students' response to the virtual world modality was overwhelmingly positive. The mean rating of the experience of learning in the virtual world environment was 3.9, on a scale from 1 to 5, where a 5 = excellent. This was significantly higher than their rating of the traditional environment, which placed at 3.5 on the same scale, $t(43) = 2.248$, $p < .05$

Eighty-percent (80%) of the students thought it was easier and 84% reported that it was more fun to learn in the virtual environment. 71% believed they learned more in the virtual environment than they did in the traditional environment. 85% of the students said they would recommend Jumping Genes to other students.

Virtual Worlds' Accessibility

Seventy-four percent (74%) said they would be able to explain the Jumping Genes program to other people. 85% stated that it was easy to navigate in the virtual world. 28% said they never got lost, while 61% admitted to getting lost "once or twice."

Continued Interest in Virtual Worlds

70% said they were interested in exploring the various areas of Jumping Genes, including the ones that were not were specifically used in class. 78% reported that they would like to learn other subjects in a computer-based virtual world.

Ideal Learning Environment

When asked to select the "ideal" learning environment (i.e., mix of virtual and traditional approaches), not one student chose 100% traditional. Nine percent favored a 25% virtual environment, 38% favored a 50% virtual environment, 40% favored a 75% virtual environment and 13% said a 100% virtual learning environment was ideal. These findings were consistent among males and females and students with varying attitudes toward science. See Figure 9.

Limitations

Several factors limit this study. With respect to knowledge of genetics, the groups were not equal at any point during the study, with the virtual world group being the less knowledgeable of the two. While there is no reason to believe that there is an order effect, it is possible that learning may be better facilitated when a traditional presentation of new science material is followed by a virtual exploration/reinforcement. Additional studies are needed to make this determination.

An unforeseen complication was the time lost (i.e., approximately 15 minutes per 45 minute class period) walking the students to the computer lab, regrouping, logging into the computers and then into the environment before finally getting started. This resulted in less time being spent in the virtual world itself. It is possible that if the time spent working had been held constant between the two conditions, the rate of demonstrated knowledge gain between the two groups might have been closer to equal. In addition to additional time,

the students in the traditional group received more modes of learning (i.e., lecture, worksheets and models), experiences that address multiple learning styles. It is not clear to what extent these unanticipated variables affected the students' performance.

DISCUSSION

This study demonstrates that a significant amount of learning can take place in a virtual environment. With appropriate design considerations, the curriculum content can be adapted to the needs of the teacher. To scale such a program, additional interfaces are needed for teacher input and for assessment. Because students rate the experience significantly higher than a traditional teaching environment, there is good reason to invest in this effort. Students believe they learn more, have more fun learning and would recommend learning in a virtual world to other students.

Most of the students found the program easy to use, felt comfortable describing it to others and expressed a desire to explore more and use the medium for other classes. The students' stated "ideal mix" of modalities is especially important, because it validates Hidi & Harackiewicz's (2000) assertion that a variety of activities, ideas and

Figure 9. Ideal Learning Environment by Sex

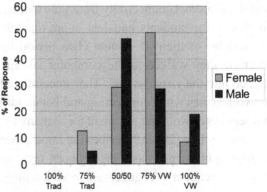

materials is powerful in building student interest and self-motivation. This study further validates the Self-Determination Theory of Motivation (Deci et al, 1991) finding that teaching environments supportive of student autonomy produce a higher level of intrinsic motivation, perceived competence and self-esteem. The students in this study thought that it was not only easier to learn in the virtual environment, but they also learned more in it.

The fact that girls were so enthusiastic, describing an ideal mix of modalities that included virtual worlds more often than boys, is telling. It would seem that this medium holds special appeal for girls, perhaps due to the social aspects of the multi-user environment. This observation holds promise for the continued use of virtual worlds and other new media to engage girls in subjects such as science and mathematics.

The Tree of Life activity takes place in a multi-user environment, which is a fundamentally social space. While we have conducted preliminary analyses of chat interactions between students and mentors (Rosen et al, 2003) in SciCentr programs, there is also a need to understand the impact and dynamic of team interactions and the potential impact of NPC or live guides on the learning experience.

An important consideration for the development of new teaching technologies is the potential for time loss and unpredictability of using computers in the classroom. Many of the schools that we work with have experienced network problems and slow Internet connectivity from time to time. In this study, students had lost approximately 15 minutes of their 45 minute class period by the time they walked to the computer lab and logged into the virtual world. They encountered network issues while connecting and bandwidth bottlenecks downloading content for so many users at once. Lee (2006) describes the importance of having efficient transitions between tasks to improve academic engagement and learning. Losing one-third of a class period in transition

from a traditional to virtual world environment is a great loss. The differences in students' learning between traditional and computing mediums observed in this study should reduce as technology use becomes better integrated in schools and transitions become more fluid.

The present study was conducted in 2007 and has since been replicated with the same result. Researchers in Spain (Wrzesien & Raya, 2010) compared traditional teaching methods with an immersive 3D virtual world experience concerning the ecosystem of the Mediterranean Sea. While there was not a significant difference in the amount learned, the virtual world group reported significantly more enjoyment, engagement and intention to participate than the traditional classroom group (p. 183).

CONCLUSION

This project represents a deep partnership with a teacher. The teacher understood the challenges of designing the study and the research team respected his need to balance the learning experiences of all students and to accomplish his teaching goals. In addition, extra effort was made on both sides to allow for the teacher to control the focus of the activity through oversight of questions and answers and development of worksheets. Thus, the "game" was customized to the classroom, which is similar to a teacher assigning textbook readings, selecting homework questions and writing quizzes. This kind of flexibility is important in developing game-like educational tools focused on content mastery. Design-based research is one way to approach this challenge.

New, effective computer-based tools that go beyond using computer games as alternatives to textbooks are needed to inspire students. One challenge is to leverage the rich knowledge base that commercial developers have amassed around player support and engagement while avoiding the pitfall of static content that quickly becomes outdated or doesn't precisely meet a teacher's needs. Neal Stephenson published his vision of the ultimate teaching tool, the Young Lady's Illustrated Primer, in *Diamond Age* (1995). The Primer responds to the learner's needs through artificial intelligence and human response, customizing its story and activities to the learner at every step, always actively linked to an all-encompassing network. Further research into the design of teacher-customization tools, including useful assessments, will be essential if we are to find real-world applications for such a vision.

ACKNOWLEDGMENT

The Jumping Genes project work was funded by the National Science Foundation under award #0107416. General operating support for SciCentr has been provided from a variety of sources: Cornell University, New York State, the GE Foundation, Microsoft, Intel, USDA, community foundations, participating educational and community organizations. Any opinions, findings, conclusions or recommendations expressed in this material are those of the authors and do not necessarily reflect those of the National Science Foundation or any other sponsor. We gratefully acknowledge key Cornell students involved in the development of the Tree of Life. David Peth and Dan White conceived of and designed the majority of the world's features. Caitlin Ramsey researched and developed the Web content available to players in the Tree. Cornell University Professor of Plant Breeding Susan McCouch provided scientific oversight and expertise for this project.

Active Worlds is a trademark of Active Worlds, Inc. Xelagot was created by Alex Grigny de Castro (XelaG).

REFERENCES

Barab, S. A., Gresalfi, M., & Arici, A. (2009). Why educators should care about games. *Educational Leadership, 67*(1), 76–80.

Barab, S. A., Scott, B., Siyahhan, S., Goldstone, R., Ingram-Goble, A., Zuiker, S. J., & Warren, S. (2009). Transformational play as a curriculum scaffold: Using videogames to support science education. *Journal of Science Education and Technology, 18*, 305–320. doi:10.1007/s10956-009-9171-5

Bellotti, F., Berta, R., De Gloria, A., & Primavera, L. (2010). Supporting authors in the development of task-based learning in serious virtual worlds. *British Journal of Educational Technology, 41*(1), 86–107. doi:10.1111/j.1467-8535.2009.01039.x

Clark, J. (1999). *Minorities in science and math.* Columbus, OH: ERIC Clearinghouse for Science, Mathematics and Environmental Education.

Corbit, M. (2005). Game worlds for learning. *Knowledge Quest. Journal of the American Association of School Librarians, 34*(1), 18–22.

Corbit, M., Kolodziej, S., & Bernstein, R. (2005). SciFair: A multi-user virtual environment for building science literacy. *Proceedings of the PCST Working Symposium*, Beijing, China.

Corbit, M., & Norton, C. (2007). A constructionist approach to using virtual worlds to motivate in the classroom. *Proceedings of the 2007 NYSCATE Conference*, Rochester, NY.

De Freitas, S., Rebolledo-Mendez, G., Liarokapis, F., Magoulas, G., & Poulovassilis, A. (2010). Learning as immersive experiences: Using the four-dimensional framework for designing and evaluating immersive learning experiences in a virtual world. *British Journal of Educational Technology, 41*(1), 69–85. doi:10.1111/j.1467-8535.2009.01024.x

Deci, E., & Ryan, R. (1985). *Intrinsic motivation and self-determination in human behavior*. New York, NY: Plenum.

Deci, E., Vallerand, R., Pelletier, L., & Ryan, R. (1991). Motivation and education: The self-determination perspective. *Educational Psychologist, 26*(3-4), 325–346. doi:10.1207/s15326985ep2603&4_6

Dede, C., Clarke, J., Ketelhut, D., Nelson, B., & Bowman, C. (2005). Students' motivation and learning of science in a multi-user virtual environment. *Proceedings of the American Educational Research Association*, Montreal, Canada.

Dede, C., Clarke, J., Ketelhut, D., Nelson, B., & Bowman, C. (2005). Fostering motivation, learning, and transfer in multi-user virtual environments. *Proceedings of the American Educational Research Association*, Montreal, Canada.

Dede, C., Ketelhut, D., & Nelson, B. (2004). Design-based research on gender, class, race and ethnicity in a multi-user virtual environment. *Proceedings of the International Conference on Learning Science*, Mahweh, NJ

Dede, C., Ketelhut, D., & Ruess, K. (2003). Designing for motivation and usability in a museum-based multi-user virtual environment. *Proceedings of the American Educational Research Association*, Chicago, IL

Dicintio, M., & Gee, S. (1999). Control is the key: Unlocking the motivation of at-risk students. *Psychology in the Schools, 36*(3), 231–237. doi:10.1002/(SICI)1520-6807(199905)36:3<231::AID-PITS6>3.0.CO;2-#

Gee, J. (2005). Good video games and good learning. *Phi Kappa Phi Forum, 85*(2), 33–37.

Hidi, S., & Harackiewicz, J. (2000). Motivating the academically unmotivated: A critical issue for the 21st century. *Review of Educational Research, 70*(2), 151–179.

Jones, T., & Clarke, V. (1994). A computer attitude scale for secondary students. *Computers & Education, 4*(22), 315–318. doi:10.1016/0360-1315(94)90053-1

Lee, D. (2006). Facilitating transitions between and within academic tasks: An application of behavioral momentum. *Remedial and Special Education, 27*(5), 312–317. doi:10.1177/07419325060270050601

Lim, C. P., Nonis, D., & Hedberg, J. (2006). Gaming in a 3D multiuser virtual environment: Engaging students in Science lessons. *British Journal of Educational Technology, 37*(2), 211–231. doi:10.1111/j.1467-8535.2006.00531.x

Rosen, D., Woelfel, J., Krikorian, D., & Barnett, G. (2003). Procedures for analyses of online communities. *Journal of Computer-Mediated Communication, 8*(4). Retrieved December 1, 2008, from http://jcmc.indiana.edu/vol8/issue4/rosen.html

Smalley, N., Graff, M., & Saunders, D. (2001). A revised computer attitude scale for secondary students. *Educational and Child Psychology, 18*(3), 47–57.

Steinkuehler, C., & Duncan, S. (2008). Scientific habits of mind in virtual worlds. *Journal of Science Education and Technology, 17*(6), 530–543. doi:10.1007/s10956-008-9120-8

Stephenson, N. (1995). *The diamond age*. New York, NY: Bantam.

Warren, S. J., Stein, R. A., Dondlinger, M. J., & Barab, S. A. (2009). A look inside a MUVE design process: Blending instructional design and game principles to target writing skills. *Journal of Educational Computing Research, 40*(3), 295–321. doi:10.2190/EC.40.3.c

Wrzesien, M., & Raya, M. A. (2010). Learning in serious virtual worlds: Evaluation of learning effectiveness and appeal to students in the E-Junior project. *Computers & Education, 55*, 178–187. doi:10.1016/j.compedu.2010.01.003

Chapter 19
Playing Myself or Playing to Win?
Gamers' Strategies of Avatar Creation in Terms of Gender and Sex

Sabine Trepte
Hamburg Media School, Germany

Leonard Reinecke
Hamburg Media School, Germany

Katharina-Maria Behr
Hamburg Media School, Germany

ABSTRACT

Who do people want to be in virtual worlds? Video game players can create their avatars with characteristics similar to themselves, create a superhero that is predominantly designed to win, or chose an in-between strategy. In a quasi-experimental study, players were expected to prefer their avatars to have their sex, but to create avatars with gender attributes that best meet the requirements of the game. In the main study, participants created an avatar they would like to play with by choosing from a list of (pre-tested) masculine and feminine avatar features. Additionally, participants chose their avatars' biological sex. The results reveal a mixed strategy: On the one hand, the avatar's features are chosen in accordance with the game's demands to facilitate mastery of the game. On the other hand, players strive for identification with their avatar and thus prefer avatars of their own sex. Participants rated those game descriptions and gaming scenarios more entertaining which require avatar features in line with their own sex role.

DOI: 10.4018/978-1-60960-565-0.ch019

INTRODUCTION

Avatars and agents have become a crucial interface between media users and virtual environments. Via an avatar, the player can elicit all kinds of social interactions. Thus, "avatar-mediated communication", the communication and the social interaction between users and avatars as well as its potential effects, seems to be one crucial issue in the studies of human-computer interaction, virtual environments, and video games. Avatars will increasingly be the "face" of computer mediated communication in games, the internet or learning software (Donath, 2007; Nowak & Rauh, 2008). Studies on avatars and agents indicate that people get a more emotional access to computer based environments by communicating with an avatar or agent (Dryer, 1999; McQuiggan & Lester, 2007; Rizzo et al., 2001). This has several implications. With avatars and agents, people concentrate easier, learn better, and find computer mediated communication more enjoyable and fun (Gaggioli et al., 2003; Ku et al., 2005; Whalen et al., 2003).

In video and computer games, avatars are not limited to the visual characteristics of the interface players use to navigate through games. Game avatars are also embedded into the game narratives and may have different personalities and histories, offering different roles players may take. An increasing number of games like massively multiplayer online role playing games allow their users to create the avatars' visual appearance, but also skills and personality. With their avatars, players can engage in social interaction and even behave like human beings. Thus, communication between players and avatars evolves to a new form and it has potential effects on user identity as well as on the experience of video and computer gaming (Bailenson, 2006; Bailenson & Beall, 2005; Bessière et al., 2007; Hsu et al., 2007; Hsu et al., 2005). Depending on the game's features and the player's skills, the player may experience enormous autonomy in the interaction

with an avatar. Players can create avatars with characteristics similar to themselves, create virtual superheroes with attributes far beyond reality or choose an in-between strategy. Consequently, the manner in which a player designs an avatar triggers two questions: Who do people want to be in virtual worlds? If they have the freedom to create their avatars, do they prefer to resemble themselves in real life or to be somebody else, e.g. a virtual superhero? To answer these questions, this chapter will deal with the similarity between avatars and players and will explore the impact of the similarity between the player and the avatar on game enjoyment.

Avatar-player-similarity is a multifaceted construct, and many avatar or player characteristics, such as outer appearance or physical strength, can be taken into account. A particularly prevalent issue in research on players and avatar characteristics is gender (Hartmann & Klimmt, 2006a; Lucas & Sherry, 2004; Ogletree & Drake, 2007; Smith, 2006).[1] Content analyses demonstrate that many video games portray women in a sex-stereotyped manner (Dietz, 1998; Ivory, 2006; Jansz & Martis, 2007; Smith, 2006)—a great part of video gaming is still "a man's world", particularly in the action genre. Consequently, many games do not meet female users' entertainment needs because of their violent content and the predominantly male gender stereotypes represented in the games (Hartmann & Klimmt, 2006a; see also Lucas & Sherry, 2004). Beyond affecting user's affinity for games, the features of video game characters can impact player cognition and behavior (Yee & Bailenson, 2007). For example, playing as a female (i.e., playing a female avatar) against a male avatar increases aggressive thoughts, whereas playing as a male against a female opponent consistently and significantly decreases aggressive thoughts (Eastin, 2006). Sexually stereotyped portrayals of video game characters influence the players' understanding of gender roles (Eastin, 2006) as well as attitudes toward and beliefs about women

(Behm-Morawitz & Mastro, 2009; Dill, Brown & Collins, 2008; Fox & Bailenson, 2009). Also, research indicates that sex-stereotyped and aggressive games affect female players by rendering sex-stereotyped role-behavior (Anderson et al., 1996; Bartholow & Anderson, 2002; Chumbley & Griffiths, 2006; Dietz, 1998; Eastin, 2006; Jansz & Martis, 2007; Norris, 2004; Quaiser-Pohl et al., 2006; Reinhard, 2006).

A more thorough understanding of how players relate to video game avatars and how specific avatar characteristics impact video game playing experiences will therefore contribute to our understanding of video game use and effects in general. In this chapter, a study on the similarity between players and their avatars and the impact of avatar-player similarity on video game enjoyment will be presented.[2]

In the following section, previous research on gendered video game content and playing will be reviewed. Based on this review, hypotheses regarding players' strategies of avatar creation will be proposed. To test these hypotheses, a quasi-experimental study on the choice of gender-related avatar features will be presented. Finally, the results will be discussed with regard to avatar-mediated communication as well as video game research and design.

Gendered Video Game Content

The content and use of video games are impacted by various gender-related factors. Video games are primarily designed by males and for a primarily male audience (Heeter, Egidio, Mishra, Winn & Winn, 2009). They often convey gender stereotypes and are used differently by male and female players. Several content analyses have demonstrated that the portrayal of male and female characters differs considerably in video games (Smith, 2006). Female characters tend to appear less frequently in video games than male characters. For example, Downs and Smith (2010) analyzed the top 20, best-selling console games

(Microsoft Xbox, Sony PlayStation2, Nintendo Game-Cube) from the U.S. market for the fiscal year 2003. In these 60 games, 86% of the characters with an identifiable sex were male, compared to 14% female characters. Williams, Martins, Consalvo, and Ivory (2009) found a similar ratio of 85% male versus 15% female characters in their analysis of 133 top-selling games for nine major game systems sold in the U.S. from March 2005 to February 2006. These studies mirror earlier findings (Beasley & Standley, 2002; Children Now, 2000, 2001; Dietz, 1998; Dill, Gentile, Richter & Dill, 2005).

Moreover, content analyses show that female game characters are depicted in a more sexualized way than male characters (Beasley & Standley, 2002; Haninger & Thompson, 2004) and their roles within the game are often limited to being sex objects or the damsel in distress awaiting male rescue (Dietz, 1998). Downs and Smith (2010) report that in their content analysis 41% of the female characters were portrayed in sexually revealing clothing compared to 11% of the male characters. Furthermore, 43% of the female characters were portrayed partially or totally nude compared to 4% of the male characters. Female characters were also more likely to be shown with unrealistic body proportions (e.g., large breasts and thin waist) than male characters. Martins, Williams, Harrison and Ratan (2009) compared female video game characters to anthropometric data (e.g., height, head, chest, waist, hip measures) from a representative sample of American women and found that at high levels of photorealism (as in current video games), female game characters are systematically thinner than the average American woman. Such stereotyped portrayal of male and female game characters can also be found in video game magazines (Dill & Thill, 2007; Miller & Summers, 2007), in game reviews (Ivory, 2006), and on video game covers (Burgess, Stermer & Burgess, 2007).

Gendered Video Game Playing

Men and women play differently in terms of genre, frequency, duration, their motivations, and how they are affected by games (Ambady & Gray, 2002; Digital Trends, 2006; Hartmann & Klimmt, 2006a; Information Solutions Group, 2007; Lucas & Sherry, 2004). Games not only do have different effects on men and women, they also affect gender as well as sex roles (Bem, 1974; Smith, 2006).

67% of the American households play computer or video games, and six out of ten players are male (Entertainment Software Association, 2010). In contrast to the high proportion of males in the general population of video game users, 64% of online gamers (Digital Trends, 2006) and 53% of social gamers (The NPD Group, 2010) are women. Also, the overall audience for casual games is predominantly female (Information Solutions Group, 2007). However, the percentage of women under the age of 40 who play casual games (25%) is smaller than men (37%). Men choose casual game genres such as sports, war, role-playing, and other simulations, whereas women enjoy puzzle, word-games, arcade, and card games (Information Solutions Group, 2007).

Apart from content preferences, men and women also differ in their motives to play video games. While some gratifications of video games are equally attractive for men and women alike (e.g., control and challenge), preference for other gratifications (e.g., competition or social interaction) are more gender-specific. Controlling the game environment and the course of events is a primary aspect of playing video and computer games for both male as well as female players (Grodal, 2000; Lucas & Sherry, 2004). It addresses the players' effectance motivation and feelings of causal agency, which in turn increases video game enjoyment (Klimmt & Hartmann, 2006; Trepte & Reinecke, in press). Also, both men and women are equally motivated to play video games in order to experience feelings of challenge (Lucas & Sherry, 2004). Lucas and

Sherry (2004) argue that both men and women strive for inclusion, affection, and control, and that both men and women engage in behavior seen as gender-typical to fulfill these needs. Video games are seen as a "boy domain" (Lucas & Sherry, 2004, p. 507), and for men, playing video games is a gender-typical activity. Thus, men are more likely than women to play video games with other peers because it provides means to fulfill their need for inclusion and affection. Moreover, males are more motivated to play video games to engage in competition (playing against another person or computer controlled opponents) than are women. On the contrary, female players are more motivated by challenge than by competition. For online games, Yee (2006) reports that achievement and competition are significantly more important to males than to females, whereas women value social aspects of game playing like relationship and teamwork more than men do. Taken together, these results emphasize that video game play is strongly influenced by the players' gender. In the following section, we outline possible strategies for avatar creation and derive hypothesis regarding male and female players' choice of gender attributes for video game avatars.

Similarity and Success: Game Players' Strategies of Avatar Creation

The possibility to customize one's avatar is a game feature that is likely to increase video game playing (cf. Weber & Shaw, this volume). Whether or not players have the option to use a customized video game avatar impacts the playing experience. Lim and Reeves (2009) demonstrated that the option to pick the character that will represent the player in the game leads to greater arousal, especially for male players. Playing with a customized avatar is associated with higher physiological arousal and subjective presence than playing with a pre-determined or assigned avatar (Bailey, Wise & Bolls, 2009). But what determines the features and characteristics players choose to customize their video game characters?

The results of a number of studies suggests that video game players show a general preference for games that allow them to play with avatars that are similar to themselves (Hsu, Kao, & Wu, 2007; Hsu, Lee, & Wu, 2005; Ogletree & Drake, 2007; Trepte & Reinecke, 2010). One motive for choosing a similar avatar may be the attempt to transfer real life social cognition to virtual worlds in order to make the virtual world easier to comprehend. Similarity might make it easier for the player to feel "at home" in the game. Hsu, Lee and Wu (2005) conducted a qualitative study with 16 frequent buyers of computer games. Participants assigned 28 different "Pac-Man" games to three groups in terms of perceived fun. Afterwards they compared games from different groups according to design features. Hsu, Lee, and Wu (2005) report that players especially enjoy games with characters that are similar to themselves. According to their results, apart from having dramatic scenarios, the avatar's similarity to the player was the second most important criterion for liking a game. Accordingly, Hsu, Kao and Wu (2007) reveal that both the players' similarity and familiarity to heroic roles allow for predicting the preference for these heroic roles in role playing games. Furthermore, users most likely experience identification phenomena such as emotional release, when feeling similar to their avatar (Cohen, 2001).

The importance of avatar-player similarity for the gaming experience is also demonstrated by data from a study by Trepte and Reinecke (2010). The authors hypothesized that avatar-player similarity determines identification with the avatar, which in turn was suggested to enhance the enjoyment experience. In a quasi-experimental study, ($N = 666$) participants were asked to choose the personality features of an avatar for six different game scenarios. The results confirmed the hypotheses. Avatar-player similarity showed a positive relationship with identification with the avatar which in turn was strongly related to game enjoyment.

Taken together the research results reviewed above demonstrate that players prefer playing with similar avatars and experience more enjoyment in games that feature avatars that are similar to themselves. Furthermore, the preference for a high player-avatar similarity also relates to gender-specific avatar features: According to Ogletree and Drake (2007), women are more likely to choose female characters and men are more likely to choose male characters when they play computer games. In line with this research, H1 states that women as well as men will experience more enjoyment in games with avatars that are similar to themselves in terms of gender-specific attributes.

H1: Female players will find games requiring avatars with female attributes more enjoyable and male players will find games requiring avatars with male attributes more enjoyable.

However, we suspect that not all players will design their avatars similar to themselves in all games. Instead, how people create their avatar may also be driven by rational choice considerations. Vasalou, Joinson, Baenziger, Goldie, and Pitt (2008) investigated how users customize avatars for different social media contexts such as online gaming or online dating. Users primarily created avatars that accurately reflected their offline self. But they also concealed or emphasized attributes of their own personality in their avatars in order to address the avatar's purpose (e.g., winning an online game vs. meeting another person online).

We argue that similar mechanisms apply to the creation of video game characters. Successful mastery of a game and control over the gaming environment are crucial gratifications of game play and significantly contribute to video game enjoyment (Grodal, 2000; Klimmt & Hartmann, 2006; Tamborini et al., in, press). Control and the chance to succeed in the game may be maximized by choosing an avatar that meets the game requirements as well as possible. Many video games are embedded in a context necessitating attributes such as physical strength or aggressiveness. Mastery and control in these games may only be reached by creating an avatar with attributes dissimilar to the player. Thus, control is achieved by designing an avatar according to features required for game achievements and not according to the player's preference for similar avatars (cf. H1). The better an avatar is equipped in terms of success-enhancing features, the more control can be executed during challenges faced in the game. Moreover, players may want to try out different identities and use the game as a virtual playground to probe social interactions they would not dare to exhibit in the real world (Bessière et al., 2007).

By creating a dissimilar avatar that fits into a game and meets game requirements, the primary goal of control can be accomplished (Grodal, 2000; Klimmt & Hartmann, 2006; Lucas & Sherry, 2004). Also, players can use a "borrowed" identity and try out behavior that is out of reach in real life.

Summing up, previous research suggests that players like same sex games requiring same sex avatars (see H1). However, in some games players might not be successful with avatars that resemble them. In the second and third hypotheses we therefore propose that players want to play with avatars that meet a game's requirements. Accordingly, for games that can be considered "masculine" in terms of their requirements, players design masculine avatars. "Feminine" games will lead to the creation of feminine avatars.

H2: In "masculine" games (pretest-rated), players of both sexes will create avatars with male attributes and in "feminine" games (pretest-rated), players will create avatars with female attributes independent of their own sex.

H3: In "masculine" games (pretest-rated), players of both sexes will create an avatar with male attributes and in "feminine" games (pretest-rated), players will create an avatar with female attributes independent of their own sex role orientation.

In H1 it was assumed that players like to play games requiring avatars of their own gender. Furthermore, H2 and H3 proposed that this preference is inhibited if the game requirements demand a dissimilar avatar. It will now be suggested in H4 that, even when forced to create dissimilar avatars for the sake of maximizing control and game success, players will stick to their gender-identity in terms of biological sex. By creating avatars with matching biological sex, players have the chance to pursue their aim to play with avatars reflecting attributes of their own gender and simultaneously being able to meet the game requirements and to be successful. It is thus posited that players choose a mixed strategy to satisfy their need for similarity while simultaneously maximizing their chance for success: On the one hand players may create an avatar with their own *biological sex* with the aim to increase similarity and on the other hand choose *gender attributes* meeting the game requirements (e.g., physical strength) to increase the chance of winning (cf. H2 and H3).

Apart from similarity in terms of gender attributes, assigning a "biological" sex to an avatar seems to be crucial to players. Even though avatars do not have biological mechanisms (in terms of a genotype), they can have traits and conditions (similar to a phenotype) that would be causally biologically linked to being male or female (Gentile, 1993, p. 120), such as secondary sexual characteristics (e.g., breasts of female avatars). Most empirical work gathered on this issue demonstrates that players commonly choose same-sex avatars (Eastin, 2006; Hsu et al., 2005; Nowak & Rauh, 2005). For the inhabitants of *Second Life* it was shown that only very few females choose to be playing a male character (4%) and not many men choose to be a girl (14%). Most users (42% men, 40% women) stay with their real world gender (Rymaszewski et al., 2007). First exploratory studies reveal that gamers might try out gender swapping (Hussain & Griffiths, 2008). However, when it comes to the "main" character, a gender match between the real world and the

Table 1. Pretest One: Stimulus material

	M	SD	T	df	p
Game One: *The Sims*	4.42	1.30	2.293	49	.026
Game Two: *My Animal Hospital*	5.36	1.27	7.549	49	< .001
Game Three: *GTA: San Andreas*	2.52	1.33	-7.877	49	< .001
Game Four: *Crysis*	1.90	0.91	-16.333	49	< .001
Game Five: *Urban Chaos*	2.32	1.39	-8.537	49	< .001
Scenario One: Pursuit	1.98	1.04	-13.737	49	< .001
Scenario Two: Interviewing a witness	5.84	1.24	10.536	49	< .001

Note. Scales range from 1 = "requires primarily male features" to 7 = "requires primarily female features". One-sample *t* tests were conducted to test for significant deviations from the scale midpoint (4.0). Descriptions rated significantly lower than 4.0 were considered "masculine"; descriptions rated significantly higher than 4.0 were considered "feminine".

virtual world seems to be more likely (Eastin, 2006; Hsu et al., 2005; Nowak & Rauh, 2005). Consequently, in terms of biological sex, players are expected to assign their own sex to avatars regardless of game requirements.

H4: Game players will prefer to assign their own sex to the avatar rather than creating an avatar with the biological sex that seems to match the game requirements.

METHOD

Pretest One: Stimulus Material

In a pretest, 50 participants (36% men, 64% women; mean age = 27.84, *SD* = 8.70) rated descriptions of five computer games and two gaming scenarios according to the features an avatar should have to fulfill the situational demands required by the respective game.

The five game descriptions resemble authentic descriptions of existing computer games (*The Sims, My Animal Hospital, Grand Theft Auto: San Andreas, Crysis,* and *Urban Chaos*) and were obtained from the official product websites. All cues referring to the original games (e.g., titles or character names) were excluded from the de-

scriptions. The two gaming scenarios depict two different situations within a crime video game (see Appendix 1 and Appendix 2 for exact wording of game descriptions and scenarios respectively).

Participants received the instruction to imagine an avatar for every description that optimally matches the requirements of the respective game or gaming scenario. For every game description and gaming scenario, participants indicated whether an avatar should have "primarily male attributes" or "primarily female attributes" to perfectly meet the respective situational demands on a 7-point Likert scale. See Table 1 for the summarized results.

One-sample *t* tests were computed to test for significant deviations from the scale midpoint (4.0). Descriptions rated significantly lower than 4.0 were categorized as "masculine" games because they were perceived as requiring primarily male avatar attributes by the pretest participants. Analogously, descriptions rated significantly higher than 4.0 were considered "feminine" games. Accordingly, Game One (*The Sims*), Game Two (*My Animal Hospital*) and Scenario Two (Interviewing a witness) were categorized as "feminine", whereas Game Three (*GTA: San Andreas*), Game Four (*Crysis*), Game Five (*Urban Chaos*) and Scenario One (Pursuit) were categorized as "masculine".

Table 2. Pretest Two: Avatar features

	M	SD	t	df	p
analytical	2.35	0.81	-6.031	56	< .001
warm	3.93	0.65	10.787	56	< .001
athletic	2.59	0.60	-5.155	56	< .001
ambitious	2.93	0.68	-0.782	56	.438
forceful	1.72	1.41	-6.852	56	< .001
affectionate	3.81	0.72	8.485	56	< .001
beautiful	3.84	0.82	7.761	56	< .001
has leadership abilities	2.68	0.81	-2.961	56	.004

Note. Scales range from 1 = "masculine" to 5 = "feminine". One-sample *t* tests were conducted to test for significant deviations from scale midpoint (3.0). Features rated significantly lower than 3.0 were considered "masculine"; features rated significantly higher than 3.0 were considered "feminine".

Pretest Two: Avatar Features

In a second pretest, 57 participants (19 men and 38 women) rated eight adjectives: analytical, warm, athletic, forceful, ambitious, affectionate, beautiful, has leadership qualities. These features were derived from literature on sex role stereotyping (Bem, 1974) and they represent typical masculine or feminine attributes. The features were pretested to verify their stereotypical gender character. Participants received the instruction to indicate for every adjective whether it resembles a rather masculine or rather feminine feature. Participants rated each adjective on a 5-point Likert scale ranging from 1 = "masculine" to 5 "feminine". The results are presented in Table 2.

One-sample *t* tests were computed to test for significant deviations from the scale midpoint (3.0). Features rated significantly lower than 3.0 were categorized as masculine features and features rated significantly higher than 3.0 were considered feminine features. Accordingly, the attributes "analytical", "athletic", "forceful" and "has leadership qualities" were categorized as masculine features, whereas "warm", "affectionate" and "beautiful" were rated as feminine features. No significant deviation from the scale midpoint was found for "ambitious", which is

why this feature was excluded from data analysis in the main study.

MAIN STUDY

Participants

A total of 142 undergraduate students from a large German university participated in this quasi-experiment.

Sub-sample one: In a first step, 108 participants (38 men and 70 women) were recruited in introductory psychology classes and received course credits for participation.

Sub-sample two: To equalize the ratio of male and female participants, 34 additional male participants were added to the sample. This second male sample was part of a follow-up study which addressed the effects of satisfaction with life on avatar choice. The results of this study are presented elsewhere (Trepte & Reinecke, 2010). Participants of sub-sample two received exactly the same instructions as participants of the first sample, only the measures of entertainment value slightly differed in both samples (see procedure section for further information).

The final sample comprised 72 Men (50.7%) and 70 women (49.3%). Their ages ranged from

18 to 48 years (M = 24.6 yrs.; SD = 6.05 yrs). None of the participants of pretests one or two participated in the main study.

Procedure

In a 2 (gender) x 2 (male vs. female situational setting) quasi-experimental design, the choice of avatar features was investigated. All experimental sessions were conducted in a computer laboratory with six open cubicles, and data were collected using a computer-aided procedure.

Participants received the five previously rated computer game descriptions in random order. After a game description was presented, participants were asked to create an avatar "*they would like to play with*" for the respective game by choosing from a list of the eight pretested attributes (analytical, warm, athletic, ambitious, has leadership qualities, beautiful, strong, affectionate). Participants were allowed to distribute a total of 40 points among these attributes and up to 10 points for one, i.e. they had to assign a value between 0 and 10 to every attribute. After configuring the avatar's features, participants were requested to choose the avatar's biological sex (1 = "male"; 2 = "female"). After receiving all five game descriptions and configuring an avatar for each one, participants obtained the two gaming scenario descriptions used in the pretest in random order and they were requested to develop another two avatars using the same procedure.

To control for participants' prior experience with the games used as experimental stimuli, participants in sub-sample one were asked to indicate for each description whether they were familiar with the respective game (1= "yes"; 2 = "no"; 3 = "I don't know").

Participants were then asked to judge the games' entertainment value by indicating their approval of the statements: (a) "This game [scenario] sounds exciting", (b) "I could entertain myself well with this game [scenario]" and (c) "I would like to play this game [scenario]". Judgments

were given on a five-point Likert scale ranging from 1 "not right at all" to 5 "absolutely right". The three items used to measure entertainment value showed satisfactory internal consistency for all game descriptions and gaming scenarios (for all: Cronbach's α > .908) and they were summed to form a single entertainment value index. In the case of the 34 additional male participants of sub-sample two, entertainment value was assessed using the item "I could entertain myself well with this game [scenario]" on a six-point scale ranging from 1 "not right at all" to 6 "absolutely right". To make entertainment scores of both groups of participants comparable, scores were standardized using a z-transformation in both sub-samples.

After rating the games' entertainment value, participants completed the Bem Sex Role Inventory (BSRI, Bem, 1974). At the end of the experiment, participants reported age, sex, the average number of times they play video or computer games per week and the average length of a usual gaming session.

Measures

Bem Sex Role Inventory (BSRI). The Bem Sex Role Inventory (Bem, 1974) was used to assess the participants' sex role orientation. The BSRI consists of 60 adjectives forming three scales of 20 items each: (a) the masculinity scale (acts like a leader, aggressive, ambitious, analytical, assertive, athletic, competitive, defends own beliefs, dominant, forceful, has leadership qualities, independent, individualistic, makes decisions easily, masculine, self-reliant, self-sufficient, strong personality, willing to take a stand, willing to take risks), (b) the femininity scale (affectionate, cheerful, childlike, compassionate, does not use harsh language, eager to soothe hurt feelings, feminine, easy to flatter, gentle, gullible, loves children, loyal, sensitive to the needs of others, shy, soft spoken, sympathetic, tender, understanding, warm, yielding) and (c) the social desirability scale (adaptable, conceited, conscientious, con-

Table 3. Mean scores for entertainment value ratings by male and female participants

	Mean rating of entertainment value		*t*	*df*	*p*
	men	women			
Game One: *The Sims* (feminine)	-0.168	0.172	-2.056	140	.042
Game Two: *My Animal Hospital* (feminine)	-0.179	0.172	-2.109	140	.037
Game Three: *GTA: San Andreas* (masculine)	0.194	-0.200	2.393	140	.018
Game Four: *Crysis* (masculine)	0.330	-0.340	4.238	140	< .001
Game Five: *Urban Chaos* (masculine)	0.248	-0.251	3.058	140	.003
Scenario One: Pursuit (masculine)	0.170	-0.198	2.216	140	.028
Scenario Two: Interviewing a witness (feminine)	-0.037	0.038	-0.447	140	*n.s.*

Note. To assure comparability, scores in sub-sample one and two were standardized using a z-transformation.

ventional, friendly, happy, helpful, inefficient, jealous, likable, moody, reliable, secretive, sincere, solemn, tactful, theatrical, truthful, unpredictable, unsystematic). Participants were requested to indicate how well each quality describes them on a 7-point scale ranging from 1 ("never or almost never true") to 7 ("always or almost always true"). Both the masculinity scale (Cronbach's α = .79) as well as the femininity scale (Cronbach's α = .76) showed satisfactory internal consistencies. For this study, the self-rating means for all masculine and all feminine items were calculated (ranging from 1 to 7). Participants who scored higher on the masculinity scale than on the femininity scale were considered to have a predominantly masculine sex role orientation. Those who scored higher on the femininity scale were considered to have a predominantly feminine sex role orientation.

RESULTS

Hypothesis 1

To test for differences in perceived entertainment value between men and women, independent-

samples *t* tests were conducted for the entertainment value ratings of male and female participants for all game descriptions and gaming scenarios. The results are summarized in Table 3.

Rated masculine in the pretest, Game Three (*GTA: San Andreas*), Game Four (*Crysis*), Game Five (*Urban Chaos*) and Scenario One (Pursuit) were judged significantly higher by men than by women regarding entertainment value. Game One (*The Sims*) and Game Two (*My Animal Hospital*), both rated feminine in the pretest, were judged significantly higher in entertainment value by women than by men. No significant differences were found for Scenario Two (Interviewing a witness). Thus, women rated those games categorized as "feminine" in the pretest higher in entertainment value than men. Moreover, men gave higher ratings to gaming Scenario One and those games rated "masculine" in the pretest. Obviously, the participants' gender and the dominance of male versus female avatar attributes required in the described situation influenced the perceived entertainment value. Thus, Hypothesis 1 is supported by the data.

To control for the influence of game experience on the evaluation of the presented game descrip-

Table 4. Mean scores for masculine and feminine avatar attributes by male and female participants.

		M masculine avatar attributes	*M* feminine avatar attributes	*t*	*df*	*p*
Game One: *The Sims* (feminine)	men	4.52	5.57	-3.453	67	.001
	women	4.12	5.79	-6.161	64	< .001
Game Two: *My Animal Hospital* (feminine)	men	4.27	5.60	-3.540	65	.001
	women	4.09	5.65	-4.581	66	< .001
Game Three: *GTA: San Andreas* (masculine)	men	6.12	2.82	10.248	65	< .001
	women	5.67	3.44	5.972	65	< .001
Game Four: *Crysis* (masculine)	men	7.29	1.52	17.860	68	< .001
	women	7.10	1.69	20.037	68	< .001
Game Five: *Urban Chaos* (masculine)	men	7.12	1.82	15.239	66	< .001
	women	6.85	1.82	18.230	67	< .001
Scenario One: Pursuit (masculine)	men	6.95	1.59	17.253	65	< .001
	women	6.86	1.42	20.543	67	< .001
Scenario Two: Interviewing a witness (feminine)	men	3.78	6.52	-9.803	70	< .001
	women	3.75	6.49	-9.219	68	< .001

Note. Differences between the mean scores of masculine and feminine avatar attributes were tested with paired-sample *t* tests separately for male and female participants. Varying degrees of freedom are due to missing data.

tions, ANCOVAs with sex as a fixed factor, the frequency of playing games per week as covariate and the entertainment ratings as dependent variables were computed for all five games and the two game descriptions. With the exception of Game Three (*GTA: San Andreas*) where no significant main effect of sex could be replicated ($F(1,142) = 3.856, p = .052, \eta^2 = .026$) the pattern of results remained unchanged when controlling for game experience which again supports Hypothesis 1.

To control for the influence of the participants' prior experience with the games used as experimental stimuli on the evaluation of the entertainment value of the respective games, ANOVAS with participants' sex and prior experience with the game as fixed factors and the entertainment ratings as dependent variables were computed. The significant effect of the participants' sex on the ratings of entertainment value was replicated only for Game Two (*My Animal Hospital*) ($F(1,108) = 4.822, p = .030, \eta^2 = .042$), Game Four (*Crysis*) ($F(1,108) = 4.728, p = .016, \eta^2 = .044$), and Game

Five (*Urban Chaos*) ($F(1,108) = 5.556, p = .011, \eta^2 = .052$) when controlling for prior experience with the games.

Hypothesis 2

Both male and female participants created avatars with feminine attributes in Game One (*The Sims*) and Game Two (*My Animal Hospital*), and avatars with masculine attributes in Game Three (*GTA: San Andreas*), Game Four (*Crysis*) and Game Five (*Urban Chaos*; see Table 4). Both men and women created avatars in gaming Scenario One (Pursuit) primarily with masculine attributes, while they designed avatars in Scenario Two (Interviewing a witness) mainly with feminine attributes (see Table 4).

According to these findings, the participants' sex did not have an influence on the choice of avatar features. For all games and gaming scenarios, male and female participants set the same priorities in avatar design. They created avatars with male attributes for those games and gaming scenarios rated "masculine" in the pretest and avatars with female attributes for games and gaming scenarios rated "feminine". According to these results, the situational requirements expressed in the respective descriptions primarily regulated the participants' choice of avatar features. This occurred independent of their sex, which supports Hypothesis 2.

In the analysis presented above, participants' strategy for avatar design was tested using paired-samples t tests separately for all games and gaming descriptions. To evaluate the overall selection strategy and all avatar design decisions simultaneously, a 2-factor MANOVA was computed with participant sex and the stimulus pretest result ("game requires primarily masculine features" = 1; "game requires primarily feminine features" = 2) as the fixed factors and the sum of masculine and feminine avatar features as dependent variables. The data were therefore restructured. Every avatar designed by the participants was taken as a separate unit of analysis in that 2-factor MANOVA. Thus, the scores of avatar features of all seven avatars designed by each participant were taken as separate cases for the analysis, resulting in 994 cases. The MANOVA showed a significant main effect of participant sex on the scores of masculine ($F(1, 979) = 5.147$, $p = .023$, $\eta^2 < .001$) but not on feminine ($F(1, 979) = .462$, $p = .497$, $\eta^2 < .001$) avatar features. Furthermore, a significant main effect was found for the game requirements (pretest rated) on the scores of masculine ($F(1, 979) = 649.550$, $p < .001$, $\eta^2 = .050$) as well as feminine ($F(1, 979) = 1044.341$, $p < .001$, $\eta^2 = .179$) avatar features. No interaction effects between participants' sex and game requirements were found for the scores of masculine ($F(1, 979) = .001$, $p = .979$, $\eta^2 < .001$) and feminine avatar features ($F(1, 979) = .307$, $p = .580$, $\eta^2 < .001$). As reported above, the data demonstrate a significant main effect of participant's sex on the choice of masculine avatar features. Although significant, the effect size of the influence of

sex on the choice of male avatar features is very small ($\eta^2 < .001$). In contrast, both significant main effects of game requirements on the choice of masculine and feminine avatar features show substantial effect sizes. Accordingly, participants' overall strategy for choosing avatar features was primarily influenced by the situational requirements in the given descriptions. Hypothesis 2 is supported by the results.

To control for the influence of general game experience on the overall selection strategy of avatar features ANCOVAs with game requirements (pretest rated) as fixed factor, the frequency of playing games per week as covariate and the sum of masculine and feminine avatar features as dependent variables were computed. The effect of game requirements on the choice of masculine ($F(1, 979) = 646.196$, $p < .001$, $\eta^2 = .050$) and feminine $F(1, 979) = 1048.556$, $p < .001$, $\eta^2 = .179$) avatar features remained significant when controlling for game experience.

To test for the effects of prior experience with the games used as experimental stimuli, a MANOVA with game experience as fixed factor and the sum of masculine and feminine avatar features as dependent variables was computed. Prior experience neither had a significant main effect on the sum of masculine ($F(2, 756) = 2.750$, $p = .065$, $\eta^2 = .001$) nor on the sum of feminine avatar features ($F(2, 756) = .768$, $p = .464$, $\eta^2 < .001$).

Hypothesis 3

To test for the effect of sex role on the choice of avatar features, participants were categorized according to their femininity and masculinity scores assessed with the BSRI. For this purpose, separate self-rating means for all masculine and for all feminine items were calculated (ranging from 1 to 7) for every participant. Individuals scoring higher on the femininity scale than on the masculinity scale were considered to have a predominantly feminine sex role orientation whereas those scoring higher on the masculinity scale were considered to have a predominantly masculine sex role orientation. Consequently, 57 participants were classified as having a masculine sex role orientation and 83 as having a feminine sex role orientation. Two participants were excluded from the analysis because their femininity and masculinity scores were identical, making categorization impossible. Paired-samples t tests were computed for the mean sums of masculine and feminine avatar attributes for participants with masculine and feminine sex role orientation separately for every game and gaming scenario (results are provided in Table 5).

Both participants with masculine and feminine sex role orientation created avatars with feminine attributes in Game One (*The Sims*) and Game Two (*My Animal Hospital*) and with masculine attributes in Game Three (*GTA: San Andreas*), Game Four (*Crysis*) and Game Five (*Urban Chaos*; see Table 5). In gaming Scenario One (Pursuit)

mainly avatars with masculine attributes were created, whereas in Scenario Two (Interviewing a witness) subjects predominantly created avatars with feminine attributes independent of participant sex role orientation.

Accordingly, avatar feature choice was not influenced by the participants' sex role orientation. Instead, situational requirements expressed in the respective descriptions primarily impacted participants when they chose their avatars' features, independent of their individual sex role orientation. Thus, the results found for male and female participants were replicated for those with masculine and feminine sex role orientation.

Similar to the data analysis conducted for Hypothesis 2 and in order to test the overall selection strategy of avatar features, a 2-factor MANOVA was computed with participant sex role orientation (1 = masculine; 2 = feminine) and the stimulus pretest result (1 = "game requires primarily mas-

Table 5. Mean scores for masculine and feminine avatar attributes by participants with masculine or feminine sex role orientations

	Participants' sex role orientation	M masculine avatar attributes	M feminine avatar attributes	t	df	P
Game One: *The Sims* (feminine)	masculine	4.36	5.65	-4.604	53	< .001
	feminine	4.28	5.71	-4.887	76	< .001
Game Two: *My Animal Hospital* (feminine)	masculine	4.23	5.71	-3.663	52	.001
	feminine	4.14	5.58	-4.289	77	< .001
Game Three: *GTA: San Andreas* (masculine)	masculine	5.95	2.97	9.765	54	< .001
	feminine	5.86	3.26	6.835	74	< .001
Game Four: *Crysis* (masculine)	masculine	7.24	1.67	17.370	54	< .001
	feminine	7.15	1.55	19.581	80	< .001
Game Five: *Urban Chaos* (masculine)	masculine	6.81	2.04	12.792	53	< .001
	feminine	7.11	1.65	20.174	78	< .001
Scenario One: Pursuit (masculine)	masculine	6.95	1.41	18.889	54	< .001
	feminine	6.87	1.56	18.794	76	< .001
Scenario Two: Interviewing a witness (feminine)	masculine	3.66	6.59	-9.404	54	< .001
	feminine	3.81	6.50	-9.985	82	< .001

Note. Differences between the mean scores of masculine and feminine avatar attributes were tested with paired-sample t tests separately for participants with masculine or feminine sex role orientations. Varying degrees of freedom are due to missing data.

culine features"; 2 = "game requires primarily feminine features") as the fixed factors and the sum of masculine and feminine avatar features as dependent variables. Therefore the data were restructured in the same manner reported for Hypothesis 2, again resulting in 994 cases. The MANOVA showed no main effect for participant sex role orientation on the scores of feminine ($F(1, 965) = .087, p = .768, \eta^2 < .001$) or masculine ($F(1, 965) = .023, p = .879, \eta^2 < .001$) avatar features. In contrast, a significant main effect was found for the game requirements (pretest rated) on the scores of feminine ($F(1, 965) = 991.885, p < .001, \eta^2 = .174$) as well as masculine ($F(1, 965) = 615.122, p < .001, \eta^2 = .049$) avatar features. No interaction effects between participant sex role and game requirements were found for the scores of feminine ($F(1, 965) = .024, p = .877, \eta^2 < .001$) and masculine avatar features ($F(1, 965) = .078, p = .780, \eta^2 < .001$). Accordingly, participants' overall strategy for avatar feature choice was independent

of their own sex role, but significantly influenced by the situational requirements expressed in the descriptions. Thus, Hypothesis 3 was supported.

Hypothesis 4

Mann-Whitney U tests were computed for every game description and gaming scenario to detect differences in the choice of the avatars' biological sex between male and female participants (see Table 6). The results indicate that men chose male avatars significantly more often than women did. Further, women chose female avatars significantly more often than men did. These findings hold for all game descriptions as well as for Scenarios 1 and 2.

Accordingly, the participants' sex significantly influenced the choice of their avatars' biological sex, resulting in a preference for same-sex avatars. Thus, Hypothesis 4 is supported.

Table 6. Mean ranks for avatars' biological sex chosen by male and female participants

	Participants' sex	N	Mean rank of avatars' biological sex	Man-Whitney U	p
Game One: *The Sims* (feminine)	men	72	54.21	1275	<.001
	women	70	89.29		
Game Two: *My Animal Hospital* (feminine)	men	72	61.99	1835	.001
	women	70	81.29		
Game Three: *GTA: San Andreas* (masculine)	men	72	61.86	1826	<.001
	women	70	81.41		
Game Four: *Crysis* (masculine)	men	72	63.92	1974	.001
	women	70	79.30		
Game Five: *Urban Chaos* (masculine)	men	72	63.93	1975	.001
	women	70	79.29		
Scenario One: Pursuit (masculine)	men	72	65.94	2120	.006
	women	70	77.21		
Scenario Two: Interviewing a witness (feminine)	men	72	61.49	1799	<.001
	women	70	81.80		

Note. The scale ranges from 1 = "male" to 2 "female". Higher mean ranks indicate a higher tendency to choose avatars with the female biological sex.

DISCUSSION

The purpose of this study was to examine which strategy participants apply to create avatars in computer and video games. Altogether, the results illustrate the noteworthy interdependence between game contexts, participants' sex, strategies for avatar creation, and entertainment experience. Confirming our first hypothesis, participants evaluated the presented game and gaming scenario descriptions to be more entertaining if they encompassed a context designed to be mastered by an avatar with attributes of their own gender. Regarding avatar features, participants designed their ideal game character according to the requirements presented in the game and gaming scenario descriptions. Supporting the second and third hypotheses, these results occurred independently of participant sex and sex role orientation. Both men and women chose avatar features previously rated male when they expected to play games prejudged as "masculine". Conversely, both men and women preferred female features for avatars in games previously rated as feminine. These results suggest that in terms of avatar attributes, video game players prefer avatars designed to meet the requirements of the games. Yet when it comes to biological sex, men preferred male avatars and women favored female avatars, thus supporting the fourth hypothesis.

The results of this study allow for a wider generalization on computer mediated communication. Previous studies show that people react differently to different types of avatars and agents (Nowak & Rauh, 2008; Yee & Bailenson, 2007). The user's learning results and their interest as well as emotional variables such as empathy are influenced by the avatars' and agents' character and their visual representation (Bailenson, 2006; Bailenson & Beall, 2005; Ku et al., 2005; McQuiggan & Lester, 2007). The study presented in this chapter accordingly shows that the avatars' sex and their gender attributes are crucial for effects in computer mediated communication: If players

have the freedom to alter an avatar's sex and to influence their character in terms of gender, they prefer an avatar similar to their own sex role orientation. This might allow for the conclusion that computer mediated communication with same sex agents and avatars leads to better results in terms of learning, collaborating and acceptance of virtual representations.

Also, the results of our study contribute to a better understanding of entertainment experiences and of the relationship between game players and avatars. In the increasingly popular segment of casual games, many games such as puzzle or card games do not feature avatars (International Game Developers Association, 2006). But for other game genres, the variability of avatars is of growing importance. For massively multiplayer online role playing games (MMORPGs) such as "World of Warcraft", avatars—and the possibility to create individual avatars—play an important role for their popularity (Chan & Vorderer, 2006).

In line with previous studies, our results support the assumption that similarity between players and game characters can enhance the player's entertainment experience (Hsu et al., 2005). In addition to the work of Ogletree and Drake (2007) who demonstrated that men are more likely to select male avatars, whereas women are more likely to choose female avatars, our study shows that games are rated more entertaining if they require game characters with attributes that are perceived as being typical for one's own gender. The positive effect of gender similarity on entertainment is not only due to the sex of the avatar, but also depends on the game context requiring masculine or feminine attributes.

This result is particularly interesting from the perspective of game design. Content analyses show that the majority of video and computer games feature male characters, and that female characters are often presented in a sex-stereotyped way and as victims or subordinate to male characters (Children Now, 2001; Dietz, 1998). If female characters appear in a leading role in video games such as Lara Croft in "Tomb Raider" or Sonya Blade in "Mortal Combat", they often face tasks and challenges that require primarily masculine attributes like physical strength. The results of our study offer an explanation why such games are not more popular among women than similar games with male main characters: Even though the sex and appearance of game characters like Lara Croft is female, they have to act like male characters in order to be successful in these games. Graner Ray (2004) states that women are not satisfied playing manly characters for various reasons. First, they are not familiar with the dominant and very physical roles masculine characters very often play in computer games. Second, women are primarily interested in activity based games instead of goal oriented games. They might reach a feeling of accomplishment by transferring real life cognitions to a virtual world. Our results underline that games do not necessarily become more interesting to women by the appearance of female game characters as long as the game still requires primarily masculine attributes.

Furthermore, this may explain the preference of women for role playing aspects of games compared to the achievement and competition aspect of games (Hartmann & Klimmt, 2006a; Lucas & Sherry, 2004; Yee, 2007; Yee & Bailenson, 2007), and the increasing number of women playing MMORPGs (Griffiths et al., 2003, 2004). (Online) role playing games such as "The Elder Scrolls IV: Oblivion" (Bethesda Softworks/2kGames) or "World of Warcraft" (Blizzard Entertainment/ Vivendi) allow players to choose male or female characters and to change their appearance according to individual preferences (Chan & Vorderer, 2006). Moreover, players can choose among several classes of characters featuring different attributes and various professions requiring different skills. This means that in many (online) role playing games, players can decide to develop characters with other than primarily masculine attributes, e.g. healing skills. Role playing games also allow players to choose among a considerable

number of main and side quests. These quests (e.g., locating hidden items in the game environment, defeating an enemy) vary in terms of the skills or attributes required to master them. Thus players cannot only adjust the game character, but also the basic nature of the game demands. This may attract women in particular, because they do not have to focus on tasks that require primarily masculine attributes.

A similar explanation can be found for the enormous popularity of *The Sims* (Maxis/Electronic Arts) series among women. In these games, players can design their characters with respect to sex and physical appearance, and also with respect to personality traits. Female "sims" do not only look like females, but can act according to female sex roles, too.

Of course, game requirements as well as the players' own sex do not fully determine the experience of entertainment and the strategies applied to avatar creation. Prior research shows that the exposure to computer and video games depends on a variety of factors, e.g. motivations and expected gratifications (Sherry et al., 2006; Yee, 2007) or personality traits (Hartmann & Klimmt, 2006b; Slater, 2003). Motivation or personality traits also impact what kind of game content is perceived as entertaining, and can influence strategies of avatar creation as well. For example, the motivation to engage in social interaction in online gaming could override the requirements of an otherwise competitive game and lead to the design of a particularly attractive avatar instead of an avatar with high physical strength or magic abilities (cf. Yee & Bailenson, 2007). The interdependence between possible factors determining avatar creation is a promising direction of future research on the use of video and computer games and virtual worlds.

There are some limitations to this study and a hint of caution should be given when interpreting results: Participants received game descriptions as stimuli and they were subsequently asked to imagine an avatar they would like to play with. Although investigating the creation of avatars in *real* games could assess avatar choice behavior more directly, we decided to use this type of experimental manipulation for reasons of internal and external validity. Regarding internal validity, games allowing avatar creation often encompass very distinct features. In some games players can only change their avatar's appearance, in others appearance and biological sex, and in less restricted games even personality traits and physical attributes can be adjusted. Using existing games would thus limit stimulus comparability, because games have different contexts and task requirements in terms of their scope of avatar feature choices. Moreover, the influence of the presented game context on entertainment ratings would have been confounded with features such as graphics, game control mechanisms or sound, which differ from game to game.

In order to assure high external validity, game descriptions were based on existing games. We tried to remove all cues leading to an identification of the games, because recognizing the games behind the description may have influenced the participants' choices. Nevertheless, some game descriptions might be familiar to experienced game players even without direct identification cues. Thus we asked the participants whether the game descriptions sounded familiar to them and whether they had played such games before. It turned out that for *The Sims* and *GTA: San Andreas* the effect of sex on the rating of entertainment value was no longer significant when controlling for prior knowledge. Thus, additional knowledge about games may reduce the effect of sex on entertainment ratings. The presented descriptions highlight masculine or feminine task contexts as cues for the evaluation of the games' entertainment potential. The effect of these cues obviously decreases if the games are very popular like *The Sims* and *GTA: San Andreas* and if the participants possess additional information about the games. In this case, the participants might have rated the entertainment value of the games not only based on the described masculine or feminine task context,

but also based on additional information about the games such as graphics, humor, or story. Game playing experience in terms of individual playing time (hours per week) was also controlled for. The main effects remained significant except for the entertainment ratings of Game Three (*GTA: San Andreas*).

In sum, the results of our study shed light on who users of video and computer games want to be in these games. Similarity between players and their avatars increases entertainment experience, but only as far as similarity does not prevent from successful play. From that notion, the question arises whether people apply different strategies to create an alter ego for virtual worlds like Second Life or for games with a less competitive setting. In the absence narrowly defined game requirements, it might be of minor importance to create an avatar with features designed to master goals set by the context. Moreover, besides gendered attributes, other aspects such as personality traits may come into play. To this end, further research is needed to answer these questions.

REFERENCES

Ambady, N., & Gray, H. M. (2002). On being sad and mistaken: Mood effects on the accuracy of thin-slice judgments. *Journal of Personality and Social Psychology, 83*(4), 947–961. doi:10.1037/0022-3514.83.4.947

Anderson, D. R., Collins, P. A., Schmitt, K. L., & Smith Jacobvitz, R. (1996). Stressful life events and television viewing. *Communication Research, 23*(3), 243–260. doi:10.1177/009365096023003001

Bailenson, J. N. (2006). Transformed social interaction in collaborative virtual environments . In Messaris, P., & Humphreys, L. (Eds.), *Digital media: Transformations in human communication* (pp. 255–264). New York, NY: Peter Lang.

Bailenson, J. N., & Beall, A. C. (2005). Transformed social interaction: Exploring the digital plasticity of avatars. In Schroeder, R., & Axelsson, A. (Eds.), *Avatars at work and play: Collaboration and interaction in shared virtual environments* (pp. 1–16). Heidelberg, Germany: Springer.

Bailey, R., Wise, K., & Bolls, P. (2009). How avatar customizability affects children's arousal and subjective presence during junk food-sponsored online video games. *CyberPsycholgy & Behavior, 12*(3), 277–283. doi:10.1089/cpb.2008.0292

Bartholow, B. D., & Anderson, C. A. (2002). Effects of violent video games on aggressive behavior: Potential sex differences. *Journal of Experimental Social Psychology, 38*(3), 283–290. doi:10.1006/jesp.2001.1502

Beasley, B., & Standley, T. C. (2002). Shirts vs. skins: Clothing as an indicator of gender role stereotyping in video games. *Mass Communication & Society, 5*, 279–293. doi:10.1207/S15327825MCS0503_3

Behm-Morawitz, E., & Mastro, D. (2009). The effects of the sexualization of female video game characters on gender stereotyping and female self-concept. *Sex Roles, 61*(11-12), 808–823. doi:10.1007/s11199-009-9683-8

Bem, S. L. (1974). The measurement of psychological androgyny. *Journal of Consulting and Clinical Psychology, 42*(2), 155–162. doi:10.1037/h0036215

Bessière, K., Seay, F., & Kiesler, S. (2007). The ideal elf: Identity exploration in World of Warcraft. *Cyberpsychology & Behavior, 10*(4), 530–535. doi:10.1089/cpb.2007.9994

Burgess, M. C. R., Stermer, S. P., & Burgess, S. R. (2007). Sex, lies, and video games: The portrayal of male and female characters on video game covers. *Sex Roles, 57*(5-6), 419–433. doi:10.1007/s11199-007-9250-0

Chan, E., & Vorderer, P. (2006). Massively multiplayer online games. In Vorderer, P., & Bryant, J. (Eds.), *Playing video games. Motives, responses, and consequences* (pp. 77–88). Mahwah, NJ: Lawrence Erlbaum.

Children Now. (2000). *Girls and gaming: A console video game content analysis*. Oakland, CA: Children Now.

Children Now. (2001). *Fair play? Violence, gender, and race in video games*. Oakland, CA: Children Now.

Chumbley, J., & Griffiths, M. (2006). Affect and the computer game player: The effect of gender, personality, and game reinforcement structure on affective responses to computer game-play. *Cyberpsychology & Behavior, 9*(3), 308–316. doi:10.1089/cpb.2006.9.308

Cohen, J. (2001). Defining identification: A theoretical look at the identification of audiences with media characters. *Mass Communication & Society, 4*(3), 245–264. doi:10.1207/S15327825MCS0403_01

Diamond, M. (2002). Sex and gender are different: Sexual identity and gender are different. *Clinical Child Psychology and Psychiatry, 7*(3), 320–334. doi:10.1177/1359104502007003002

Dietz, T. L. (1998). An examination of violence and gender role portrayals in video games: Implications for gender socialization and aggressive behavior. *Sex Roles, 38*(5-6), 425–442. doi:10.1023/A:1018709905920

Digital Trends. (2006). *Nielsen: Video games getting more social*. Retrieved February 13, 2008, from http://news.digitaltrends.com/news/story/11464/nielsen_video_games_getting_more_social

Dill, K., Gentile, D., Richter, W., & Dill, J. (2005). Violence, sex, race and age in popular videogames. In Cole, E., & Daniel, J. (Eds.), *Featuring females: Feminist analysis of the media* (pp. 115–130). Washington, DC: American Psychological Association. doi:10.1037/11213-008

Dill, K. E., Brown, B. P., & Collins, M. A. (2008). Effects of exposure to sex-stereotyped video game characters on tolerance of sexual harassment. *Journal of Experimental Social Psychology, 44*(5), 1402–1408. doi:10.1016/j.jesp.2008.06.002

Dill, K. E., & Thill, K. P. (2007). Video game characters and the socialization of gender roles: Young people's perceptions mirror sexist media depictions. *Sex Roles, 57*(11-12), 851–864. doi:10.1007/s11199-007-9278-1

Donath, J. (2007). Virtually trustworthy. *Science, 317*, 53–54. doi:10.1126/science.1142770

Downs, E., & Smith, S. L. (2010). Keeping abreast of hypersexuality: A video game character content analysis. *Sex Roles, 62*(11-12), 721–733. doi:10.1007/s11199-009-9637-1

Dryer, D. C. (1999). Getting personal with computers: How to design personalities for agents. *Applied Artificial Intelligence, 13*, 273–295. doi:10.1080/088395199117423

Eastin, M. S. (2006). Video game violence and the female game player: Self- and opponent gender effects on presence and aggressive thoughts. *Human Communication Research, 32*, 351–372. doi:10.1111/j.1468-2958.2006.00279.x

Entertainment Software Association. (2010). *Sales, demographic and usage data. Essential facts about the computer and video game industry.* Retrieved September 16, 2010, from http://www.theesa.com/facts/pdfs/ESA_Essential_Facts_2010.PDF

Fox, J., & Bailenson, J. N. (2009). Virtual virgins and vamps: The effects of exposure to female characters' sexualized appearance and gaze in an immersive virtual environment. *Sex Roles, 61*(3-4), 147–157. doi:10.1007/s11199-009-9599-3

Gaggioli, A., Mantovani, F., Castelnuovo, G., Wiederhold, B., & Riva, G. (2003). Avatars in clinical psychology: A framework for the clinical use of virtual humans. *Cyberpsychology & Behavior, 6*(2), 117–125. doi:10.1089/109493103321640301

Gentile, D. A. (1993). Just what are sex and gender, anyway? *Psychological Science, 4*(2), 120–122. doi:10.1111/j.1467-9280.1993.tb00472.x

Graner Ray, S. (2004). *Gender inclusive game design. Expanding the market.* Hingham, MA: Charles River Media.

Griffiths, M. D., Davies, M. N. O., & Chappell, D. (2003). Breaking the stereotype: The case of online gaming. *Cyberpsychology & Behavior, 6*(1), 81–91. doi:10.1089/109493103321167992

Griffiths, M. D., Davies, M. N. O., & Chappell, D. (2004). Online computer gaming: A comparison of adolescent and adult gamers. *Journal of Adolescence, 27*, 87–96. doi:10.1016/j.adolescence.2003.10.007

Grodal, T. (2000). Video games and the pleasures of control. In Zillmann, D., & Vorderer, P. (Eds.), *Media entertainment. The psychology of its appeal* (pp. 197–213). Mahwah, NJ: Lawrence Erlbaum Associates.

Haninger, K., & Thompson, K. M. (2004). Content and ratings of teen-rated video games. *Journal of the American Medical Association, 291*, 856–865. doi:10.1001/jama.291.7.856

Hartmann, T., & Klimmt, C. (2006a). Gender and computer games: Exploring females' dislikes. *Journal of Computer-Mediated Communication, 11*(4). doi:10.1111/j.1083-6101.2006.00301.x

Hartmann, T., & Klimmt, C. (2006b). The influence of personality factors on computer game choice . In Vorderer, P., & Bryant, J. (Eds.), *Playing computer games: Motives, responses, and consequences* (pp. 115–131). Mahwah, NJ: Lawrence Erlbaum Associates.

Heeter, C., Egidio, R., Mishra, P., Winn, B., & Winn, J. (2009). Alien games: Do girls prefer games designed by girls? *Games and Culture*, *4*(1), 74–100. doi:10.1177/1555412008325481

Hsu, S. H., Kao, C.-H., & Wu, M.-C. (2007). Factors influencing player preferences for heroic roles in role-playing games. *Cyberpsychology & Behavior*, *10*(2), 293–295. doi:10.1089/cpb.2006.9955

Hsu, S. H., Lee, F. L., & Wu, M.-C. (2005). Designing action games for appealing to buyers. *Cyberpsychology & Behavior*, *8*(6), 585–591. doi:10.1089/cpb.2005.8.585

Hussain, Z., & Griffiths, M. D. (2008). Gender swapping and socializing in cyberspace: An exploratory study. *Cyberpsychology & Behavior*, *11*(1), 47–53. doi:10.1089/cpb.2007.0020

Information Solutions Group. (2007). *Women choose "casual" videogames over TV. 100 million+ women now play regularly, for different reasons than men*. Retrieved February 13, 2008, from http://www.infosolutionsgroup.com/press_release_A.htm

International Game Developers Association. (2006). *2006 casual games whitepaper*. Retrieved June 29, 2007, from http://www.igda.org/casual/IGDA_CasualGames_Whitepaper_2006.pdf

Ivory, J. D. (2006). Still a man's game: Gender representation in online reviews of video games. *Mass Communication & Society*, *9*(1), 103–114. doi:10.1207/s15327825mcs0901_6

Jansz, J., & Martis, R. G. (2007). The Lara phenomenon: Powerful female characters in video games. *Sex Roles*, *56*, 141–148. doi:10.1007/s11199-006-9158-0

Klimmt, C., & Hartmann, T. (2006). Effectance, self-efficacy, and the motivation to play video games . In Vorderer, P., & Bryant, J. (Eds.), *Playing video games: Motives, responses, and consequences* (pp. 133–145). Mahwah, NJ: Lawrence Erlbaum Associates.

Ku, J., Jang, H. J., Kim, K. U., Kim, J. H., Park, S. H., & Lee, J. H. (2005). Experimental results of affective valence and arousal to avatar's facial expressions. *Cyberpsychology & Behavior*, *8*(5), 493–503. doi:10.1089/cpb.2005.8.493

Lim, S., & Reeves, B. (2009). Being in the game: Effects of avatar choice and point of view on psychophysiological responses during play. *Media Psychology*, *12*, 348–370. doi:10.1080/15213260903287242

Lucas, K., & Sherry, J. L. (2004). Sex differences in video game play: A communication-based explanation. *Communication Research*, *31*, 499–523. doi:10.1177/0093650204267930

Martins, N., Williams, D. C., Harrison, L., & Ratan, R. A. (2009). A content analysis of female body imagery in video games. *Sex Roles*, *61*(11-12), 824–836. doi:10.1007/s11199-009-9682-9

McQuiggan, S. W., & Lester, J. C. (2007). Modeling and evaluating empathy in embodied companion agents. *International Journal of Human-Computer Studies*, *65*(4), 348–360. doi:10.1016/j.ijhcs.2006.11.015

Miller, M. K., & Summers, A. (2007). Gender differences in video game characters' roles, appearances, and attire as portrayed in video game magazines. *Sex Roles*, *57*(9-10), 733–742. doi:10.1007/s11199-007-9307-0

Norris, K. O. (2004). Gender stereotypes, aggression, and computer games: An online survey of women. *CyperPsychology & Behavior*, *7*(6), 714–727. doi:10.1089/cpb.2004.7.714

Nowak, K. L., & Rauh, C. (2005). The influence of the avatar on online perceptions of anthropomorphism, androgyny, credibility, homophily, and attraction. *Journal of Computer-Mediated Communication*, *11*(1), 153–178. doi:10.1111/j.1083-6101.2006.tb00308.x

Nowak, K. L., & Rauh, C. (2008). Choose your "buddy icon" carefully: The influence of avatar androgyny, anthropomorphism and credibility in online interactions. *Computers in Human Behavior*, *24*, 1473–1493. doi:10.1016/j.chb.2007.05.005

Ogletree, S. M., & Drake, R. (2007). College students' video game participation and perceptions: Gender differences and implications. *Sex Roles*, *56*, 537–542. doi:10.1007/s11199-007-9193-5

Pryzgoda, J., & Chrisler, J. C. (2000). Definitions of gender and sex: The subtleties of meaning. *Sex Roles*, *43*(7/8), 553–569. doi:10.1023/A:1007123617636

Quaiser-Pohl, C., Geiser, C., & Lehmann, W. (2006). The relationship between computer-game preference, gender, and mental-rotation ability. *Personality and Individual Differences*, *40*(3), 609–619. doi:10.1016/j.paid.2005.07.015

Reinhard, C. L. D. (2006, June 21-24). *Hypersexualized females in digital games: Do men want them, do women want to be them?* Paper presented at the 56th Annual Meeting of the International Communication Association, Dresden, Germany.

Rizzo, A. A., Neumann, U., Enciso, R., Fidaleo, D., & Noh, J. Y. (2001). Performance-driven facial animation: Basic research on human judgments of emotional state in facial avatars. *Cyberpsychology & Behavior*, *4*(4), 471–487. doi:10.1089/109493101750527033

Rymaszewski, M., Wagner, J. A., Wallace, M., Winters, C., Ondrejka, C., & Batstone-Cunningham, B. (2007). *Second Life-The official guide*. New Jersey: Wiley Publishing.

Sherry, J. L., Lucas, K., Greenberg, B. S., & Lachlan, K. (2006). Video game uses and gratifications as predictors of use and game preferences . In Vorderer, P., & Bryant, J. (Eds.), *Playing video games. Motives, responses, and consequences* (pp. 213–224). Mahwah, NJ & London, UK: Lawrence Erlbaum.

Slater, M. D. (2003). Alienation, aggression, and sensation seeking as predictors of adolescent use of violent film, computer, and website content. *The Journal of Communication*, *53*(1), 105–121. doi:10.1111/j.1460-2466.2003.tb03008.x

Smith, S. L. (2006). Perps, pimps, and provocative clothing: Examining negative content patterns in video games . In Vorderer, P., & Bryant, J. (Eds.), *Playing video games: Motives, responses, and consequences* (pp. 57–75). Mahwah, NJ: Lawrence Erlbaum Associates.

Tamborini, R., Grizzard, M., Bowman, N. D., Reinecke, L., Lewis, R., & Eden, A. (in press). Media enjoyment as need satisfaction: The contribution of hedonic and non-hedonic needs. *The Journal of Communication*.

The, N. P. D. Group. (2010). *20 percent of the U.S. population, or 56.8 million U.S. consumers, reports having played a game on a social network*. Retrieved September 16, 2010, from http://www.npd.com/press/releases/press_100823.html

Trepte, S., & Reinecke, L. (2010). Avatar creation and video game enjoyment: Effects of life-satisfaction, game competitiveness, and identification with the avatar. *Journal of Media Psychology*, *22*, 171–184. doi:10.1027/1864-1105/a000022

Trepte, S., & Reinecke, L. (in press). The pleasures of success: Game-related efficacy experiences as a mediator between player performance and game enjoyment. *Cyberpsychology, Behavior, and Social Networking.*

Unger, R. K. (1979). Toward a redefinition of sex and gender. *The American Psychologist, 34*(11), 1085–1094. doi:10.1037/0003-066X.34.11.1085

Vasalou, A., Joinson, A., Baenziger, T., Goldie, P., & Pitt, J. (2008). Avatars in social media: Balancing accuracy, playfulness and embodied messages. *International Journal of Human-Computer Studies, 66*(11), 801–811. doi:10.1016/j.ijhcs.2008.08.002

Whalen, T. E., Petriu, D. C., Yang, L., Petriu, E. M., & Cordea, M. D. (2003). Capturing behaviour for the use of avatars in virtual environments. *Cyberpsychology & Behavior, 6*(5), 537–544. doi:10.1089/109493103769710569

Williams, D., Martins, N., Consalvo, M., & Ivory, J. D. (2009). The virtual census: Representations of gender, race and age in video games. *New Media & Society, 11*(5), 815–834. doi:10.1177/1461444809105354

Yee, N. (2006). Motivations for play in online games. *Cyberpsychology & Behavior, 9*(6), 772–775. doi:10.1089/cpb.2006.9.772

Yee, N., & Bailenson, J. (2007). The proteus effect: The effect of transformed self-representation on behavior. *Human Communication Research, 33*, 271–290. doi:10.1111/j.1468-2958.2007.00299.x

ENDNOTES

1. Although often used interchangeably by lay persons and scientists alike (Pryzgoda & Chrisler, 2000), the terms *sex* and *gender* have distinct connotations. While the term *sex* is focused on biological differences between men and women, *gender* refers to the socially and culturally based differences in traits and behaviors of males and females (Diamond, 2002; Gentile, 1993; Pryzgoda & Chrisler, 2000; Unger, 1979). Accordingly, the term *sex* implies biological mechanisms (Unger, 1979) and encompasses "traits or conditions that are causally biologically linked to the condition of being male or female" (Gentile, 1993, p. 120) whereas *gender* comprises "nonphysiological components of sex that are culturally regarded as appropriate to males or to females" (Unger, 1979 p. 1086). The term *sex role* refers to the degree an individual has "internalized society's sex-typed standards of desirable behavior for men and women" (Bem, 1974, p. 155), i.e. the individual's self-concept with respect to masculine and feminine behaviors.

2. This study was first published as Trepte, S., Reinecke, L., & Behr, K.-M. (2009). Creating virtual alter egos or superheroines? Gamers' strategies of avatar creation in terms of gender and sex. *International Journal of Gaming and Computer-Mediated Simulations, 1*(2), 52-76. The present chapter provides an updated version of this journal article.

APPENDIX 1

Descriptions of the computer games used in this study. The official names (in parentheses) were not presented to participants.

Game One (*The Sims*)

In this game it is your job to manage a neighborhood inhabited by a variety of different game characters – their lives are in your hand. Create a character and build a house for it. Help your character to make a career, earn money, make friends and fall in love – or turn its life upside down! There is no right or wrong in this game. Test your character's skills by confronting it with the blows of life - challenging and entertaining situations. Family and friends, career and chaos – you're the only one who can help your character to get through all of this!

Game Two (*My Animal Hospital*)

This is an exciting game where you can run your own *animal hospital*. You examine and medicate fully-grown and baby animals, from puppies to foals. Bit by bit, you can build and equip new vivariums, buy new medical instruments and even found a horse clinic. While building your career you can earn lots of awards.

Game Three (*Grand Theft Auto: San Andreas*)

Five years ago you managed to escape from the problems of Los Santos, a city in the state of San Andreas that is drowning in gang wars, drugs and corruption. A city in which movie stars and millionaires try to get out of the way of dealers and gangs as much as they can. Now – we're in the early 90ies – you have to go back. Your mother has been murdered, your family has broken apart and your old friends are on the road to perdition. But shortly after returning to your old home, a bunch of corrupt cops are chasing you for a murder you didn't commit. You have to get away and the trip must lead you through San Andreas to rescue your family and gain control over the streets.

Game Four (*Crysis*)

In the year 2019, a massive asteroid crashes into an island chain belonging to North Korea. The country's government isolates the whole island chain immediately, claiming the secrets of the mysterious asteroid for themselves. The United States send an elite team of the Delta Force Operators to analyze the situation and to send a report to the Pentagon. As the tensions between the USA and North Korea start to escalate, the asteroid bursts open and reveals a huge, extraterrestrial spaceship, more than 2 kilometers high. It is surrounded by a huge dome of energy which freezes most parts of the island. The invasion of the earth has begun. The two rivaling nations form an alliance to stop the aliens and to save the human race. The allies fight epic battles against the aggressive aliens. While hope is waning rapidly, you are guiding an elite troupe through the deep jungle, frozen landscapes and, eventually, into the heart of the aliens' ship where the ultimate battle with the enemy forces is fought in zero gravity.

Game Five (*Urban Chaos*)

A city at the verge of total chaos is terrorized by a gang. You and your elite crew T-Zero, especially trained for the war against terror, are the last hope in this fast-paced game. Take over the role of a T-zero member, get a reputation, expand your armory and make life miserable for the gang members. Intense hostage scenarios: Keep your nerves to place the perfect shot. Take over control and command America's best firemen, paramedics and policemen.

APPENDIX 2

Descriptions of gaming situations. The titles (in parentheses) were not presented to participants.

Scenario One (Pursuit)

You are about to arrest a wanted criminal. The suspect is fleeing through the cellars and backyards of the neighborhood. You can't follow him with your car and you are on your own with no backup in sight. To arrest him, you will have to chase him on foot. Hurry up: The suspect is aggressive and will resist his arrest; he is probably even carrying a gun!

Scenario Two (Interviewing a Witness)

You have to interview a witness in a homicide, the victim's widow. The old lady has observed the murder. During the first encounter with the police right after the deed, she was very scared and not willing to provide any information. Obviously she doesn't like the police. However, the information is very important. Hence you have to contact the old lady again and try talk to her.

Chapter 20
Investigating Perceptions of Avatar Creation for Use in Educational MUVEs

Joseph DiPietro
University of Florida, USA

ABSTRACT

The purpose of this qualitative inquiry is to extend the investigation of perceptions and experiences of users creating avatars for interactions in online learning environments. Using Linden Lab's Second Life, volunteers created three-dimensional representations of themselves, called avatars, under the premise of participating in a hypothetical online class. Avatar creation sessions were book-ended with pre- and post- interviews focused on participant perceptions of various elements of self-representation and interactions as situated in online environments. Human computer interactions (HCI) of avatar creation were also explored. Findings indicate users created avatars that mirrored their respective physical appearances as closely as possible and were collectively adamant in feeling morally obliged to do so.

INTRODUCTION

Multi User Virtual Environments (MUVEs) and Massive Multiplayer Online Role Playing Games (MMORPGs) are exponentially growing sectors of a billion dollar industry (Entertainment Software Association, 2009). Worldwide fervor for online, subscription-based titles like Blizzard Entertainment's *World of Warcraft* (*WoW*) clearly exemplifies the demand as, according to their Web site (2008), the company boasted over 11.5 million active accounts just a month after *WoW*'s fourth anniversary. Interaction within subscription-based worlds requires users to purchase software and pay an additional monthly fee, usually ranging between US$10 and US$15 per month (Cyber

DOI: 10.4018/978-1-60960-565-0.ch020

Creations Inc., 2009). This fee entitles access to new content that is added via downloadable software patches on a regular basis.

Unlike subscription-based applications, free-to-play (F2P) titles provide the core software at no cost and do not require recurring monthly fees. Rather, these games and simulations sell various perks to their users that are not necessarily required but are usually highly desired by their respective populations. *Runescape* is a F2P game boasting over 120 million registered accounts since 2001 with an average 8.5 million of those still active each month (Gibson, 2008). Another F2P application is Linden Lab's *Second Life* (*SL*), an online simulation focused on social interaction. Some recent reports from Linden Lab have claimed as many as 16 million "residents" inhabiting the virtual world, yet only around a million of these users log in each month (2009a).

Jonassen, Carr, and Yueh (1998) refer to these virtual spaces as "microworlds" and purport they "are perhaps the ultimate example of active learning environments, because the users can exercise so much control over the environment" (p. 27). Participants in MUVEs interact with each other and their virtual surroundings through self-representations called avatars. Users are free to create their avatars as they see fit and are limited only by whatever constraints or restrictions may be set in place by the software manufacturers. As online learning environments continue to shift from text-based, direct instruction models to more immersive and engaging polymodal paradigms, educational institutions are seeking to incorporate various aspects of MUVEs, namely avatars, into their academic programs.

SL is a prime example of a F2P MUVE being employed as a tool for distance learning (Conklin, 2007). The Open University, Harvard, Texas State, and Stanford are examples of major research institutions that own virtual real estate in *SL* where users create avatars in order to interact with one another, their instructors, as well as academic content (Linden Lab, 2009b). Picciano and Seaman

(2009) reported a 47% increase in K-12 student participation in online courses between 2005–2006 and 2007–2008 and most colleges and universities with online programs exceed this growth. The logical conclusion is that all instructors, regardless of grade level focus or subject area expertise, should be as informed as possible regarding their respective student populations. Academia has held its watchful gaze on first-world and F2F interactions for centuries, and only recently has this focus shifted to the exploration of text-based online interactions.

A void exists within academic literature related to self-representation within MUVEs and the decision-making processes behind avatar creation. Further investigation within this realm could lead to the answering of important questions of equity and to the determination of whether people are treated differently in MUVEs based on personal choices of self-representation. Akin to seminal research focusing on first-world interactions between teacher and pupil (Clark & Clark, 1950; Rosenthal & Jacobson, 1992), human-avatar interactions must be investigated in hopes of adding to the scientific body of knowledge concerning effective instruction in virtual environments. As distance-based models of education grow in popularity and number, the need for further research in this emerging realm is paramount in order to ensure equitable, high quality instruction for all students. If the exponential growth of distance education continues, online courses and virtual learning environments could well become the dominant form of instruction in the very near future.

The vast majority of interactions inherent to MUVEs are analogous to first-world ones. Users can synchronously chat via text or voice, congregate within virtual spaces, and even collaborate to accomplish common goals, tasks, or quests. An important difference between reality and its virtual counterpart is that users often have greater control over personal appearance within online spaces given the ability to self-represent via an avatar. As Turkle (1995) explained, "You can be whoever you want to be. You can completely redefine yourself if you want. You can be the opposite sex. You can be more talkative. You can be less talkative. Whatever..." (p. 184). There is little we can do to alter most aspects of our first-world physical forms without extensive effort and/or surgery, yet MUVE participants are free to assume physical representations drastically different from their first-world ones with minimal effort or expense. This freedom makes it possible for light-skinned people to create avatars with very dark skin tones, for women to assume male personas (and vice versa), and for near infinite possibilities regarding the alteration of one's self-representation for use in MUVEs.

Important research studies have investigated aspects of avatars from various perspectives including effect on physical behavior (Yee, 2007), perceptions of attractiveness (Nowak & Rauh, 2005), and methodological analysis of user creation (DiPietro & Black, 2008). The body of knowledge is growing, but there is a dire need in regards to research of perceptions of self-representation in online environments. If MUVEs, and/or elements thereof, are going to be used for educational purposes, we would do well to explore how users create themselves within these virtual spaces and why they make the choices that they do regarding self-representation.

The qualitative inquiry investigates why people choose to represent themselves in particular fashions within online learning environments in hopes of better understanding the social dynamics of educational MUVEs. Since interactions within virtual environments most frequently occur between avatars, research and discussion in this area will advance the scientific body of knowledge focused on using MUVEs and MMORPGs for academic purposes. In order to distance the researcher from the data, as well as to gain the participants' respective insights into the avatar creation process, a series of phenomenological interviews were conducted with participants of varying technological expertise focused around

the research question: "How do users perceive the avatar creation process intended for use in educational online environments?"

METHODS

Subjectivity and Bias

The researcher's primary bias is rooted in the theoretical concept of a false perception of impunity and/or anonymity exhibited by the vast majority of computer users operating in online environments. Whether simply perusing the Web for news articles or battling orcs online, the researcher believes that most users are novices in terms of many technical aspects related to computing. They may fail to realize that surfing the Internet, making online transactions, and communicating with others via synchronous or asynchronous modalities leaves a unique trial of identifiers that are as easily traceable as fingerprints. It is the belief of the researcher that this false sense of anonymity bolsters expectations of impunity and affords individuals with the opportunity to behave and express themselves in ways they may typically avoid in real life situations.

A secondary researcher bias relates to avatars themselves. Avatars are digital representations of self used for a variety of online activities. They can be anything from pictures, emoticons or smiley faces, to multi-dimensional characters like those created in this study. This fundamental tenet manifests in the researcher's belief that avatars will match the purpose for which they will be used. For example, an avatar intended for use in a gaming environment would tend to be much less formal than an avatar created for interaction in a distance education program.

Theory

Phenomenology was employed as an interview framework for this study in hopes of best distancing researcher from participants. In order to most efficiently, effectively, and impartially observe and understand the creation process through the eyes and minds of volunteers, this theoretical framework proved the most logical fit. Schwandt (2001) purports phenomenology is "more oriented toward describing the experience" of subjects thus reducing researcher bias (p. 115). Examining respective perceptions of self-representation through avatars in this study likened itself to Crotty's (1998) concept of exploring conscious phenomena due to the learning curve associated with the avatar creation task engaged in by participants (p. 78). The incorporation of "bracketing" (Crabtree & Miller, 1992; Hatch, 2002) was a crucial step in implementing this phenomenological methodology helping to separate the researcher's preconceived notions or hypotheses from actual findings or implications gleaned from collected data.

Description of Participants

Participants included three White female graduate students attending a large, southeastern university. Recruitment procedures were basic and consisted only of placing 8.5 x 11-inch signs around high traffic areas within the college of education on the university's campus. The study's focus was concisely described on the recruitment signage, but all individuals that expressed interest were then given a complete explanation of all related procedures via e-mail. Word of mouth proved beneficial and three volunteers offered to participate and agreed to Institutional Review Board requirements within the first week of sign placement. The first three volunteers agreeing to all study requirements were selected. Participants exhibited varying degrees of technological expertise, and all had participated in at least one online course. None had any prior experience with *SL*.

Participant 1: "Angela"

The first volunteer was assigned the pseudonym "Angela." She was friendly and open regarding the task presented to her despite her self-professed novice level of technological savvy. Angela frequently asked questions when new ideas or concepts were presented to her, and she often furrowed her brow as if deep in thought. She seemed surprised by the concept of avatar usage in MUVEs and shared that she did not see much value in game and simulation environments. She shared prior knowledge of online self-representation through the use of two-dimensional photographs but not through three-dimensional means. Angela described online environments as functional tools best exemplified by e-mail or the Internet *in toto*.

Angela regarded her family as her number one priority in life and dismissed the possibility of using online environments for communication or socialization unless her family co-inhabited said environments. When asked about interacting through an avatar within MUVEs like *SL*, Angela expressed little interest stating she would consider it only if "my family were here and this was the only way I got to interact with them." Angela also shared a lack of personal time as the biggest factor limiting her personal exploration of various technological tools including *SL*. She shared, "For me, time is of the essence so I have to be real careful about where I deposit that time." When asked about using MUVEs, and *SL* in general, she added, "I wouldn't deposit a lot of time here."

Participant 2: "Barbara"

The second volunteer, "Barbara," was outgoing and positive about engaging in this study. She was inquisitive to the extreme bordering on bubbly. Barbara was talkative throughout both interviews and was noticeably excited about creating her avatar and also about discussing it during her post-creation interview. She understood how MUVEs could be used for entertainment as well as education, but expressed no interest in exploring virtual worlds on her own time. She expressed a keen disinterest in fantasy and saw little value in engaging in MUVEs outside of an educational setting.

She listed e-mail, the Internet, online games, and synchronous online chat as primary examples of possible online environments. She had experience in online courses from both ends describing those she engaged in as a student and polycombased courses she had taught. When initially asked about her experiences with online environments, Barbara went into great detail recounting the story of meeting her husband as she excitedly shouted, "Online? I met my husband online!"

Participant 3: "Cathy"

The final participant, "Cathy," was quiet and reserved throughout her interviews and avatar creation session. She was intense, noticeably concentrating on wording her responses to individual questions and was equally methodical regarding her avatar modifications. Cathy initially seemed guarded about sharing her personal experiences with online environments, but this reluctance waned throughout the session. She expressed a possible interest in participating in MUVEs but was unsure of how and where to begin.

Cathy defined online environments to include e-mail, the Internet, teaching applications, synchronous online chat, and online games (including several MUVEs). She shared a variety of past teaching experiences including polycom-based courses, blended models, as well as fully online ones. When asked about previous experiences representing herself online she shared stories of using two-dimensional photographs of her pets in lieu of avatar-based self-representation.

Data Collection

In order to most effectively separate the researcher from data collection, and to glean participants' own perceptions of the avatar creation process, a series of semi-structured interviews were conducted built around the research question, "How do users perceive the avatar creation process intended for use in educational online environments?" The interview sessions were divided into a pre-creation interview, an avatar creation session, and a post-creation interview. No time limits were enacted for any phase of data collection and appropriate probing questions were used when necessary.

Following the pre-creation interview, participants were asked to create an avatar using *SL*. Volunteers were informed that all aspects of their human-computer interaction (HCI) would be recorded using a screen capture program called *Camtasia* (2005). HCI was recorded in *.avi format at 30 frames per second allowing clear and fluid view of all actions carried out by participants during avatar creation; this is explained fully in the *HCI FINDINGS* section of this article. While volunteers were interacting with the *SL* avatar creation software, observational journal notes were taken. Information discussed during pre-creation interview sessions, body language, and all questions asked in relation to the *SL* application (and research process in general) were also recorded.

As a follow up, the researcher again recorded observational journal notes after volunteers left their respective sessions. Aspects related to post-creation interviews or researcher afterthoughts

Table 1. Pre-creation interview questions

| 1) Describe your past experiences with online environments. |
| 2) Describe characteristics of yourself you would represent in an online environment. |
| 3) Describe characteristics of yourself you would not represent in an online environment. |

Table 2. Post-creation interview questions

1) Describe the impressions and feelings you experienced during the creation of your avatar.
2) Describe your perceptions of this avatar as an ideal representation of yourself for use in an online environment.
3) Describe how you could modify your avatar to maximize your comfort level with using it as a self-representation in an online environment.

were documented during this time and referenced when necessary during follow-up member checks.

Data Analysis

Upon completion of interview transcription (roughly 90 minutes total), all raw text was formatted using a word processing program into a series of three text boxes. The left text box was simply used for line numbering, the center box for verbatim transcription data, and the right text box was used for research notes, annotations, and coding. Coding emerged from an inductive approach (Hatch, 2002) and data from each participant's interviews and observational reflection journal entries were viewed as a whole in order to help draw out overarching themes or trends. Codes took shape in the following form:

The category of "Expectations – self" refers to the volunteers sharing that intrinsic factors and motivation have an effect on the creation of avatars. All participants were aware of and referred to internal motivations driving their choices of creation and selection. For example, Barbara shared her goal in avatar creation was, "To make sure that it was more like me. So, um, I guess to make it more accurate." This "right-or-wrong" style of thinking is echoed throughout participant interviews in relation to "Expectations – self."

Conversely, "Expectations – others" implies participants discussing extrinsic factors placed on individuals also has an effect on choices regarding avatar creation. Participants spoke of wanting to be favorably viewed by other members of the hypothetical online class despite the lack of face-to-face (F2F) interactions. A powerful instance of this was shared by Angela who offered, "I wouldn't want people to get an impression of me that's not what I am or … or to learn too much about me."

Also interwoven throughout the interviews was the concept of "Uses." This concept refers to the intended functionality of the avatar from the perspective of the creator. Participants were aware of the designed intent for their avatar's interactions in this study as it was presupposed that participation was intended to take place in a hypothetical online class. Participants collectively operated within this set context. Succinctly, "Uses" comes from the perspective of the avatar creator and relates to those comments where the user felt empowered. Participants were fully aware of the virtual system in which their avatars would exist yet often discussed the effects of first-world social pressures on choices regarding self-representation. They also referred to their avatars by the gender-specific pronouns "she" and "her" rather than the gender-neutral "it."

Interview Findings

Findings discussed in this section highlight only similarities shared between participants. Given the homogenous nature of the volunteer sample and strict adherence to interview protocols, differences between subject perceptions failed to emerge.

Table 3. Codes used in transcript and observational journal analysis

Expectations – self	Expectations – others	Uses

1. Participants Sought to Create Avatars that Mirrored Themselves

Despite varied levels of technological expertise and familiarity with online environments, there were significant commonalities present between interview participants. Perhaps the most notable of the findings was the inherent desire for avatars to mirror the creator. Realism was a clear focus for all participants and deviations from a state of actual representation was frowned upon greatly. When asked about what personal characteristics she would be comfortable sharing online, Angela noted, "I've pretty much represented myself by who I am. I guess my name, my name is out there. My professional credentials are out there." Following her avatar creation, she offered:

That's a personality thing. I mean, I think it's important for a person to see you are who you get not that you have to hide behind some kind of façade of who you'd like to be or something. I think that's just that I don't need to pretend to be something I'm not.

Barbara added her own perspective following avatar creation by sharing, "I wanted to be able to be honest and represent who I was so that their impression would be 'that's who this girl is' and 'that's what she looks like.'" This desire for realistic self-representation was also shared by Cathy in her musing that:

Well, if you like your good qualities then you wouldn't want to change them. But if there is something that you don't necessarily favor then you would project that so I guess that this is really my fantasy self.

The knowledge that one could alter their self-representation was clearly shared between participants. The willingness to deviate from a photorealistic self, however, did not manifest itself in any creation session. The shared meme existed

that this avatar was to be used for an academic setting and should thus be as accurate to one's true self as possible with absolutely no exception.

2. Intrinsic Motivations Stressed Openness and Honesty through Avatar-Representation

It is also of note that given the purpose of interaction for this hypothetical online environment, volunteers were willing to share more information than they normally would in F2F environments. F2F interactions place responsibility on the participant at all times and relationships must be constantly given effort. Some online interactions allow users to escape these complications and this was a clear theme shared by participants. Few factors were offered by interview subjects relating to information they would not share.

Barbara met her husband of two years through the use of an online dating site, yet professed that she would not share personally identifying information such as:

Social Security number. I wouldn't put my actual address. I would say [city name omitted], [state name omitted] though. But I wouldn't put my street address. I wouldn't put my phone number. It actually took me a long time to buy anything online too because I was a little leery of credit card numbers going across the Internet, but I've given in to that.

Cathy jokingly laughed about what she considered taboo. She would not share information about, "Weight, politics, or religion." She rhetorically grinned, "Aren't those the big three?"

Angela was staunch in her views and discussed her desire to eschew misleading others. She shared her need to avoid doing anything that:

Would cause people to get a false impression of me or to learn too much about me that's not what I want to put forth. I guess, like, I probably wouldn't put my age because I don't think that's relevant, whatever that is, but, um, I probably wouldn't put, um, I was going to say my location but the fact that it says [university name omitted]. edu gives it away.

3. The Purposes for Which Avatars are Ceated with Help Shape Participant Choices Regarding Creation

The final common belief exhibited by participants in this study is that the purpose of online interactions helps to shape volunteers' choices regarding exactly how they want to represent themselves. This may seem commonsensical, but the richness of data offered by interview subjects is truly telling.

Angela mused that:

Who you present really determines your purpose for participating because I guess if I were a single person I would be there thinking I might have done it a little bit differently thinking that maybe I'm looking for a partner or something like that so I might have made myself a little different. But, I'm not, so I wanted to project myself as my true self.

Barbara offered:

It was fun playing around to see what it would look like with bigger boobs or a bigger butt. That was funny. I guess I just identified with it. I thought it was me so like I'm saying I saw the bigger butt and was like oh that's funny.

Cathy told of the first time she was asked to choose an avatar for self-representation for use in an online course. She shared, "I wasn't comfortable putting up a picture so I put up a picture of my cat." She felt her choice of representation offered professional insight into her compassionate nature and love of animals. During her post-creation interview, however, Cathy expressed her comfort at digital self-representation through her

avatar emphatically smiling and nodding as she asserted, "I think she looks like me."

Participants as a whole wanted to represent themselves professionally and as accurately as possible for use in an online educational environment. Although they were not completely satisfied with the outcome of their avatar, all agreed that their creations would be acceptable self-representations to be used in an educational setting. All participants were also open in admitting that they would be willing to share more personal information within an online environment as opposed to a F2F settings but ambiguity surfaced in terms of whether this was due to the hypothetical educational setting framing the study or the use of a self-representative avatar. Finally, participants agreed that the purpose of an online environment is a critical element shaping the avatar creation process and that there are no exceptions or deviations to be made when considering this rule.

HCI Findings

HCI for all participants was gathered using a screen recording program as users created their respective avatars. Avatar creation is rooted in HCI whereby the user inputs decisions of how to represent their virtual appearance into an avatar creation engine. The avatar engine in *SL* is highly robust and affords an exhaustive number of variables for manipulation. The researcher wanted to view the actions of each participant as they engaged with the avatar creation engine in the least obtrusive possible fashion. This information was analyzed through inductive methods (Hatch, 2002) in a similar fashion to interview analysis.

Research regarding the analysis of HCI screen capture data and its application to online environments is sparse at best. Dutton and Consalvo (2006) note that "previous empirical work in the area of game studies has taken two main approaches" investigating only "the audience for games (the players) or critiques of the games themselves" (p. 1). Studies conducted by researchers such as

Figure 1. Avatar creation samples

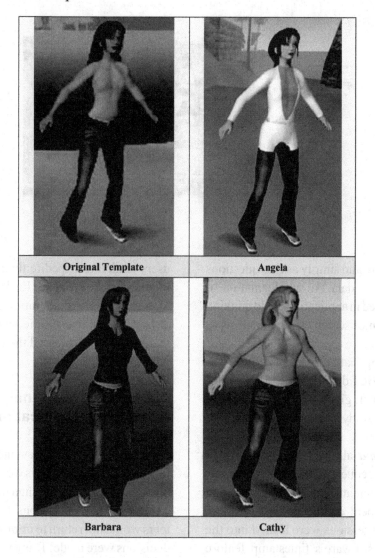

Fabricatore, Nussbaum, and Rosas (2002) adhere to this convention as they investigate the quality of games, but not the way people interact or how they choose the represent themselves within the game environment. Researchers such as Holliday (2000) question and explore reasons why video, and indeed visual representations more generally, have been largely ignored in the social sciences, and why the possibilities of video as an empirical source have been sidelined by cultural studies. Pink (2001a) explores the potential of video for a reflexive approach to qualitative research in sociology and anthropology; she also examines how recent interdisciplinary exchanges have portrayed the founding disciplines in visual research and representation through a focus on visual anthropology.

Combining the collective works of Pink (2001b, 2004) along with other researchers such as Grbich (2007) proved a most logical foundation for analysis. Employing inductive, reflexive, and critical inquiry into HCI via ethnographic content analysis is a research-based and practical method of inquiry. More simply, looking at an avatar in the

Figure 2. Transana in action

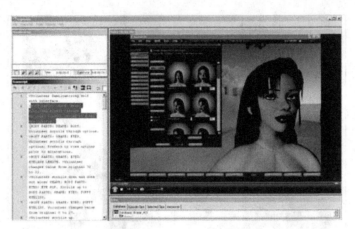

context of this study and simply asking questions afforded a wealth of data. An amalgamation of perspectives resulted in application of old thinking to the new medium of screen capture analysis as a video data source.

The software application *Transana* (2007) was used to facilitate HCI data analysis. It is of importance to note that, given the low numbers of participants in this study and its depth not breadth style of inquiry, only overarching themes are discussed. *Transana* allowed for the thorough examination of the sequence in which participants interacted with avatar attribute manipulation and overall time on spent on the task of creation. Recorded creation sessions were loaded into the program and the software's timestamp feature allowed for the addition of coded annotations to supplement mouse movements and participant interaction with their respective avatars. The end result was a real-time and synergistic data source providing a variety of findings.

1. Time-on-Task Reduced Over Time

The first finding relates to users' time on task. It is clear that volunteers spent a great deal of time at the beginning of a creation session familiarizing themselves with the software interface, general presentation, and ordering of character attribute data. As their creation session continued, however,

users tended to expedite their movements making them more efficient. Lack of familiarity with *SL*'s slider-style of alteration proved an obstacle at first, but all users' time on task for individual manipulations decreased the longer they worked with the application.

2. Choices Were Final and Users Did Not Revisit Modifications Once Made

Secondly, users seldom revisited alterations made to their avatars. Volunteers would view a particular attribute, change it, and then move on to the next. There were few exceptions, but generally volunteers would not return to implement changes once decisions were made. There was no commonality shared between the few factors participants did revisit within respective creation sessions. Great hesitance was often observed by the researcher as participants tilted their heads and/or squinted at their computer monitors as if trying to view their avatar from a different perspective.

3. The Creation Process was Viewed as Linear and was Directed by the Second Life Avatar Creation Software

A third finding could be best described as volunteers viewing avatar creation as a linear process.

Users chose to alter attributes in the order that they were presented rather than in the order of their own choosing. They were never instructed to complete the creation in any particular way, yet all users formed their avatars in the order set forth by *SL*'s user interface. Participants sequentially progressed through the modification of each individual aspect of their avatars as if checking off items on a list.

4. Participants Focused Most Attention on Modifying Gender-Based Sexual Characteristics

Finally, volunteers spent the most time altering their faces, hair, and primary sex characteristics, such as breast size and hip dimensions, as opposed to the host of secondary traits available in the avatar creation software. Little attention was given to tertiary factors like ear or foot size. The *SL* avatar creation software is incredibly detailed and allows users to customize the most seemingly insignificant of minutia, from factors such as ear lobe attachment level to shin length. Volunteers unanimously focused on the qualities of self for their virtual representations that they deemed most important for communication followed by those they most closely identified with in their first-world existences.

IMPLICATIONS

Given the growth and evolution of distance education, coupled with the transitioning trend of text-based to three-dimensional online learning environments, avatar studies are quickly becoming an important area of research. Developing a framework for exploring avatar creation and self-representation in online environments is a critical component in ensuring that high quality learning environments are made available for all students. Studies, like the one described in this article, are forming the framework for this

to take place. Continuing the discussion of and exploration into avatars and their creators is a vital component if we are to bridge the distance between current online education and the virtual classrooms of the future.

This study is only a first step in encouraging researchers to turn their attention toward the virtual and begin developing procedures and processes that will help create viable online educational content that best meets the needs of tomorrow's diverse learning populations. If participants creating avatars for online educational environments insist upon realism, first-world biases may affect how students are treated and how MUVE interactions take place. Clearly, more inquiry is needed to ensure the needs of students are actually being met and that best practices of online education continue to evolve along with corresponding technologies. Continued study into self-representation in online environments will allow for the development of best practices regarding instructional strategies in MUVEs. This research hopes to fill in some of the gaps about how we represent ourselves online and highlight why those choices of representation matter.

The current shift in various presentation modalities places great responsibility on instructors and researchers alike. Once hailed cutting edge technologies are becoming ubiquitous and arguably expected elements of the modern classroom. MUVEs such as *SL* may encourage collaboration and the fostering of individuality but they also require that instructors using them be informed of the choices users are making in regards to self-representation in order to ensure positive interactions for all participants. Seminal educational research on F2F perceptions and interactions in the classroom, such as Jane Elliott's *Blue Eyes Brown Eyes Exercise* (Bloom, 2005), has demonstrated the power of categorizing and dangers of stereotyping learners.

Rapport building is an integral part of successful teaching and avatar-to-avatar interactions must be better understood if we hope to foster relationship building and instructional efficacy in MUVEs. Simply transposing past F2F educational findings to online environments is not an option. It is critical to consider how choices in representation may affect online interactions if we are to ensure all students are equitably educated with maximum efficacy. Researchers and instructors alike would do well to consider what elements of assumption, bias, and/or innate first-world tendencies of prejudgment transfer into online environment and to better understand user choices regarding self-representation in online environments.

In MUVEs, instructors and students alike are afforded great freedom regarding self-representation through avatar creation. Future studies focused on investigating time on task and proportional distribution of attention to specific characteristics will help to refine superfluous avatar creation engines intended for educational use. Heterogeneous populations will be investigated to broaden the applicability of avatar creation studies like this one. Continued inquiry will also better inform instructors on aspects of avatars requiring the most attention in order to best connect with the widest spectrum of learners. For example, if users pay most attention to facial features when creating avatars, course instructors would do well to mimic this trend in creation of their own. Once we know more about avatars and avatar-based interactions, we can help to shape best practices for implementation for the classrooms of tomorrow.

REFERENCES

Blizzard Entertainment. (2008). *Media alert*. Retrieved June 3, 2009, from http://www.blizzard.com/us/press/081121.html

Bloom, S. G. (2005). Lesson of a lifetime: Her bold experiment to teach Iowa third graders about racial prejudice divided townspeople and thrust her onto the national stage. Decades later, Jane Elliott's students say the ordeal changed them for good. *Smithsonian, 36*(6), 82–93.

Camtasia Studio 3.0 [Computer software]. (2005). Okemos, MI: TechSmith. Retrieved from http://www.techsmith.com

Clark, K. B., & Clark, M. P. (1950). Emotional factors in racial identification and preference in Negro children. *The Journal of Negro Education, 19*(3), 341–350. doi:10.2307/2966491

Conklin, M. (2007). *101 uses for Second Life in the college classroom*. Retrieved June 3, 2009, from http://facstaff.elon.edu/mconklin/pubs/glshandout.pdf

Crabtree, B. F., & Miller, W. L. (1992). *Doing qualitative research*. Newbury Park, CA: Sage.

Crotty, M. (1998). *The foundations of social research*. London: Sage.

Cyber Creations Inc. (2009). *MMORPG Gamelist*. Retrieved June 3, 2009, from http://www.mmorpg.com/gamelist.cfm

DiPietro, J., & Black, E. (2008). Visual analysis of avatars in gaming environments. In R. E. Ferdig (Ed.), *Handbook of research on effective electronic gaming in education* (pp. 606-620). Hershey, PA: IGI Global.

Dutton, N., & Consalvo, M. (2006). Game analysis: Developing a methodological toolkit for the qualitative study of games. *The International Journal of Computer Game Research, 6*(1). Retrieved June 3, 2009, from http://gamestudies.org/0601/articles/consalvo_dutton

Entertainment Software Association. (2009). *The essential facts about the computer and video game industry*. Retrieved June 3, 2009, from http://www.theesa.com/facts/econdata.asp

Fabricatore, C., Nussbaum, M., & Rosas, R. (2002). Playability in action videogames: A qualitative design model. *Human-Computer Interaction, 17*(4), 311–368. doi:10.1207/S15327051HCI1704_1

Gibson, N. (2008). *IP profile: Runescape*. Retrieved June 3, 2009, from http://www.developmag.com/interviews/200/IP-profile-RuneScape

Grbich, C. (2007). *Qualitative data analysis: An introduction*. London: Sage.

Hatch, A. (2002). *Doing qualitative research in education settings*. Albany, NY: State University of New York Press.

Holliday, R. (2000). We've been framed: Visualising methodology. *The Sociological Review, 48*(4), 503–522. doi:10.1111/1467-954X.00230

Holstein, J., & Gubrium, J. (Eds.). (2003). *Inside interviewing: New lenses, new concerns*. Thousand Oaks, CA: Sage.

Jonassen, H. D., Carr, C., & Yueh, H.-P. (1998). Computers as mindtools for engaging learners in critical thinking. *TechTrends, 43*(2), 24–32. doi:10.1007/BF02818172

Linden Lab. (2009a). *Second Life economic statistics*. Retrieved June 3, 2009, from http://secondlife.com/whatis/economy_stats.php

Linden Lab. (2009b). *How education enterprises use virtual worlds*. Retrieved June 3, 2009, from http://secondlifegrid.net/slfe/education-use-virtual-world

Nowak, K. L., & Rauh, C. (2005). The influence of the avatar on online perceptions of anthropomorphism, androgyny, credibility, homophily, and attraction. *Journal of Computer-Mediated Communication, 11*(1), Article 8.

Picciano, A., & Seaman, J. (2009). *K–12 online learning: A 2008 follow-up of the survey of U.S. school district administrators*. Retrieved June 3, 2009, from http://www.sloan-c.org/publications/survey/pdf/k-12_online_learning_2008.pdf

Pink, S. (2001a). More visualising, more methodologies: On video, reflexivity and qualitative research. *The Sociological Review, 49*(4), 586–599. doi:10.1111/1467-954X.00349

Pink, S. (2001b). *Doing visual ethnography: Images, media and representation in research*. London: Sage.

Pink, S. (2004). Conversing anthropologically: Hypermedia as Anthropological Text. In S. Pink, L. Kürti, & A. I. Afonso (Eds.), *Working images: Visual research and representation in ethnography* (pp. 166-184). New York: Routledge.

Rosenthal, R., & Jacobson, L. (1992). *Pygmalion in the classroom*. New York: Irvington.

Schwandt, T. (2001). *Dictionary of qualitative inquiry* (2nd ed). Thousand Oaks, CA: Sage.

Second Life [Computer software]. (2008). San Francisco, CA: Linden Labs. Retrieved from http://secondlife.com

Silverman, D. (1993). *Interpreting qualitative data: Methods for analyzing talk, text, and interaction*. London: Sage.

Transana 2.20 [Computer software]. (2007). Madison, WI: The Board of Regents of the University of Wisconsin System. Retrieved from http://www.transana.org

Turkle, S. (1995). *Life on the screen: Identity in the age of the Internet*. New York: Simon & Schuster.

Yee, N. (2007). *The Proteus Effect: Behavioral modification via transformations of digital self-representation*. Retrieved June 3, 2009, from http://www.nickyee.com/pubs/Dissertation_Nick_Yee.pdf

This work was previously published in International Journal of Gaming and Computer-Mediated Simulations, Volume 1, Issue 4, edited by Richard E. Ferdig, pp. 50-62, copyright 2009 by IGI Publishing (an imprint of IGI Global).

Compilation of References

Abrash, M. (2000). *Inside Quake: Visible-surface determination.* GameDev.net. Retrieved February 10, 2008, from http://www.gamedev.net/reference/articles/article981.asp

Ageia Phys, X. SDK documentation. (2007a). *Collision detection, meshes, cooking.* [Electronic version]. Mountain View, CA: Ageia.

Ageia Phys, X. SDK documentation. (2007b). *Lesson 305–Raycast report.* Mountain View, CA: Ageia.

Ajs15822 (forum name). (2007, May 24). *Navi.* Retrieved from http://www.ogre3d.org/forums/viewtopic.php?t=32384

Albrecht, R. (1997, May 28). *General considerations for clinical studies... from protocol to results.* Retrieved Aug 20, 2008, from http://www.fda.gov/cder/present/genconra/sld009.htm

Alexandrov, O. (2007). *Surface normal.* Retrieved March 4, 2008, from http://en.wikipedia.org/wiki/Surface_normal

Alvermann, D. E., Moon, J. S., & Hagood, M. C. (1999). *Popular culture in the classroom: Teaching and researching critical media literacy.* Newark, DE: International Reading Association.

Amarelo, M. (2008, May 22). *Fixing the education digital disconnect one video game at a time–FAS launches immune attack.* Retrieved May 28, 2008, from http://www.fas.org/press/news/2008/may_ialaunch.html

Ambady, N., & Gray, H. M. (2002). On being sad and mistaken: Mood effects on the accuracy of thin-slice judgments. *Journal of Personality and Social Psychology, 83*(4), 947–961. doi:10.1037/0022-3514.83.4.947

Anderson, D. R., Collins, P. A., Schmitt, K. L., & Smith Jacobvitz, R. (1996). Stressful life events and television viewing. *Communication Research, 23*(3), 243–260. doi:10.1177/009365096023003001

Annetta, L. A., Murray, M. R., Laird, S. G., Bohr, S. C., & Park, J. C. (2006). Serious games: Incorporating video games in the classroom. *EDUCAUSE Quarterly, 29*(3), 16–22.

Antti, K., Tuula, N., & Marja, K. (2007, September 24-28). *Team structure in the development of game-based learning Environments.* Paper presented at DiGRA 2007, Tokyo, Japan. Retrieved May 20, 2008, from http://www.digra.org/dl/db/07344.35576.pdf

Appiah, K. A. (2007). *Cosmopolitanism: Ethics in a world of strangers.* London, UK: Penguin Books.

Austin, J. L. (1975). *How to do things with words* (2nd ed.). Cambridge, MA: MIT Press.

Autodesk Software. (2006). *Autodesk Maya.* Retrieved January 20, 2009, from http://usa.autodesk.com/adsk/servlet/index?id=7635018&siteID=123112

Baddeley, A. D. (1986). *Working memory.* New York, NY: Oxford University Press.

Bailenson, J. N. (2006). Transformed social interaction in collaborative virtual environments. In Messaris, P., & Humphreys, L. (Eds.), *Digital media: Transformations in human communication* (pp. 255–264). New York, NY: Peter Lang.

Bailenson, J. N., & Beall, A. C. (2005). Transformed social interaction: Exploring the digital plasticity of avatars. In Schroeder, R., & Axelsson, A. (Eds.), *Avatars at work and play: Collaboration and interaction in shared virtual environments* (pp. 1–16). Heidelberg, Germany: Springer.

Bailey, R., Wise, K., & Bolls, P. (2009). How avatar customizability affects children's arousal and subjective presence during junk food-sponsored online video games. *CyberPsycholgy & Behavior*, *12*(3), 277–283. doi:10.1089/cpb.2008.0292

Bakhtin, M. M. (1981). *The dialogic imagination: Four essays*. Austin, TX: University of Texas Press.

Balicer, R. (2007). Modeling infectious diseases dissemination through online role-playing games. *Epidemiology (Cambridge, Mass.)*, *18*(2), 260–261. doi:10.1097/01.ede.0000254692.80550.60

Bandura, A. (1986). *Social foundations of thought and action: A social cognitive theory*. Englewood Cliffs, NJ: Prentice Hall.

Bandura, A. (1997). *Self-efficacy: The exercise of control*. New York, NY: W.H. Freeman.

Bandura, A. (2001). Social cognitive theory of mass communications. In Bryant, J., & Zillmann, D. (Eds.), *Media effects: Advances in theory and research* (2nd ed., pp. 121–153). Hillsdale, NJ: Lawrence Erlbaum.

Banks, J. A. (2008). Diversity, group identity, and citizenship education in a global age. *Educational Researcher*, *37*(3), 129–139. doi:10.3102/0013189X08317501

Barab, S. A., Gresalfi, M., & Arici, A. (2009). Why educators should care about games. *Educational Leadership*, *67*(1), 76–80.

Barab, S. A., Scott, B., Siyahhan, S., Goldstone, R., Ingram-Goble, A., Zuiker, S. J., & Warren, S. (2009). Transformational play as a curriculum scaffold: Using videogames to support science education. *Journal of Science Education and Technology*, *18*, 305–320. doi:10.1007/s10956-009-9171-5

Barab, S., Thomas, M., Dodge, T., Carteaux, R., & Tuzun, H. (2005). Making learning fun: Quest Atlantis, a game without guns. *Educational Technology Research and Development*, *53*(1), 86–107. doi:10.1007/BF02504859doi:10.1007/BF02504859

Barad, K. (2003). Posthumanist performativity: Toward an understanding of how matter comes to matter. *Signs: Journal of Women in Culture and Society*, *28*(3), 801–831. doi:10.1086/345321

Barnard, A., & Spencer, J. (Eds.). (2002). *Encyclopedia of social and cultural anthropology*. New York, NY: Routledge.

Bartholow, B. D., & Anderson, C. A. (2002). Effects of violent video games on aggressive behavior: Potential sex differences. *Journal of Experimental Social Psychology*, *38*(3), 283–290. doi:10.1006/jesp.2001.1502

Bartle, R. A. (2004). *Designing virtual worlds*. Berkeley, CA: New Riders.

Bartle, R. (2006). Hearts, clubs, diamonds, spades: Players who suit MUDs. In Salen, K., & Zimmerman, E. (Eds.), *The game design reader* (pp. 754–787). Cambridge, MA: MIT Press.

Bartle, R. (1990). *Interactive multi-user computer games*. MUSE Ltd, British Telecom, December.

Bates, J. E. (1989). Concepts and measures of temperament. In Kohnstamm, G. A., Bates, J. E., & Rothbart, M. K. (Eds.), *Temperament in childhood* (pp. 3–26). New York, NY: John Wiley & Sons.

Bateson, G. (1979). *Mind and nature: A necessary unity*. New York, NY: Bantam Books.

Battalio, R., Fisher, E. Jr, Kagel, J., Basmann, R., Winkler, R., & Krasner, L. (1974). An experimental investigation of consumer behavior in a controlled environment. *The Journal of Consumer Research*, *1*(2), 52–60. doi:10.1086/208591

Battalio, R., Kagel, J., Rachlin, H., & Green, L. (1981). Commodity-choice behavior with pigeons as subjects. *The Journal of Political Economy*, *89*(1), 67–91. doi:10.1086/260950

Battalio, R., Kagel, J., & Reynolds, M. (1977). Income distributions in two experimental economies. *The Journal of Political Economy*, *85*(6), 1259–1271. doi:10.1086/260636

Baumeister, R. F., & Leary, M. R. (1995). The need to belong: Desire for interpersonal attachments as a fundamental human motivation. *Psychological Bulletin*, *117*(3), 497–529. doi:10.1037/0033-2909.117.3.497

BBC. (2004, August 11). Video games "good for children". *BBC News*. Retrieved April 30, 2008, from http://news.bbc.co.uk/go/pr/fr/-/1/hi/scotland/3553352.stm

Beasley, B., & Standley, T. C. (2002). Shirts vs. skins: Clothing as an indicator of gender role stereotyping in video games. *Mass Communication & Society, 5,* 279–293. doi:10.1207/S15327825MCS0503_3

Beck, J. C., & Wade, M. (2004). *Got game: How the gamer generation is reshaping business forever.* Boston, MA: Harvard Press.

Becker, K., & Parker, J. R. (2005, Oct 13-15). *All I ever needed to know about programming, I learned from re-writing classic arcade games.* Paper presented at the Future Play: The International Conference on the Future of Game Design and Technology, East Lansing, MI.

Becker, L. (2000). *Effect size.* Retrieved December 9, 2008, from http://web.uccs.edu/lbecker/ Psy590/es.htm

Behm-Morawitz, E., & Mastro, D. (2009). The effects of the sexualization of female video game characters on gender stereotyping and female self-concept. *Sex Roles, 61*(11-12), 808–823. doi:10.1007/s11199-009-9683-8

Bellotti, F., Berta, R., De Gloria, A., & Primavera, L. (2010). Supporting authors in the development of task-based learning in serious virtual worlds. *British Journal of Educational Technology, 41*(1), 86–107. doi:10.1111/j.1467-8535.2009.01039.x

Bem, S. L. (1974). The measurement of psychological androgyny. *Journal of Consulting and Clinical Psychology, 42*(2), 155–162. doi:10.1037/h0036215

Bencina, R. (2008). *Portable cross-platform audio API.* Retrieved January 20, 2009, from http://www.portaudio.com/

Bentham, J. (1882). *The theory of legislation.* London, UK: Trubner.

Berg, J., Bradshaw, B., Carbone, J., Chojnacky, C., Conroy, S., Cleaves, D., et al. (1999). *Decision protocol 2.0.* Washington, DC: USDA Forest Service.

Berger, A. (2006, January 31). Neverwinter nights in the classroom. *University of Minnesota News.* Retrieved April 30, 2008, from http://www1.umn.edu/umnnews/Feature_Stories/22Neverwinter_Nights22_in_the_classroom.html

Berkley Software. (2008). *BSD license definition.* Retrieved January 20, 2009, from http://www.linfo.org/bsdlicense.html

Bessière, K., Seay, F., & Kiesler, S. (2007). The ideal elf: Identity exploration in World of Warcraft. *Cyberpsychology & Behavior, 10*(4), 530–535. doi:10.1089/cpb.2007.9994

BetaJaen (forum name). (2006, November 7). *BetaGUI: BetaGUI 2.5 update - Style system added.* Retrieved from http://www.ogre3d.org/forums/viewtopic.php?f=11&t=25853&start=275

Betrancourt, M. (2005). *The animation and interactivity principles in multimedia learning.* New York, NY: Cambridge.

Bilas, S. (2007). *A data-driven game object system.* [Electronic version]. Retrieved from http://www.drizzle.com/~scottb/gdc/game-objects.ppt

Biocca, F., Harms, C., & Burgoon, J. K. (2003). Criteria for a theory and measure of social presence. *Presence (Cambridge, Mass.), 12*(5), 456–480. doi:10.1162/105474603322761270

Bisco. (2008). *Tools.* Retrieved January 20, 2009, from http://www.ogre3d.org/index.php?option=com_content&task=view&id=413&Itemid=133

Blender. (2009). *Blender.* Retrieved January 15, 2009, from http://www.blender.org/

Blizzard Entertainment. (2008). *Media alert.* Retrieved June 3, 2009, from http://www.blizzard.com/us/press/081121.html

Bloom, S. G. (2005). Lesson of a lifetime: Her bold experiment to teach Iowa third graders about racial prejudice divided townspeople and thrust her onto the national stage. Decades later, Jane Elliott's students say the ordeal changed them for good. *Smithsonian, 36*(6), 82–93.

Botturi, L., & Loh, C. S. (2009). Once upon a game: Rediscovering the roots of games in education. In C. Miller (Ed.), *Games: Their purpose and potential in education* (pp. 1-22). New York: Springer Publishing Company.

Bounds, J. (2007, April 6). Game on! *Dallas Business Journal.* Retrieved February 2, 2009, from http://dallas.bizjournals.com/dallas/stories/2007/04/09/focus1.html

Brown, S. (1999). Play as an organizing principal: Clinical evidence and personal observations. In Beckoff, M., & Byers, J. A. (Eds.), *Animal play: Evolutionary, comparative and ecological perspectives* (pp. 247–248). Cambridge, UK: Cambridge University Press.

Brown, E., & Cairns, P. (2004). *A grounded investigation of game immersion*. ACM CHI 2004, (pp. 1297-1300). Retrieved November 11, 2008, from http://complexworld. pbwiki.com/f/Brown+and+Cairns+(2004).pdf

Brünken, R., Plass, J. L., & Leutner, D. (2003). Direct measurement of cognitive load in multimedia learning. *Educational Psychologist*, *38*, 53–61. doi:10.1207/ S15326985EP3801_7

Brünken, R., Steinbacher, S., Plass, J. L., & Leutner, D. (2002). Assessment of cognitive load in multimedia learning using dual-task methodology. *Experimental Psychology*, *49*, 109–119. doi:10.1027//1618-3169.49.2.109

Bryant, J., & Davis, J. (2006). Selective exposure to video games. In Vorderer, P., & Bryant, J. (Eds.), *Playing video games - Motives, responses, and consequences* (pp. 181–194). Mahwah, NJ: Lawrence Erlbaum.

Buckingham, D. (Ed.). (2008). *Youth, identity, and digital media*. Cambridge, MA: MIT Press.

Burgess, M. C. R., Stermer, S. P., & Burgess, S. R. (2007). Sex, lies, and video games: The portrayal of male and female characters on video game covers. *Sex Roles*, *57*(5-6), 419–433. doi:10.1007/s11199-007-9250-0

Calleja, G. (2007). Digital game involvement: A conceptual model. *Games and Culture*, *2*, 236–260. doi:10.1177/1555412007306206

Camtasia Studio 3.0 [Computer software]. (2005). Okemos, MI: TechSmith. Retrieved from http://www. techsmith.com

Carlson, R., Chandler, P., & Sweller, J. (2003). Learning and understanding science instructional material. *Journal of Educational Psychology*, *95*(3), 629–640. doi:10.1037/0022-0663.95.3.629

Carlson, M. (2004). *Performance: A critical introduction*. New York, NY: Routledge.

Carnegie Mellon Entertainment Technology Center. (2006). *Welcome to Panda3D!* Retrieved January 20, 2009, from http://panda3d.org/

Carver, C. S., & Scheier, M. F. (1981). The self attention-induced feedback loop and social facilitation. *Journal of Experimental Social Psychology*, *17*, 545–568. doi:10.1016/0022-1031(81)90039-1

Cassell, J., & Jenkins, H. (Eds.). (1998). *From Barbie to Mortal Kombat: Gender and computer games*. Cambridge, MA: MIT Press.

Castillo, T., & Novak, J. (2008). *Game level design*. Clifton Park, NY: Delmar Cengage Learning.

Castronova, E. (2005). *Synthetic worlds: The business and culture of online games*. Chicago, IL: University of Chicago Press.

Castronova, E. (2006). On the research value of large games: Natural experiments in Norrath and Camelot. *Games and Culture*, *1*(2), 163–186. doi:10.1177/1555412006286686

Castronova, E. (2007). *Exodus to the virtual world: How online fun is changing reality*. New York, NY: Palgrave/ MacMillan.

Castronova, E., Williams, D., Shen, C., Ratan, R., Xiong, L., & Huang, Y. (2009). As real as real? Macroeconomic behavior in a large-scale virtual world. *New Media & Society*, *11*(5), 685–707. doi:10.1177/1461444809105346

Castronova, E. (2001). *Virtual worlds: A first-hand account of market and society on the cyberian frontier*. CESifo Working Paper No. 618.

Casual Games Market Report. (2007). *All about casual*. Retrieved April 11, 2009, from Casual Connect web site: http://www.casualconnect.org/newscontent/11-2007/ CasualGamesMarketReport2007_Summary.pdf

Chan, E., & Vorderer, P. (2006). Massively multiplayer online games. In Vorderer, P., & Bryant, J. (Eds.), *Playing video games. Motives, responses, and consequences* (pp. 77–88). Mahwah, NJ: Lawrence Erlbaum.

Chandler, P. (2004). The crucial role of cognitive processes in the design of dynamic visualizations. *Learning and Instruction*, *14*, 353–357. doi:10.1016/j.learninstruc.2004.06.009

Chapman, E. (2003). Alternative approaches to assessing student engagement rates. *Practical Assessment, Research and Evaluation, 8*(13). Retrieved May 11, 2009, from http://PAREonline.net/getvn.asp?v=8&n=13

Charmaz, K. (2006). *Constructing grounded theory: A practical guide through qualitative analysis*. Thousand Oaks, CA: Sage Publications.

Chartrand, T. L., & Bargh, J. A. (1999). The chameleon effect: The perception-behavior link and social interaction. *Journal of Personality and Social Psychology, 76*(6), 893–910. doi:10.1037/0022-3514.76.6.893

Chase, W. G., & Simon, H. A. (1973). Perception in chess. *Cognitive Psychology, 4*, 55–81. doi:10.1016/0010-0285(73)90004-2

Chee, Y. S. (2007). Embodiment, embeddedness, and experience: Game-based learning and the construction of identity. *Research and Practice in Technology Enhanced Learning, 2*(1), 3–30. doi:10.1142/S1793206807000282

Chee, Y. S. (2010a). Possession, profession, and performance: Epistemological considerations for effective game-based learning. In Cai, Y. (Ed.), *Interactive and digital media for education in virtual learning environments* (pp. 7–24). New York, NY: Nova Science Publishers.

Chee, Y. S. (2010b). *Learning as becoming through performance, play, and dialog, and performance: A model of game-based learning with the game Legends of Alkhimia.* Manuscript submitted for publication.

Chen, S., & Michael, D. (2005). Proof of learning: Assessment in serious games. *Gamasutra*. Retrieved from http://www.gamasutra.com/features/20051019/chen_01.shtml

Chesney, T., Chuah, S., & Hoffmann, R. (2009). Virtual world experimentation: An exploratory study. *Journal of Economic Behavior & Organization, 72*(1), 618–635. doi:10.1016/j.jebo.2009.05.026

Chew, O. A. J. (1998). Civics and moral education in Singapore: Lessons for citizenship education? *Journal of Moral Education, 27*(4), 505–524. doi:10.1080/0305724980270405

Chi, M. T. H., Glaser, R., & Rees, E. (1982). Expertise in problem solving. In Sternberg, R. (Ed.), *Advances in the psychology of human intelligence* (*Vol. 1*, pp. 17–76). Hillsdale, NJ: Erlbaum.

Chiba, N., Muraoka, K., Takahashi, H., & Miura, M. (2006, October). Two-dimensional visual simulation of flames, smoke and the spread of fire. *The Journal of Visualization and Computer Animation, 5*(1), 37–53. doi:10.1002/vis.4340050104

Children Now. (2000). *Girls and gaming: A console video game content analysis*. Oakland, CA: Children Now.

Children Now. (2001). *Fair play? Violence, gender, and race in video games*. Oakland, CA: Children Now.

Chumbley, J., & Griffiths, M. (2006). Affect and the computer game player: The effect of gender, personality, and game reinforcement structure on affective responses to computer game-play. *Cyberpsychology & Behavior, 9*(3), 308–316. doi:10.1089/cpb.2006.9.308

Clancey, W. J. (1997). *Situated cognition: On human knowledge and computer representations*. New York, NY: Cambridge University Press.

Clark, J. M., & Paivio, A. (1991). Dual coding theory and education. *Educational Psychology Review, 3*(3), 149–210. doi:10.1007/BF01320076

Clark, J. (1999). *Minorities in science and math*. Columbus, OH: ERIC Clearinghouse for Science, Mathematics and Environmental Education.

Clark, K. B., & Clark, M. P. (1950). Emotional factors in racial identification and preference in Negro children. *The Journal of Negro Education, 19*(3), 341–350. doi:10.2307/2966491

Clark, R. E. (2007, May-June). Point of view: Learning from serious games? *Educational Technology, 47*, 56–59.

Clayman, S., & Maynard, D. (1995). Ethnomethodology and conversation analysis. In ten Have, P., & Psathas, G. (Eds.), *Situated order: Studies in the social organization of talk and embodied activities* (pp. 1–30). Washington, DC: University Press of America.

Cohen, J. (2001). Defining identification: A theoretical look at the identification of audiences with media characters. *Mass Communication & Society, 4*(3), 245–264. doi:10.1207/S15327825MCS0403_01

Collen, A. (2003). *Systemic change through praxis and inquiry*. New Brunswick, NJ: Transaction Publishers.

Collins, A., & Ferguson, W. (1993). Epistemic forms and epistemic games: Structures and strategies to guide inquiry. *Educational Psychologist*, *28*(1), 25–42. doi:10.1207/s15326985ep2801_3

Collins, A., Brown, J. S., & Newman, S. E. (1989). Cognitive apprenticeship: Teaching the crafts of reading, writing, and mathematics. In Resnick, L. B. (Ed.), *Knowing, learning and instruction: Essays in honor of Robert Glaser* (pp. 453–494). Hillsdale, NJ: Lawrence Erlbaum Associates.

Conklin, M. (2007). *101 uses for Second Life in the college classroom*. Retrieved June 3, 2009, from http://facstaff.elon.edu/mconklin/pubs/glshandout.pdf

Corbit, M. (2005). Game worlds for learning. *Knowledge Quest. Journal of the American Association of School Librarians*, *34*(1), 18–22.

Corbit, M., & Norton, C. (2007). A constructionist approach to using virtual worlds to motivate in the classroom. *Proceedings of the 2007 NYSCATE Conference*, Rochester, NY.

Corbit, M., Kolodziej, S., & Bernstein, R. (2005). SciFair: A multi-user virtual environment for building science literacy. *Proceedings of the PCST Working Symposium*, Beijing, China.

Corsaro, W. (1985). *Friendship and peer culture in the early years*. Norwood, NJ: Abex.

Cottrell, N. B. (1972). Social facilitation. In McClintock, C. G. (Ed.), *Experimental social psychology* (pp. 185–235). New York, NY: Holt, Rinehart & Winston.

Crabtree, B. F., & Miller, W. L. (1992). *Doing qualitative research*. Newbury Park, CA: Sage.

Creative Labs. (2008). *OpenAL*. Retrieved January 20, 2009, from http://connect.creativelabs.com/openal/default.aspx

Creative Technology. (2008). *Sound blaster*. Retrieved January 20, 2009, from http://www.soundblaster.com/

Crotty, M. (1998). *The foundations of social research*. London: Sage.

Cruz, D., Wieland, T., & Ziegler, A. (2006). Evaluation criteria for free/open source software products based on project analysis. *Software Process Improvement and Practice*, *11*(2), 107–122. doi:10.1002/spip.257

Csikszentmihaly, M., Rathunde, K., & Whalen, S. (1996). *Talented teenagers: The roots of success and failure*. New York, NY: Cambridge University Press.

Csikszentmihalyi, I., & Csikszentmihalyi, M. (1988). *Optimal experience: Psychological studies of flow in consciousness*. New York, NY: Cambridge University Press.

Csikszentmihalyi, M. (1975). *Beyond boredom and anxiety*. San Francisco, CA: Jossey-Bass.

Csikszentmihalyi, M. (1990). *Flow: The psychology of optimal experience*. New York, NY: Harper and Row.

Cyber Creations Inc. (2009). *MMORPG Gamelist*. Retrieved June 3, 2009, from http://www.mmorpg.com/gamelist.cfm

Dawson, C. R., Cragg, A., Taylor, C., & Toombs, B. (2007). *Video games: Research to improve understanding of what players enjoy about video games, and to explain their preferences for particular games. British Board of Film Classification*. BBFC.

De Freitas, S., Rebolledo-Mendez, G., Liarokapis, F., Magoulas, G., & Poulovassilis, A. (2010). Learning as immersive experiences: Using the four-dimensional framework for designing and evaluating immersive learning experiences in a virtual world. *British Journal of Educational Technology*, *41*(1), 69–85. doi:10.1111/j.1467-8535.2009.01024.x

De Groot, A. D. (1965). *Thought and choice in chess*. The Hague, The Netherlands: Mouton.

de Jong, T., & van Joolingen, W. R. (1998). Scientific discovery learning with computer simulations of conceptual domains. *Review of Educational Research*, *68*(2), 179–201.

De Jong, T., van Joolingen, W., Scott, D., de Hoog, R., Lapied, L., & Valent, R. (1994). SMISLE: System for multimedia integration simulation learning environments. In de Jong, T., & Sarti, L. (Eds.), *Design and production of multimedia and simulation based learning material* (pp. 133–167). Dordrecht, The Netherlands: Kluwer Academic Publishers.

de Kort, Y. A. W., & IJsselsteijn, W. A. (2008). People, places and play: A research framework for digital game experience in a socio-spatial context. *ACM Computers in Entertainment, 6*(2), Article No. 18.

de Kort, Y. A. W., IJsselsteijn, W. A., & Poels, K. (2007). Digital games as social presence technology: Development of the social presence questionnaire (SPGQ). *Proceedings of Presence 2007 Conference*, October 25-27, Barcelona.

Deacon, T. W. (1997). *The symbolic species: The co-evolution of language and the brain* (1st ed.). New York, NY: W.W. Norton.

Deci, E. L., & Ryan, R. M. (2002). *Handbook of self-determination research*. Rochester, NY: University of Rochester Press.

Deci, E., & Ryan, R. (1985). *Intrinsic motivation and self-determination in human behavior*. New York, NY: Plenum.

Deci, E., Vallerand, R., Pelletier, L., & Ryan, R. (1991). Motivation and education: The self-determination perspective. *Educational Psychologist, 26*(3-4), 325–346. doi:10.1207/s15326985ep2603&4_6

Dede, C., Clarke, J., Ketelhut, D., Nelson, B., & Bowman, C. (2005). Students' motivation and learning of science in a multi-user virtual environment. *Proceedings of the American Educational Research Association*, Montreal, Canada.

Dede, C., Clarke, J., Ketelhut, D., Nelson, B., & Bowman, C. (2005). Fostering motivation, learning, and transfer in multi-user virtual environments. *Proceedings of the American Educational Research Association*, Montreal, Canada.

Dede, C., Ketelhut, D., & Nelson, B. (2004). Design-based research on gender, class, race and ethnicity in a multi-user virtual environment. *Proceedings of the International Conference on Learning Science*, Mahweh, NJ

Dede, C., Ketelhut, D., & Ruess, K. (2003). Designing for motivation and usability in a museum-based multi-user virtual environment. *Proceedings of the American Educational Research Association*, Chicago, IL

Deitel, H., & Deitel, P. (2001). *C++ how to program* (3rd ed.). New Jersey: Upper Saddle River.

Despain, W. (Ed.). (2008). *Professional techniques for video game writing*. Wellesley, MA: A. K. Peters, Ltd.

Dewey, J. (1938). *Experience and education*. New York, NY: Macmillan.

Diamond, M. (2002). Sex and gender are different: Sexual identity and gender are different. *Clinical Child Psychology and Psychiatry, 7*(3), 320–334. doi:10.1177/1359104502007003002

Dicintio, M., & Gee, S. (1999). Control is the key: Unlocking the motivation of at-risk students. *Psychology in the Schools, 36*(3), 231–237. doi:10.1002/(SICI)1520-6807(199905)36:3<231::AID-PITS6>3.0.CO;2-#

Dietz, T. L. (1998). An examination of violence and gender role portrayals in video games: Implications for gender socialization and aggressive behavior. *Sex Roles, 38*(5-6), 425–442. doi:10.1023/A:1018709905920

Digital Trends. (2006). *Nielsen: Video games getting more social*. Retrieved February 13, 2008, from http://news.digitaltrends.com/news/story/11464/nielsen_video_games_getting_more_social

Dill, K. E., Brown, B. P., & Collins, M. A. (2008). Effects of exposure to sex-stereotyped video game characters on tolerance of sexual harassment. *Journal of Experimental Social Psychology, 44*(5), 1402–1408. doi:10.1016/j.jesp.2008.06.002

Dill, K. E., & Thill, K. P. (2007). Video game characters and the socialization of gender roles: Young people's perceptions mirror sexist media depictions. *Sex Roles, 57*(11-12), 851–864. doi:10.1007/s11199-007-9278-1

Dill, K., Gentile, D., Richter, W., & Dill, J. (2005). Violence, sex, race and age in popular videogames. In Cole, E., & Daniel, J. (Eds.), *Featuring females: Feminist analysis of the media* (pp. 115–130). Washington, DC: American Psychological Association. doi:10.1037/11213-008

Dillenbourg, P., Baker, M., Blayne, A., & O'Malley, C. (1996). The evolution of research on collaborative learning. In Spada, H., & Reimann, P. (Eds.), *Learning in humans and machine: Towards an interdisciplinary learning science* (pp. 189–211). Oxford, UK: Elsevier.

DiPietro, J., & Black, E. (2008). Visual analysis of avatars in gaming environments. In R. E. Ferdig (Ed.), *Handbook of research on effective electronic gaming in education* (pp. 606-620). Hershey, PA: IGI Global.

Doise, W., & Mugny, G. (1984). *The social development of the intellect- International series in experimental social psychology* (*Vol. 10*). Pergamon Press.

Donath, J. (2007). Virtually trustworthy. *Science, 317*, 53–54. doi:10.1126/science.1142770

Downs, E., & Smith, S. L. (2010). Keeping abreast of hypersexuality: A video game character content analysis. *Sex Roles, 62*(11-12), 721–733. doi:10.1007/s11199-009-9637-1

Draucker, C. B., Martsolf, D. S., Ross, R., & Rusk, T. B. (2007). Theoretical sampling and category development in grounded theory. *Qualitative Health Research, 17*, 1137–1148. doi:10.1177/1049732307308450

Dryer, D. C. (1999). Getting personal with computers: How to design personalities for agents. *Applied Artificial Intelligence, 13*, 273–295. doi:10.1080/088395199117423

Dubbels, B. R. (2008). Video games, reading, and transmedial comprehension. In Ferdig, R. E. (Ed.), *Handbook of research on effective electronic gaming in education* (pp. 251–276). Hershey, PA: Information Science Reference. doi:10.4018/9781599048086.ch015

Ducheneaut, N., Yee, N., Nickell, E., & Moore, R. J. (2006). Alone together? Exploring the social dynamics of massively multiplayer online games. In R. Grinter, T. Rodden, P. Aoki, E. Cutrell, R. Jeffries, & G. Olson, (Eds.), *Proceedings of the SIGCHI Conference on Human Factors in Computing Systems*, (pp. 407-416). Montreal, Quebec, Canada, April 22 - 27, 2006. New York, NY: ACM.

Dutton, N., & Consalvo, M. (2006). Game analysis: Developing a methodological toolkit for the qualitative study of games. *The International Journal of Computer Game Research, 6*(1). Retrieved June 3, 2009, from http://gamestudies.org/0601/articles/consalvo_dutton

Dweck, C. (2000). *Self-theories: Their role in motivation, personality, and development*. Philadelphia, PA: Taylor & Francis.

Dweck, C. (2006). *Mindset: The new psychology of success*. New York: Random House.

Dweck, C. S., & Leggett, E. L. (1988). A social-cognitive approach to motivation and personality. *Psychological Review, 95*, 256–273. doi:10.1037/0033-295X.95.2.256

Eastin, M. S. (2006). Video game violence and the female game player: Self- and opponent gender effects on presence and aggressive thoughts. *Human Communication Research, 32*, 351–372. doi:10.1111/j.1468-2958.2006.00279.x

Edelman, G. M. (1992). *Bright air, brilliant fire: On the matter of the mind*. New York, NY: Basic Books.

Elliot, E. S., & Church, M. A. (1997). A hierarchal model of approach and avoidance achievement motivation. *Journal of Personality and Social Psychology, 72*, 218–232. doi:10.1037/0022-3514.72.1.218

Elshout, J. J., & Veenman, M. V. (1992). Relation between intellectual ability and working method as predictors of learning. *The Journal of Educational Research, 85*(3), 134–143. doi:10.1080/00220671.1992.9944429

Entertainment Software Association. (2008). *The essential facts about the computer and video game industry*. Retrieved April 6, 2008, from http://www.theesa.com/facts/ sales_genre_data.php

Entertainment Software Association. (2010). *Video games in the 21st century*. Retrieved September 3, 2010, from http://www.theesa.com/facts/pdfs/VideoGames21stCentury_2010.pdf

Entertainment Software Association. (2010). *Sales, demographic and usage data. Essential facts about the computer and video game industry*. Retrieved September 16, 2010, from http://www.theesa.com/facts/pdfs/ESA_Essential_Facts_2010.PDF

Entertainment Software Association. (2009). *The essential facts about the computer and video game industry*. Retrieved June 3, 2009, from http://www.theesa.com/facts/econdata.asp

Epic Software. (2008). *Unreal technology*. Retrieved January 20, 2009, from http://www.unrealtechnology.com/

Ermi, L., & Mäyrä, F. (2005). Fundamental components of the gameplay experience: Analysing immersion. In S. de Castell & J. Jenson (Eds.), *Changing views: Worlds in play* (pp. 15-27). Retrieved November 11, 2008, from http://www.uta.fi/~tlilma/gameplay_experience.pdf

Espe, H., & Seiwert, M. (1986). European television-viewer types: A six-nation classification by programme interests. *European Journal of Communication, 1*(3), 301–325. doi:10.1177/0267323186001003004

Fabricatore, C., Nussbaum, M., & Rosas, R. (2002). Playability in action videogames: A qualitative design model. *Human-Computer Interaction, 17*(4), 311–368. doi:10.1207/S15327051HCI1704_1

Fairclough, N. (2003). *Analysing discourse*. New York, NY: Routledge.

Federation of American Scientists. (2006). *Summit on Educational Games 2006: Harnessing the power of video games for learning*. Washington, DC: Author.

Ferdig, R. E. (Ed.). (2008). *Handbook of research on effective electronic gaming in education*. Hershey, PA: Information Science Reference.

Fernando, R. (2004). *GPU gems: Programming techniques, tips, and tricks for real-time graphics*. Canada: Addison-Wesley Professional.

Ferré, F. (1996). *Being and value: Toward a constructive postmodern metaphysics*. New York, NY: SUNY Press.

Ferré, F. (1998). *Knowing and value: Toward a constructive postmodern epistemology*. New York, NY: SUNY Press.

Ferster, C. B., & Skinner, B. F. (1957). *Schedules of reinforcement*. New York, NY: Appleton-Century-Crofts. doi:10.1037/10627-000

Festinger, L. (1957). *A theory of cognitive dissonance*. Stanford: CA Stanford: University Press.

Fiedler, G. (2007). *Clients approximate server physics locally*. Retrieved January 20, 2009, from. http://www.gaffer.org/game-physics/networked-physics/

Firelight Technologies. (2008). *FMOD music and sound effects system*. Retrieved January 20, 2009, from http://www.fmod.org/

Fox, J., & Bailenson, J. N. (2009). Virtual virgins and vamps: The effects of exposure to female characters' sexualized appearance and gaze in an immersive virtual environment. *Sex Roles, 61*(3-4), 147–157. doi:10.1007/s11199-009-9599-3

Freebody, P., & Luke, A. (1990). Literacies programs: Debates and demands in cultural context. *Australian Journal of TESOL, 5*(7), 7–16.

Freebody, P. (1992). A socio-cultural approach: Resourcing four roles as a literacy learner. In Watson, A., & Badenhop, A. (Eds.), *Prevention of reading failure* (pp. 48–60). Sydney, Australia: Ashton-Scholastic.

Gaggioli, A., Mantovani, F., Castelnuovo, G., Wiederhold, B., & Riva, G. (2003). Avatars in clinical psychology: A framework for the clinical use of virtual humans. *Cyberpsychology & Behavior, 6*(2), 117–125. doi:10.1089/109493103321640301

Gajadhar, B. J., de Kort, Y. A. W., & IJsselsteijn, W. A. (2008a). Shared fun is doubled fun: Player enjoyment as a function of social setting. In Markopoulos, P., de Ruyter, B., IJsselsteijn, W., & Rowland, D. (Eds.), *Fun and games* (pp. 106–117). New York, NY: Springer. doi:10.1007/978-3-540-88322-7_11

Gajadhar, B. J., de Kort, Y. A. W., & IJsselsteijn, W. A. (2008b). *Influence of social setting on player experience of digital games*. Works in progress paper CHI'08 Extended Abstracts, April 5-10, Florence, Italy. (ACM 978-1-60558-012-8/08/04).

Gajadhar, B. J., de Kort, Y. A. W., & IJsselsteijn, W. A. (2009b). See no rival, hear no rival: The role of social cues in digital game settings. *Proceedings of CHI Nederland 2009*, (pp. 25-31). June 11, Leiden, the Netherlands.

Gajadhar, B. J., de Kort, Y. A. W., IJsselsteijn, W. A., & Poels, K. (2009a). Where everybody knows your game: The appeal and function of game cafés in Western Europe. *Proceedings of ACE 2009*, (pp. 28-35). October 29-31, Athens, Greece.

Garfinkel, H. (1967). *Studies in ethnomethodology*. Malden, MA: Blackwell Publishing.

Gee, J. (2007). *Good video games + good learning: Collected essays on video games, language, and learning*. New York: Peter Lang.

Gee, J. P. (2003). *What video games have to teach us about learning and literacy*. New York, NY: Palgrave Macmillan.

Gee, J. P. (1996). *Social linguistics and literacies, ideology in discourses*. Bristol, PA: Taylor & Francis.

Gee, J. P. (2005). Semiotic social spaces and affinity spaces: From The Age of Mythology to today's schools. In Barton, D., & Tusting, K. (Eds.), *Beyond communities of practice* (pp. 214–232). New York, NY: Cambridge University Press. doi:10.1017/CBO9780511610554.012

Gee, J. P. (2007). *What video games have to teach us about learning and literacy* (rev. and updated ed.). New York, NY: Palgrave Macmillan.

Geertz, C. (1973). Deep play: Notes on a Balinese cockfight. In Geertz, C. (Ed.), *The interpretation of cultures: Selected essays*. New York, NY: Basic Books.

Gentile, D. A. (1993). Just what are sex and gender, anyway? *Psychological Science*, *4*(2), 120–122. doi:10.1111/j.1467-9280.1993.tb00472.x

Gergen, K. J. (1999). *An invitation to social construction*. London, UK: Sage.

Gibson, J. (1979). *The ecological approach to visual perception*. New Jersey, USA: Lawrence Erlbaum Associates.

Gibson, J. (1977). The theory of affordances. In Shaw, R., & Bransford, J. (Eds.), *Perceiving, acting, and knowing*. Hillsdale, NJ: Lawrence Erlbaum Associates.

Gibson, N. (2008). *IP profile: Runescape*. Retrieved June 3, 2009, from http://www.developmag.com/interviews/200/IP-profile-RuneScape

Gilbert, B. (2009, March 5). *American library association goes gaming*. Retrieved March 9, 2009, from http://www.joystiq.com/2009/03/05/american-library-association-goes-gaming

Glaser, B., & Strauss, A. (1967). *Discovery of grounded theory: Strategies for qualitative research*. Piscataway, NJ: Transaction Publishers.

Goffman, E. (1959). *The presentation of self in everyday life*. New York, NY: Anchor Books.

Gogg, T. J., & Mott, J. R. (1993). *Improve quality & productivity with simulation*. Norcross, GA: Industrial Engineering Management Press.

Goldstein, J. (2007). Games and society: The engine of digital lifestyle. *Proceedings of ISFE Expert 2007 Conference*, (pp 24–28). June 26&27, Brussels.

Google. (2008). *Google summer of code*. Retrieved January 20, 2009, from http://code.google.com/soc/2008

Graner Ray, S. (2004). *Gender inclusive game design. Expanding the market*. Hingham, MA: Charles River Media.

Grbich, C. (2007). *Qualitative data analysis: An introduction*. London: Sage.

Griffiths, M. D. (1991). Are computer games bad for children? *The Psychologist: Bulletin of the British Psychological Society*, *6*, 401–407.

Griffiths, M. D., Davies, M. N. O., & Chappell, D. (2003). Breaking the stereotype: The case of online gaming. *Cyberpsychology & Behavior*, *6*(1), 81–91. doi:10.1089/109493103321167992

Griffiths, M. D., Davies, M. N. O., & Chappell, D. (2004). Online computer gaming: A comparison of adolescent and adult gamers. *Journal of Adolescence*, *27*, 87–96. doi:10.1016/j.adolescence.2003.10.007

Grodal, T. (2000). Video games and the pleasures of control. In Zillmann, D., & Vorderer, P. (Eds.), *Media entertainment. The psychology of its appeal* (pp. 197–213). Mahwah, NJ: Lawrence Erlbaum Associates.

Gruber, H., Graf, M., Mandl, H., Renkl, A., & Stark, R. (1995). *Fostering applicable knowledge by multiple perspectives and guided problem solving*. Paper Presented at the Conference of the European Association for Research on Learning and Instruction, Nijmegen, The Netherlands.

Guthrie, J. T., Weber, S., & Kimmerly, N. (1993). Searching documents: Cognitive processes and deficits in understanding graphs, tables, and illustrations. *Contemporary Educational Psychology*, *18*, 186–221. doi:10.1006/ceps.1993.1017

Haertel, G. D., & Means, B. (Eds.). (2003). *Evaluating education technology: Effective research designs for improving learning*. New York: Teachers College Press.

Hämäläinen, R., Manninen, T., Järvelä, S., & Häkkinen, P. (2006). Learning to collaborate: Designing collaboration in a 3-D game environment. *The Internet and Higher Education*, *9*(1), 47–61. doi:10.1016/j.iheduc.2005.12.004doi:10.1016/j.iheduc.2005.12.004

Haninger, K., & Thompson, K. M. (2004). Content and ratings of teen-rated video games. *Journal of the American Medical Association, 291*, 856–865. doi:10.1001/jama.291.7.856

Harris, M. (2004). *Fast fluid dynamics simulation on the GPU* (pp. 637–655). GPU Gems. Addison Wesley.

Hartmann, T., & Klimmt, C. (2006a). Gender and computer games: Exploring females' dislikes. *Journal of Computer-Mediated Communication, 11*(4). doi:10.1111/j.1083-6101.2006.00301.x

Hartmann, T., & Klimmt, C. (2006b). The influence of personality factors on computer game choice. In Vorderer, P., & Bryant, J. (Eds.), *Playing computer games: Motives, responses, and consequences* (pp. 115–131). Mahwah, NJ: Lawrence Erlbaum Associates.

Hastings, N. B., & Tracey, M. W. (2004). Does media affect learning: Where are we now? *TechTrends, 49*(2), 28–30. doi:10.1007/BF02773968doi:10.1007/BF02773968

Hatch, A. (2002). *Doing qualitative research in education settings*. Albany, NY: State University of New York Press.

Hatfield, E., Cacioppo, J. T., & Rapson, R. L. (1992). Primitive emotional contagion. In Clark, M. S. (Ed.), *Emotion and social behavior* (pp. 151–177). Thousand Oaks, CA: Sage.

Heeter, C., Egidio, R., Mishra, P., Winn, B., & Winn, J. (2009). Alien games: Do girls prefer games designed by girls? *Games and Culture, 4*(1), 74–100. doi:10.1177/1555412008325481

Heeter, C., & Winn, B. (2008). Implications of gender, player type and learning strategies for the design of games for learning. In Kafai, Y., Heeter, C., Denner, J., & Sun, J. (Eds.), *Beyond Barbie and Mortal Kombat: New perspectives on gender and gaming*. Cambridge, MA: MIT Press.

Heeter, C. (2000). Interactivity in the context of designed experiences. *Journal of Interactive Advertising, 1*(1). Retrieved September 30, 2008, from http://www.jiad.org/article2

Heeter, C., Winn, B., Winn, J., & Bozoki, A. (2008, October). The challenge of challenge: Avoiding and embracing difficulty in a memory game. *Meaningful Play Conference*. East Lansing, Michigan.

Hegarty, M., & Just, M. A. (1993). Constructing mental models of machines from text and diagrams. *Journal of Memory and Language, 32*(6), 717–742. doi:10.1006/jmla.1993.1036

Hewitt, D. (2008, June 23). *Use of video game technology in the workplace increasing*. Retrieved Oct 20, 2008, from http://www.theesa.com/newsroom/release_detail.asp?releaseID=24

Hidi, S., & Harackiewicz, J. (2000). Motivating the academically unmotivated: A critical issue for the 21st century. *Review of Educational Research, 70*(2), 151–179.

Höffler, T., & Leutner, D. (2007). Instructional animation versus static pictures: A meta-analysis. *Learning and Instruction, 17*, 722–738. doi:10.1016/j.learninstruc.2007.09.013

Holland, D., Lachicotte, W. Jr, Skinner, D., & Cain, C. (1998). *Identity and agency in cultural worlds*. Cambridge, MA: Harvard University Press.

Holliday, R. (2000). We've been framed: Visualising methodology. *The Sociological Review, 48*(4), 503–522. doi:10.1111/1467-954X.00230

Holstein, J., & Gubrium, J. (Eds.). (2003). *Inside interviewing: New lenses, new concerns*. Thousand Oaks, CA: Sage.

Homer, B. D., & Nelson, K. (2005). *Seeing objects as symbols and symbols as objects: Language and the development of dual representation*. Mahwah, NJ: Erlbaum.

Homer, B. D., & Plass, J. L. (2010). Expertise reversal for iconic representations in science simulations. *Instructional Science, 38*, 259–276. doi:10.1007/s11251-009-9108-7

Hopson, J. (2006). We're not listening: An open letter to academic game researchers. *Gamasutra*. Retrieved from http://www.gamasutra.com/features/20061110/hopson_01.shtml

Howard, G. S. (1980). Response shift bias: A problem in evaluating interventions with pre/post self-reports. *Evaluation Review, 4*(1), 93–106. doi:10.1177/0193841X8000400105

Hsu, S. H., Kao, C.-H., & Wu, M.-C. (2007). Factors influencing player preferences for heroic roles in role-playing games. *Cyberpsychology & Behavior, 10*(2), 293–295. doi:10.1089/cpb.2006.9955

Hsu, S. H., Lee, F. L., & Wu, M.-C. (2005). Designing action games for appealing to buyers. *Cyberpsychology & Behavior, 8*(6), 585–591. doi:10.1089/cpb.2005.8.585

Huizinga, J. (1938). *Homo Ludens: A study of the play element in culture*. Boston, MA: Beacon Press.

Hussain, Z., & Griffiths, M. D. (2008). Gender swapping and socializing in cyberspace: An exploratory study. *Cyberpsychology & Behavior, 11*(1), 47–53. doi:10.1089/cpb.2007.0020

Hustwit, J. R. (2007). Process philosophy. *The Internet Encyclopaedia of Philosophy*. Retrieved November 18, 2008, from http://www. iep.utm.edu/p/processp.htm

IJsselsteijn, W. A., de Kort, Y. A. W. & Poels, K. (forthcoming). *The game experience questionnaire: Development of a self-report measure to assess the psychological impact of digital games.*

Information Solutions Group. (2007). *Women choose "casual" videogames over TV. 100 million+ women now play regularly, for different reasons than men*. Retrieved February 13, 2008, from http://www.infosolutionsgroup.com/press_release_A.htm

International Game Developers Association. (2006). *2006 casual games whitepaper*. Retrieved June 29, 2007, from http://www.igda.org/casual/IGDA_CasualGames_Whitepaper_2006.pdf

Ivory, J. D. (2006). Still a man's game: Gender representation in online reviews of video games. *Mass Communication & Society, 9*(1), 103–114. doi:10.1207/s15327825mcs0901_6

Jakobsson, M., & Taylor, T. (2003). The Sopranos meets EverQuest: Socialization processes in massively multi-user games. *FineArt Forum, 17*(8).

Jansz, J., & Martens, L. (2005). Gaming at a LAN event: The social context of playing video games. *New Media & Society, 7*, 333–355. doi:10.1177/1461444805052280

Jansz, J., & Martis, R. G. (2007). The Lara phenomenon: Powerful female characters in video games. *Sex Roles, 56*, 141–148. doi:10.1007/s11199-006-9158-0

Jefferson, G. (1984). Transcript notation. In Heritage, J. (Ed.), *Structures of social interaction*. New York, NY: Cambridge University Press.

Jenkins, K. (2008). *Jenkins software*. Retrieved January 20, 2009, from http://www.jenkinssoftware.com/

Jensen, S. (2008). *JamPlus*. Retrieved January 20, 2009, from http://redmine.jamplex.org/projects/show/jamplus

Jinks, J., & Morgan, V. (1999). Children's perceived academic self-efficacy: An inventory scale. *Clearing House (Menasha, Wis.), 72*, 224–230. doi:10.1080/00098659909599398

Johnson, R. T., & Johnson, D. W. (1994). An overview of cooperative learning. In Thousand, J., Villa, A., & Nevin, A. (Eds.), *Creativity and collaborative learning*. Baltimore, MD: Brookes Press.

Johnson, D., & Johnson, R. (2009). *What is cooperative learning?* Retrieved May 11, 2009, from http://www.co-operation.org/pages/cl.html

Jonassen, H. D., Carr, C., & Yueh, H.-P. (1998). Computers as mindtools for engaging learners in critical thinking. *TechTrends, 43*(2), 24–32. doi:10.1007/BF02818172

Jones, T., & Clarke, V. (1994). A computer attitude scale for secondary students. *Computers & Education, 4*(22), 315–318. doi:10.1016/0360-1315(94)90053-1

Jordan, B., & Henderson, A. (1995). Interaction analysis: Foundations and practice. *Journal of the Learning Sciences, 4*(1), 39–103. doi:10.1207/s15327809jls0401_2

Junker, G. (Xavier, forum name). (2007, January 31). *Movable object listener*. Retrieved from http://www.ogre3d.org/phpBB2/viewtopic.php?=&p=200435

Kalyuga, S. (2006). *Instructing and testing advance learners: A cognitive load approach*. New York, NY: Nova Science.

Kalyuga, S. (2008). Relative effectiveness of animated and static diagrams: An effect of learner prior knowledge. *Computers in Human Behavior, 24*, 852–861. doi:10.1016/j.chb.2007.02.018

Kalyuga, S., Ayres, P., Chandler, P., & Sweller, J. (2003). Expertise reversal effect. *Educational Psychologist, 38*, 23–31. doi:10.1207/S15326985EP3801_4

Kenny, D. A., Kashy, D. A., & Cook, W. L. (2006). *Dyadic data analysis*. New York, NY: Guilford Press.

Khronos Group. (2008). *Collada—3D asset exchange schema*. Retrieved January 20, 2009, from http://www.khronos.org/collada/

Kim, M. C., & Hannafin, M. J. (2010a). Scaffolding problem solving in technology-enhanced learning environments (TELEs): Bridging research and theory with practice. *Computers & Education*. doi:.doi:10.1016/j.compedu.2010.08.024

Kim, M. C., & Hannafin, M. J. (2010b). Scaffolding 6th graders' problem solving in technology-enhanced science classrooms: A qualitative case study. *Instructional Science*. doi:.doi:10.1007/s11251-010-9127-4

Kim, M. C., Hannafin, M. J., & Bryan, L. A. (2007). Technology-enhanced inquiry tools in science education: An emerging pedagogical framework for classroom practice. *Science Education*, *91*(6), 1010–1030. doi:10.1002/sce.20219

Kimble, C. R., & Rezabek, J. (1992). Playing games before an audience: Social facilitation or choking. *Social Behavior and Personality: An International Journal*, *20*(2), 115–120. doi:10.2224/sbp.1992.20.2.115

Kipfer, P., Segal, M., & Westermann, R. (2004). Uberflow: A GPU-based particle engine. *Proceedings of the ACM SIGGRAPH/Eurographics Conference Workshop on Graphics Hardware* (pp. 115–122).

Kirschner, P. A., Sweller, J., & Clark, R. E. (2006). Why minimal guidance during instruction does not work: An analysis of the failure of constructivist, discovery, problem-based, experiential, and inquiry-based teaching. *Educational Psychologist*, *41*(2), 75–86. doi:10.1207/s15326985ep4102_1doi:10.1207/s15326985ep4102_1

Klimmt, C., & Hartmann, T. (2006). Effectance, self-efficacy, and the motivation to play video games. In Vorderer, P., & Bryant, J. (Eds.), *Playing video games: Motives, responses, and consequences* (pp. 133–145). Mahwah, NJ: Lawrence Erlbaum Associates.

Ko, S. (2002). An empirical analysis of children's thinking and learning in a computer game context. *Educational Psychology*, *22*(2), 219–233. doi:10.1080/01443410120115274

Koschmann, T., Zemel, A., Conlee-Stevens, M., Young, N., Robbs, J., & Barnardt, A. (2005). How do people learn? In Bromme, R., Hesse, F. W., & Spada, H. (Eds.), *Barriers and biases in computer-mediated knowledge communication and how they may be overcome*. Dordrecht, The Netherlands: Springer. doi:10.1007/0-387-24319-4_12

Koschmann, T., Stahl, G., & Zemel, A. (2005). The video analyst's manifesto (or the implications of Garfinkel's policies for studying practice within design-based research). In Derry, S., & Pea, R. (Eds.), *Video research in the learning sciences*. Mahwah, NJ: Lawrence Erlbaum Associates.

Kosslyn, S. M. (1989). Understanding charts and graphs. *Applied Cognitive Psychology*, *3*(3), 185–225. doi:10.1002/acp.2350030302

Ku, J., Jang, H. J., Kim, K. U., Kim, J. H., Park, S. H., & Lee, J. H. (2005). Experimental results of affective valence and arousal to avatar's facial expressions. *Cyberpsychology & Behavior*, *8*(5), 493–503. doi:10.1089/cpb.2005.8.493

Kuarnes, T. (2008). *Ogre bullet forum index*. Retrieved January 20, 2009, from http://www.ogre3d.org/addonforums/viewforum.php?f=12&start=0

KungFooMasta (forum name). (2008). *QuickGUI forum index*. Retrieved January 20, 2009, from. http://www.ogre3d.org/addonforums/viewforum.php?f=13

Larkin, J. H., & Simon, H. A. (1987). Why a diagram is (sometimes) worth ten thousand words. *Cognitive Science*, *11*, 65–99. doi:10.1111/j.1551-6708.1987.tb00863.x

LaRose, R., & Eastin, M. S. (2004). A social cognitive theory of Internet uses and gratifications: Toward a new model of media attendance. *Journal of Broadcasting & Electronic Media*, *48*(3), 358–377. doi:10.1207/s15506878jobem4803_2

Lastowka, F., & Hunter, D. (2004). The laws of the virtual worlds. *California Law Review*, *92*(1). doi:10.2307/3481444

Lave, J., & Wenger, E. (1991). *Situated learning: Legitimate peripheral participation: Learning in doing: Social, cognitive and computational perspectives*. Cambridge, UK: Cambridge University Press.

Lazzaro, N. (2007). The 4 most important emotions of game design. *Game Developers Conference*. San Francisco.

Lee, H., Plass, J. L., & Homer, B. D. (2006). Optimizing cognitive load for learning from computer-based science simulations. *Journal of Educational Psychology, 98*(4), 902–913. doi:10.1037/0022-0663.98.4.902

Lee, O., Buxton, C., Lewis, S., & LeRoy, K. (2006). Science inquiry and student diversity: Enhanced abilities and continuing difficulties after an instructional intervention. *Journal of Research in Science Teaching, 43*(7), 607–636. doi:10.1002/tea.20141

Lee, F. K., Sheldon, K. M., & Turban, D. B. (2003). Personality and the goal striving process: The influence of achievement goal patterns, goal level, and mental focus on performance and enjoyment. *The Journal of Applied Psychology, 88*, 256–265. doi:10.1037/0021-9010.88.2.256

Lee, D. (2006). Facilitating transitions between and within academic tasks: An application of behavioral momentum. *Remedial and Special Education, 27*(5), 312–317. doi:10.1177/07419325060270050601

Lenhart, A., Kahne, J., Middaugh, E., Macgill, A. R., Evans, C., & Vitak, J. (2008). *Teens, video games and civics: Teens' gaming experiences are diverse and include significant social interaction and civic engagement*. Washington, DC: Pew Internet & American Life Project.

Lepper, M. R., & Henderlong, J. (2000). Turning "play" into "work" and "work" into "play": 25 years of research on intrinsic versus extrinsic motivation. In Sansone, C., & Harackiewicz, J. M. (Eds.), *Intrinsic and extrinsic motivation: The search for optimal motivation and performance* (pp. 257–307). San Diego: Academic Press. doi:10.1016/B978-012619070-0/50032-5

Lepper, M. R., Aspinwall, L. G., Mumme, D. L., & Chabay, R. W. (1990). Self-perception and social perception processes in tutoring: Subtle social control strategies of expert tutors. In J. Olson & M. P. Zanna (Eds.), *Self inference processes: The Sixth Ontario Symposium in Social Psychology* (pp. 217-237). Hillsdale, NJ: Erlbaum.

Leue, W. H. (2005). *Metaphysical foundations for a theory of value in the philosophy of Alfred North Whitehead*. Ashfield, MA: Down-to-Earth Books.

Leutner, D. (1993). Guided discovery learning with computer-based simulation games: Effects of adaptive and non-adaptive instructional support. *Learning and Instruction, 3*(2), 113–132. doi:10.1016/0959-4752(93)90011-N

Levie, W. H., & Lentz, R. (1982). Effects of text illustrations: A review of research. *Educational Communication & Technology Journal, 30*(4), 195–232.

Levie, W. H. (1987). Research on pictures: A guide to the literature. In Willows, D. M., & Houghton, H. A. (Eds.), *The psychology of illustration: I. Basic research* (pp. 1–50). New York, NY: Springer.

Lewis, E. L., Stern, J. L., & Linn, M. C. (1993). The effect of computer simulations on introductory thermodynamics understanding. *Educational Technology, 33*, 45–58.

Lewis, M. L., Weber, R., & Bowman, N. D. (2008). They may be pixels, but they're my pixels: Developing a metric of character attachment in role-playing video games. *Cyberpsychology & Behavior, 11*(4), 515–518. doi:10.1089/cpb.2007.0137

Lim, C. P., Nonis, D., & Hedberg, J. (2006). Gaming in a 3D multiuser virtual environment: Engaging students in Science lessons. *British Journal of Educational Technology, 37*(2), 211–231. doi:10.1111/j.1467-8535.2006.00531.x

Lim, S., & Reeves, B. (2009). Being in the game: Effects of avatar choice and point of view on psychophysiological responses during play. *Media Psychology, 12*, 348–370. doi:10.1080/15213260903287242

Lim, S., & Lee, J. R. (2007). *Effects of coplaying on arousal and emotional responses in videogame play*. International Communication Association Conference. San Francisco.

Lim, S., & Reeves, B. (2006). *Responses to interactive game characters controlled by a computer versus other players*. International Communication Association Conference, San Francisco, CA, USA.

Linden Lab. (2009a). *Second Life economic statistics*. Retrieved June 3, 2009, from http://secondlife.com/whatis/economy_stats.php

Linden Lab. (2009b). *How education enterprises use virtual worlds*. Retrieved June 3, 2009, from http://secondlifegrid.net/slfe/education-use-virtual-world

Linn, M. C., & Burbules, N. C. (1991). Construction of knowledge and group learning. In Tobin, K. G. (Ed.), *The practice of constructivism in science education* (pp. 91–119). Washington, DC: AAAS Press.

Locke, B., Moore, M., & Burton, J. (2001). Old concerns with new distance education research. *EDUCAUSE Quarterly*, *24*(2), 60–62.

Lockee, B. B., Burton, J. K., & Cross, L. H. (1999). No comparison: Distance education finds a new use for 'No significant difference.'. *Educational Technology Research and Development*, *47*(3), 33–42. doi:10.1007/BF02299632doi:10.1007/BF02299632

Lofgren, E., & Fefferman, N. (2007). The untapped potential of virtual game worlds to shed light on real world epidemics. *The Lancet Infectious Diseases*, *7*(9), 625–629. doi:10.1016/S1473-3099(07)70212-8

Loh, C. S. (2006). *Tracking an avatar: Designing data collection into online games.* Paper presented at the annual conference of the Association for Educational Communications and Technology (AECT 2006), Dallas, TX.

Loh, C. S. (2008). Designing online games assessment as "Information Trails." In V. Sugumaran (Ed.), *Intelligent information technologies: Concepts, methodologies, tools, and applications* (Vol. 1, pp. 553-574). Hershey, PA: Information Science Reference.

Loh, C. S., & Byun, J. H. (2009). Modding neverwinter nights into serious games. In D. Gibson & Y. K. Baek (Eds.), *Digital simulations for improving education: Learning through artificial teaching environments* (pp. 408-426). Hershey, PA: Information Science Reference.

Loh, C. S., Anantachai, A., Byun, J., & Lenox, J. (2007, November 21-23). *Assessing what players learned in serious games: In situ data collection, information trails, and quantitative analysis.* Paper presented at the Computer Games: AI, Animation, Mobile, Educational & Serious Games (CGAMES 2007), Louisville, KY.

Lombard, Y. (2002a, November 11). Combining octrees and BSP trees... is it possible? Retrieved from http://www.gamedev.net/community/forums/topic.asp?topic_id=123169

Lowe, R. (1993). Constructing a mental representation from an abstract technical diagram. *Learning and Instruction*, *3*(3), 157–179. doi:10.1016/0959-4752(93)90002-H

Lowe, R. K. (1999). Extracting information from an animation during complex visual learning. *European Journal of Psychology of Education*, *14*(2), 225–244. doi:10.1007/BF03172967

Lowe, R. K. (2003). Animation and learning: Selective processing of information in dynamic graphics. *Learning and Instruction*, *13*(2), 157–176. doi:10.1016/S0959-4752(02)00018-X

Lucas, K., & Sherry, J. L. (2004). Sex differences in video game play: A communication-based explanation. *Communication Research*, *31*(5), 499–523. doi:10.1177/0093650204267930

Lucas, R. E. (1986). The behavioral foundations of economic theory. *The Journal of Business*, *59*(4), S401–S426.

Lucas, K., & Sherry, J. L. (2004). Sex differences in video game play: A communication-based explanation. *Communication Research*, *31*, 499–523. doi:10.1177/0093650204267930

LucasArts Entertainment Company (2002). *Jedi knight II: Jedi outcast* [CD-ROM].

Macromedia. (2004). *Flash MX 2004* [Software application]. Mountain View, CA.

Magerko, B. (2008). Adaptation in digital games. Entertainment Computing Column. *IEEE Computer Magazine*, *41*(6), 87–89.

Magerko, B., Heeter, C., Medler, B., & Fitzgerald, J. (2008). Intelligent adaptation of digital game-based learning. In *Proceedings of the Future Play Conference*, Toronto.

Mahncke, H. (2006, August 15). Memory enhancement in healthy older adults using a brain plasticity-based training program: A randomized, controlled study. *Proceedings of the National Academy of Sciences of the United States of America*, *103*(33). doi:10.1073/pnas.0605194103

Malaby, T. (2006). Parlaying value: Capital in and beyond virtual worlds. *Games and Culture*, *1*(2), 141–162. doi:10.1177/1555412006286688

Mandinach, E. B., & Honey, M. (2008). *Data-driven school improvement: Linking data and learning*. New York: Teachers College Press.

Mandl, H., & Levin, J. R. (1989). *Knowledge acquisition from text and pictures*. Amsterdam, The Netherlands: Elsevier.

Mangels, J. A., Butterfield, B., Lamb, J., Good, C. D., & Dweck, C. S. (2006). Why do beliefs about intelligence influence learning success? A social-cognitive-neuroscience model. *Social Cognitive and Affective Neuroscience, 1*, 75–86. doi:10.1093/scan/nsl013

Martins, N., Williams, D. C., Harrison, L., & Ratan, R. A. (2009). A content analysis of female body imagery in video games. *Sex Roles, 61*(11-12), 824–836. doi:10.1007/s11199-009-9682-9

Mayer, R. E., & Sims, V. K. (1994). For whom is a picture worth a thousand words? Extensions of a dual-coding theory of multimedia learning. *Journal of Educational Psychology, 86*(3), 389–401. doi:10.1037/0022-0663.86.3.389

Mayer, R. E. (2001). *Multimedia learning*. New York, NY: Cambridge

Mayer, R. E. (2005). *The Cambridge handbook of multimedia learning*. New York, NY: Cambridge.

McGrath, S. (2004). *Developer's blog: September 8th, 2004 – Post processing framework, HDR pipeline*. Project Offset. Retrieved September, 2007, from http://www.projectoffset.com/blog.php?id=15

McKenna, K., & Lee, S. (1995). *A love affair with MUDs: Flow and social interaction in multi-user dungeons*. International Communication Association Conference, Chicago, IL, USA. Retrieved June 6th, 2008, from http://fragment.nl/mirror/various/McKenna_et_al.nd.A_love_affair_with_muds.html

McQuiggan, S. W., & Lester, J. C. (2007). Modeling and evaluating empathy in embodied companion agents. *International Journal of Human-Computer Studies, 65*(4), 348–360. doi:10.1016/j.ijhcs.2006.11.015

McShaffrey, M. (2003). *Game events and scripting languages. Game coding complete* (2nd ed.). Scottsdale, AZ: Paraglyph Press Inc.

Mesle, C. R. (2008). *Process-relational philosophy: An introduction to Alfred North Whitehead*. West Conshohocken, PA: Temple Foundation Press.

Michael, D., & Chen, S. (2006). *Serious games: Games that educate, train, and inform*. Boston: Thomson Course technology PTR.

Microsoft Developer Network. (2009). *DDS*. Retrieved January 20, 2009, from http://msdn.microsoft.com/en-us/library/bb943990(VS.85).aspx

Miller, G. A. (1956). The magical number seven, plus or minus two: Some limits on our capacity for processing information. *Psychological Review, 63*, 81–97. doi:10.1037/h0043158

Miller, M. K., & Summers, A. (2007). Gender differences in video game characters' roles, appearances, and attire as portrayed in video game magazines. *Sex Roles, 57*(9-10), 733–742. doi:10.1007/s11199-007-9307-0

Miller, C. T. (Ed.). (2008). *Games: Purpose and potential in education* (1st ed.). New York: Springer Science+Business Media, LLC.

Milne, I., & Rowe, G. (2005). Interpreting computer code in a computer-based learning system for novice programmers. *Software, Practice & Experience, 35*(15), 1477–1493. doi:10.1002/spe.680

Mohamed, M. (2006, April). *Stop your physics simulation*. Retrieved November 3, 2007, from http://reality.artificialstudios.com/twiki/bin/view/Main/RigidActors

Moore, R. J., Ducheneaut, N., & Nickell, E. (2007). Doing virtually nothing: Awareness and accountability in massively multiplayer online worlds. *Computer Supported Cooperative Work, 16*, 265–305. doi:10.1007/s10606-006-9021-4

Moreland, R. L., & Zajonc, R. B. (1982). Exposure effects in person perception: Familiarity, similarity and attraction. *Journal of Experimental Social Psychology, 18*, 395–415. doi:10.1016/0022-1031(82)90062-2

Mozilla Foundation. (2008). *Mozilla code licensing*. Retrieved January 20, 2009, from http://www.mozilla.org/MPL/

Mumford, L. (1945). *The myth of the machine: Technics and human development.* New York, NY: Harcourt, Brace, & World.

Murray, M., Mokros, J., & Rubin, A. (1998). Where's the math in computer games? *Hands On, 21*(2), 8–11.

Nardi, B., & Harris, J. (2006). *Strangers and friends: Collaborative play in World of Warcraft.* 20th Anniversary Conference on Computer Supported Cooperative Work (pp. 149-158). New York, NY: ACM.

National Institute for Play. (2009). *Play deprived life - Devastating result.* Retrieved April 16, 2009, from http://nifplay.org/whitman.html

Newton. (2008). *Newton game dynamics.* Retrieved January 20, 2009, from http://www.newtondynamics.com/index.html

Nguyen, H. (2004). *Fire in the "Vulcan" demo* (pp. 87–105). GPU Gems. Addison Wesley.

Nielsen Interactive Entertainment. (2005). *Video gamers in Europe - 2005. Research Report Prepared for the Interactive Software Federation of Europe.* ISFE.

Nielsen, J. (1994). Heuristic evaluation. In Nielsen, J., & Mack, R. L. (Eds.), *Usability inspection methods.* New York, NY: John Wiley & Sons.

Njoo, M., & De Jong, T. (1993). Exploratory learning with a computer simulation for control theory: Learning processes and instructional support. *Journal of Research in Science Teaching, 8,* 821–844. doi:10.1002/tea.3660300803

Norman, D. A. (1988). *The design of everyday things.* New York, NY: Doubleday.

Norris, K. O. (2004). Gender stereotypes, aggression, and computer games: An online survey of women. *CyperPsychology & Behavior, 7*(6), 714–727. doi:10.1089/cpb.2004.7.714

Nowak, K. L., & Rauh, C. (2005). The influence of the avatar on online perceptions of anthropomorphism, androgyny, credibility, homophily, and attraction. *Journal of Computer-Mediated Communication, 11*(1), 153–178. doi:10.1111/j.1083-6101.2006.tb00308.x

Nowak, K. L., & Rauh, C. (2008). Choose your "buddy icon" carefully: The influence of avatar androgyny, anthropomorphism and credibility in online interactions. *Computers in Human Behavior, 24,* 1473–1493. doi:10.1016/j.chb.2007.05.005

Nowak, K. L., & Rauh, C. (2005). The influence of the avatar on online perceptions of anthropomorphism, androgyny, credibility, homophily, and attraction. *Journal of Computer-Mediated Communication, 11*(1), Article 8.

Nvidia. (2009). *NVIDIA PhysX.* Retrieved January 20, 2009, from http://www.nvidia.com/object/nvidia_physx.html

Ogletree, S. M., & Drake, R. (2007). College students' video game participation and perceptions: Gender differences and implications. *Sex Roles, 56,* 537–542. doi:10.1007/s11199-007-9193-5

Ogre3D API. (2008a). *Ogre: String interface class reference.* Retrieved January 20, 2009, from http://www.ogre3d.org/docs/api/html/classOgre_1_1StringInterface.html

Ogre3D API. (2008b). *Ogre: Entity class reference.* Retrieved January 20, 2009, from http://www.ogre3d.org/docs/api/html/classOgre_1_1Entity.html

Oliver, M., & Pelletier, C. (2005). *The things we learned on Liberty Island: Designing games to help people become competent game players.* DiGRA 2005: the Digital Games Research Association's 2nd International Conference, Changing Views: Worlds in Play, Vancouver, British Columbia, Canada, June 16-20.

OSG. (2008). *Welcome to the OpenSceneGraph website.* Retrieved January 20, 2009, from http://www.openscenegraph.org/projects/osg

Pajares, F. (1996). Self-efficacy beliefs and mathematical problem solving of gifted students. *Contemporary Educational Psychology, 21,* 325–344. doi:10.1006/ceps.1996.0025

Palmgreen, P. C., Wenner, L. A., & Rosengreen, K. E. (1985). Uses and gratification research: The past ten years. In Rosengreen, K. E., Wenner, L. A., & Palmgreen, P. C. (Eds.), *Uses and gratifications research: Current perspectives* (pp. 11–37). Beverly Hills, CA: Sage.

Parker, J. R., Becker, K., & Sawyer, B. (2008, January/February). Re-reconsidering research on learning from media: Comments on Richard E. Clark's point of view column on serious games. *Educational Technology, 48,* 39–43.

Peirce, C. S. (1955). Logic as semiotic: The theory of signs. In Buchler, J. (Ed.), *The philosophical writings of Peirce* (pp. 98–110). New York, NY: Dover Books.

Peppler, K. A., & Kafai, Y. B. (2007, September 24-28). *What videogame making can teach us about literacy and learning: Alternative pathways into participatory culture.* Paper presented at DiGRA 2007, Tokyo, Japan. Retrieved May 20, 2008, from http://www.digra.org/dl/db/07311.33576.pdf

Petkovsek, C. (2007). *Quaternion and rotation primer.* Retrieved January 15, 2007, from http://www.ogre3d.org/wiki/index.php/Quaternion_and_Rotation_Primer

Phillips, C. A., Rolls, S., Rouse, A., & Griffiths, M. D. (1995). Home video game playing in schoolchildren: A study of incidence and patterns of play. *Journal of Adolescence, 18,* 687–691. doi:10.1006/jado.1995.1049

Piaget, J., & Inhelder, B. (1956). *The child's conception of space.* London, UK: Routledge & Paul.

Picciano, A., & Seaman, J. (2009). *K–12 online learning: A 2008 follow-up of the survey of U.S. school district administrators.* Retrieved June 3, 2009, from http://www.sloan-c.org/publications/survey/pdf/k-12_online_learning_2008.pdf

Pink, S. (2001a). More visualising, more methodologies: On video, reflexivity and qualitative research. *The Sociological Review, 49*(4), 586–599. doi:10.1111/1467-954X.00349

Pink, S. (2001b). *Doing visual ethnography: Images, media and representation in research.* London: Sage.

Pink, S. (2004). Conversing anthropologically: Hypermedia as Anthropological Text. In S. Pink, L. Kürti, & A. I. Afonso (Eds.), *Working images: Visual research and representation in ethnography* (pp. 166-184). New York: Routledge.

Pintrich, P. R., & De Groot, E. V. (1990). Motivational self-regulated learning components of classroom academic performance. *Journal of Educational Psychology, 82,* 33–40. doi:10.1037/0022-0663.82.1.33

Plass, J. L., Chun, D. M., Mayer, R. E., & Leutner, D. (2003). Cognitive load in reading a foreign language text with multimedia aids and the influence of verbal and spatial abilities. *Computers in Human Behavior, 19*(2), 221–243. doi:10.1016/S0747-5632(02)00015-8

Plass, J. L., Homer, B. D., & Hayward, E. (2009). Design Factors for Educationally Effective Animations and Simulations. *Journal of Computing in Higher Education, 21*(1), 31–61. doi:10.1007/s12528-009-9011-x

Plass, J. L., & Kalyuga, S. (2010). Individual differences and cognitive load theory. In Plass, J. L., Moreno, R., & Brünken, R. (Eds.), *Cognitive Load Theory.* New York, NY: Cambridge University Press.

Plass, J. L., Goldman, R., Flanagan, M., Diamond, J., Song, H., Rosalia, C., & Perlin, K. (2007). *RAPUNSEL: How a computer game designed based on educational theory can improve girls' self-efficacy and self-esteem.* Paper presented at the 2007 Annual Meeting for the American Educational Research Association (AERA), Division C-5: Learning Environments, in Chicago.

Plass, J. L., Homer, B. D., Milne, C., & Jordan, T. (2007). *Optimizing cognitive load in simulations for science education.* Paper presented at the 2007 Annual Meeting for the American Educational Research Association (AERA), Division C-4: Science, in Chicago.

Playyoo (2008). *Snacking on casual games.* Retrieved April 11, 2009, from Playyoo Blog: http://blog.playyoo.com/tags/casual-games/

Poels, K., de Kort, Y. A. W., & IJsselsteijn, W. A. (2007). It is always a lot of fun! Exploring dimensions of digital game experience using focus group methodology. *Proceedings of Futureplay 2007 Conference,* (pp. 83-89). Toronto, Canada.

PopCap Games. (2006). *Study: Women choose "casual" videogames over TV; 100 Million+ women now play regularly, for different reasons than men.* Retrieved April 11, 2009, from Popcap Games web site: http://www.popcap.com/press/release.php?gid=2006-10-02

Pratchett, R., & Harris, D. (2005). *Gamers in the UK. Digital play, digital lifestyles*. London, UK: BBC Audience Research.

Preacher, K. J., & Hayes, A. F. (2004). SPSS and SAS procedures for estimating indirect effects in simple mediation models. *Behavior Research Methods, Instruments, & Computers, 36*(4), 717–731. doi:10.3758/BF03206553

Prensky, M. (2005). *Engage me or enrage me: What today's learners demand*. Retrieved July 25, 2005, from http://www.marcprensky.com/writing/Prensky-Engage_Me_or_Enrage_Me.pdf

Prensky, M. (2007). *Digital game-based learning*. St. Paul, MN: Paragon House Publishers.

Project, G. N. U. (2008a). *GNU general public license*. Retrieved January 20, 2009, from http://www.gnu.org/copyleft/gpl.html

Pryzgoda, J., & Chrisler, J. C. (2000). Definitions of gender and sex: The subtleties of meaning. *Sex Roles, 43*(7/8), 553–569. doi:10.1023/A:1007123617636

Putnam, H. (2002). *The collapse of the fact/ value dichotomy*. Cambridge, MA: Harvard University Press.

Quaiser-Pohl, C., Geiser, C., & Lehmann, W. (2006). The relationship between computer-game preference, gender, and mental-rotation ability. *Personality and Individual Differences, 40*(3), 609–619. doi:10.1016/j.paid.2005.07.015

Quake Engine. (2007). *id software*. [Electronic version]. http://www.idsoftware.com/games-/quake/quake3-teamarena/

Quinn, J., & Alessi, S. M. (1994). The effects of simulation complexity and hypothesis-generation strategy on learning. *Journal of Research on Computing in Education, 27*, 75–91.

Radford, R. (1945). The economic organisation of a POW camp. *Economica, 12*(48), 189–201. doi:10.2307/2550133

Raghunathan, R., & Corfman, K. (2006). Is happiness shared doubled and sadness shared halved? Social influence on enjoyment of hedonic experiences. *JMR, Journal of Marketing Research, 43*(August), 386–394. doi:10.1509/jmkr.43.3.386

Ramey, R. (2004). *Serialization overview*. Retrieved January 20, 2009, from http://www.boost.org/doc/libs/1_37_0/libs/serialization/doc/index.html

Ravaja, N. (2009). The psychophysiology of digital gaming: The effect of a non co-located opponent. *Media Psychology, 12*, 268–294. doi:10.1080/15213260903052240

Ravaja, N., Saari, T., Turpeinen, M., Laarni, J., Slaminen, M., & Kivikangas, M. (2006). Spatial presence and emotions during video game playing: Does it matter with whom you play? *Presence (Cambridge, Mass.), 15*, 381–392. doi:10.1162/pres.15.4.381

ReedBeta. (2008). *Kd-trees*. Retrieved January 20, 2009, from. http://en.wikipedia.org/wiki/Kd-tree

Reeves, R. (1983, April). Particle systems—A technique for modeling a class of fuzzy objects. *ACM Transactions on Graphics, 2*(2), 91–108. doi:10.1145/357318.357320

Reeves, B., & Nass, C. (1996). *The media equation: How people treat computers, television, and new media like real people and places*. Cambridge, UK: Cambridge University Press.

Reinhard, C. L. D. (2006, June 21-24). *Hypersexualized females in digital games: Do men want them, do women want to be them?* Paper presented at the 56th Annual Meeting of the International Communication Association, Dresden, Germany.

Rescher, N. (2000). *Process philosophy: A survey of basic issues*. Pittsburgh, PA: University of Pittsburgh Press.

Rescher, N. (2008). Process philosophy. *Stanford Encyclopaedia of Philosophy*. Retrieved November 4, 2008, from http://plato.stanford.edu/entries/process-philosophy/

Resinari, R. (2007). *WoodPong*. DoubleR Software.

Rieber, L. P. (1990). Using computer animated graphics with science instruction with children. *Journal of Educational Psychology, 82*(1), 135–140. doi:10.1037/0022-0663.82.1.135

Rieber, L. P. (1991). Effects of visual grouping strategies of computer-animated presentations on selective attention in science. *Educational Technology Research and Development, 39*(4), 5–15. doi:10.1007/BF02296567

Rieber, L. P., & Parmley, M. W. (1995). To teach or not to teach? Comparing the use of computer-based simulations in deductive versus inductive approaches to learning with adults in science. *Journal of Educational Computing Research, 13*(4), 359–374. doi:10.2190/M8VX-68BC-1TU2-B6DV

Rieber, L. P., Smith, M., Al-Ghafry, S., Strickland, B., Chu, G., & Spahi, F. (1996). The role of meaning in interpreting graphic textual feedback during a computer-based simulation. *Computers & Education, 27*(1), 45–58. doi:10.1016/0360-1315(96)00005-X

Rieber, L. P., Tzeng, S., & Tribble, K. (2004). Discovery learning, representation, and explanation within a computer-based simulation: Finding the right mix. *Learning and Instruction, 14*, 307–323. doi:10.1016/j.learninstruc.2004.06.008

Rizzo, A. A., Neumann, U., Enciso, R., Fidaleo, D., & Noh, J. Y. (2001). Performance-driven facial animation: Basic research on human judgments of emotional state in facial avatars. *Cyberpsychology & Behavior, 4*(4), 471–487. doi:10.1089/109493101750527033

Roberts, N. (2007). *Naughty's MEL scripts, modeling scripts*. Retrieved September 1, 2007, from http://www.naughtynathan.supanet.com/data/mel.htm

Robertson, J., & Good, J. (2005). Story creation in virtual game worlds. *Communications of the ACM, 48*(1), 61–65. doi:10.1145/1039539.1039571d oi:10.1145/1039539.1039571

Rockwell, S. K., & Kohn, H. (1989). Post then pre evaluation. *Journal of Extension, 27*(2), 19–21.

Rogoff, B. (1993). Children's guided participation and participatory appropriation in sociocultural activity. In Wozniak, R. H., & Fischer, K. W. (Eds.), *Development in context: Acting and thinking in specific environments* (pp. 121–153). Hillsdale, NJ: Lawrence Erlbaum.

Rosen, D., Woelfel, J., Krikorian, D., & Barnett, G. (2003). Procedures for analyses of online communities. *Journal of Computer-Mediated Communication, 8*(4). Retrieved December 1, 2008, from http://jcmc.indiana.edu/vol8/issue4/rosen.html

Rosengreen, K. E. (1974). Uses and gratifications: A paradigm outlined. In Blumler, J. G., & Katz, E. (Eds.), *The uses of mass communications: Current perspectives of gratification research* (pp. 269–286). Beverly Hills, CA: Sage.

Rosenthal, R., & Jacobson, L. (1992). *Pygmalion in the classroom*. New York: Irvington.

Ross, T. L., & Cornell, R. D. (2010). *Towards an experimental methodology of virtual world research*. Paper presented at the 2010 Second International Conference on Games and Virtual Worlds for Serious Applications.

Ryan, R. M., & Deci, E. L. (2000). Self-determination theory and the facilitation of intrinsic motivation, social development, and well-being. *The American Psychologist, 55*, 68–78. doi:10.1037/0003-066X.55.1.68

Ryan, R. M., Rigby, C. S., & Przybylski, A. (2006). The motivational pull of video games: A self-determination theory approach. *Motivation and Emotion, 30*(4), 347–363. doi:10.1007/s11031-006-9051-8

Rymaszewski, M., Wagner, J. A., Wallace, M., Winters, C., Ondrejka, C., & Batstone-Cunningham, B. (2007). *Second Life-The official guide*. New Jersey: Wiley Publishing.

Salzman, L. (2008). *Enet*. Retrieved January 20, 2009, from http://enet.bespin.org/

Sandford, R., Ulicsak, M., Facer, K., & Rudd, T. (2006). *Teaching with games: Using commercial off-the-shelf computer games in formal education*. Harbourside, United Kingdom: Futurelab.

Sawyer, B. (2005). The state of serious games. *Gamasutra*. Retrieved from http://www.gamasutra.com/features/20051024/sawyer_01.shtml

Schnotz, W., & Bannert, M. (2003). Construction and interference in learning from multiple representation. *Learning and Instruction, 13*(2), 141–156. doi:10.1016/S0959-4752(02)00017-8

Schnotz, W., Böckler, J., & Grzondziel, H. (1999). Individual and co-operative learning with interactive animated pictures. *European Journal of Psychology of Education, 14*, 245–265. doi:10.1007/BF03172968

Schnotz, W., & Kulhavy, R. W. (1994). *Comprehension of graphics*. Amsterdam, The Netherlands: North-Holland/Elsevier Science Publishers.

Schnotz, W., Picard, E., & Hron, A. (1993). How do successful and unsuccessful learners use texts and graphics? *Learning and Instruction, 3*, 181–199. doi:10.1016/0959-4752(93)90003-I

Schwandt, T. (2001). *Dictionary of qualitative inquiry* (2nd ed). Thousand Oaks, CA: Sage.

Second Life [Computer software]. (2008). San Francisco, CA: Linden Labs. Retrieved from http://secondlife.com

Seldin, T. (2008). *Montessori 101: Some basic information that every Montessori parent should know*. Retrieved April 11, 2009, from Montessori web site: http://www.montessori.org/sitefiles/Montessori_101_nonprintable.pdf

Selnow, G. W. (1984). Playing videogames: The electronic friend. *The Journal of Communication, 34*(2), 148–156. doi:10.1111/j.1460-2466.1984.tb02166.x

Selwyn, N. (2002). *Literature review in citizenship, technology and learning* (Report No. 3). Bristol, UK: Futurelab.

Semetsky, I. (2006). *Deleuze, education, and becoming*. Rotterdam, The Netherlands: Sense Publishers.

Shaffer, D. W., & Gee, J. P. (2006). *How computer games help children learn*. New York, NY: Palgrave Macmillan. doi:10.1057/9780230601994

Shaffer, D. W. (2006). Epistemic frames for epistemic games. *Computers & Education, 46*(3), 223–234. doi:10.1016/j.compedu.2005.11.003

Shah, P., & Carpenter, P. A. (1995). Conceptual limitations in comprehending line graphs. *Journal of Experimental Psychology. General, 124*(1), 43–61. doi:10.1037/0096-3445.124.1.43

Shah, P., & Hoeffner, J. (2002). Review of graph comprehension research: Implications for instruction. *Educational Psychology Review, 14*, 47–69. doi:10.1023/A:1013180410169

Sharritt, M. J. (2008). Forms of learning in collaborative game play. *Research and Practice in Technology Enhanced Learning, 3*(2), 97–138. doi:10.1142/S1793206808000471

Sharritt, M. J. (2010b). An open-ended, emergent approach for studying serious games. In Annetta, L., & Bronack, S. (Eds.), *Serious educational game assessment*. Rotterdam, The Netherlands: Sense Publishers.

Sharritt, M. J. (2010c). Evaluating video game design and interactivity. In Van Eck, R. (Ed.), *Interdisciplinary models and tools for serious games: Emerging concepts and future directions*. Hershey, PA: IGI Global. doi:10.4018/978-1-61520-719-0.ch008

Sharritt, M. J. (2010a). Designing game affordances to promote learning and engagement. *Cognitive Technology Journal, 14*(2)-*15*(1), 43-57.

Shelton, B. E., Stowell, T., Scoresby, J., Alvarez, M., Capell, M., & Coats, C. (2010). A Frankenstein approach to open-source: The construction of a 3D game engine as meaningful educational process. *IEEE Transactions on Learning Technologies, 3*(2). http://doi.ieeecomputersociety.org/10.1109/TLT.2010.3

Sherlock, L. M. 2007. When social networking meets online games: the activity system of grouping in World of Warcraft. In *Proceedings of the 25th Annual ACM international Conference on Design of Communication*, (pp. 14-20). El Paso, Texas, USA, October 22 - 24, 2007. New York, NY: ACM.

Sherry, J. L. (2001). Toward an etiology of media use motivations: The role of temperament in media use. *Communication Monographs, 68*(3), 274–288. doi:10.1080/03637750128065

Sherry, J. L. (2004). Flow and media enjoyment. *Communication Theory, 14*(4), 328–347. doi:10.1111/j.1468-2885.2004.tb00318.x

Sherry, J. L., Lucas, K., Greenberg, B., & Lachlan, K. (2006). Video game uses and gratifications as predictors of use and game preference. In Vorderer, P., & Bryant, J. (Eds.), *Playing video games - Motives, responses, and consequences* (pp. 213–224). Mahwah, NJ: Lawrence Erlbaum.

Sherry, J. L., Lucas, K., Greenberg, B. S., & Lachlan, K. (2006). Video game uses and gratifications as predictors of use and game preferences. In Vorderer, P., & Bryant, J. (Eds.), *Playing video games. Motives, responses, and consequences* (pp. 213–224). Mahwah, NJ & London, UK: Lawrence Erlbaum.

Sidorkin, A. M. (1999). *Beyond discourse: Education, the self, and dialogue*. New York, NY: SUNY Press.

Silicon Graphics. (2008). *Open inventor*. Retrieved January 20, 2009, from http://oss.sgi.com/projects/inventor/

Silverman, D. (1993). *Interpreting qualitative data: Methods for analyzing talk, text, and interaction*. London: Sage.

Singapore Ministry of Education. (2008). *Desired outcomes of education*. Retrieved November 27, 2008, from http://www.moe.gov.sg/education/desired-outcomes/

Skinner, E. A., & Belmont, M. J. (1993). Motivation in the classroom: Reciprocal effects of teacher behavior and student engagement across the school year. *Journal of Educational Psychology, 85*(4), 571–581. doi:10.1037/0022-0663.85.4.571

Slater, M. D. (2003). Alienation, aggression, and sensation seeking as predictors of adolescent use of violent film, computer, and website content. *The Journal of Communication, 53*(1), 105–121. doi:10.1111/j.1460-2466.2003.tb03008.x

Slavin, R. (1990). An introduction to cooperative learning. In Slavin, R. E. (Ed.), *Cooperative learning: Theory research and practice* (2nd ed., pp. 1–46). Boston, MA: Allyn and Bacon.

Smalley, N., Graff, M., & Saunders, D. (2001). A revised computer attitude scale for secondary students. *Educational and Child Psychology, 18*(3), 47–57.

Smart, J. (2008). *What is wxWidgets?* Retrieved January 20, 2009, from http://www.wxwidgets.org/

Smith, S. L. (2006). Perps, pimps, and provocative clothing: Examining negative content patterns in video games. In Vorderer, P., & Bryant, J. (Eds.), *Playing video games: Motives, responses, and consequences* (pp. 57–75). Mahwah, NJ: Lawrence Erlbaum Associates.

Sobel, M. E. (1982). Asymptotic confidence intervals for indirect effects in structural equation models. In Leinhardt, S. (Ed.), *Sociological methodology* (pp. 290–312). Washington, DC: American Sociological Association.

Sobel, M. E. (1986). Some new results on indirect effects and their standard errors in covariance structure models. In Tuma, N. (Ed.), *Sociological methodology* (pp. 159–186). Washington, DC: American Sociological Association.

SpaceDude (forum name). (2007, March 31). *Ragdolls*. Retrieved from http://www.ogre3d.org/phpBB2addons/viewtopic.php?t=3949&highlight=ragdoll

Squire, K., & Steinkuehler, C. (2006). Generating CyberCulture/s: The case of Star Wars Galaxies. In Gibbs, D., & Krause, K. (Eds.), *Cyberlines2: Languages and cultures of the Internet* (2nd ed.). Albert Park, Australia: James Nicholas Publishers.

Squire, K. (2003). Video games in education. *International Journal of Intelligent Games & Simulation, 2*(1).

Squire, K. (2005). Changing the game: What happens when video games enter the classroom? *Innovate, 1*(6).

Steinkuehler, C., & Duncan, S. (2008). Scientific habits of mind in virtual worlds. *Journal of Science Education and Technology, 17*(6), 530–543. doi:10.1007/s10956-008-9120-8

Steinkuehler, C., & Johnson, B. Z. (2009). Computational literacy in online games: The social life of mods. *International Journal of Gaming and Computer-Mediated Simulations, 1*(1), 53–65.

Stenning, K., & Oberlander, J. (1995). A cognitive theory of graphical and linguistic reasoning: Logic and implementation. *Cognitive Science, 19*(1), 97–140. doi:10.1207/s15516709cog1901_3

Stephenson, N. (1995). *The diamond age*. New York, NY: Bantam.

Stowell, T. (trs79, forum name). (2006, November 6). *Custom projection matrix changes RaySceneQuery?* Retrieved from http://www.ogre3d.org/forums/viewtopic.php?f=2&t=25673

Streeting, S. (2007). *DevMaster.net. 3D engines database, Ogre 3D*. Retrieved August 1, 2006, from http://www.devmaster.net/engines/engine_details.php?id=2

Streeting, S. (2009). *What is Ogre?* Retrieved January 20, 2009, from http://www.ogre3d.org/index.php?option=com_content&task=view&id=19&Itemid=105

Suter, J. (1999). *Introduction to octrees.* Retrieved January 20, 2009, from http://www.flipcode.com/archives/Introduction_To_Octrees.shtml

Suthers, D. D. (2001). Towards a systematic study of representational guidance for collaborative learning discourse. *Journal of Universal Computer Science, 7*(3), 254–277.

Suthers, D. D. (2006). Technology affordances for intersubjective meaning-making: A research agenda for CSCL. *International Journal of Computer-Supported Collaborative Learning, 1*(2), 315–337. doi:10.1007/s11412-006-9660-y

Suthers, D. D., & Hundhausen, C. (2003). An empirical study of the effects of representational guidance on collaborative learning. *Journal of the Learning Sciences, 12*(2), 183–218. doi:10.1207/S15327809JLS1202_2

Sutton-Smith, B. (1997). *The ambiguity of play.* Boston, MA: Harvard University Press.

Swaak, J., Van Joolingen, W., & De Jong, T. (1998). Supporting simulation-based learning- The effects of model progression and assignments on definitional and intuitive knowledge. *Learning and Instruction, 8*(3), 235–252. doi:10.1016/S0959-4752(98)00018-8

Sweetser, P., & Wyeth, P. (2005). GameFlow: A model for evaluating player enjoyment in games. *ACM Computers in Entertainment, 3*, Article 3A.

Sweller, J. (1999). *Instructional design in technical areas.* Camberwell, Australia: ACER Press.

Szafron, D., Carbonaro, M., Cutumisu, M., Gillis, S., McNaughton, M., Onuczko, C., et al. (2005). Writing interactive stories in the classroom. *Interactive Multimedia Electronic Journal of Computer-Enhanced Learning, 7*(1).

Szell, M., Lambiotte, R., & Thurner, S. (2010). Multirelational organization of large-scale social networks in an online world. *Proceedings of the National Academy of Sciences of the United States of America, 107*(31), 13636. doi:10.1073/pnas.1004008107

Tamborini, R., Bowman, N. D., Eden, A., Grizzard, M., & Ogan, A. (in press). Defining media enjoyment as the satisfaction of intrinsic needs. *The Journal of Communication.*

Tamborini, R., Grizzard, M., Bowman, N. D., Reinecke, L., Lewis, R., & Eden, A. (in press). Media enjoyment as need satisfaction: The contribution of hedonic and nonhedonic needs. *The Journal of Communication.*

Tan, T. W., & Chew, L. C. (2004). Moral and citizenship education as statecraft in Singapore: A curriculum critique. *Journal of Moral Education, 33*(4), 597–606. doi:10.1080/0305724042000315644

Tan, E. S., & Jansz, J. (2008). The game experience. In Schifferstein, H. N., & Hekkert, P. P. (Eds.), *Product experience.* San Diego, CA: Elsevier. doi:10.1016/B978-008045089-6.50026-5

Tarr, D. (1976). Experiments in token economies: A review of the evidence relating to assumptions and implications of economic theory. *Southern Economic Journal, 43*(2), 1136–1143. doi:10.2307/1057338

Teasley, S. D., & Roschelle, J. (1993). Constructing a joint problem space: The computer as a tool for sharing knowledge. In Lajoie, S. P., & Derry, S. J. (Eds.), *Computers as cognitive tools* (pp. 229–258). Hillsdale, NJ: Lawrence Erlbaum Associates.

The, N. P. D. Group. (2010). *20 percent of the U.S. population, or 56.8 million U.S. consumers, reports having played a game on a social network.* Retrieved September 16, 2010, from http://www.npd.com/press/releases/press_100823.html

Thomas, A., & Chess, S. (1977). *Temperament and development.* New York, NY: Brunner & Mazel.

Thompson, A. D., Simonson, M. R., & Hargrave, C. P. (1992). *Educational technology: A review of the research.* Washington, DC: Association for Educational Communications and Technology.

Towne, D. M. (1995). *Learning and instruction in simulation environments.* Englewood Cliffs, NJ: Educational Technology Publications.

Transana 2.20 [Computer software]. (2007). Madison, WI: The Board of Regents of the University of Wisconsin System. Retrieved from http://www.transana.org

Transana. (2008). *Jefferson transcript notation*. Retrieved January 9, 2008, from http://www.transana.org/support/OnlineHelp/Team1/transcriptnotation1.html

Trepte, S., & Reinecke, L. (2010). Avatar creation and video game enjoyment: Effects of life-satisfaction, game competitiveness, and identification with the avatar. *Journal of Media Psychology*, *22*, 171–184. doi:10.1027/1864-1105/a000022

Trepte, S., & Reinecke, L. (in press). The pleasures of success: Game-related efficacy experiences as a mediator between player performance and game enjoyment. *Cyberpsychology, Behavior, and Social Networking*.

Turkle, S. (1995). *Life on the screen: Identity in the age of the Internet*. New York: Simon & Schuster.

Turner, P. (CrazyEddie, forum name). (2008). *Welcome to crazy Eddie's GUI system*. Retrieved January 20, 2009, from http://www.cegui.org.uk/wiki/index.php/Main_Page

Unger, R. K. (1979). Toward a redefinition of sex and gender. *The American Psychologist*, *34*(11), 1085–1094. doi:10.1037/0003-066X.34.11.1085

Vallius, L., Manninen, T., & Kujanpää, T. (2006). Sharing experiences - Co-experiencing three experimental collaborative computer games. *Proceedings of Futureplay 2006 Conference*, London, Ontario, Canada.

Valve Software. (2008). *Source multiplayer networking*. Retrieved January 20, 2009, from http://developer.valvesoftware.com/wiki/Source_Multiplayer_Networking

Van der Meij, J., & deJong, T. (2006). Supporting students' learning with multiple representations in a dynamic simulation-based learning environment. *Learning and Instruction*, *16*(3), 199–212. doi:10.1016/j.learninstruc.2006.03.007

van Eck, R. (2007). Building intelligent learning games. In D. Gibson, C. Aldrich, & M. Prensky (Eds.), *Games and simulation in online learning: Research and development frameworks*. Hershey, PA: Idea Group, Inc.

Van Manen, M. (1997). *Researching lived experience*. London, Ontario, Canada: Althouse Press.

Vasalou, A., Joinson, A., Baenziger, T., Goldie, P., & Pitt, J. (2008). Avatars in social media: Balancing accuracy, playfulness and embodied messages. *International Journal of Human-Computer Studies*, *66*(11), 801–811. doi:10.1016/j.ijhcs.2008.08.002

Villagrana, J. (2007). *Downloads*. ABT. Retrieved April 10, 2007, from. http://www.3dgloom.net/html/downloads.html

Volca (forum name). (2007). *CVS code repository*. Retrieved April 3, 2007, from http://opde.cvs.sourceforge.net/opde/opde/src/

Vorderer, P., Steen, F. F., & Chan, E. (2006). Motivation. In Bryant, J., & Vorderer, P. (Eds.), *Psychology of entertainment* (pp. 3–17). Mahwah, NJ: Lawrence Erlbaum Associates.

Vorderer, P., Hartmann, T., & Klimmt, C. (2003). Explaining the enjoyment of playing video games: The role of competition. In *Proceedings of 2nd International Conference on Entertainment Computing, ICEC 2003*, ACM Digital Library.

Vorderer, P., Hartmann, T., & Klimmt, C. (2003). Explaining the enjoyment of playing video games: The role of competition. In D. Marinelli (Ed.), *Proceedings of the 2nd International Conference on Entertainment Computing (ICEC 2003), Pittsburgh* (pp. 1–8). New York, NY: ACM.

Vygotsky, L. S. (1978). *Mind in society: The development of higher psychological processes* (Cole, M., John-Steiner, V., Scribner, S., & Souberman, E. (Trans. Eds.)). Cambridge, MA: Harvard University Press.

Wade, B. (1998). *BSP tree frequently asked questions (FAQ)*. Retrieved January 20, 2009, from http://www.gamedev.net/reference/articles/article657.asp

Warren, S. J., Stein, R. A., Dondlinger, M. J., & Barab, S. A. (2009). A look inside a MUVE design process: Blending instructional design and game principles to target writing skills. *Journal of Educational Computing Research*, *40*(3), 295–321. doi:10.2190/EC.40.3.c

Weber, R., Bates, C., & Behr, K.-M. (2010). *Developing a metric of interactivity in video games*. Paper presented at the 96th Annual Convention of the National Communication Association November 14-17, 2010, San Francisco.

Wenger, E. (1998). *Communities of practice: Learning, meaning, and identity.* Cambridge, UK: Cambridge University Press.

Whalen, T. E., Petriu, D. C., Yang, L., Petriu, E. M., & Cordea, M. D. (2003). Capturing behaviour for the use of avatars in virtual environments. *Cyberpsychology & Behavior, 6*(5), 537–544. doi:10.1089/109493103769710569

Whitehead, A. N. (1926). *Religion in the making.* New York, NY: Macmillan.

Whitehead, A. N. (1978). *Process and reality: An essay in cosmology* (Corrected ed.). New York, NY: Free Press.

Wigand, R. T., Borstelmann, S. E., & Boster, F. J. (1985). Electronic leisure: Video game usage and the communication climate of video arcades. *Communication Yearbook, 9,* 275–293.

Wiley, J., & Jensen, M. (2006). When three heads are better than two. *Proceedings of the Annual Conference of the Cognitive Science Society.* Retrieved April 18, 2007, from http://litd.psch.uic.edu/personal/jwiley/Wiley_Jensen_06.pdf

Williams, A., & Walker, J. (1993). Computerized laboratory exercises for microeconomics education: Three applications motivated by experimental economics. *The Journal of Economic Education, 24*(4), 291–316. doi:10.2307/1183043

Williams, D., Martins, N., Consalvo, M., & Ivory, J. D. (2009). The virtual census: Representations of gender, race and age in video games. *New Media & Society, 11*(5), 815–834. doi:10.1177/1461444809105354

Williams, D. (2006). A brief social history of game play. In Vorderer, P., & Bryant, J. (Eds.), *Playing video games - Motives, responses, and consequences* (pp. 197–212). Mahwah, NJ: Lawrence Erlbaum.

Willows, D. M., & Houghton, H. A. (Eds.). (1987). *The psychology of illustration – Vol. I basic research.* New York, NY: Springer-Verlag.

Wilson, K. (2007). *Game object structure: Inheritance vs. aggregation.* Retrieved July 18, 2007, from http://gamearchitect.net/Articles/GameObjects1.html

Windle, M. (1992). Revised dimensions of temperament survey (DOTS-R): Simultaneous group confirmatory factor analysis for adolescent gender groups. *Psychological Assessment, 4,* 228–234. doi:10.1037/1040-3590.4.2.228

Windle, M., & Lerner, R. M. (1986). Reassessing the dimensions of individuality across the life span: The revised dimensions of temperament survey (DOTS-R). *Journal of Adolescent Research, 1,* 213–230. doi:10.1177/074355488612007

Winn, W. (1991). Learning from maps and diagrams. *Educational Psychology Review, 3*(3), 211–247. doi:10.1007/BF01320077

Winn, B. (2008). The design, play, and experience framework. In Ferdig, R. (Ed.), *Handbook of research on effective electronic gaming in education.* Hershey, PA: IGI Global. doi:10.4018/9781599048086.ch058

Winn, W. (1994). Contributions of perceptual and cognitive processes to the comprehension of graphics. In Schnotz, W., & Kulhavy, R. (Eds.), *Comprehension of graphics* (pp. 3–27). Amsterdam, The Netherlands: Elsevier. doi:10.1016/S0166-4115(09)60105-9

Wouters, P., Tabbers, H. K., & Paas, F. (2007). Interactivity in video-based models. *Educational Psychology Review, 19*(3), 327–342. doi:10.1007/s10648-007-9045-4

Wrzesien, M., & Raya, M. A. (2010). Learning in serious virtual worlds: Evaluation of learning effectiveness and appeal to students in the E-Junior project. *Computers & Education, 55,* 178–187. doi:10.1016/j.compedu.2010.01.003

wxWidgets. (2007). *wxWidgets book.* Retrieved August 1, 2006, from http://www.wxWidgets.org

Wyeld, T. G., Leavy, B., Carroll, J., Gibbons, C., Ledwich, B., & Hills, J. (2007, September 24-28). *The ethics of indigenous storytelling: Using the torque game engine to support Australian Aboriginal cultural heritage.* Paper presented at DiGRA 2007, Tokyo, Japan. Retrieved April 30, 2007, from http://www.digra.org/dl/db/07312.11188.pdf

Yee, N. (2006). The demographics, motivations and derived experiences of users of massively multi-user online graphical environments. *Presence (Cambridge, Mass.), 15*(3), 309–329. doi:10.1162/pres.15.3.309

Yee, N., & Bailenson, J. (2007). The Proteus effect: The effect of transformed self representation on behavior. *Human Communication Research*, *33*(3), 271–290. doi:10.1111/j.1468-2958.2007.00299.x

Yee, N. (2006). Motivations for play in online games. *Cyberpsychology & Behavior*, *9*(6), 772–775. doi:10.1089/cpb.2006.9.772

Yee, N., & Bailenson, J. (2007). The proteus effect: The effect of transformed self-representation on behavior. *Human Communication Research*, *33*, 271–290. doi:10.1111/j.1468-2958.2007.00299.x

Yee, N. (2008). Maps of digital desires: Exploring the topography of gender and play in online games. In Kafai, Y., Heeter, C., Denner, J., & Sun, J. (Eds.), *Beyond Barbie and Mortal Kombat: New perspectives in gender and gaming*. Cambridge, MA: MIT Press.

Yee, N. (2007). *The Proteus Effect: Behavioral modification via transformations of digital self-representation*. Retrieved June 3, 2009, from http://www.nickyee.com/pubs/Dissertation_Nick_Yee.pdf

Zajonc, R. B. (1980). Compresence. In Paulus, P. B. (Ed.), *Psychology of group influence* (pp. 35–60). Hillsdale, NJ: Erlbaum.

Zillmann, D. (1988). Mood management: Using entertainment to full advantage. In Donohue, L., Sypher, H. E., & Higgins, E. T. (Eds.), *Communication, social cognition and affect* (pp. 147–171). Hillsdale, NJ: Lawrence Erlbaum Associates.

Zillmann, D., & Bryant, J. (1985). Affect, mood, and emotion as determinant of selective exposure. In Zillmann, D., & Bryant, J. (Eds.), *Selective exposure to communication (pp. 157-190)*. Hillsdale, NJ: Lawrence Erlbaum Associates.

Zimbardo, P. (2007). *The Lucifer effect: Understanding how good people turn evil*. Random House Inc.

Zimmerman, B. J. (2000). Attaining self-regulation: A social cognitive perspective. In Boekaerts, M., Pintrich, P., & Zeidner, M. (Eds.), *Self-regulation: Theory, research, and applications* (pp. 13–39). Orlando, FL: Academic Press.

About the Contributors

Richard E. Ferdig is the RCET Research Professor and Professor of Instructional Technology at Kent State University. He works within the Research Center for Educational Technology and also the School of Lifespan Development and Educational Sciences. He earned his PhD in educational psychology from Michigan State University. At Kent State University, his research, teaching, and service focus on combining cutting-edge technologies with current pedagogic theory to create innovative learning environments. His research interests include online education, educational games and simulations, and what he labels a deeper psychology of technology. In addition to publishing and presenting nationally and internationally, Ferdig has also been funded to study the impact of emerging technologies such as K-12 Virtual Schools. Rick is the editor of the International Journal of Gaming and Computer Mediated Simulations, the Associate Editor of the Journal of Technology and Teacher Education, and currently serves on the Development Editorial Board of ETRD and on the Review Panel of the British Journal of Educational Technology.

* * *

Pavlo (Pasha) Antonenko is an Assistant Professor of Educational Technology at Oklahoma State University. He earned his BS degree in English and German Language/Literature and an MS in Linguistics from Nizhyn State University, Ukraine. He also holds a PhD in a) Curriculum and Instructional Technology and b) Human-Computer Interaction from Iowa State University. Pavlo's present research and teaching interests include (meta)cognitive scaffolding of learning in serious games, optimization of cognitive load in educational hypermedia, and application of open source tools to the design of computer-based learning environments.

Elizabeth Bagley is a graduate student at the University of Wisconsin-Madison in the Educational Psychology department and the Gaylord Nelson Institute for Environmental Studies. Before coming to the University of Wisconsin, Elizabeth spent a year studying in Kenya through the Minnesota Studies in International Development program and during that time, became interested in the disconnect between people and their environment. She taught 8-12th grade sciences for two years in South Louisiana through Teach For America. While teaching, she became interested in exploring students' understandings of ecology and how their understandings shaped their world. She is currently working with Dr. David Williamson Shaffer on the Urban Science epistemic game in which players engage in the professional practices of urban planners and learn how to become ecological thinkers in the process.

Mark W. Bell is a student in Telecommunications at Indiana University.

Erik W. Black is a doctoral fellow and candidate in the School of Teaching and Learning at the University of Florida. His research blends contemporary psychological and educational theory in the analysis and representation of data derived from virtual and technology-rich environments. Erik is a graduate of Virginia Tech with a B.S. in marketing management. Prior to initiating his doctoral studies in educational technology at the University of Florida, he received an M.A. in Human Services from The College of New Jersey.

Michael R. Capell received an MFA degree in graphic design from Utah State University in 2007, a BFA degree, Magna Cum Laude, from Utah State University in 2002, and an AA from Brigham Young University-Idaho in 1999. He is serving as a consultant for the HEAT project. He has worked as an Instructor at Utah State University in Animation and Design. He has created several virtual 3D characters for a computer-based interactive learning environment called MATHGIRLS. Current research includes a study on perception, which was presented as an award-winning poster at the 10th Annual Intermountain Posters and Paper Symposium. He has art directed sequences of animation for the Utah Jazz, Portland Trailblazers, and Houston Rockets; additionally, his work has been written about on www.planit3d.com.

Edward Castronova (PhD, Economics, Wisconsin, 1991) is an Associate Professor in the Department of Telecommunications at Indiana University, Bloomington. He is an expert on the economies of large-scale online games and has numerous publications on that topic. His latest is a book, Exodus to the Virtual World.

Yam San Chee is an Associate Professor in the Learning Sciences & Technologies Academic Group and the Learning Sciences Lab at the National Institute of Education, Nanyang Technological University, Singapore. He obtained his BSc (Econ) Hons from the London School of Economics and Political Science, University of London, and his PhD from the University of Queensland, Australia. Dr. Chee's research focuses on new literacies and new media in education, with a special emphasis on game-based learning. Recent games developed for research include *Space Station Leonis*, *Escape from Centauri 7*, and *Ideal Force*. Dr. Chee also conducts research on the interaction between online virtual life and real life and how this interaction impacts the construction of self identity. Dr. Chee was the Founding Executive Editor of *Research and Practice in Technology Enhanced Learning*, the journal of the Asia-Pacific Society for Computers in Education.

Robert Cornell is a student in Telecommunications at Indiana University.

James J. Cummings is a student in Telecommunications at Indiana University.

Chris Dede is the Timothy E. Wirth Professor of Learning Technologies at Harvard's Graduate School of Education. His fields of scholarship include emerging technologies, policy, and leadership. His funded research includes a grant from the National Science Foundation to aid middle school students learning science via shared virtual environments and a Star Schools grant from the U.S. Department of Education to help high school students with math and literacy skills using wireless mobile devices to create augmented reality simulations. Chris has served as a member of the National Academy of Sciences Committee on Foundations of Educational and Psychological Assessment, a member of the U.S. Department of Education's Expert Panel on Technology, and International Steering Committee member for the Second International Technology in Education Study. He serves on Advisory Boards and Commissions for PBS TeacherLine, the Partnership for 21st Century Skills, the Pittsburgh Science of Learning Center, and several federal research grants. In addition, Chris is a member of the Board of Directors of the Boston Tech Academy, an experimental small high school in the Boston Public School system, funded by the Gates Foundation. His co-edited book, Scaling Up Success: Lessons Learned from Technology-based Educational Improvement, was published by Jossey-Bass in 2005. A second volume he edited, Online Professional Development for Teachers: Emerging Models and Methods, was published by the Harvard Education Press in 2006. He is an experienced presenter in many types of settings.

Joseph C. DiPietro is a doctoral fellow and PhD candidate in the School of Teaching and Learning at the University of Florida. His research interests include exploring self-representation and bias in online environments and their applications to educational games and simulations. Prior to initiating his doctoral studies, Joseph worked as a public school teacher, countywide technology coordinator, and college instructor affording a diverse perspective of K-20 education. He has earned BAE and MEd degrees from the University of Florida and is an avid gamer.

Brock R. Dubbels has worked since 1999 as a professional in education and instructional design. His specialties include reading comprehension and instruction and assessment. His current focus is on the role of embodied cognition connected with digital literacies, game design, and play. From these perspectives he designs face-to-face, virtual, and hybrid learning environments, exploring new technologies for assessment, delivering content, creating engagement with learners, and investigating ways people approach learning. He is currently a research associate at the Center for Cognitive Science at the University of Minnesota. He is also the founder and principal learning architect at www.vgalt.com.

Will Emigh is the Motive Force at game company Studio Cypher, LLC.

Matthew Falk is a student in Telecommunications at Indiana University.

Michael Fatten is a student in Telecommunications at Indiana University.

Joe Fitzgerald is a MA student in the department of Telecommunications, Information Studies & Media at Michigan State University. He received his BA in Telecommunication, Information Studies, and Media from Michigan State University with a specialization in video game design and development. He is enrolled in the Serious Games Masters Program at MSU. Joe is currently conducting research and developing serious games for cultural heritage learning and outreach at Matrix: The Center for Humane Arts, Letters & Social Sciences Online at MSU.

Nick Fortugno is Co-Founder and President of Rebel Monkey, Inc., a NYC-based casual game entertainment company. CampFu, Rebel Monkey's forthcoming casual MMO, is launching in open beta in February 2009. Before Rebel Monkey, Fortugno was the Director of Game Design at gameLab, where he was a designer, writer, and project manager on dozens of commercial and serious games, and served as lead designer on the downloadable blockbuster Diner Dash and the award-winning serious game Ayiti: The Cost of Life. Nick teaches game design and interactive narrative design at Parsons, The New School of Design, and has participated in the construction of the school's game design curriculum. Nick is also a co-founder of the Come Out and Play street games festival hosted in New York City and Amsterdam since 2006.

Brian Gajadhar is currently a PhD student at the Eindhoven University of Technology. In 2002 he completed a Bachelor's degree in Applied Physics, including a final project, Reducing Sound within a MRI-scanner. He worked as an all-round metrologist on the length department of the Nederlands Meetinstituut (NMi) and then studied Human Technology and Interaction at the Eindhoven University of Technology. In 2006, he earned a Master of Science degree including the final project, Change Blindness as a Function of Role Variations using Road Traffic Scenarios. His doctoral research examines the social context of playing digital games, focusing on measurable differences between the experiences of solitary play and social play. The aim is to understand social behavior in game environments which will extend the existing models and will contribute to the science of game experience measurement.

Stephen Guynup has, for more than 15 years, been considered one of the most creative and controversial designers of online virtual worlds. His past efforts include numerous conference presentations, including SIGGRAPH 1998, 1999, 2000, 2003, 2004, 2009, and he will Chair the Web3D Art Gallery at SIGGRAPH 2010. He currently teaches Game Design for the Art Institute of Pittsburgh - Online Division.

Carrie Heeter is a Professor of serious game design in the department of Telecommunication, Information Studies, and Media at Michigan State University. She is co-editor of *Beyond Barbie and Mortal Kombat: New Perspectives in Gender, Gaming, and Computing* and creator of *Investigaming.com,* an online gateway to research about gender and gaming. Heeter's innovative software designs have won more than 50 awards, including Discover Magazine's Software Innovation of the Year. She has directed software development for 32 projects. Her research looks at the experience and design of meaningful play. Current work includes design of learning and brain games which adapt to fit player mindset and motivation and persuasive games where the designer goal is to engender more informed decision-making on complex socio-scientific issues. Heeter also serves as creative director for MSU Virtual University Design and Technology. For the last 12 years she has lived in San Francisco and telecommuted to MSU.

Bruce D. Homer is an Associate Professor of Educational Psychology at the Graduate Center, City University of New York, Director of Research of the Consortium for Research and Evaluation of Advanced Technologies in Education, and Director of the Interdisciplinary Postdoctoral Research Training Fellowship in the Educational Science (IPoRT) program. His research examines the role of cognitive and affective factors in multimedia learning environments. He also investigates the ways in which children learn to use "cultural tools" to store and transmit knowledge (e.g., language, literacy, and Information Technologies), and how the acquisition of these tools transforms cognitive and developmental processes. He has reviewed for a number of child development and education journals, including Child Development, Computers and Human Behavior, and Psychological Science.

Wijnand IJsselsteijn is Associate Professor at the Human-Technology Interaction group of Eindhoven University of Technology. He has a background in psychology and artificial intelligence, with an MSc in cognitive neuropsychology from Utrecht University, and a PhD in media psychology/HCI from Eindhoven University of Technology on the topic of telepresence. His current research interests include social digital media, immersive media technology, and digital gaming. His focus is on conceptualizing and measuring human experiences in relation to these advanced media. Wijnand is significantly involved in various nationally funded as well as EU funded projects. He is associate director of the Media, Interface, and Network Design labs (http://www.mindlab.org/cgi-bin/default.pl), and co-director of the Game Experience Lab (http://www.gamexplab.nl). He has published over 100 journal and conference papers and co-edited five books. He is highly active as an organizer of conferences and workshops, and as a reviewer and editor. Homepage: http://www.ijsselsteijn.nl.

Barbara Z. Johnson is co-owner and Chief Executive Officer of an investment and project management company and has twenty years experience in software development and Information Technology in both industry and academia. She has taught classes, seminars and workshops in academic writing, Web page authoring, and classroom technology integration. Currently, she is a doctoral student in Teaching and Learning at the University of Minnesota, studying how to include games and simulations as virtual experiences that enhance and encourage learning.

Catherine Johnston is an advanced doctoral student at Harvard and a research assistant on the HARP project.

Trace Jordan is Associate Director of the Morse Academic Plan - NYU's general education curriculum – with responsibility for the Foundations of Scientific Inquiry program. This program provides science education courses for over 1400 students each semester who are majoring in the arts, humanities, social sciences, education, or business. He regularly teaches courses on Energy and the Environment, Human Genetics, and Molecules of Life and has twice won NYU's Outstanding Teaching Award (in 1999 and 2006). His research interests encompass the development of effective computer simulations for science teaching, the investigation and improvement of students' 3D visualization skills in the context of molecular structures, and the cognitive methods that students employ to analyze complex issues with both a scientific and societal dimension. He serves on the Programming Committee for the Chemical Education Division of the American Chemical Society, a Senior Fellow for the NSF-Funded SENCER project, and a Faculty member for the 21st century in Project Kaleidoscope. Dr. Jordan holds a B.Sc. degree (honors) in Applied Physics (University of Essex), an M.A. in History and Philosophy of Science (University of Toronto), and a Ph.D. in Chemistry (Princeton University).

Slava Kalyuga is Senior Lecturer at the University of New South Wales (UNSW) in Sydney, Australia where he has worked since 1995. He received a Ph.D. in Education from UNSW in 1998 and was awarded an Australian Research Council Postdoctoral Research Fellowship (2001-2003). His research interests are in cognitive processes and evidence-based instructional design principles for multimedia learning environments. His specific contributions include detailed experimental studies of the role of learner prior knowledge in multimedia learning (the expertise reversal effect), the redundancy effect in multimedia learning, the development of rapid online diagnostic assessment methods, and studies of the effectiveness of different adaptive procedures for tailoring instruction to levels of learner expertise. He is the author of the book Instructing and Testing Advanced Learners: A Cognitive Load Approach (2006) and 35 research articles and chapters. During his previous work in Russia (until 1991), he published more than 30 articles and several books and textbooks.

Minchi C. Kim is an Assistant Professor of Educational Technology at Purdue University. Previously, she served as postdoctoral scholar in the Consortium for Research and Evaluation of Advanced Technologies in Education (CREATE) at New York University. She worked on several National Science Foundation and Department of Education funded projects as a research assistant at the Learning and Performance Support Laboratory at the University of Georgia. Her research focuses on scaffolding students' scientific problem solving with technology-enhanced learning environments, advancing pedagogical frameworks for learning and teaching in technology-enhanced classes, and integrating emergent technologies into K-12 classes. Her research has been published in numerous journals such as Journal of Computing in Higher Education, Quarterly Review of Distance Education, Instructional Science, Distance Learning, and Science Education.

Yvonne de Kort is Assistant Professor environmental psychology and co-director of the Game Experience Lab at Eindhoven University of Technology. She received her PhD in 1999 and since then has been working in the Human-Technology Interaction Group. She specializes in the interaction between humans and their socio-physical environment. Yvonne's research focuses on two domains. The first comprises spaces, technology, and social interaction (e.g., situated social interaction in and around digital games, locatedness in mediated social interaction). The second lies at the intersection of spaces, technology, and health (restorative effects of mediated environments, effects of lighting on people's health, mood, and mental restoration). Yvonne is involved in several European projects under the sixth and seventh framework. She supervises PhD students and postdocs, has published over 70 papers, has co-organised scientific workshops and conferences, and reviews for various journals and conferences.

Paul LaFourest is a student in Music Composition at Indiana University.

Hyunjeong Lee is an Assistant Professor and Director of the Center for Teaching and Learning at the University of Seoul. Her research explores instructional design based on a cognitive approach in multimedia environments. Currently, she participates in the research and development of digital textbooks at the national level of Korea; she contributes to the development of prototype digital textbooks in math, science, sociology, language, music, and arts for fifth grade students. Her research interests are in the relations among cognitive load, learning expansion, and learners' aptitude, especially in technology-based environments. Her specific contribution to this area is the experimental study of the manipulation of cognitive load through visual scaffolding and restructuring of information and investigating the interaction effect between cognitive load and learners' aptitude. In addition to K12 settings, she has applied Information Technology to human resource development for corporate workers: Virtual Practice Firm. Hyunjeong Lee is on the editorial board of Asia Pacific Educational Research.

Feng Liu is a doctoral fellow in the School of Teaching and Learning at the University of Florida. Originally from Nanjing, China, Mr. Liu received a B.S. in computer science education from Nanjing

Normal University and a M.Ed. in educational technology from Georgia College and State University. His research focuses on contemporary issues in multiculturalism and multicultural online education.

Christian Sebastian Loh wears many hats in real life. He is a researcher, an educator, a gamer, and a father. Professionally, he is an Assistant Professor of Instructional Design Technology and one of the coordinators of the Collaboratory for Interactive Learning Research (C.I.L.R.) at the Southern Illinois University Carbondale. He also serves as President (2008-2009) for the Multimedia Production Division (MPD) of the Association for Educational Communications and Technology (AECT), reviews articles for the *IJGCMS* as Associate Editor, and judges professional serious game competitions. His publications include many journal articles and book chapters on and about serious games, assessment, and emerging technology. Currently, he is pioneering the research on "Information Trails," a user behavior analysis framework for *in situ* assessment within multi-user virtual environments, including serious games and virtual worlds.

Swee Kin Loke is a Lecturer (Research) in the Learning Sciences Laboratory at the National Institute of Education, Singapore, and a trained schoolteacher. His specific contribution to the *Space Station Leonis* project was the design and construction of learning activities to support the game-based learning. He worked previously in the Educational Technology Division of the Ministry of Education, Singapore, where he was part of the team designing and implementing a national level policy, the Baseline ICT Standards.

Brian Magerko is an Assistant Professor of Digital Media in the School of Literature, Communication, and Culture at the Georgia Institute of Technology. He received his B.S. in Cognitive Science from Carnegie Mellon University and a M.S. and Ph.D. in Computer Science and Engineering from the University of Michigan. As head of the Adaptive Digital Media Lab, his work has focused on how to create digital media experiences that create experiences tailored to individuals for pedagogical gain, entertainment value, or both. His current research focuses on adaptive games for learning, cognitive modeling of improvisational acting, and creating virtual ecosystems for scientific collaboration, education, and historical preservation. Dr. Magerko has also been a pioneer in the field of interactive narrative, working on several systems that have used an intelligent story director agent to guide a user through a narrative experience in a virtual world.

Ben Medler is a second year doctoral student at Georgia Institute of Technology studying Digital Media. Ben earned a B.S. in Computer Science in 2005 and an M.A. in Digital Media in 2007, both from Michigan State University. His research focus is tied to the study/production of digital games and how they impact our society. Current projects include a) studying the creative and communication skills improvisational actors use during performances in order to build digital improvisational agents for games, b) building game systems that monitor and adapts to a player's play style in order to better suit that player's needs, and c) theorizing about conflicts found in digital games and how neutral or peaceful activities can be used for gameplay. Other research interests include storytelling/interactive drama, building authoring tools, user interfaces in games, machinima production and social networks.

Catherine Milne is an Associate Professor of science education within the Department of Teaching and Learning in the Steinhardt School of Culture, Education and Human Development at New York

University. Her research interests include the nature of engagement in learning science, the role of representations in science education, urban science education, and the role of the history and philosophy of science in science education. She has made contributions to the nature of analogies in laboratory simulations, the nature of individual and collective engagement, and the role of stories in learning science. Catherine Milne is on the editorial boards of the Journal of Research in Science Education and Research in Science Education. Currently she is also working on a book for Sense Publishers, Science as Separate and Connected Knowing: Understanding Inquiry in the Science Classroom.

Nathan Mishler is a cofounder of Studio Cypher, LLC.

Rebecca Mitchell is an advanced doctoral student at Harvard and a research assistant on the HARP project.

Patrick O'Shea is the Director of the Handheld Augmented Reality Project at Harvard University's Graduate School of Education. This project is focused on studying the potential of GPS-enabled handheld computing in educational settings to improve academic and non-academic outcomes. In addition, Dr. O'Shea has more than 15 years of experience working at every level of education. Among his accomplishments, Dr. O'Shea has consulted internationally for the Bill and Melinda Gates Foundation, built online testing protocols, designed, implemented, and evaluated large-scale university-level projects, and has extensive experience with practical applications of technology in the educational setting.

Jan L. Plass is an Associate Professor and coordinator of the Ph.D. program in Educational Communication and Technology at New York University, as well as the Director of the Consortium for Research and Evaluation of Advanced Technologies in Education. His research explores the intersection of cognitive science, technology, and design to further our understanding of the design of effective digital technologies for learning and instruction. He has made contributions to the study of cognitive and emotional factors in the design of educational games, simulation, and Web-based materials, with a particular focus on visual learning and the effects of specific learner characteristics, as well as to second language acquisition with multimedia. Jan Plass is on the editorial boards of the Journal of Educational Psychology, Computers in Human Behavior, Educational Technology Research and Development, Journal of Research on Technology in Education, and International Journal on E-Learning and is a contributing editor for the Wiley Visualizing series.

Justin Reynard is currently a gameplay programmer at Obsidian Entertainment.

Sarah "Intellagirl" Robbins is a doctoral candidate at Ball State University.

Travis Ross is a student in telecommunications at Indiana University.

William Ryan is a doctoral candidate in Human-Computer Interaction at Indiana University.

Jon Scoresby holds a BS degree in Information Systems/business management from Brigham Young University, a MEd degree in instructional technology from the University of Georgia, and is currently pursuing a PhD degree in the same field from Utah State University. While in Georgia, he worked as a graduate assistant for the Office of Instructional Support and Development, helping design and develop instructional CD ROMs and DVDs. Jon is currently a graduate assistant in the Center for Open and Sustainable Learning at Utah State University, researching and developing learning problems for a 3D physics simulation and developing the instructional design for the HEAT project. His research interests include educational games and simulation, and the effects of game player point-of-view.

David Williamson Shaffer is a Professor at the University of Wisconsin-Madison in the departments of Educational Psychology and Curriculum and Instruction. Before coming to the University of Wisconsin, Dr. Shaffer taught grades 4-12 in the United States and abroad, including two years working with the Asian Development Bank and US Peace Corps in Nepal. His M.S. and Ph.D. are from the Media Laboratory at the Massachusetts Institute of Technology, and he taught in the Technology and Education Program at the Harvard Graduate School of Education. He was a founding member of the Games and Professional Practice Simulations (GAPPS) research group at the University of Wisconsin. Dr. Shaffer studies how new technologies change the way people think and learn. His particular are of interest is in the development of epistemic games: computer and video games in which players become professionals to develop innovative and creative ways of thinking. His most recent book is How Computer Games Help Children Learn.

Matthew Sharritt is a recent graduate of the interdisciplinary Communication and Information Sciences doctoral program at the University of Hawai'i at Manoa (2008). Previously, Dr. Sharritt earned his M.S. (2003) from the Department of Information and Computer Sciences at the University of Hawai'i, where he served as a teaching assistant for the introductory Java programming courses for six years. Prior, he obtained his B.S. from Marquette University in Computer Engineering (2001) while serving as webmaster at Time Warner Telecom. Dr. Sharritt's research examines way of maximizing flow and the self-efficacy of the user experience through the design of cutting-edge video games, which can engage current and future generations on a level of which they are capable. This research has supported the idea that learning can be fun while teaching concepts that can be explored and tested through play. In his spare time Dr. Sharritt enjoys gaming, cooking, and photography.

Patrick Shaw is lead designer at Reactor Zero in Ann Arbor, Michigan and is working on simulations for the United States military and unannounced next generation video games. He has over ten years of game development experience in variety of roles (senior technical artist, senior producer, and lead game designer) and projects (ranging from Star Wars edutainment to "The Sims"). Patrick has a Bachelor's degree in Environmental Studies from the University of Chicago and recently earned his Master's of Telecommunication from Michigan State University.

Brett E. Shelton has a PhD degree in educational technology from the University of Washington, an M.T. degree in industrial management and supervision from Arizona State University and a BS degree in computer engineering from the University of Idaho. He is currently an Assistant Professor of Instructional Technology and Learning Sciences at Utah State University. He uses a variety of mixed-method research approaches to study vision, perception, cognition, and the design and assessment of innovative technologies for learning. Other interests include immersive and interactive learning environments, data visualizations, instructional simulations, and educational gaming. He is the Director of the Center for

Open and Sustainable Learning. The mission of this group is to make educational resources available and accessible to as many people as possible.

Miguel Sicart is Assistant Professor at the IT University of Copenhagen, where he teaches game design. He received his Ph.D. in game studies in December 2006. His 3-year research project focused on providing a multidisciplinary approach to ethics and computer games, focusing on issues such as game design, violence and videogames, and the role of age-regulation codes. His research has now crystallized into a book, The Ethics of Computer Games to be published by MIT Press in Spring 2009. His current research focuses on developing a design framework for implementing ethical gameplay in digital games. E-mail: miguel@itu.dk.

Rory Starks is a graduate of the Master of Immersive Mediated Environments program at Indiana University.

Constance Steinkuehler is an Assistant Professor in the Educational Communication & Technology program in the Curriculum & Instruction department at the University of Wisconsin–Madison. Her research is on cognition, learning, and literacy in massively multiplayer online games (MMOs). Current interests include "pop cosmopolitanism" in online worlds and the intellectual practices that underwrite such a disposition, including informal scientific reasoning, collaborative problem solving, media literacy (as production, not just consumption), computational literacy, and the social learning mechanisms that support the development of such expertise (e.g., reciprocal apprenticeship, collective intelligence).

Tim Stowell received am MS degree in instructional technology in 2006, and a BFA degree in art with a minor in computer science in 2004, all from Utah State University. While at Utah State, Tim worked as a Web developer for the College of Natural Resources and the Accommodating Students with Disabilities in Higher Education Project. He also did some freelance illustration. For his Master's thesis, Tim modified the Quake 3 game engine to work for a 3D version of the Voices of Spoon River instructional game. He is currently working on the HEAT project for the Center for Open and Sustainable Learning, and has interests in instructional games, 3D virtual environments, and visual design.

Dan Suthers is Professor in the Department of Information and Computer Sciences at the University of Hawai'i at Manoa, and is chair of the interdisciplinary Communication and Information Sciences program. Dr. Suthers obtained his Bachelor of Fine Arts (1979) from Kansas City Art Institute, studied Psychology at the graduate level at Northern Arizona University, 1982-1985, and then earned M.S. (1988) and Ph.D. (1993) degrees in Computer Science from the University of Massachusetts. Dr. Suthers' research is generally concerned with cognitive, social, and computational perspectives on designing and evaluating software for learning, collaboration, and community. His current research focus is on how software interfaces influence collaborative learning and problem solving processes in small groups and the formation of relationships and social capital in online communities. He is presently Editor for the journal Research and Practice in Technology Enhanced Learning and associate editor for the International Journal of Computer Supported Collaborative Learning.

Ek Ming Tan is a trained schoolteacher on secondment to the National Institute of Education, Singapore, as a Lecturer (Research). He obtained his BArts from the National University of Singapore and a Master's in Education from the University of Western Australia. Prior to his current position, he was a Level Head in a Singapore Secondary School and Acting Head of Department for English Language and Literature.

Paul A. D. Waelchli is the current Information Literacy & Instruction Librarian for St. Norbert College where he is charged with building a library instruction program applying video game strategies as pedagogy. In his former position at the Charles C. Myers Library at the University of Dubuque, Paul developed lesson plans incorporating gaming strategies into the classroom. Paul has authored chapters for both American Library Association (ALA) and the Association of College & Research Libraries (ACRL) publications on using video games and gaming strategies to teach information literacy. Since 2006, Paul has written about video games strategies, information literacy, and education on his blog Research Quest. He was recognized by the ACRL in August of 2007 as a featured member profile and was recently appointed to a position on the ALA's Libraries, Literacy, and Gaming Expert Group. In addition to his work in libraries, Paul has collaborated on research with Andrew Bub, creator of Gamerdad.com. He holds a Master's of Arts in Teaching from Clarke College and a Master's of Library and Information Science from the University of Wisconsin – Milwaukee.

René Weber is an Assistant Professor in the Department of Communication at the University of California, Santa Barbara. He holds a Bachelor/Master's degree in both Communication and Quantitative Economics, a PhD in Psychology, and an MD in Cognitive Neuroscience. In his recent research he focuses on cognitive and emotional effects of television and new technology media, including new generation video games. He develops and applies both traditional social scientific and neuroscientific methodology (fMRI) to test media related theories. He earned several awards and honors such as Michigan State University's "New Faculty Award" for the study "Neurophysiology of Entertainment" or "Best Dissertation Award" of the German and Swiss Marketing Associations for his work on "TV Audience Prediction".

Baird Whelan is a post-graduate researcher and the founder of the non-profit, cognitive research group, Synappsys, located in San Francisco, CA. The recipient of an M.A.E. in Educational Technology from the University of Florida, Mr. Whelan has led Synappsys in collaborations with Bay Area Biotechnology organizations. His research concerns are in the fields of cognitive development, immersive technology and brain function, artificial life simulations, and the development of open educational resources.

Brian M. Winn is Associate Professor in the Telecommunication, Information Studies, and Media Department and Director of the Games for Entertainment and Learning (GEL) Lab at Michigan State University. Winn designs, creates, and researches interactive media design, including game design, digital game-based learning, and interactive health communication. Winn's expertise is in designing engaging serious games that balancing learning, pedagogical, and gameplay objectives. Winn's award-winning interactive media work has been presented, exhibited, and experienced around the world. Winn is also an accomplished teacher who became an Apple Distinguished Educator in 2001 and a Lilly Teaching Fellow in 2005. Winn is a co-founder and co-director of the undergraduate Game Design and Development Specialization and the Serious Game Design Master of Arts program at Michigan State University. Winn serves as faculty advisor of the MSU SpartaSoft game developers student group and a coordinate of the Michigan Chapter of the International Game Developers Association.

Index

A

Agency for Mining Zone Redevelopment (ANDZM) 76, 81

Agricultural Electronics 164

Agricultural Fleet Management 152, 154, 158, 162, 166, 170

Agricultural Governance 172-179, 181

agricultural policy 21, 37, 90, 131, 174, 181, 183, 247, 252, 254, 256, 291, 294, 340, 447-449, 452-453, 460, 463-467, 469

agricultural sector 9-10, 93, 97, 116, 128, 148, 172, 174, 176, 196, 263-264, 266, 273, 277, 280, 404, 447, 463, 466, 468-469

Agriculture Land Use Change 358

Agri-Environment 23-24, 32-35, 131, 259-260, 355-357

Agri-Environmental Schemes (AES) 21, 23-25, 31, 34-38, 81, 259, 340, 358

Agrifood Industry 196

Agrifood Organization Structures 206

Agriport A7 103

Agroecosystems Analysis (AEA) 261

Alternatives 29, 38, 58, 154, 184, 189, 195, 243, 252, 299-301, 304-307, 309-310, 313-317, 322, 383, 390, 396, 400, 416, 426, 428-430, 433-434, 436, 440, 443, 445, 451, 469

Analytic Hierarchy Process (AHP) 304, 316

ARIMA Models 327-328, 338

artificial intelligence (AI) 427

Asset Specificity 6, 9, 14, 183-185, 189, 191, 194

Australian Department of Agriculture, Fisheries and Forestry (AFFA) 176, 266

autocorrelation function (ACF) 327

autoregressive distributed lag (ARDL) 364

Auto-Regressive Integrated Moving Average (ARIMA) 320, 326-328, 332, 334-335, 338

B

Bank of Regional Data (BDR) 47

Bergerden 103

Biodiversity conservation 289, 292-295, 297, 341, 350, 353, 355, 358

Birds Directive 342, 358

Black Sea 299-300, 302-303, 305, 315-317, 346

Box-Jenkins method 327-328

Business Process Automation (BPA) 268, 271

Business Process Execution Language (BPEL) 269, 275, 277, 282, 285-286

Business Process Execution Language for Web Services (BPEL4WS) 269, 282, 286

Business Process Improvement (BPI) 268, 271, 274

Business Process Management (BPM) 140, 221, 268, 275

Business Process Modeling Notation (BPMN) 275

Business Process Reengineering (BPR) 268, 271

C

Campania 93-97

Capacity-Objectives-Processes-Impacts (COPI) 288, 292

Capacity-Objectives-Processes-Impacts framework 288

CAP-IRE project 187

CAP Reform 182, 187, 192, 194, 356, 466

Capture Fisheries 336, 338

Centers for Disease Control and Prevention (CDC) 214

Central Statistical Office (GUS) 47-48, 50

Climate Change 8, 87-93, 95-100, 294, 300, 355, 357, 362, 372-373, 401, 407, 421

Cointegration 359-366, 368-376

Collaborative Mapping (CM) 380, 391-392